Eighth Witness

Witness

The Biography of
John Whitmer

Eighth Witness

The Biography of John Whitmer

By Ronald E. Romig

John Whitmer Books

Independence, Missouri

2014

Published by John Whitmer Books

John Whitmer Books is a trademark of the
John Whitmer Historical Association

ISBN-13: 978-1-934-90128-1

View our complete catalog online at www.JohnWhitmerBooks.com

Learn more about the John Whitmer Historical Association
at www.JWHA.info

Cover and interior design and typesetting by John Hamer

PRINTED IN THE UNITED STATES OF AMERICA

This book is dedicated to family:
My mother, Goldie (Spriggle) Romig, in acknowledgement of an
exemplary life and distant shared ethnic, cultural, and ancestral
connections with the Whitmer family.

I am also greatly indebted to my wife, Anne (Holmes) Romig, and
my daughter, Rene, who have both provided endless encouragement
throughout this project.

CONTENTS

Introduction xi

Chapters

1　The Whitmer Family in Fayette 1

2　Encountering Joseph Smith: June 1829 19

3　Completing the Book of Mormon Translation 35

4　First Calling: Missionary and Witness 48

5　Organizing the Church 65

6　The Great Commission: John Whitmer in Ohio 84

7　Kirtland: The Gathering Place 102

8　First Church Historian 122

9　Preparing to Publish the Revelations: Fall 1831 136

10　John Whitmer in Missouri 151

11　The Printing Business in Independence 161

12　Whitmer Settlement: 1832 179

13　Kirtland–Independence Relations 192

14　Violence in Independence: 1833 206

15　Expulsion from Jackson County 224

16　Return to Ohio 248

17　Editing the *Messenger and Advocate* 256

18　Tension and Reconciliation 269

19   Return to Missouri: 1836 292

20   A Gathering to Missouri: A Ragged Break 314

21   Competing Visions 326

22   Exclusion 340

23   New Beginnings 359

24   The Mormon War in Missouri 364

25   Reclaiming Far West 378

26   Life after the Mormons 393

27   Succession Questions 403

28   Building a Legacy 422

29   Consolidating the John Whitmer Farm 433

30   A Passing Generation 445

31   Death of the Eighth Witness 465

32   The Last Witness 479

33   The Whitmer Documents and Artifacts 488

Appendix A: Provenance of The Book of John Whitmer 507

Appendix B: John Whitmer's First and Last Editorials 516

Appendix C: John Whitmer's Patriarchal Blessing 523

Appendix D: John Whitmer's Missouri Mormon War Trial
Testimony 524

Appendix E: John Whitmer and David Whitmer Interviews by
P. Wilhelm Poulson, 1878 526

Appendix F: William E. McLellin: Our Tour West in 1847 528

Appendix G: Far West 538

Appendix H: William Lewis, 1877 553

Appendix I: Orson Pratt and Joseph F. Smith, Visit to Far West,
1878 555

Appendix J: Sketches of Christopher F. Kerr and Jacob D. Whitmer 558

Appendix K: James Williams: Far West Seventy-Five Years Ago, Written in 1911 560

Appendix L: A Revelation received at Far West, July 26, 1861 563

Appendix M: John Whitmer to Dear Children, 1 March 1871 566

Appendix N: C. J. Hunt, "An Acknowledgement to John Whitmer" 568

Appendix O: Ethel Johnson Lewellen to C. Edward Miller, 1932 571

Appendix P: Evan A. Fry to Ella Turner, 1949 573

Appendix Q: Samuel Russell, Correspondence, 1882 576

Appendix R: William B. Smith, 1879 Invitation to Gather at Far West 580

Appendix S: Arthur B. Deming, 1888 585

Appendix T: George W. Schweich to O. R. Beardsley, 1900 587

Appendix U: Edmund C. Brand, Letter to Joseph Smith III, 1875 588

Appendix V: Joseph F. Smith, Letter to Samuel Russell, 1901 589

Appendix W: Last House in Far West Destroyed, 1913 591

Appendix X: Ronald E. Romig, Review of *From Historian to Dissident* by Bruce N. Westergren 592

Appendix Y: Published Reproductions of Book of Mormon Caractors 595

Bibliography 597

Index 654

INTRODUCTION

"JOHN WHITMER" IS one of the most familiar names in early Mormonism. As one of Joseph Smith's earliest supporters and associates, John was a member of one of the founding families of Smith's Restoration movement. He was also one of the eight witnesses to the authenticity of the Book of Mormon, Mormonism's founding document. His name is reproduced in each of the millions of copies of that work that exist in dozens of different editions. Many know no more than his name, but the better informed likewise know that he also became wary of Joseph Smith and Mormonism, turned his back on what had been a sublime adventure, and thus became a cautionary tale to the faithful.

John Whitmer's rise and fall within Mormonism is an exhilarating narrative, his conversion very much a movement of his family into the new church. Paralleling this movement, his exodus out of Mormonism was also a clan movement as the Whitmers, after less than a decade, experienced difficulties with Joseph's leadership.

These best-known facts are, of course, only shallow stereotypes of John Whitmer and the extended Whitmer family. Many perspectives may be found of the Whitmer family's experience with Mormonism. James Henry Moyle encountered David Whitmer in 1885. In response to a question from Moyle, David Whitmer provided the following rationale for the extended family's departure from the mainstream movement. Moyle wrote, "I asked him ... why he had left the Church. He said he had not, but the Church had left him."[1]

---

1. David Whitmer, interview by James Henry Moyle, June 28, 1885, cited in Moyle, "Address by Elder James H. Moyle before the Ensign Stake conference," and reproduced in Hinckley, *James Henry Moyle*, 366–67. Moyle also stated: "I asked him why he had left the Church. He replied that he had never left the Church, that he had continued with the branch of the Church that was originally organized in Richmond, and still presided over it." Moyle, "Statement," reprinted in *Desert News*, and reproduced in, Cook, *David Whitmer Interviews*, 161–64.

Martin Harris, another Book of Mormon witness experienced similar difficulties with the early Mormon church. Harris also later voiced a
parallel perspective, saying, "I never did leave the Church; the Church left
me."[2]

But this perspective typically is powerfully overshadowed by more
orthodox institutional views of church history. Reinforcing what has become the predominant perspective of the Whitmers' experience in northern Missouri, Alexander L. Baugh, a professor of LDS church history at
Brigham Young University, observes:

> In Kirtland, [Ohio], Mormon expatriates were eventually successful
> in forcing the Church leadership to leave the community. However,
> Mormon leaders were not about to let this happen in Far West, [Mis-
> souri]. In June 1838, with the exception of [William E.] McLellin,
> all of the dissenters were still living in Far West where, in spite of
> their minority status, they continued to conduct their subversive ac-
> tivities in an attempt to undermine the Mormon leadership. It was at
> this time that the Mormon leadership perceived if they allowed their
> former associates to carry out their lawsuits and deviant operations
> unchecked, "they would destroy the Church," so a decision was made
> to encourage them to leave Far West.[3]

This familiar story of betrayal and intrigue, with the blame clearly
assigned and motives clearly delineated, is an instance of what historian
Jan Shipps has termed the politics of definition, which is—structuring
truth conducive to dominance.[4] Baugh's language strongly slants events in
northwestern Missouri in 1838, decidedly favoring orthodox LDS church
perspectives. This story is integral to a larger institutional narrative in
which apologist authors adopt Mormons-against-the-world shorthand.
Carefully selected words plainly differentiate the victims from the villains.
Baugh's treatment marginalizes John Whitmer, his family, and friends,
while justifying and defending the actions of Joseph Smith and his friends
who now saw the Whitmers as a threat. This perspective serves Mormons

---

2. Homer, "'Publish It Upon the Mountains': The Story of Martin Harris," 505.

3. Baugh, "A Community Abandoned," 22. The internal quotation is from Corrill, *Brief
    History of the Church of Christ*, 30.

4. Shipps, "Telling the Whole Story of Mormonism."

well, making their past legible and retrievable for LDS institutional purposes.[5]

But there is more to John's story than revealed by these contrasting perspectives. Born to a humble farm family at the beginning of the nineteenth century, John Whitmer gained notice and notoriety during the nineteenth century for his role in early Mormonism.[6] He served as the movement's first historian (1831–38) and proved to be a careful steward of important Mormon documents. He also served competently as a counselor in the presidency of the Mormon church in Missouri (1834–38) and was one of the co-founders of Mormondom's northern Missouri headquarters city at Far West in Caldwell County. Whitmer's manuscript history of the 1830s Church of Christ, called "The Book of John Whitmer," has provided scholars and students with important insights into the early life of the faith.

This biographical exploration of John's life is also intended to supplement established understandings of the activities of early sojourners of the Mormon movement. Each participant experienced the story differently. This work provides a perspective upon how an individual, such as John Whitmer, as well as his extended family, experienced the development of early Mormonism. It is also offers a perspective of the continuing influence Mormonism had upon the lives of the Whitmer clan.

Just as biography is a reflection of all of human experience, it is also the particular as experienced by a unique individual. Though discovering John's particular experiences has proven harder than I imagined and John, as a person, has proven exceptionally elusive, his life is a unique window into the experience of early Mormonism.

I was privileged to oversee the stewardship of and provide for the care of several original John Whitmer documents while serving as the Community of Christ archivist (1988–2009). While seeking to better understand these documents, my interest in John's life was piqued. More than this, because of some similar aspects of our roles within the movement, I began to identify with John.

5. For a discussion of this dynamic at work, see Gaddis, *Landscape of History*, 139.
6. Harold Barchers of Richmond, Missouri, a descendant of Jacob Whitmer, states that John's middle name was "David" but does not identify the source of this information. Barchers, "The Descendants and History of the Peter Whitmer Family," 42.

My interest intensified when I learned of plans in 1995 to repub-
lish John Whitmer's manuscript history, The Book of John Whitmer, by
scholar Bruce N. Westergren, through Signature Books. I had at that point
already completed my own transcription of Whitmer's manuscript history,
endeavoring to correct it to the original.

When asked to prepare a review of Westergren's book for the *John
Whitmer Historical Association Journal*, I am afraid I used the occasion to
vent a bit. By this point, I had already come to respect John Whitmer as a
man of integrity. The presentation of the Westergren book, itself, perhaps
more than the conscious efforts of Bruce as the author, seemed to challenge my emerging perception of John Whitmer. I wrote:

> *From Historian to Dissident* attempts to emphasize Whitmer's per-
> ceived rebellious nature. As such, it seeks to capitalize on what has
> become a somewhat popular theme in recent years. The book strives to
> create a somber mood. The selection of title, the colors and illustration
> for the cover, the manufacture and insertion of chapter headings in the
> text, and choice of excerpts displayed on the back cover, all reinforce
> this theme. Whether this was the author's or the publisher's intent
> is unclear. For inside the covers, the book contains little to support
> this view. The effort to cast Whitmer's writings as a dissenting work
> appears more a reflection of what might be politely described as bias.
> Except for the presence of occasional comments to this effect within
> the author's annotations, an outside reader, not knowing the ortho-
> dox LDS view, might very likely conclude that rather than Whitmer
> leaving the church, the church left Whitmer. This bias implies that
> Whitmer both initiated and proved to be the ultimate cause of this
> unfortunate split. I believe the judgment of history remains open as
> to whether Whitmer chose a dissenting role or whether it was forced
> upon him and his family.[7]

I wrote this statement out of a growing awareness that participants
in the early Mormon movement have a tendency to be treated unequally by
the larger church historical community. I perceived that, had Westergren
perhaps revealed more of John Whitmer the man, scholars and readers
could strip away such bias. Of Westergren's documentary efforts I wrote:

---

7.   Romig, review of *From Historian to Dissident*, 145. To read the complete review, see ap-
     pendix X in this book.

This edition makes available a reasonably careful rediscovery of the original wordings of the "Book of John Whitmer." And each new generation of scholars is benefited in making the effort to reclaim and reinterpret such standard works, as with new eyes. Given that, this new "Book of John Whitmer" is somewhat disappointing. It seems an opportunity was missed. Republication could have provided an occasion for a thoughtful reevaluation of the person of John Whitmer and his Mormon experience. Apparently this was not the author's purpose. Thus far there has been no truly novel effort to explore the life of John Whitmer. Treatment of the "essential Whitmer" is sketchy at best. In this vein, this book provides little more than a dull glaze as context for Whitmer's life. Despite evidence of meticulous work, I sense that the author never really got to know John Whitmer, nor those he chronicled. Annotations draw heavily from other published reference works. One might also expect to see more revealed of the process by which the history was originally created.[8]

With this present effort to chronicle the life of John, my criticism has come full circle. Taking up my own challenge has proven more difficult than I expected. I now realize that despite my best efforts, John will remain largely hidden from history.

Regrettably, John's writings divulge far too little of the man himself, his interests, and his accomplishments. But, I feel that my efforts to pull back the shadowy covering will benefit readers to a degree. And, hopefully this work will encourage a wider perception of the various motivations that compelled individuals to participate in the early Mormon movement. This volume attempts to recapture the reality of John Whitmer's experience behind the familiar preconceptions, reconstructing what is known and making judicious guesses, where warranted, when the surprisingly numerous gaps in the historical record leave questions.

Today, John's primary source documents and writings about his life experiences are widely scattered. Community of Christ is fortunate to exercise stewardship and care over a significant representation of John's official writings. Items in the Community of Christ Archives in Independence, Missouri, include not only John's manuscript history that he himself named "The Book of John Whitmer," but also a number of manuscripts

8.   Romig, review of *From Historian to Dissident*, 144–45.

associated with Joseph Smith's Bible revision. When he separated from the Latter Day Saints in 1838, John retained possession of these official records and papers of the church.

The Community of Christ Archives also has a significant collection of Whitmer papers, primarily associated with David Whitmer and Richmond, Missouri, as well as copies of the Book of Commandments associated with the family and Whitmer family seer stones. In addition, the Community of Christ Archives also cares for copies of some significant visual materials relating to the John Whitmer family. Though now assigned as director of the Kirtland Temple Visitor Center, in Kirtland, Ohio, I continue to experience a profound sense of appreciation for the opportunity to be associated with the Community of Christ Archives as well as for the genuine support and encouragement of staff and administrators.

The Church History Library of The Church of Jesus Christ of Latter-day Saints in Salt Lake City, Utah, has also gathered an important collection of originals and copies of holograph letters, publications, administrative documents, and some personal materials, such as John Whitmer's family Bible. Its archive also maintains a significant collection of visual materials. I am deeply indebted to the LDS church, its professional staff, and its fine historical facilities for furnishing access to these important resources, including former church historian Marlin K. Jensen, assistant historian Rick E. Turley, Ronald O. Barney, Robin Jensen, Steven Sorensen, Ron D. Watt.

The L. Tom Perry Special Collections repository in the Harold B. Lee Library at Brigham Young University, Provo, Utah, also cares for a significant gathering of John Whitmer primary sources, including letters and John Whitmer's copy of the Book of Mormon. Again, Russ Taylor and the staff and facilities of this important repository have been essential in the process of reviewing and interpreting the historical reflection of John Whitmer.

I am also very appreciative of the professionalism and help received from Stan Larson, curator of manuscripts at the J. Willard Marriott Library, University of Utah. The Marriott cares for important holographs, such as the John Logan Traughber Papers, as well as many copies of Whitmer family-related documents.

The Huntington Library, in San Marino, California, has the important Oliver Cowdery letter book that establishes a significant context for the larger Whitmer family. The Huntington also has John Whitmer's Book of Commandments. I express my thanks to this unique facility for their persistent support of the wider historical and cultural endeavor.

My thanks also go to Lewis Crandall, of the Crandall Historical Printing Museum, Provo, Utah, for his invaluable and generous help with printing-related issues.

And, equally important, descendants of the Whitmers continue to play an important role in preserving and maintaining significant artifactual holdings. Most notable have been John Whitmer descendant Lorene Pollard; Jacob Whitmer descendant Harold Barchers and his wife, Kay; and Hiram Page descendant Bonnie Page Damon. Such a work as this could not be possible without their significant input and encouragement.

I also wish to express my thanks and appreciation to and for the many scholars and researchers who have explored in the past and who even now continue to explore the life of John Whitmer, the extended Whitmer clan, as well as related parts of the history of the extensive Mormon movement. Those making notable contributions through the years within the extended RLDS/Community of Christ context include: Barbara Bernauer, Alma Blair, Robert B. Flanders, Wayne Ham, John Hamer, Richard P. Howard, David Howlett, Henry K. Inouye Jr., Warren Jennings, Danny Jorgensen, Rachel Killebrew, Roger D. Launius, Lachlan Mackay, Mark McKiernan, Isleta Pement, William D. Russell, Paul M. Edwards, Mark Scherer, Heman C. Smith, Lee Updike, Barbara Walden, and Biloine Young.

From the LDS community, I recognize the influence of George Edward Anderson, Paul L. Anderson, Richard Lloyd Anderson, Valeen Tippetts Avery, Philip L. Barlow, Alexander L. Baugh, Susan Easton Black, Richard L. Bushman, Donald Q. Cannon, Todd M. Compton, Lyndon W. Cook, Jill Mulvey Derr, Ron Esplin, Scott H. Faulring, William G. Hartley, Richard Neitzel Holzapfel, Andrew Jenson, Richard L. Jensen, Dean C. Jessee, Clark V. Johnson, Steven Knecht, Glen M. Leonard, Robert J. Matthews, Linda King Newell, Max H Parkin, Larry C. Porter, Eric Paul Rogers, Bruce G. Stewart, Richard S. Van Wagoner, Bruce Westergren, and Lavina Fielding Anderson who did the major editing and indexing of this work.

I can in no way adequately express the importance of Lavina Fielding Anderson's encouragement and contribution to this project. I am thankful to be one of the many researchers and writers who have benefitted from Lavina's commitment to the encouragement of historical scholarship and publication.

Independent researchers include: R. Jean Addams; Harold D. Barchers; Helen Van Cleave Blankmeyer; Fred Collier; William and Annette Curtis; Cleora Dear; Mario S. De Pillis; Vivian Graybill; Stephen LeSueur; S. Reed Murdock; H. Michael Marquardt; Jeffrey S. O'Driscoll; Lorene E. Burdick Pollard and her son Roger Pollard; D. Michael Quinn; Michael S. Riggs; Jan Shipps; Alta Short; Dan Vogel, whose *Early Mormon Documents* series has been an invaluable aid; and Pearl G. Wilcox.

Without the model and example of such scholars, colleagues, and friends as these, I would not have been able to pursue this passion.

Thanks also to the John Whitmer Historical Association and the staff of its publishing imprint, John Whitmer Books. I am especially indebted to John Hamer and Mike Karpowicz who helped launch this endeavor, William D. Russell, Peter Judd, Jan Marshall, Erin B. Jennings Metcalfe, whose thorough knowledge of the Whitmers helped avoid many mistakes, and Vickie Cleverley Speek, final editor of this work.

And, of course, I am profoundly appreciative of the support I have received from my family, especially my wife, Anne, and daughter, Rene, who both helped with proofreading and chapter rewrites. They have been a source of endless encouragement.

John Whitmer, 1802–78

CHAPTER ONE

The Whitmer Family in Fayette

JOHN WHITMER WAS born into the second founding family of Mormonism. Despite their significant contributions to this movement, historically there has been little interest about the Whitmer family's origins. Contradictory opinions about John Whitmer's family heritage abound. The traditional Mormon history story encounters the Peter Whitmer Sr. family residing in the Harrisburg, Pennsylvania, area.[1] It was here, during the first decade of the nineteenth century, that John and Jacob Whitmer, later to become Book of Mormon witnesses, were born. Around 1808, Peter Whitmer Sr. and Mary Musselman resettled their young family in central New York, helping set the stage for the emergence of Mormonism.

Their origins seem equally unclear to members of the Whitmer family. Whitmer descendant Harold Barchers posits that John's father, Peter Whitmer Sr., was named after his father and grandfather, which made three men in a row named "Peter."[2]

Recently, there has been more curiosity about earlier generations of the Whitmer family and their Germanic ethnic heritage. Mormon-movement historian Dan Vogel observes that the Whitmer's "ancestry on both sides of the family was German or German speaking, and [members of] the family spoke with a German accent." Vogel suggests that John Whitmer's grandfather, named George Whitmer, was born in Prussia and George's father was born in Switzerland.[3] Though Vogel may be incorrect in identifying Peter Whitmer's father as George, it is more probable that Vogel's assertion is true that John Whitmer's paternal lineage may be traced to Switzerland.

1. *History of the LDS Church*, 1:48, 49 notes.

2. Barchers, "The Descendants and History of the Peter Whitmer Family," 14, 16.

3. Introduction, David Whitmer Collection, in Vogel, *Early Mormon Documents*, 5:9n1.

As Richard W. Davis, noted Mennonite researcher, explains, "The W[h]itmers ... and Musselmans all had their origin in Switzerland ... these families were exiled from Switzerland for their religious beliefs in the late 1600s."[4] Whitmer family researcher Erin Jennings Metcalfe has recently elaborated a thorough Whitmer genealogy, rooted in, and building upon the published findings of Richard Davis of Provo, Utah.[5] Jennings identifies John's grandfather as Christian Herr Witmer, born about 1747 in Lancaster County, Pennsylvania, and John's great-grandfather as Peter Wittmer, who was born around 1710–12.[6]

Since Erin's groundbreaking findings, a suggested lineage for Peter has further emerged, via Internet research, which connects Peter Wittmer to his father, Peter Hiestand Widmer (1659–?), of Richterswil, Zürich, Switzerland. In turn, Widmer's father was Heinrich Widmer (1630–?), descending from Jakob Widmer (1606–?), also both from Richterswil, Zürich.[7]

Immigrant Peter Wittmer (also Widmer and Witmer) arrived with a group of Mennonites and Amish in the Americas in 1744.[8] Peter apparently settled near distant relatives in Manor Township, Lancaster County, Pennsylvania.[9] Lancaster County is southeast of Harrisburg, Pennsylvania, along the Susquehanna River. Peter Wittmer became acquainted with

4. Richard W. Davis, e-mail to author, February 26, 2011.

5. Erin proposed this alternative family genealogy in her "The Whitmer Family Beliefs and Their Church of Christ," which built upon Davis, *Emigrants, Refugees, and Prisoners*, 2:421–22.

6. Erin describes Peter Wittmer as a cordwainer by profession and a dedicated Mennonite in "Whitmer Family Beliefs and Their Church of Christ," 26. A cordwainer, a common name for a shoemaker, works with cordovan leather. *Merriam–Webster's Collegiate Dictionary*, 11th ed., s.v. "cordwainer."

7. "Peter Widmer [Wittmer] tree," Geni, accessed July 2013, http://www.geni.com/people/Peter-Widmer/6000000001788681854.

8. Peter left Europe from Germany on the *Muscliffe Galley* and docked in Philadelphia on December 22, 1744. Rupp, *A Collection of Upwards of Thirty Thousand Names*, 173. Peter signed his name on the passenger list as Petter Wittmer with all "t's" uncrossed. Strassberger and Hinke, *Pennsylvania German Pioneers*, 2:379. However, Davis, *Emigrants, Refugees, and Prisoners*, 2:421, and others, including me, prefer "Peter."

9. Brackbill, "Family Data in Pennsylvania Land Patents," 94. Conestoga Manor was later divided, a land transaction also reported in Rupp, *History of Lancaster, Pennsylvania*, 132.

and married Elizabeth Herr Brubaker (ca. 1717–47), the widow of Hans Brubaker and a daughter of Isaac Herr and Elizabeth Lotscher Herr.[10] The couple had two children, Elizabeth and Christian. Christian was born around 1747. Christian's mother, Elizabeth, died shortly after Christian's birth in 1747. After Elizabeth's death, Peter married Magdalena Shellenberger (ca. 1732–55), a daughter of Ulrich Shellenberger.[11] This marriage occurred around 1749. Three children, Magdalena, Peter, and Mary were born from this union. Peter's wife, Magdalena, died around 1755, and Peter married his third wife, Catharina Brechbill Engle (ca. 1739–1807), a daughter of Ulrich Engle and Anna Brechbill.[12] Peter and Catharina had thirteen children.

Steven M. Nolt, assistant professor of history at Goshen College in Goshen, Indiana, finds a strong probability that Peter and his wives "were Mennonite church members. Judging by the names of their children's spouses and the names of their friends who witnessed their wills, the family at least had exclusively Mennonite social ties and connections.... The same goes for the next generations too."[13]

In February 1745, Peter Wittmer purchased 132 acres of land in Manor Township, Lancaster, from Jacob Brubaker,[14] and apparently settled down to farming. Peter was still living in Manor Township in 1792, when he died at age eighty. By his three wives, Peter Wittmer fathered eighteen children. Peter Wittmer's will, prepared November 20, 1784, lists seventeen of his eighteen children. It also names one grandson, Peter, the only child of his son, Christian, who had died in 1776 or 1777.[15] This Peter (Peter Whitmer Sr., hereinafter called Peter Sr.) is John Whitmer's father.

10. Best, "Martin Kendig's Swiss Relatives," 2–18, cited in Jennings, "Whitmer Family Beliefs and Their Church of Christ," 26.

11. McKellar, "Shellenbarger Family," cited in Jennings, "Whitmer Family Beliefs and Their Church of Christ," 27.

12. Brechbill, "History of the Old Order River Brethren," 12, cited in Jennings, "Whitmer Family Beliefs and Their Church of Christ," 27.

13. Steven M. Nolt, e-mail to Andrew Bolton, February 5, 2002, printout in my possession.

14. Brackbill, "Family Data in Pennsylvania Land Patents," 94; Rupp, *History of Lancaster, Pennsylvania*, 132.

15. Peter Wittmer will dated November 20, 1784, F–370, Wills, Lancaster County Archives, Lancaster County, Pennsylvania.

Very little is known about Peter Sr.'s father and John Whitmer's grandfather, Christian Witmer. It is known that in 1771, Christian Witmer married Barbara Ebersohl (1748–?), a daughter of Abraham Ebersohl and Barbara Detweiler Ebersohl. The couple apparently made their home near the Ebersohls in Donegal Township, Lancaster County, Pennsylvania, about fifteen miles from Christian's father.[16]

Donegal Township was named for Donegal, Ireland, by early Irish immigrants to the area. Here, on April 14, 1773, Christian and Barbara's only child, Peter (Sr.) (1773–1854) was born.[17] Erin Jennings Metcalfe suggests that Christian was highly spiritual and committed to God as manifested by his involvement in the formation of a group that would formally organize years later as the "Old Order River Brethren" in Donegal Township. Jacob Engle, a brother of Christian's stepmother Catherine (Catherina), was also a founding member of the "River Brethren" Mennonites. Jennings documents that Christian was associated with Engle, perhaps later in life, in an experiment with triune baptism, a practice at variance from the beliefs of rank-and-file Mennonites.[18] Jennings's research also places Christian as living near the Engles, close to Conoy Creek in what is today East Donegal Township, Lancaster, Pennsylvania. When Christian died in 1776 or 1777, Barbara married John Baughman. What happened to John and Barbara is not clear; but by 1792, Christian's son Peter Whitmer Sr. became the ward of Frederick Sweitzer,[19] about whom nothing is currently known. At that time, a young man was permitted to select his own guardian at age fourteen.[20]

16. Christian Witmer will dated February 14, 1776, and probated February 7, 1777, cited in Davis, *Emigrants, Refugees, and Prisoners*, 422.

17. Peter Sr. was born in Donegal Township, Lancaster County, Pennsylvania, according to Davis, *Emigrants, Refugees, and Prisoners*, 2:421–22. See also Wevodau, *Abstracts of Lancaster County, Pennsylvania, Orphans Court Records*, 93. Whitmer descendant Harold Barchers gives Peter Sr.'s birth information as April 14, 1773, at Harrisburg, Pennsylvania. Barchers, "The Descendants and History of the Peter Whitmer Family," 16.

18. Trine immersion means baptism three times in the names of the members of the Trinity. Jennings, "Whitmer Family Beliefs and Their Church of Christ," 30–31.

19. Frederick Sweitzer, guardian of Peter Whitmer Sr., Petition, Orphan Court Record, Court of Common Pleas for the County of Lancaster, December 11 and 31, 1792, and March 26, 1793, cited in Davis, *Emigrants, Refugees, and Prisoners*, 2:422.

20. Curry, "Frederick Schott," 10.

Peter Sr. grew to manhood in southeastern Pennsylvania during a period of great change on the American frontier. Lorene Pollard, a John Whitmer descendant, observed, "The British occupation of Philadelphia was scarcely a hundred miles away from the Whitmer home.... Valley Forge was even less than that."[21] Of course, in 1776, Peter Sr. would have been only three—ten when the Treaty of Paris ended hostilities on September 3, 1783. No details have survived about his childhood and youth.

In 1797, when Peter Sr. was twenty-four, he married nineteen-year-old Mary Musselman. Mary was born August 27, 1778, in Strasburg, Lancaster, Pennsylvania, and died January 1856.[22] Little is known about Mary's parents or family. Mary's father Jacob Musselman (1747–98) immigrated to the United States, arriving in Philadelphia, Pennsylvania, on the *Minerva*, on October 13, 1769.[23] Even less is known about his wife, Elizabeth. She apparently did not emigrate with Jacob, so they must have met and married in Pennsylvania. It has been suggested that Jacob Musselman initially settled with relatives in Lancaster County, Pennsylvania. Elizabeth may have also been raised in this area.

21. Pollard's statement in Pollard and Woods, *Whitmer Memoirs*, 5. According to David Whitmer, in an interview with an unidentified reporter, Peter served in the Revolutionary War, but since Peter was born in 1773, such service was impossible. David Whitmer, interview by the *Chicago Tribune*, December 15, 1885, in Cook, *David Whitmer Interviews*, 172.

22. Mary Musselman's birth location given as a result of original research by Erin Jennings Metcalfe, "Outline Descendant Report of Jacob Musselman," 1, unpublished, copy in my possession courtesy of Erin Jennings Metcalfe. It is a Whitmer family tradition that Mary was born in Strasburg, Germany. See Barchers, "The Descendants and History of the Peter Whitmer Family," 16. Harold Barchers indicates Mary Musselman was born in Germany and this appears to correlate with Peter Page family data, Richmond Township, 1880 census. At the time, Mary Musselman's daughter Catherine Whitmer Page was living with her son Peter Page. The census listed Catherine's age as seventy-three, her occupation as "keeping house," her birthplace as Pennsylvania, her father's birthplace also as Pennsylvania, and her mother's as Germany. Elsa appears as her middle name on "Peter Whitmer Sr.," *Wikipedia,* accessed September 15, 2007, http://en.wikipedia.org/wiki/Peter_Whitmer%2C_Sr. Mary Musselman's older sister, Elizabeth, was born September 30, 1775, and married Andrew Schenk, born November 13, 1777, in Millersville, Lancaster County, Pennsylvania. See Ancestry.com, accessed September 15, 2007, http://awt.ancestry.com/cgi-bin/igm.cgi?op=GET&db=familyhart&id=I349575.

23. Phelan, "Descendants of Christian Musselman," 17.

```
                        JakobWidmer
                          1606–?
                            |
                      Heinrich Widmer
                          1630–?
                            |
                  Peter Hiestand Widmer
                          1659–?
                            |
```

Elizabeth ══ (1) Petter   (2) ══ Magdalena   (3) ══ Catharina
Herr   Wittmer   Shellenberger   Brechbill
Brubaker   1710–92   1732–55   Engle
1717–47   ca. 1739–1807

3 children   *13 children*

Christian ══ (1) Barbara (2) ══ John   Elizabeth
Herr Witmer   Ebersohl   Baughman   Witmer
1747–77   1748–?   1745–?   1746–?

Peter ══ Mary
Whitmer Sr.   Musselman
1773–1854   1778–1856

Christian   John   Catherine   Nancy
Whitmer   Whitmer   Whitmer   Whitmer
1798–1835   1802–78   1807–80   1812–13

Jacob   David D.   Peter   Elizabeth
Whitmer   Whitmer   Whitmer Jr.   Ann
1800–56   1805–88   1809–36   Whitmer
                                                     1815–92

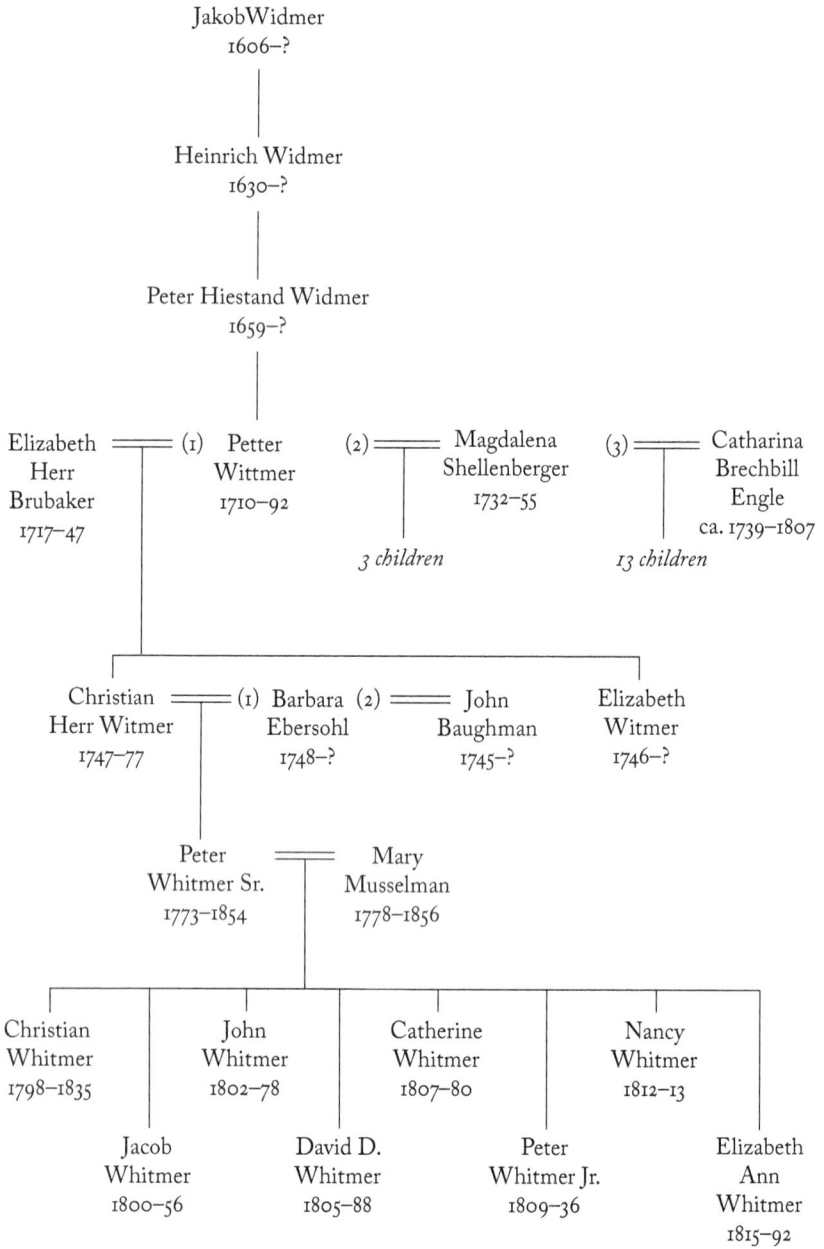

Fig. 1.1. Whitmer Family Ancestry

Jacob and Elizabeth's marriage date is not known, but the couple's first child, Christian Musselman, was born in 1770. He was followed by John in 1773, and Elizabeth, born September 30, 1775. Mary was born August 1778, in Strasburg, Lancaster County, Pennsylvania. Mary also had seven younger siblings. By the time of their births, Jacob and Elizabeth Musselman had relocated to Donegal Township, Lancaster, Pennsylvania. Mary's younger siblings were Jacob born in 1779, Henry born in 1782, Daniel born in 1784, David born in 1788, Michael born in 1790, and two girls, possibly named Catherine and Nancy, born in 1792 and 1794.[24]

Mary Musselman must have met and married Peter Whitmer Sr. while living in Donegal Township, Lancaster, Pennsylvania. However, early in their marriage they packed up and moved west. Peter Sr. apparently set out to make his own life in either York or Dauphin County in the vicinity of Harrisburg, all of which were part of a large fertile agricultural region in southcentral Pennsylvania along the Susquehanna River. Both York and Dauphin Counties were formed from a part of what had been Lancaster County. York was created on August 19, 1749, and was named either for the Duke of York, an early patron of the Penn family, or for the city and shire of York in England. Dauphin County was created on March 4, 1785, and "was named after Louis-Joseph, Dauphin of France, the first son of Louis XVI."[25] Peter Sr.'s ancestors had made their homes in Lancaster County before it was subdivided. David Whitmer's family Bible sheds no light on Peter Sr.'s birth place but documents the birth of John Whitmer and several of his siblings.[26]

The young family may have been attracted to the area by the presence of distant relatives. Census records indicate that both Whitmers and Musselmans lived in York County during this period. Peter Sr.'s uncle, Da-

---

24. Metcalfe, "Outline Descendant Report of Jacob Musselman," 1.

25. "Dauphin County, Pennsylvania," *Wikipedia*, accessed January 20, 2008, http://en.wikipedia.org/wiki/Dauphin_County,_Pennsylvania. "Dauphin," a French title, signifies the heir apparent to the throne.

26. David Whitmer, Bible, family record, in the interests of simplicity, in footnotes I will consistently cite this repository as CofC Archives; see also Journal History, introduction, 26. This family Bible should not be confused with the Whitmer Family Bible, in which the births of most of Peter and Mary's children are listed, or with John Whitmer's family Bible. See bibliography.

vid Engle Whitmer, was a Mennonite minister in Spring Garden Township, York County, Pennsylvania, during this period.[27]

Five of Peter and Mary's eight children were apparently born in York County across the Susquehanna River from Harrisburg. Christian, their eldest, was born January 18, 1798,[28] followed by Jacob in 1800. The family was clearly living in York County in 1802, when John, their third child, was born on August 27, 1802.[29] Also born during this period, apparently closer to Harrisburg, were two additional siblings: David, on January 7, 1805, and Catharine, on April 22, 1807.

David Whitmer's family Bible, containing birth information for the Peter and Mary (Musselman) Whitmer family. Courtesy of Community of Christ Archives.

Almost all sources agree that the Whitmer heritage, like the Musselmans, was "Pennsylvania Dutch." The "Wittmer" surname is common among those of German ancestry throughout Pennsylvania, and the Susquehanna River Valley in the Harrisburg region is still predominantly Mennonite, making a strong circumstantial case that Peter Sr. and Mary were cultural Mennonites, as well as their parents. They had Mennonite relatives and social ties. Richard W. Davis, webmaster of Mennosearch.com, observed, "It is clear that both Peter Whitmer Sr. and his wife Mary Musselman

27. Gibson, *Biographical History of York County, Pennsylvania*, 194.

28. The name is given as Christopher in the Whitmer Family Bible (1851–1914), but all records after he became an adult use the name Christian.

29. John Whitmer family Bible, MS 13505 and Whitmer Family Bible, CofC Archives. John was born across the river from Harrisburg in York County, rather than in Dauphin County, Pennsylvania, according to the John Whitmer family Bible.

were closely associated with Mennonites in their early years."[30] They were influenced by Mennonite cultural values, probably including a high commitment to religious values and an aversion to the use of force in conflict resolution.[31]

According to Lorene Pollard, Peter Sr. "worked as a 'pathfinder' in Pennsylvania and New York ... trying to find better trails and roads.... Ultimately, these travels took him to Seneca County, New York. Grandfather Peter noticed that crops grew more abundantly there above the Five Fingers Lakes area. They called it 'black dirt land.' Fruit trees were a great crop for the area as well, so in 1809 he moved his family north to New York."[32]

Although no details of their journey have survived, a travel narrative of Andrew Schott, a Whitmer neighbor, describes the route he traveled in 1805 from Derry Township, Dauphin County, Pennsylvania, to Fayette a couple of years before the Whitmers. During the summer, the Schotts traveled up the Susquehanna River by water and on foot, taking about six weeks. Members of the Schott family, and perhaps the Whitmers, may have been motivated to leave the Harrisburg area of Pennsylvania because of an outbreak of a deadly fever.[33]

The Whitmer Family Bible does not identify Peter Jr.'s birthplace, but it seems likely that the family was already in New York by the time he was born on September 27, 1809. The last of the eight children were daughters: Nancy, born December 24, 1812 (she lived less than six months), and Elizabeth Ann, born January 22, 1815.[34]

---

30. Richard W. Davis, webmaster of http://www.mennosearch.com, e-mail to author, February 26, 2011.

31. Nolt, e-mail to Andrew Bolton, February 5, 2002.

32. Pollard and Woods, *Whitmer Memoirs*, 5.

33. "Andrew Schott, a Pioneer," undated clipping from unidentified newspaper in scrapbook, "Index Rerum," Waterloo Library and Historical Society, Waterloo, New York, quoted in Porter, "A Study of the Origins," 226. See also, Curry, "Frederick Schott," 11.

34. Nancy Whitmer's birth and death dates are December 24, 1812, and April 19, 1813, Whitmer Family Bible. According to Curtis, "Whitmer Family," 7–11, a possible youngest son, Dan Whitmer, was reportedly born January 1, 1817, and died in 1847, but his record does not appear in the Whitmer Family Bible. More likely, this child is Daniel E. Whitmer, son of Jacob Whitmer and Elizabeth Schott Whitmer, born January 7, 1847, in Richmond, Ray County, Missouri. He died January 7, 1877. "Glory's

John was about six at the time of this move. The family settled "at a point midway between the northern extremities of Lakes Cayuga and Seneca, two miles from Waterloo, New York, seven miles from Geneva, and twenty-seven miles from Palmyra."[35] This area was originally part of Washington Township, Seneca County, New York, and was renamed Fayette on April 6, 1808.[36] This location was then a well-populated concentration of adjacent farms. Almost certainly the Whitmers fit comfortably into their new neighborhood, as Fayette's inhabitants were principally of German extraction from Pennsylvania.[37] The Whitmers settled in the area by 1809, and Peter Sr. appears in the 1810 census.[38]

The family was in the area for a decade before they finally acquired their own land in April 1819.[39] Larry C. Porter of Brigham Young University's history department suggests that "the family entered into a purchase agreement and began to work the land where the present Whitmer farm is located."[40] This farm was located on a beautiful elevation, the southeast corner of Military Lot Number 13 in Fayette Township.[41] As they could afford it, they picked up neighboring parcels. Between 1819 and 1827, Peter Sr. amassed one hundred acres of farm land in four installment purchases.[42] An 1824 local gazetteer describes the area as "having the advantages of

---

Family Tree," *Rootsweb*, accessed September 10, 2007, http://worldconnect.genealogy. rootsweb.com/cgi-bin/igm.cgi?op=AHN&db=glory43&id=I1893.

35. David Whitmer, "Mormonism: Authentic Account," 197–99; reprint of interview, *Kansas City Journal*, June 5, 1881, 197. Since the *Herald* has been variously titled the *True Latter Day Saints' Herald* (January 1860–December 1876), the *Saints' Herald* (January 1, 1877–May 1972), *Saints Herald* (June 1972–March 2001) and *Herald* (April 2001–), in the interests of simplicity, I will consistently cite this periodical as *Herald*.

36. Porter, "A Study of the Origins," 224, 225.

37. Spafford, *Gazetteer of the State of New York* (1813), 171.

38. David Whitmer reported that the family's move to New York occurred in 1809. David Whitmer, interview by the *Kansas City Daily Journal*, June 5, 1881; 1810 Census, Fayette Township, Seneca County, New York.

39. Porter, "A Study of the Origins," appendix F: "Land Records of the Peter Whitmer, Sr., Farm," 367–70.

40. Ibid., 227.

41. Willers Jr., *Centennial Historical Sketch of the Town of Fayette*, 47.

42. Seneca County, New York, Clerk's Office, Deed Record Books, M:430, Q:134, R:124, S:567, cited in Porter, "A Study of the Origins," 367–70.

good streams and lake navigation. The surface of this Town is but moderately uneven, or quite level, the lands are ... very productive. Gypsum and Limestone are known to abound."[43]

The Whitmers' economic circumstances seem to have been modest. David later remembered that their first cabin, constructed by Peter Sr., was "a primitive and poorly designed structure."[44] The family also hand-dug a well in the yard.[45] However, as the family prospered, they built a larger log house nearby, probably of square-hewn logs with chinking between. The house was apparently twenty feet square and a story and a half. There were two rooms on the first floor and one or two rooms upstairs under a slanting clapboard or shingle roof.[46] Dale Berge, assistant professor of archaeology and anthropology at Brigham Young University, provided an imaginative reconstruction of its interior:

> The floor would be made of hand-hewn lumber. Overhead would be cross beams and rafters, hand-sawn roof boards covered with either a split-shingle roof or bark roof. There would be an open fireplace with a big pole and trammel, while alongside was probably a bake-oven. The thick log wall would most likely be plastered with mud to keep out the cold.
>
> Furniture and equipment which adorned the cabin might consist of wooden hooks, from which were suspended flint lock rifles, a shot gun and a musket. Along with these weapons there would be shot power-horn, bullet-pouch, and shot bag. Shelves would contain plates and platters and cups of pewter, and pottery of various types. In a corner there would be a wooden water-bucket with a gourd for drinking water. In the fireplace would hang iron pots and kettles for

---

43. Spafford, *A Gazetteer of the State of New York* (1824), 171, cited in Porter, "A Study of the Origins," 224.

44. David Whitmer, interview by the *Chicago Tribune*, December 15, 1885, in Cook, *David Whitmer Interviews*, 173; also Orson Pratt, 29 January 1860, *Journal of Discourses*, 7:372, cited in Porter, "A Study of the Origins," 227.

45. Jenson, journal, 2 October 1888, cited in Grant, "Peter Whitmer's Log House," 349.

46. Grant, "Peter Whitmer's Log House," 365; Anderson, "The House Where the Church Was Organized," 19. A man named Webster, who lived on the farm until the 1920s, remembered the log house's location because his father, born in 1836, pointed out the site to Webster. In the 1970s, the younger Webster helped Porter locate the house's exact site. Porter, untitled presentation, 2006.

Peter and Mary Whitmer home (reconstruction) in Fayette, Seneca County, New York. Photograph ca. 2010, courtesy of Ron Romig.

cooking. Also, bake kettles, skillets and spiders, a gridiron, a toasting iron, ladles, skimmers, a toasting fork, fire dogs or andirons, and a heavy shovel and tongs would be present. There might be a wooden bread trough for kneading bread dough, along with a braided straw bread-basket. In another part of the house there would be a flax wheel and hatchel, and perhaps bed-warming pans. From the beams there might hang strings of dried apples, pumpkins, or other foods stuffs.[47]

Over the years, fields were cleared, fences built and a complement of requisite outbuildings constructed.

Peter Sr. enjoyed a local reputation as "a worthy and industrious citizen,"[48] John's brother David characterized their father as "a hard working, God-fearing man ... a strict Presbyterian ... [who] brought his chil-

---

47. Berge, "Archaeology at the Peter Whitmer Farm, Seneca County, New York," 200–201.

48. Willers Jr., *Centennial Historical Sketch of the Town of Fayette*, 49.

dren up with rigid sectarian discipline."[49] Peter Sr. was elected overseer of district highways in 1826 and 1827 and also served as a trustee of the local school.[50]

The Peter Whitmer Sr. family remained close, almost clannish in nature. The five sons helped their father work his farm until they arrived at the age of manhood, their combined efforts producing an adequate, if not affluent livelihood. Each apparently received some education, although it is less clear whether the daughters were also schooled.[51] Christian and Jacob evidently also received some specialized training in shoemaking or served an apprenticeship, since that was their trade as adults.[52] Peter Jr. was a tailor.[53]

The family was religiously inclined, and several of them, including Peter Sr., were for a time members of the German-speaking Christ's Church, a Reformed German church that met in Bearytown, in the Fayette neighborhood.[54] Pastor Diedrich Willers Sr. documents the Whitmer family's participation in his congregation.[55] Willers described Peter Sr. as "a quiet, unpretending, and apparently honest, candid, and simple-minded

---

49. "Presbyterian" probably indicated having an organizational structure and polity derived from the larger Presbyterian tradition, not a formal congregation. David Whitmer, interview by the *Chicago Tribune*, December 15, 1885, reprinted in Cook, *David Whitmer Interviews*, 172.

50. Anderson, "Five Who Handled the Plates," 39.

51. John J. Snyder to Paul Hanson, 13 January 1923.

52. *History of Ray County, Missouri*, 529. In Jackson County, Missouri, Christian earned his livelihood making shoes and farming. Harold Barchers, a descendant of Jacob Whitmer, recalled that Christian's surviving brother Jacob later operated a shoe shop on South Street in Richmond, Missouri. Barchers, untitled presentation.

53. According to Alexander W. Doniphan, interview by the *Kansas City Daily Journal*, June 12, 1881, cited in Anderson, "Five Who Handled the Plates," 40, Peter Whitmer Jr. was an accomplished tailor who opened his own shop in Independence in 1831. Doniphan was one of his clients.

54. Christ's Church was located in nearby Bearytown, Fayette, Seneca County. *Manual of the Churches of Seneca County*, 102; see also Buckley, *Diedrich Willers [Jr.]: Local Historian of the Centennial Years 1879–1904*, 89, quoted in Backman, *Eyewitness Accounts of the Restoration*, 134n6.

55. Willers [Jr.], "Pennsylvania German Settlers Fayette," in *Centennial Historical Sketch of Fayette, Seneca County, New York, 1800–1900*, 49, 150–52.

man."[56] On April 5–7, 1822, three of Peter's and Mary's children—Christian, Jacob, and John—asked for instruction in and communion with Christ's Church. Reverend Willers noted their membership in his ledger: "Johannas [John], Christian, and Jacob Whittmer [*sic*] were received into communion." Willers ledger notes: "At my first confirmation services of a class after instruction in the Heidlberg [Heidelberg] Catechism, I find among the names of the thirty-eight young persons then confirmed by me those of John Whitmer, Christian Whitmer, and Jacob Whitmer. My recollection is that I baptized one or more of the Whitmer family as adults, according to the custom of the Reformed Church."[57] At some point, the Whitmers also attended a second Reformed church organized about a mile and a half from their home at West Fayette, in 1811.[58]

The German Reformed movement, like the Mennonites, had its origins in the Protestant Reformation, principally reflecting the theology of Ulrich Zwingli. Zwingli's ideas provided the grist for the development of most of the strict and radical forms of Protestantism. Willers, affiliated with the German Reformed Synod of the United States, started his term as pastor of Christ's Church in April 1821.[59]

As a young man, Christian, being recognized as a natural leader, was commissioned as an officer in the 102nd New York Militia in 1825 and served as Fayette Township constable in 1828–29 when he would have been thirty or thirty-one.[60] On February 2, 1825, at the age of twenty-eight, he

56. Diedrich Willers Sr. to Ellen E. Dickinson, 19 January 1882, in Vogel, *Early Mormon Documents*, 5:282; Willers Jr., *Centennial Historical Sketch of the Town of Fayette*, 49. Diedrich Willers Sr. was born in Germany and came to the United States after having served with the Hanoverian forces at the Battle of Waterloo. *Guide to the Willers Family Papers, 1820–1908*.

57. Diedrich Willers [Sr.] et al., "Ledger of the Reformed Church, Bearytown, Seneca County, New York," quoted in Porter, "A Study of the Origins," 228–29.

58. *Manual of the Churches of Seneca County*, 123, cited in Porter, "A Study of the Origins," 228.

59. Willers served as pastor of this church (Christ Reformed Congregation, Bearytown, Seneca County, New York) until January 1, 1882, when he resigned—a period of sixty years and eight months. Willers also preached at Zion's church to discourage others in the neighborhood from taking Mormonism seriously. Willers to Dickinson, 19 January 1882, in Vogel, *Early Mormon Documents*, 5:282–84.

60. Anderson, "Five Who Handled the Plates," 39.

married Anne Schott, the daughter of Frederick and Anna Schott, from the neighboring farm to the north.[61] Anne was born in 1800, in Derry Township, Lancaster (later Dauphin) County, Pennsylvania. Christian and Anne had no children.[62] Their first home was apparently near the Whitmer farm in Fayette.

Indeed, 1825 turned out to be a year of marriages for the family. On September 29, twenty-five-year-old Jacob married Elizabeth Schott (born in 1803, in Fayette, New York), Anne's younger sister. Eighteen-year-old Catharine, the oldest Whitmer daughter, married Hiram Page on November 10 in Fayette. Jacob and Elizabeth moved into the Whitmers' first log cabin, just across the yard from the newer one-and-a-half story log house.

David D. (no record spells out a middle name for him) Whitmer, the fourth son,

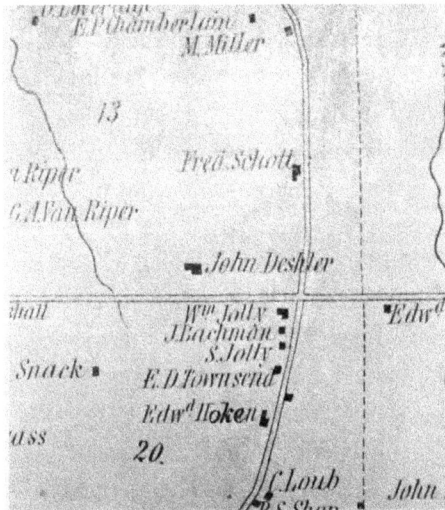

The location of the Peter and Mary (Musselman) Whitmer farm, with the Schott farm to the north and the Jolly home to the south.

grew up working on the family's hundred-acre farm. Like Christian, David also served in the military, becoming a sergeant in 1825 in Fayette's newly organized militia, the "Seneca Grenadiers."[63] Peter Jr., the youngest of the five sons, had the same farm-oriented youth and probably assumed he would follow a farmer's life. But before Peter Jr. turned twenty, his brother David traveled to Harmony, Pennsylvania, partly out of religious curiosity,

61. Anna Schott Hulet, Biography, accessed August 7, 2013, http://josephsmithpapers. org/person?name=Anna+Schott+Hulet; see also, Curry, "Frederick Schott." Dear, *Two Hundred Thirty-eight Years of the Whitmer Family*, 9.

62. Dear, *Two Hundred Thirty-eight Years of the Whitmer Family*, 9.

63. Barchers, "The Descendants and History of the Peter Whitmer Family," 58. The date of organizing the Grenadiers is given in the *Seneca Farmer* (Waterloo, NY) as March 23, 1825, cited in Richard L. Anderson, "Five Who Handled the Plates," 39.

and was accompanied on his return by a young school teacher named Oliver Hervy Pliny Cowdery,[64] and another intriguing guest—twenty-three-year-old Joseph Smith. The trio also brought along a partially translated manuscript of the Book of Mormon. This occurrence would change the course of the Whitmer family.

The two Whitmer sisters who survived to adulthood, Catharine and Elizabeth Ann, both became part of the Mormon story, not only through their parents and brothers, but by marriage to believing husbands. Catharine's husband, Hiram Page, was, according to Reverend Willers, "an itinerant botanic or root doctor." Willers, writing with obvious skepticism, presented Page as something of a charlatan and related that Catharine's father was "opposed to the marriage until convinced by Page that Miss Whitmer was consumptive, and that he alone, by the extraction of a certain root, the location of which he alone knew, could effect a cure.... The pretended cure was reputed to have been effected through Page's agency, and the marriage took place."[65] Four years later, Hiram became one of eleven Book of Mormon witnesses with his five brothers-in-law.[66]

Elizabeth Ann later married Oliver Cowdery, Joseph Smith's scribe and "second elder" in the church, on December 18, 1832, in Jackson County, Missouri. She was not quite seventeen, and Cowdery was twenty-six at the time of the marriage.[67] David's Whitmer's great-granddaughter Helen Van Cleave Blankmeyer described Elizabeth Ann Whitmer as "a tiny bird-like creature, sympathetic, practical, resourceful, and a fountain of fun."[68]

In the spring of 1829, at the time of Joseph and Oliver's arrival, the Whitmer family formed a close grouping. In the home were parents Peter Sr. and his wife, Mary; their eighteen-year-old unmarried hired girl, Sarah Conrad; and four of the Whitmer children: twenty-six-year-old John; twenty-four-year-old David; nineteen-year-old Peter Jr.; and fourteen-year-old Elizabeth. Jacob and Elizabeth were living just a few steps away

64. "Oliver Cowdery," *Geni*, accessed February 19, 2011, http://www.geni.com/people/Oliver-Cowdery/6000000001679175478.

65. Willers Sr. to Dickinson, 19 January 1882, in Vogel, *Early Mormon Documents*, 5:283.

66. Hiram Page was born in 1800 in Vermont. Curtis, "Whitmer Family," 10.

67. Richardson, "David Whitmer," 8. The marriage is documented in Jackson County, Missouri, Marriage Record, Book A, p. 44, October 14, 1832, Book 1:39.

68. Blankmeyer, *David Whitmer, Witness for God*, 8.

in the old Whitmer cabin. Christian and Anne may have been living with Frederick and Anna Schott one farm to the north. Hiram and Catharine, also, probably lived in the immediate neighborhood.[69]

In the spring of 1829, the family was drawn into some unusual excitement for their area. Peter Sr. was selected to serve as a juror in a sensational trial in which George Chapman, a local citizen, was tried for murder and convicted. The trial concluded April 16, 1829, and Chapman was hanged six weeks later, on May 28, 1829, before a crowd estimated at between fifteen thousand and twenty thousand people.[70] But such public events were rare. National news filtered into the area slowly and usually weeks after it happened. For the most part, the family moved within its own circle of farming work, weekly religious services, a wedding, the birth of a grandchild, or the cautious and long-planned-for addition of another piece of land to the family farm. The spring of 1829 would have been predictably busy for any farm family in the region. Great-great-granddaughter Lorene Pollard and her co-writer Rebecca Woods noted, "The country was just coming out of the long recession of the 1820s and a sense of more prosperous times was in the air."[71] Pollard further observed:

> Grandfather Peter ... of New York, taught all the family to plant potatoes way back in the early 1800s.... The garden was what many a family lived or died by, and there is a man's part to the garden, absolutely, especially when it comes to planting potatoes. Using a single shovel plow with a small white mule, a row would be laid off across the garden and then covered the same way. By plowing time, the potatoes would already have been cut into pieces with about three eyes on each piece.... Three pieces would be put into each potato hill, eighteen inches apart.... When the potato plants came up to about nine inches, once again the mule, and this time a double shovel plow appeared, and pronto, the weeds disappeared. Grandfather Peter of Waterloo, New York, taught all the family to plant potatoes way back in the early

69. My reconstruction of locations. In 1897, Oliver B. Huntington interviewed Sally Heller Conrad who later married David Edwin Bunnell. Huntington, "History of the Life of Oliver B. Huntington," 49–50. Sarah also affiliated with the new movement.

70. Becker, *A History of The Village of Waterloo*, 117–18, quoted in Porter, *A Study of The Church*, 93.

71. Pollard and Woods, *Whitmer Memoirs*, 9.

1800s. If Grandmother wasn't looking he would try some of the other rows and invariably some of the plants would be covered with soil. Everyone would then be called for to go through all the garden and gently uncover the delicate plants.[72]

But such domestic concerns would soon be pushed into the background by the arrival of Joseph Smith, a relative stranger with a strange tale and a strange book—mobilizing and redirecting the family's energies.

72. Ibid., 53.

CHAPTER TWO

Encountering Joseph Smith: June 1829

THE LARGER REGION that the Whitmers called home proved to be a hotbed of emerging and competing cultures. Religious denominations, sects, and seekers associated, resulting in a tumble of ideas and interests. From this mix, a new religion was born in western New York, founded by a youthful farmer named Joseph Smith. The Whitmers came to be key participants in a group that enthusiasts described as "True Followers of Christ," a church that disbelievers derisively called "Mormon" or "Mormonite" after its most distinctive feature, a volume of new scripture.[1]

With the exception of a young teacher named Oliver Cowdery, as Mormon researcher Lyndon Cook notes, the original "body of believers essentially consisted only of three extended families—the Smiths, the Whitmers, and the Joseph Knights of Colesville, Broome County, New York. And, although Joseph Smith was accorded special recognition as leader, the group was initially, in its social and political attitudes, remarkably homogeneous, communal, and democratic."[2]

How and why did the Whitmers, and especially John, become involved in the Restoration story? John apparently first came into contact with Joseph Smith Jr. and the early Restoration through his brother David, and friend Oliver Cowdery.

David had apparently first met Oliver on a business trip to Palmyra in 1828. The business, of an unspecified nature, was an errand he was performing for "My Brother [Christian who] was Sheriff of our county in

---

1. Diedrich Willers Sr. to Reverend Brethren, 1830, in Vogel, *Early Mormon Documents*, 5:277.

2. Cook, *David Whitmer Interviews*, xv.

Western New York. He got crippled and had business in the neighborhood of where the Smiths lived and sent me to attend to it, while transacting the business I first heard of the Smiths, and the translation."[3] In a different, 1881 interview, he identifies Cowdery as his contact: "A great many people in the neighborhood were talking about the finding of certain golden plates by one Joseph Smith, Jr., a young man of that neighborhood. Cowdery and I, as well as others, talked about the matter, but at that time I paid but little attention to it, supposing it to be only the idle gossip of the neighborhood. Cowdery said he was acquainted with the Smith family, and he believed there must be some truth in the story of the plates, and that he intended to investigate the matter."[4]

According to Stanley Gunn, an Oliver Cowdery biographer, "Talk upon the subject had been so free that there is little doubt but that David Whitmer was led into the discussions at first by mere idle curiosity."[5] However, several months later, Cowdery told the Whitmer family that he was going to Harmony, Pennsylvania, "whither Joseph Smith had gone with the plates on account of persecutions of his neighbors—and see him about the matter."[6] Gunn states that Cowdery "purposely routed to take him through the town of Fayette in order that he might call upon the Whitmer family. David, upon hearing of Oliver's purpose, obtained a promise from him (Oliver) that after he had visited the Prophet, he would write the Whitmers in regards to his impression of the truth or untruth of Joseph Smith's having the authentic ancient records."[7]

Cowdery, who had been teaching school and boarding with the Smith family during the winter of 1828–29 left Palmyra on April 5, 1829, with Joseph's younger brother, Samuel Harrison Smith (March 13, 1808–July 30, 1844). The two apparently walked to Harmony in northeastern Pennsylvania.[8]

3.   David Whitmer, quoted in Kimball, "Missouri Mormon Manuscripts," 485.

4.   David Whitmer, "Mormonism: Authentic Account," 197.

5.   Gunn, *Oliver Cowdery*, 33.

6.   David Whitmer, "Mormonism: Authentic Account," 197.

7.   Gunn, *Oliver Cowdery*, 33.

8.   Anderson, *Lucy's Book*, 437–38.

According to Linda King Newell and Valeen Tippetts Avery, "Cowdery was twenty-two. About five feet, five inches tall, he carried his slight frame with a loose easy walk. His Roman nose gave balance to his clean-shaven face with its prominent lower jaw. He had dark brown eyes, a high forehead, and a quick smile."[9]

Oliver was immediately struck with Joseph, persuaded that he was, in fact, in possession of the promised record, and promptly agreed to serve as Joseph's scribe, thus assisting with the translation. As promised, Oliver reported to David: "Joseph had told him his (Oliver's) secret thoughts, and all he had meditated about going to see him, which no man on earth knew."[10]

Cowdery was among the first scribes to help Smith prepare his religious narrative. Emma and one of her brothers, Reuben, were the first scribes, but only temporarily.[11]

Becoming an intimate of the Smith family and their son Joseph Jr., beginning about 1826, Martin Harris, a resident of Palmyra, New York, also participated in many of the founding events of Mormonism. About forty-five at the time, Harris was a well-to-do farmer and respected resident in Palmyra. Harris stood about five feet, eight inches tall and had a light complexion with brown hair and blue eyes. During much of his life, Martin sported a Greek-style beard fringing the edge of his chin.

Harris was naturally curious when Joseph Smith mentioned visits from angelic beings. Martin's interest peaked when Smith claimed to have recovered ancient American artifacts from a neighboring hill. Principal among these was a book of hieroglyphics said to be inscribed on plates having the appearance of gold. Harris financially assisted Joseph and his wife, Emma Hale Smith, to relocate from Palmyra to Harmony, Pennsylvania, where Emma's family lived. Although the Hales were dubious about Joseph's account of the Book of Mormon, and assumed that he would settle down to farming, Joseph had other plans. He lived at Harmony, ex-

---

9. Newell and Avery, *Mormon Enigma*, 28.

10. Jenson, *Latter-day Saint Biographical Encyclopedia*, 1:267.

11. Joseph Smith III wrote, "Mrs. Emma Bidamon, formerly Emma Smith nee Hale ... informed me that she ... wrote for Joseph Smith during the work of translation, as did also Reuben Hale, her brother, and O. Cowdery." Joseph Smith III to James T. Cobb, 14 February 1879.

cept for brief trips back to Palmyra, from December 1827 to May 1830, a period during which much of what was later published as the Book of Mormon emerged.

Harris came to visit in the spring of 1828 and was Joseph's primary scribe from April 12 through June 14, 1828. By that point, Smith's manuscript had more than 116 holograph pages. Wishing to share this accomplishment with his wife and friends, Harris persuaded Joseph Smith to allow him to take the document to Palmyra. To Joseph's great distress, the manuscript disappeared. It has been reported that Lucy Harris feared Martin's involvement would lead to their financial ruin, so she burned the pages in their stove one night.[12] After this setback, which occurred simultaneously with the difficult birth and subsequent death of Joseph and Emma's first child, Joseph was unable to continue. He said that the means of translation were taken from him, and, almost certainly, the remorse and grief at the double loss were equally paralyzing.

When the project picked up again in the fall of 1829, Emma began writing a second time for her husband. But Joseph informed his mother Lucy that "the Lord would send ... a scribe."[13] That scribe was Oliver Cowdery, who arrived with young Samuel H. Smith in the spring of 1829. Twenty-one-year-old Samuel helped Joseph "with the tilling and planting,"[14] but probably did most of it himself, since Oliver and Joseph almost immediately began working full time on the manuscript.

According to David Whitmer's later account, Oliver soon wrote him a second letter "in which he gave me a few lines of what they had translated, and he assured me that he knew of a certainty that he [Smith] had a record of a people that inhabited this continent, and that the plates they were translating gave a complete history of these people ... and ... he [Cowdery] had revealed knowledge concerning the truth of them."[15] David showed Oliver's letters to his parents, brothers, and sisters; and "the news

12. According to Pomeroy Tucker (1802–70), an acquaintance of the Harris family, Lucy Harris took the manuscript while Martin was asleep and burned it. Tucker, *Origin, Rise and Progress of Mormonism*, 46.

13. Anderson, *Lucy's Book*, 428.

14. Newell and Avery, *Mormon Enigma*, 28.

15. David Whitmer, interview by the *Kansas City Journal*, June 1, 1881; also his "Mormonism: Authentic Account," 197–98.

created no small stir with the Whitmers, as the entire family, sensing the magnitude of such a discovery, became anxious to learn more."[16]

On May 15, 1829, Joseph and Oliver, then about halfway through the Book of Mormon, encountered in the narrative the prophet Alma's organization of a church in which baptism figured prominently. Both were familiar with the rite, not only from the Bible, but also from the common practice of contemporary churches. It is believed that neither young man had been previously baptized. So, they decided to pray about it. As later reported, this led to a divine encounter. This was not Oliver's first experience with prayer, but it was his first encounter with a messenger from heaven, perhaps in the form of a shared open vision. Both of them later described the appearance of John the Baptist, who invested them with heavenly authority and instructed them to baptize one another.[17] Samuel Smith also became convicted of the truth of their divine encounter and the necessity for his own baptism. On May 15, Oliver officiated in this ordinance, making Samuel the third person to be baptized, even though no church existed as yet.[18]

As David recalled, the Whitmers then received a third letter from Oliver "telling me to come down into Pennsylvania and bring him and Joseph to my father's house, giving as a reason therefore that they had received a commandment from God to that effect."[19] This letter coincided with David's supernatural speed in preparing his fields—even the assistance of angels—as reported in Lucy Mack Smith's narration of the account.[20]

16. Pollard and Woods, *Whitmer Memoirs,* 9.

17. Oliver Cowdery to W. W. Phelps, 7 September 1834, p. 15. A decade later, in 1839, an official account of Joseph and Oliver's May 1829 experience was prepared under Joseph Smith's direction. Manuscript History, Book A–1:17–18. See Jessee, *Papers of Joseph Smith,* 1:290–91.

18. *History of the LDS Church,* 1:39–41, 44.

19. Whitmer, "Mormonism: Authentic Account," 198.

20. Lucy Mack Smith reported: "One morning ... [Joseph] was commanded to write a letter to one David Whitmer, who lived in Waterloo. This man Joseph had never seen, but he was instructed to say to him that he must come with his team immediately, in order to convey Joseph and Oliver back to his house, that they might remain with him there until the translation should be completed, as an evil-designing people were seeking to take away Joseph's life in order to prevent the work of God from going forth among the world. The letter was written and delivered, and Mr. Whitmer showed it

John Whitmer would have known about the letters and the miracles, but he left no record or description, then or later. In any case, Peter Sr. and Mary's interest was sufficiently stirred to urge David to fulfill the request.

Nor did the supernatural events cease. According to Lucy Mack Smith's later account, David "was soon on his way and in 2 days he arrived

---

to his father, mother, sisters, and brothers, asking their advice as to what it would be best for him to do. His father said, 'Why, David, you know you have sowed as much wheat as you can harrow in tomorrow and the next day, and then you have a quantity of plaster of paris to spread that is much needed on your land. You cannot go unless you get an evidence from God that it is very necessary.' This suggestion pleased David, and he asked the Lord for a testimony that it was his will that he should go. He was told by the voice of the Spirit to harrow in his wheat, and then go straightway to Pennsylvania. The next morning David went to the field and found that he had two heavy days' work before him. He then asked the Lord to enable him to do this work sooner than the same work had ever been done on the farm before—and he would receive it as an evidence that it was God's will that he should do all in his power to assist Joseph Smith in the work in which he was engaged. He then fastened his horses to the harrow, and instead of dividing the field into what is, by farmers, usually termed bands, he drove round the whole of it, continuing thus till noon, when, on stopping for dinner, he looked around, and discovered to his surprise that he had harrowed in full half, the wheat. After dinner he again went on as before, and by evening he finished the whole two days' work. When he informed his father of the fact, his father could not believe it till he examined for himself and ascertained that it was actually true. 'Well,' said his father, 'there must be some overruling power in this thing, and I think you had better go as soon as you get your plaster of paris sown and bring up the man with his scribe.' To this also David agreed. The next morning, as soon as breakfast was over, he took the half-bushel measure under his arm and went out to the place where he supposed the plaster to be, as he knew exactly where he had left it twenty-four hours earlier. But when he came to look for it, behold, it had entirely disappeared! Every vestige of it was gone from the spot where he left it. He ran to his sister's house a few yards distant and inquired if she knew what had become of it.' 'Why?' she said, in surprise. 'Was it not all spread yesterday?' 'Not to my knowledge,' answered David. 'I am astonished at that,' replied his sister, 'for the children came to me in the forenoon and begged of me to go out and see the men sow plaster in the field, saying that they never saw anybody sow plaster so fast in their lives. I accordingly went and saw three men at work in the field, as the children said, but, supposing that you had hired some help on account of your hurry, I went immediately into the house and gave the subject no further attention.' David made considerable inquiry in regard to the matter, both among his relatives and neighbors, but was not able to learn who had done it. However, the family were [*sic*] convinced that there was an exertion of supernatural power connected with this strange occurrence." Proctor and Proctor, *History of Joseph Smith by His Mother*, 192–94.

there [in Harmony] without injuring his horses in the least although the distance was 135 miles."[21]

Joseph Smith's account of this experience omits Oliver's crucial role in providing the introduction and instead attributes the invitation to David Whitmer's interest:

> [In June 1829,] David Whitmer came to the place where we were residing, and brought with him a two horse waggon [*sic*], for the purpose of having us accompany him to his father's place and there remain until we should finish the work. He proposed that we should have our board free of charge, and the assistence [*sic*] of one of his brothers to write for me, as [and] also his own assistance when convenient. Having much need of such timely aid in an undertaking so arduous, and being informed that the people of the neighborhood were anxiously awaiting the opportunity to enquire into these things, we accepted the invitation.[22]

In an 1884 interview, David recounted many impressive details that confirmed his positive first impression of the young seer:

> Oliver told me they knew just when I started, where I put up at night and even the name on the sign board of the hotel where I stayed each night, for he had asked Joseph to look in the Seer stone, that he did so, and told him all these particulars of my journey, which Oliver had carefully noted in his book. Oliver asked me where I first met them, when I left home, where I stayed on the road, and the names of the persons keeping the hotels. I could not tell the names but as we returned I pointed out the several houses where I had stopped, when he pulled out his book and found it to be correct even to the names.[23]

Whitmer also gave a corroborating account to a reporter in 1878: "Before his (Whitmer's) arrival, Joseph Smith also detailed for Cowdery the wagon Whitmer would arrive in, 'with two long poles on it at each end

21. Anderson, *Lucy's Book,* 449.

22. "History of Joseph Smith," *Times and Seasons* 3:884–85.

23. David Whitmer, interview by James H. Hart, March 18, 1884, "About the Book of Mormon," 14. Apparently Oliver's book did not survive.

across the end gates of the wagon box, and then two boards laid across that for seats on those hickory poles."[24]

For unknown reasons, possibly because of Joseph's haste to leave or lack of space, Emma remained in Harmony. Samuel Smith also stayed in Harmony, perhaps until July or August.[25]

David took Joseph and Oliver and started on the 135-mile trip to Fayette. According to an 1885 interview David gave Zenas Gurley Jr: "On our way I conversed freely with them upon this great work they were bringing about."[26]

The Whitmer family immediately welcomed Smith and Cowdery, and John met the young Joseph Smith. According to the Pollard and Woods family history, "The people of Fayette treated Joseph kindly and were extremely interested in the work he was doing with the translation. Before long, neighbors began to fill the Whitmer home.... The visitors seemed to come in a never ending stream, trying to get a glimpse of the new prophet.... They all had to be fed, and the subsequent dishes cleaned, the cow had to be milked and the butter churned, the bread baked, the beans soaked, and the floor swept."[27] This heavy burden of hospitality naturally fell on Mary and fourteen-year-old Elizabeth Ann.

While each member of the Whitmer family, in his or her own way, assisted with Joseph's work, three of the brothers—John, David, and Christian—developed the closest ties. Of the three, David's education may have been the most limited, with the result that John or Christian, but seldom David, took Cowdery's place as scribe while Joseph Smith continued to dictate the Book of Mormon narrative, now in its final stages. Nonetheless, Joseph formed the deepest friendship with David, perhaps because they were closest in age. Joseph Smith was nearly twelve months younger than

24. David Whitmer, interview by Orson Pratt/Joseph F. Smith, September 7–8, 1878, in Cook, *David Whitmer Interviews*, 49.

25. Anderson, *Lucy's Book*, 440.

26. David Whitmer, interview by Zenas H. Gurley Jr., January 14, 1885; see also Cook, *David Whitmer Interviews,* 154. Gurley's father, Zenas H. Gurley Sr., was a seventy in Joseph Smith Jr.'s church and, later played a crucial role in mobilizing a core of believers for Joseph Smith III's Reorganization, in which, after its 1852–60 organization, he served as an apostle. Zenas Gurley Jr. also later served as an apostle in Joseph III's organization.

27. Pollard and Woods, *Whitmer Memoirs,* 11.

David, while Christian was almost eight years Joseph's senior, and John was three years and four months older than Joseph.

Late in life, David recalled Joseph Smith as "a man of great magnetism, made friends easily, was liberal and noble in his impulses, tall, finely formed and full of animal life, but sprung from the most humble of circumstances. The first good suit of clothes he had ever worn was presented to him by [my brother] Christian Whitmer."[28]

Friendship was important to Joseph Smith. According to Rodger I. Anderson, a Smith biographer, "As many seemed drawn to him, Joseph sharpened his discernment as a useful guide in establishing enduring friendships and personal commitment. Joseph Rogers, knowing Joseph Smith as a youth, recalled, 'He could read the character of men readily.'"[29] This appraisal, unfortunately, was not universally true; examples are his spectacularly misplaced confidence in John C. Bennett and Joseph H. Jackson in Nauvoo, Illinois. Although he was also quick to forgive a repentant friend, he also demanded immense personal loyalty and obedience to a stream of revelatory instructions and organizational requirements. When such obedience and loyalty were not forthcoming, he was quick to repudiate former friends, a dynamic that would play out with Oliver Cowdery and the Whitmers as well as others. Steve Epperson, a religious studies scholar, identifies friendship as one of Joseph's "grand fundamental principles" that he foresaw would "revolution[ize] the world." Epperson observes, "Smith correctly perceived how friendships provided a setting for the identification, display, and exercise of virtues essential for the difficult work of creating and maintaining an alternative religious community.... In and by the virtues embodied in friends ... the Saints would come to know and live virtuous lives and commit themselves to sustaining the work of community building."[30] The Whitmers would experience both the warmth and intimacy of friendship with Joseph and also chilling alienation and punishment. Smith began to refine his understanding of the powerful potential of friendship in Fayette, living and working with the Whitmers. His intense emphasis on personal loyalties harked back to an earlier genera-

28. David Whitmer, "David Whitmer Interviewed," 347.

29. Anderson, *Joseph Smith's New York Reputation Reexamined*, 162.

30. Epperson, "The Grand, Fundamental Principle," 96.

tion; but US "political and economic philosophy [was] calibrated to secure and protect competitive and acquisitive rights rather than promote the 'common wealth.'"[31]

The Whitmers were not just taken with Joseph as a friendly young man, worthy in turn of their friendship. They were impressed by Joseph's claims of religious authority. As a young man—just twenty-three at the time—Smith did not present the sobriety, prudence, and stability expected of typical clergymen and, in fact, reportedly sometimes displayed "a spirit of lightness and levity."[32] A strong affinity developed between the whole Whitmer clan and Joseph Smith, and Joseph wisely involved all the members of the Whitmer family in many aspects of his religious pursuits. Such engagement reinforced their exertions in his behalf and their personal loyalty to him, while the rapidly evolving religious work itself became a strongly shared interest.

Each party received something valuable from this union. Joseph received needed physical sustenance and support from the Whitmers. In turn, his presence among the Whitmers endowed daily chores with a sense of excitement and purpose that gave them greater significance and a larger scope. Joseph's very presence seemed to stimulate singular experiences. Despite—or perhaps because of—his departure from the norm expected of a spiritual leader, Joseph's teachings and actions fostered a creative religious expectation within the Whitmers. In a sense, Joseph was more the visionary artist than the enunciator of religious truths. He articulated the opening of a window between the spiritual and natural worlds. He did not construct logical arguments or appeal to reason as much as he captured some universal subjective truth that resonated within each listener. Drawn into such an animated atmosphere, the Whitmers, no doubt, sensed that remarkable events would be regular occurrences. Such heightened awareness complemented the desire of these humble and sincere people for increased spiritual intimacy with the Divine. Joseph's spiritual propensities seemed to portray a pathway to God.

Along with the rest of the family, John enjoyed and encouraged the evolution of this symbiotic exchange. With Joseph's encouragement, John

31. Ibid., 79.
32. Ezra Booth to Edward Partridge, 20 September 1831; see also Ezra Booth to Mr. Partridge, 20 September 1831, in Howe, *Mormonism Unvailed*, 203.

participated in a number of events that reinforced such high expectations. Peter Sr. and Mary were apparently fully convinced of Joseph's gifts and committed to the work. Their new intimacy with the marvelous work God seemed to be accomplishing though them may have contrasted favorably with any earlier feelings of social or economic privation. Joseph's enthusiasm allowed the Whitmers to transcend possible concerns of religious inadequacy, "replacing them with feelings of religious privilege" or chosenness.[33] With enthusiasm, they embraced this new, superior religious identity.

Twenty-seven-year-old John, unmarried and still living at home, seemed to need the security of close ties with his family and religious group. Although friendly, he was thought to be reserved and rather private. Neighbors may have perceived him as a loner. But these characteristics made him a valuable observer of others' actions and motives.

A strong aspect of John's personality was a firm attachment to his large, extended family. He did not chafe under its demands, express unwillingness to devote his labor to its welfare, or seek opportunities for autonomy. As Joseph succeeded in forging family-like bonds between the Smith and Whitmer clans, John was already predisposed to play a supporting role in an extended sacred fellowship. Early shared experiences reinforced an expanded sense of kinship among participants. As the group successfully surmounted one new difficulty after another, their shared bonds grew stronger. As a result, the extended Smith and Whitmer families furnished a strong nucleus of fervent and committed disciples.

The developing family of co-believers provided John with what every person desires: an identity, significant work, and a secure place in the world. John's involvement in what his kin also perceived as a great, even divine, work provided a great deal of personal satisfaction, reinforced in turn by his family's deepening involvement. In such a clan-like setting, unity was particularly urgent. Every family member needed to be part of, support, and advance family beliefs. With the family so intimately engrossed in the religious movement, each sibling had an interconnected impulse to join and thereafter remain part of the "in" group through the secret religious knowledge that Joseph offered in a friendly and appreciative way.

---

33. Jennings, "City in the Garden," 111.

The combination of religious motivations and familial incentive led John to become Joseph's enthusiastic friend.

In his *The Burned-Over District,* historian Whitney Cross states, "The fundamental condition leading to [Mormonism] was the credulity and spiritual yearning which made people anxious to follow a prophet, whoever he might be."[34] David Whitmer relates two stories, one immediately before, and the other immediately after meeting Joseph Smith, that shed light on the family's willingness to entertain unconventional spiritual happenings. One such story, the already mentioned account of angels who helped David Whitmer harrow and fertile his spring crop, was a favorite in the Whitmer family. Helen Van Cleave Blankmeyer, David Whitmer's great-granddaughter, tells this somewhat romanticized but colorful version:

> When Peter [Whitmer Sr.] heard David planning to go off to meet Oliver [and Joseph Smith in Harmony], and in mid-week too, he protested: "Na, na,—not till the south field is harrowed and the plaster spread! That is your job, as you know, and it will not take less than two full days, maybe more. Duty first, duty first." David agreed, but he was sad, and the little Elizabeth ... grieved for her brother's disappointment. She watched him through the next day as he drove the harrow hard, his long body and broad shoulders contesting with the earth as with a strong wrestler, but at evening the task was scarcely half done. Rising early on the second day to prepare his breakfast, she stepped into the yard and glanced toward the field. To her amazement it was all evenly harrowed, and the lime neatly spread, while two strange men, just visible through the morning mist, were leaving the place at the far side. David came out of the house, and stood entranced beside her. "Elizabeth? ... Elizabeth! ... It must be, it can only be ...." "Yes," she breathed ... "angels."[35]

A second similar incident occurred within a matter of days as David Whitmer drove Oliver Cowdery and Joseph Smith back toward his parents' home. Edward Stevenson, who joined the movement almost a decade later, interviewed David in December 1877, and took rapid notes:

34. Cross, *Burned-Over District,* 143.

35. Blankmeyer, *David Whitmer, Witness for God,* 7.

Oliver, & The Prophet, & I were riding in a wagon, & an aged man about 5 feet 10, heavy Set & on his back an old fashioned Armey [*sic*] knapsack Strapped over his Shoulders & Something Square in it, & he walked along side of the Wagon & Wiped the Sweat off of his face, Smileing [*sic*] very Pleasant David asked him to ride and he replied I am going across to hill Comorah [*sic*]. Soon after they passed they felt strangely & Stopped, but could See nothing of him all arround [*sic*] was clear & they asked the Lord about it he Said that the Prophet Looked as White as a Sheet & Said that it was one of the Nephites & he had the Plates. on arriveing [*sic*] at home they were impressed that the Same Person was under the bed [shed] & again they were informed that it was So. they Saw where he had been & the next morning David's Mother Saw the Person at the Shed and he took the plates from A Box & showed them to her She Said that they Were fastened with Rings thus D [Stevenson has drawn the shape of a capital D] he turned the leaves over this was a Sattisfaction [*sic*] to her.[36]

The Whitmer family readily accepted these stories about the intervention of supernatural visitors in ordinary human events. Obviously the entire family had no difficulty believing that God could and would interact with human beings. Several members of the family subsequently claimed to participate in experiences that transcend common understanding. For John, seeing Smith translate while looking into a hat was an uncommon experience in itself.[37] Oliver Cowdery set the stage, heightening the Whitmer family's expectation of the marvelous when he testified that Joseph had seen the details of Oliver's trip to Harmony through supernatural means. One or more Whitmers were present at various times when Joseph received divine revelations. Hyrum Smith related the wondrous tale of accompanying Joseph, along with Oliver Cowdery and an unnamed Whitmer brother to the Hill Cumorah. "As the men were walking up the hill, a door opened and they walked into a room that was about sixteen feet square. In the room, they beheld an angel and saw a trunk on which rested a Book of Mormon, the plates from which it was translated, Laban's sword,

---

36. Cook, *David Whitmer Interviews*, 13; see also David Whitmer, interview by Edward Stevenson, Saturday, December 22, 1877.

37. Bushman, *Joseph Smith: Rough Stone Rolling*, 72, describes this process: "By any measure, transcription was a miraculous process, calling for a huge leap of faith to believe."

and Aaron's breastplate."[38] While plowing in the field after Joseph Smith's arrival, David heard a voice and saw a personage who told him, "Blessed is the name of the Lord & they who keep his commandments." Almost immediately, Joseph interrupted his work and invited him to become one of the witnesses of the Book of Mormon.[39]

On another occasion, related without any details about time and place but probably during these weeks at Fayette, David, Oliver, and Joseph saw "one of the three Nephites." Reinforcing this marvelous tale was their observation that "Joseph's countenance became almost transparent."[40]

Such experiences gave the Whitmers a sense that they were part of a chain of divinely initiated experiences related to the translation of the gold plates. If, as some claim, Joseph deceived early witnesses by imposing this and later experiences upon them in some way, the Whitmers' subsequent actions confirm that they perceived such experiences as genuine manifestations of divine interaction. Despite the inherent subjectivity of such experience and the likelihood that family acceptance strongly dampened impulses toward skepticism, the Whitmers seemed predisposed to accept these creative religious experiences as real. Once they perceived such experiences as literal, they would have followed human nature in confirming and internalizing such beliefs, as well as denying contrary evidence. That is why the early affiliation of the Whitmers to the Restoration, followed by their painful disassociation, provides a story so gripping in human drama.

These early events that brought Joseph and the Whitmer family together coincided with a blossoming of genuine inquiry that was sweeping larger American society. Forces of democratization and industrialization promoted an increase of individualism and religious liberalism. Many thoughtful people were resisting what they perceived as excessive religious control over common people. The era invited intellectual individuality with a new emphasis on the opportunities afforded by education. The Whitmers, by casting their lot with Joseph Smith, initially turned away from this movement, viewing the new liberal awakening as a human-centered emphasis that displaced and even denied God. Alarmed, they opposed

---

38. O'Driscoll, *Hyrum Smith: A Life of Integrity*, 29.

39. Edward Stevenson interview of February 9, 1886, as recorded in his journal. See also Cook, *David Whitmer Interviews*, 181.

40. Edward Stevenson to John Taylor, 7 January 1878, Journal History.

these liberalizing tendencies by working to preserve social traditions and maintain the historic role of religion. John Whitmer's personal philosophy at his time of contact with the Restoration is not known; but as an able and active individual, he appears to have stood at the intersection of these two conflicting movements. In that context, he asked—and eventually answered—the major questions of his time.

Joseph Smith's values and actions ran counter to this growing common liberalism. He reacted strongly against the divisions of society resulting from the Protestant Reformation, capitalism, and nationalism. Society appeared to be flying out of balance. Economic forces were stressing the American middle class, rewarding individualism and ambition at the expense of cooperation, self-sacrifice, and social order.[41] Joseph Smith sensed that his own family's social isolation and poverty were rooted in society's rampant pursuit of materialism, political corruption, and religious pluralism. Joseph also found himself at odds with the religious establishment of his day. Smith was concerned by "the diminishing role of religion in an emerging democratic, competitive and increasingly secular world," notes Marvin Hill. He perceived the influences of Calvinism, revivalism, and professional clergy as being out of touch with the needs of the poor.[42] Joseph wished to refashion the fabric of this world into a garment that recognized the worth of every individual.[43] Yet Joseph seemed to simultaneously believe that this true freedom he envisioned was possible only when an individual was firmly rooted in a system of social and moral authority. Security for humanity existed only within the kingdom of God, and then only when theocratic dominion maintained order.[44]

John seemed to be comfortable at once with these conservative views. Indeed, the Whitmers' Anabaptist religious background may account for their openness to Smith's own evolving radical Christianity. Whether John's openness is a reflection of his natural predisposition or deference to Joseph is unclear. However, even though the extended Whitmer clan

41. The first epoch of the American middle class was coming to an end in 1830. Hartmann, *Screwed: The Undeclared War against the Middle Class.*
42. Hill, *Quest for Refuge,* front flyleaf, introduction, xii, and 16.
43. Adapted from Zehr, *Sing the Journey! Hymnal: A Worship Book Supplement 1,* 24.
44. Jennings, "City in the Garden," 116. Smith longed to see the end of the present order and the ultimate triumph of God. See Hill, *Quest for Refuge,* 13.

readily gave their initial loyalty to Joseph Smith, their developing individuality would one day erode the bonds of these shared experiences with Joseph. Over the next few years, the Whitmers found that keeping pace with Joseph demanded increasing conformity to a conservative worldview. Before the decade was over, John and David would contest the form of the prophet's envisioned earthly kingdom, and the entire Whitmer family would find itself on another, less socially divergent path.

CHAPTER THREE

Completing the Book of Mormon Translation

THE SHARED COMMON experience of helping to produce the scripture known as the Book of Mormon further cemented participant relationships. Joseph probably asked one of the Whitmers to also move Emma and some of their belongings to New York. Before long, Emma and Joseph were reunited at Fayette, where they occupied an upstairs bedroom at the Whitmer home while the Book of Mormon translation was being completed.

The Whitmer house, probably not much larger than about twenty-feet square sheltered a surprising number of people. In addition to the parents, Peter Sr. and Mary, residents included the Whitmers' housekeeper, a young unmarried woman named Sarah Conrad, brothers John and David Whitmer, Peter Jr., Elizabeth Ann, Oliver Cowdery, and the Smiths. By now, Christian, Jacob, and Catherine Whitmer were married and living nearby in separate households.

In an 1885 interview, David Whitmer recalled: "Each time before resuming the work [on the Book of Mormon] all present would kneel in prayer and invoke the divine blessing on the proceeding. After prayer Smith would sit on one side of a table and the amanuenses, in turn as they became tired, on the other. Those present and not actively engaged in the work seated themselves around the room and then the work began."[1]

LDS historian Kenneth W. Godfrey notes that David Whitmer, the most frequently interviewed of all the witnesses, "was not always consistent in the way he remembered Latter-day Saint beginnings." Godfrey's essay,

---

1. David Whitmer, interview by the *Chicago Tribune*, December 15, 1885, in Cook, *David Whitmer Interviews*, 174.

"The Shaping of Latter-day Saint History," identifies a number of such contradictions among extant interviews.[2] For example, Godfrey notes:

> With respect to the translation of the Book of Mormon, David Whitmer ... said that while Joseph and Oliver resided at the Whitmer home, "a blanket which served as a portiere, was stretched across the family living room to shelter the translators and the plates from the eye of any who might call at the house while the work was in progress." The purpose of the blanket, said Whitmer, was not to conceal the plates or the translator from the amanuensis. However, in another account, Whitmer told Nathan Tanner Jr. that a blanket separated Joseph from his scribe.[3]

Despite inconsistencies, David provides an important alternative perspective for reconstructing many of the day-to-day experiences of key participants.

Oliver continued to serve as Joseph's primary scribe throughout this period, and the Book of Mormon manuscript progressed rapidly. However, Smith's official history also notes that, beginning in early June 1829, John Whitmer "assisted us very much in writing during the remainder of the work."[4] Analyzing the dictated Book of Mormon manuscript, Joseph Smith specialist Dean C. Jessee tentatively identified John Whitmer and an additional unknown scribe as having written the first fifteen chapters of 1 Nephi.[5] Myron Bond, an RLDS missionary, heard John himself testify

2.   Godfrey, "The Shaping of Latter-day Saint History," 223–56.

3.   Ibid., 235; Cook, *David Whitmer Interviews*, 174; David Whitmer, interview by Nathan Tanner Jr., April 13, 1886, cited in Cook, *David Whitmer Interviews*, 191.

4.   *History of the LDS Church*, 1:49. Speaking in 1859 in Salt Lake City, Orson Pratt recalled that on November 4, 1830, "I went into the chamber of father Whitmer, in whose house the Lord manifested himself in the organization of this Church, consisting of six members. I went into that chamber with the Prophet Joseph Smith, to inquire of the Lord; and he received a revelation for my benefit, which was written from the mouth of the Prophet by John Whitmer." Orson Pratt, 18 September 1859, *Journal of Discourses*, 7:308–13.

5.   It was John Whitmer's "especial pride and joy that he had written sixty pages of the Book of Mormon." Gurley, "Synopsis of a Discourse Delivered at Lamoni, Iowa," 370. According to Jessee, in "The Original Book of Mormon Manuscript," 273, 276–78, scribe 2 of the dictated manuscript might be John Whitmer. A later analysis by Jessee, Anderson, Faulring, and Skousen noted consistent variations between John Whitmer's known writings and the pages written by scribe 2 in the dictated manuscript (1 Nephi

in 1877 "that he knew ... that Joseph translated the ancient writing which was upon the plates which he 'saw and handled,' and which, as one of the scribes, he helped to copy, as the words fell from Joseph's lips, by supernatural or almighty power."[6]

Apparently, Joseph translated in the same room that he and Emma occupied as a bedchamber. Emma later commented to her son Joseph Smith III, "Though I was an active participant in the scenes that transpired, and was present during the translation of the plates, and had cognizance of things as they transpired, it is marvelous to me, 'a marvel and a wonder,' as much so as to anyone else."[7]

David Whitmer, who did not act as a scribe, was frequently present while the work was pursued. But in such cramped quarters, the task did not always go smoothly. David related in 1882 that he once observed Joseph in a domestic difficulty with Emma that impeded the translation process:

> He could not translate unless he was humble and possessed the right feeling towards every one. To illustrate, so you can see. One morning when he was getting ready to continue the translation, something went wrong about the house and he was put out about it. Something that Emma, his wife, had done. Oliver and I went upstairs, and Joseph came up soon after to continue the translation, but he could not do anything. He could not translate a single syllable. He went downstairs, out into the orchard and made supplication to the Lord; was gone about an hour—came back to the house, asked Emma's forgiveness and then came up stairs where we were and the translation went on all right.[8]

3:7 to 1 Nephi 4:14, 1 Nephi 12:9 to 1 Nephi 16:1, LDS versification): "But overall the hand looks the same." Royal Skousen, e-mail to author, October 18, 2007.

6. John Whitmer, quoted in Myron Bond to Henry Stebbins, 2 August 1878, 253: "I do think tithing." "Myron H. Bond was born August 2, 1843, at Kirtland, Ohio, and joined the [RLDS] church in his twenty-fifth year, at Manti, Iowa, July 26, 1868. He has been an ordained minister since April 10, 1886, being considered one of the most deeply philosophical preachers the church has produced." "Elder Myron H. Bond Passes Away," 564.

7. Emma Smith Bidamon, interview by Joseph Smith III, February 4–10, 1879; see also "Last Testimony of Sister Emma," 289–90.

8. David Whitmer, interview by William H. Kelley, 68.

With other scribes at hand, Emma was freed from the time-consuming translation process, although "the larger part of this labor was done in her presence, and where she could see and Know what was being done."[9] Almost certainly as a well-trained housewife and considerate guest, she spent most of her time working with Mary and Elizabeth Ann to keep the household running smoothly and to minimize the labor caused by these guests. When occasion dictated, she felt free to move the plates when necessary for cleaning. Emma later related: "The plates often lay on the table without any attempt at concealment, wrapped in a small linen tablecloth, which I had given him to fold them in. I once felt of the plates, as they thus lay on the table, tracing their outline and shape. They seemed to be pliable like thick paper, and would rustle with a metallic sound when the edges were moved by the thumb, as one does sometimes thumb the edges of a book."[10] She does not say when this happened—certainly during their months in Harmony, but not improbably during the Fayette months as well.

The translation process itself occasioned great interest within the extended family circle. David said, "It was a laborious work for the weather was very warm, and the days were long and they [Joseph and Oliver] worked from morning till night. But they were both young and strong and were soon able to complete the work."[11]

The actual process of translation and the use of such aids as spectacles and seer stones have become the subject of endless debate. All students of the movement have had to struggle with the inconsistencies extant in historical descriptions of the method and mechanism of the translation. Even assuming that their words were recorded correctly, John, David, and other early witnesses appear at times to use these terms with considerable variation.[12]

---

9.   Joseph Smith III to James T. Cobb, 14 February 1879.

10. Emma Smith Bidamon, interview by Joseph Smith III, February 4–10, 1879, 290.

11. David Whitmer, interview by James H. Hart, March 18, 1884, 14.

12. David Whitmer's great-granddaughter Helen Van Cleave Blankmeyer, *David Whitmer, Witness for God*, 4, observes: "Oddly enough, these 'seer stones,' the Urim and Thummim, apparently set together, were always referred to by the church in the singular, as 'the stone.'" David Whitmer, *An Address to All Believers in Christ*, 32, also refers to the stone as singular: "After the translation of the Book of Mormon was finished,

Joseph Smith himself said very little about the translation process, except for the simple explanation that he interpreted the ancient record "by the gift and power of God."[13] Once when asked to describe the translation process in Far West, Joseph declined, saying: "It was not intended to tell the world all the particulars of the coming forth of the Book of Mormon; and ... it was not expedient for him to relate these things."[14]

Next to Joseph, Oliver Cowdery was perhaps in the best position to describe it. In April 1831, he "testified under oath, that ... Smith found with the plates, from which he translated his book, two transparent stones.... Through these, he was able to read in English, the reformed Egyptian characters."[15] David Whitmer, who would have been an observer rather than a scribe, claimed throughout his life that the process involved a literal word-for-word translation of characters into English words.[16]

Obviously, some associated with the early translation process apparently believed that, by looking into his stone, Joseph Smith was able to see and read aloud English words—in other words, that the translation of the ancient text occurred through some mechanical process or even within the stone itself.[17] This very perception had been put to the test shortly before Joseph and Emma came to the Whitmers. Between April and June 1828 in Harmony, Joseph Smith translated 116 pages of manuscript text with the aid of Martin Harris, a family friend from Palmyra, New York. Movement scholar Grant Palmer observes, "Critics who sought to test this claim stole [the] 116 pages of the Book of Mormon transcript, then apparently waited to see if Joseph 'should bring forth the same words again.' Smith avoided this test altogether by translating a different version of the same story from

---

early in the spring of 1830, before April 6th, Joseph gave the stone to Oliver Cowdery and told me as well as the rest that he was through with it, and did not use the stone any more." Commentators have seemingly agreed in adopting the singular form of the term.

13. Book of Mormon, copyright/title page, drafted June 11, 1829.

14. Cannon and Cook, *Far West Record*, 23; also *History of the LDS Church*, 1:220.

15. A[bram]. W. Benton, "Mormonites," 120, quoted in Palmer, *An Insider's View of Mormon Origins*, 6.

16. David Whitmer "Mormonism: Authentic Account," 198; Cook, *David Whitmer Interviews*, 62.

17. See Palmer, *An Insider's View of Mormon Origins*, 5–7.

a different set of plates."[18] If the English translation of the Book of Mormon text was appearing directly as a result of Smith's stone gazing, then reproducing the missing portion verbatim would have been possible, so clearly the translation process was more complex. The fact that the Book of Mormon included a second set of plates covering approximately the same time period that Mormon had included without abridgement let Smith make a new beginning with the translation, avoiding what by revelation was identified as a plot to impugn the translation by inconsistency.

Reminiscences of those who assisted during this period continue to suggest that the translation involved a somewhat mechanical process. The earliest newspaper account of the discovery of the plates, the *Palmyra Freeman* of August 11, 1829, reported that "the [Gold] Bible was found, together with a huge pair of spectacles!... By placing the spectacles in a hat, and looking into it, Smith could ... interpret these characters."[19]

Many years later, William W. Blair, a member of the RLDS First Presidency, questioned Michael Morse, husband of Emma Smith's sister, Tryal, about the translation process. Morse had observed the translation during its early stages while the Smiths were still at Harmony. According to Blair:

> Michael was present during the translation. He further states that when Joseph was translating the Book of Mormon, he, (Morse), had occasion more than once to go into his immediate presence, and saw him engaged at his work of translation.
>
> The mode of procedure consisted in Joseph's placing the seer stone in the crown of a hat, then putting his face into the hat, so as to entirely cover his face, resting his elbows upon his knees, and then dictating, word after word while the scribe—Emma, John Whitmer, O. Cowdery, or some other, wrote it down.[20]

But even prominent witnesses do not always agree. At times, their stories appear to conflate distinct elements of the story. Apparently the

---

18. Ibid.

19. Jonathan A. Hadley, letter, 11 August 1829, reprinted as "Golden Bible," 18.

20. Blair, "Editors Herald," May 22, 1879, 190–91. John Whitmer was not present in Harmony when Morse would have observed the Book of Mormon translation process. Probably, Blair, knowing that John was deeply involved, injected this error into the narrative.

story has been shared in snapshot fashion, each representing a different perspective of the process and a slightly different view of a larger scene. Some, like Emma, Oliver, and John, were full participants in the process. John and David Whitmer could know only what occurred during the months in Harmony from stories told by others. Martin Harris had been in Harmony, but he could not have known firsthand what occurred while Joseph resided with the Whitmers. Others who also left accounts, including William B. Smith and Elizabeth Ann Whitmer, were merely observers.

In 1890, RLDS members J. W. Peterson and W. S. Pender interviewed eighty-two-year-old William B. Smith (March 13, 1811–November 13, 1893), the only brother of Joseph Smith to live past 1844. William, who died three years after the interview, was nine during the Book of Mormon translation, but his version of the story of the translation is perhaps the most elaborate. Peterson records meeting the elderly William Smith on July 4:

> Most of the two or three days that followed was spent in asking the old man questions concerning his father's family and his brother Joseph in particular, being at that time especially interested in the Urim and Thummim with which his brother Joseph translated the Book of Mormon.... He said he had hefted the plates as they lay on the table [in Palmyra] wrapped in an old frock or jacket in which Joseph <h>ad brought them home. That he had thum[b]ed them through the cloth and ascertained that they were thin sheets of some kind of metal. When asked why he had not uncovered them he said they were told not to do so unless the Lord would give permission, that they were the property of an angel and had received strict command[ments] with regard to that matter.... Explaining the expression as to the stones in the Urim and thummim being set in two rims of a bow he said: A silver bow ran over one stone, under the other, around over that one and under the first in the shape of a horizontal figure 8 much like a pair of spectacles. That they were much too large for Joseph and he could only see through one at a time using sometimes one and sometimes the other. By putting his head in a hat or some dark object it was not necessary to close one eye while looking through the stone with the other. In that way sometimes when his eyes grew [tired] he relieved them of the strain. He also said the Urim and Thummim was attached to the breastplate by a rod which was fastened at the outer shoulde[r]

edge of the breastplate and to the end of the silver bow. This rod was just the right length so that when the Urim and thummim was removed from before the eyes it woul<d> reac<h> to a pocked [pocket?] on the left side of the breastplate where the instrument was kept when not in use by the Seer.[21]

Peterson adds more details in a second statement about this interview confirming William's youthful perspective of his interaction with his brother during the translation process: "William informed us that he had himself, by Joseph's direction, put the Urim and Thummim before his eyes, but could see nothing, as he did not have the gift of a Seer. He also informed us that the instruments were too wide for his eyes, as also for Joseph's, and must have been used by much larger men."[22]

Another RLDS church member, Eri Mullin, received a similar impression of the translation process from a conversation with David Whitmer: "Mr. D. Whitmer told me in the year 1874, that Joseph Smith used the Urim and Thummim when he was translating.... I asked him how they looked. He said they looked like spectacles, and he (Joseph) would put them on and look in a hat, or put his face in the hat and read."[23] Whitmer was here describing the translation of the 116 pages, for which he was not present; but he corroborated the use of the spectacles or interpreters in two interviews.[24] However, after the loss of the 116 pages, according to Whitmer, Joseph used a small stone rather than the spectacles or interpret-

21. William B. Smith, interview by J. W. Peterson and W. S. Pender, July 4, 1890, in Vogel, *Early Mormon Documents*, 1:507–9.

22. William B. Smith, quoted in J. W. Peterson, "The Urim and Thummim," in Sheldon, *The Rod of Iron*, 6–7.

23. Eri B. Mullin to Dear Brethren, 76.

24. Cook, *David Whitmer Interviews*, 200. See also "The Last Witness Dead," *Herald* 35:94–95 reprinted from the *Richmond Democrat*, January 26, 1888. The conflation of "spectacles" and "interpreters" is also problematic. Oliver Cowdery suggested that the Nephite term for the translation device was "Interpreters." Cowdery to W. W. Phelps, 7 September 1834, 14. William E. McLellin, who was not present during any of the Book of Mormon translation, offers his own perception: "The Urim was used alone for <the> purpose of inquiring of God. The Interpreters were used alone for the purposes of interpreting languages. They were not used interchangeably. Now by this we see how all L.D. Saints have been deceived, and believed erroneously in this item." William E. McLellin to Joseph Smith III, [31?] July, and 8 September 1872.

ers.[25] In another instance, Whitmer said Smith "had the Urim and Thummim, and a chocolate colored stone, which he used alternately, as suited his convenience."[26] Martin Harris also described two different translation media: "The seer stone differed in appearance entirely from the Urim and Thummim that was obtained with the plates, which were two clear stones set in two rims, very much resembling spectacles, only they were larger."[27] Emma Smith, a participant during both stages of translation, also described two translation media: "Now the first that my husband translated, was translated by the use of the Urim and Thummim, and that was the part that Martin Harris lost, after that he used a small stone, not exactly black, but was rather a dark color."[28]

Although all three of these participants (David Whitmer, Martin Harris, and Emma Smith) call the spectacles the "urim and thummim," the term is anachronistic. In his *Restoration Scriptures*, RLDS church historian Richard Howard observes that the first occurrence in early church literature of the biblical term "urim and thummim" appeared in an 1833 article by W. W. Phelps. By 1835, Joseph had also adopted this term.[29] Members began to generally associate this term with the translation process. Its use immediately helped harmonize apparent inconsistencies in statements by key participants. Over time, Joseph Smith came to see the use of the term "urim and thummim" as inclusive of all devices or methods for revealing the mind and will of God.[30]

25. David Whitmer, interview by Zenas H. Gurley, January 14, 1885, in Cook, *David Whitmer Interviews*, 156–58. Joseph Smith's official 1838 history indicates, that after losing the 116 pages, he was "forgiven" and the plates and the urim and thummim were returned for further use. *History of the LDS Church*, 1:23. This early use of the term "urim and thummim" appears to be supported by its appearance in CofC D&C 3, LDS D&C 10; however, the term does not appear in the original reading of this revelation (chapter 9), as published in the 1833 Book of Commandments.

26. David Whitmer, interview by Nathan Tanner Jr., in Cook, *David Whitmer Interviews*, 191–92.

27. Martin Harris, sermon, September 4, 1870, quoted in Jenson, "The Three Witnesses: Martin Harris," 216.

28. Emma Smith to Mrs. [Emma] Pilgrim, 27 March, 1876.

29. Howard, *Restoration Scriptures*, 152–53.

30. Lancaster, "By the Gift and Power of God," 806.

In 1879, J. L. Traughber Jr., an RLDS resident of Ray County, Missouri, rather aggressively explained the introduction of this term into church vernacular:

> I am aware of the fact that the "Urim and thummim" story has long been foisted upon the world as the true account of the origin of the Book of Mormon; but the times demand, and, the interest of truth demands, that the truth should be told. We need not be afraid of truth; and I greatly doubt if anybody will be ultimately benefited by the perpetuation of a falsehood, which was invented for the purpose of gaining prestige, in the minds of the people, for ambitious leaders. The proofs are clear and positive that the story of Urim and Thummim Translation does not date back, for its origin, further than 1833, or, between that date and 1835; for it is not found in any printed document of the Church of Christ up to the latter part of the year 1833, or the year 1834. The "Book of Commandments" to the Church of Christ, published in Independence, Mo., in 1833, does not contain any allusion to Urim and Thummim; though the term was inserted in some of the revelations in their reprint in the "Book of Doctrine and Covenants" in 1835.... It is proper to notice what it is claimed the Urim and Thummim was. P. P. and O. Pratt both say it was an instrument composed of two clear or transparent stones set in the two rims of a bow. It is also confounded with the "Interpreters," which were shaped something like a pair of ordinary spectacles, though larger.[31]

Clearly, the terms "spectacles," "interpreters," and "urim and thummim" have often been conflated in testimonies. However, witnesses consistently indicate that Smith employed some type of stone to complete the translation process at the Whitmer home. Some sources suggest that Joseph used two stones during this period. Only once out of all of his interviews was David Whitmer quoted as referring to the stones in the plural. "I, as well as all of my father's family, Smith's wife, Oliver Cowdery, and Martin Harris were present during the translation. The translation was by Smith, and the manner as follows: 'He had two small stones of a chocolate color, nearly egg shaped and perfectly smooth, but not transparent, called interpreters, which were given him with the plates. He did not

31. Traughber, "Testimony of David Whitmer," 341.

use the plates in the translation, but would hold the interpreters to his eyes and cover his face with a hat, excluding all light.'"[32]

Perhaps the most authoritative recounting of David's experience appears in Traughber's account:

> With the sanction of David Whitmer, and by his authority, I now state that he does not say that Joseph Smith ever translated in his presence by aid of Urim and Thummim; but by means of one dark colored, opaque stone, called a "Seer Stone," which was placed in the crown of a hat, into which Joseph put his face, so as to exclude the external light. Then, a spiritual light would shine forth, and parchment would appear before Joseph, upon which was a line of characters from the plates, and under it, the translation in English; at least, so Joseph said.[33]

David also left several accounts describing Joseph receiving revelations by means of a seer stone while living with the Whitmers.[34]

Elizabeth Ann Whitmer, age fourteen when Joseph and Emma Smith moved to the Whitmer farm, must have passed her early teen years in constant wonder as miraculous events unfolded. She must have crept up the stairs to peek into the bedroom occupied by Joseph and Emma, marveling at the grown men who spent from early morning until late at night sitting at a table and working, not with shovel or pitchfork, but pen and paper. She must have hovered, fascinated in the doorway as Oliver, Christian, John, and others were scribing for Joseph, either on the Book of Mormon text or writing out revelations. Downstairs in the parlor, she must have hurried back and forth at her mother's bidding to entertain visitors or paused, wide-eyed, as Joseph related one of his amazing stories.

In 1870 when Elizabeth Ann was fifty-five and had been widowed for two decades, William McLellin, one of Joseph's original apostles, asked her to describe the translation process. She responded willingly, he recorded:

32. David Whitmer, interview by the *Kansas City Journal*, June 5, 1881, in Cook, *David Whitmer Interviews*, 62. David Whitmer also suggested to Nathan Tanner Jr. that the plates were not necessarily present while Joseph dictated. Kenneth Godfrey asks this interesting question: "If this information is correct, then why were the plates preserved in the first place? Godfrey, "The Shaping of Latter-day Saint History," 236.

33. Traughber, "Testimony of David Whitmer," 341.

34. Whitmer, *An Address to All Believers in Christ*, 53, 55.

She gave me a certificate And this is the copy. [Elizabeth Ann (Whitmer) Cowdery, affidavit], Richmond, Ray Co., Mo. Feb 15th 1870—

I cheerfully certify that I was familiar with the manner of Joseph Smith's translating the book of Mormon. He translated most of it at my Father's house. And I often sat by and saw and heard them translate and write for hours together. Joseph never had a curtain drawn between him and his scribe while he was translating. He would place the director in his hat, and then place his <face in his> hat, so as to exclude the light, and then [read] off to his scribe the words (he said) as they appeared before him [bottom of page missing][35]

David Whitmer stated that the "translation at my father's occupied about one month, that is from June 1, to July 1, 1829."[36] John Whitmer's involvement with the production of the Book of Mormon occurred primarily near the end of the project.[37] At age seventy-six, John told RLDS church member Zenas H. Gurley in 1878 that it was his "especial pride and joy that he had written sixty pages of the Book of Mormon." Gurley further related: "When the work of translation was going on he [John] sat at one table with his writing materials and Joseph at another with the breast-plate and Urim and Thummim. The latter were attached on the breast-plate and were two crystals or glasses, into which he looked and saw the words of the book. The words remained in sight till correctly written, and mistakes of the scribe in spelling the names were corrected by the seer without diverting his gaze from the Urim and Thummim."[38]

This recollection is at odds with the current scholarly understandings discussed above that Joseph used a seer stone in the later translation process. Exactly how John Whitmer understood the translation process is not clear, as he provided but little additional comment about it.

Oliver Cowdery, as primary scribe, probably recognized better than the others that the interpretive process was not translation in the common sense. In 1839 he wrote, "I have sometime had seasons of skepticism, in

35. William E. McLellin, copy of affidavit, quoted in letter to My dear Friends, February 1870. The original of this affidavit is not extant.

36. David Whitmer, *Kansas City Daily Journal*, June 5, 1881, in Cook, *David Whitmer Interviews*, 62.

37. Jenson, "The Three Witnesses: John Whitmer," 6:612.

38. John Whitmer, quoted in Zenas H. Gurley, "Synopsis of a Discourse," 370.

which I did seriously wonder whether the prophet and I were men in our sober senses, when he would be translating from the plates, through the 'Urim and Thummim' [interpreters, or spectacles, or stones] and the plates not be in sight at all."[39] Yet only five years earlier in 1834, Cowdery had averred: "These were days never to be forgotten—to sit under the sound of a voice dictated by the inspiration of heaven."[40] Of the extended Whitmer clan, Oliver Cowdery seemed to appreciate best that the translation was ultimately a process of mentally studying a theme and receiving inward confirmation.[41]

39. Cowdery, *Defense*, 229–30. The authenticity of Cowdery's *Defense* remains under debate, but the basis of this statement is substantiated by others' reminiscences. The translation process reflected traditional folk magic techniques. As observers described the process, Joseph placed a seer stone, sometimes called a peepstone, in a hat, to exclude the light and read aloud the text that appeared. Many early revelations to individuals associated with the Restoration were also received in this way. Joseph's methodology grew more sophisticated as the movement evolved. Smith's move away from instruments of folk magic was a bit problematic for some early Mormon folk believers. "Members of the Whitmer family were so devoted to the importance of seer stones that David Whitmer, John Whitmer, and Hiram Page later dated the beginning of their own disenchantment with Mormonism at the time when Joseph Smith stopped using the seer stone as an instrument of revelation." Stewart, "Hiram Page," 140–46, quoted in Quinn, *Early Mormonism and the Magic World View*, 201.

40. Oliver Cowdery to W. W. Phelps, 7 September 1834, p. 14.

41. Doctrine and Covenants, Community of Christ edition (Independence, MO: Herald House, 1962), 9:3b, c, hereafter cited as CofC D&C. Compare LDS D&C 9:8. RLDS member E. M. Wildermuth in "1883 or 1884" asked Joseph Smith III his understanding of the translation process. Smith answered, "I am told it was translated partly by the Urim and Thummim, partly by a peep stone, and partly by inspiration (he closing his eyes, his hand to his forehead, and the words would come to him)." When David Whitmer's relative James R. B. Van Cleave asked Joseph Smith III his opinion about seer stones, Joseph III answered: "My experience, and my Knowledge of the means of communication employed by the Deity to reach man, warrants the belief that communications received through the stones referred to by you are not reliable.... I am not favorably impressed with the 'seer stones' as being from God; while at the same time, I have no objection to them if they be, nor would I feel dissatisfied should they prove so to be." Joseph Smith III to James R. B. Van Cleave, 27 September 1878.

CHAPTER FOUR

First Calling:
Missionary and Witness

JUNE 1829 SAW an explosion of activities within the new movement: baptisms, ordinations, and revelations giving personalized
instructions. Toward its end, once the translation was finished, Joseph
Smith called David Whitmer, Oliver Cowdery, and Martin Harris as three
witnesses to bear testimony to the truth of the Book of Mormon. Within
five days, John and seven others were called to also serve as witnesses. It
was a heady time.[1]

In June 1829, John, David, and Peter Whitmer Jr. were called to
the Restoration work through revelation (CofC D&C 12–14; LDS D&C
14–16). David Whitmer remembered, "In this month [June 1829] I was
baptized, confirmed, and ordained an Elder in the Church of Christ by
Bro. Joseph Smith."[2] At the same service, Joseph also baptized his brother
Hyrum,[3] and Oliver baptized Peter Whitmer Jr. The timing of subsequent
events indicates that John was also baptized about this same time. Historian Lyndon Cook places John's baptism in June 1829, performed by Oliver Cowdery.[4] All three Whitmers were baptized by immersion in nearby
Seneca Lake. Although the exact baptismal dates of the three Whitmer

---

1. Chronology, 1771–1831, appendix B, in Vogel, *Early Mormon Documents,* 5:421–22.

2. David Whitmer, *An Address to All Believers in Christ,* 32. Note David's anachronistic
reference to the Church of Christ before its organization on April 6, 1830.

3. *History of the LDS Church,* 1:51; see also Smith, "Biography of David Whitmer," 301.

4. Cook, *Revelations of the Prophet Joseph Smith,* 25.

brothers have not been recorded, John Whitmer was thus definitely among the first seven individuals to receive this ordinance.[5]

The revelation to Oliver Cowdery and David Whitmer, in what is now Doctrine and Covenants 16, received in June 1829, suggests equal callings to apostolic duty: "You are called even with that same calling with which he [Paul mine apostle] was called." In these earliest days, the spiritual authority of Joseph, Oliver, John, David, and Peter Jr. were apparently seen as equal.

As John became ever more intimately associated in the task of translation, he began to glimpse a larger personal calling. In June 1829, with his interest in the work deepening, John sought to better understand the life choices being presented to him. He told Joseph that he wished to know "that which would be of the most worth" for him to do. In response, between June 5 and June 8, 1829, Joseph received a revelation, through the seer stone, counseling John to "declare repentance" and bring souls unto Christ (CofC D&C 13, LDS D&C 15). Early participants had an understandable urge to share the good news with others, drawing them into the exciting and spiritually intense fellowship they enjoyed. David recalled: "In August, 1829, we began to preach the gospel of Christ. The following six Elders had then been ordained: Joseph Smith, Oliver Cowdery, Peter Whitmer, Samuel H. Smith, Hyrum Smith and myself."[6] Though John was also ordained an elder by Joseph Smith on June 9, 1830,[7] the concept of priesthood was still amorphous. Still, the main message was unmistakable: John was being called to preach the gospel.

John Whitmer apparently never aspired to a central role in the evolving church. Nevertheless, he became a full participant in events that shaped the movement. His experiences in relation to the founding of the church became an important element of his identity, defining the man throughout his life.

---

5. Earliest members: Joseph Smith and Oliver Cowdery, baptized May 1829, Hyrum Smith, David Whitmer, Peter Whitmer Jr., June 1829, *History of the LDS Church,* 39, 51; Samuel H. Smith—May 21, 1829, John Whitmer—June 1829, Cook, *The Revelations of the Prophet Joseph Smith,* 34, 25.

6. Whitmer, *An Address to All Believers in Christ,* 32.

7. John Whitmer, elder's license; see also Vogel, *Early Mormon Documents,* 5:357.

The Book of Mormon narrative described a church of Christ among the Nephites of the New World, both before and after Christ's visit to them. Joseph Smith clearly became interested in the possibility of restoring this organization for his own day, especially since the communication received during his First Vision at about age fourteen declared "the world lieth ~~and~~ in sin at this time and none doeth good no not one they have turned aside from the gospel and keep not <my> commandments."[8]

In mid-June, Joseph, Oliver, and David petitioned God for "instructions about building up the church of Christ, according to the fullness of the gospel."[9] In answer, they received what became chapter 15 in the Book of Commandments, directing them to reflect upon "the things which are written [in the Book of Mormon]."[10] Joseph noted in his draft 1839 history: "We continued to receive instruction concerning our duties from time to time, and among ~~the~~ many things the following directions, fixing the time of our anticipated meeting together <for the purpose of being organized> were given by the Spirit of prophecy and revelation."[11] The "anticipated meeting" was scheduled to occur on April 6, 1830, about six months in the future.[12]

About July 1, 1829, the landmark event of completing the translation was achieved, followed immediately by another. The Whitmer family furnished the nucleus of the select group of men and women who gathered around the family hearth to hear the Book of Mormon read from the completed manuscript for the first time.

LDS historian Marvin Hill described the premise of the narrative:

> The text described a society of ancient Americans faced with social disintegration, brought on by religious disbelief, rampant materialism, indifference toward the poor, political corruption, and war, all of which threatened their survival. Book of Mormon society was divided into two main factions: Nephites who were true Christians and who established a theocratic government to offset social disintegration, and

---

8. Jessee, *Personal Writings of Joseph Smith,* 11.

9. Book of Commandments, heading to chapter 15.

10. Ibid.; see also CofC D&C 16:1c; LDS D&C 18:3.

11. 1839 Draft History, in Jesse, *Papers of Joseph Smith,* 1:239.

12. Faulring, "An Examination of the 1829 'Articles,'" 64.

the Lamanites who were atheists and who waged a war of extermination on God's elect.... Nephite society thrived only at times when prophet-statesmen controlled the government and sustained the support of the faithful. Thus Nephite society was anti-pluralistic, for dissent and diversity were always atheistic and destructive.[13]

Emma Smith biographers Linda King Newell and Valeen Tippetts Avery summarize the story line of the Book of Mormon as:

> An account of an ancient people who migrated to America from Jerusalem about 600 B.C., drifting with the prevailing ocean and wind currents. They divided into two major factions called the Lamanites and the Nephites. Wars and contentions persisted throughout their history. They kept meticulous records of their conflicts, social structure, economic life, religious beliefs, and faith. At one time [after his resurrection] Jesus Christ visited and taught the Nephites, and for two hundred years thereafter peace prevailed. Later devastating wars almost annihilated the Nephites, but one man remained to write the final words of this ancient record. This was Moroni, last keeper of the record and son of Mormon, after whom the book would be named. Joseph explained that the Lamanites were ancestors of the American Indians and the book's purpose was to be a witness for Christ.[14]

Religious scholar Nathan O. Hatch, provides this assessment: "The Book of Mormon is a document of profound social protest, an impassioned manifesto by a hostile outsider against the smug complacency of those in power and the reality of social distinction based on wealth, class, and education."[15]

As early as March 1829, Martin Harris had asked to see the plates (D&C 5). One day in July 1829, following the usual morning family worship held in the Whitmer home, Joseph Smith confirmed the privilege of finally seeing the golden records and sacred artifacts upon Harris, Oliver Cowdery, and David Whitmer. Joseph's mother and father were also present on this occasion. Lucy Mack Smith recalled that her son expressed

---

13. Hill, *Quest for Refuge*, xii. Hill further observes, "The Book of Mormon was a history of ancient America, but its primary purpose was to warn Americans in the 1830s" (21).

14. Newell and Avery, *Mormon Enigma*, 29.

15. Hatch, *Democratization of American Christianity*, 121–22.

concern about Martin Harris's attitude, telling him, "You have got to humble yourself before your God this day, that you may obtain a forgiveness of your sins. If you do, it is the will of God that you should look upon the plates in company with Oliver Cowdery and David Whitmer."[16]

As the prospective witnesses stepped out of the door of the Whitmer home, they embarked upon a transformative experience. By agreeing to become witnesses to the facticity of the Book of Mormon, their lives would be forever changed. Joseph invited the three to accompany him to a grove near the Whitmer home. Joseph prayed aloud, followed by each of the others in turn. After the second round of prayers, Martin withdrew, believing that his presence prevented the anticipated experience.

Soon after Martin's departure, an angel appeared and showed the men plates with the appearance of gold and inscribed with strange characters. They repeated hearing a voice that spoke out of a bright light above them saying: "These plates have been revealed by the power of God, and they have been translated by the power of God. The translation of them which you have seen is correct, and I command you to bear record of what you now see and hear."[17] Martin Harris, the third witness, had a similar experience later the same day.

David Whitmer's account is the most explicit:

It was in June, 1829—the latter part of the month, and the Eight Witnesses saw them, I think, the next day or the day after (i.e. one or two days after). Joseph showed them the plates himself, but the angel showed us (the Three Witnesses) the plates, as I suppose to fulfill the words of the book itself. Martin Harris was not with us at this time; he obtained a view of them afterwards (the same day). Joseph, Oliver and myself were together when I saw them. We not only saw the plates of the Book of Mormon but also the brass plates, the plates of the Book of Ether, the plates containing the records of the wickedness and secret combinations of the people of the world down to the time of their being engraved, and many other plates. The fact is, it was just as though Joseph, Oliver and I were sitting just here on a log, when we were overshadowed by a light. It was not like the light of the sun nor like that of a fire, but more glorious and beautiful. It extended

16. *History of the LDS Church*, 1:55 note.
17. Ibid.

away round us, I cannot tell how far, but in the midst of this light about as far off as he sits (pointing to John C. Whitmer, sitting a few feet from him), there appeared as it were, a table with many records or plates upon it, besides the plates of the Book of Mormon, also the Sword of Laban, the Directors—i.e., the ball which Lehi had—and the Interpreters. I saw them just as plain as I see this bed (striking the bed beside him with his hand), and I heard the voice of the Lord, as distinctly as I ever heard anything in my life, declaring that the records of the plates of the Book of Mormon were translated by the gift and power of God.[18]

Throughout his life, David bore faithful witness of the reality of this encounter. Undoubtedly he perceived this experience as genuine, though some historians have raised questions about both the language of the written testimony and the setting.[19] Movement historian Dan Vogel surveys various documentary sources recounting the witnesses' experience, including many interviews with the witnesses themselves, analyzes the reliability of the available accounts and what they reveal about the nature of their encounter, and characterizes the experience of both the three and eight witnesses as "internal and subjective and in the fullest sense a vision."[20] In examining the evidence of the witnesses' statements, Vogel observes that the experience of the three witnesses was not as spiritual and that of the eight witnesses not as physical as has been commonly assumed. "Given the fact that the three witnesses saw a vision and that the experience of the eight witnesses seems to have been similarly visionary, there is no compelling evidence that Joseph Smith actually possessed anciently constructed plates."[21]

David Whitmer granted approximately seventy interviews that have been preserved in either print or holograph. After his initial 1829 witness, they span from 1838 to 1888, the last given on his deathbed. They all assert the divine origin and truthfulness of the Book of Mormon.

18. David Whitmer, interview by elders Orson Pratt and Joseph F. Smith, published as "Report of Elders Orson Pratt and Joseph F. Smith," 771–74.
19. Vogel, "The Validity of the Witnesses' Testimonies," 86.
20. Ibid., 86.
21. Ibid., 108.

One of the earliest newspaper reports, republished in the Painesville *Telegraph* in 1831, challenges the basic claim that the witnesses were shown the plates by an angel:

> [David] Whitmar [*sic*] … [has] been of late permitted, not only to see and handle it [the plates], but to examine the contents. Whitmar relates that he was led by Smith into an open field, on his [Whitmer's] father's farm near Waterloo, when they found the book lying on the ground; Smith took it up and requested him to examine it, which he did for the space of half an hour or more, when he returned it to Smith, who placed it in its former position, alleging that the book was in the custody of *another*, intimating that some divine agent would have it in safe keeping. This witness describes the book as being something like eight inches square, the leaves were plates of metal of a *whitish yellow* color, and of the thickness of tin plate—the back was secured with three small rings of the same metal, passing through each leaf in succession.[22]

Of course, Whitmer witnessed about his angelic encounter in numerous interviews. Whether he physically handled the plates is a more interesting question. In at least two interviews, David seems to suggest that he did. J. W. Chatburn reported Whitmer saying, "These hands handled the plates, these eyes saw the angel, and these ears heard his voice." And James H. Moyle recalled David saying "that he did see and handle the plates; that he did see and hear the angel and heard the declaration that the plates had been translated correctly."[23] Like many of our own day, Moyle noted that Whitmer "was somewhat spiritual in his explanation and not as materialistic as I wished."[24]

---

22. Howe, "The Gold Bible Fever," 2. Howe prepared an introductory paragraph ending with: "The following is from the last number of the *Reflector*, published near Smith's quarry." The remainder of the article reproduces a portion of Abner Cole, "Gold Bible, No. 6."

23. David Whitmer, interview by J. W. Chatburn, in "Bro. J. W. Chatburn, of Harlan, Iowa," 189; David Whitmer, interview by James H. Moyle, *Deseret News*, August 2, 1941, reprinted in Cook, *David Whitmer Interviews*, 163; for the correct dating of the *Deseret News* article, see Anderson, "Review of *David Whitmer Interviews*," 188.

24. David Whitmer, interview by Moyle, June 1885, in Cook, *David Whitmer Interviews*, 166–67.

Only a few days after the experience of the three witnesses, John Whitmer, who had served as a scribe for the Book of Mormon's translation during at least some of the previous month, was selected as one of eight additional witnesses to view and testify of the plates. Joseph was anxious to share with his own family the good news that the translation was finished. Joseph traveled to his brother Hyrum's home in Manchester, New York, about twenty-five miles from Fayette in company with the Whitmer brothers, Christian, Jacob, John, Peter Jr., and Hiram Page, all of whom became part of the group known as the eight witnesses. According to Lucy Mack Smith, one of the ancient Nephites brought the plates to a nearby grove where "the male part of the company, with my husband, Samuel, and Hyrum ... looked upon them and handled them."[25] The eight witnesses were thus five from the Whitmer clan (Christian, Jacob, Peter Jr., John Whitmer, and Hiram Page) and three Smiths (Joseph Sr., Hyrum, and Samuel H.).

In April 1878, John Whitmer told Danish LDS convert and physician Peter Wilhelm Poulson that he was among a group of three witnesses who saw the plates in the Smith home and that "at another time he [Smith] showed them to four persons more." According to this 1878 account, John saw the uncovered plates, touched them, and turned the leaves.[26] If this

25. This visitation may have occurred in the "sacred grove" where Joseph had earlier experienced what is known as the First Vision, but Lucy identifies it only as "a little grove where it was customary for the family to offer up their secret prayers." Lucy Smith, preliminary manuscript, 1844–45. Printed versions are readily available in Anderson, *Lucy's Book*, 455–56, and "Lucy Smith History, 1845," in Vogel, *Early Mormon Documents*, 1:395–96.

26. Poulson, "Death of John Whitmer," *Deseret News*, August 14, 1878, 2. Peter Wilhelm Poulson, Count Fagerstjerna, was born in Copenhagen, Denmark, in 1841, a descendant of Lutheran priests and Scandinavian nobility. As a young man, he received military schooling and earned doctorates in theology and medicine. He affiliated with the Mormons in Denmark, serving as administrator over the LDS Copenhagen District. He was an officer in the party of Mormon emigrants whom he accompanied to the United States. His arrival coincided with the conclusion of the Civil War. Poulson presented his medical credentials to the New York Medical Society and was accorded a diploma and license to practice medicine and surgery. He also studied homeopathic medicine and practiced as a physician in Council Bluffs, Iowa, and Salt Lake City, then, suffering from ill health, in San Francisco. He recrossed the continent to Council Bluffs, Iowa, as one of the first passengers on the newly completed Union Pacific and Central Pacific Railroad. After injuring his knee in a railroad accident in 1874, he pursued an extended

report is correct, however, the eight witnesses may have been two groups of four, rather than eight simultaneously.

Mormon critic Eber D. Howe, who exerted strenuous efforts to discredit the movement before it was five years old, wrote in 1831:

> There appears to be a great discrepancy, in the stories told by the famous three witnesses to the Gold Bible; and these *pious* reprobates, individually, frequently gave different versions of the same transaction. In the first place it was roundly asserted that the plates on which Mormon wrote his history, (in the reformed Egyptian language) were of gold, and hence its name—gentlemen in this vicinity were called on to estimate its value from its weight, (something more than 20 lbs.) Smith and Harris gave out, that no mortal save Jo could look upon it and live; and Harris declared, that when he acted as *amanuenses,* and wrote the translation, as Smith dictated, such was his fear of the Divine displeasure, that a screen (sheet) was suspended between the prophet and himself.[27]

The published testimony of the eight witnesses affirms that they had "seen and hefted" the plates.[28] Of the eight witnesses, summarizes Vogel, "Christian Whitmer, Peter Whitmer Jr., Jacob Whitmer, and Joseph Smith Sr. left no commentary regarding their testimonies. Both Hyrum

---

recuperation in Salt Lake City, where he again practiced medicine but also lectured frequently at the Liberal Institute, which formed a social center and political club, primarily for non-Mormons in Utah. Joseph Smith III and his brothers also lectured at this institute on their periodic missions to Utah. During this period Poulson developed interests in psychoanalysis and spiritualism. In April 1878, he traveled to northern Missouri where he interviewed John and David Whitmer. During this period, he also pursued a friendship with David H. Smith, brother of Joseph Smith III, who described Poulson as "a man of ability and learning, [who] is and has been for some years, a Spiritualist." But Joseph III expressed concern about Poulson's friendship with David: "I fear his influence would not be for David's good. Of this I am assured, Poulson is crazy enough to fancy that he can cure David." In 1886 Poulson moved to California where he built Fruitvale Hospital as a sanitarium for the treatment of mental, nervous, and chronic diseases. *The Bay of San Francisco: The Metropolis of the Pacific Coast and Its Suburban Cities,* 2:91–93. See also Jenson, *History of the Scandinavian Mission,* 156, 177, 494; Joseph Smith III to Dr. E. A. Kilbourne, 11 March 1879, 135.

27.   Howe, "Gold Bible Fever," 2.

28.   Statement of the eight witnesses, Book of Mormon.

and Samuel Smith left brief accounts stating that they saw and handled the plates. Hiram Page only testified that he saw the plates."[29]

In 1847, Hiram Page, in asserting the truthfulness of the Book of Mormon, added a testimony of the ministry of angels to his knowledge of the plates:

> As to the Book of Mormon, it would be doing injustice to myself and to the work of God of the last days, to say that I could know a thing to be true in 1830, and know the same thing to be false in 1847. To say my mind was so treacherous that I have forgotten what I saw, to say that a man of Joseph's ability, who at that time did not know how to pronounce the word Nephi, could write a book of six hundred pages, as correct as the Book of Mormon without supernatural power. And to say that those holy Angels who came and showed themselves to me as I was walking through the field, to confirm me in the work of the Lord of the last days—three of whom came to me afterwards and sang an hymn in their own pure language; yes, it would be treating the God of heaven with contempt, to deny these testimonies.[30]

Almost nine years later when the church was relocating to Missouri, Hyrum Smith stayed at the home of Sally Parker in Ohio and told her, "Wee wass talking about the Book of Mormon which he is one of the witnesses he said he had but too hands and too eyes he said he had seen the plates with his eyes and handled them with his hands."[31] Hyrum also published a statement in the church's Nauvoo newspaper, *Times and Seasons,* about having seen and handled the plates: "I had been abused and thrust into a dungeon ... on account of my faith.... However—I thank God that I felt a determination to die, rather than deny the things which my eyes had seen, which my hands had handled, and which I had borne testimony to, wherever my lot had been cast; and I can assure my beloved brethren that I was enabled to bear as strong a testimony, when nothing but death presented itself, as ever I did in my life."[32]

29. Vogel, "Validity of the Witnesses' Testimonies," 99.

30. Hiram Page to William E. McLellin, 30 May 1847, *Ensign of Liberty,* 1:63.

31. Sally Parker to John Kempton, 26 August 1838, quoted in Anderson, "Attempts to Redefine the Experience of the Eight Witnesses," 18–31.

32. Smith, "To the Saints Scattered Abroad," 23.

Convert Daniel Tyler said that Joseph's younger brother Samuel, one of the eight witnesses, told him in 1832: "He knew his brother Joseph had the plates, for ... [Joseph] had shown them to him, and he had handled them and seen the engravings thereon."[33]

These encounters with the plates provide intriguing supplemental detail to the published testimony of the eight witnesses, found in every printing of the work from the first edition on.

John and his family apparently shared a cultural worldview that readily harmonized religious and folk beliefs. On June 18, 1830, the Whitmers' former pastor, Diedrich Willers Sr., wrote disapprovingly to his colleagues, Lewis Mayer and Daniel Young, professors at the Theological Seminary of the Reformed church in York, Pennsylvania: "I am acquainted with the Whitmers.... They are gullible to the highest degree and even believe in witches. Hiram Page is equally full of superstition."[34] He was not just slandering the Whitmers. According to Edward Miller Fogel, who published *Beliefs and Superstitions of the Pennsylvania Germans* in 1915, folk beliefs and superstitions were an integral part of the German-American ethnic culture.[35] Willers continued: "When it became known to me that Peter Whitmer and his family were becoming the dupes of Smith and his co-workers, I called upon Mr. Whitmer, in order to remonstrate with him and to warn him of the errors and delusions and the false doctrines promulgated by these men. My conversation, however, apparently made no impression upon him, his only reply to my arguments being the repeated quotations in the German language of the words 'Jesus Christ, yesterday, to-day, and forever.'"[36]

Influenced by Joseph Smith's use of a seer stone, some of the Whitmers acquired similar stones. Hiram Page and Jacob Whitmer are known

---

33. Daniel Tyler was converted to the faith in 1832, in part by hearing Samuel Smith tell his story, quoted in Anderson, *Investigating the Book of Mormon Witnesses*, 140.

34. Diedrich Willers to Reverend Brethren, 18 June 1830, quoted in Vogel, *Early Mormon Documents*, 5:278; see also Quinn, "The First Months of Mormonism," 317–33.

35. Fogel, *Beliefs and Superstitions of the Pennsylvania Germans*, 18, noted that the assumption that Pennsylvania Germans were extremely superstitious "is hardly correct. Their superstition has simply not taken a form sanctioned by other strata of society."

36. Diedrich Willers Sr. to Ellen E. Dickinson, 19 January 1882, in Dickinson, *New Light on Mormonism*, 249–52, quoted in Vogel, *Early Mormon Documents*, 5:284.

to have possessed such stones. Jacob's remained in his family until the 1950s.[37] John may have also acquired a stone while serving as Joseph's scribe. The Whitmers were reportedly "so devoted to the importance of seer stones that David Whitmer, John Whitmer, and Hiram Page later dated the beginning of their own disenchantment with Mormonism at the time when Joseph Smith stopped using the seer stone as an instrument of revelation."[38] Michael Quinn continues: "Their interest in seer stones continued long after their association with Smith. David Whitmer's family preserved their grandfather's artifacts," including an oblong stone with two holes, now in the possession of the Community of Christ in Independence, Missouri.[39]

A variety of seekers and critics have entertained suspicions about the witnesses' cultural worldview. A recent historian posits that, rather than having experienced a physical manifestation, the witnesses actually perceived the plates through their spiritual eyes or as some kind of self-induced hallucination.[40] Others have characterized early church members

37. Jacob Whitmer's granddaughter, Mayme Janetta Whitmer Koontz (1879–1961), wrote, "As to how this Seer stone came into my possession, it has been handed down through one generation of the Whitmer family to the next generation until it finally was given to me, and I consider it a very great honor to have such a sacred trust in my possession." Mayme Koontz to Alvin R. Dyer, 12 June 1955, partially quoted in Dyer, *The Refiner's Fire*, 263. In 1970, Mayme Koontz's daughters Lillian Merle Barchers, Gladys Evelyn DeMint, and Beulah Elizabeth Hayes sold this stone to David C. Martin who placed it in "the vault of the Marine First National Bank, Janesville, Wisconsin, where it lay forgotten for a decade." Martin sold it to rare book dealer Rick Grunder of New York. Grunder sold it to Steven F. Christensen who owned it from February 1984, until shortly before he was murdered by Mark W. Hofmann. Grunder reacquired the stone and sold it again. Today, "it remains in private hands." A photograph of the stone can be seen online at Rick Grunder Books website: "Whitmer Family Seer Stone," Treasures Past, accessed May 2, 2012, http://www.rickgrunder.com/HistoricalArchive/whitmerstone.htm.

38. Stewart, "Hiram Page," 140–46, quoted in Quinn, *Early Mormonism and the Magic World View*, 201.

39. Quinn, *Early Mormonism and the Magic World View*, illustrations, figures 11, 12. This object (Stone 1) is a Native American artifact of the class known as gorgets. The holes are hand drilled with perhaps the intent of suspending it upon a thong.

40. McElveen, *The Mormon Illusion*, 8. When Anthony Metcalf questioned David Whitmer about whether his viewing of the plates was "spiritual" or "natural," Whitmer responded in writing:

as a society of "folk believers."[41] Peter W. Williams, a historian of popular religion in early America, concluded that Smith's "natural constituency was among those who saw the world through the categories of the folk—those to whom special providences and spectral appearances are inherently plausible."[42]

Most of the eleven witnesses to the Book of Mormon were familiar with an unconventional form of pre-Enlightenment Christianity—what John L. Brooke calls "the Radical tradition." However, he acknowledged, "Despite the experience in treasure-hunting and Freemasonry of many early Mormons, their frame of reference was overwhelmingly traditional and biblical."[43] This unique blend of perspectives admits a broad context for a ready acceptance of Mormonism's heady doctrines and practices.[44]

John Whitmer lived the longest of the eight witnesses, affording the opportunity to leave the most detailed record of the experience of this group. Although John Whitmer signed the testimony of the eight witnesses, his later statements are sometimes ambiguous about the amount of direct physical contact he had with the plates themselves. During Whitmer's April 1839 encounter at Far West with Theodore Turley, a believing

---

> In regards to my testimony to the visitation of the angel, who declared to us Three Witnesses that the Book of Mormon is true, I have this to say: Of course we were in the spirit when we had the view, for no man can behold the face of an angel, except in a spiritual view, but we were in the body also, and everything was as natural to us, as it is at any time. Martin Harris, you say, called it "being in vision." We read in the Scriptures, Cornelius saw, in a vision, an angel of God. Daniel saw an angel in a vision, also in other places it states they saw an angel in the spirit. A bright light enveloped us where we were, that filled at noon day, and there in a vision, or in the spirit, we saw and heard just as it is stated in my testimony in the Book of Mormon.

David Whitmer to Anthony Metcalf, March 1887, in Metcalf, *Ten Years before the Mast*, 74, partially quoted in Anderson, *Investigating Book of Mormon Witnesses*, 87.

41. Quinn, *Early Mormonism and the Magic World View*, 226.

42. Williams, *Popular Religion in America*, 86, quoted in Quinn, *Early Mormonism and the Magic World View*, 194.

43. Brooke, *Refiner's Fire*, 58, 209, quoted in Quinn, *Early Mormonism and the Magic World View* (1998), 241.

44. Old Testament references to the urim and thummim (Exod. 28:30, KJV) and mention in the book of Revelation of a "white stone" to be received by believers (Rev. 2:17 KJV) may have opened Mormonism to the use of divining stones.

Mormon who had not yet left Missouri for Nauvoo, John said: "I handled those plates; there were fine engravings on both sides."[45] RLDS church member Myron Bond wrote, "John Whitmer told me last winter...[that he] 'saw and handled' [the plates and]...helped to copy [the Book of Mormon manuscript] as the words fell from Joseph's lips by supernatural or [A]lmighty power."[46] Interviewers from an increasingly science-oriented culture obviously struggled about how to interpret John's pre-scientific understandings and experiences.

The eight, plus three witnesses, and Joseph Smith, were perhaps collectively intended to represent twelve disciples, invested with special apostolic significance.[47] David Marks, an itinerant preacher who stayed with the Whitmer family March 29, 1830, elaborated this possibility. The Whitmers told him "that twelve apostles were to be appointed, who would soon confirm their mission by miracles."[48] A revelation through Joseph Smith in June 1829 communicated the information to John, David, and Oliver that "you are called even with that same calling with which he [Paul] was called" (CofC D&C 16:3b; LDS D&C 18:9). In other words, they were apostles. John's elder's license, dated June 9, 1830, communicates the same information: "Given to John Whitmer signifying & proveing [sic] that he is an Apostle of Jesus Christ [and] an Elder in this Church."[49] Although Jesus had not selected Paul as an apostle during his mortal ministry, the New Testament portrays that fervent preacher as a charismatic apostle and special witness, and he certainly asserted an apostolic identity.

Apparently throughout early 1831, the twelve founding disciples, by virtue of their role as special witnesses to the Book of Mormon, saw themselves as apostles. Smith reportedly told the Kirtland School of the Prophets in 1833 "that the title 'apostle' applied to those who had received

---

45. Theodore Turley, memoranda, 5 April 1839.

46. Myron Bond, letter, Cadillac, Michigan, 2 August 1878, *Herald* 25:253. Peter Wilhelm Poulson visited John Whitmer at Far West shortly before John's death, as well as David Whitmer in Richmond, Missouri, in 1878; Poulson, "Interview with David Whitmer," *Deseret News*, August 21, 1878, 13; Poulson, "Correspondence: Death of John Whitmer," *Deseret News*, August 14, 1878, 2.

47. For an extended discussion, see Quinn, *Mormon Hierarchy: Origins of Power*, 10–14.

48. Marks, *Memoirs of the Life of David Marks*, 236–37.

49. John Whitmer, elder's license.

a vision."[50] Furthermore, during this charismatic period, early participants saw themselves as Joseph's equals. David Whitmer described their relationship in these first two years of their association. "Brother Joseph gave many true prophesies [*sic*] when he was humble before God: but this is no more than many of the other brethren did."[51]

With the Book of Mormon translation completed, attention turned to getting the book into print. John Gilbert, a typesetter in the print shop of Egbert B. Grandin in Palmyra recalled in 1877, "One pleasant day in the summer of 1829, Hiram Smith, Joe's brother, came to the office to negotiate for the printing of the book."[52] Martin Harris's financial commitment persuaded Grandin to undertake the project, one so lengthy and ambitious that Grandin needed to purchase a new font of type.[53] Possibly as a result of the lost 116 pages, Joseph ordered strict precautions to safeguard the manuscript during the printing process. According to Lucy Smith:

> A revelation came to Joseph commanding him to see that Oliver transcribed the whole work a second time and never take both transcripts to the office but leave one and carry the other so that in case one was destroyed the other would be left furthermore Peter ~~whi~~ Whitmer was commanded to remain at our [the Hyrum Smith] house to assist in guarding the writing and also ~~for the purpose of~~ to accompany Oliver to the Office and back when no other person could be spared from the place to go and come with him as it was necessary that oliver [*sic*] should be accompanied by some one for the purpose of protecting him in case of danger, that if this <precaution> was not ~~the case~~ taken his enemies would be likely to ~~to~~ waylay him in order to get the manuscript away from him.[54]

Thus, during the printing, Cowdery daily produced enough copy to keep the printer busy the next day. The majority of this printer's manu-

50. Graffam, *Salt Lake School of the Prophets*, 71, quoted in Quinn, *Mormon Hierarchy: Origins of Power*, 12n58.

51. David Whitmer, *An Address to All Believers*, 32.

52. Gilbert, "Joe Smith," 3, quoted in O'Driscoll, *Hyrum Smith: A Life of Integrity*, 30.

53. Gilbert, memorandum, 8 September 1892.

54. Anderson, *Lucy's Book*, 459.

script is in Oliver's hand, but several others also assisted with the copying.[55] Hyrum Smith and Cowdery often both spent the day at Grandin's,[56] and the work progressed rather rapidly. One impediment was that, despite Joseph's instructions, the manuscript was left at the print shop one weekend. Abner Cole, who rented the facility on weekends, began printing the text in his newspaper, the *Reflector,* and Joseph had to come from Harmony and threaten legal action before Cole desisted. Also, according to Lucy, some Palmyra residents organized a boycott, vowing not to purchase the book and assuring Grandin that he would never be paid. Martin Harris's mortgage on his farm relieved Grandin's apprehensions, and the project went forward.

A description of the book and its translation appeared in the *Fredonia* [New York] *Censor:*

> *New Bible*—A fellow by the name of Joseph Smith, who resides in the upper part of Susquehanna county, has been, for the last two years we are told, employed in dictating, as he says, by inspiration, a new *Bible.* He pretended that he had been entrusted by God with a golden bible which had been always hidden from the world. Smith would put his face into a hat in which he had a *white stone,* and pretend to read from it, while his coadjutor transcribed. The book purports to give an account of the "ten tribes" and strange as it may seem, there are some who have full faith in his divine commission.[57]

The Book of Mormon became available to the public on March 26, 1830. Less caution was necessary now that the Book of Mormon manuscript was in print. Joseph set the dictated manuscript safely aside and gave Oliver Cowdery, his faithful scribe, the second copy, which had served as the printer's manuscript. David Whitmer, who was present, described that

---

55. Skousen, *Original Manuscript of the Book of Mormon,* 14, has identified the following scribes in the extant portions of the dictated Book of Mormon manuscript: Oliver Cowdery (LDS versification) 1 Nephi 2:2–3:6, 1 Nephi 15–20, 1 Nephi 16:1–Enos 1:14, Alma 10:31–45:22, Alma 45:22–Ether 15:17; Joseph Smith Alma 45:22; Scribe 2 (unknown—possibly John Whitmer) 1 Nephi 3:7–4:14, 1 Nephi 12:9–16:1; Scribe 3 (unknown) 1 Nephi 4:20–12:8.

56. O'Driscoll, *Hyrum Smith: A Life of Integrity,* 30–31.

57. "New Bible," *Fredonia (New York) Censor,* June 2, 1830, reprinted from the *Wayne County Republican,* accessed May 2, 2012, http://www.sidneyrigdon.com/dbroadhu/NY/miscNYS1.htm.

Joseph handed the printer's manuscript over to Oliver, placing him under sober obligation: "O, it was such a solemn charge. He (Joseph) said, I feel it in my bones that there will be a division in the Church, like it was with the Nephites and Lamanites, and if these manuscripts are not preserved, I fear that the church may be injured, and when you deliver them up to others, be sure they are left in good hands."[58]

Joseph, now free to turn his attention to other matters, energetically began to work on a plan to revise the Holy Scriptures, even while moving to formally organize a quickly coalescing movement. During the preparation of the Book of Mormon, Joseph came to believe that the Bible had become corrupted as it was transmitted over the generations by religious leaders who deliberately departed from biblical truth and that many plain and precious things had been lost from Bible texts (CofC Book of Mormon, 1 Nephi 3:171; LDS 1 Nephi 13:24–28). Even while the Book of Mormon was being printed, Smith prepared to launch an ambitious project intending to restore the Holy Scriptures' original content. Toward this end, on October 8, 1829, Joseph Smith and Oliver Cowdery purchased a copy of an 1828 Phinney edition of the King James Bible at the E. B. Grandin Bookstore, Palmyra, Wayne County, New York.

Just as had been the case since 1829, John Whitmer was at Joseph's side even as Smith prepared to launch a new phase of Mormonism.

58. *History of the RLDS Church*, 4:446–47.

CHAPTER FIVE

Organizing the Church

O NE URGENT ACTIVITY, the organization of a church, had been postponed until the Book of Mormon's publication. Smith had, six months earlier, identified April 6, 1830, as the preferred date. Ironically, there is considerable uncertainty about this central event. Scholars cannot agree where and by whom the church was officially organized. In 1881, more than fifty years after the fact, David Whitmer listed John as among the six elders who met on April 6, 1830, in the Whitmer home at Fayette, Seneca County, New York, in the organizational meeting.[1]

However, there is no agreement among early sources about who participated in the organization of the church nor even that the event was held in Fayette.[2] Currently, an 1862 list compiled by Joseph Knight Jr., who

---

1. On June 5, 1881, David gave a *Kansas City Journal* reporter a list of seven elders: Joseph Smith, Oliver Cowdery, Martin Harris, Hyrum Smith, John Whitmer, Peter Whitmer, and David Whitmer. Harris had not been ordained an elder at this point; David Whitmer, interview by the *Kansas City Daily Journal*, June 5, 1881, in Cook, *David Whitmer Interviews*, 58–71; David later repudiated portions of the *Kansas City Journal* interview, although the list of seven was not one of the misquoted items. David Whitmer to S. T. Mouch, 18 November 1882; David Whitmer to *Kansas City Journal*, corrections to 1 June 1881 interview, in Cook, *David Whitmer Interviews*, 71–72. Vogel suggests that David Whitmer was attempting to name the elders who were present rather than the six founders of the church and concludes: "Whitmer's lists of 'elders' should, therefore, not be confused with Joseph Knight, Jr.'s naming of six founding 'members.'" Vogel, *Early Mormon Documents*, 4:67–68. On January 2, 1887, David told Edward Stevenson that the six elders were Joseph Smith, Oliver Cowdery, David Whitmer, John Whitmer, Peter Whitmer, and Hyrum Smith. Stevenson, journal, 2 January 1887, in Cook, *David Whitmer Interviews*, 214.

2. Vogel, *Early Mormon Documents*, 4:67, summarizes these extant lists of founders. Anderson, "Who Were the Six Who Organized the Church on 6 April 1830?," 44–45, identifies seven lists. Jessee, *Papers of Joseph Smith*, 1:241, adds a list created by William McLellin. Marquardt, "An Appraisal of Manchester as Location for the Organization

was then fifty-four, has become more or less authoritative.[3] Knight identifies the six as Joseph Smith, Oliver Cowdery, Samuel H. Smith, Hyrum
Smith, Peter Whitmer Jr., and David Whitmer—but not John.[4] Joseph
Knight's father, Joseph Knight Sr., sometime between 1835 and 1847, placed
the organizational meeting in Manchester, New York.[5] William E. McLellin, who was not present, later wrote, "THE CHURCH OF CHRIST was
organized on the 6th day of April, 1830, in the township of Manchester,
and State of New York, with only six members, viz. Joseph Smith; sen.,
Lucy Smith his wife, Joseph Smith, jr., Oliver Cowdery, David Whitmore

---

of the Church," 50, identifies an additional founders' list from Turner, *Mormonism in
All Ages*, 22. "On the 6th of April, 1830; the first Mormon church was organized in
Manchester, N. Y., with only six members, viz., Joseph Smith, Hyrum Smith, Samuel
Smith, the father and brothers of the prophet, Oliver Cowdery, scribe to Smith, Joseph
Knight, and the prophet: Of these, of course, Joseph Smith, jun., the prophet." Steven
C. Harper, informed by his excellent research related to the discovery and publication
of the Book of Commandments manuscript, argues that scholars interested in the
question of the location of the organization of the church may have to take a further
look at evidence in this manuscript. The headnote of the 17th commandment reads
"17th Commandment AD 1829, <April <6> 1830>." Jensen, Woodford, and Harper,
Revelations and Translations, 27. The revelation's internal text alludes to the organization of the church in the past tense, so Book of Commandments editors struck through
John's original dating of 1829. At some point, Oliver Cowdery inserted April 1830.
John apparently later still inserted the "6." For more of Harper's argument on behalf
of Fayette, see Harper, "Historical Headnotes and the Index of Contents in the Book
of Commandments and Revelations," 58–59. While Harper's observations are percep-
tive, I do not see the evidence emerging from this editorial revision process, nor accept
Harper's argument on this issue, as definitive. It is equally plausible this revelation
may have been given preceding the organization of the church as suggested by John's
initial dating. During the scribal process, John may have simply shifted away from
the initial tense while copying this revelation into the "Book of Commandments and
Revelations" manuscript, causing the wording to conform to the familiar terminology
"Organized and established ...," which regularly appears in official documents of the
church of that time.

3. Joseph Knight Jr., quoted in Porter, "A Study of the Origins of the Church," 249n69.
   John does not appear on Knight's list. See also Joseph Knight Jr., statement, 11 August
   1862, in Vogel, *Early Mormon Documents*, 4:66.

4. Joseph Knight Jr., statement, 11 August 1862, in Vogel, *Early Mormon Documents*, 4:66.

5. Jessee, "Joseph Knight [Sr.]'s Recollection of Early Mormon History," 36–37; see also
   Vogel, *Early Mormon Documents*, 4:21–22. However, Porter, in his "A Study of the Origins," 248, surmises that Joseph Knight Sr. was not actually present during the organizational meeting.

[*sic*], and Martin Harris."[6] This list differs drastically from Joseph Knight's by including all three Book of Mormon witnesses and also by including a woman, Joseph's mother. But he is almost certainly mistaken in naming Lucy. The New York State law in force in 1830 reads, "Every male person of full age who has either worshipped with the Church, congregation or society and has formerly been considered as belonging thereto is given the right to vote."[7] Therefore, the six members who established the church were probably not only men, but also apparently had been previously ordained to the priesthood. An appraisal of the minutes of early church conferences suggests that church business was conducted by priesthood holders, a more restricted participation than the every-male-member regulation enunciated in New York law.

David Whitmer identified another set of founding elders in his 1887 *An Address to All Believers in Christ*: Joseph Smith, Oliver Cowdery, Peter Whitmer, Samuel H. Smith, Hyrum Smith, and David Whitmer. David observed, "We attended to our business of organizing," on April 6, 1830, "according to the laws of the land, the church acknowledging us six elders as their ministers."[8]

Scholars now hypothesize that David Whitmer's recollections about the organizational meeting, dating more than fifty years after the fact, are also less than reliable.[9] He apparently blended the organizational meeting on April 6 with the first conference, which was definitely held at the Whitmer home in Fayette on June 9.

6. McLellin, "A Special Conference of All the Ministerial Authorities," 2.

7. Attorney George H. Mortimer, regional representative of the twelve for the Niagara Falls and New York regions of the LDS church to Larry Porter, 28 January 1970, quoted in Porter, "A Study of the Origins," 382.

8. David Whitmer, *An Address to All Believers in Christ*, 32, 33.

9. "It is important, too, to note that Whitmer himself was not always consistent in the way he remembered Latter-day Saint beginnings." Godfrey, "The Shaping of Latter-day Saint History," 225. David Whitmer considered himself frequently misquoted: "I am not responsible for what men Say in regard to their conversations with me. It is Seldom that my Statements are correctly reported. And when I write Even then what I Say is not always printed as I have written." David Whitmer to S. T. Mouch, 18 November 1882.

The organization of the Church of Christ on April 6, 1830. Edited image courtesy of Community of Christ.

Though John Whitmer was baptized prior to the church's organization and may have been in attendance, he was apparently not among the six who officially organized the church.

At the organizational meeting on April 6, probably in Manchester Township, New York,[10] Oliver Cowdery was assigned by revelation to keep the church's records.[11] Five days later on April 11 at the Whitmer home, Cowdery delivered "the first <real> public sermon, which was delivered by any <member> of our Church, we had a crowded audience." Afterward, he baptized Hiram Page, Catherine Whitmer Page, Christian Whitmer, Anne/Anna Schott Whitmer (Christian's wife), Jacob Whitmer, Elizabeth Ann Schott Whitmer (Jacob's wife), and Mary Page (relationship to Hi-

10. As I appraise the evidence, I give more credence to sources indicating that the church was organized in the Smith home in Manchester Township, Wayne County, New York.

11. The revelation says "a record shall be kept" without naming Cowdery, but Oliver clearly began serving as the church's first recorder. See Book of Commandments 22; 1835 D&C 42; CofC D&C 19; LDS D&C 21. Several people were baptized following this service, including Joseph Smith Sr., Lucy Mack Smith, Orrin Porter Rockwell, and Martin Harris. *History of the LDS Church*, 1:79.

ram Page unknown) in Seneca Lake.[12] As with the Book of Mormon's translation, the Whitmer home continued to serve as a primary gathering place. One week later on April 18, a second preaching service was held. Cowdery again delivered the sermon and afterward baptized in Seneca Lake seven more people: Peter Sr. and Mary Whitmer, William and Elizabeth Jolly, Vincent Jolly, Richard B. "Ziba" Peterson, and Elizabeth Ann Whitmer, John's younger sister and Oliver's future wife.[13]

The Whitmer family's former pastor, Diedrich Willers Sr., identified the locations of subsequent meetings. "Preaching services were held in 1830 and 1831 at Peter Whitmer's house, and at Whitmer's school house, in District No. 17, Fayette.... Another preaching point was at the school house in school district No. 15, in the locality known as 'The Beach,' in northeast Fayette."[14]

Although early baptisms were conducted in nearby Seneca Lake, during the months following the church's organization, small streams and creeks in the area also became baptismal settings. Jacob Shiley, a young man in his twenties who lived in the

Diedrich Willers Sr., the Whitmer family's pastor when they lived in the Fayette, Seneca County, New York, area.

Whitmer neighborhood and attended early services held at the Whitmer and William Jolly homes, reported that baptisms were performed in the nearby Thomas and Kendig Creeks.[15]

As the new organization unfolded, individuals stepped forward to fill ministerial roles. John and David were among the six elders who con-

---

12. Jessee, *Papers of Joseph Smith*, 1:244. The Sunday after the organizational meeting at Manchester, the Fayette Branch was established. Marquardt, "An Appraisal of Manchester," 54.

13. *History of the RLDS Church*, 1:84–85, 88.

14. Willers Jr., *Centennial Historical Sketch of the Town of Fayette*, 48, quoted in Porter, "A Study of the Origins," 254.

15. Jacob Shiley, quoted in Diedrich Willers Sr. to Ellen E. Dickinson, 19 January 1882, quoted in Vogel, *Early Mormon Documents*, 5:284. See also Porter, "A Study of the Origins," 256–58.

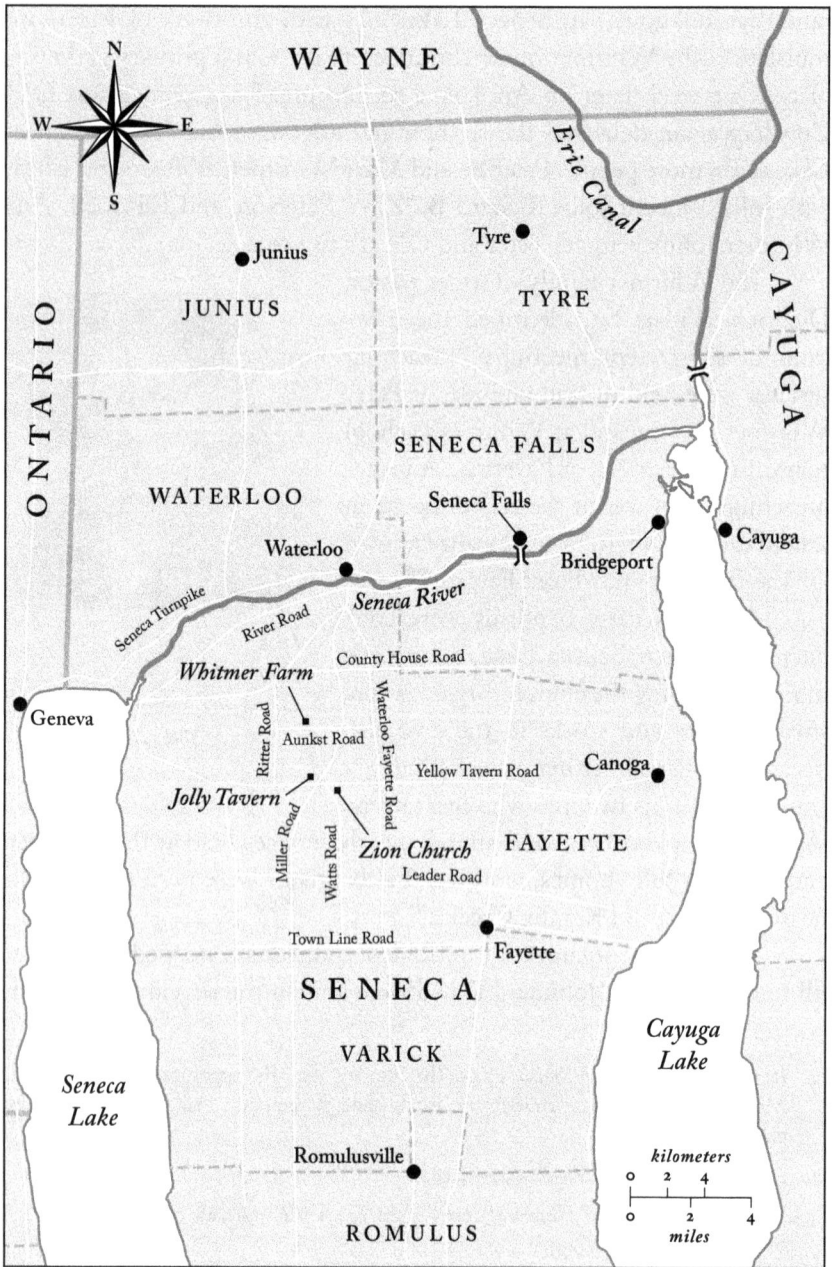

Fig. 5.1. Vicinity of the Whitmer Farm in Fayette, New York.

vened the first church conference (as opposed to a preaching service) on June 9, 1830. Having been recognized by the body as its first elder, Joseph took the lead of the meeting.[16] Here, an early version of the articles and covenants, prepared by Oliver Cowdery, was read and adopted as the church rule.[17] They confirmed newly baptized members, administered the sacrament, and ordained and licensed most of the male members as elders, priests, and teachers. It was at this conference that John received a written license identifying him as both an apostle and an elder.[18] LDS church history observes, "Much exhortation and instruction was given," during the June 9 conference "and the Holy Ghost was poured out upon us in a miraculous manner."[19]

Joseph and Emma were preparing to move back to Harmony, Pennsylvania, to resume their residence near Emma's parents on the Hale family farm. Accompanied by Oliver, David, and John, Joseph and Emma left immediately after the June 9 conference. The three young single men were planning an extended stay.[20]

Almost immediately after reaching Harmony, Joseph, Emma, Oliver, David, and John paid a crucial visit to the large Knight family at Colesville in Broom County, New York. Here they were successful in establishing a branch in late June 1830, despite considerable local opposition.[21] Newel Knight, Joseph Knight's second son, who was then twenty-nine, wrote, "There were many in our neighborhood who believed, and were anxiously waiting for an opportunity to be baptized. Meeting was appointed for the Sabbath [June 27, 1830], and on Saturday afternoon we erected a dam across a stream which was close by."[22] John, no doubt familiar with such farm-related work, helped construct the dam. On Sunday morning, they

16. As an early item of business, the conference of six elders approved the articles and covenants. Minutes of conference held 9 June 1830, in Cannon and Cook, *Far West Record*, 1. The text of the articles and covenants identified Joseph Smith as first elder. "Articles of the Church," [1–2].

17. Faulring, "An Examination of the 1829 'Articles,'" 57–91.

18. Cannon and Cook, *Far West Record*, 1; John Whitmer, elder's license.

19. *History of the LDS Church*, 1:84–85.

20. Ibid., 1:86.

21. Jenson, *LDS Biographical Encyclopedia*, 1:251.

22. Knight, "Newel Knight's Journal," 53.

discovered that someone had demolished the dam, leaving the stream too shallow for baptism by immersion. Regardless, Oliver preached to a good audience. Early on Monday morning, June 28, 1830, they repaired the dam; and Oliver baptized Emma Smith and twelve members of the extended Joseph Knight Sr. family: Hezekiah Peck and his wife, Martha Long Peck; Joseph Knight Sr. and Polly Peck Knight and their unmarried children Polly and Joseph Jr.; William Stringham and Esther Knight Stringham; Aaron Culver and Ester Peck Culver; and Levi Hale [Hall].²³ Before the new members could be confirmed, Joseph Smith was arrested on charges of disorderly conduct and held for trial before the magistrate's court in Broom County. In describing this event in his 1839 history, Joseph took pains to gratefully note the support of "my former faithful friends and lawyers" who "were again at my side."²⁴ Clearly it was a source of consolation to Joseph that John and the others remained supportive during this exhausting and irritating interruption, which involved a second arrest immediately after the first. In the end, Joseph was acquitted.²⁵

Another source of solace during Joseph's arrest was a revelation that Joseph described as a "precious morsel." During June [13–30] 1830, Joseph received an expanded version of Moses's call to deliver the children of Israel from Egypt. "For behold, this is my work and my glory—to bring to pass the immortality and eternal life of man."²⁶ In the midst of his own tribulation, Joseph found strength through this reminder of God's deliverance: "line upon line of knowledge–here a little and there a little."²⁷

After the Bainbridge trial and alarmed by threats of more judicial action, John returned to the Smith home in Harmony with Joseph, Emma, David, and Oliver, leaving the newly baptized converts at Colesville unconfirmed.²⁸

23. Jessee, *Papers of Joseph Smith*, 1:251.

24. Ibid., 1:255.

25. *History of the LDS Church*, 1:86–96.

26. For dating the revelation, see Vogel, chronology, *Early Mormon Documents*, 5:433. Joseph Smith Jr., The Holy Scriptures: Inspired Version, forepart, page 9; CofC D&C 22:23b; Joseph Smith, the Book of Moses in the Pearl of Great Price, 1:39.

27. *History of the LDS Church*, 1:98.

28. Jessee, *Papers of Joseph Smith*, 1:251–58.

With the vision of Moses still fresh in his mind, Joseph was eager to begin the formal revision of the Bible with Oliver as scribe. Robert J. Matthews, a scholar of Joseph Smith's *New Translation of the Holy Scriptures*, cites the Book of Mormon passage that, when the Bible proceeded forth from the mouth of the Jews, "it contained the plainness of the gospel of the Lamb." However, "through the centuries it became deficient, because 'there are many plain and precious things taken away from the book'" (CofC 1 Nephi 3:171; LDS 1 Nephi 13:24–28). The Book of Mormon itself and Smith's revelations not only informed him "that the Bible was imperfect, but also that at least some of the missing parts would be restored. In addition, the inference was certainly strong that he would be the one to restore them."[29]

Even as early as 1830, scholarly versions of the King James Bible informed by textual criticism were available attempting to restore original readings.[30] Smith's textual revision effort, occurring between June and September 1830, was not a conventional scholarly production or a retranslation from older manuscripts in Hebrew and Greek.[31] Instead, Joseph based his work upon the copy of the Phinney edition of the King James Bible that had been purchased with Oliver Cowdery in October 1829.[32] Smith did not use his seer stone but planned to identify mistakes of translation by careful contemplation and direct inspiration. Orson Pratt, who subsequently associated with Smith's movement, "once asked him [Smith] why he did not resort to the ancient instruments. He was told that the translation of the Book of Mormon had made him 'so well acquainted with the spirit of

---

29. Robert J. Matthews, *"A Plainer Translation,"* 4, 5.

30. Examples of such works include: Campbell, *Sacred Writing of the Apostles*; Palfrey, *New Testament in the Common Version*; Greaves, *Gospel of God's Anointed*.

31. Lorenzo Brown in 1880 says he heard Joseph describe his translation: "After I got through translating the Book of Mormon, I took up the Bible to read with the Urim and Thummim. I read the first chapter of Genesis and I saw the things as they were done. I turned over the next and the next, and the whole passed before me like a grand panorama; and so on chapter after chapter until I read the whole of it. I saw it all!" Brown, "Sayings of Joseph," quoted in Matthews, *"A Plainer Translation,"* 25.

32. Handwritten note on title page of the Phinney, or "Marked Bible," CofC Archives.

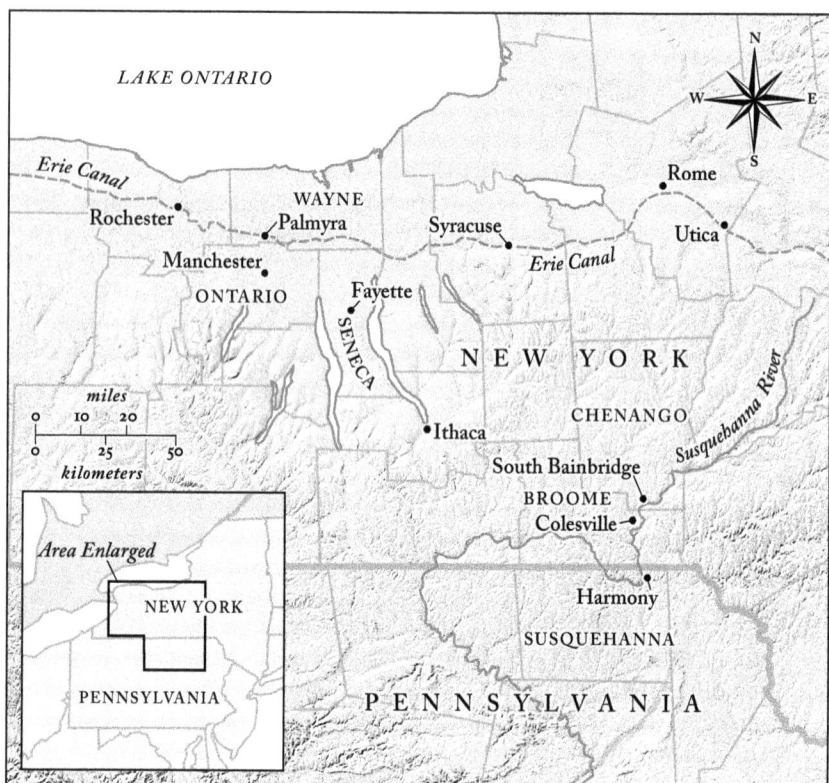

Fig. 5.2. The region around Fayette, New York, and Harmony, Pennsylvania.

revelation and prophecy, that in the translation of the New Testament he did not need its aid."[33]

Despite their anxiety to begin the project, Joseph and Oliver made little progress beyond the mid-June 1830 expansion of Moses's call to deliver the children of Israel. Instead of continuing the Bible revision, Joseph took time to arrange and copy revelations he had already received. In this project, he wrote, "I was assisted by John Whitmer, who now resided with me."[34]

---

33. Orson Pratt, minutes of the School of the Prophets, 14 January 1871, quoted in Matthews, *A Plainer Translation*, 40.

34. *History of the LDS Church*, 1:104.

Also in early or mid-July 1830, Joseph received a revelation that instructed him, Oliver, and John: "You shall let your time be devoted to the studying of the scriptures, and to preaching, and to confirming the church at Colesville; and to performing your labors on the land, such as is required, until after you shall go to the west [Fayette], to hold the next conference [on September 26, 1830] and then it shall be made known what you shall do."[35] Church members at Fayette also needed pastoral care, so soon after this revelation in early July, Oliver, and apparently David, returned to the Whitmer home in Fayette while John stayed on with the Smiths.

Joseph received the "Elect Lady" revelation in July, as well, directing Emma, "You shall be ordained under his [Joseph's] hand to expound Scriptures, and to exhort the church according as it shall be given thee by my Spirit." Emma was also instructed to compile a selection of sacred hymns for use by the church and to serve as Joseph's scribe.[36] This fourth direction was intended to free Oliver for other activities, especially preaching. In what would become a typical pattern, John filled in as needed. He continued writing Joseph's correspondence and eventually took over primary scribal duties. Emma must have devoted any time beyond household responsibilities to identifying hymns. As the translation of the scriptures progressed, John, rather than Emma, became Joseph's primary scribe. Indeed, many of the manuscript copies of the early church's scripture were eventually recorded in John Whitmer's sure and even handwriting.

During this period, the extended Whitmer family was caught up in one of the earliest of frequent administrative controversies. In Fayette, the zealous and confident Oliver Cowdery, who had been designated second elder at the April organizational meeting, felt free to express disagreement and dissatisfaction over the wording of one of Smith's recent commandments.[37] Joseph received word of this dispute by a letter from Oliver, "the contents of which gave me both sorrow and uneasiness."[38] The questionable passage reads: "and truly manifest by their works that they have received of the Spirit of Christ unto the remission of their sins." According to his-

35. Book of Commandments 49; 1835 D&C 49:1; CofC D&C 25; LDS D&C 26.

36. CofC D&C 24:2–3; LDS D&C 25:6–13.

37. 1835 D&C 2; CofC D&C 17; LDS D&C 20.

38. Jessee, *Papers of Joseph Smith*, 1:260.

torian Dean Jessee, Oliver, perhaps believing God's creation was saved by grace, "averred that the quotation 'was erroneous.'" Oliver then added "[I] command you in the name of God, To erase those words from that commandment,' that no priestcraft be amongst us.'"[39]

John assisted Joseph in drafting an immediate reply, asking by what authority Oliver "took upon him to command me to alter or erase, to add to or diminish from, a revelation or commandment from Almighty God."[40] Joseph and John immediately visited Fayette in late July 1830 to reason with Oliver and the Whitmers. Apparently the key to Joseph's regaining control was when Christian Whitmer became convinced that the reference to works was reasonable. Ultimately, Joseph's original rendition prevailed.[41]

During these early months, administrative or doctrinal issues were resolved by a participatory process that eventually led to a shared consensus. Cowdery, Hiram Page, and others felt free to question Smith's expression of religious ideas and to share their own insights about God's will with the group. This process of building group agreement is referred to as "common consent" in the church's articles and covenants, although, later, the meaning became more closely associated with the process of deliberative conference action. As this example shows, however, "common consent" was already becoming a mechanism to enforce top-down decision making, with "consent" meaning that members had the obligation to sustain decisions made by their hierarchical superiors—and the hierarchy was rapidly becoming more clearly defined.

By early August 1830, Joseph and John returned to Harmony. During this stay, Joseph concluded a land transaction with his father-in-law, Isaac Hale. Joseph and Emma were living in a small house on Hale's farm. Joseph made the final payment for the house and thirteen and one-half acres

---

39. Ibid., 1:260. Early Mormonism researcher Scott H. Faulring suggests, "It is possible that Oliver associated the requirement of 'manifest by their works' as being too closely akin to the requirement that a believer must prove before the congregation that he or she has received God's grace before being admitted into full fellowship, but the basis of his objection remains unstated and obscure." Faulring, "An Examination of the 1829 'Articles,'" 73.

40. Vogel, *Early Mormon Documents*, early-mid July 1830 (B), 5:437.

41. *History of the LDS Church*, 1:104–5.

of land. Isaac executed a deed for this property on August 25, 1830. John Whitmer was present and signed as one of two witnesses to the contract.[42]

Joseph and John intended to return to Colesville on August 21 to confirm baptized members but were again delayed. They were expecting Hyrum Smith and David Whitmer, who had not yet arrived.

On August 28, John took Joseph's dictation for a letter to Joseph Knight Sr:

> We have the more earnest desire to come to see you, but our friends from the West have not yet come [Hyrum Smith and David Whitmer],[43] and we can get no horse and wagon, and we are not able to come afoot so far, therefore we cannot come this saturday, but we look for our friends from the West every day and with safety we can promise to come next saturday, if the Lord will; therefore our desire is that ye should assemble yourselves together next saturday So that all things will be in order when we come.[44]

Probably during these last few days of August, "Brother Knight" (probably Newel) visited Harmony where, according to Joseph, "persecutions ... had been got up against us" and "invited us to go live with him" in Colesville.[45] Joseph quickly accepted the invitation to leave but changed the destination to the Whitmer home in Fayette, some measure of his fear of legal or physical harassment in Colesville.

This visit by "Brother Knight" was probably the occasion on which Joseph received a revelation to regulate the administration of the sacrament.[46] Joseph wrote in his 1839 history, "Early in the month of August [*sic;* September 1830], Newel Knight and his wife paid us a visit, at my place at Harmony, Penn; and as neither his wife nor mine had been as yet con-

---

42. Ibid., 4:425–26.

43. Journal History, 29 August 1830.

44. Joseph Smith and John Whitmer to Dearly Beloved in the Lord, 28 August 1830; also reproduced as Joseph Smith and John Whitmer to Colesville Saints, 28 August 1830, in Vogel, *Early Mormon Documents*, 1:13–14.

45. Ibid., 1:322.

46. Jenson, "John Whitmer," 612.

firmed, it was proposed that we should confirm them, and partake together of the sacrament, before he and his wife should leave us."[47]

Joseph recalled, "In order to prepare for this I set out to procure some wine for the occasion, but had gone only a short distance when I was met by a heavenly messenger, and received the following revelation: Wherefore, a commandment I give unto you, that you shall not purchase wine, neither strong drink of your enemies; Wherefore, you shall partake of none except it is made new among you."[48] Newel Knight recalled, "We prepared some wine of our own make, and held our meeting, consisting of only five persons namely, Joseph Smith and wife, John Whitmer, and myself and wife. We partook of the sacrament, after which we confirmed the two sisters into the Church."[49] As a result of this experience, grape juice, rather than wine, became standard for observing the sacrament.

The group, including John, quickly prepared for departure and arrived safely at the Whitmers' home during the last week of August 1830. Sometime between September 5 and 10, 1830, Joseph Smith, accompanied by John, Hyrum, and David, traveled to Colesville with obvious apprehension. Joseph's 1839 history relates:

> Well knowing the determined hostility of our enemies in that quarter, we also knowing that it was our duty to visit the church, we had called upon our Heavenly Father in mighty prayer, that he would grant us an opportunity of meeting with them; that he would blind the eyes of our enemies, so that they would not know us, and that we might on this occasion return unmolested.—Our prayers were not in vain, for, when within a little distance of Mr Knights place, we encountered a large company at work upon the public road, among <whom> were several of our most bitter enemies. They looked earnestly at us, but not knowing us. We passed on with out interruption. We that evening assembled the church, and confirmed them, partook of the sacrament,

---

47. Jessee, *Papers of Joseph Smith*, 1:320–21.

48. *History of the LDS Church*, 1:106.

49. Newel Knight, in Journal History, [between 5–10] August 1830. Vogel explains that the compilers of Joseph's History incorrectly dated the beginning of the September 1830 conference as September 1, 1830, rather than September 26–28. This misunderstanding caused dating issues in Joseph's History. Vogel, *Early Mormon Documents*, 4:442–43.

and held a happy meeting, having much reason to rejoice in the God of our salvation, and sing Hosannas to his holy name.[50]

Returning to New York, Smith discovered another challenge to his authority. Hiram Page had been receiving revelations through his seer stone. None have survived, but they sought to instruct the church about the "upbuilding of Zion" and apparently threatened the church's organization as established by the June 9 conference. Because of their family ties to Page, the Whitmers and Oliver Cowdery naturally leaned toward Page's interpretation. Ezra Booth, who joined the church by May 1831 and had disaffiliated by October 1831, provides the most detailed description of the Page episode:

> Hiram Page, one of the eight witnesses, and also one of the "money diggers," found a smooth stone, upon which there appeared to be a writing, which when transcribed upon paper, disappeared from the stone, and another impression appeared in its place. This when copied, vanished as the former had done, and so it continued, alternately appearing and disappearing; in the meanwhile, he continued to write, until he had written over considerable paper. It bore most striking marks of a Mormonite revelation, and was received as an authentic document by most of the Mormonites.[51]

In 1856, Martin Harris's brother Emer recounted this incident with some additional details at a Utah stake conference in Provo, Utah: "Br. Hiram Page dug out of the earth a black stone put it in his pocket when he got home he looked at it it contained a sentence on paper to exce[rpt] it it as soon has [*sic*] he rote one sentence another sentence came on the stone until he rote 16 pages."[52] Joseph, without directly confronting Page's revelation, announced that the second church conference would be held in about a month on September 26, 1830.

Meanwhile, a new investigator, Parley P. Pratt, who would become a dazzling missionary, made his appearance in Fayette. Following Pratt's conversion and ordination as an elder, on Sunday, September 5, 1830, he

50. Joseph Smith, "History, 1839," in Vogel, *Early Mormon Documents*, 1:131–32.

51. Ezra Booth, letter no. 8, to Reverend Ira Eddy, 29 November 1831, pp. 2–3, quoted in Howe, *Mormonism Unvailed*, 215–16, cited in Tamez, "The Hiram Page Stone," 4.

52. Emer Harris, statement, 6 April 1856.

addressed a large audience at the home of Philip Burroughs in neighboring Seneca Falls, not far from Waterloo, Fayette, New York.[53] As a result of Pratt's preaching, four heads of families were baptized.[54]

According to Stephen Knecht, a student of Joseph Smith's efforts with the text of the Bible, Joseph returned to his biblical revision at some point before the September 26, 1830, conference. The first manuscript, of what is now known as Joseph's New Translation, revised Genesis chapters 1–5. Smith started by dictating the content while Oliver wrote out the text.[55]

> This [first part of the] text was written by Oliver Cowdery in two sections into a large folio that already contained the June, 1830 Revelation. Section one, comprising the text of Genesis chapters 1–3 was entitled: "A Revelation given to the Elders of the Church of Christ On the first Book of Moses Given to Joseph the Seer [date lost due to the manuscript's deterioration].... Chapter First." When the work resumed the second section was written having the title: "Chapter 2—A Revelation concerning Adam after he had been driven out of the garden of Eden." This undated translation of chapter 4, which was written into the folio before September 26, 1830, ceased abruptly in the middle of verse 18.[56]

Perhaps because of Joseph's revision to the translation, a role in which he obviously felt confident, he came to a firm conclusion to repudiate Hiram Page's competing role as a revelator. A few days before the conference, Joseph Smith received a revelation that commanded Cowdery to continue his labor with Page:

> Thou shalt take thy brother, Hiram Page, between him and thee alone, and tell him that those things which he hath written from that stone

53. Porter, "A Study of the Origins," 255.

54. Cook, *Revelations of the Prophet Joseph Smith*, 42 note, indicates that both Peter Burroughs and his wife were members. See also Pratt, *Autobiography of Parley Parker Pratt*, 42–43. Phillip Burroughs had "a nice Farm in what is called the Burgh," in the town of Fayette. Diedrich Willers to Lee Yost, 18 May 1897, in Vogel, *Early Mormon Documents*, 5:289; also quoted in Porter, "A Study of the Origins," 262.

55. Knecht, *The Story of Joseph Smith's Bible Translation: A Documented History* (1984 ed.), both editions of this work hereafter cited: *Joseph Smith's Bible Translation*, 1.

56. Ibid., (1977 ed.), 15.

are not of me, and that Satan deceiveth him, for behold, these things have not been appointed unto him, neither shall anything be appointed unto any of this church contrary to the church covenants. For all things must be done in order, and by common consent in the church, by the prayer of faith. And thou shalt assist to settle all these things, according to the covenants of the church, before thou shalt take thy journey among the Lamanites. (CofC D&C 27:4b–5a; LDS D&C 28:11–14)

These instructions to deflate Page's claims came after an opening section that validated Oliver in his role "as Aaron" to speak "with power and authority unto the church" and "to speak and teach ... by the way of commandment unto the church" whenever he was "led ... by the Comforter" (CofC D&C 27:1–2c; LDS D&C 28:3–4). He was, however, forbidden to "write by way of commandment" because "no one shall be appointed to receive commandments and revelations ... excepting my servant Joseph Smith" whom the revelation compared to "Moses" (CofC D&C 27:2a; LDS D&C 28:5, 2).

The middle section of this revelation also held out a glittering promise to Oliver: "You shall go unto the Lamanites and preach my gospel to them," then continued by evoking probably the most glamorous image in Christendom: the city of Zion. Smith's revelation declared that "it is not revealed, and no man knoweth where the city of Zion shall be built, but it shall be given hereafter" (CofC D&C 27; LDS D&C 28:8–9).

When the three-day conference began at the Whitmer farm on September 26, 1830, Joseph Smith was "appointed by the voice of the conference to receive and write Revelations and Commandments for this Church." During their deliberations, Smith successfully convinced Page and the priesthood of the church to renounce Page's stone and "all things connected therewith."[57] As a result, according to Emer Harris, Page's stone "was broke to powder and the writings burnt."[58]

This contest of authority could have resulted in a schism before the church was three months old; but Smith emerged from the crisis as primary spokesperson for the movement with his inspired directives characterized as revelations of God's will to the church. Ezra Booth, a later

57. *History of the LDS Church,* 1:115.
58. Emer Harris, statement, 6 April 1856.

member-turned-critic, disparaged Smith's revelations as one-man rule: "The Mormonite church depends principally upon the commandments.... These commandments come from Smith, at such times and on such occasions as he feels disposed to speak.... They are received by the church as divinely inspired, and the name of the Lord is substituted for that of Smith. They are called 'The Commandments of the Lord.'"[59]

Official members probably still felt free to share their insights but now added the step of awaiting Joseph's validation on doctrinal points. On matters where Joseph spoke first, "common consent" meant strong pressure to agree or disagree with Joseph's perceptions. This model of ecclesial polity was quickly routinized. After the Page episode, no one who took public issue with Smith's pronouncements could remain in good standing. At the time, it seemed like only a small adjustment; and because of the intimate relationships in the church, most members felt that they had as much say in church affairs as before by direct discussions with their friend Joseph.

According to the minutes of this September 26 conference, the church now numbered sixty-two.[60] Soon afterward, Joseph sent his brother Hyrum to Colesville. Hyrum and his wife, Jerusha, stayed with the Newel Knight family.[61] With Oliver Cowdery slated for a long mission to the West, David Whitmer was assigned to keep the church records until the next conference,[62] which was held at the Whitmer home, January 2, 1831.

Cowdery's contribution to Genesis chapter 4:1–18a, was his last direct involvement with the project.[63] Oliver immediately began preparing for his mission to the Lamanites, the Book of Mormon term applied to American Indians by Mormons who saw them as descendants of the house of Israel.

Happy to be back in Fayette again, John resumed his scribal duties. A second assignment came at the end of the September 26–28, 1830, conference when Joseph received a revelation directing John to tour the

---

59. Ezra Booth, letter no. 8, 29 November 1831.

60. Cannon and Cook, *Far West Record*, 3.

61. Newel Knight, journal, 65, partially quoted in O'Driscoll, *Hyrum Smith: A Life of Integrity*, 41.

62. Cannon and Cook, *Far West Record*, 3.

63. Knecht, *Joseph Smith's Bible Translation* (1977), 11, 15.

neighborhood and "proclaim my gospel, as with the voice of a trump. And your labor shall be at your brother Philip Burroughs', and in that region round about: yea, wherever you can be heard."[64] John thus became one of only sixteen individuals known to have engaged in missionary activities on behalf of the new church movement before the end of 1830.[65] Their combined efforts succeeded in building a membership of about seventy, from Colesville to Canandaigua in New York.[66]

This same revelation, however, reproved David Whitmer. The Hiram Page incident may not have been completely resolved. Rather than receiving further ministry and the status that went with it, the revelation told David that he needed to quit listening to others and give "heed unto my Spirit, and to those who were set over you"—clear references to Joseph Smith.[67]

64. Book of Commandments 52; CofC D&C 29; LDS D&C 31. Despite the earlier meetings that Parley P. Pratt held at Phillip Burroughs's home in September 1830, Burroughs was apparently never baptized. Black, *Membership of the Church of Jesus Christ of Latter-day Saints*, 7:837, quoted in McCune, *Personalities in the Doctrine and Covenants*, 23. Lee Yost, a Fayette resident, told Diedrich Willers that "quite a number of men pretty well off refused to give their Property to the mormons So did mrot <not> become members." "Oran Chamberlain owning property between Waterloo and Seneca Falls was one[.] Philip Burrows [another]." Yost to Diedrich Willers Jr., 18 May 1897, quoted in Vogel, *Early Mormon Documents*, 5:289.

65. Journal History, December 1830. The September 26, 1830, conference appointed David Whitmer to keep church records, sent Hyrum Smith to preside over the Colesville Branch, and instructed the Joseph Smith Sr. family to move to Waterloo. Right after the conference, Joseph, accompanied by Emma, went on a preaching tour to Macedon while Samuel went to Livonia, New York, and the four "Lamanite missionaries"—Oliver Cowdery, Parley P. Pratt, Peter Whitmer Jr., and Ziba Peterson—set out about October 17, 1830. Journal History, 26 September–17 October 1830.

66. *History of the LDS Church*, 1, chap. 12 (October–December 1830).

67. CofC D&C 29:2a, c; LDS D&C 30:5.

CHAPTER SIX

The Great Commission: John Whitmer in Ohio

IN LATE SEPTEMBER 1830, the Mormon movement became part of the great trend westward, already well underway in the United States. Following the September 26–28 conference, Peter Whitmer Jr. was called to "take your journey with your brother Oliver; for the time has come that it is expedient in me that you shall open your mouth to declare my gospel ... to build up my church among the Lamanites."[1] Around October 15–17, 1830, Ziba Peterson and Parley P. Pratt were also appointed to accompany Oliver Cowdery on the church's most important mission to date: to share the Mormon message with the "Lamanites." Dartmouth College in Hanover, New Hampshire, and perhaps other New England institutions had successfully promoted the ideals of Christianizing and educating Native Americans.[2] The content of the Book of Mormon further affirmed the value of such an effort in the minds of church members.

On October 17, 1830, key adherents gathered in Manchester, New York, anticipating the departure of the four missionaries, who signed a "Missionaries Covenant." The covenant acknowledged that participants were "commanded of the Lord God to go forth unto the Lamanites to proclaim glad tidings of great joy unto them by presenting unto them the fullness of the gospel of the only begotten son of God, and also to rear up a pillar as a witness where the temple of God shall be built in the glorious New Jerusalem."[3] Joseph Smith and David Whitmer signed as witnesses.[4]

1. CofC D&C 29:2a, c; LDS D&C 30:5.
2. Behrens, "Dreams, Visions and Visitations," 179.
3. "Missionary Covenant," *BYU Studies,* 36:2, 226.
4. "Missionaries Covenant," in Vogel, *Early Mormon Documents,* 3:504–6.

One might anticipate that John would have also signed the covenant had he also been present to see his brother Peter off on this adventure. The day after the missionaries' departure, Joseph and David returned to Fayette. An investigator named Peter Bauder called at the Peter Whitmer Sr. home sometime between October 18 and 31, 1830. Bauder wrote, "I called at P[eter]. Whitmer's house, for the purpose of seeing Smith ... and had the privilege of conversing with him alone, several hours, and of investigating his writings, church records, &c." Joseph also showed Bauder the manuscript of the Bible revision. Bauder described it as:

> Another manuscript which he was then preparing for publication, which I also saw. He told me no man had ever seen it except a few of his apostles: the publication intended was to be the Bible!!! The manner in which it was written is as follows:—he commenced at the first chapter of Genesis, he wrote a few verses of scripture, than added delusion, which he added every few verses of scripture, and so making a compound of scripture and delusion. On my interrogating him on the subject, he professed to be inspired by the Holy Ghost to write it.[5]

Oliver's departure once again positioned John by Joseph's side. Oliver had been Joseph's right-hand man and Joseph's spokesperson since the organization of the church. Cowdery preached at all important gatherings, and did much of the baptizing. In Oliver's absence, Joseph turned to John to fill the void, with the result that significant duties fell to John.

Joseph quickly picked up his revision of the Bible, beginning on October 21 at Genesis 4:18b. He dictated seventeen lines (verses 18b–24) to John. Then came an interruption that lasted more than a month. The next session, on November 31, continued the text to Genesis 5:11. New Translation historian Robert J. Matthews sums up John's contributions between October and December 1830 as recording Joseph Smith's editorial revisions from Genesis 4:19 to approximately Genesis 5:20.[6] On December 1, 1830, the text was extended to Genesis 5:21, but Emma Smith[7] served as the

5. Bauder, *Kingdom and Gospel of Jesus Christ*, 35, 36, cited in Vogel, *Early Mormon Documents*, 1:17–18.

6. Matthews, "Joseph Smith's Translation of the Bible," 2:763–69.

7. Faulring, Jackson, and Matthews, *Joseph Smith's New Translation of the Bible*, 63. The scribe had not been identified earlier.

scribe for this portion since John was absent, presumably preaching nearby. By the time of the next session, between December 1 and December 10, probably around December 8, 1830, John returned, extending the text an additional sixty-one lines concluding at RLDS Genesis 7:1.[8]

Orson Pratt also provides a glimpse of John's important role as scribe during Joseph's revelations. Pratt had been baptized by his brother, Parley, on September 19, 1830,[9] and called on Joseph at the Peter Whitmer Sr. residence on November 4, 1830:

> He asked Joseph whether he could not ascertain what his mission was, and Joseph answered him that he would see, & asked Pratt and John Whitmer to go upstairs with him, and on arriving there Joseph produced a small stone called a seer stone, and putting it into a Hat soon commenced speaking and asked Elder P. to write as he would speak, but being too young and timid and feeling his unworthiness he asked whether Bro. John W. could not write it, and the Prophet said that he could: Then came the revelation to the Three named [above] given Nov. 4th 1830 as can be found in the book of D. & Covenants.[10]

John served in this way throughout this period. Writing down Smith's revelations became a natural outgrowth of John's work as scribe on the Bible revision. John no doubt approached both tasks with similar methodology and may, at the same time, have started gathering the various revelations previously written on loose sheets of paper.

Meanwhile in New York, between October 7 and November 5, 1830, Lucy and the younger Smith children moved from Manchester to Waterloo, Seneca County, near the Whitmers. They settled temporarily midway between Waterloo and Seneca Falls, in a community known as the "King-

---

8. Knecht, *Joseph Smith's Bible Translation* (1984), 14, 15.

9. "In conversation with Brother John Van Cott, yesterday, he informed us that he is the only living witness of the baptism of the late Apostle Orson Pratt, which event occurred 51 years ago last September 19th. He was acquainted with Elder Pratt when he was quite a young boy, several years before he joined the Church. Brother Van Cott was also present when Elder Pratt first heard the gospel preached by Parley P. Pratt and Ziba Peterson." "Local and Other Matters: Old Times," *Deseret News*, December 21, 1881, 1.

10. James R. B. Van Cleave to Joseph Smith III, 29 September 1878.

dom" on the Seneca River.[11] Joseph Smith Sr. was incarcerated for debt in the jail at Canandaigua, Ontario County, on about November 5, 1830.[12]

Serendipitously, what the Lamanite missionaries intended as a brief stop in northern Ohio turned into an extended and productive layover. Oliver Cowdery, Peter Whitmer, Parley Pratt, and Ziba Peterson reached Mentor, Ohio, in early November 1830 and were welcomed by Pratt's friend, the noted regional minister Sidney Rigdon, and his disciples in the Kirtland area. Lyman Wight, one of Sidney Rigdon's flock, remembered attending a meeting where "one [Oliver Cowdery] testified that he had seen angels, and another [Peter Whitmer Jr.] that he had seen the plates."[13]

Inquiries from surrounding communities flooded in. Mormonism quickly became a big story in local papers as a result of its success among Rigdon's former flock. Parley Pratt reported: "The interest and excitement now became general in Kirtland, and in all of the region round about. The people thronged us night and day, insomuch that we had no time for rest and retirement.... In two or three weeks from our arrival in the neighborhood with the news, we had baptized one hundred and twenty-seven souls, and this number soon increased to one thousand."[14]

Sidney Rigdon initially resisted the message of the missionaries; but after reading the Book of Mormon, he "became fully convinced of the truth of the work by a revelation from Jesus Christ."[15] Rigdon was baptized in early November 1830, probably on November 7.[16]

Solomon Hancock, a resident of Euclid Township and subsequent convert to the church, wrote about a meeting at Mayfield that apparently occurred between Sidney Rigdon's conversion and the departure of the Lamanite missionaries for Missouri:

> Four men came to the city of Mayfield, where they held meetings, proclaiming that they had a book which was a history of a people who

11. "Lucy Smith History, 1845," in Vogel, *Early Mormon Documents*, 1:214, 440n288.

12. Porter, "A Study of the Origins of the Church," 104–5; see also Vogel, *Early Mormon Documents*, 5:446–47, chronology, appendix B.

13. Wight, journal, no longer extant, quoted in *History of the RLDS Church*, 1:153.

14. Pratt, *Autobiography of Parley Parker Pratt*, 48.

15. "History of Joseph Smith," 4:290.

16. Van Wagoner, *Sidney Rigdon*, 62.

once inhabited this land. My brother, Levi took my mother to one of these meetings on horseback. Parley P. Pratt was the speaker and Sidney Rigdon asked the people to hear the words of Brother Pratt. At the close of the sermon, Parley P. Pratt asked if anyone wished to be baptized? Alta joined in and was baptized, followed by her father-in-law Thomas [Adams] and his daughter, Clarissa.[17]

The missionaries stayed until November 15. According to Peter Whitmer Jr., at Kirtland "we declared the fullness of the gospil [*sic*] and had much sucksess [*sic*] we Baptised [*sic*] one 100 and thirty members."[18] While visiting Mayfield in Cuyahoga County, Oliver Cowdery apparently experienced some kind of involvement with a young woman. Although the details of this episode are not known, he may have been thinking of marriage; and some later saw this behavior by a missionary as inappropriate.[19]

Despite their success, the missionaries were anxious to continue their journey. Around November 15, 1830, they wrote Joseph Smith, asking, according to Lucy Mack Smith, for "an Elder to preside over the branch which they had raised up."[20] They then continued on toward Missouri.[21] According to Peter Whitmer, the four missionaries went "to upper Sandusky but no admitence [*sic*] because of Priest craft from thence to cincinate [Cincinnati] from thence to shipings Port [Shipingport] from thence to saint lewis [St. Louis] and from thence to visit the tribes of the delawares and the tribe Shawneyes [*sic*] we came to independence on the twelfth month on the 13d. of the month."[22]

Unwilling to wait for a response to the letter, Sidney Rigdon, accompanied by Edward Partridge, a prosperous hatter from neighboring Painesville, set out for New York to meet Joseph in person and learn more

---

17. "Solomon Hancock," extracted from *Testimonies of the Hancocks,* 154, accessed May 10, 2012, http://www.scribd.com/doc/32227869/Testimony-of-the-Hancocks. This same meeting was apparently also described by Judge John Barr, a one-time sheriff of Cuyahoga County, Ohio. Mather, "Early Days of Mormonism," 206–7.

18. Peter Whitmer Jr., journal, 13 December 1831.

19. Ezra Booth, letter no. 7, to Reverend Ira Eddy, 21 November 1831, 1–2.

20. "Lucy Smith History, 1845," in Vogel, *Early Mormon Documents,* 1:444.

21. "The Golden Bible," (Painesville) *Telegraph* 3; "The Book of Mormon," 3.

22. Peter Whitmer Jr., journal, 13 December 1831.

about this new faith. They apparently made good time traveling by stage and reached Fayette in early December 1830.[23]

There on December 2, 1830, John penned a letter that Joseph dictated to the Colesville Saints. The letter served as a letter of introduction for newly ordained Orson Pratt. It also warned that perilous times of destruction were coming to their neighborhood, encouraged all to repent and be baptized, and instructed them to gather together in order to prepare the way of the Lord.[24] On December 3, John was in the process of writing pages 14–15 of the Bible manuscript.[25] Then, on December 10, 1830, Joseph and John were conducting a meeting at Joseph's parents' house in Waterloo.[26] With almost dramatic timing, Rigdon and Partridge entered this meeting, introduced themselves, and pledged their faith in the new movement. Partridge asked for baptism on the spot but agreed to wait until the next day. Their arrival changed everything for John Whitmer.

Rigdon and Partridge remained in New York for about a month and a half. Joseph, with a keen eye for talent, immediately invited Rigdon to take over John's scribal duties of managing correspondence and producing the Bible manuscript, an invitation that was formalized in a revelation naming Rigdon as scribe on December 7, 1830.[27] Rigdon accompanied them to Fayette and commenced writing where Whitmer left off—page 15, line 16—and continued through Genesis 5:22–23.[28] After about a month and a half in New York, Rigdon became fully convinced of Joseph's claims as a prophet. The energetic and vivid Rigdon, whom Elizabeth Ann Smith Whitney remembered as "a great Campbellite preacher,"[29] also displaced John as Joseph's second in command in dealing with daily church activities

23. Journal History, 15 November and [n.d.] December, 1830.

24. Joseph Smith and John Whitmer to Colesville Saints, 2 December 1830, in Vogel, *Early Mormon Documents*, 1:19–21.

25. Knecht, *Joseph Smith's Bible Translation* (1984), 15.

26. Anderson, *Lucy's Book*, 504.

27. CofC D&C 34:5a–b; cf. LDS D&C 35:2.

28. Knecht, *Joseph Smith's Bible Translation* (1984), 15.

29. Whitney, "Leaf from an Autobiography," 51. Rigdon had actually broken with Campbell's movement earlier in the year claiming that New Testament teachings required a community of goods. Hayden, *Early History of the Disciples in the Western Reserve*, 298–99.

and special events. Rigdon's conversion permanently changed John's future in the movement.

John never mentioned whether this abrupt displacement was unwelcome or hurt his feelings; but he would have had to be unusually mature not to regret the change. He received, and faithfully carried out, the unglamorous task of copying the dictated Bible manuscript to this point, including the June 1830 introductory revelation.[30]

Edward Partridge had accompanied Rigdon to New York to investigate for himself the claims of this new religion. On December 11, Edward Partridge asked for baptism and immediately wrote the news of his conversion to his family and friends in Ohio.[31]

On January 2, 1831, at the third significant conference held in New York, members gathered at the Whitmer home. Newel Knight recalled: "It was at this conference that we were instructed as a people, to begin the gathering of Israel, and a revelation was given to the prophet on this subject."[32] Joseph's pronouncement advised his followers, "You should go to the Ohio; and there I will give unto you my law; and there you shall be en-

---

30. This manuscript is now known as Manuscript 3 (OT 3) even though earlier scholars, including Richard P. Howard and Robert J. Matthews, denominated this manuscript as Old Testament Manuscript 1 (OT 1). Manuscript 3 is John Whitmer's copy of portions of the Old Testament manuscript, including Smith's June 1830 revelation and a revision of Genesis materials. Manuscript 3 is nearly sixteen pages in length. Smith Bible translation scholar Stephen R. Knecht, *The Story of Joseph Smith's Bible Translation: A Documented History* (1984), 16, believes OT 3 was written as John's personal copy. Smith Bible scholar Robert J. Matthews observes that John's handwriting "is small, with generally fifty-three to fifty-seven lines to a page, and is written on both sides of the paper. Full use is made of each page, for the writing extends to the very edges with no margins left or right, top or bottom.... There is little punctuation, no division into chapters or verses, and scarcely any into sentences." Matthews, *"A Plainer Translation,"* 62. Manuscript 3 may have been prepared as a duplicate printer's copy in anticipation of its publication, or it may be the copy John carried with him to Ohio in late December, as referred to in the Painesville *Telegraph.* Matthews, *"A Plainer Translation,"* 63, 64. The manuscript remained in the Whitmer family's possession until 1903 when the RLDS church acquired it. See Walter W. Smith to First Presidency, 14 September 1925.

31. Edward Partridge quoted by Philo Dibble in 1882, cited in Vogel, *Early Mormon Documents,* 5:450; see also Anderson, *Lucy's Book,* 505.

32. Knight, "Newel Knight's Journal," 68. The revelation is in Book of Commandments 80; CofC D&C 37:1a; LDS D&C 36:1.

dowed with power from on high" (CofC D&C 38:7b, c; LDS D&C 38:32). Joseph stopped his work on the Bible in preparation for his own departure.

But John Whitmer was the first to make the move. Either from Rigdon or from the slower mail, Smith had received word about the need for a presiding elder in Ohio and promptly assigned the task to John. John noted in his history, "After Joseph and Sidney returned from Colesville to Fayette. The Lord manifested himself to Joseph the Revelator and gave commandment for me to go to Ohio, and carry the commandments and revelations, with me, to comfort and strengthen my brethren in that land."[33] It was an excellent solution; John, displaced by the more exciting Rigdon, was available; furthermore, as a Book of Mormon witness, apostle, elder, and missionary, he was one of the most seasoned Mormons around, qualifications that would communicate to the Ohio congregation how seriously Joseph was taking their membership.

Rigdon prepared a letter to the Ohio disciples, announcing: "I send you this letter by John Whitmer. Receive him, for he is a brother greatly beloved, and an Apostle of this church. With him we send all the revelations which we have received."[34]

Twenty-eight-year-old John immediately left for Kirtland, probably traveling by stage, and carrying a manuscript copy of the recent commandments and revelations.[35] He arrived in mid-January, as noted by a sarcastic announcement in the *Telegraph* on January 18, 1831: "A young gentleman by the name of Whitmer arrived here last week from Manchester, N. Y., the seat of wonders, with a new batch of revelations from God, as he pretended, which have just been communicated to Joseph Smith."[36]

According to John's own history, "The Lord ... worked and many embraced the work the Ohio," having "increased in numbers [to] about

33. Whitmer, Book of John Whitmer, chap. 1, p. 10; also McKiernan and Launius, *An Early Latter Day Saint History*, 36.

34. Sidney Rigdon to the Brethren in Ohio, January 1831, reprinted in Howe, *Mormonism Unvailed*, 110.

35. Whitmer, Book of John Whitmer, chap. 1, p. 10; McKiernan and Launius, *An Early Latter Day Saint History*, 36. "To the Editor," *Reflector* (Palmyra, NY), February 1, 1831: indicates that Sidney Rigdon returned to Ohio by stage. Because John Whitmer's trip occurred between January 3 and 18, 1831, he probably also traveled by stage.

36. "Mormonism," *Telegraph*, January 18, 1831.

three hundred."[37] No record exists of where he found lodging; but, apparently, the Ohio converts met his needs. John shared the church's sacred writings and administrative guidelines with this body of new believers. He understood his task to be establishing some leadership structure among the scattered members, most of whom he was meeting for the first time. He had also been instructed to prepare a place for church members from New York who would soon be gathering to Kirtland.

Overseeing Rigdon's former disciples proved to be a handful. John's experiences left him unprepared to deal with the disciples' expressions of religious and economic fervor, some of whom were attempting to live by the New Testament ideals expressed in Acts 2. Sidney Rigdon had already influenced many who were attracted to the new religious expression and who had initiated a communal society called "the Family." This economic experiment had already triggered Rigdon's break from his former friend Alexander Campbell and from the Campbellite movement.

Believing that an ideal Christian lifestyle would be based on the scriptural example, in February 1830, Rigdon had persuaded Lyman Wight and eight other families to move into homes located on seventy-six acres on the north half of lot 6 northeast of the Kirtland Flats. This was the farm of Isaac Morley, a prosperous disciple of Rigdon's. Isaac and his wife, Lucy Gunn Morley, "threw open [their] doors in welcome to all who chose to enter and make this their common home."[38] Here they implemented an economic reordering called common stock or "all things common," consistent with their understanding of New Testament principles. They established a covenant with each other condemning private property and proclaiming that all of their goods would be shared in common.[39] They

37. Whitmer, Book of John Whitmer, chap. 1, p. 10; McKiernan and Launius, *An Early Latter Day Saint History*, 36.

38. McKiernan, *The Voice of One Crying in the Wilderness*, 29. According to *History of Geauga and Lake Counties*, 46, "Rigdon sometimes branched off on 'common stock.' The idea met with coldness at Mentor, but at Kirtland it soon kindled to a blaze, Isaac Morley being the first converted." An 1827 Geauga County, Ohio, tax duplicate (local county certification of real estate assessments) shows that Morley paid tax on a frame house in the northeast part of lot 6, house and land valued at $250. Elizabeth G. Hitchcock, "Houses along the East Branch," 2–3. The names of those who first engaged in this experiment are not known, but they numbered about a hundred in October 1830.

39. McKiernan, *Voice of One Crying in the Wilderness*, 29.

"sought to implement equal distribution and community of property or possessions. Each individual was afforded the opportunity of equally giving, or being equally willing to give, his or her possessions and talents for the common good."[40]

According to Lyman Wight, about November 1, 1830, "five families concluded to join us in the town of Mayfield, about seven miles up the [Chagrin] river. They each owning a good farm and mills, it was concluded best to establish a branch there. Accordingly, I was appointed to go and take charge of this branch."[41] Still others lived in Chardon.[42]

An enthusiastic convert, Solomon Hancock, had joined the church in January 1831 and promptly left on a mission around northern Ohio. During this mission, Hancock visited Strongsville, Cuyahoga County, Ohio, and converted Seymour Brunson, whom he baptized "sometime between the 15th and 20th days of January, 1831." To complete the conversion process, on January 21, 1831, John Whitmer confirmed Seymour Brunson and also ordained him an elder.[43]

Before John's arrival, individuals joining the Family, as the group on the Morley farm was known, had begun selling their individual farms to facilitate a centralized gathering. John did not discourage gathering but advised against selling any more land. The *Telegraph* in Painesville reported in mid-January: "Orders were also brought to the brethren to sell no more land, but rather buy more. Joseph Smith and all his forces are to be here soon to take possession of the promised land."[44] Some of their communitarian ideals may have been derived from association with the Shakers, who also had several communities in the area. The *Telegraph* added that,

---

40. Cook, *Joseph Smith and the Law of Consecration*, 6.

41. Wight, journal, quoted in *History of the RLDS Church*, 1:153.

42. Benjamin Shattuck to Mr. Howe, p. 3, discusses a "Family" at Chardon whose leader was Edison Fuller. Philo Dibble owned several "speculation" town lots in Chardon. Geauga County Records, Deed Books 12:369–705, 792, 13:159, 352, 15:133, 17:48. According to the Book of John Whitmer, the Chardon Saints "teased" to go to Zion. Book of John Whitmer, chap. 8, p. 30; McKiernan and Launius, *An Early Latter Day Saint History*, 76.

43. Lewis Brunson, statement, 1861. This is apparently the first documented priesthood ordinance John Whitmer performed.

44. "Mormonism," *Telegraph*, January 18, 1831.

for a time, individuals associated with the Family took to wearing Shaker hats, "by which they distinguish themselves and exhibit their humility."[45]

Most of those in the Family who had not previously joined the new movement soon followed Rigdon's example and were baptized when the four missionaries to the Lamanites arrived. Most, if not all, of the church's new converts in the Kirtland area were somehow involved in or aware of this experiment. Despite their good intentions, however, John was appalled at their practices: They "were going to destruction very fast as to temporal things; for they considered from reading the scripture that what belonged to a brother, belonged to any of the brethren."[46]

Perhaps even more troubling were extreme manifestations of the biblical gifts of the Spirit. Lyman Wight recalled that the Lamanite missionaries had promoted openness to the gifts. During the first meeting he attended, "one testified that he had seen angels, and another that he had seen the plates, and that the gifts were back in the church again, etc."[47] However, according to J. J. Moss, an interested observer, the missionaries did not encourage such actions but, when they occurred, "said it was the Holy Ghost."[48]

John Corrill, an early Ohio convert, wrote:

> During the fall and winter of A.D. 1830 and '31 [after the missionaries to the Lamanites had departed for Missouri] ... many improprieties and visionary notions crept into the church, which tried the feelings of the more sound minded. Many young persons became very vision-ary, and had divers operations of the spirit, as they supposed. They saw wonderful lights in the air and on the ground, and would relate many great and marvelous things which they saw in their visions. They conducted themselves in a strange manner, sometimes imitating In-dians in their manoeuvres [*sic*], sometimes running out into the fields, getting on stumps of trees and there preaching as though surrounded by a congregation,—all the while so completely absorbed in visions as to be apparently insensible to all that was passing around them. I

---

45. Clapp, "Mormonism," 1.

46. This letter is no longer extant but is quoted in Whitmer, Book of John Whitmer, chap. 2, p. 11; McKiernan and Launius, *An Early Latter Day Saint History*, 37.

47. Heman C. Smith, letter to the editor, 16 May 1882, *Herald*, 29:192.

48. *Braden and Kelley Debate*, 386.

would here remark, however, that it was but a very few of the Church who were exercised in that way. The more substantial minded looked upon it with astonishment, and were suspicious that it was from an evil source.[49]

After the missionaries' departure, preaching meetings characterized by similar manifestations were frequently held at Isaac Morley's farm. William S. Smith (not related to the prophet's family), who resided in Kirtland as a young man, stated:

> I have attended the meetings at Mr. Morley's.... The buildings were upon a little flat, and if my memory serves me, when the people began to come there they put up a cabin or small addition to the house part.... My first attendance was when it began to be generally noised around that there was strange things done, and we young folks were curious to see what it was.... I have seen Black Pete [an African American adherent], as we called him, as he went over the hills hallowing and making strange noises, and the common report was that he was speaking in tongues and making speeches. And in the house I have seen young men and women seemingly unconscious and the folks said they had lain so for two days.

He also recalled, "They were wholly unconscious, and some roguish boys would stick a pin into the arm and there was no manifestation of sensation."[50]

These manifestations were in full bloom when John Whitmer arrived in January 1831, but he regarded them with dismay:

> The enemy of all righteousness had got hold of some of those who professed to <be> his followers, because they had not sufficient knowledge to detect him in all of his devices. But He took anotion [*sic*] to blind the minds of some of the weaker ones, and made them think that an angel of God appeared to them, and showed them writings ond [*sic*] the outside cover of the Bible, and on parchment, which flew through the air, and on the back of their hands, and many such foolish and vain things, others lost their strength, and some seated <slid> ond

---

49. Corrill, *Brief History of the Church of Christ*, 16–17.

50. William S. Smith, quoted in *Braden and Kelley Debate*, 388, 390. See the early chapters in Staker, *Harken, O Ye People*, for information about this former slave's involvement in early Mormonism in Ohio.

[*sic*] the floor, and such like maneuvers, which proved greatly to the injury of the cause.[51]

Local opponent Eber, or E. D., Howe contended:

They pretended that the power to work miracles was about to be given to all who embraced the new faith, and commenced communicating the spirit by laying their hands on the heads of the converts, which produced an instantaneous prostration of body and mind. Many fell on the floor, and would lie for a long time, apparently lifeless.... Young men and women were peculiarly subject to this delirium.... Preaching to the Indians, the Lamanites, converting the Lamanites was the hobby of Mormonism at first.... Many would have fits of speaking all Indian dialects.[52]

John Whitmer's efforts to regulate the spiritual gifts and channel them in a productive and more decorous direction largely failed. In January 1831, John appealed to Joseph in New York for his immediate attention to the branch in Ohio. Still, he saw that "the honest in heart stood firm and immovable. It was very nessary [*sic*] that this people should have instructions, and learn to discern between the things of God and the works of Satan. For the inhabitants of the earth knew nothing of the working of the Spirit of the Lord, in these days."[53]

Meanwhile, back in New York, Smith and Rigdon traveled to the Colesville area immediately after the January 2, 1831, conference. John Whitmer, based on reports he must have heard from them later, recorded that hostility greeted them:

After these things were done Joseph and Sidney went to Colesville to do the will of the Lord in that part of the land; and to strengthen the disciples in that part of the vineyard, and preach the gospel to a hardened and a wicked people; and it is fearful that they are all delivered over to hardness of heart and blindness of [sight,] so that they cannot be brought to repentance. For when Sidney and the Revelator

---

51. Whitmer, Book of John Whitmer, chap. 1, p. 10; McKiernan and Launius, *An Early Latter Day Saint History*, 36.

52. Howe, *Mormonism Unvailed*, 104–6; see also *Braden and Kelly Debate*, 368.

53. McKiernan and Launius, *An Early Latter Day Saint History*, 36; Whitmer, Book of John Whitmer, chap. 1, pp. 10–11.

arrived there, they held prayer meetings, among the disciples, and they also held public meetings, but it was all in vain, they threatened to kill them. Therefore, they knew that they were not fit for the kingdom of God, and well nigh ripe for destruction. The Spirit of the Lord fell upon Sidney, and he spoke with boldness, and he preached the gospel in its purity; but they laughed him to scorn, he being filled, with the Holy Spirit, he cried aloud, O ye heavens give ear and ye angels attend, I bear witness in the name of Jesus Christ that this people is sealed up to everlasting destruction. And immediately he left them and escaped out of their hands. And his enemies were astonished and amazed at the doctrines which he preached, for they taught as men having authority and not as hireling priests.[54]

Rigdon's pronouncement reinforced an emerging perception that those who failed to gather would be visited by God's wrath, soon to be poured out upon the wicked. Rigdon reiterated this message within the month. A January 26, 1831, unsigned letter from a Waterloo correspondent to the Palmyra *Reflector* reported:

> He [Rigdon] delivered a discourse at the Court House immediately preceding his departure [for Ohio], where he depicted in strong language, the want of "charity and brotherly love" among the prevailing sects and denomiantions [*sic*] of professing Christians.... After denouncing dreadful vengeance on the whole state of New York, and this village [Waterloo] in particular, and recommending to all such as wished to flee from "the wrath to come," to follow him beyond the "eastern waters" ... Their first place of destination is understood to be a few miles west of Painesville, Ohio, which is just within the east bounds of this new land of promise, which extends from thence to the Pacific Ocean.[55]

Marvin Hill, a Mormon scholar, probes the question of communalism among Mormons in New York and concludes: "The meager sources of early Mormonism in New York reveal little of the depth and breadth in the Mormon search for social seamlessness which would later become so apparent. It is clear, however, that some of the Mormon emigrants who fled

---

54. Whitmer, Book of John Whitmer, chap. 1, pp. 9–10; McKiernan and Launius, *An Early Latter Day Saint History*, 35–36.

55. Unsigned letter to the editor, *Reflector*, February 1, 1831.

New York for Kirtland, Ohio, pooled their material wealth on the eve of departure."⁵⁶ For example, Newel Knight described making "great sacrifices of our property. The most of my time was occupied in visiting the brethren, and helping to arrange their affairs, so that we might travel together in one company."⁵⁷

This move constituted the first "sifting" of the earliest converts, since some were unwilling to make the move. On March 9, 1831, the *Reflector* in Palmyra announced that "our Waterloo correspondent" had passed on word that "two of the most responsible *Mormonites*, as it respects property, in that vicinity, have *demurred* to the divine command, through Jo Smith, requiring them to sell their property and put it into the common *fund*, and repair with all convenient speed to the New Jerusalem, lately located by Cowdery somewhere in the western region." One of these members refused "a requisition of *twelve hundred* dollars, in cash," demanded because "the Lord ha[d] need of it."⁵⁸

Sensitive about the consequences of his own decision in leaving for Ohio, John saw such resistance as rebellion against God: "After the Lord had manifested the above words, through Joseph the Seer, there were some divisions among the congregations, some would not receive the above as the word of the Lord: But that Joseph had invented it himself to deceive the people that in the end he might get gain. Now this was because, their hearts were not right in the sight of the Lord."⁵⁹

During this month of heightened religious tension, twenty-six-year-old David Whitmer, by then six months an elder, married sixteen-year-old Julia Ann Jolly ("Juliann" in family records) on January 9, 1831. David had baptized her in June 1830.⁶⁰ This happy event was an opportunity that the whole neighborhood, regardless of religious feelings, could join in cel-

---

56. Hill, *Quest for Refuge,* 31.

57. "Newel Knight's Journal," 68.

58. "Mormonism," *Reflector,* March 9, 1831, emphasis in original.

59. Whitmer, Book of John Whitmer, chap. 1, p. 9; McKiernan and Launius, *An Early Latter Day Saint History,* 34–35.

60. Julia Ann Jolly was born February 7, 1815, in New York and was baptized by David Whitmer on June 9, 1830. Curtis, "Whitmer Family," 10; Porter, "A Study of the Origins," 261.

ebrating. Great-granddaughter Helen Van Cleave Blankmeyer described the occasion vividly:

> An outdoor festival scene set in glistening snow, as villagers of Fayette, New York gathered to welcome the newly wed Juliann and David, who had slipped off over the line into ... Pennsylvania, "to be married without any fuss." ... David must have been delighted.... My great-grandmother (Juliann) was the most correct female who ever wore long stays and a Lyons velvet pelisse. She had character, as her whole life confirmed. She had "manner," a poise worthy of the most select drawing rooms, and she had the most exquisite taste, evidenced by her choices in china, glass, silver and lace, and furnishings not merely expensive but really beautiful. Her own sewing was so delicate that on fine pieces not a stitch could be seen. Yet she could wear a sunbonnet with grace.
>
> The Whitmer farm was noted for its abundance and hospitality.... There was ample food on hand. Juliann's family would be sent for, the neighbors brought in, and after dining and wining there would be fiddle music for dancing.... Happy young people facing without doubt or fear the challenge of a change in their lives far beyond the ordinary adjustments of marriage. For already they knew that they were called upon to move out into the western wilderness (called by this enticing new religion).[61]

Attending to his important pastoral duties in Kirtland, Ohio, area, John missed out on this significant family event.

Meanwhile, Joseph had received John's letter appealing for assistance in late December, "inquired of the Lord and received a commandment to go straightway to Kirtland with his family and effects."[62] Joseph had already, in the January 2, 1831, conference, designated "the Ohio" as the new gathering place, so this letter probably only hastened his departure. Lucy Mack Smith wrote, "It was but a short time till Joseph and Emma were on their way, accompanied by Sidney Rigdon, Edward Partridge, Ezra

---

61. Blankmeyer, *David Whitmer, Witness for God,* 22, 23; terminal punctuation and capitalization standardized. Larry Porter, speaking at the Whitmer Family Celebration, October 6, 2006, Richmond, Missouri, indicated that David and Julia Ann's wedding took place at 6 a.m.; notes in my possession.

62. "Lucy Smith History, 1845," in Vogel, *Early Mormon Documents,* 1:446. The original draft, cited in the same work, dates John Whitmer's letter as December 1830.

Thayre [Thayer], and Newel Knight. When they were about starting, they preached at our house on the Seneca River [Kingdom]; and on their way, they preached at the house of Calvin Stodard [Stoddard], and likewise at the house of Preserved Harris."[63] Corroboration that Joseph Smith's party started hastily comes from Joseph Knight Jr.'s 1862 reminiscence: "The persecution was so great that my Father [Joseph Knight Sr.] and Joseph started in the Winter with my sleigh, which cost me fifty dollars; the rest of us [stayed] till Spring and sold what property we could."[64]

According to the Palmyra *Reflector* of February 1, 1831:

> Elder S. Rigdon left this village [Waterloo] on Monday morning last [probably January 21, 1831] in the stage, for the "Holy Land," where all the "Gold Bible" converts, have recently received a written command-ment from God, through Jo Smith, junior, to repair with all conve-nient speed after selling off the[ir] property. This command was at first resisted by such as had property, (the brethren from the neighboring counties being all assembled by special summons,) but after a night of fasting, prayer and trial, they all consented to obey the holy mes-senger.—Rigdon has for some time past been arranging matters with Smith for the final departure of the faithful for the "far west."

This *Reflector* article also reported the sale of the Whitmer farm shortly after Smith's departure for Ohio: "The Prophet, spouse, and whole 'holy family' (as they style themselves,) will follow Rigdon, so soon as their deluded or hypothetical followers, shall be able to dispose of what little real property they possess in this region: one farm (Whitmers) was sold a few days ago [January 1831] for $2,300. Their first place of destination is un-derstood to be a few miles west of Painesville, Ohio."[65] However, this first

---

63. Ibid., 171. She is mistaken about the makeup of the party. Rigdon and Partridge trav-eled separately to reach Ohio more swiftly. Furthermore, according to another source, it was not Newel Knight, but Joseph and Polly Knight, and their daughter Lucy, who accompanied Joseph and Emma to Kirtland. Meader, "The Shakers and the Mor-mons," 91, cited in Flake, "A Shaker View of a Mormon Mission," 94–99. Apparently the group, totaling eight, traveled in two sleighs. Hartley, *"Stand by My Servant Joseph,"* 105.

64. Knight, "Joseph Knight's Incidents of History from 1827–1844," p. 2.

65. "Plain Truth" [pseud.], letter to the editor, *Reflector*, February 1, 1831. The pseudonym, "Plain Truth," suggests an association with an anticlerical newspaper by the same title in Canandaigua, New York.

sale may have fallen through because, on April 1, 1831, Peter sold his entire hundred-acre farm to a local resident named Charles Stewart by warranty deed for $2,200.[66]

Rigdon, anxious to prepare his former followers in Ohio for Joseph's arrival, left January 24, 1831, with Edward Partridge.[67] They probably traveled on the Pioneer Stage Line, which regularly advertised in the Painesville *Telegraph*. In operation since 1828, it ran "from Niagara through Lockport and Rochester, to Canandaigua, where it unites with the line from Buffalo."[68] From there, they could have obtained passage on a boat to Cleveland or Fairport Harbor, near Kirtland.[69] The Painesville *Telegraph* reported that Rigdon arrived at his home in Mentor on February 1, 1831. Mormon antagonist E. D. Howe, a resident of Painesville, corroborates that Rigdon returned home February 1, 1831, "followed in a few days ... by the prophet and his connections."[70] No record has survived of the meeting between Joseph Smith and John Whitmer, his faithful deputy in Ohio, but it must have been a glad one.

66. About five weeks later, John Deshler acquired the property from Stuart. Deed Book W, 318, and Deed Book X, 25, Seneca County Courthouse, Waterloo, New York, cited in Porter, "A Study of the Origins," 312. See also Fayette Township, Seneca County, New York plat map, cited in Barchers, "The Descendants and History of the Peter Whitmer Family," 7, 22.

67. Unidentified correspondent from Waterloo, New York, letter to editor, *Reflector*, February 1, 1831.

68. Merrill, "Pioneer Stages," 3.

69. Advertisement for the Lake Erie Steam-Boat Line, Buffalo to Detroit, with stops at Cleveland, *Telegraph and Geauga Free Press*, June 22, 1830.

70. Clapp, "Mormonism," 1; Howe, *Mormonism Unvailed*, 112–13.

CHAPTER SEVEN

Kirtland: The Gathering Place

PETER SR. AND Mary Whitmer apparently remained in New York until May 1831, wrapping up their business affairs. Lucy Mack Smith's familiar account of departing for Ohio with a company of about fifty individuals, in April or May 1831, does not mention the Whitmers. A second company of about thirty under the leadership of Thomas B. Marsh left at the same time. Both companies traveled east to Seneca Falls, then went west on the Erie Canal to Buffalo.[1] According to a newspaper story on May 27, a third group of fifty, which included Martin Harris, left from Palmyra.[2] John's history notes the arrival of this third group in early June: "About these days [early June 1831] the disciples arrived from the State of New York. To this place Kirtland State of Ohio."[3] Perhaps this group included John's parents and, out of modesty, he did not single them out for attention.

Joseph Smith's February 1831 arrival in Ohio immediately altered John's role, as Joseph assumed all presiding responsibilities. John may have felt relieved, or he may have felt rebuffed at being so summarily replaced. However, he makes no mention of his feelings. It is true that the church's sudden success in Ohio ushered in a series of new administrative challenges: the need for a flexible but firm church organization, definitions of acceptable behavior during worship services, the articulation of core beliefs, and the regulation of the community's economic life. Smith urgently

1. Barben, "Cayuga and Seneca Canal, 1813–1963," cited in Porter, "A Study of the Origins of the Church," 316; see also Porter, untitled presentation, Whitmer Family Celebration, October 6, 2006.

2. "Mormon Emigration," *Wayne Sentinel* (Palmyra, NY), May 27, 1831, 38.

3. Whitmer, Book of John Whitmer, chap. 7, p. 27; McKiernan and Launius, *An Early Latter Day Saint History*, 65. Modestly, John might not wish to make too much of the arrival of his own family.

sought to gain control over the religious excesses that John had encountered among Ohio believers.

An unidentified Presbyterian observer from Chester, Ohio, described Ohio Mormonism in early 1831:

> Joseph Smith, jr. author of the new revelation, is now head man in the big family. He pretends that he goes to the Lord occasionally for advice, and they think, yea they *know* they have all their orders from head quarters, even from the Lord Almighty, through the mouth of his prophet. Jo pretends to cast out devils, to give the Holy Ghost by laying on of hands, to heal the sick, &c. He has 10 years translating to do; he looks in a small stone he has, and there reads the will of the Lord and writes it for the good of his fellow-men; he can read a person's heart by looking in his face. Some lie in trances a day or two and visit the unknown regions in the meantime; some are taken with a fit of terrible shaking which they say is the power of the Holy Ghost.[4]

This same correspondent added: "I presume there are not less than 5[00] or 600 of these deluded beings in the towns north and west of this. They have ... what is called the 'big family,' where no one says that ought of the things that he possesses is his own; they have all things in common."[5] Joseph hoped to quickly assert control over Rigdon's former adherents.

John, along with the whole church, was part of a long-term, ongoing struggle over church authority. At the outset, Joseph Smith's authority to act in God's name was implicit rather than explicit. His primary concern about his own status with God at the beginning of his religious journey had been limited to a remission of his sins, then obtaining and translating the plates. Conferred authority was not needed, either divine or human; but this situation changed in April 1829. Motivated by passages they were translating from the Book of Mormon, Smith and Cowdery "went to the waters of the Susquehanna River in anticipation of baptism and received authority to baptize each other" at the hand of an angelic messenger.[6] Such

4. "A Presbyterian," letter dated February 22, 1831, "The Mormon Delusion," *New-Hampshire Patriot & State Gazette*, May [16], 1831. Uncle Dale's Readings in Early Mormon History, accessed May 9, 2012, http://www.sidneyrigdon.com/dbroadhu/NE/miscne01.htm.

5. Ibid.

6. Prince, *Origins and Development of Priesthood*, 16–19.

conferred authority prompted the formal organization of a church with an initial structure consistent with that described in the Book of Mormon. The church started out with elders, priests, and teachers. With the organization's relocation to Ohio, its infrastructure needs expanded. At the same time, Joseph moved away from his earlier charismatic leadership style toward a more authoritative model. The church's ecclesiology reflected Joseph Smith's need to exercise careful oversight over every aspect of the life of the church.

But the initial situation Joseph encountered in Ohio was chaotic. At this point, Joseph faced serious challenges to his leadership. Unanticipated events, resistance, and opposition—some of it intensely personal—threatened his ability to achieve acceptance for his ideas and administrative innovations. The large number of almost-instant Ohio converts, while a boon in some ways, also brought unanticipated consequences. Joseph set out at once to forge a new sense of community among his followers.

Sidney Rigdon biographer Richard S. Van Wagoner observed, "Joseph Smith's communal vision began evolving within days of meeting Rigdon, who discussed with Smith the range of his own religious experience, including communitarianism."[7] Sidney Rigdon no doubt observed that the new organization lacked the New Testament office of bishop.

Following their initial conversations, Smith's revelations turned to economic matters. Community and economics necessarily go hand in hand, so even before leaving New York, Smith hinted that the church would also regulate community relationships. "Certain men among you" should be appointed to "look to the poor and the needy, and administer to their relief, that they shall not suffer."[8] No doubt Rigdon informed Joseph of his extensive community experiment, known as the Family, already functioning in several locations near Kirtland, Ohio. Sidney had been a church bishop himself while associated with religious innovator Alexander Campbell.[9] However, Rigdon separated from Campbell in 1830 in a dis-

---

7. Van Wagoner, *Sidney Rigdon*, 79.

8. CofC D&C 38:8a, b; LDS D&C 38:34–35, as described in ibid., 84–85.

9. "Bishops Scott, Rigdon, and Bentley, in Ohio, within the last six months have immersed about eight hundred persons." *Christian Baptist*, June 2, 1828, quoted in Van Wagoner, *Sidney Rigdon*, 46n30. "Saturday, August 30, 1828.... Voted, That the following brethren be appointed to preach on tomorrow, viz. Bishops Alexander Campbell, Walter Scott,

pute over the implications of Acts 2:44–45 in the New Testament. During the 1830 annual meetings of the Mahoning Baptist Association, Sidney argued, "Our pretensions to follow the apostles in all their New Testament teachings, required a community of goods; that as they [early Christians] established their order in the model church at Jerusalem, we were bound to imitate their example."[10] Campbell disagreed, believing New Testament communitarianism to be a "special circumstance." This breach ended Rigdon and Campbell's association. Sidney returned to Mentor, Ohio, where he shepherded several congregations, determined to implement common stock. In February 1830, Sidney convinced Lyman Wight and Isaac Morley to launch a collective experiment. "Morley and Wight, along with Titus Billings and three other families covenanted with each other to renounce private property and share all goods. They called their order the 'Family.'"[11] Rigdon himself served as their spiritual and temporal head, filling the New Testament role of bishop. However, his decision to join Smith's Church of Christ considerably altered his responsibilities.

In January 1831, Smith and Rigdon suspended community planning while the church moved to Ohio. But almost immediately upon reaching Ohio, Joseph revealed his own communitarian program. Mormon economic historians Leonard Arrington, Feramorz Y. Fox, and Dean L. May, describe Smith's idea: "The beginning of Mormon communitarianism, the Law of Consecration and Stewardship, was first outlined in a revelation to Joseph Smith dated February 9, 1831. Briefly, the law was a prescription for transforming the highly individualistic economic order of Jacksonian America into a system characterized by economic equality, socialization of surplus incomes, freedom of enterprise, and group economic self-sufficiency."[12]

As part of the consecration package, Smith introduced a new priesthood function to his followers—that of bishop. This was an entirely new

and Sidney Rigdon." Jacob Gaskill, clerk, *Minutes of the Mahoning Baptist Association*, 4. See also William Whitsitt, *Sidney Rigdon: The Real Founder of Mormonism, 1885*, SidneyRigdon.com, accessed May 21, 2012, http://sidneyrigdon.com/wht/1891WhtB.htm.

10. Hayden, *Early History of the Disciples in the Western Reserve*, quoted in Van Wagoner, *Sidney Rigdon*, 53.

11. Van Wagoner, *Sidney Rigdon*, 50.

12. Arrington, Fox, and May, *Building the City of God*, 15.

role within the organization, and there was little internal precedent beyond revelation by which to frame this function.[13] John Corrill observed, "I joined the Church on the tenth of January, 1831, and in the course of three or four days I was ordained an elder. Shortly after this, the Church from the State of New York removed to Kirtland Ohio.... Shortly after he arrived at Kirtland, Smith received a Revelation appointing Edward Partridge Bishop of the Church. This was the first time that I knew or even thought that there was to be a Bishop in the Church, but on reflection I knew that there were bishops in old times, and I said nothing against it."[14]

Like the bishop's ministerial role in other religious bodies such as the Campbellites and Shakers, the Mormon bishop managed the life of a congregation or religious community, functioning as both a spiritual leader and as chief financial officer. On February 4, 1831, partly in response to the urgings of Sidney Rigdon, Joseph named Edward Partridge, a man with proven business skills, as bishop of the church.

Five days later on February 9, 1831, Joseph announced the "Law of the Church." The law was an elaborate new church economic initiative since known as the "law of consecration" and canonized as Doctrine and Covenants section 42. This revelation also clarified Partridge's new duties.

Joseph's all-encompassing goal with this initiative was nothing less than the realization of God's kingdom upon the earth. Smith's envisioned kingdom merged several related concepts that had coalesced in his thinking as he worked on the Book of Mormon. According to social anthropologist Rex Cooper, Smith's thought relied on two main concepts: first, "his belief [that] the scriptures contained a Divine Heavenly Pattern of living—which he could discern"; and second, "that through his correct ac-

---

13. The articles and covenants of the church, as organized on April 6, 1830, described only the priesthood offices of elder, priest, and teacher. Vogel, *Religious Seekers and the Advent of Mormonism*, 218, makes the interesting argument that the introduction of additional offices may have reflected a shift from a perspective of congregational and spiritual charismatic authority toward an institutionalization of a lineal authority ideologically dependent upon heavenly restoration and angelic endowment. "The early emphasis on charisma, the lack of a clear priesthood restoration concept in the Book of Mormon and in the 'Articles and Covenants of the Church of Christ,' the additions made to the 1835 Doctrine and Covenants concerning angelic ordinations, and statements of early leaders all demonstrate the shift to accommodate evolving notions of authority and governance."

14. Corrill, *Brief History of the Church of Christ*, 17.

tion he could assume the necessary Heavenly authority needed to claim the divine promises revealed in the Scriptures and resolve the details of the envisioned Kingdom."[15]

Joseph's ideal of a heavenly lifestyle on earth sought to harmonize every aspect of life in the early church. Smith's vision of Christian discipleship incorporated several related concepts into one powerful package:

1. Restoration of authority and heavenly power

2. Spiritual vision leading to the rediscovery of scriptural precedents

3. Stewardship

4. Gathering to a physical place/extended family/patriarchal ministry

5. Community/social justice

6. Temple building/collective salvation

7. Fulfillment of the great commission via evangelism throughout the world[16]

Cooper suggests that Smith's whole idealistic package was intended to "complement the primacy of the institutions of a sacred city and consecrated economic relations as public vehicles of salvation with 'a new covenantal system' based on consanguineous and constructed ties of kinship."[17]

The law of consecration was a key component of Joseph's overall initiative. Smith used consecration as a tool with which to intentionally restructure the Kirtland community life around the major themes in Acts. These themes include: gathering, communal economics, awareness of the signs of the latter days, preaching the gospel to all nations, building a temple for worship and education, and a Pentecostal endowment of the Holy Spirit.[18] Consecration was Joseph's attempt to place the emerging church squarely within a radical Christian economic tradition.

15. Cooper, *Promises Made to the Fathers*, 100–101.

16. Romig, "Perceptions of Discipleship within the Early Restoration Movement, 1830s."

17. Cooper, *Promises Made to the Fathers*, 100–101, 132–49.

18. Bolton, "Pentecost and All Things Common," 6.

Like the Family, Smith drew heavily from the model in Acts 2, but gave "consecration" his own unique twist, by emphasizing early Christian practices as described in Acts 4:31–33 rather than Acts 2, thus differentiating it from Rigdon's Family. Not only did consecration ask adherents to give their all to God but also one-tenth of their annual increase. Smith intended the law of consecration to replace the "all things in common" stewardship practice of Rigdon's Family. He was pleased with the plan's initial reception, "The plan of 'common stock,' which had existed in what was called 'the family' ... was readily abandoned for the more perfect law of the Lord."[19]

Early 1831 was a difficult period for Smith. He wanted to devote more of his time to the task of revising the scriptures. To do this, he needed more consistent financial support from the disciples. Joseph thought his system of consecration would allow this adjustment. Smith also anticipated that his followers would provide for all of his own and Sidney's living needs so they could continue the revision full time and without interruptions. Along this same line, Joseph also hoped that the plan would generate sufficient surplus to fund the clerical costs of the project and other church administrative needs.

Although John Whitmer was not the primary scribe, the Bible revision kept him busy. John also became, in a sense, an employee of the church. Consecration was intended to furnish a livelihood for John, so he could copy Joseph's Bible manuscripts and attend to his duties as church clerk and historian. Later, in David Whitmer's 1887 book, part autobiography and part doctrinal argument, David would remember that "John Whitmer was clerk of the Church of Christ, built upon the Book of Mormon and Bible alone."[20]

Early Kirtland disciples were remarkably dynamic, accommodating a grand influx of creative energy and ideas coming from many directions. Members wanted to participate in shaping the emerging community through their spiritual gifts and personal revelations. Although this enthusiasm provided a remarkably lively and appealing community, rarely

19. *History of the LDS Church*, 1:146–47.

20. David Whitmer, *An Address to Believers in the Book of Mormon*, 2.

a day passed without someone urging the community toward a different direction than the one Smith envisioned.

John Whitmer commented rather restrainedly for this period that the church "had some difficulty because of some that did not continue faithful; who denied the truth and turned into fables."[21] John may be referring to a young New York convert, Northrop Sweet, who came on to Ohio after he joined the church. Soon after Sweet's arrival, one of Rigdon's converts, Wycom Clark, claimed to receive a revelation naming Sweet as "the true revelator instead of Joseph Smith." Sweet joined Clark and four others in organizing the "Pure Church of Christ" in February or March 1831, "but that was the extent of the growth of this early schism."[22]

John Whitmer made special note in his history of a woman named Laura Hubble:

> who professed to be a prophetess of the Lord and professed to have many revelations, and knew the Book of Mormon was true; and that she should become a teacher in the Church of Christ. She appear[ed] very sanctimonious and deceived some, who were not able to detect her in her hypocrisy: others however had the spirit of discernment, and her follies and abominations were made manifest. The Lord gave Revelation that the Saints might not be deceived which reads as follows: O hearken, ye elders of my church, and give ear to the words which I shall speak unto you: for behold, verily, verily I say unto you, that ye have received a commandment for a law unto my church, through him whom I have appointed unto you, to receive commandments and revelations from my hand. And this ye shall know assuredly, that there is none other appointed unto you to receive <commandments and> revelations until he be taken if he abide in me.[23]

This firm revelatory declaration apparently quashed Hubble's attempt. Other individuals also challenged Joseph's control during this early

21. Whitmer, Book of John Whitmer, chap. 7, p. 27; McKiernan and Launius, *An Early Latter Day Saint History,* 65. The reference that some turned to fables may also suggest that the timing of the Whitmer family's removal from New York and trip to Ohio may have been impacted by the decisions or actions of other members.

22. George A. Smith, 15 November 1864, *Journal of Discourses,* 11:3; quoted in Parkin, "Conflict at Kirtland," 91–92.

23. Whitmer, Book of John Whitmer, chap. 3, p. 18; CofC D&C 43:1a–b, LDS D&C 43:1–3. See also Staker, *Hearken, O Ye People,* 111–14.

period with no better results, including John Noah, and a man named Horton.[24] Although Joseph succeeded in retaining control and remained the single source of authoritative pronouncements, it was becoming harder to locate unswerving converts in this turbulent climate.

At this point, Smith's authority remained based on charisma. Powerful manifestations of the Holy Ghost were an important part in early conversion experiences. Smith knew that continuing missionary success depended upon the active exercise of the gifts of the Spirit, which confirmed the movement's religious authority. However, Joseph quickly learned that the gifts could be a double-edged sword. It was apparent that their unregulated function could seriously threaten organizational stability. Through a series of revelations, Smith orchestrated a transition to a more hierarchal administration and a promised "endowment" experience for those ordained to the priesthood, thus successfully subordinating dangerous aspects of charisma.

Joseph began by implementing a set of administrative innovations. They were not meant to be only minor changes to the status quo. Rather, he wished to set the stage for a more comprehensive social reordering. What is known today as Doctrine and Covenants section 42, received on February 9, 1831, provided for evangelistic outreach, economic reform, and measures of social reform. The revelation urged every available elder out into the field, saying, "Ye shall go forth in my name, every one of you, excepting my servants Joseph Smith, Jr., and Sidney Rigdon."[25] It also established guidelines by revelation regulating expected behaviors during a mission:

> The elders, priests, and teachers of this church shall teach the principles of my gospel which are in the Bible and the Book of Mormon, in which is the fullness of the gospel; and they shall observe the covenants and church articles to do them, and these shall be their teachings, as they shall be directed by the Spirit; and the Spirit shall be given unto you by the prayer of faith, and if ye receive not the Spirit ye shall not teach. And all this ye shall observe to do as I have commanded concerning your teaching, until the fullness of my Scriptures

24. George A. Smith, 15 November 1864, *Journal of Discourses*, 11:6; quoted in Parkin, "Conflict at Kirtland," 92.

25. CofC D&C 42:4a; LDS D&C 42:4.

is given. And as ye shall lift up your voices by the Comforter, ye shall speak and prophesy as seemeth me good; for, behold, the Comforter knoweth all things, and beareth record of the Father and of the Son.[26]

Joseph used this revelation to create a little space for himself by dispatching all available elders on proselytizing missions. In addition to spreading the gospel, Smith realized that giving these energetic elders something important to do and getting them out of Kirtland would quiet things considerably. Smith calculated that, with some of the contending voices away in the missionary field, he and Rigdon could redirect the attention of the body of believers to their higher callings as Christians.

Besides its evangelistic initiatives, Doctrine and Covenants 42 provided for the necessary infrastructure for a comprehensive social re-visioning. Smith's revelation identified which social behaviors would be expected of proper followers of Christ. Following the example of Moses in dealing with disorderly Israelites, much of Joseph Smith's "Law of the Church" restated counsel found in the letters of Paul and Ten Commandments, i.e., "do not kill" and "do not steal," etc. Powerful community mores were established through a combination of promises, modeled behaviors, and perceived rewards. The lifestyle enjoined by section 42 was akin to that advocated by radical Christian seekers of past centuries. Joseph's quest was for a scriptural, social, and economic Christian society.

Section 42 also commanded the recommencement of the Bible translation. Joseph devoted more time to his Bible project with Rigdon serving as primary scribe. This session of scriptural revisions continued from February 9, 1831, until March 7, 1831, this time stopping at Genesis 19:29.[27] Section 42 explains the importance of Smith's revision of the Bible and directs its eventual publication and dissemination.[28] Beginning around

---

26. D&C 42, received February 9, 1831.

27. Knecht, *Joseph Smith's Bible Translation* (1984), 23; CofC D&C 45:11a; LDS D&C 45.

28. Ibid., 16, 17. For references to the New Translation, see CofC D&C 42:5a–c, 15a–b; LDS D&C 42:13–15, 43–44. Elders, priests, and teachers, were to hold their "peace concerning them (corrected Bible scriptures), and not teach them until thou hast received them in full" (CofC D&C 42:15a; LDS D&C 42:43). Smith had previously claimed that the Book of Mormon contained the fullness of the gospel. Section 42 hints that the goal of Smith's revision of the Holy Scriptures was to restore therein the fullness of the gospel, which would re-elevate the Bible to the same status that the Book of Mormon enjoyed within the movement.

March 8, 1831, John began preparing a printer's copy of the manuscript in anticipation of its publication.[29]

Doctrine and Covenants section 42 actually added to John's work-load. Although he was among those expected to take a mission, John need-ed to stay close to Kirtland, attending to his increasing clerical duties. It was John's job to help equip the church's expanded ministerial force as they prepared for their missionary journeys. Before leaving Kirtland, would-be church ambassadors needed credentials in case they encountered someone who questioned their authority to preach. Each missionary was furnished with his priesthood license. Some of Smith's revelations (sections CofC 17 [LDS 20] and 42), in addition to proclaiming doctrine, also symbol-ized the church's ecclesial authority. The church's articles and covenants—which became Doctrine and Covenants section 17 (LDS 20)—described the structure of the church and its governance, explained church beliefs, and outlined the duties of members.[30] Every missionary, naturally, wanted to have his own copy of such documents. Producing the licenses and copies of the revelations, probably kept John busy between February 9, 1831, and the end of the month.

Following the announcement of section 42, all available priesthood holders, including John, left Kirtland on short missions. Sometime around the first of March, John and Lyman Wight performed a short mission to neighboring Portage County, about forty miles south of Kirtland. Dur-ing March 1831, they organized a branch in Nelson Township.[31] Many in Portage County were already familiar with Sidney Rigdon as a visiting preacher, so John and Lyman found considerable interest among county residents. One of the most significant conversions in this county was that of the John Johnson family who lived near Hiram. Much taken with the report of a new prophet, John and Elsa Johnson visited Kirtland to meet Joseph Smith, and, during this visit, Elsa experienced a dramatic healing. Their son, Luke Johnson, a future apostle, described the incident: "Soon after Joseph Smith moved from the state of New York, my father, mother, and Ezra Booth, a Methodist minister, went to Kirtland to investigate

29. Jackson and Jasinski, "The Process of Inspired Translation," 38.

30. Faulring, "An Examination of the 1829 'Articles,'" 71–73.

31. Cannon and Cook, *Far West Record*, 12.

Mormonism. My mother had been laboring under an attack of chronic rheumatism in the shoulder, so that she could not raise her hand to her head, for about two years; the Prophet laid hands upon her, and she was healed immediately."[32] Mormon missionary efforts throughout northern Ohio began bearing good fruit, indeed.

Despite the many immediate demands upon his attention caused by the revelation canonized as Doctrine and Covenants section 42, Joseph's scriptural revision of the Bible remained his highest priority. Between February 9, 1831, and March 7, 1831, Smith and Rigdon worked on the Old Testament again.[33] In reworking Genesis 14, Joseph "added several verses describing an ancient order to which Melchisedec had been ordained as a high priest, which possessed immense this-worldly powers." Thereby, Smith came to forcefully associate the term "endowment" with "the ancient order to which Melchizedek was ordained as a high priest and through which he possessed tangible power."[34] In Joseph's mind, the concept of endowment pertained to ministerial preparation and, therefore, to priesthood empowerment as missionaries.

Smith continued to take advantage of this period of adjustment to further rein in his more unruly adherents. Wisely, instead of reacting to such spiritual and administrative challenges directly, Joseph took the initiative on February 9 by announcing the revelation (now D&C 43), intended to channel his followers' spiritual energies into more useful directions. Outdoing his competition, Smith hinted that a remarkable endowment of spiritual power would soon occur. In exchange for continuing organizational and financial support, Joseph offered members hope for eternal glories: "If ye desire the glories of the Kingdom, appoint ye my Servant Joseph Smith Jr. and uphold him before me by the prayer of faith. And again, I say unto you, that if ye desire the mysteries of the Kingdom, provide for him food and raiment and whatsoever he needeth to accomplish the work, wherewith I have commanded him; and if ye do it not, he shall remain unto them who have received him, that I may reserve unto myself a pure people before me" (CofC D&C 43:3d–f; LDS 43:11–14). With section

32. Johnson, "History of Luke Johnson," 1.

33. Knecht, *Joseph Smith's Bible Translation* (1984), 107.

34. Prince, *Power from On High*, 16.

43, he hoped to persuade them to abandon their own pursuit of individual spiritual empowerment and adopt his vision of a corporate endowment.

Also in February 1831, he received another revelation, now Doctrine and Covenants section 44. Many of the elders had been away from Kirtland on their mandated missions (D&C 42). Ill-equipped for their task, they were not experiencing the empowerment of the Holy Ghost as they had been led to expect, but this revelation moved quickly to meet that need:

> Behold, thus saith the Lord, unto you my Servants, it is expedient in me that the elders of my Church should be called together; from the east, and from the west, from the north and from the South, by letter or otherwise. And it shall come to pass, that I will pour out my Spirit upon them, in the day that they assemble themselves together; and it shall come to pass, that they shall go forth into the regions round about; and preach repentance unto the people, and many shall be converted.
>
> Behold I say unto you, that ye must visit the poor and the needy, and administer to their relief, that they may be kept until all things may be done according to my law, which ye have receiv[e]d. Amen.[35]

Perhaps Joseph's work on the Bible, along with feedback from disappointed missionaries returning from the field, prompted this summons to be "taught from on High" (CofC D&C 43:4c; LDS D&C 43:16). Some of the missionaries out in the field, including John, returned immediately to Kirtland, but still had to wait a couple of months for the endowment.

John summarized their experience: "Some of the Elders returned from their missions, to gain some rest and instructions. They rehearsed some of the wickedness which they had seen among this generation: while they were proclaiming the gospel, and warning the people, some would cry false prophets, false christ [*sic*] &c. Some would receive the word gladly, until their priests would cry delusion! delusion!!"[36]

Also, Rigdon had been troubled when the four missionaries to the Lamanites were unable to heal sick believers and had discussed this situ-

35. February 1831, Book of Commandments 46:2, p. 100; 1835 D&C 62; D&C 44.
36. Whitmer, Book of John Whitmer, chap. 3, p. 22.

ation with Joseph Smith during his New York visit.[37] It was Smith's belief that, once Mormon elders were "endowed with power from on high," these deficiencies would be rectified.

Some indication that converts were still seeking spiritual empowerment in unprofitable places appears in revelations received on March 8 and May 9, 1831: "Beware, lest ye are deceived, and that ye may not be deceived, seek ye earnestly the best gifts ... that all may be benefited."[38] Joseph was still repeating this caution in Nauvoo: "We believe in it [the Holy Ghost] in all its fullness, and power, and greatness, and glory: but whilst we do this we believe in it rationally, reasonably, consistently, and scripturally, and not according to the wild vagaries, foolish, notions and traditions of men."[39] However, he simultaneously affirmed in his March 8, 1831, revelation that the "gifts come from God, for the benefit of the children of God" (CofC D&C 46:7f; LDS D&C 46:26) and had a place in the church. Though cautioning against false spirits, the revelation stated that "it is given to some to speak with tongues, and to another it is given the interpretation of tongues" (CofC D&C 46:7e; LDS D&C 46:24–25).

On the one hand, Smith wanted his missionary force to be empowered through the gifts of the Holy Ghost, enabling them to serve as mighty witnesses and convert many to the new religion. But in pursuing this course, he was also taking a risk that the endowment might only end up producing a whole new cadre of independent prophets, everyone flying off in his own direction. But the risk seemed to pay off.

John Corrill, in describing this period in his history of the early church, records Joseph's ultimate victory over unchanneled religious enthusiasm: "Those visionary spirits spoken of before continued in the church; and rose to such height that the elders became so dissatisfied with them that they determined to have something done about it. Accordingly, they called upon the prophet and united in prayer, and asked God to give them light upon the subject. They received a revelation (sections 46 and 50) through the prophet, which was very gratifying, for it condemned these

---

37. Clapp, "Mormonism," 1–2.

38. CofC D&C 46:4a, b; LDS D&C 46:8, and "That which doth not edify, is not of God," CofC D&C 50:6b; LDS D&C 50:23.

39. "Gift of the Holy Ghost," 823.

visionary spirits, and gave rules for judging of spirits in general. After a while these spirits were rooted out of the Church."[40]

In Nauvoo, Joseph later reflected on these experiences:

> Soon after the gospel was established in Kirtland, and during the absence of the authorities of the church, many false spirits were introduced, many strange visions were seen, and wild enthusiastic notions were entertained; men run [*sic*] out of doors under the influence of this spirit, and some of them got upon the stumps of trees and shouted, and all kinds of extravagances were entered into by them; one man pursued a ball that he saw flying in the air, until he came to a precipice when he jumped into the top of a tree which saved his life, and many miraculous things were entered into, calculated to bring disgrace upon the church of God; to cause the spirit of God to be withdrawn; and to uproot and destroy those glorious principles which had been developed for the salvation of the human family. But when the authorities returned the spirit was made manifest, those members that were exercised with it were tried for their fellowship; and those that would not repent and forsake it were cut off.[41]

When Joseph Smith "stepped out of a sleigh at Kirtland's main crossroad … he introduced himself to a congregation that included a number of shouters and religious enthusiasts," wrote Kirtland-era historian, Mark Lyman Staker. The chapter, "Joseph Smith and the Gifts of the Spirit," in Staker's *Harken, O Ye People: The Historical Setting of Joseph Smith's Ohio Revelations*, provides an excellent analysis of Smith's response to ecstatic expressions of gifts.

Smith took steps to reduce conditions among his new followers that fostered excesses. For example, revelation received by Smith on March 7 and 8, 1831, offered an alternative eschatology which better equipped disciples to evaluate the immanence of Christ's return and the End Times. Smith noted that many things needed to be accomplished before the end would come. "Jacob shall flourish in the wilderness, the Lamanites shall blossom as a rose" (CofC D&C 46:4b–5b; LDS D&C 49:23–25). Much of

---

40. Corrill, *Brief History of the Church of Christ*, 17–18.

41. Joseph Smith, "Try the Spirits," 747. Joseph added, "At a subsequent period a Shaker spirit was on the point of being introduced, and at another time the Methodist and Presbyterian falling-down power; but the spirit was rebuked."

Smith's guidance "focused on the gifts of the Spirit," providing a methodology that equipped disciples to discern appropriate and inappropriate behavior. Also, "the bishop ... [and] elders unto the church," were given authority to evaluate the appropriateness of expressions of the gifts (CofC D&C 46:7g; LDS D&C 46:27). Joseph also stopped excluding nonmembers from sacrament services and suspended the late-night worship events that exacerbated the situation. Further, revelation reaffirmed the value of spiritual gifts previously identified in the Book of Mormon.

Also, responding to concern expressed by some of the elders, such as Parley P. Pratt, John Murdock, and John Corrill, Joseph received a revelation on May 9, 1831, condemning inappropriate behavior and providing rules for judging spiritual phenomena by the Spirit (CofC D&C 50:1–2a and 5–6a; LDS D&C 50:1–4 and 17–23). While not successful in completely resolving the place of gifts in the life of the church, Joseph managed to impose a great deal more control over the situation.[42]

Meanwhile, anticipation concerning an upcoming endowment experience continued to build throughout March and May. And finally the important endowment conference was scheduled for early June.

Through May 1831, Joseph devoted considerable energy to ensuring the successful implementation of his new economic policy. As church members from New York continued to gather to Ohio, Smith struggled to integrate them into the fabric of the life of the Kirtland church. When the extended Knight family—numbering about sixty—arrived from Colesville on May 14, 1831, the beleaguered Smith shifted the responsibility for providing accommodations and food for this branch to Bishop Partridge. The bewildered Partridge pushed back, requesting detailed guidance.[43] What later became Doctrine and Covenants section 51, received May 20, 1831, became the roadmap for organizing the Colesville Branch and implementing the law of consecration simultaneously[44]:

> Hearken unto me saith the Lord your God and I will speak unto my servant Edward and give unto him directions for it must needs be that he receive directions how to organize this people [Colesville Branch] for it must needs be that they are organized according to my laws....

42. Staker, *Harken, O Ye People*, 137–38.

43. Journal History, 25 July 1831; Knight, "Newel Knight's Journal," 69.

44. Jensen, Woodford, and Harper, *Revelations and Translations*, 145.

Wherefore let my servant Edward receive the properties of this people which have covenanted with me ... and go and obtain a deed or article of this land [acreage in Thompson, Ohio owned by a convert named Lemon Copley] unto himself.... Wherefore let my servant Edward ... appoint unto this people their portion every man alike according to their families according to their wants and their needs. And ... give unto him a writing that shall secure unto him his portion that he shall hold it of the church until he transgresses.... And again let the Bishop appoint a storehouse unto this church and let all things both in money and in meat which is more than needful for the wants of this people be kept in the hands of the Bishop.... [B]ehold this shall be an example unto my servant Edward in other places in all churches [branches].[45]

The conversion of Leman Copley coincided fortuitously with the arrival of the Colesville Branch.[46] Copley was a former Shaker in Ohio who was attracted by Mormonism's communitarian ideas. Wishing to experiment with consecration, Copley promised to make available to the church approximately seven hundred acres in Thompson, a neighboring township in Geauga County, not far from an existing Shaker community. Apparently, Copley did not actually consecrate this acreage but offered to sell it to the church at less than its assessed value. Joseph saw settling Colesville members on this land as a solution to two problems: caring for the needs of the Colesville Branch and implementing his new economic policy.

Whether Edward Partridge had formulated an alternative proposal is not known; but apparently, based on his business experience, he foresaw problems with this proposal. Joseph dismissed his concerns. Ezra Booth, whose trajectory through the church lasted for only a few months, later observed: "The law of the church enjoins that no debt with the world should be contracted. But a Thousand Acres of land in the town of Thompson could be purchased for one half its value, and he [Bishop Partridge] was commanded to secure it, and in order to do it he was under the necessity to contract a debt with the world, to the amount of several hundred dollars.

45. Tanner and Tanner, *Joseph Smith's Kirtland Revelation Book,* 87–89. The wording in this version is somewhat different from the revised language published in the 1835 Doctrine and Covenants. Terminal punctuation and capitalization added where needed.

46. Hartley, *"Stand by My Servant Joseph,"* 115.

He hesitated and the command was repeated, 'You must secure the land.'"[47] The exact arrangements have not survived; but Partridge entered into some kind of contract for the land on behalf of the church.[48] As Partridge had foreseen, the arrangement did not work out well, Copley reclaimed his land, and Joseph solved the problem by sending the Colesville Branch to Missouri in June 1831.

The regional press, eager to attract readers, had not overlooked the occasional contradictions and colorful possibilities of Smith's new religion. Even before the Lamanite missionaries had reached Ohio, the *Cleveland Herald* cautioned readers that the "Book of Mormon ... better known to some as the Golden Bible ... [was] one of the veriest impositions of the day."[49] Some indication of how widespread publicity had been appears in the letter of an unidentified Presbyterian from Chester, Geauga County, Ohio, who observed in February 1831: "The public mind is awake in this region; go where we will we hear little except Mormonism."[50]

A host of local voices warned citizens of this dangerous religious delusion. Editor John St. John, in the *Cleveland Herald* accused Cowdery of engaging in a money-making scheme: "We had known Cowdry [*sic*] some seven or 8 years ago, when he was a dabbler in the art of Printing, and principally occupied in writing and printing pamphlets, with which as a pedestrian pedlar, he visited the towns and villages of eastern N. York and Canada."[51] The *Telegraph* in Painesville, Ohio, characterized the Book of Mormon as "a pretended new revelation from God."[52] Levi Hancock, a convert from Rome, Ashtabula County, Ohio, writing of 1830, recalled: "Lies began to circulate through the land concerning the church; this caused the people to be more cold."[53]

47. Ezra Booth, letter no. 9, to Reverend Ira Eddy, 6 December 1831, 2–3.

48. Knight, "Newel Knight's Journal," 69.

49. "The Golden Bible," *Special Collections: Early Mormonism Collection 2, Cleaveland [sic] Herald* November 25, 1830, accessed May 9, 2012, http://www.solomonspalding.com/docs/1830oh11b.htm.

50. A Presbyterian, "The Mormon Delusion," *New-Hampshire Patriot & State Gazette* 3 (May [16], 1831).

51. "The Golden Bible," *Cleveland Herald*.

52. Howe, "The Book of Mormon," 3.

53. Levi Ward Hancock, journal, fall 1830, p. 37.

Eber D. Howe, editor of the *Telegraph* published in Painesville, Ohio, took a special interest—all of it negative—in Mormonism. He had previously pursued a policy of giving but little notice to religion in his columns; however, in mid-February, Howe reversed his course, explaining: "But when any subject becomes a matter of general enquiry and conversation through the whole community, with but few exceptions, that community will call upon the Press to speak—and a free press will speak. We therefore declare our columns open, and free to the investigation of the divine pretensions of the 'Book of Mormon,' and its 'Author and Proprietor, Joseph Smith.'"[54]

Other local papers followed a similar hard line, including the local *Geauga Gazette, Ravenna Courier*, and *Ohio Star* (also published in Ravenna). Howe published Smith's "Article and Covenants" revelation in his September 13, 1831, issue, commenting, "They [the Mormons] have also manuscripts among them sufficient to make several [copies] of similar (revelations), which are, however, kept from the view of the weaker brethren."[55] As time went on, Smith began to employ code names in his revelations in an effort to minimize public ridicule; but the effort, though concealing the identity of persons named in the revelation, presented an array of such unusual names (i.e., Joseph was "Baurak Ale") that they merely gave the skeptical new ammunition.[56]

Throughout early 1831, Joseph and Sidney Rigdon—but not John— devoted a significant amount of their time to correcting and revising the Bible. John's shift back into a lesser role may have caused some private difficulties, since Rigdon's influence stimulated its own wave of organizational adjustment and change. Well-versed in the Bible and biblical argument, Rigdon thoroughly supplanted Oliver Cowdery, John, and David Whitmer, as Joseph's most intimate advisor. In 1887, David characterized Rigdon as gifted but dangerous:

> Rigdon was a thorough Bible scholar, a man of fine education, and a
> powerful orator. He soon worked himself deep into Brother Joseph's

54. Clapp, "Mormonism," 1.

55. Howe, "Secret Bye Laws of the Mormonites," 1.

56. For the code names used in the Doctrine and Covenants, see Whittaker, "Substituted Names in the Published Revelations of Joseph Smith," 111.

affections, and had more influence over him than any other man living. He was Brother Joseph's private counselor, and his most intimate friend and brother for some time after they met. Brother Joseph rejoiced, believing that the Lord had sent to him this great and mighty man Sydney [*sic*] Rigdon, to help him in the work. Poor Brother Joseph! He was mistaken about this, and likewise all of the brethren were mistaken, for we thought at the time just as Brother Joseph did about it.[57]

Neither David nor John left any account of his feelings during this period; but they must have found private ways of dealing with the dissonance occasioned by their misgivings about Rigdon's growing influence with Joseph. Perhaps, they considered it a test of loyalty and simply suppressed their own negative feelings, or, perhaps, they found ways of seeing the situation positively. In retrospect, however, Joseph would have been well advised to find ways to invite broader and more candid participation.

During 1831, as Joseph and Rigdon encountered perceived biblical scriptural problems or inconsistencies, Sidney helped Joseph uncover exciting new possibilities within the texts. As a result, Rigdon significantly impacted the church's scriptural innovation. Together, they laid the foundation of an evolving doctrinal tradition. Recast scripture further expanded Smith's alternative visions for society. A scholar of the Bible translation process, Stephen Knecht, observes: "From our vantage point in time, Joseph is interjecting his understanding into texts that did not support his doctrine,"[58] reshaping them to provide that missing support.

---

57. David Whitmer, *An Address to All Believers in Christ*, 35.

58. Knecht, *Joseph Smith's Bible Translation* (1984), 162.

CHAPTER EIGHT

First Church Historian

O N March 8, 1831, Joseph Smith initiated measures to gather and maintain vital records about the church and its members, calling John to function as church historian. John was dutiful but not enthusiastic about his new responsibility. "I would rather not do it," he commented, "but observed that the will of the Lord be done, and if he desires it, I desire that he would manifest it through Joseph the Seer."[1] Joseph therefore sought inspired counsel and received this revelation:

> Behold it is expedient in me that my servant John should write and keep a regular history, and assist you, my servant Joseph, in transcribing all things which shall be given you, until he is called to further duties. Again, verily I say unto you, that he can also lift up his voice in meetings, whenever it shall be expedient. And again, I say unto you, that it shall be appointed unto him to keep the Church record and history continually, for Oliver Cowdery I have appointed to another office. Wherefore it shall be given him, inasmuch as he is faithful, by the Comforter, to write these things.[2]

With this authoritative reassurance, John apparently started gathering sources for his history immediately. Although the extant manuscript, now housed in the Community of Christ Archives in Independence, Missouri, is obviously a later draft, the first seven chapters are written in contemporaneous style. John noted in chapter 6, "Oliver Cowdery has written the commencement of the church history, commencing at the time of the finding of the plates up to June 12, 1831,"[3] but wrote in his own opening lines:

1. Whitmer, Book of John Whitmer, chap. 6, p. 24.

2. Book of Commandments, 50, p. 114; D&C 47.

3. Whitmer, Book of John Whitmer, chap. 6, p. 25; McKiernan and Launius, *An Early Latter Day Saint History,* 56.

"I shall proceed to continue this record."[4] John's initial entry in chapter 1 is dated June 12, 1831. Chapters 1–8 quickly summarize events up through early 1831, leading to his assumption of keeping the church record. From that point on, his entries are brief. John characterizes them as "a mere sketch of the things that have transpired, they are however all that seemed to me wisdom to write—many things happened that are to be lamented because of the weakness and instability of man."[5] Like every good historian, John shaped the church narrative by what he chose to include or omit.

The March 8, 1831, revelation also reconnected John to the Bible translation project by instructing him to assist "my servant Joseph, in transcribing all things which shall be given you, until he is called to further duties." At this point, Joseph laid aside Genesis, which was revised up to chapter 19, verse 29, to begin working on the New Testament. John Whitmer began making a copy of the dictated Old Testament manuscript. New Translation scholar Stephen Knecht observes, "Smith assigned John the task of preparing the Old Testament Dictated Manuscript for the printer. This was to be done by supplying biblical chapters and subheadings while he copied the entire text over."[6] John worked at this project for almost a month—between March 8 and April 4, 1831. That same day, March 8, Joseph and Sidney turned their attention to the New Testament, their first venture beyond the Old Testament. Over the next four weeks, they proceeded as far as Matthew 9.[7]

On April 4, 1831, John completed his Old Testament transcription and began copying the recently dictated New Testament: Matthew 1–9:1. On April 4, 1831, while John was at work with the New Testament manuscript, Joseph and Sidney switched their attention back to the Old Testament, completing up through Genesis 24:41a. The next day, April 5, John completed his transcription of Matthew 1–9:1 and recommenced copying and emending the Old Testament printer's copy. He brought the text in this manuscript up to Genesis 24:41a.[8]

---

4. Whitmer, Book of John Whitmer, chap. 1, p. 1.

5. Ibid., chap. 6, p. 25.

6. Knecht, *Joseph Smith's Bible Translation* (1977), 25.

7. Ibid., 24.

8. Ibid., 25.

Having been diverted from the New Testament translation for two days, on April 7, 1831, Joseph and Sidney picked up their work at Matthew 9:2 and continued through Matthew 26:71a.[9] They then laid it aside for a planned trip to Missouri, departing on June 19, 1831.

Joseph continued to prepare the church's missionaries to receive the promised endowment of "power from on high." In both March and May 1831, Joseph had received revelations (D&C 46 and 50), encouraging adherents to seek "the best gifts" and explaining how to differentiate between positive and negative spiritual manifestations. "Solomon and Levi Hancock, two brothers who had preached across Ohio's countryside, arrived in Kirtland at the end of May [1831] and learned that on June 4, 'there was to be an indowment [*sic*] of some Elders.'"[10]

The anticipated fourth general conference of the church convened June 3–6, 1831. Mark Staker, a scholar of the Kirtland period, theorizes that the conference was actually a four-day event. "A preparatory meeting convened on Friday, June 3, [1831], at which its [the conference's] agenda was given by revelation. A special ordination meeting on Saturday, June 4, introduced the high priesthood. A general meeting for the entire membership followed on Sunday, June 5. A concluding session on Monday, June 6, issued calls to numerous missionaries."[11]

Levi Hancock recalled that "the fourth of June came and we all met in a little string of buildings under the hill near Isaac Morley's in Kirtland.... We all went to a school house on the hill about one fourth of a mile, ascending all the way. It was built of logs. This was filled with benches. Here the Elders were seated. The meeting was opened as usual."[12] "Ezra Booth indicated: "The 4th of June ... was appointed for the sessions of the conference.... Smith, the day before the conference [June 3, 1831], profess-

9.   Ibid., 24.

10. Hancock, autobiography, p. 23, quoted in Staker, *Hearken, O Ye People*, 139.

11. Staker, *Hearken, O Ye People*, 155–56. The conference minutes in the Far West Record combined the events of the first two days of this conference under the date of June 3, 1831.

12. Hancock, autobiography, p. 23.

ing to be filled with the spirit of prophecy, declared that 'not three days should pass away, before some should see their Savior, face to face.'"[13]

This conference event was the culmination of weeks of anticipation and preparation. Participants expected to be empowered from "on high" so that they, like their New Testament counterparts, could claim the undeniable stamp of divine authority. They hoped that this bestowal of spiritual gifts would enable them to spread the gospel message "among all nations."[14] During this conference, on June 4, 1831, John was selected as one of the first group of elders ordained to the high priesthood.[15] And participants did experience something of a Pentecostal outpouring, although some of the manifestations were alarming. Church member John Corrill wrote:

> The meeting was conducted by Smith. Some curious things took place. The same visionary and marvelous spirits spoken of before, got hold of some of the elders; it threw one from his seat to the floor; it bound another, so that for some time he could not use his limbs nor speak; and some other curious effect were experienced, but, by a mighty exertion, in the name of the Lord, it was exposed and shown to be from an evil source. The Malchisedec [*sic*] priesthood was then for the first time introduced, and conferred on several of the elders. In this chiefly consisted the endowment.... Some doubting took place among the elders, and considerable conversation was held on the subject. The elders not fairly understanding the nature of the endowments, it took some time to reconcile all their feelings.[16]

Ezra Booth, a member who remained with the church only a short time, summarized the anticipated endowment: "It was a Pentecost, consisting of revelation, prophecy, vision, healing, casting out of evil spirits,

---

13. Ezra Booth, letter no. 4, to Ira Eddy, 31 October 1831, "Mormonism, No. 4," 2.

14. Book of Commandments 40:28; CofC D&C 38:7c; LDS D&C 38:32–33.

15. David Whitmer also participated in this conference on June 3–6, 1831, at Kirtland, when the first high priests were ordained, but, according to the minutes, he was not specifically listed among those ordained to the high priesthood. Cannon and Cook, *Far West Record*, 6–7. The June 3 [4], 1831, minutes of this meeting, as recorded in the Far West Record, listed forty-four elders, four priests, and fourteen teachers present, twenty-three of whom were ordained to the high priesthood. Ibid., 6–7.

16. Corrill, *Brief History of the Church of Christ*, 18.

speaking in unknown tongues, and, according to one witness, an unsuccessful attempt to raise a dead child."[17]

The conference's concluding activity occurred Monday, June 6, 1831. "Joseph Smith presented ... [a] revelation he had received in vision to the body of priesthood holders along with ... mission calls."[18] Rather than sending the newly empowered missionaries abroad, Smith roused expectations even higher by announcing plans to send them on a mission to discover the New Jerusalem, in western Missouri. John Murdock noted, "I with others received a command as recorded in Book of Cov. ... to journey to Mi[ssouri] preaching by the way."[19]

In all, this conference initiated the high priesthood within the new movement, clarified concepts of priesthood, and also provided an expanded authority mechanism to control excesses of religious ecstasy.

Meanwhile, during this exciting period, despite Bishop Partridge's best efforts, the Thompson, Ohio, experimental community flagged and faltered. Inevitably, divisions developed between Leman Copley, Newel Knight, and other participants. When what Copley perceived as an important missionary effort among neighboring Shakers failed, perhaps coupled with other disappointments, his interest in Mormonism evaporated.[20] According to John Whitmer, Copley's subsequent activities "confused the whole church."[21] Copley asked Ashbel Kitchell, a Shaker elder at North Union, Cuyahoga County, Ohio, to accept him back into the Shaker Society and sought Kitchell's help in regaining control of his land.[22]

17. Ezra Booth, letter no. 4, to Ira Eddy, 31 October 1831, "Mormonism, No. 4," 3.

18. Staker, *Hearken, O Ye People*, 161.

19. John Murdock, journal, p. 13.

20. Porter, "The Colesville Branch in Kaw Township," 282–83.

21. Whitmer, Book of John Whitmer, chap. 8, p. 29.

22. Ashbel Kitchell's account apparently foreshortened the sequence of events, for it did not become apparent until the end of May that Copley intended to break the agreement, prompting Newel Knight's visit to Kirtland for Joseph's advice. An entry in Kitchell's journal observes that Copley "had a large farm, and about 100 Mormons were living with him, on it. When he got home [immediately returning from the Shaker mission, suggesting the month of March 1831] he found the Mormons had rejected him, & could not own him for one of them, because he had deceived them with the idea of converting us. He felt very bad;—was not able to rest;—came back to us and begged for union." Although the main body of the Colesville Branch had

Somewhere during this period, John encountered a newly converted family, John and Martha F. Jackson, who apparently lived near Kirtland.[23] The Jacksons may have been part of the Family movement under Rigdon's leadership with Lyman Wight as pastor. In that case, John probably met the Jacksons at a conference. John Jackson was born in 1780 in Pennsylvania where he was a farmer.[24] He and Martha apparently once lived in Monroe County in southeastern Ohio, where their third child, Eliza, was born between 1810 and 1820.[25] Eliza's older siblings were Sarah M. and Andrew J.; James, Thomas J., and Lewis were younger, and there may have been other children as well. Twenty-nine-year-old John found himself particularly attracted to twenty-two-year-old Sarah Maria/Mariah (1809–73).[26]

The missionaries to the Lamanites—Oliver Cowdery, Peter Whitmer Jr., Parley P. Pratt, Ziba Peterson, and Frederick G. Williams, an en-

---

not yet arrived from New York, several church members had been living at Thompson on Copley's farm since March, including Joseph and Polly Knight, and their daughter Lucy, who had, by one account, come to Kirtland with Joseph and Emma Smith in January 1831. Kitchell noted further, "After some consultation we concluded to give him [Copley] union, and help him through; and to accomplish this, I went home with him, and held a meeting in the dooryard, among the Mormons.... A lively exchange, lasting until the next day followed. I stayed all [next] day, and assisted them to settle their affairs.—I wrote for them two or three hours; and after I was thro' I took hold of the Elder [Newel Knight] and walked the floor, ameuseing [*sic*] him with a number of pleasant things." Kitchell, quoted in Meader, "The Shakers and the Mormons," 91, quoted in Flake, "A Shaker View of a Mormon Mission," 94–99; see also Kitchell, "A Mormon Interview."

23. A John Jackson family is listed in Mayfield Township, Cuyahoga County, Ohio, in the 1820 and 1830 federal censuses. Whitmer descendant Lorene Pollard believed that the Jackson family lived in the area of Euclid (Mayfield), Ohio. Pollard, conversation with the author, Whitmer Family Celebration, October 6, 2006.

24. 1850 census, Chariton Township, Appanoose County, Iowa.

25. Sherry Case, posting on "John H. Zimmer," GenForum, Genealogy.com, 1998, accessed May 10, 2012, http://genforum.genealogy.com/cgi-bin/pageload.cgi?Jackson::zimmer ::72.html. See also 1840 census, Rockport Township, Caldwell County, Missouri. John and his son Andrew are listed as farmers in the 1850 Iowa census for Chariton Township, Appanoose County.

26. "Sarah M. Whitmer, nee Jackson ... from Ohio, in which state Mrs. W. was born and brought up." "Jacob D. Whitmer," in *History of Caldwell and Livingston Counties*, 340, quoted in Curtis, "Whitmer Family," 17. Erin Jennings Metcalfe gives Sarah Jackson's birth date as October 13, 1809. Jennings, "Outline Descendant Report for Jacob Musselman," 1. This date is confirmed in the John Whitmer family Bible.

thusiastic convert who joined the group in Ohio—had arrived safely in Missouri in late December or early January 1831, despite record cold and deep snow. Although government agents thwarted their attempts to gain access to Native Americans on reserves in what later became Kansas, they succeeded in converting a number of white residents in Jackson County, Missouri. Pratt set out alone to return to Kirtland on February 14, 1831, to report their experience.

News of the Lamanite missionaries' accomplishment prompted the church's second great missionary journey. During the conference held June 3–6, 1831, in Kirtland, Joseph Smith designated fourteen teams of missionaries to travel to Missouri during the summer of 1831. Joseph paired David Whitmer with Harvey Whitlock for the thousand-mile journey to the West. Joseph and Sidney also undertook this journey. John's assignment was to remain in Kirtland to complete transcriptions of Smith's scriptural revision.

Shortly before the conference, a new convert, William Wines Phelps, appeared in Kirtland. Before affiliating with Joseph Smith's movement, Phelps had played a prominent role in New York state politics as editor of a partisan paper.[27] Smith immediately called Phelps into the ministry because of his communication and printing skills. His bold style equipped him to be a strong spokesperson for Smith's religious initiatives. In coming years, Phelps's editorial endeavors and hymn writing would capture much of the spirit of the movement, and he promptly became part of the group planning to travel to Missouri.

But within days of their departure, the already deteriorating situation with the Colesville Branch in Thompson completely broke down. John recorded in his history, "At this time the Church at Thompson Ohio was embroiled in difficulty, because of the rebellion of Leman Copley. Who would not do as he had previously agreed ... finally the Lord spoke unto Joseph Smith Jr the prophet." This revelation advised all involved to "repent of all their sins; and become truly humble ... and contrite." The revelation chastised them: "The covenant which they made unto me, has been broken, even so it has become void and of none effect."[28]

---

27. Linn, *Story of the Mormons*, 167.

28. Whitmer, Book of John Whitmer, chap 8, pp. 29–30.

Joseph promptly advised the displaced Colesville members at Thompson, composed primarily of the extended Knight family—some sixty individuals—to travel to western Missouri. In revelatory language, he counseled: "Go to now and flee the land, lest your enemies come upon you; and take your journey into the regions westward, and appoint whom you will to be your leader, and to pay moneys for you. And thus you shall take your journey <into the regions> westward, unto the land of Missouri, unto the borders of the Lamanites. And after you have done journeying, behold I say unto you, seek ye a living like unto men, until I prepare a place for you."[29]

According to John, "The Church at Thompson made all possible haste to leave for Missouri, and left and none of their enemies harmed them."[30] Three members of the Knight family—Joseph Sr., Joseph Jr., and Newel—left several accounts of the Thompson experience, which I have combined and harmonized here:

> Now this spring Joseph received a number of revelations. One was to purchase a thousand acres of land which was claimed by Lemon [*sic*] Copley and not paid for. He had a little before come into the church and appeared to be zealous and faithful. It was advised that the Colesville Branch remain together, and go to a neighboring town called Thompson, as ... Copley had a considerable tract of land there which he offered to let the saints occupy, consequently a contract was agreed upon and we commenced work in good faith—preparing houses and my folks came on. We all went to work and made fence and planted and sowed the fields. About this time we were called upon to consecrate our properties. In a short time [about five weeks] Copley broke the engagement. Copley would not consecrate his property, therefore he was cut of[f] from the church. He began to persecute us and we had to leave his farm. We sold what we could but Copley took the advantage of us [sued in Geauga County Court] and we could not git [*sic*] anything for what we had done. [We had to] pay sixty dollars damage for fitting up his houses and planting his ground. We then had a revelation [from Joseph Smith]. We was commanded to take up

29. Book of Commandments 56; 1835 D&C 67; LDS D&C 54.
30. Whitmer, Book of John Whitmer, chap. 8, p. 30.

our journey to the region westward to the borders of the Lamanites. So we left Copley's in June, 1831.[31]

Eber D. Howe's *Telegraph* in Painesville took note of the Colesville Branch's departure on June 28: "Before Jo left [for Missouri], he had a special command for all those of his followers who had located themselves in the township of Thompson, to depart forthwith for Missourie [*sic*], and all those who did not obey were to be deprived of all the blessings of Mormonism. There were in that township about twenty families, the most of whom started last week for the Ohio River, leaving their spring crops all upon the ground."[32]

On June 19, 1831, Joseph Smith, Sidney Rigdon, William W. Phelps, Martin Harris, Edward Partridge, Joseph Coe, Ezra Booth, Algernon Sidney Gilbert, and his wife, Elizabeth Van Benthusen Gilbert, also set out for Missouri. They traveled by wagon, canal boat, and stagecoach to Cincinnati, Ohio, and from there to Louisville, Kentucky, by steamboat. When their steamer was delayed, Smith, Harris, Phelps, Partridge, and Coe continued on by foot to Independence, arriving July 14, 1831. The rest of the party followed by water, joining them a few days later.[33] During this initial visit to Jackson County, Smith launched a number of important initiatives for the Mormon settlement.

Meanwhile, the other designated missionary teams made their own way to Missouri. David Whitmer and Harvey Whitlock visited Paris, Illinois, en route where they taught Mormonism to a schoolteacher named William E. McLellin. McLellin, who had already heard a sermon about Joseph Smith and the Book of Mormon a few days earlier from another team of missionaries, responded positively to their message. He described these "Mormonite" beliefs in a letter to relatives:

> Some time in July 1831. Two men came to Paris & held an evening meeting, only a few attended, but among the others, I was there. They

31. My synthesis of the Knight family recollections about Thompson, Geauga County, Ohio, taken from Knight, "Joseph Knight's Recollection of Early Mormon History," p. 35; Knight, "Incidents from History"; and Knight, "Newel Knight's Journal," 69–70.

32. Howe, "We mentioned two weeks since," 3. This source dates the departure of the Colesville Branch around June 21, 1831; Freeborn Demill wrote, "Coleville April [June] 21st 1831 on thursday [*sic*] Set out." Demill, itinerary.

33. Van Wagoner, *Sidney Rigdon*, 98–99.

delivered some ideas which appeared very strange to me at that time. They said that in September 1827 an Angel appeared to Joseph Smith (in Ontario Co. New York) and showed to him the confusion on the earth respecting true religion. It also told him to go a few miles distant to a certain hill and there he should find some plates with engravings, which (if he was faithful) he should be enabled to translate. He went as directed and found plates (which had the appearance of fine Gold) about 8 inches long 5 or 6 wide and all together about 6 inches thick; each one about as thick as thin paste Board fastened together and opened in the form of a book containing engravings of reformed Egyptian Hieroglyphical characters: which he was inspired to translate and the record was published in 1830 and is called the book of Mormon. It is a record which was kept on this continent by the ancient inhabitants. Those men had this book with them and they told us about it, and also of the rise of the church (which is now called Mormonites from their faith in this book &c.) They left Paris very early next morning and pursued their journey Westward. But in a few days two others came into the neighbourhood proclaiming that these were the last days, and that God had sent forth the book of Mormon to show the times of the fulfillment of the ancient prophecies when the Saviour shall come to destroy iniquity off the face of the earth, and reign with his saints in Millennial Rest. One of these was a witness to the book and had seen an angel which declared its truth (his name was David Whitmer). They were in the neighbourhood about a week. I talked much with them by way of enquiry and argument. They believed Joseph Smith to be an inspired prophet. They told me that he and between 20 & thirty of their Preachers were on their way to Independence. My curiosity was roused <up> and my anxiety also to know the truth.[34]

McLellin hastily decided to follow the missionaries after they departed from Paris and subsequently was baptized by Hyrum Smith on August 20, 1831, after his arrival in Jackson County.[35]

Joined by some of the missionary teams, Smith proclaimed Jackson County as the church's "land of Zion," to be a righteous city, a gathering place where disciples might fully live Christ's teachings and thereby assist

34. William E. McLellin to Beloved Relatives, 4 August 1832.

35. Shipps and Welch, *Journals of William E. McLellin*, 34.

in ushering in God's kingdom on earth. On August 3, church officiants dedicated a temple site in Independence. Revelations received during July and August assigned primary responsibility for the settlement's oversight to Edward Partridge, Sidney Gilbert, Oliver Cowdery, and W. W. Phelps. Phelps was to "be planted in this place [Zion] and be established as a printer unto the church."[36]

The first conference in Missouri was held on August 4, 1831, at the home of Joshua Lewis in Kaw Township. Joseph Smith Jr., Samuel H. Smith, Sidney Rigdon, Frederick G. Williams, Oliver Cowdery, Reynolds Cahoon, Sidney Gilbert, W. W. Phelps, Joseph Coe, Ezra Booth, and Peter Whitmer Jr. all left Independence for Ohio on August 9, 1831.[37] Phelps also left, traveling east to wrap up his business and relocate his family to Missouri. In early October, an Ohio conference instructed Phelps to purchase a press "for the purpose of establishing a monthly paper [in Missouri] to be called the *Evening and [the] Morning Star.*"[38]

Although John did not participate in this mission to Missouri, neither was he left out of its flurry. He remained in Ohio, obedient to a revelation that instructed, "Let the residue of the elders watch over the churches, and declare the word in the regions among them, and let them labor with their own hands" (CofC D&C 52:9a–b; LDS D&C 52:38–39). While so many of the elders were away, John provided pastoral ministry. In July 1831, he traveled to neighboring Amherst, Ohio, where he preached in a Mr. Barna's barn. Jared Carter, who attended this meeting, observed what he felt was miraculous protection:

> While Elder [John] Whitmer was preaching, a shower of rain came up. I thought at first that this would interrupt the meeting, as I saw the roof of the barn was only shingled in parts; but after a few minutes it appeared to me that the Lord was willing to part the rain, so that the congregation should not be disturbed. Consequently, I began to pray to the Lord, that the rain might not annoy us. My prayer was heard. It rained considerably around the barn, but not on the barn itself sufficient to wet us. After the rain was over, I took particular notice of

36. Tanner and Tanner, *Joseph Smith's Kirtland Revelation Book,* 90–91.

37. Jessee, *Papers of Joseph Smith,* 1:361n5.

38. *History of the RLDS Church,* 1:219.

how the rain had fallen and saw that the storm had actually parted where the barn stood.[39]

Also, just before leaving for Missouri, Joseph turned the dictated New Testament manuscript over to John so that he could transcribe the newly dictated material into the printer's copy of the New Testament. John essentially completed this assignment during Smith's absence, between June 1831 and September 26, 1831. John apparently quit when he ran out of paper at Matthew chapter 26, which coincided with the end of the folio on which he was working. For some reason, John was unable to procure more paper and finish the transcription of Matthew beyond the middle of chapter 26.[40]

The second week in August, Joseph Smith, Sidney Rigdon, and Reynolds Cahoon returned from Missouri, traveling partway by canoe and partway by stage. On August 13, 1831, at Chariton, Missouri, they encountered some of the western missionaries still struggling to reach Missouri: Hyrum Smith and John Murdock, who formed one team, and the second team of David Whitmer and Harvey Whitlock.[41] Hyrum Smith and John Murdock had fallen behind because Murdock had become ill. By revelation, Joseph exhorted the four missionaries to continue on to Jackson County and complete their mission. The two teams pooled their meager resources and purchased a horse so Murdock could ride. His illness only intensified; so arranging for his care, they left him and continued on, reaching Jackson County about August 18.[42]

David Whitmer participated in a second conference on August 24, 1831, in Kaw Township, Jackson County, Missouri, and explored possible settlement locations. On August 25, 1831, he, Hyrum Smith, Martin Harris, Harvey Whitlock, Simeon Carter, and William McLellin started for Ohio. On August 27, 1831, Whitlock learned that his wife was en route, so he returned to Independence to wait for her. On August 31, David Whitmer and Martin Harris left the main group and returned to Kirtland via St.

39. Carter, "Manuscript History of the Great Lakes Mission," July 1831.

40. Knecht, *Joseph Smith's Bible Translation* (1977), 25.

41. Reynolds Cahoon, journal, quoted in Journal History, 13 August 1831.

42. John Murdock, journal, quoted in Murdock, *John Murdock: His Life and His Legacy*, 78–79.

Louis, Vandalia, Terre Haute, and Indianapolis. Simeon Carter also left the party, traveling by himself. Hyrum Smith and William McLellin traveled by land, crossing the Mississippi River at Louisiana, Missouri. Then they traveled on, stopping briefly in Paris, Illinois, William McLellin's home. They were soon on their way again, taking four more weeks to reach Kirtland, by way of Terre Haute and Indianapolis, Indiana.[43] On reaching Kirtland, McLellin wrote, "Here I first saw brother Joseph [Smith] the Seer, also brothers Oliver [Cowdery], John [Whitmer] & Sidney [Rigdon].[44]

Smith, Rigdon, and Cowdery reached Ohio by stage on August 27, 1831. On September 1, John's brother, Peter, who had been absent since leaving on his mission to the Lamanites from New York in October 1830, reached Kirtland with Frederick G. Williams, Samuel H. Smith, Reynolds Cahoon, Joseph Coe, and the disgruntled Ezra Booth. Booth wrote: "At St. Louis we took passage in a steam-boat, and came to Wellsville; and from thence in the stage home. We traveled about eight hundred miles farther than the three who took their passage in the stage, and arrived at our homes but a few days later."[45] Booth resented that he and the second-tier missionaries had been left to make their own way back, depending on the help of strangers, even though Joseph and Sidney, who had gone at least partway in a canoe, were obviously not traveling in luxury.

Nor had Booth and the others suffered undue delay, reaching Kirtland within five days of the Joseph Smith party. Joseph Smith, Sidney Rigdon, and Oliver Cowdery met with Booth several times, apparently trying to deal with his objections; but they failed to achieve reconciliation. On September 6, 1831, less than a week after his arrival, Booth was relieved of his elder's license and was excommunicated.[46]

Booth and fellow Portage County, Ohio, convert, Symonds Ryder, publicly renounced their faith in Mormonism at a Methodist camp meet-

---

43. Shipps and Welch, *Journals of William E. McLellin*, August 25–28, 1831, 36–45; see also, O'Driscoll, *Hyrum Smith: A Life of Integrity*, 52–53.

44. Shipps and Welch, *Journals of William McLellin*, 44–45.

45. Ezra Booth, letter no. 7, 20 September 1831.

46. Van Wagoner, *Sidney Rigdon*, 109.

ing at Shalersville, Trumbull County, Ohio, on September 6, 1831.[47] Booth promptly started writing a series of nine letters reflecting his skepticism, which appeared in the *Ohio Star,* a Ravenna, Ohio, newspaper, between October 13 and December 8, 1831.[48] These letters, obviously literate and written from an inside perspective, negatively impacted Smith's work. George A. Smith, Joseph's younger cousin, later recalled, "It was generally believed by our enemies, at the time, that the apostasy and revelations of Ezra Booth would put an utter end to 'Mormonism.'"[49]

Compounding the problems with Booth, Smith found that, during his two months' absence, several converts had withdrawn from fellowship. Simeon Carter noted that, at a conference in Orange on October 25, soon after Joseph's return, he "mourned because of the falling away [in Kirtland] since he took his journey to the Land of Zion."[50]

Because of the revelation designating Jackson County as Zion, church members anticipated a general move to Missouri during the next spring and summer when travel would be easiest. But Smith had been un-favorably impressed with the quality of life on the frontier. On September 11, 1831, he announced that Kirtland should be retained as a "stronghold ... for the space of five years" (CofC D&C 64:4c; LDS D&C 64:21).[51]

47. Carter, "Manuscript History of the Great Lakes Mission," September 6, 1831; Booth and Ryder, *Warren* (Ohio) *News Letter and Trumbull County Republican,* 1831, cited in Parkin, *Conflict at Kirtland,* 116; also Hayden, *Early History of the Disciples in the Western Reserve,* 252.

48. Van Wagoner, *Sidney Rigdon,* 110.

49. George A. Smith, 10 January 1858, *Journal of Discourses* 7:112–13.

50. Simeon Carter, statement during conference, Minutes of a General Conference, Orange, Cuyahoga County, Ohio, in Cannon and Cook, *Far West Record,* 22.

51. Van Wagoner, *Sidney Rigdon,* 105.

CHAPTER NINE

Preparing to Publish the Revelations: Fall 1831

I N LATE SEPTEMBER 1831 or early October 1831, Joseph, Sidney, their families, and other key church leaders, including John and his parents, moved away from Kirtland. This move allowed Joseph in particular to avoid the mounting administrative distractions at Kirtland and concentrate on his Bible revision, for which John had prepared complete copies as far as Matthew 26. They relocated forty miles south of Kirtland at the John Johnson farm at Hiram, in Portage County, Ohio. Local resident Hartwell Ryder, son of Symonds Ryder, who was briefly a Mormon convert, recalled, "They soon began preaching and gained many converts. They built a dam across the creek on the property now owned by Mr. Vaughn, and thither they went to baptize converts, sometimes to the number of 15 or 20."[1] At this point, Emma, who had given birth to twins who had not survived, was caring for the adopted Murdock twins, Joseph and Julia. Their mother had died in childbirth on May 1, 1831, and their father was an ardent missionary.

The entire Whitmer family seems to have moved to the Johnson farm. Hartwell Ryder further recalled, "Mr. [John] Johnson owned several log houses which he offered to them to occupy. Joe Smith and wife settled in part of ... [the Johnson's] home. Sidney Rigdon and family settled just across the street in a small log house. The Whitmers, Smiths, Cowderys, and Poormans occupied another house."[2]

---

1. Ryder, "A Short History," 3.
2. The Johnson farmhouse was not spacious and part of the summer kitchen at the back of the house served as Joseph's and Emma's bedroom. Ibid., 3, 4. See also Staker, "The Relationship between Oral Tradition and Latter-day Saint Material Culture." John Poorman was Father Whitmer's neighbor in New York; David Whitmer baptized him

Around the end of September, 1831, the Smith, Whitmer, Rigdon, and other church families moved forty miles south of Kirtland to the John Johnson farm at Hiram, Portage County, Ohio. Photograph ca. 2011, courtesy of Ron Romig.

John probably moved in with his parents and sixteen-year-old Elizabeth Ann, and they no doubt eagerly welcomed Peter Jr., who turned twenty-two in September, when he returned from Missouri. No doubt both sons helped the parents provide for their daily necessities and probably were engaged in the fall harvest, which would have provided plenty of work for all hands. But, John's primary duty was to assist with church administrative affairs, and to copy revelations and Bible manuscripts as needed.

Hiram, Ohio, was in Ezra Booth's backyard. Booth lived in nearby Mantua in Portage County. According to Hartwell Ryder, "When Mr. Booth returned from Missouri, he called on my father and after talking together they began to undo what they had done in the way of influencing people to join the Mormons. In a short time there were only a few pro-

---

in Seneca Lake on June 9, 1830. When the Whitmers relocated to Hiram, apparently so did the Poormans. *History of the LDS Church,* 1:86.

fessed followers of the Mormon religion left in Hiram. These, however, still continued their meetings at the Johnston [*sic*] house."[3]

Joseph, by moving to Hiram, was in a position to respond to those most directly impacted by Booth's critiques. Also in Hiram, Smith apparently considered Eber D. Howe's criticism that the revelations were not available to those deemed "weaker" in the faith by deciding that the church should publish them. Since some were getting into the press anyway, the church's publishing would ensure their correctness and allay suspicions that they were being kept secret. A church-owned press could also respond to dissidents like Booth.

On September 26, 1831, Joseph began recording his Bible revisions on a new folio forty-eight pages in length. Page 1 of this new manuscript reads "September 26th 1831 Capt [chapter] 26."[4] This time, Joseph dictated a new text for Matthew 26:1–71a that differs significantly from the revisions previously made on the same chapter in June 1831.[5] Because Rigdon had apparently not yet settled in, John once again briefly served as the project's primary scribe. He took Joseph's dictation for Matthew 26 through Mark 8 in the manuscript known today as New Testament Manuscript 2, folio 2.[6] "Throughout the process," notes scholars Kent P. Jackson and Peter M. Jasinski in their study of the New Translation, "John was a faithful copyist whose transcriptions diverged intentionally from the originals only in very rare cases" when he occasionally ventured to correct what he felt were apparent grammatical or writing errors in the originals.[7] This revision phase lasted until late September or early October 1831.[8]

John Whitmer wrote more of the New Translation manuscript materials than any other scribe with the exception of Sidney Rigdon— eighty-five of the 180 pages of the Old Testament holograph manuscript, not including his personal copy of the early Old Testament revision. Other scribes whose handwriting has been identified (including notes pinned to

3. Ryder, "A Short History," 3.
4. New Translation, New Testament Manuscript 2, folio 2, Matthew 26:1, page 1.
5. Knecht, *Joseph Smith's Bible Translation* (1984), 24, 25.
6. Ibid., 35.
7. Jackson and Jasinski, "The Process of Inspired Translation," 40.
8. Knecht, *Joseph Smith's Bible Translation* (1984), 35.

the manuscript) are Oliver Cowdery (ten pages Old Testament), Sidney Rigdon (176 pages Old Testament and nineteen New Testament), Jesse Gause (eight pages New Testament), Frederick G. Williams (sixty-three pages Old Testament and five pages New Testament), Emma Smith (four pages Old Testament), Joseph Smith (four pages Old Testament), and possibly others.[9]

On October 5, 1831, Joseph's younger brother, William Smith, was ordained to the office of teacher, at Hiram, Ohio. As clerk, John wrote and signed William's priesthood license.[10]

By this point, Sidney had rejoined Joseph in Hiram, but a funding crisis interrupted the reworking of the Bible. They were unable to adequately provide for their families, having devoted the bulk of their energies to the revision. By October 11, 1831, David Whitmer and Martin Harris had rejoined the disciples in northern Ohio, and Joseph Smith immediately asked David and Reynolds Cahoon to solicit contributions from local congregations.[11] Joseph's financial embarrassment continued through the end of October. A main topic of discussion at the October 25, 1831, conference held at Irenus (Serenus) Burnett's home at Orange, Cuyahoga County, was the importance of the New Translation and the urgency of securing means to support the "writing [being done by Sidney Rigdon] and copying [being done by John Whitmer of] the fullness of the scriptures."[12] During the conference, many participants bore testimonies of the impact of the church on their lives.

When his turn came, John expressed his concern "that a certain clause in the Church Covenants was too much neglected he feared by

---

9. Page counts are only approximate. An exact count of pages per scribe is difficult to ascertain, because some scribes wrote a part of a page and another the other part. There are 446 holograph pages of Old and New Testament manuscripts. Faulring, Jackson, and Matthews, *Joseph Smith's New Translation of the Bible,* 63–73; Jennings, "The Consequential Counselor," 183.

10. John Whitmer and Joseph Smith Jr. to William Smith, certificate of ordination to the office of teacher.

11. Knecht, *Joseph Smith's Bible Translation* (1984), 35.

12. Cannon and Cook, *Far West Record,* 23–24.

the brethren [—and it was] read accordingly."[13] Although the clause is not specified, it was presumably about branch statistical reporting, which had been mandated by the articles and covenants (CofC D&C 17; LDS D&C 20). Teachers were to attend conferences of elders and report on the status of their branch. This requirement was evidently being overlooked. For example, at this October 25, 1831, conference, only three teachers were present, and the minutes report no statistics, nor do subsequent extant conference minutes of early meetings. As recently appointed church historian, John was obviously sensitive to this lacuna in the official record that would only become more serious as time passed.

In the evening conference session, Orson Hyde, Simeon Carter, Emer Harris, and Hyrum Smith were assigned and ordained to join David and Reynolds in soliciting money to support the scripture project. They were to promise members that God would bestow his greatest blessings on those who helped support the work of the translation of the Bible.[14]

The four new missionaries undertook this assignment in November. Hyrum and recent convert William E. McLellin had reached Kirtland from Missouri on October 18, and this conference was John's first meeting with a man who would have a significant impact on his future religious life and beliefs. McLellin wrote, "I attended a general conference in the town of Orange, about 20 miles distant. Here I first met and formed an acquaintance with Joseph Smith, Jr., Oliver Cowdery, Sidney Rigdon, John Whitmer, etc. About 40 ministers attended the conference. During its sittings, I, with nine others, was pointed out again by the spirit of revelation, as having the gifts and callings to the office of High Priest, and was ordained thereunto under the hands of Pres. Oliver Cowdery."[15]

W. W. Phelps, designated "printer for the church" in June, was also destined to figure prominently in John's future. He was briefly in Ohio, en route to New York to conclude his business affairs and move his family to

13. Ibid., 20. For background on the historical development of the articles and covenants (CofC D&C 17; LDS D&C 20), see Faulring, "The Book of Mormon: A Blueprint for Organizing the Church"; and Faulring, "An Examination."

14. Cannon and Cook, *Far West Record*, 17; see also Knecht, *Joseph Smith's Bible Translation* (1984), 37.

15. McLellin, "Our Views Relative to the Legal Successor of Joseph Smith in the First Presidency," 60. John had been ordained as a high priest during the June 1831 conference.

Independence, where he would operate the church press. His instructions became more specific at the October 11, 1831, conference, which authorized Phelps to purchase a press (source of funding not specified) to print the monthly *Evening and the Morning Star*. Soon after the conference, Phelps and his family left for Missouri, passing through Cincinnati, where he purchased the printing press.[16]

Meanwhile in Missouri, a small group headed by bishop Edward Partridge was working hard to facilitate the press's operation. The Partridge family was now in Missouri, and the Colesville Branch had moved to what the church began calling "Zion" during the summer. Anticipating the forthcoming gathering of members, Partridge began purchasing land in Jackson County, Missouri, eventually acquiring nearly two thousand acres for church use. Though the bulk of this land was located to the west in Kaw Township, close to the Kansas border, Independence was the center of church operations. The town of Independence had been originally platted in 1827. On August 8, 1831, Partridge purchased lot 76 in the town's plat. Here the printing office would be located.[17]

Although Joseph was emphasizing his revision of the Bible, he simultaneously launched an intensive period of corporate and hierarchical expansion through a series of conferences and business meetings conducted at Hiram. They foreshadowed profound changes in the church's previously simple and egalitarian structure, accelerating the movement's transition from a "simple to more complex organization."[18] At the same time, the infusion of converts in Ohio was helping to crystallize the movement's nature and ideals. Friendship continued as an important guiding principle in forging the bonds of community, and Joseph consistently drew older skilled men into leadership positions.

16. Jessee, *Papers of Joseph Smith*, 1:364; see also *History of the RLDS Church*, 1:215–19; Sanford C. Gladden, in "An Early Printing Press Used in Colorado," wrote that Phelps purchased a Washington press, in common use at this time. It had a lever instead of a screw, which increased its printing speed. Several companies made similar presses, with a silhouette of George Washington on the side and featuring cast-iron parts.

17. Partridge purchased lot 76 from James Gray for fifty dollars. Jackson County Land Records, Book A, 114.

18. Cook, *David Whitmer Interviews*, xvii.

The room in the Johnson house, Hiram, Ohio, where a series of conferences and business meetings were held to approve the church's printing activities in Independence, Missouri. Photo ca. 2011, courtesy of Ron Romig.

In November 1831, Smith scheduled a series of meetings and conferences to coordinate planning to advance the Mormon settlement of Missouri. Joseph identified the establishment of a printing press in Missouri as an important priority, particularly with the view of publishing his revelations.

On the premise that the whole church would soon move to Jackson County, Joseph assigned early New York supporters to key leadership roles in Jackson County. David Whitmer and Newel Knight would, in coming years, receive presiding roles. In addition to the assignments already given to Phelps and Partridge, he now directed Oliver and John to assist with publishing the church's sacred writings. To this point, John Whitmer had been primarily the creator and custodian of the volume of Smith's manuscript revelations known as the Book of Commandments and Revelations. Decisions made during these meetings would significantly impact John's role and relationship with this volume of revelations.

On November 1, 1831, at Hiram, Joseph Smith asked church members to endorse his plan to publish his revelations as the Book of Commandments. He read a preface to this work, which he had received by revelation, and several participants volunteered "to testify to the world that they knew that they [Smith's revelations] were of the Lord."[19] The conference approved and accepted both the preface and the revelations that would become the Book of Commandments as scripture for the benefit of the church.[20]

But later reminiscences disclose some disagreement among the participants. A familiar story of William McLellin attempting and failing to satisfactorily replicate the revelatory process is associated with this conference. Some who participated in the conference initially hesitated to affirm the revelations. Joseph responded by receiving a revelation on November 2, 1831, inviting the conference to "appoint him that is the most wise among you" to produce a revelation like unto Smith's commandments. When William E. McLellin was selected to make an attempt, his effort apparently failed to impress conference participants. The November 2 revelation further reasoned, "If you cannot make one like unto it ye are under condemnation if you do not bear [record] that it is true for ye know that there is no unrighteousness in it." This revelation apparently satisfied initial objections. In the end, participants subscribed their names, testifying that Smith's commandments were "given by inspiration of God & are profitable for all men."[21]

There is no contemporary evidence that David Whitmer objected to or challenged Smith's plan to publish the revelations. However, much later in 1887, David Whitmer said that he opposed the decision—primarily made by Joseph and Sidney, as he recalled it—to print the revelations.

19. Cannon and Cook, *Far West Record*, 27.

20. Knecht, *Story of Joseph Smith's Bible Translation* (1984), 37. When printed, the Book of Commandments' "Preface" revelation was included as chapter 1, pp. 3–6. The preface is now Doctrine and Covenants 1 in both Community of Christ and LDS scripture.

21. November 2, 1831, Book of Commandments and Revelations, 114–15. While the testimony of the witnesses to the Book of Commandments was dictated November 1, 1831, it may not have been signed until after the November 2, 1831, revelation and William McLellin's subsequent attempt to produce an equivalent revelation. The testimony of the witnesses was copied into the manuscript following the Book of Commandments preface given November 3, 1831 (CofC D&C 108; LDS D&C 133).

David believed that the revelations were intended for private individuals. "A few of the brethren—including myself—objected to it seriously. We told them that if the revelations were published, the world would get the books, and it would not do; that it was not the will of the Lord that the revelations should be published. But Brothers Joseph and Sydney would not listen to us, and said they were going to send them to Independence to be published. I objected to it and withstood Brothers Joseph and Sydney to the[ir] face."[22] David prophesied that, if the church printed the revelations, "the people would come upon them and tear down the printing press, and the church would be driven out of Jackson county."[23] Of course, by the time David wrote this reminiscence, it described exactly what had happened; although it is not at all clear that the cause for the demolition and expulsion was the publication of the revelations.

John Whitmer did not record his position on the desirability of publishing the revelations, but he apparently did not dig in his heels nor voice any resistance. Not until later, along with all of his Whitmer relatives, would John adopt David's concern about their publication. Instead in November 1831, he implemented the conference's decisions. He began by reviewing his compilation of revelations to ensure that it was complete and up to date. His volume would serve as a printer's copy of the revelations to be used during printing.

As such, John's compilation of manuscript revelations was an important extension of his work as historian and should be recognized as a "history," just as we have come to view his primary work of history since known as "The Book of John Whitmer." The creation of the Book of Commandments manuscript was the result of Whitmer's call to "write & keep a regular history, and assist my servant Joseph in transcribing all things which shall be given."[24]

Only four sheets (eight pages) of the Book of Commandments printer's manuscript, all in John's hand, were known to have survived to our day. These four double-sided sheets have been available for scholarly research for many years at the Community of Christ Archives in Inde-

22. David Whitmer, *An Address to All Believers in Christ,* 54–55.

23. Ibid., 55.

24. March 8, 1831; D&C 47.

pendence.[25] Students of history had hoped that more of the manuscript survived and were excited when, in late 2008, Marlin K. Jensen, of the LDS seventy, church historian and recorder, announced the discovery of the bulk of the remainder of the Book of Commandments printer's manuscript. The manuscript had apparently for years been overlooked in the LDS Church History Library's collection. Jensen explained, "By at least March of 1831, John Whitmer began copying this early collection of revelation manuscripts into what he titled the 'Book of Commandments and Revelations.' This manuscript book, which [Joseph Smith] Papers [project] editors have designated as Revelation Book 1, contains items that were copied from around March 1831 to the middle of 1835."[26]

After the conference on November 2, 1831, at which church leaders ratified a preface for the Book of Commandments, Joseph convened four additional conferences (November 8–12), probably in the John Johnson home. Rather than preaching services, they were more like management meetings, clarifying the changing roles of key leaders and planning future church programs and policies. John clerked for two of them.[27]

The first special conference, November 8, was devoted to ensuring that the revelations were as correct as possible before publication: "Remarks by Brother Sidney Rigdon suggested that the errors or mistakes which are in [the] commandments and revelations [were] made either

25. Book of Commandments, manuscript fragments, CofC Archives. In the fall of 2007, the CofC Archives and the LDS Church History Department initiated a cooperative agreement that both expanded scholarly access and provided for conservation of these fragments.

26. Jensen, "Joseph Smith Papers," 46–51; Jensen, "From Manuscript to Printed Page," 20, provided the following description: "The Book of Commandments and Revelations was originally a ledger book of about 205 pages, marked with pre-printed horizontal and vertical lines.... The volume likely contained nine gatherings of twelve leaves, with the pages measuring about 12 ½ x 7 inches. A label currently adorns the spine of the volume, reading 'Book of Commandments and Revelations,' which is a shortened version of the full title contained on page 1: 'A Book of Commandments and Revelations of the Lord Given to Joseph the Seer & Others by the Inspiration of God & Gift & Power of the Holy Ghost Which Beareth Re[c]ord of the Father & Son Which Is One God Infinite & Eternal World without End Amen.' Pages 3–10, 15–22, and 25–26 are missing from the volume and their location is unknown." Pages 111–12, 117–20, and 139–40 are also missing from the volume and are housed in the CofC Archives.

27. Cannon and Cook, *Far West Record,* 16–17, 26–28.

by the translation in consequence of the slow way of the scribe at the time of receiving or by the scribes themselves." The conference resolved "that Brother Joseph Smith Jr. correct these errors or mistakes which he may discover by the Holy Spirit while reviewing the revelations and commandments and also the fullness of the scriptures."[28] Oliver Cowdery had been tasked with helping correct print copy and selecting projects "to go to the world through the Printing Press."[29] But the minutes of this meeting make it clear that Joseph had the final say about the content of the revelations and commandments. Clearly, the final round of corrections to the revelations needed to be completed—with Joseph Smith's direct involvement—before publication. He spent the next two weeks reviewing and revising the revelations.[30] In the Book of Commandments manuscript, revisions for this period are in Sidney's handwriting, rather than Joseph's. Book of Commandments researcher Robin Jensen notes, "Joseph Smith's handwriting is not prominent among" Rigdon's editorial changes.[31] Possibly the two reviewed the manuscript together, and Sidney wrote down Joseph's corrections. However, the revisions are less a matter of returning the manuscript to the form of the original revelation than of improving the style and grammar.[32] Thus, it is also possible that Joseph delegated the task of revision to Rigdon, who worked his way through the manuscript, correcting spelling and grammar but also introducing an occasional rephrasing or wording change. In short, while Joseph may have overseen the

28. Ibid., 29.

29. The conference affirmed Smith's July 20, 1831, revelation received in Missouri, and Cowdery was to assist printer W. W. Phelps, by copying, correcting, and selecting "all the writings which go forth to the world through the Printing Press." Ibid., 28–29.

30. *History of the LDS Church*, 1:229, 235.

31. Jensen, "From Manuscript to Printed Page," 34.

32. For example, see Book of Commandments 68, p. 112, received October 29, 1831, CofC Archives. The manuscript reads: "keep these Sayings, true & faithfull & thou Shalt magnify thine office & push many people to Zion." Sidney inserted above the line: "for they are" between "Sayings: and "true & faithful"; struck through: thou Shalt magnify thine; and inserted "you shall" above the line in front of "magnify" and also inserted "your" after "magnify."[...] keep these Sayings <for they are true & faithful>, & <you shall> magnify <your> office. [...] However, it appears that, during printing, Rigdon's second insertion was also crossed out and subsequently printed so as to more closely reflect the original manuscript.

process, it seems that he left the actual labor initially to Sidney Rigdon and, subsequently during printing, to John and Oliver.

The second and third conferences, held November 9 and 11, diverted the decision-makers' attention, at least in part, from the Bible revisions to church administration and infrastructure issues that would support the gathering to Missouri. John clerked for the November 9 conference but was not present for the November 11 meeting, which discussed elders' duties and whether Reynolds Cahoon should move to Zion the next spring. The fourth special conference, on November 12, identified key leaders entitled to financial support from church colonization efforts in Missouri. Smith believed that a church press in Missouri could provide a sound financial basis for the whole settlement. Phelps had already left Ohio, but church leaders in Kirtland retained financial control over the printing operation. Undaunted by his own limited business experience, Joseph announced the revelation that is now Doctrine and Covenants section 70, sketching out the foundational business principles for the church printing operation. Having articulated the law of consecration as a basis of church economy half a year before, Smith could not institute the printing operation as a private venture. Its economic underpinning must be consistent with the principles of the law of consecration.

Joseph Smith saw the press's operation as both a means and an end. In addition to generating income to support personnel and programs, the press could provide a necessary communication link between church centers in Ohio and Missouri. It would also serve institutional and missionary purposes—standardizing, publishing, promoting, and also publicizing church doctrine and organization.[33] Further, a press could be a wonderful tool to favorably impress the public mind. In the end, Smith hoped that, by promoting church organization and doctrine, the press might be a literal and physical means of guiding the church into realizing his vision of Zion.

Joseph initially hoped that Martin Harris would make a significant consecration of resources to provide start-up capital for the venture, much

---

33. When the *Star* finally appeared, Phelps wrote: "We promised [in the prospectus] to correct as many falsehoods as we could, for all the statements that have been published in the newspapers of the day concerning this church not one has reached us but what in a greater or less degree was untrue." Phelps, "Rise and Progress of the Church of Christ," [4].

as Martin had financed the publication of the Book of Mormon. Smith anticipated that Martin would move to Missouri during the spring or summer of 1832, buying paper on the way for the church press. Instead, Martin, apparently, went on a mission to the East with his brother Emer.[34] In 1832, Martin Harris did help with the printing venture when he was inducted into a group of leaders assigned to finance and supervise church publications.[35]

On November 12, 1831, Smith delivered what became Doctrine and Covenants section 70, which furnished a preliminary solution for obtaining needed capital by outlining the rudiments of a cooperative business model based on joint stewardships. He optimistically saw it as supporting several families, most of them Smith's core New York supporters. Joseph himself, Martin Harris, Oliver Cowdery, John Whitmer, Sidney Rigdon, and W. W. Phelps formed a special stewardship relationship with the collective task of underwriting, inaugurating, and managing the church's printing venture—and also managing the anticipated profits. Surpluses would be turned over to the bishop's storehouse just as the law of consecration provided. Smith denominated this collective venture the "Literary Firm." In Smith's view, firms united individuals with skills and those with capital into joint stewardships for the collective benefit of the church. Smith foresaw that other essential church projects could also be promoted as "firms," and church leaders subsequently adapted this economic pattern to launch a variety of church-related business ventures. For example, Sidney Gilbert, a former Kirtland merchant, used this model to establish a church mercantile business in Independence.

34. Oliver Cowdery to Joseph Smith, 28 January 1832; see also Cannon and Cook, *Far West Record*, appendix A, 238; "Copies of Revelations to Joseph Smith in the Handwriting of Frederick G. Williams, Orson Hyde, Joseph Smith, Oliver Cowdery, and Others, Kirtland Revelations Book," quoted in Collier, *Unpublished Revelations*, 1:60–61. Emer Harris was called on a mission. LDS D&C 75:30. See also Emer Harris, letter, 7 May 1833.

35. Black, "The Unheralded Role of Martin Harris in Missouri." It is believed that Martin (Doctrine and Covenants code name "Mehemson") was named as part of the united firm (CofC D&C 81; LDS D&C 82) during Smith's visit to Independence on April 26, 1832. However, historian Erin Jennings Metcalfe asserts that Martin Harris's name was later substituted for that of Jesse Gause. Gause was in Missouri at the time, while Harris was not.

On November 12–13, Joseph Smith, Martin Harris, Oliver Cowdery, John Whitmer, Sidney Rigdon, and W. W. Phelps were appointed and ordained as "stewards over the revelations and commandments … to manage them according to the Laws of the Church & the Commandments of the Lord."[36] In light of previous commitments of labor and financial support, Joseph urged the conference to compensate key participants. The conference decreed that, in light of their long history in assisting with these sacred writings, Joseph Smith Jr., Oliver Cowdery, Martin Harris, John Whitmer, and Sidney Rigdon "have claim on the Church for recompense."[37] The conference further granted inheritances in Zion to Joseph, Oliver, John, and Sidney; to the four other Smith brothers (Hyrum, Samuel, William, and Don Carlos); and the five other Whitmer brothers (David, Peter, Christian, Jacob, and Peter Jr.); along with Hiram Page, and associated families, for their roles in assisting "in bringing to light by grace of God these sacred things [writings]."[38] The minutes read: "Voted by this Conference that the above named brethren be recommended to the Bishop in Zion as being worthy of inheritances among the people of the Lord according to the laws of said Church."[39] At first, participants in these meetings entrusted Oliver Cowdery with the responsibility of carrying the Book of "commandments [manuscript] and the moneys [for the printing business]" to Missouri; but before the meetings ended, John Whitmer was also commanded to accompany Oliver to Missouri (D&C 69). Smith dedicated and consecrated Oliver and John along with the manuscripts to this end.[40]

Joseph's revelation also augmented John's role as historian. In a way, by acting as clerk of the conference, John was already fulfilling the intent of counsel. He was to note "all the important things which he shall observe and know concerning my church; and also that he receive counsel and assistance from my servant Oliver Cowdery, and others … [in] writing, copying, selecting, and obtaining all things which shall be for the good of the

---

36. Cannon and Cook, *Far West Record*, 32; CofC D&C 70:1b; LDS D&C 70:3.

37. Ibid.

38. Conference minutes, 12–13 November 1831, Hiram, Ohio, in ibid. This blessing might have come in response to David Whitmer's strenuous objections about printing the revelations which he voiced days earlier.

39. Ibid.

40. Ibid., 31.

church, and for the rising generations." Furthermore, John was to record the church's activities and progress in all locales:

> And also, my servants who are abroad in the earth, should send forth the accounts of their stewardships to the land of Zion; for the land of Zion shall be a seat and a place to receive and do all these things; nevertheless, let my servant John Whitmer travel many times from place to place, and from church to church, that he may the more easily obtain knowledge: preaching and expounding, writing, copying, selecting, and obtaining all things which shall be for the good of the church, and for the rising generations, that shall grow up on the land of Zion, to possess it from generation to generation, forever and ever.[41]

41. Book of Commandments 28, p. 60; D&C 69.

CHAPTER TEN

John Whitmer in Missouri

C ARRYING MANUSCRIPT COPIES of revelations and money earmarked
for Bishop Partridge's use (CofC D&C 69:1a; LDS D&C 69:1), John
Whitmer and Oliver Cowdery left Ohio on November 20, 1831, less than
a week after the conclusion of the special conference on November 12–13.[1]
They also carried with them an important volume of minutes; either John
or Oliver had clerked at most of these meetings, and the volume contained
the official record of many of the church's most important decisions. As
church clerk and historian, John anticipated that he would continue recording important meetings in Zion, which he did. Oliver also added more
records during his stay in Jackson, Clay, and Caldwell Counties (1831–38),
at which point John and Oliver both parted company with the church. This
record book eventually came to be known as the Far West Record, a title
that does not reflect the numerous important records it contained that had
been generated in Ohio.

As soon as the conference ended, Joseph and Sidney resumed work
on Mark chapter 9 and were into the book of Luke before they laid the
work aside in early December 1831.[2] They spent until mid-January on a mission to surrounding communities, trying to counteract the negative impact
of Ezra Booth's critical letters, which were printed in October and November in the *Ohio Star* of Ravenna.

Meanwhile, on November 29, 1831, John Whitmer and Oliver
Cowdery stopped at a small Mormon branch in Winchester, Randolph
County, Indiana, to handle some local business. Another visiting missionary, Seymour Brunson, who was en route to Jackson County, asked that
the two help settle difficulties among elders in the branch. According to

1. Whitmer, Book of John Whitmer, chap. 10, p. 37.

2. Knecht, *Joseph Smith's Bible Translation* (1984), 38.

brief minutes in the Far West Record, Henry Jackson charged Isaac Fallis with misrepresenting scriptures in Acts and the Book of Mormon that depicted disciples living with all things common. The issue was apparently an intransigent one since, even with Oliver and John's help, it took through December 7 to reconcile the disputants and bring their understandings into line with Joseph Smith's Christian economic principles as embodied in the law of consecration. Oliver led out in these negotiations while John took minutes.[3]

John and Oliver resumed their journey in late December and reached Independence on January 5, 1832.[4] John left little information about his arrival, his first impressions of Independence, or his initial activities. He probably became the guest or boarder of one of the Mormon families, perhaps former acquaintances from New York. Construction on an office building for the printing press had not yet begun, even though W. W. and Sally Phelps, their six children, and their press had reached Independence in October 1831. In addition to the lack of a print shop, the printer also had no printing supplies, paper, ink, or staff. The Phelpses had stayed temporarily with another Mormon family, perhaps the Partridges. Bishop Partridge initially rented a farm in Independence, then built a home on the northeast corner of the Temple Lot after Edward purchased sixty-three acres at that location for the church.

In 1827, Jackson County residents had erected a log courthouse east of the square at the corner of present-day East Lexington and Lynn Streets on part of lot 59, comprising one-and-a-half acres. The building's massive walnut logs were hand-hewn by Sam Sheppard, a slave. Before the Mormon missionaries had made their first appearance in Independence in December 1830 or early January 1831, the county had also started work on a permanent court building on the square. This two-story brick building was completed in 1830. On February 20, 1832, Sidney Gilbert, on behalf of the firm of Gilbert and Whitney, acquired the recently vacated log courthouse from Smallwood V. Noland for $371.00. Jackson County land records sug-

---

3.   Cannon and Cook, *Far West Record,* 33–38. Henry Jackson's relationship, if any, to Sarah Jackson is not known.

4.   Whitmer, Book of John Whitmer, chap. 10, p. 38; McKiernan and Launius, *An Early Latter Day Saint History,* 85.

gest that Gilbert's purchase also included a house and a saddler's shop.⁵ The Gilberts made their home in the former courthouse, setting aside a portion of the structure for the church store. Acquiring this additional property for church use may have also afforded John and Oliver an opportunity to move to better living quarters. The ensuing January 24, 1832, conference, held at the home of Newel Knight in Kaw Township, voted to ask bishop Edward Partridge to "establish a house of entertainment in the Town of Independence to accommodate the traveling Elders of this Church and other brethren whose circumstances may require."⁶

Ezra Booth, who visited Independence in July 1831, described it as "a new Town, containing a courthouse, built of brick, two or three merchant stores, and fifteen or twenty dwelling houses, built mostly of logs hewed on both sides."⁷ William McLellin, another Mormon convert who was also in Independence during the same summer, left this description: "Independence is situated on a high rise 3 miles south of the Missouri river, 12 miles from the west line of the state nearly 300 miles above St. Louis. The local situation of the country round about it, for health, richness of soil, good spring water, and other conveniences—is as good, it seems to me, as heart could wish."⁸

In January 1832, the church had not yet grown much beyond its small beginnings since Oliver's initial visit in early 1831. John would have known most of the approximately sixty members of the Colesville Branch, who had moved to Missouri the previous summer; but they lived in Kaw Township, about ten miles by road. Members of the Knight family may have come to town occasionally for supplies or meetings; but, other than that, John probably saw very little of them. The same was true for Parley P. Pratt whom John had met only briefly prior to the departure of the missionaries to the Lamanites in October 1830. Pratt and his wife, Thankful, settled near the Prairie Branch, on the extreme western edge of Missouri, about twelve miles from Independence. But most of the members were new con-

5. Jackson County Land Records, Book B, 32.

6. Minutes of a meeting held January 28, 1832, suggest that the church was to provide a house for traveling members. Cannon and Cook, *Far West Record*, 234; also *Evening and the Morning Star Extra*, February 1834, 1.

7. Ezra Booth, letter no. 6, to Reverend Ira Eddy, 14 November 1831, 2.

8. William E. McLellin to Samuel McLellin, 4 August 1832.

verts from many different points of origination. Without pressing family or social obligation, John was free to focus on his primary duties. Within eight days, on January 12, 1832, John completed transcribing a copy of the "Articles, Covenants, and Law of the Church of Christ," for missionaries Zebedee Coltrin and Harvey Whitlock, who were the last of the fourteen teams of missionaries to Missouri sent forth in June 1831.[9]

Levi Ward Hancock, an elder from Ohio, was a skilled brick mason who had also come to Missouri as part of the fourteen teams of missionaries in the summer of 1831. He undertook the responsibility of constructing the print shop, a two-story building. The Phelps family lived on the first floor and the printing works occupied the entire second floor.

Hancock's journal indicates that, after Oliver and John's arrival, "Oliver Cowdery and David [it should be John] Whitmer came and [Sidney] Gilbert told them I was just the man to build the printing works. I told them if they knew how they wanted it done, I could do it. Oliver gave me the plans and I began to work on it and was soon finished."[10]

John and Oliver participated in three January conferences held shortly after their arrival. The meetings focused on plans for the church colony and organizational concerns. The opening of the church store was taking longer than anticipated but arrangements for putting the printing press into operation were coming together. Hope was expressed that Martin Harris would soon be able to supply paper for the press. Also, Partridge reported that he had acquired twelve hundred acres of woodland costing more than $8,000 for gathering church members.[11]

From temporary surroundings on February 1832, Phelps issued a prospectus for the *Evening and the Morning Star,* a monthly newspaper whose

9. The revelation was written in booklet form on a small gathering of folded sheets. On the cover sheet, John wrote: "The Articles Covenants and Law of the Church of Christ Independence Jackson County Missorie [*sic*] January 12th 1832 Copied by J. Whitmer for Zebidee Coltrin Harvey Whitlock Sum [*sic*] Elders of the Church of Christ."

10. Hancock, journal, pp. 46–47. An alternative account suggests that a two-story brick house had already been built on lot 76 when Partridge purchased it in August 1831. I find Levi Hancock's narrative more plausible. On August 8, 1831, Partridge "purchased from Mr. James Gray a brick home and a lot ... for $50.... In the upper room of the brick home the printing press was installed." Wilcox, "Early Independence in Retrospect, Part 8," 178.

11. Oliver Cowdery to Joseph Smith, in Cannon and Cook, *Far West Record,* 231–38.

subscriptions cost one dollar per year. Its highly symbolic name revealed Phelps's and the church's strong millennial outlook. He explained, "As the forerunner of the night of the end, and the messenger of the day of redemption ... the Star will borrow its light from sacred sources."[12]

On behalf of the literary firm, William, Oliver, and John forwarded a copy of the *Evening and the Morning Star's* prospectus to Joseph Smith and reminded him of the need for paper. During March 1832, Joseph received the prospectus for the *Star* along with word that William, John, and Oliver had "arrived at Independence, Missouri, in good health and spirits, with a printing press and store of goods [for Sidney Gilbert's mercantile]."[13]

On March 1, 1832, Joseph Smith, announced the formation of a "United Firm" to manage all church business ventures. The revelation proposed the creation of a new "Mercantile Firm" as a companion establishment to the existing "Literary Firm." Joseph Smith, Sidney Rigdon, and Newel K. Whitney, were also added to the management pool. The revelation reads: "For verily, I say unto you that the time has come and is now at hand, and behold and lo, it must needs be that there be an organization of the literary and mercantile establishments of my church both in this place and in the land of Zion for a permanent and everlasting establishment and firm unto my church to advance the cause which ye have espoused."[14]

These parallel firms were meant to assist each other; but both were severely undercapitalized. Phelps had no resources with which to purchase paper—hence his appeal to Joseph Smith. On March 20, 1832, Joseph announced God's directive: "It is expedient ... that the paper shall be purchased for the printing of the books of the Lord's commandments and it must needs be that you [Joseph Smith] take it [to Independence] with you.... Let the purchase be made by the Bishop if it needs must be by hire

12. Phelps, prospectus, *Evening and the Morning Star,* quoted in "History of Joseph Smith," *Times and Seasons* 5, no. 15 (August 15, 1844): 609. For a history of the printing press, see Crawley, *A Descriptive Bibliography of the Mormon Church,* 1:18–19; see also Pearson, "Historic Press of the First Newspaper in Independence," 3.

13. *History of the LDS Church,* 1:259.

14. Jensen, Woodford, and Harper, *Revelations and Translations,* 267. The wording of this revelation in modern editions (CofC D&C 77; LDS D&C 78:3–4) obscures the fact that the united firm was intended as a commercial enterprise. The 1835 Doctrine and Covenants 75, substituted the words "storehouse for the poor of my people," in place of "Literary and Merchantile [*sic*] establishments of my church."

[borrowing money]."[15] Essentially, the revelation instructed Joseph to buy the paper and take it to Independence—then let Bishop Partridge figure out how to pay for it.

The need for funds to promote church programs was unending. The law of consecration tended to allocate incoming funds to the uses identified by revelation: buying land in Missouri, assisting the poor, and building houses of worship. Joseph's revelation had failed to provide an income to support key leaders and programs. Partridge, far away in Zion, was more or less free to establish his own priorities on spending church money. This administrative arrangement left Joseph free to devote his attention to re-working the Bible; but over time, he began to regret the level of autonomy in the bishop's office. Ezra Booth intimates that, in the summer of 1831, Partridge had felt it his duty to refuse to pay for Joseph's and Sidney's return trip from Missouri out of consecrated funds. Booth, in a letter to Partridge, wrote: "The method by which Joseph and Co. designed to proceed home, it was discovered, would be very expensive. 'The Lord don't care how much *money* it takes to get us home,'" said Sidney. "Not satisfied with the money they received from you, they used their best endeavors to exact money from others, who had but little, compared with what they had; telling them in substance, 'you can beg your passage, on foot, but as we are to travel in the stage, we must have money.'"[16] This exchange suggests that Smith and Rigdon asked Partridge for stagecoach fare but had been denied, prompting their departure from Independence by canoe. Joseph returned to Ohio believing he needed more control over Bishop Partridge and church affairs in Missouri.

On January 25, 1832, Joseph began to establish the differentiated ranks of the high priesthood—in part to correct this administrative lapse. Orson Pratt wrote that during the conference at Amherst, Lorain County, Ohio: "The Prophet Joseph was acknowledged President of the High Priesthood, and hands were laid on him by Elder Sidney Rigdon."[17] On March 8, 1832, Jesse Gause, a convert from a nearby Shaker group, and Sidney Rigdon were set apart as Smith's counselors in the presidency of the high priest-

---

15. Jensen, Woodford, and Harper, *Revelations and Translations,* 273; also in Collier, *Unpublished Revelations,* 1:60–61.

16. Ezra Booth, letter no. 7, to Reverend Ira Eddy, 21 November 1831, 1–2.

17. Watson, *Orson Pratt Journals,* 11.

hood, an innovation that once again centralized Joseph's authority over the entire church.[18] This innovation would seriously impact Edward Partridge's role as bishop in Missouri.

After the fall's busy flurry of administrative activity, Joseph and Sidney settled down during the winter in Hiram, Ohio, and made progress on the revision of the scriptures. But the spring brought a serious setback. On Saturday night, March 24–25, 1832, their routine was suddenly interrupted when Portage County neighbors burst into Joseph's and Sidney's rooms during the night, dragged the two men out, and tarred and feathered both. Joseph attributed this vigilantism to mob persecution; but local resident Hartwell Ryder, the son of Symonds Ryder, attributed their anger to the negative impact of Ezra Booth's letters in the *Ohio Star*, published in Ravenna. In addition to Booth, Symonds Ryder, Eli Johnson, Edward Johnson, and John Johnson Jr., had also left the church. Ryder also suggested that an economic component had triggered the violence. Local converts "found the papers of the church and among them was a revelation [on consecration] that all who had property should give it over into the hands of Smith for the good of the Hiram church."[19]

Although Joseph calmly preached a sermon on Sunday morning after their ordeal, both he and Sidney decided to leave Hiram. Sidney, who had been dragged across frozen ruts by the feet and had suffered injury to his head, was slow to recover. When Smith visited him on Monday morning, he "found him crazy, and his head highly inflamed."[20] Sidney's family subsequently returned to Kirtland around March 28, 1832. "On Wednesday, four days after the mobbing, she [Phebe Rigdon] bundled the family into an open wagon and moved them to Kirtland. Sidney never returned to Hiram. After arriving in Kirtland, 'on account of the mob [in Kirtland], he went to Chardon on Saturday, March 31st.'"[21] Joseph remained in Hiram while he prepared to go to Jackson County, Missouri.[22] Joseph and Emma's

18. Tanner and Tanner, *Joseph Smith's Kirtland Revelation Book*, 10–11. Smith ratified this ordination through the receipt of what became CofC D&C 80; LDS D&C 81, about one week later on March 15, 1832.

19. *History of the LDS Church*, 1:260. Ryder, "A Short History," 3.

20. *History of the LDS Church*, 1:265.

21. Staker, *Hearken, O Ye People*, 355, citing *History of the [LDS] Church*, 1:265.

22. Backman, *Heavens Resound*, 100.

adopted baby boy twin, Joseph Murdock Smith, feverish from measles and exposed to the cold air on March 24, 1832, the night Joseph and Sidney were tarred and feathered, died of pneumonia on Thursday, March 29, 1832. He was buried in the Johnson family cemetery.[23]

On April 1, 1832, Smith set out for Missouri, accompanied by Peter Whitmer Jr., Newel K. Whitney, and Jesse Gause, Joseph's new counselor in the first presidency. Joseph noted, "Brother George Pitkin took us in his wagon by the most expeditious route to Warren, where we arrived the same day, and were there joined by Elder Rigdon."[24] They then traveled to Steubenville, Ohio, and took passage on a steamboat for Wheeling, Virginia (now West Virginia), where they bought paper for the press.[25]

Winter was ending in Missouri. John, still a farm boy at heart, anxiously waited for spring. Having consumed preserved foods over the

Cover of John Whitmer's Account Book, 1832–78. Courtesy of the LDS Church History Library.

cold season, he looked forward to something fresh. Wherever he was staying, he must have furnished his own board. Almost as soon as he arrived in Independence, he purchased a bound account book in which to keep track of income and expenses. He made his first entry on January 8, 1832. That same month, he bought venison, the next month "Flower [flour]." And with great optimism on April 5, he purchased a "garden spade & seeds."[26]

23. Staker, *Hearken, O Ye People*, 354–55.

24. *History of the LDS Church*, 1:265–66.

25. *History of the RLDS Church*, 1:244.

26. Whitmer, account book, p. 3.

Title page of John Whitmer's Account Book, started on January 5, 1832, in Missouri. Courtesy of the LDS Church History Library.

John stopped making entries in his account book a year later, on January 25, 1833, for some time. Apparently, he also used this period to reflect on his experiences. He does not date his entries into his history; but chapter 10 of the Book of John Whitmer, which covers the winter of 1831–32, consists of typically terse or hurried items, suggesting that John was busy or preoccupied while writing. Of his earliest days in Jackson County, he writes:

> We left Ohio, on the 20 of Nov, 1831 and arrived in Zion Mo, Jan. 5, 1832.
>
> When we arrived at Zion we found the saints in as good situation as we could reasonably expect.
>
> Jan 23, 1832, held a conference in Zion, attended to the business of the church.
>
> In March 1832, the enemies held a council in Independence Jackson County Mo, how they might destroy the saints but did not succeed at this time. But continued their broils until they had expelled us from the county as you will hereafter see.[27]

This last entry was obviously written sometime after November 1833. During the next twelve months, members in Missouri experienced the young church's most idealistic and strenuous effort to fashion a Christlike society. The ultimate collapse of that effort, which ended in the Saints' forced exile from Jackson County, north across the Missouri River into Clay County, in no way dims the sincerity of their desire and the extent to which individuals sacrificed personal goals for the perhaps unreachable goal of perfect unity. Believing that God's celestial city of Zion could be built only through human effort, participants saw themselves as founders of an earthly kingdom of God.

27.   Whitmer, Book of John Whitmer, chap. 10, p. 38; McKiernan and Launius, *An Early Latter Day Saint History*, 85–86.

CHAPTER ELEVEN

The Printing Business in Independence

I N MARCH 1832, Joseph Smith was still looking for a way to underwrite the colonization of Jackson County, Missouri, including capitalizing a new church store and printing office. The intent of Smith's revelation on March 1, 1832 (CofC D&C 77; LDS D&C 78), was to link the envisioned printing and store operations in Jackson County, allowing one entity to assist with the finances of the other. Smith anticipated that the printing operation would immediately generate income from which directors of the united firm could underwrite envisioned store operations.[1] Moreover, income from these combined ventures was intended to provide for the living expenses of firm directors, as well as to supplement consecration resources from members gathering from Ohio to Missouri.

Joseph Smith, Newel K. Whitney, and Sidney Rigdon were instructed to go to Zion and "organize," as the revelation commanded. After a remarkably quick trip by water—only twenty days—Joseph Smith, his counselors Jesse Gause and Sidney Rigdon, and Newel K. Whitney, reached Independence on April 24, 1832.[2] With this second visit by Smith and Rigdon, members of the literary firm received the precious supply of paper. In order to print just the Book of Commandments, W. W. Phelps needed fifteen thousand sheets of 11" x 18" paper.

Joseph wanted the leadership system in Zion to echo the pattern of church operations in Ohio, and he promptly moved to initiate a new organizational structure that would reassert his direct authority over Missouri

---

1. Jensen, Woodford, and Harper, *Revelations and Translations*, 267.

2. The party was composed of Smith, Newel K. Whitney, Peter Whitmer Jr., and Jesse Gause. *History of the LDS Church*, 1:266.

affairs as the president of the newly instituted order of high priests. His underlying motives were to establish a better method of administering the affairs of Zion, to better regulate the program of consecration, to organize a Missouri branch of the new mercantile firm,[3] and to work out a difficulty that had developed long distance between Rigdon and Partridge.[4] John noted in his history: "It came to pass that Joseph the Seer and Sidney the Scribe, and N. K. Whitney and one Jesse Gause came to Zion to comfort the Saints and Settle some little difficulties, and regulate the church and affairs concerning it."[5]

Two days after arriving, Smith convened a church conference. The Missouri church acknowledged Joseph Smith as "President of the High Priesthood, according to commandment and ordination in Ohio" on January 25, 1832. And the right hand of fellowship was given him "by the Bishop, Edward Partridge, in behalf of the Church."[6] This role allowed Joseph to reassert control over the bishop and all church affairs in Missouri. But one consequence of this hierarchical innovation was that John, and other early supporters, found themselves even further distanced from Smith.

The Missouri visit also included a series of "councils" by which Joseph clarified leadership roles in the settlement. During Joseph's previous visit to Missouri, in July and August 1831, Edward Partridge, Oliver Cowdery, W. W. Phelps, and Sidney Gilbert had been assigned specific responsibilities on behalf of the outpost.[7] But Smith was dissatisfied with the results of this arrangement.

In July 1831, Smith had charged bishop Edward Partridge with the supervision of the Missouri church. But nearly a year later, during Joseph's April 1832 visit, Joseph began an overhaul of the colony's management structure. By revelation on April 26, 1832, Joseph named nine individuals who were to be responsible "to manage the affairs of the poor, and all things pertaining to the bishopric both in the land of Zion and in the

---

3. Cannon and Cook, *Far West Record,* 46. Though operating in Missouri (Zion), the administration of the literary firm was still partly managed from Ohio, with inevitable conflicts over the allocation of skimpy funds.

4. Cook, *Revelations of the Prophet Joseph Smith,* 313.

5. Whitmer, Book of John Whitmer, chapter 10, p. 38.

6. *History of the LDS Church,* 1:267.

7. These four and their assignments are identified in Doctrine and Covenants 57.

land of Shinehah [Kirtland]." This initiative removed the "overall tempo-ral policy consideration from the province of the bishop."[8] The "presiding" bishopric became a subset of a committee of high priests. This new council was composed of Joseph Smith, Newel K. Whitney, Sidney Rigdon, Jesse Gause (soon replaced by Martin Harris), Oliver Cowdery, William W. Phelps, John Whitmer, Sidney Gilbert, and Edward Partridge.[9]

It is not clear whether Oliver Cowdery headed the council. He might seem to be the natural leader, given his prominent history as second elder and leader of the Lamanite mission. However, a cloud hung over him during this period. On May 26, 1832, Cowdery was brought before a church court in Independence, for either a sexual transgression or at least an impropriety with a young woman, which apparently occurred in the fall of 1830 at Mayfield, Ohio. Booth wrote, "While descending the Missouri river [August 1831], Peter [Whitmer Jr.] and Frederick [G. Williams], two of my company, divulged a secret respecting Oliver, which placed his con-duct on a parallel with Ziba's; for which Ziba [Peterson] was deprived of his Elder and Apostleship."[10]

The charges against Oliver Cowdery were resolved when, "after some discussion," according to the minutes of the May 26, 1832, trial, as recorded in the Far West Record, Cowdery "frankly confessed the same to the sat-isfaction of all present."[11]

This new council of high priests was also charged with the oversight of business affairs in Zion.[12] In response to the April 26, 1832, revelation, the council created a "United Firm." To manage all of the church's business initiatives, the united firm combined four business leader-directors from Ohio with five Missouri brethren into a "united" or overarching joint-

8. Arrington, Fox, and May, *Building the City of God*, 31.

9. Stewardship scholar Joseph Geddes inferred that the council was to be composed of only Missouri-based leaders: Oliver Cowdery, William W. Phelps, John Whitmer, Sidney Gilbert, Edward Partridge, Isaac Morley, and John Corrill. "These men were members of two governing bodies: a council, or committee of Seven High Priests, and a Bishopric [in Zion] of three members." Geddes, *United Order among the Mormons*, 22.

10. Ezra Booth, letter no. 7, to Reverend Ira Eddy, 21 November 1831, 1–2.

11. Cannon and Cook, *Far West Record*, 49. Cowdery's trial was held in Independence on May 26, 1832, after Smith's return to Ohio.

12. Arrington, Fox, and May, *Building the City of God*, 31.

stewardship. The move unified the control of church business operations in both Ohio and Missouri. As cooperative stewards, firm members managed church publications, established and operated merchandising stores in Ohio and Missouri, held properties in trust, and assisted the poor.[13] The firm was composed of Joseph Smith, Sidney Rigdon, Oliver Cowdery, Sidney Gilbert, Edward Partridge, Newel K. Whitney, John Whitmer, W. W. Phelps, and Jesse Gause.[14]

Though its purpose was to manage church-oriented business, researcher Lyndon Cook characterizes the firm as "essentially a private business concern…. They [firm members] were to benefit personally from the profits of the firm, [and] the surplus profits were to be used for the operation and blessing of the whole church."[15]

The committee's second act was the creation of a "united" mercantile firm. Lyndon Cook explains, "During their [Joseph Smith's and the Ohio leaders'] visit in Missouri, an April 27, 1831, meeting of the united firm essentially incorporated" a branch of the mercantile firm in Missouri.[16] Its members were the same as those who composed the united firm.[17] Known as the Gilbert and Whitney Store, it was the Missouri component of the united mercantile firm. Its Ohio counterpart was doing business as the Newel K. Whitney Store at Kirtland.

Before moving to Independence, Sidney Gilbert and Newel K. Whitney had been associated in business ventures in Michigan, and at Mentor

---

13. Ibid.

14. The members of the firm were to be "bound together by a bond and covenant that cannot be broken by transgression except judgment shall immediately follow, in your several stewardships, to manage the affairs of the poor, and all things pertaining to the bishopric both in the land of Zion and in the land of Shinehah [Kirtland]…. This order I have appointed to be an everlasting order unto you and unto your successors, inasmuch as you sin not: and the soul that sins against this covenant, and hardeneth his heart against it, shall be dealt with according to the laws of my church, and shall be delivered over to the buffitings of satan until the day of redemption…. Make unto yourselves friends with the mammon of unrighteousness, and they will not destroy you." CofC D&C 81:4a–b, 5a, b, 6a; LDS D&C 82:11–12, 20–22. Martin Harris later replaced Jesse Gause when Gause withdrew from the church.

15. Cook, *Revelations of the Prophet Joseph Smith*, 168.

16. Ibid.

17. Ibid., 48n2.

and Kirtland, Ohio.[18] Whitney remained in Ohio, continuing the store's operation as N. K. Whitney & Co. At the inception of the united firm, the Kirtland store was the firm's only real economic asset. To get Gilbert, Whitney & Co., into operation in Independence, Whitney was instructed to borrow $15,000 for five years, using the Kirtland store as collateral, and to purchase on credit the goods needed to stock the new enterprise.[19]

Next, the directors of the united firm turned their attention to the operation of the "Literary Firm." Members of the literary firm were: "Joseph Smith Jr., Prisident [sic], Sidney Rigdon, John Whitmer, Oliver Cowdery, William W. Phelps, Jesse Gause, one of the President's councilors [sic]."[20] On April 30, 1832, they voted to reduce the number of Book of Commandments to be printed from the extravagant number of ten thousand authorized by the Hiram conference of November 1, 1831, to the still-ambitious number of three thousand.[21]

Rather uncharacteristically, Joseph relinquished some control over the Book of Commandments project by appointing Phelps, Cowdery, and John Whitmer as a committee to "select for printing such as shall be deemed by them proper, as dictated by the spirit & make all necessary verbal corrections."[22] The literary firm was also to publish "Hymns selected by sister Emma."[23] Further, the publication of "an alminack [sic] for Zion

---

18. Staker, *Harken, O Ye People,* 202, 217.

19. Cannon and Cook, *Far West Record,* 45, 48n2, 48n4.

20. Ibid., 46.

21. Ibid., 27, 46. The 1830 Palmyra edition of the Book of Mormon had a print run of five thousand copies; the next printing, at Kirtland before September 1837, consisted of three thousand. Crawley, *A Descriptive Bibliography,* 1:29, 67.

22. "Minutes of a Council of the litterary [sic] Firm, Zion, April 30, 1832," in Cannon and Cook, *Far West Record,* 46. Smith essentially authorized the committee to select which of the revelations Oliver and John had brought to Missouri in January 1832 should appear in print.

23. Ibid. This meeting authorizing publication occurred ten months after Emma was appointed to select hymns; but it is not completely clear when she actually made her selections. Some hymns had apparently been identified and sent to Jackson County by the time of this April 30 meeting. W. W. Phelps partially rewrote some texts to reflect Restoration doctrines, and printed hymns (texts without musical notations) in the earliest numbers (June and July 1832) of the *Evening and the Morning Star.* They are introduced with the heading: "Hymns, selected and prepared for the Church of Christ, in these last days." When Emma's first hymnal was actually printed during the winter

this season [was to] be left at the option of brs. William Oliver & John."[24] Other long-term projects included publishing a children's and youth education curriculum, Joseph's translation of the Bible, and a second edition of the Book of Mormon.[25]

Though undercapitalized and over ambitious, the publishing program proved quite successful in several respects. As soon as the print shop had been completed and the supply of paper had finally arrived, Phelps energetically went to work. The first issue of the church's first periodical, the *Evening and the Morning Star*, appeared in June 1832 and continued for a year. Phelps also printed the locally oriented *Upper Missouri Advertiser* from the church press between June and July 1833.[26] Typesetting on A Book of Commandments had progressed to the sixty-fifth chapter, with five large uncut galley sheets, each containing thirty-two pages—sixteen on either side—having been printed and awaiting folding and cutting. But before the process could be completed, the printing office was destroyed in July by angry Missourians. After the destruction of the press, Cowdery returned to Ohio. The *Star* was in such demand that the literary firm se-

---

of 1835–36, it contained ninety hymns, none of which are attributed to Emma herself. Most of her selections were borrowed from the Baptists or the Campbellites. Peter Crawley and Chad J. Flake, *A Mormon Fifty: An Exhibition in the Harold B. Lee Library in Conjunction with the Annual Conference of the 1984 Mormon History Association,* 9–10, item 6, suggests: "The predominance of Baptist hymns among those borrowed suggests that the hymnal was probably based on a Baptist book, possibly one in use by the Campbellites. The hymnal contains at least 33 hymns of Mormon authorship, twenty-six by Phelps himself, three by Parley P. Pratt, one by Thomas B. Marsh and Parley Pratt, and one each by Eliza R. Snow, Edward Partridge, and Philo Dibble."

24. Cannon and Cook, *Far West Record,* 46. Almanacs in the 1830s typically contained practical wisdom of a local and general nature and often described expected weather patterns. An almanac featuring information of specific interest to emigrating church members would have been a good resource.

25. Cook, *Revelations of the Prophet Joseph Smith,* 196, 321; *History of the RLDS Church,* 1:299.

26. Only one issue of the *Upper Missouri Advertiser* is known to be extant, that of June 27, 1833. Crawley, *A Descriptive Bibliography,* 1:34–35. Editor W. W. Phelps informed his readers, "The disciples should loose [*sic*] no time in preparing schools for their children, that they may be taught as is pleasing unto the Lord and brought up in the way of holiness. Those appointed to select and prepare books for the use of schools, will attend to that subject, as soon as more weighty matters are finished." Phelps, "Common Schools," [6].

cured another press and continued its publication in 1834, also reprinting earlier issues to supply the demand from members who had joined the church after 1833. However, the printing office in Independence was unable to begin Emma's hymnal, the almanac, or the religious curriculum for church youth.[27]

Despite Joseph Smith's optimistic plans, it became clear, following these meetings of the united firm in Missouri, that the literary firm could not generate enough money to finance its printing ventures; and, unfortunately, the interim solution—of assigning Whitney to use his store as collateral to negotiate a $15,000 loan for "five years or longer" did not prove particularly realistic.[28]

An immediate benefit of the united firm arrangement was that it allowed Joseph and other Kirtland leaders to reassert control over economic activities in Zion. But it also instigated an unintended weakness. The arrangement essentially created a two-tier economic system in the church intended to function concurrently and somewhat at odds with the law of consecration in Zion. The primary system, or the law of consecration, pertained to the typical member, while the economic arrangements of the firm served the leaders. Members of the united firm were apparently never required to consecrate. Indeed, Joseph Smith, Sidney Rigdon, Oliver Cowdery, Sidney Gilbert, John Whitmer, and W. W. Phelps had been promised inheritances in Zion during the Hiram, Ohio, meetings.[29]

The little colony of Mormons struggled to implement its economic system. Cowdery had noted, "The store not getting opened as soon as we expected has injured us verry [sic] much in the purchase of provisions."[30] On April 28–29, 1832, Smith visited the settlements above the Big Blue River in Kaw Township where he encouraged the brethren to work hard and be "united as one in the same faith" for each other's benefit.[31] In an effort to ensure the equitable application of consecration, Joseph received a

27. Regarding plans to print Emma's hymnal, see *History of the LDS Church*, 1:270.

28. Cannon and Cook, *Far West Record*, 48.

29. Ibid., 32.

30. Oliver Cowdery to Joseph Smith, 28 January 1832, in Cannon and Cook, *Far West Record*, appendix A, 237.

31. *History of the LDS Church*, 1:269.

revelation confirming the rights of widows and their children to the benefits of the storehouse (CofC D&C 82; LDS D&C 83). While this commitment to equity was admirable, the church's financial situation could not
then support it.

The meetings also afforded an opportunity for Rigdon and Partridge
to resolve a long-standing interpersonal difficulty. Although extant documents do not define the issue, it may have been Partridge's refusal to fund
Joseph and Sidney's return trip to Ohio the previous summer (CofC D&C
60:2d, 3c; LDS D&C 60:5, 10). (See chapter 10.) Rigdon may have taken
umbrage at Partridge's perceived impudence for thinking he was Smith
and Rigdon's equal in decision making, or it may have been Rigdon's resistance to Partridge's understanding of a bishop's job description, since
Rigdon had originally suggested the job to Joseph. At any rate, the issue
was resolved, at least temporarily, and Smith received a congratulatory revelation in early May 1832 near the conclusion of the visit: "Inasmuch as you
have forgiven one another your trespasses, even so I, the Lord forgive you"
(CofC D&C 81:1a; LDS D&C 82:1).

After conducting business at a blistering pace for nine days (April
26–May 5), Smith departed for Ohio on May 6, 1832. But Smith's new
counselor, Jesse Gause, remained in Independence until at least the first
week in June. During this stay, Gause coached John Whitmer in grammar. Gause was certainly qualified. Researcher Erin Jennings Metcalfe
has found that Jesse served twice, from 1812 to 1813 and 1824 to 1825, as
"the principal of the Wilmington Friends School on the corner of Fourth
and West in Wilmington, Delaware."[32] John noted in his account book on
June 4: "Paid Jesse Gause for Lectures in Grammar $3.00."[33] Although the
date of Gause's return to Ohio is not known, he became disaffected and
was excommunicated by December 2, 1832, after his return to Ohio.[34] One
wonders if he and John ever paused in their study of grammar to discuss
concerns about the movement.

32. "Teachers Supported by the Wilmington Monthly Meeting, 1794–1842," cited in Jennings, "The Consequential Counselor," 190.

33. Whitmer, account book, 4 June 1832, p. 3.

34. "Held a conference in the Evening. Br Jes[s]e [Gause] and Mo[r]gan and William
McLel[l]en was excommunicated from the Church," Faulring, *An American Prophet's
Record,* 10.

However, the immediate effect of the new leadership arrangement was positive. John now participated regularly in council meetings and local conferences devoted to organizational and administrative matters.[35]

The print shop, which was nearing completion in May 1832, was the church's first major building project. It formed a focus for the members who lived in Independence; and, as a sturdy, two-story building in the same material as the courthouse, it was an ornament to the city.

The facility was dedicated on May 29, 1832. "W. W. Phelps & Company" began operations the same day. According to the dedication minutes in the Far West Record, "Several appropriate commandments were read by br. John Whitmer, after which some explanatory remarks were made by brs. Phelps Oliver & others in relation to rules & regulations of the office & the important duties devolving upon those whom the Lord has designated to preach his truths & revelations in these last days to the inhabitants of the earth. After which the Bishop proceeded Solemnly to dedicate the building for Printing & all materials appertaining thereto unto the Lord."[36]

Phelps proudly described the new venture in the first issue of the *Evening and the Morning Star*, which appeared only a few days later: "The Star office is situated within twelve miles of the west line of the state of Missouri:—which at present, is the western limits of the United States, and about 120 miles west of any press in the state—In about 39 degrees of North Latitude, and about 17½ degrees of West Longitude; 2½ miles south of Missouri River; 280 miles by land, or 500 by water, west of St. Louis; nearly 1,200 miles west of Washington; 1,300 miles from New-York, and more than 1,500 miles from Boston."[37] The June issue was, like other issues that first year, an eight-page royal quarto (35 cm). Subscriptions were a dollar a year. The only paper in Independence at the time, the *Star* was also, as Phelps had proudly noted, the westernmost newspaper published in Missouri.

The building immediately began serving as a de facto church office and locale for church meetings, such as the administrative council, the

---

35. Meetings of May 26, July 3, July 13, October 2, and October 5, 1832 in Cannon and Cook, *Far West Record*, 48–52, 55, 56–57.

36. Ibid., 49–50.

37. "To Agents and the Public," *Evening and the Morning Star* 1, no. 1 (June 1832): 6.

bishopric, the mercantile firm, and branch officers. Phelps, Cowdery, and Whitmer assumed the responsibility for managing the facility, which employed seven altogether.[38] Cowdery helped Phelps write monthly articles and set type. William Holbert, a young employee, set type and operated the press.[39] John may have helped with the actual typesetting and physical work of inking the press, printing the sheets, and hanging them to dry for the various printing projects, including the newspaper and the Book of Commandments. Almost certainly, however, he was largely occupied as church clerk, as bookkeeper in the printing office, and as church historian. His responsibilities as clerk required attending the numerous meetings where he took minutes. He also made out membership forms and licenses,[40] and copied manuscript materials and revelations for traveling missionaries as necessary.

John's clerking duties also no doubt involved the management of church correspondence. On January 31, he purchased "one box of wafers," costing 6¼ cents.[41] William G. Hartley, a church history professor at Brigham Young University, explains how wafers were used to seal letters: "Letters, or letters with their covers, were folded and secured by seals or wafers. Seals were made by melting colored wax and pressing the drop on the outside of both the upper and lower flaps with a small round stamper. An alternative was closing the letter with a moistened paste wafer, often colored, near the inside edge of the final flap and then pressing the flap

---

38. *History of the LDS Church*, 1:411–12.

39. Holbert died October 31, 1833. His obituary, printed when the publication resumed in Kirtland, Ohio, praised his excellent typography. *Evening and the Morning Star* 2, no. 15 (December 1833): 117. Perhaps there were additional employees in the Independence printing office. Oliver Cowdery to Ambrose Palmer, 30 October 1833, mentions sending "for one of our former apprentices from Zion" to help with the *Star* in Kirtland.

40. The Far West Record lists John Whitmer as clerk for many of the early conferences (1831–37). Oliver Cowdery quoted Joseph Smith's reasons for keeping these vital records: "It is necessary to keep the names of the Saints, and when a child is brought forward to be blessed by the elders, it is then necessary to take their name upon the Church Record. Put down the name of the man, his place of birth, and when, etc., and also of his family. If he begets children after that and they do not come into the Church their names are not known with their brethren in the book of remembrance. The names of the Saints are to be kept in a book that contains the laws of God." Oliver Cowdery to Dear Brother John, 1 January 1834; also cited in Gunn, *Oliver Cowdery*, 233–34.

41. Whitmer, account book, 31 January 1832, p. 3 (counting from the title page with the title page counted as page 1).

down so that the wafer was on the inner side. Such precut round wafers were sold in boxes. A drawer or compartment in inkstands held wafers."[42]

Employees of the printing firm were doubly motivated to succeed, not only to advance the kingdom of God, but also to support themselves and families. John must have also been considering the prospects of marriage and a family. Although no documentation or family stories have survived, he and Sarah Jackson had parted in Ohio near the end of 1831. Possibly they had an informal commitment or at least an "understanding." On March 16, 1832, John noted paying twenty-five cents postage on a letter from Sarah's father, John Jackson.[43] It would have been most unconventional in the early nineteenth century for a young woman to write directly to a young man, so perhaps this letter from Sarah's father contained welcome news from or about Sarah and family. Furthermore, letter writing, given the undeveloped state of the US mail system, was an ambitious and expensive undertaking. Thus, the very fact of the letter's existence suggests a stronger relationship between John and Sarah than mere acquaintance.

During the period that the church had a presence in Jackson County, John Whitmer's account book recorded additional payments of 25 cents and 18¾ cents and for "letter postage." Mormon historian Dean Jessee provided this explanation of the postal system in his *Personal Writings of Joseph Smith:* "Between 1816 and 1845, the cost for sending a single sheet letter less than 30 miles was six cents; not over 80 miles, ten cents; not over 150 miles, 12½ cents; and not over 400 miles, 18¾ cents. Greater distances cost 25 cents. Letters of two or more sheets required additional postage in proportion." As a result, he concludes, "For many, postal communication was a luxury."[44]

Hartley adds: "In the early 1830s, a letter sent by regular mail service between Independence and Kirtland, either direction, averaged three to four weeks travel time.... Postage could be paid in advance by the writer, collected from the addressee upon delivery, or paid partially in advance and partially upon delivery. Most often the recipient had to pay the postage."[45]

42. Hartley, "Letters and Mail between Kirtland and Independence," 177.

43. Whitmer, account book, 16 March 1832, p. 3.

44. Jessee, *Personal Writings of Joseph Smith,* 126.

45. Hartley, "Letters and Mail between Kirtland and Independence," 176, 180, 181. Quoted inflation values could not be verified, seee www.westegg.com/inflation/infl.cgi,

A dollar in 1833 was roughly equivalent to $23 in 2012, so the postage cost the equivalent of nearly six of our dollars.[46]

Between monthly issues, Phelps could give attention to printing Smith's commandments, and many of the revelations intended for publication in the Book of Commandments were printed first in the newspaper for the eagerly waiting Saints. The new availability of Smith's teachings, however, proved a mixed blessing, "In this paper, their faith and doctrines were fully set forth, and through this vehicle, the inhabitants of Jackson county became acquainted with them," comments Phelps.[47] Fifty-five years later, David Whitmer, who had been opposed to publication, said in an "I told-you-so" tone: "The world got hold of some of them. From that time the ill-feeling toward us began to increase."[48]

John's account book, although it does not contain much personal material, gives some glimpses of his association with W. W. Phelps and Oliver Cowdery as equal partners in the literary firm.[49] For example, on January 10, 1832, John bought quills and ink powder. Ink powder came in a little package of paper, rolled up with the ends twisted. A suitable amount would be placed in a container and mixed to the desired consistency with water. A scribe or clerk would typically mix enough for a day of writing. Those with access to the basic ingredients and a few weeks to allow the gallo-tannic acid to hydrolyze could compound their own ink. A recipe for producing such ink began with grinding the gallnuts to a fine powder and immersing in half of the water. In a few weeks, mold (*penicillia*) would cover the surface. The instructions continue: "Skim off the mold and pour the liquid through a filter. Dissolve gum Arabic in a small amount of water and add it to the liquid. Dissolve the ferrous sulfate in water and add it to the liquid. Add 1 gram of carbolic acid to keep mold from forming."[50]

---

accessed March 22, 2013.

46. See www.westegg.com/inflation/infl.cgi, accessed March 22, 2013.

47. Phelps, *Star Extra,* February 1834, reproduced in Crawley, "Two Rare Missouri Documents," 502–15; and also in Flake, *A Mormon Bibliography, 1830–1930,* 226.

48. David Whitmer, *An Address to All Believers in Christ,* 55.

49. Whitmer, account book, p. 3.

50. "Old Ink Recipes," Evan Lindquist website, accessed May 3, 2012, http://evanlindquist. com/othermedia/oldinkrecipes.html.

Sketch of Independence, Missouri, courthouse, ca. 1832. Courtesy Henry Inouye Jr.

About three months later, on June 7, 1832, John bought "a Stone Pitcher for Pr Office" for twenty-five cents. This would have been a stoneware water pitcher which would have stood in the outer clerk's office during the hot Missouri summer, providing drinking water possibly fetched from one of the abundant springs within the platted town of Independence, and also water for mixing ink powder. On September 15, 1832, John purchased paper "for history."[51]

This purchase of paper marks John's formal attempt at the historian's task. He apparently filled these pages with notes on contemporary church activities from which he later drafted the early chapters of The Book of John Whitmer, although none of these early draft pages have survived. Given the demands of his time-sensitive duties as clerk, Whitmer probably had to cram his history into disjointed moments, but he no doubt anticipated that his manuscript history would one day be printed on the Independence press as well.

The pace of church members' emigration into Jackson County increased considerably over the summer of 1832. John's commission as church historian instructed him to "travel many times from place to place, and from church to church," but getting the printing press running had probably kept John close to Independence. Once the office was functioning, John had time to conduct a census of the believers living in Zion. He

51. Whitmer, account book, entries for 18 January–15 September 1832, p. 3.

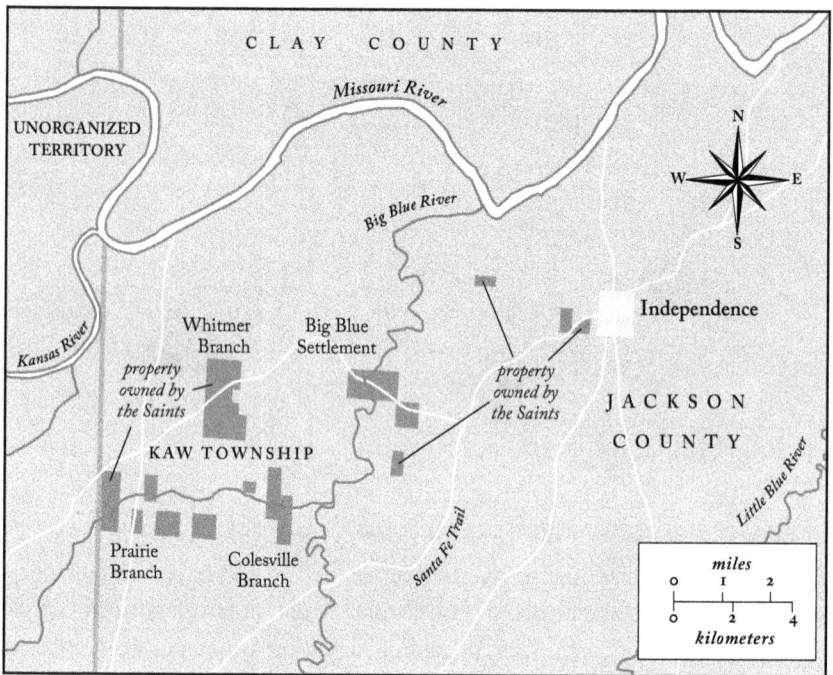

MAP BY JOHN HAMER

Fig. 11.1. Early Latter Day Saint Settlements in Jackson County, Missouri.

probably generally tracked how the church prospered. He was in a good position to watch as new families drove their teams into Independence. But Bishop Partridge had acquired cheaper land west of Independence in Kaw Township, and most new arrivals were directed to these new settlements, which covered a large area. In 1832, four branches lay west of where the Big Blue River bisected the county: Colesville Branch where Newel Knight was the presiding elder;[52] Whitmer Branch where David Whitmer presided;[53] and Big Blue Settlement, with Thomas B. Marsh, as presiding elder.[54] The farthest away was Prairie Branch, where Daniel Stanton pre-

52. Willes [Willis], "Names of the Colesville Church."

53. George A. Smith and Thomas Bullock, "Listing of the Persons Driven from Jackson Co., Mo. in 1833."

54. Marsh, "History of Thomas Baldwin Marsh."

sided, stretching along the western boundary of the state and about twelve miles away by road.[55]

A man on horseback could comfortably ride fifteen miles a day, so if John needed to travel on foot, it may have taken two days to get to Prairie, where Lyman Wight lived. On the way, John could pass through the Big Blue Settlement, where the Rockwell family resided, preparing to establish a ferry across the usually placid stream. By going a little out of his way, John could also reach the Colesville Settlement. This stop would have been a joyful visit because of John's friendship with the extended Knight family. While completing his rounds, he could also take note of other members who lived more to themselves as well as those who had bought land directly from the US government. After completing several fact-finding trips, or perhaps one extended round, in early March 1832, John noted in his history, "There are at this time 402, disciples–living in this land Zion."[56] John no doubt shared this information with Joseph Smith during his two-week visit to Jackson County.

When Joseph and his party visited church branches above the Big Blue on April 28–29, 1832, his history notes: "The Colesville branch, in particular, [had] rejoiced as the ancient Saints did with Paul."[57] John, no doubt, accompanied Smith's party, taking advantage of the opportunity to update his census figures. Following Smith's visit, John noted in his history, "Zion is prospering at present and high priests are stationed to watch over the several branches. December 1, 1832; there are now 538 individuals in this land belonging to the church."[58]

Though W. W. Phelps & Co. began issuing a regular newspaper, subscriptions did not completely defray the expenses of operation, especially given the cost of supporting the individual laborers and their several families. Many letters were exchanged in coming months, informing members of the firm in Ohio of the difficulties in Missouri, while the Ohio brethren advised from afar how to better conduct the business. In June 1833, Joseph instructed his Ohio brethren, "The order of the literary firm is a matter

55. Smith and Bullock, "Listing of the Persons Driven from Jackson Co., Mo. in 1833."
56. Whitmer, Book of John Whitmer, chap. 10, p. 38.
57. *History of the LDS Church*, 1:269.
58. Whitmer, Book of John Whitmer, chap. 10, p. 39.

of stewardship, which is of the greatest importance, and the mercantile establishment, [part of the united firm] God commanded to be devoted to the support thereof."[59] However, the financial reality was that additional sources of income were required.

Over the next year, other Ohio church leaders, "who had financial means, namely Martin Harris, Frederick G. Williams, and John Johnson were called by revelation (CofC D&C 89, 93; LDS D&C 92, 96) to become part of the united firm."[60] But such stop-gap measures had only short-term benefits, and the literary firm continued to struggle.

Furthermore, interpersonal difficulties exacerbated the financial problems. Researcher Lyndon Cook concludes that, after Rigdon's return to Ohio in May 1832, "Sidney became so disturbed over this affair [difficulties with Partridge] that he became mentally depressed and preached falsely in public in Kirtland."[61] Missouri members of the literary firm continued to feel discontented about business arrangements, and W. W. Phelps wrote to Joseph about their business woes. During December 1832, Joseph Smith also received troubling correspondence from A. Sidney Gilbert and W. W. Phelps regarding the order of the church in Missouri.[62]

Probably during the late spring or early summer of 1832, John Corrill, Partridge's counselor in the bishopric, boldly wrote Joseph a no-longer-extant letter. From Joseph's reply, it is possible to deduce that Corrill charged Smith with lacking concern for the Saints in Zion and also reported ongoing friction between Edward Partridge and Sidney Rigdon. Joseph answered:

> When Bro Sidney learned the feelings of the Brethren [in] whom he had placed so much confidence for whom he had endured so much fateague [*sic*] & suffering & whom he loved with so much love his heart was grieved his spirit failed & for a moment he became frantick [*sic*] & the adversary taking the advantage, he spake unadvisedly with his lips after receiving a severe chastisement resigned his commission

59. *History of the LDS Church*, 1:365–66.

60. Cook, *The Revelations of the Prophet Joseph Smith*, 168.

61. Ibid., 174.

62. Gilbert and Phelps's letters are mentioned in Collier and Hartwell, *Kirtland Council Minute Book*, 5.

and became a private member in the church, but has since repented ...
and ... has been restored to his high standing in the church of God.[63]

Literary firm members, hoping that the Bible revision would be a
money-making product, were growing impatient to begin setting type on
it; but Joseph was rethinking the latitude already afforded to John and
Oliver with the Book of Commandments project. Worried that they might
"alter the sense" of his Bible revision during copyediting, Smith asserted:
"You mention concerning the translation I would inform you that they will
not go from under my hand during my natural life for correction, revisal or
printing and the will of [the] Lord be done."[64]

John sensed, accurately as it turned out, that Joseph was dissatisfied
with either the quality or the quantity (or both) of his reports about the
Mormon settlements. On July 31, 1832, Joseph wrote to "the disciples in
Zion" in a letter to W. W. Phelps. It contained a paragraph reminding John
about his assignments:

> I have a partickular request to make of Bro John Whitmer that is as
> soon as you receive this letter for him to assertain the exact number of
> Deciples that have arived in Zion & how many have received there in-
> heritance and the stat[e] and standing of each branch o[f] the church
> and of this inteligence communicate to us as soon as it can be done
> by letter such as it is not wisdom to publish in the paper. I exhort Bro
> John also to remember the commandment to him to keep a history of
> the church & the gathering and be sure to shew him self approved
> whereunto he hath been called.[65]

Smith was certainly aware of the mounting discontent among the
disciples over consecration, rife as it was with administrative problems, interpersonal conflicts, and the inevitable clash between the incoming Saints'
glorious expectations and the much harsher realities. John also probably
understood that Joseph was not rebuking him as much as he was expressing concern for the welfare of the settlement as a whole, since Smith in-

63. Joseph Smith to W. W. Phelps, 31 July 1832, in Jessee, *Personal Writings of Joseph Smith,*
272–73.
64. Ibid., 273.
65. Ibid., 275–76.

cluded a line that he probably knew was of intense interest: "Sister Sarah Jackson came to live with us yesterday."[66]

Smith's letter undoubtedly prompted John to make another round of visits to the Saints, inquiring particularly about the implementation of the law of consecration and the assignment of inheritances. John almost certainly heard anxieties and frustrations from the rank and file and likely reported his findings in private letters to Joseph that are no longer extant. Unless something was done soon, the settlement's economic foundation might completely fail.

Part of John's census was not private and appeared in the November 1832 *Star.* "Since the gathering commenced, which is a little over a year," it read, "the number of the disciples which have come from the east, and which have been baptized in this region, is 465, children and those not members, about 345, total 810."[67]

Joseph had been negotiating with Bishop Partridge since his summer visit, hoping to find a way to salvage the failing consecration system. Consecration had originally been intended to place all of an adherent's worldly assets in God's control by deeding them to the bishop. Partridge used these consecrated funds to buy land which could be distributed to incoming members as "an inheritance." Such an inheritance typically included a lease on a piece of land, tools, and other necessities. Henceforth, they would live as stewards for the church. Any earnings beyond their needs would go into a common storehouse. The two assumptions—that there *would* be a surplus and that the number of inheritances available would more or less evenly match the number of those who needed them— turned out to be extremely optimistic. Disciples were not happy about the leasehold arrangement, and many who gathered to Zion refused to consecrate on this basis.

66. Ibid.

67. Phelps, "The Gathering," [5]. At this point in the life of the church, many families included nonmembers who had also moved to Zion with believing members.

CHAPTER TWELVE

The Whitmer Settlement: 1832

J OHN AND DAVID WHITMER were instrumental in helping to
build up large branches of the church around Hiram and Nelson
in Portage County, Ohio. In February 1831, the missionaries visited Nelson,
holding meetings in the home of Charles and Margaret Hulet and converting nearly the whole extended Hulet family. Charles's parents, Sylvanus
Hulet and Mary Lewis Hulet, had several married children living nearby
including: Sally, Charles, Charlotte, Rhoda, Sylvester, Francis, and Mary.

The Whitmers remained in Ohio until May 1832. During this period,
Peter Jr. returned to Ohio from his mission to the Lamanites and reunited
with his family on September 1, 1831. David Whitmer spent the early part
of 1832 engaged in missionary work and visiting branches of the church.

Joseph Smith's dream of establishing a new economic and social order
implied a literal gathering place, or Zion, for the people of the church. Smith
designated Jackson County, Missouri, as that place of gathering. But Smith's
Zion was to be more than a collection of people in a geographical spot. It
implied "a condition, a relationship between individuals, and humans and
God, best expressed in the phrase Kingdom of God."[1]

During early spring 1832, church members from Hiram and Nelson
townships in Portage County, Ohio, began preparing to gather to Missouri.
According to the law of the church that became section 42 of the church's
Doctrine and Covenants, Bishop Partridge was to receive consecrations of
property and money, and, in return, establish members and their families on
individual inheritances. In addition, the bishop was to appoint a storehouse
to receive the surplus consecrations that were "more than ... needful for the
want of this people."[2]

1.   Roberts, "History and Development of the Stewardship Idea," 13.

2.   CofC D&C 51:4a; LDS D&C 51:13.

Joseph's initial intention was that members of the church relocating to Ohio from Colesville, New York, would gather on a thousand acres of land at Thompson, Ohio. But this initial experiment did not end up as a very effective demonstration of the principles of consecration. Financial reverses, along with a growing anxiety of church members to locate in Missouri, brought an early end to the effort to establish the law at Thompson. By early summer 1831, Colesville members had moved to Missouri. Bishop Partridge was commanded to also move to the West where he could more carefully implement the stewardship law of consecration in the church colony.

Partridge had been instructed "to receive these consecrations, to allot inheritances to properly certified family heads, and to notify the church-at-large, from time to time as to the 'privileges of the land,' so that the gathering would not take place faster than lands were purchased."[3] However, Partridge's departure created a new problem. Who would receive consecrations in Ohio?

Newel K. Whitney, a local storekeeper in Kirtland, was called to serve as the bishop in Ohio. It became Whitney's job to receive consecrations of church members preparing to gather to Missouri, certify them as participants in good standing by means of a written certificate or recommend, and forward the avails of members' consecrations to Missouri for Partridge's use in acquiring land for colonization. Upon arrival in Missouri, members were to present their certificate to Partridge before receiving their land allotment, or inheritance in Zion. According to John Corrill, who served as Bishop Partridge's second counselor: "The church immediately began to gather in Jackson County, and on this subject they became quite enthusiastic. They had been commanded not to go up in haste, nor by flight, but to have all things prepared before them. Money was to be sent up to the bishop, and as fast as lands were purchased, and preparations made, the bishop was to let it be known, that the church might be gathered in. But this regulation was not attended to, for the church got crazy to go up to Zion."[4] Initially, the system failed to produce sufficient resources to adequately support the gathering.

3.　Arrington, Fox, and May, *Building the City of God*, 22.

4.　Corrill, *Brief History of the Church of Christ*, 18–19.

But, a number of adjustments were instituted over the next two years which allowed the situation to gradually improve.

The next company that moved to Missouri, after the Colesville Branch, came from Portage County, Ohio. Perhaps not fully understanding Smith's consecration expectations, the group left on May 2, 1832, and arrived in Independence, Missouri, on June 16, 1832. Their route took them to St. Louis, Missouri, by water and they completed the rest of the trip by wagon.[5]

Charles Hulet's daughter Catherine later recalled, "In 1832 my parents and I moved to Jackson County, Missouri, Father had sent money ahead with which to purchase a farm."[6] Twelve-year-old Elvira Pamela Mills, daughter of Rhoda Hulet Mills, then widowed, was also among those who left from Nelson Township. Elvira "was given an autograph album at Nelson by her aunt, Marietta Streeter Mills on May 1, 1832, apparently a bon voyage gift."[7] Elvira's album notes family events throughout their stay in Missouri.

Young Caroline Webb, whose family also left at the same time—although it is not clear if they traveled with the Hulets—included what she

5. The party numbered about a hundred, including women and children. In addition to the Whitmers, William McLellin was also with the group. They left on May 2, 1832, and arrived at Independence on June 16, 1832. William E. McLellin to Samuel McLellin, 4 August 1832. Members of the extended Hulet family known to have moved to Jackson County in 1832 include Mary Lewis Hulet, born 1763, widow of Sylvanus Hulet; Charles Hulet, born 1790, son of Mary Lewis Hulet; Margaret Ann Noah Hulet, born 1794, wife of Charles Hulet; Catherine and Melvina Hulet, born 1820, twin daughters of Charles and Margaret; Electa Fidelia Hulet, born 1823, daughter of Charles and Margaret; Sylvanus Cyrus Hulet, born 1824 [1826], son of Charles and Margaret; Sylvester Hulet, born 1800, son of Mary Lewis Hulet; Francis Hulet, born 1803 [1802], son of Mary Lewis Hulet; Schuyler Hulet, born 1824 [1826], son of Francis Hulet; Mary Hulet West, born 1804, daughter of Mary Lewis Hulet; Nathan Ayers West, born 1801, son-in-law of Mary Lewis Hulet; Rhoda Hulet Mills, born 1795, daughter of Mary Lewis Hulet; Elvira Pamela Mills, born 1820, daughter of Rhoda Hulet Mills; Robert Frederick Mills, born 1825, son of Rhoda Hulet Mills; Orrin Taylor Hulet, born 1815, son of Charles and Ann Taylor Hulet; and possibly William and Lydia Whiting. See Simmonds, "John Noah and the Hulets," 24n31.
6. Winget, "A Life Sketch of Catherine Hulet Winget," 1960, cited in Johnson, "The Life History of Charles Hulet and His Wives Anna Taylor, Margaret Noah, and Mary Lawson Kirkman," 68.
7. Mills, autograph album, cited in Simmonds, "John Noah and the Hulets," 9n32.

remembered of this trip to Missouri in a later autobiographical sketch: "My parents were James Clark Owens and Abigail Cornelia Burr Owens. When I was quite small, my parents moved to Portage Co., Ohio. Early in the spring of thirty-two my parents with my oldest brother were baptized. In May of the same year, they moved to Missouri in company of a few saints from a little town called Hiram."[8]

Church member Levi Jackman, who apparently left at the same time as the Hulets, also chronicled the journey:

> April 25 [1832] We started from Hiram, Portage Co., Ohio, for Independence, Jackson Co., Mo.
> May 2[d] left Nelson, Portage Co.
> [May 6 Bever (Beaver, Pennsylvania) on the Ohio River, chartered the Steam Boat *Messenger*.
> May 14 St. Louis, Missouri, left St. Louis by land on the 20th]
> June 7 Arrived at Chariton, Mo.[9]

At Chariton, Jackman noted, his family, and that of a fellow traveler named Shanks, "had to stop for want of teams," while the others journeyed on by wagon.[10] The main party from Hiram and Nelson arrived in Jackson County by mid-June. Margaret Ann Noah Hulet, who was pregnant, gave birth to Elizabeth, her fifth daughter and sixth child, in Independence on July 22, 1832.[11]

In responding to a letter from W. W. Phelps, Joseph Smith replied on July 31, 1832, thankful for the safe arrival of the main company from Portage County, but expressing displeasure with the Nelson Branch for not having entered into the law of consecration before leaving Ohio:

> I rejoice ... to hear that our brethren from this place and Nelson have arrived safe in Zion and as I trust without accident this is the mercy

8.   Webb, "A Short Sketch of Her Life."

9.   Jackman, record book, p. 6; bracketed items are from Jackman, "A Short Sketch of the Life of Levi Jackman," 4. Jackman noted, "August 1 Left Chariton. August 10 Arrived Independence. August 13 Left Independence and arrived at Wm. Whitings [in Whitmer Settlement]. August 14 Went to our inheritance and pitched our tent. December 9 Moved into our ho[u]se" (6).

10. I have not been able to learn anything further about the Shanks family.

11. Simmonds, "John Noah and the Hulets," 24. Simmonds mistakenly gives the birth year as 1831.

of our God, but in the discharge must inform you that they left here under the displeasure of heaven ... firstly making a mock of the profession of faith in the commandments by proceeding contrary thereto in not complying with the requirements of them in not obtaining recommends &c secondly, that the church should proceed to receive Wm. McLellin into there [*sic*] fellowship & communion on any other conditions, than the filling his mission to the South countries according to the commandment of Jesus Christ.[12]

Joseph expanded upon his concern regarding the importance of consecration in a November 27, 1832, letter to William W. Phelps, "It is contrerary [*sic*] to the will and commandment of God that those who receive not their inheritance by consecration agreeable to his law ... may be found on any of the records or hystory [*sic*] of the church.[13] Given the confusion about the consecration process, Phelps dutifully printed the relevant instructions in the *Evening and the Morning Star*: "One very important requisition for the saints that come up to the land of Zion, is, that, before they start, they procure a certificate from three elders of the church, or from the bishop in Ohio, according to the commandments; and when they arrive to present it to the bishop in Zion, otherwise they are not considered wise stewards, and cannot be received into fellowship with the church, till they prove themselves by their own goodness."[14]

According to the provisions of the law of consecration, the bishop was to grant worthy members a small allotment of land—their "inheritance in Zion." Because some from the Nelson and Hiram Branches had

12. Joseph Smith to W. W. Phelps, 31 July 1832, in Jessee, *Personal Writings of Joseph Smith*, 270. William McLellin had been appointed to fill a mission to the southern states but, instead, married and emigrated to Jackson County. Joseph saw McLellin's actions as somewhat representative of other disciples who were also failing to observe church gathering procedures, in particular, compliance with the law of consecration. Consecration called for members to place their resources in the hands of the bishop in Ohio before embarking for Missouri. Smith warned church members in Missouri not to receive McLellin into their fellowship, unless he completed his mission. The situation deteriorated to the point that McLellin was temporarily excommunicated. On December 3, 1832, McLellin was received back in good standing. He served as an initial member of the Twelve Apostles.

13. Joseph Smith to W. W. Phelps, 27 November 1832, in Jessee, *Personal Writings of Joseph Smith*, 285.

14. [Phelps], "Elders Stationed in Zion to the Churches Abroad," 111.

not consecrated their possessions to the bishop in Ohio before beginning their journey, they were not entitled to an inheritance. In contrast, because of their prominent role in bringing forth the Book of Mormon, the Whitmer clan was guaranteed a place in Zion upon their arrival. Whether the Whitmer family shared the feelings of members of the Nelson and Hiram Branches that consecration was not an absolute requirement is not clear.

John's parents, his younger sister, Elizabeth Ann, Christian and Anna, Jacob and Elizabeth and their daughter Marianne, David and Julia Ann, and Peter Jr. arrived in Zion with the main party from Hiram, Ohio. The Whitmer family was reunited again, but no documents report what must have been a happy reunion between John and his family.

Edward Partridge immediately directed the Whitmers a bit farther west, to a small cluster of church families living near the home of convert Joshua Lewis in Kaw Township. The Lewis home stood on the main trail to the west and frequently served as a temporary shelter for the gathering church community. The bishop may also have assigned a small allotment of church land to the Whitmers. The senior Whitmers, Christian's family, and Jacob's family settled along the main road leading from Independence to the unorganized territory that lay west of Missouri's border.

Following their arrival, several additional purchases of larger acreages in the vicinity were made in Jacob's name. This emerging neighborhood quickly came to be known as the Whitmer Settlement—also occasionally called Fayette, after their New York home, or sometimes, Timber Branch.[15] The group set to work establishing this family-centered settlement.

Travel between Independence and these outlying settlements was not difficult. John no doubt visited his parents frequently and helped, as he was able, to build family homes; but his administrative responsibilities kept him primarily in Independence. Peter Jr.'s profession as a tailor made it logical for him to also locate in Independence. Christian's name first appears in the minutes of a special conference held on July 3, 1832, at Edward Partridge's home in Independence. Peter Jr.'s name appears in the minutes of an August 24, 1832, meeting held in Kaw Township.[16] Two months later, Peter Jr. (1809–36) married Vashti Higley at his parents' home in Kaw

---

15. Blankmeyer, *David Whitmer, Witness for God*, 33.

16. Cannon and Cook, *Far West Record*, 53; For meetings attended by Christian and/or Peter Jr., see also Ibid., 50–51, 56.

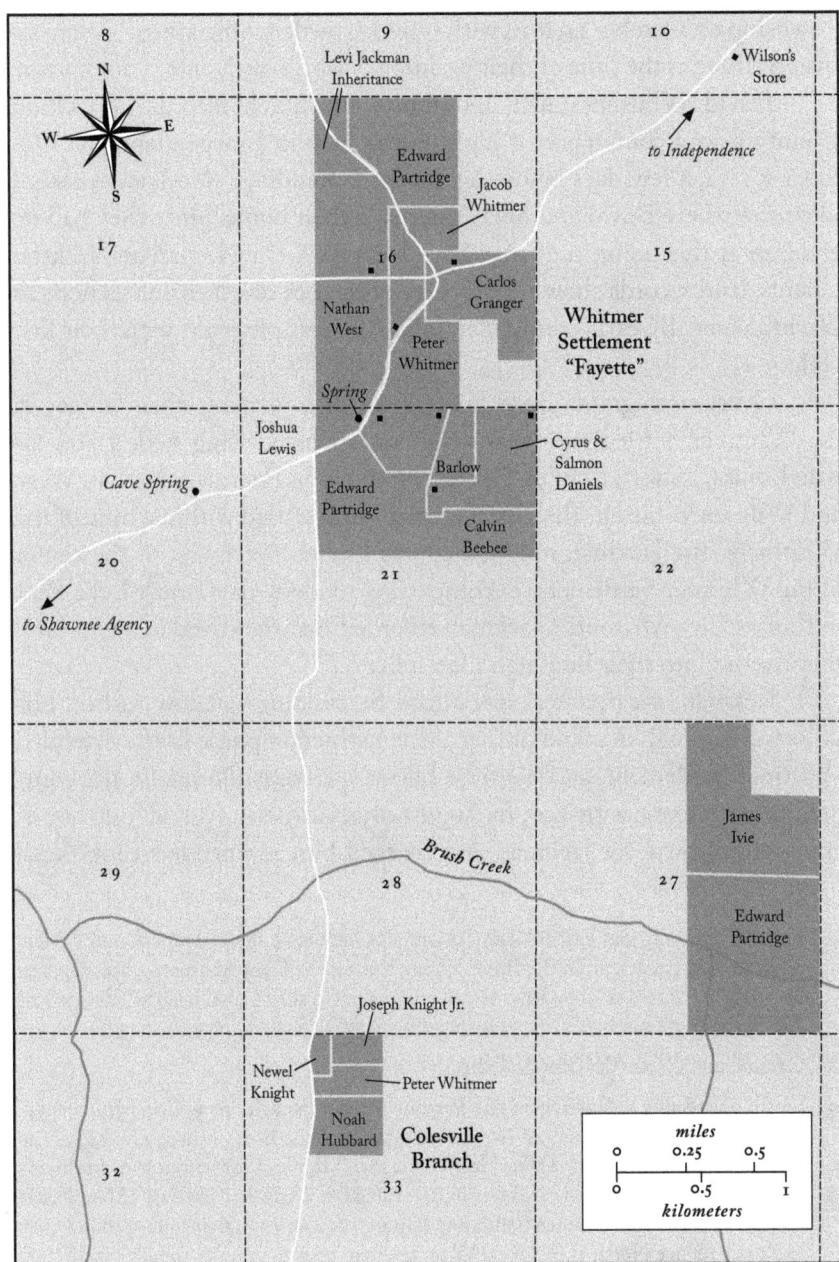

Fig. 12.1. A View of the Whitmer Settlement, Jackson County, Missouri, ca. 1833

MAP BY JOHN HAMER

Township on October 14, 1832, with Oliver Cowdery officiating.[17] Peter was twenty-three at the time of their wedding. Vashti's birth date is not known.

David Whitmer's first appearance in church records in Jackson County is at a conference of high priests held in Independence on October 5, 1832, a few days before his brother's wedding.[18] No known record identifies where David and Julia Ann made their home. Since they had no children at this point, they may have lived with David's parents. Jackson County land records show no property purchases or other transactions in David's name. By early spring 1833, Julia Ann was pregnant with their first child.

Other immigrants from Hiram and Nelson made their homes in the Whitmer Settlement. Near neighbors included King Follett and his wife Louisa, Sylvester Hulet, George Pitkin, John Poorman, Nathan West, and William Whiting. The Levi Jackmans also settled within a mile of the Whitmers. The Jackman inheritance was located northwest of the center of the Whitmer Settlement, encompassing modern-day Troost Lake Park in Kansas City, Missouri.[19] Jackman recorded that they lived in a tent until they moved into their house on December 9.[20]

Jackman, a carpenter, specialized in building window sashes. His skills were in high demand during the construction phase of the extended Whitmer Settlement, and his terse business records illuminate the community's economic activities. In August 1832, Christian hauled "one box of goods from town" for Jackman and charged him seventy-five cents "cash

---

17. Peter Whitmer Jr. and Vashti Higley, marriage. October 14, 1832, Jackson County, Marriage Record Book 1:39. In the Bible, Vashti, the wife of King Ahasuerus, was deposed because she refused to obey Ahasuerus's command "to shew ... her beauty" (Esther 1:11) and Esther replaced her.

18. Cannon and Cook, *Far West Record*, 56.

19. Smith and Bullock, "Listing of the Persons Driven from Jackson Co., Mo. in 1833." Jackman, "Battle of the 24th of November 1833 above the Blue, Jackson Co. Mo., Map Furnished [to] Historian's Office, March 25, 1871." The legal description of Jackman's inheritance reads: "Section 16, Township 49, Range 33, begin 80 rods East of Northwest corner of said Section, thence South one hundred & four rods, thence E 75 rods 8 links to a road, thence North 31 (degrees) W on the road 66 rods 21 links, thence North 7 3/4 (degrees) East 48 rods to North line of said Section, thence West on said line 44 rods to begining, [*sic*] 33 Acers." Jackman, consecration and inheritance form.

20. Jackman, record book, p. 6.

for storage." Conversely, in November 1832, Jackman worked three days for Christian, earning one dollar and fifty cents. Because Jackman had arrived late in the season, he bought three pecks of corn from Christian for eighteen cents. In December, Christian, a shoemaker, made one pair of shoes for someone in the Jackman family, charging seventy-five cents.

In December 1832, Jackman constructed twelve lights of sash for Peter Whitmer Sr.'s house. In June 1833, Jackman hired Peter Sr.'s horse "for one day to go into town." In March 1833, Jackman also produced twelve lights of sash for Christian Whitmer at a charge of one dollar and twenty cents and charged an additional fifty cents to install them, presumably in Christian's house.

In April and May 1833, Jackman credited Hiram Page for cutting 240 rails for a Mr. Swaringer, fetching potatoes from town, and loaning him his oxen for three-and-a-half days of plowing.[21]

In addition to the daily connections created by business relations, the settlement also had a strong spiritual life. David Whitmer was serving as the presiding elder by at least July 13, 1832, overseeing community-centered worship. He also baptized Levi Jackman's eight-year-old daughter, Amy Marchant, on September 15, 1833.[22]

Church members and secular settlers alike were attracted to this fertile area timbered with virgin forest. The network of tributaries around the Big and Little Blue Rivers had protected the area from prairie fires that frequently raged across the land. The resulting dense forests reminded church members of familiar lands in the New England and Ohio regions. It was universally believed that the sod on the prairie was impossible to prepare for crops, so trees, easily girdled, yielded acres of forest floor ready to accept seed for crops.

Extant land records provide a sketchy outline of the property that church members acquired in the greater Whitmer Settlement. A pleasant grouping of small homes quickly developed near the Whitmers—neat, squared-log houses that lined the wooded trails. Often the settlement is described as being on, or sometimes above, the Blue. It was actually two miles or more by road west of the Big Blue River on a gently sloping ridge

21. Ibid., pp. 10, 11, 20, 28.
22. Ibid., 15 September 1833; Willes, "The Names of the Colesville Church"; Jackson County branch boundaries are delineated in Cannon and Cook, *Far West Record*, 52.

but was watered by a small tributary or spring that fed the Blue. This location commanded a view of the extensive Blue River Valley as the settlers went to and from Independence.

Soon, a sprinkling of church settlements emerged across the Jackson County countryside. Initially, there were five principal branches. William G. Hartley, biographer of the Joseph Knight family, described the branches: "The Independence Branch served those Saints living near the temple site. Brothers Partridge, John Corrill, and Isaac Morley of the bishopric, and Elders Sidney Gilbert and W. W. Phelps lived there, with about 200 others. The Blue River Branch, with 230 members, was the largest. The Whitmer Branch, 144 members, was three miles west of the Blue [River crossing]. Two miles south of it, near Brush Creek, the Colesville Branch had seventy-nine members. West of them was the Prairie Branch with about 220 members."[23] Eventually the initial five branches were subdivided into ten church settlements.

As soon as homes and farms were established, elders set out to share the message of the church in neighboring counties. To assist in this process, in the summer of 1832, the council of high priests instituted a school of the elders, over which they called Parley P. Pratt to preside. He recalled: "This class, to the number of about sixty, met for instruction once a week. The place of meeting was in the open air, under some trees, in a retired place in the wilderness, where we prayed, preached and prophesied, and exercised ourselves in the gifts of the Holy Spirit. Here great blessings were poured out, and many great and marvelous things were manifested and taught. The Lord gave me great wisdom, and enabled me to teach and edify the Elders, and comfort and encourage them in their preparations for the great work which lay before us."[24]

John was familiar with this class, for on July 29, 1832, he commented in a letter to Oliver Cowdery and Joseph Smith, "The gifts are breaking forth in a marvelous manner.... God is pouring out his Spirit upon his people so that most all on last thurdsay [*sic*] at the school received the gift of tongues & spake & prophesied."[25] The gifts of the Spirit were seen as

23. Hartley, "*Stand by my Servant Joseph,*" 159.

24. Pratt, *Autobiography*, 93–94.

25. John Whitmer to Oliver Cowdery and Joseph Smith, 29 July 1833, cited in Cook, *Revelations of the Prophet Joseph Smith*, 188.

confirmation of God's blessing on their activity. W. W. Phelps also commented in this same letter: "Everyone that is a Saint or nearly so ... speaks in tongues. Br. David [Whitmer] says he can speak in all the tongues on earth, we shall probably begin to worship here in tongues tomorrow."[26] Mary Elizabeth Rollins, then age fourteen, concurred, recalling, "Oliver Cowdery, John Whitmer and Thomas B. Marsh often spoke in tongues in addressing the people on the Sabbath day."[27] Over-exuberant uses of the gifts eventually caused problems with some of the members of the Whitmer and Prairie Branches, namely Sylvester Hulet and Sally Crandall. Sylvester lived in the Whitmer Branch, while Sarah (or Sally) Crandall was associated with the neighboring Prairie Branch. Sarah and her husband, Daniel Crandall, were the parents of a large family, and some considered Sarah to be a visionary woman.[28]

The exercise of these spiritual gifts opened the door to the expression of increasingly excessive doctrinal ideas. By spring 1833, church leaders in Jackson County became concerned and queried church headquarters in Kirtland concerning such excesses. The prophet replied:

> Say to the brothers Hulet and to all others, that the Lord never authorized them to say that the devil, his angels or the sons of perdition, should ever be restored; for their state of destiny was not revealed to man, is not revealed, nor shall be revealed, save to those who are partakers thereof; consequently, those who teach this doctrine, have not received it of the Spirit of the Lord. Truly Brother Oliver declared it to be the doctrine of devils. We therefore command that this doctrine be taught no more in Zion. We sanction the decision of the Bishop and his council, in relation to this doctrine being a bar to communion.[29]

---

26. W. W. Phelps, statement, quoted in Cannon and Cook, *Far West Record*, 63n2. See also John Whitmer to Oliver Cowdery and Joseph Smith, 29 July 1833.

27. Lightner, "Mary Elizabeth Rollins Lightner," 195.

28. The Crandall clan included sons Patrick, Thomas, John, Simeon, and Daniel. At least John and Simeon were married during the Jackson County period. Sally (also Sarah) Crandall became very involved in the operation of tongues in the Prairie Branch in Jackson County and, later, in the Hulet Settlement in Clay County, Missouri. Cannon and Cook, *Far West Record*, 82.

29. *History of the LDS Church*, 1:366.

Oliver Cowdery and Elizabeth Ann (Whitmer) Cowdery. Courtesy of Community of Christ Archives.

Despite this attempt to control the use of gifts, their expression persisted, especially the gift of tongues. After the expulsion from Jackson County during July and August 1834 in Clay County, Missouri, the Missouri high council acted to rein in the excessive use of these gifts, although the surviving documents do not contain enough details to allow a complete determination of how the Hulet Branch activities were seen as improper. The council pronounced that "the Devil deceived them and ... they obtained not the word of the Lord as they supposed they did, but were deceived."[30]

Although John made his account book entry of December 6, 1832, in his usual black ink, it was a red-letter day for him: Sarah M. Jackson's arrival. She apparently traveled alone, since he does not mention her family; and, in fact, it is difficult to determine their whereabouts. John and Martha

30. During the Clay County period, church leaders endeavored to allay further excitement in the wake of the Jackson County expulsion by encouraging members to minimize potentially controversial activities and maintain a low profile. The high council asked Amasa Lyman and Simeon Carter, two Ohio converts, to "labor with Sally [Sarah] Crandal[l] & Sylvester Hulet and others of like faith & set forth these things in their proper light to them." Cannon and Cook, *Far West Record*, 92.

Jackson were probably still living near Elyria, Ohio, at this time.[31] Apparently they did not come to Missouri until after 1833.[32]

John was no doubt seriously considering marriage with Sarah Jackson; however, after Peter and Vashti's wedding in October, came that of Oliver Cowdery's and Elizabeth Ann Whitmer's on December 18, 1832, with W. W. Phelps performing the ceremony. Elizabeth Ann was seventeen, and Oliver was twenty-six. The new couple lived in Independence where Oliver continued his work in the printing office. Oliver and John may have been boarding with the Gilberts or Partridges, but the newlyweds probably found a place of their own in the growing community.

With young love clearly in the air, John and Sarah became engaged and were married less than two months later, on February 10, 1833. Because of the pleasant working relationship John enjoyed with W. W. Phelps, the couple invited him to perform the ceremony. They may have shared housekeeping with the Cowderys for the first few weeks or months until they could establish their own home. John suggests in his manuscript history that they were living with W. W. Phelps, or nearby.[33] John tended the garden that produced their fresh food, and Sarah added sewing to her housekeeping. Lorene Pollard, one of their great-great-granddaughters, treasured Sarah's thimble. She described thimbles as "an absolute" necessity, considering that all clothing had to be sewn by hand. "Most girls received either a silver or gold thimble with their initials engraved upon it, on about her sixteenth birthday."[34]

31. A John Jackson family was living in Jackson County, according to the 1830 census of Jackson County. Thomas Bullock's 1864 listing of Jackson County members includes a John and Elizabeth Jackson. They were apparently pre-1833 converts and younger than Sarah's parents. There is not enough evidence to determine their relationship, if any, to Sarah's family. Smith and Bullock, "Listing of the Persons Driven from Jackson Co., Mo. in 1833," 13.

32. "13 Went to Father <Jacksons> with wife." John mentions "Father Jackson" in his account book on September 13, 1834, during the Clay County period. "Father" John Jackson apparently lived in the Hulet Settlement near John's parents, a dozen or so miles west of Liberty. Whitmer, account book, 13 September 1834, p. 12. See also Whitmer, account book, 26 April 1834 and 8 October 1834, pp. 9, 15.

33. John wrote on July 20, 1833, "The whole county turned out and surrounded us came to WW Phelps, and my house and took us upon the publick Square." Whitmer, Book of John Whitmer, chap. 10, p. 43.

34. Pollard, quoted in Pollard and Woods, *Whitmer Memoirs*, 59.

CHAPTER THIRTEEN

Kirtland–Independence Relations

JOSEPH GREW INCREASINGLY concerned about consecration's deteriorating situation in Zion. As early as July 31, 1832, he expressed these concerns to W. W. Phelps.[1] The system was limping along, although some disciples continued to refuse to consecrate. A quick fix was needed for the church's troubled economic system to avoid the further hemorrhaging of funds. On December 27, 1832, Joseph dictated a revelation, the "Olive leaf ... the Lord's message of peace to us." By "us," he meant the disciples in Zion, even though he was still in Kirtland. This revelation was intended to move participants toward a more viable consensus about how consecration worked. Essentially, Smith asked members in Missouri to give consecration another chance. If they would, the bishop was authorized to convert existing inheritances, initially granted as leases, into registered deeds (CofC D&C 85; LDS D&C 88).

The revelation provided for special meetings termed "solemn assemblies" to be held in every settlement or branch of the church. Joseph Smith hoped that a compromise could be reached during these meetings that would return the Jackson County church to general compliance with consecration's fundamental provisions. The high priests' council took this matter seriously. Edward Partridge and his counselors, Isaac Morley and John Corrill, accompanied by Oliver Cowdery and John Whitmer, visited each branch during February and March 1833 where they convened these solemn assemblies. They read the "Olive Leaf" revelation, listened to participant complaints, and proposed a bargain. If members were willing to give consecration another chance, they would correct the perceived deficiencies in the church's land tenure system. Assuring members that their

1. Joseph Smith to W. W. Phelps, 31 July 1832, in Jessee, *Personal Writings of Joseph Smith,* 244.

hard work would benefit them permanently was a compelling promise. A dissatisfied inquirer with ties to the colony, Solomon Sherwood, reported news about the solemn assembly that he attended in a dissenting letter to friends in Fulton County, Missouri. He called the "Olive Leaf," which Bishop Partridge read to those assembled, "the revelation of condemnation." According to his report, "The Bishop declared ... that they must consecrate all their property in the name of [Partridge] a bishop to the Lord, or they would all be lost, and must enter into a covenant to that amount, which all that were present did."[2] Although minutes for all of the assemblies have not survived, apparently they had the desired effect in producing recommitment to the principles of consecration.[3]

While the change from lease to deed materially compromised the effects of consecration, the change permitted wider participation, and the compromise allowed retaining the concept of consecration, though with a slightly altered meaning. Church leaders succeeded in maintaining effective economic control of the Mormon settlements in Jackson County.

Only two months after this series of solemn assemblies, however, Joseph wrote Bishop Partridge on May 2, 1833, abandoning his earlier approach and precipitating a dramatic change in the method of land ownership:

> Concerning inheritances, you are bound by the law of the Lord to give a deed, securing to him who receives inheritances, his inheritance for an everlasting inheritance, or in other words to be his individual property, his private stewardship, and if he is found a transgressor and should be cut, out of the church, his inheritance is his still, and he is delivered over to the buffetings of Satan till the day of redemption. But the property which he consecrated to the poor, for their benefit and inheritance and stewardship, he cannot obtain again by the law of

2. Solomon Sherwood, *Illinois Journal*, reprinted in (Columbia) *Missouri Intelligencer and Boone's Lick Advertiser* 17, no. 43 (April 20, 1833); Uncle Dale's Readings in Early Mormon History, Dale Broadhurst's website, accessed May 4, 2012, http://www.sidneyrigdon.com/dbroadhu/MO/Miss1831.htm#042033.

3. Council of high priests, February 26, 1833, in Cannon and Cook, *Far West Record*, 60–61; see also Sherwood, *Illinois Journal*; David Pettigrew, autobiography, describing the Jackson County solemn assembly in January or February 1833, p. 15. Jenson in "A Partial Listing of Those Driven from Jackson County, Missouri, 1864," included Sherwood's widow, Laura W., on his listing of Jackson County members.

the Lord. Thus you see the propriety of this law, that rich men cannot have power to disinherit the poor by obtaining again that which they have consecrated.[4]

Sometime in early 1833, after receiving the Olive Leaf revelation and this letter, Bishop Partridge generated new agreement forms to be used for receiving consecrations and granting stewardships.[5] Members began receiving deeds for their inheritances. This new arrangement was apparently successful in alleviating many concerns about consecration and might have achieved widespread success had the experiment not been interrupted by expulsion from the county in late 1833.

Nineteen-year-old Emily Austin, a relative of the Knights, looked back on this era fondly: "The poor were provided for, as well as those who had put their money into the treasury. They were all satisfied and happy to all appearance, and all seemed to enjoy themselves."[6]

Although the number of Mormon settlers in Missouri increased steadily, it became apparent that church leaders in Ohio did not plan to move to Missouri any time soon. Rather than encouraging key leaders to continue moving to Missouri, as he had in early 1831, Joseph began designating individuals to remain in Ohio. A revelation received September 11, 1831, stated:

> I willeth not that my servant Frederick G. Williams should sell his farm, for I the Lord will to retain a strong hold in the land of Kirtland, for the space of five years, in the which I will not overthrow the wicked [in Jackson County, Missouri], that thereby I may save some; and after that day, I the Lord, will not hold any [adherents] guilty, that shall go, with an open heart, up to the land of Zion; for I, the Lord, requireth the hearts of the children of men. And it is not meet that my servants Newel K. Whitney and Sidney Gilbert should sell their store, and their possessions here, for this is not wisdom until the residue of

4. Joseph Smith to Edward Partridge, 2 May 1833, quoted in Arrington, Fox, and May, *Building the City of God*, 25–26.

5. The new form was implemented sometime after October 12, 1832, as Joseph Knight Jr.'s inheritance form of that date still uses the earlier format. Knight, deed of consecration.

6. Austin, *Mormonism; or, Life Among the Mormons*, 66–67.

the church, which remaineth in this place, shall go up unto the land of Zion.[7]

Gilbert, one of the members of the united firm, had already moved to Missouri, to open the church store, while Whitney remained in Ohio, gathering consecrations of those selected by Joseph, and some acting independently, for the purpose of gathering to Missouri. As an example of one such calling, Smith encouraged Isaac Morley to sell his farm and gather to Missouri. Smith called Morley to serve as a counselor to Bishop Edward Partridge helping advance the application of the law of consecration in Jackson County. Joseph and Emma were living at the Morley farm at the time. Mark Staker observes, "When Morley sold his farm, Joseph and Emma obviously no longer had a place to stay in Kirtland. According to Philo Dibble, 'on invitation of Father Johnson,' Joseph agreed to move Emma and the twins to Hiram."[8]

It was a time of administrative innovation and change in church structure and doctrine. The creation of the high priesthood, first introduced in June 1831, had opened the way for the enactment of new administrative structures, providing Joseph Smith both with some needed administrative support and also strengthening his authority as president of the high priesthood.

Joseph willingly shared power to a point, rapidly building up an ever-expanding network of second-tier leaders. Paradoxically, at the same time, Smith was rapidly developing the concept of high priesthood. Between June 1831 and January 1832, Joseph transformed a rather flat administrative church structure into a vibrant multi-level organization. These innovations allowed him to consolidate his own power over the expanding movement while creating new leadership roles for adherents. Joseph Smith biographer Richard Lyman Bushman writes, "How could an authoritarian religion distribute so much power to individual members?" Such a delegation of power "seems incongruous in an organization led by a man who was believed to receive revelation from the mouth of God." He further observes: "In a time when Protestant churches had lost interest in organizational forms, save to democratize them as far as possible, Joseph built

---

7.   1835 D&C 21; CofC D&C 64:4c–5c; LDS D&C 64:21.

8.   Dibble, "Philo Dibble's Narrative," 79, quoted in Staker, *Hearken, O Ye People*, 310.

an ever more elaborate structure in emulation of the ancient church as he understood it. While other churches were simplifying and flattening their structures, he erected complicated hierarchies."[9]

"Smith instituted a system of [conferences and] church councils," but did not always lead the meetings himself. "The group itself chose the moderator, shifting the responsibility from one to another of the more experienced men like Sidney Rigdon or Oliver Cowdery, but sometimes turning to new converts like William E. McLellin." As a result, "individual priesthood holders were allowed a voice in church governance, giving them ownership of the kingdom to which they had subjected themselves." One effect was more autonomy for Joseph. He "could absent himself from these meetings without crippling business. He left Kirtland for months at a time, and the councils carried on in his absence." This council system allowed the church to be self-governing.[10]

"Step by step, the hierarchy unfolded as doctrine and program required new officers," Bushman describes. "The designation of gathering cities in Independence and Kirtland created a need for governing bodies for each municipality, and high councils were formed to serve the purpose."[11] To deal with the administrative challenge of leading two geographically separated groups, Kirtland and Missouri, Joseph initiated parallel organizations in Ohio and Jackson County, a structure that opened many new managerial slots for Joseph's intimates. This result was not yet the ecclesiastical structure of the modern church, but it reflected an organizational chart that placed Smith as president of the high priesthood with two counselors at his side. As president of the newly instituted body of high priests, Joseph was able to rein in what appeared to be an autonomous bishopric in Missouri and set the stage for better coordinated leadership over the church's two centers of gathering. This arrangement of sharing power ultimately resulted in the creation of parallel administrative units or "stakes" in Kirtland and Missouri.

The introduction of multiple levels of church lieutenants also provided a welcome cushion from Smith's increasingly demanding duties.

9.   Bushman, *Joseph Smith: Rough Stone Rolling*, 253.

10.   Ibid., 252.

11.   Ibid., 254.

According to Mark Staker, "In addition to his family's need for shelter, Joseph also wanted to work in peace and quiet on the translation of the Bible. Portage County, in addition to providing a geographic buffer from Kirtland, still had the largest congregation ... [church members in several branches] anywhere." But because Joseph, Sidney Rigdon, and John Whitmer "were deeply involved in their translation work while they were at the Johnson home, they could not provide for themselves and their families financially."[12] While Joseph may have worried about leaving the church to mostly run itself in Kirtland, he may have reached a point where he could not sustain his family financially in Kirtland.

Introduction of new obedience-oriented beliefs appeared to enforce wider conformity. On February 27, 1833, Joseph disclosed the revelation on dietary principles, now known as the Word of Wisdom, which would hold great import for the Whitmers' future within the movement. David Whitmer is credited with giving the following explanation of its inception to an unidentified newspaper reporter:

> One night there was quite a little party of brethren and sisters assembled at Smith's house. Some of the men were excessive chewers of the filthy weed, and their disgusting slobbering and spitting caused Mrs. Smith (who, Mr. Whitmer insists, was a lady of predisposed refinement) to make the ironical remark that "It would be a good thing if a revelation could be had declaring the use of tobacco a sin, and commanding its suppression." The matter was taken up and joked about, one of the brethren suggesting that the revelation should also provide for a total abstinence from tea and coffee drinking, intending this as a counter "dig" at the sisters. Sure enough the subject was afterward taken up in dead earnest, and the "Word of Wisdom" advising against the use of tobacco, tea and coffee was the result.[13]

In another example of administrative realignment, on March 26, 1833, the high priests of Zion convened a conference to further consider the management of Zion. During this conference, a consensus emerged

---

12. Staker, *Hearken, O Ye People*, 310, 311.

13. "[An Anti-Polygamy] Do[cument]," *Daily Globe*; see also "[An Anti-Polygamy] Do[cument]," *Des Moines Daily News*, 20, quoted in Newell and Avery, *Mormon Enigma*, 47; photocopy of an article clipping containing identical content titled, "The Book of Mormon."

favoring a leadership model based on the seven high priests who had been sent from Kirtland "to build up Zion; viz., Oliver Cowdery, W. W. Phelps, John Whitmer, A. Sidney Gilbert, Bishop Partridge, and his two counselors, Isaac Morley and John Corrill." These men "should stand at the head of affairs, relating to the church, in that section of the Lord's vineyard."[14] The colonists seemed to favor this shift to a more diversified leadership. The management situation for the Jackson County settlement dramatically improved. But Bishop Partridge had been demoted yet again.

These seven men, with the common consent of the church branches, were to oversee the appointment of presiding elders for the several branches.[15] Under the council's direction, ten branches of the church were established September 11, 1833, formalizing the extant Jackson County settlement pattern.[16] Independence remained one of the largest branches, the center of many church activities and the focus of most members' lives.[17]

However, the council of seven apparently never functioned completely as envisioned. As a practical matter, the council lacked someone who could provide the dynamic leadership of Joseph Smith's influence and charisma. A historian of the church's economic practices, Joseph Geddes, observes, "Oliver Cowdery never exhibited the capacity to gather men around him, inspire them with confidence in himself, and at the same time to fire them with a proper conception of the importance of particular projects and draw from them the zeal and energy necessary to accomplish things in the manner which administrative work of high order requires."[18] Furthermore, effectively functioning in Joseph's long-distance shadow, they may not have felt entirely free to take the initiative.

John's own responsibilities as part of the council of seven further transformed him from a clerk into one of the primary leaders of the Jackson County settlement. John's unfailing diligence and hard work had made him a good clerk and certainly qualified him to contribute as a member of

14. Cannon and Cook, *Far West Record*, 62; *History of the RLDS Church*, 1:284.

15. *History of the RLDS Church*, 1:284.

16. Cannon and Cook, *Far West Record*, 65.

17. Independence served as the Missouri church colony's headquarters city and was understood to be the future site of the City of Zion (the New Jerusalem) and location of the temple (CofC D&C 57:1d; LDS D&C 57:3).

18. Geddes, *United Order among the Mormons*, 29.

the management team. That John wasn't forever looking for opportunities to "magnify his calling" or initiate his own innovations made him a perfect second in command.

Yet the shape of John's day-to-day life remains somewhat hazy. Between his leadership responsibilities and duties as church clerk, he had little time to pursue farming or any other ways of making a livelihood, except for the activities of the literary firm. Members of the literary firm expected to eventually "live from the profits of the sale of the publications, and even produce surpluses from the business 'which shall benefit the church at large.'"[19] Possibly, given enough time and a sufficiently large client base, this ambitious plan would have been successful; but as matters turned out, the print shop operated for only a year. During that year, the literary firm never realized a profit. John's lifestyle must have been rather Spartan.

However, some glimpses of John's personal responsibilities emerge in relation to the firm's printing of the Book of Commandments. The manuscript revelations that John had brought from Ohio had been arranged chronologically up to the point of his departure in November 1831 for Independence. In Missouri, John had continued to copy revelations into the volume but was limited by the fact that he did not have immediate or complete access to copies of revelations. After John's arrival in Independence on January 5, 1832, the revelations in John's Book of Commandments and Revelations manuscript begin to appear in the order in which John obtained them, rather than by the date in which Joseph Smith received them in Ohio.

Sidney Rigdon made some of the revisions in John's manuscript revelation volume.[20] But John, Oliver, and W. W. Phelps also made insertions, revisions, or changes. A noticeable pattern is that John often cancelled Rigdon's changes, restoring the pre-November 1831 wording. While some

---

19. Cook, *Joseph Smith and the Law of Consecration*, 44.

20. Jensen notes that before sending the Book of Commandments and Revelations manuscript to Missouri, "Smith likely delegated the responsibility of 'correcting' [it] to Rigdon, Whitmer, or Cowdery—or to all three.... Instances of Rigdon's handwriting in the majority of the Book of Commandments and Revelations were inscribed in Ohio in 1831, before the volume was carried to Missouri." Jensen, "From Manuscript to Printed Page," 34, 36.

of these changes could have been made in Ohio before John brought the manuscript to Missouri, a more likely possibility is that Whitmer and Cowdery launched a second round of editing in Missouri, with Rigdon in distant Ohio.

Robin Scott Jensen, a specialist on the Book of Commandments and Revelations, notes: "A phrase out of current section 33 reads 'remember they shall have faith in me.' Rigdon altered the reading to read: 'Remember you must have faith in me.' Whitmer cancelled Rigdon's wording and changes, inserting, 'they shall' reverting the wording back to the original." John's adjustments to this verse and many others were finalized by the printing of the Book of Commandments, perpetuating this reading in the current LDS Doctrine and Covenants 33:12. Jensen further surmises that Whitmer, Cowdery, and Phelps adopted this conservative editorial style after receiving a letter from Joseph instructing the church printer to "be careful not to alter the sense of any of [the revelations] for he that adds or diminishes to the prop[h]ecies must come under the condemnation writen therein."[21]

Jensen also demonstrates that the editors clearly worked from multiple sources. John's manuscript was not the only source available to the editorial team while preparing the revelations for print. Jensen comments: The "current [LDS] section 25 and the beginning of [section] 24 are found on the same page of the manuscript revelation book." While the editors added punctuation and versification for section 25 in the manuscript, section 24 contains no editing marks. Out of the fifty-six of John's manuscript revelations that found their way into print in the Book of Commandments, twenty-nine contain no editorial versification notations. Also, "the editors clearly accessed multiple sources from which to provide material for the printed edition of the revelations. For example, section 12 is not found anywhere in Whitmer's [manuscript] revelation book, but it is found in the Book of Commandments as chapter 11."[22]

Revisions by Cowdery and Phelps focus primarily on the mechanical process of preparing the manuscript for the printing process. For example,

---

21. Ibid., 36–37; Joseph Smith to W. W. Phelps, 31 July 1832, in Jessee, *Personal Writings of Joseph Smith*, 244.

22. Jensen, "From Manuscript to Printed Page," 37.

heavy markings introducing verse numbers and punctuation appear to be Phelps's handwriting.

While partway through the process of setting type, Phelps editorialized in the church's *Evening and the Morning Star* about the anticipated impact of the forthcoming Book of Commandments. Phelps predicted that the published work would be of great benefit to the church, and encouraged members to "lift up their heads and rejoice, and praise his holy name, that they are permitted to live in the days when he [Christ] returns to his people his everlasting covenant, to prepare them for his presence."[23]

Meanwhile, not only the printing firm, but the Mormon colony itself struggled with an uncertain future. The adoption of Smith's parallel administrative structure at the church's two centers allowed Kirtland to remain a rich economic base for the church. Consecration had not proven successful in Ohio and its provisions gradually gave way to a free enterprise system. In contrast, the stronger church economy in Ohio supported the wider church program and goals throughout this era. Trusted couriers periodically brought money to Missouri gathered by Kirtland stewards. However, too often, local needs in Kirtland prevented some earmarked resources from reaching Missouri.

Living in remote Missouri also nurtured a distinctive level of individuality among its participants. The very nature of this separation between Kirtland and Jackson County may thus have unwittingly promoted the growth of dissent, especially with the Whitmers and Oliver Cowdery. Distance freed them from Joseph's immediate oversight and tended to confirm them in their own feelings, attitudes, and actions. During this time, the Whitmer family found themselves part of a subgroup of significant church leaders and members who were developing a shared perspective that varied from Joseph's, particularly as he initiated a flood of institutional and doctrinal innovations: instituting the washing of feet (January 22, 1833),[24] announcing the dietary regulations contained in the Word of Wisdom (February 27, 1833),[25] and making Kirtland into a stake (March 23, 1833).[26]

---

23. "Revelations," *Evening and the Morning Star*, 89.

24. Collier and Harwell, *Kirtland Council Minute Book*, 6–7.

25. *History of the LDS Church*, 1:327–29; see also CofC D&C 86; LDS D&C 89.

26. *History of the LDS Church*, 1:335; CofC D&C 91; LDS D&C 94.

Despite the Olive Leaf revelation, the law of consecration proved a persistent source of difficulty. Probably the most serious stumbling block was the reluctance of new arrivals to freely consecrate all their possessions. In January 1833, Joseph Smith chastised the Missouri church for not obeying the consecration commandments, even though he did not appear to require it of members in Ohio.

On January 14, 1833, Joseph wrote W. W. Phelps a letter intended for wide dissemination among the Missouri brethren, rebuking them for "indulg[ing] in feelings towards us, which are not according to the requirement of the new covenant" but announcing with what may have been satisfaction: "yet, we have the satisfaction of knowing that the Lord approves of us, and has accepted us, and established His name in Kirtland for the salvation of the nations."[27]

Simultaneously, however, most key Missouri church leaders had already earned the right to their inheritances (meaning that their property would be secured to them by legal deeds) because of their help in bringing forth the Book of Mormon. During a special conference at Hiram, Ohio, on November 12–13, 1831, the families of "Joseph Smith Hiram [*sic*] Smith Peter Whitmer Christian Whitmer Jacob Whitmer Hiram Page & David Whitmer" were "recommended to the Bishop in Zion as being worthy of inheritances among the people of the Lord according to the laws of said Church."[28] And, of course, being prominently associated with the literary firm meant that John was also provided an inheritance. In effect, the Whitmer clan, not being required to consecrate like other members, remained apart from the provisions of the law of consecration throughout the Jackson County period.

Their situation highlights one of the major disadvantages of the firm arrangement. The united firm constituted, in essence, a second-tier economic system functioning concurrently with the law of consecration. While the typical member was involved in the primary system, or the law

27. Joseph Smith to William W. Phelps, 14 January 1833, in *History of the LDS Church*, 1:316–17.

28. Minutes of a special conference, November 12–13, 1831, in Cannon and Cook, *Far West Record*, 32. The minutes do not mention whether the Peter Whitmer in question is the father or the son. However, as Peter Whitmer Jr. was not married in 1831, the reference is probably to Peter Sr. and Mary Whitmer.

of consecration, members of the "united" economic order participated in the life of the community through the united firm.

Naturally, such bifurcation resulted in an undesirable double standard. The two economic systems did not fit well, a disparity that probably provided continual friction. A Baptist missionary to the Indians, Benton Pixley, observed in October 1832:

> The idea of equality held forth; but time will show that some take deeds of property in their own name, and those too of the most zealous and forward in the cause and prosperity of the society. And perhaps they do not pretend, like Ananias and Sapphira to have given all to the society; yet it is a point of duty they most rigidly enjoin on all their proselytes to cast their all into the common stock. Under these circumstances, it needs no prophetic eye to foresee that there will be a murmuring of the Greeks against the Hebrews. Indeed there already begins to be some feeling and some defection arising from this subject.[29]

Even after the Olive Leaf revelation, some believers still refused to participate in consecration. In 1892, John Taylor recalled that "some people who came there ... did not consecrate their substance for the good of the church, but went ahead and bought land on their own account. They brought money there for the purpose of speculating and purchasing land.... There were a few who went for that purpose, but not many; and of course they had a right to do it if they thought proper."[30]

In a later reminiscence, probably written in the 1870s, a young convert named Nathan Porter observed this tension:

> My Father resieved his inheritence in the last named Branch [Prairie Branch] under the hand of Bishop Partridge, consisting of Some 20 Acres he immediately went too building & improveing upon it Soon followed the law of consecration; which was complied with by all the Branches with one exception; there were a few in the Indipendance Branch that refused to Consecrate their propety in common with their Brethren, Notwith standing the ergent request of the Bishop on this point as there was none exempt from this Law. this was a sourse of

29. Pixley, "New Jerusalem: Letter from Independence," in Mulder and Mortensen, *Among the Mormons*, 75.

30. Temple Lot Case, 189–90.

mutch trial to the Bishop as, some were those that stood in the highest rank of the Priesthood and were set as guides to their Brethren, to
say unto them this is the way walk ye in it. therefore it is not for me
to say, as to the righteousness or unrigteousness of their course in this
matter; but will leave it with those who hold Jurisdiction over their
fellow Servants.[31]

Mormon immigrants to Jackson County had a variety of motivations
for pursuing the establishment of Zion. The movement encouraged their
feeling that God had a special purpose for their lives. Though unlikely associates, from diverse backgrounds, they were zealous in their adopted religion. On the whole, they reflected the genteel, orderly, and civilized qualities of their New England town-builder heritage. They felt that, through
hard work and adherence to the teachings of Christ, they could claim the
opportunity of implementing a Christlike lifestyle, foreshadowing a restoration of Christ's primitive church in their new home on the frontier.
They were bold about their millennial expectations. Yet as a reflection of
their New England village culture, in personal demeanor, they were more
inclined to turn the other cheek than to take up arms in the resolution of
conflict. There was also a strong expectation from their religious experience
to this point to reflect Christlike behavior when confronted.

Yet, some Mormon settlers were anything but meek and lowly. W.
W. Phelps, appointed by revelation to be "the printer unto the church"
and editor of the church's new paper, was aggressive and confrontational.
From the very beginning of his involvement with the church, Phelps had
encountered resistance and harassment from those outside the movement.
Once, he had even been jailed for reading the Book of Mormon. He also
shared Joseph Smith's perception that the new movement had been treated
badly in the public press. The *Evening and the Morning Star* was his chance
to ventilate and set the record straight.

An early nonmember resident of the county, Josiah Gregg, reflected
upon the old settlers' negative reaction to Phelps's approach: "In a little
paper printed at Independence under their immediate auspices everything

31. Porter, reminiscences, 64–65.

was said that could provoke hostility between the Saints and their worldly neighbors."[32]

Though it appears that church leaders did not anticipate such a reaction, the nonmember population of the county kept up a prejudicial agitation. Cowdery provided an overview of the troubles, writing that between the summer of 1832 and spring of 1833:

> Few acts of violence were committed openly by the populace, but continual rumors of a mischievous and wicked nature, too incredible and trifling to be named among the intelligent part of [the] community, were busily circulated ... and had the desired effect.... One report was, that "the Mormons had declared, that they would have the land of Jackson County, for the Lord had given it to them, &c."—Another that "the Mormons were tampering with the Blacks of said county; and they were colloging [*sic*] with the Indians, and exciting them to hostilities against the whites, &c.[33]

These rumors reverberated over and over as the intrusive values of church members came into conflict with the established political culture and personal values of their nonmember neighbors. Josiah Gregg further reflected of the Mormons:

> At last they became so emboldened by impunity as openly to boast of their determination to be the sole proprietors of the land of Zion; a revelation to that effect having been made to their prophet.... [This] at once roused the latent spirit of the honest backwoodsmen, some of whom were of the pioneer settlers of Missouri, and had become familiar with danger in their terrific wars with the savages. They were therefore by no means appropriate subjects for yielding what they believed to be their rights. Meetings were held for the purpose of devising means of redress.[34]

The inevitable consequences would definitively end the dream of a Mormon Zion in Missouri.

---

32. Gregg, *Commerce of the Prairies*, 165.

33. Extra, *Evening and the Morning Star*, February 1834, 1.

34. Gregg, *Commerce of the Prairies*, 165–66.

CHAPTER FOURTEEN

Violence in Independence: 1833

THROUGHOUT 1833, THE cultural divide between church members and local citizens grew more pronounced. Elias Higbee, a recent arrival in Missouri, poignantly described the situation of the disciples: "Though often persecuted and vilified for their difference in religious opinions from their fellow citizens, still [the Mormons] were happy. They saw their society increasing in numbers; their farms teemed with plenty; and they fondly looked forward to a future big with hope. That there was prejudice existing against them, they deplored: yet they felt that these things were unmerited and unjust."[1]

Despite general apprehensions, looking back on events from a later perspective, disciples saw themselves as so much the victims that they did not take adequate steps to deflect the hostility. Joseph Smith tried to warn colonists that they needed to exercise caution in both word and deed. Addressing W. W. Phelps by letter, Smith warned, "Your ignorant & unstable Sisters & weak members ... write wicked and discouraging letters to there [their] relatives who have a zeal but <not> according to knowledge and prophecy falsly [*sic*] which excites many to believe that you are putting up the Indians to slay the Gentiles which exposes the lives of the Saints evry [*sic*] where."

Church members in Missouri could sense that a tide of hostility was rising against them, yet apparently felt somewhat powerless to forestall the events that culminated in their 1833 expulsion from Jackson County. Edward Partridge's daughter Emily, who was then nine years old, remembered that disgruntled neighbors "began to gather in small parties and commit depredations by night by braking windows and shooting into the houses

---

1. Higbee, Taylor, and Smith, "To the Honorable the Senate and House of Representatives," in Johnson, *Mormon Redress Petitions*, 395.

of the Saints, and sometimes using abusive language to our people.... They were often holding meetings and forming resolutions to drive or destroy the Mormons."[2] Church colonist David Pettigrew very precisely described his non-Mormon neighbors' intent:

> I was at work in the field near the high road one day, and a man who I knew well by the name of Allen, cried out at the top of his voice, "Mr. Pettigrew, you are at work, as though you intended to remain here," to which I replied that "I thought I had a right to Stay upon my own land." He then said, "We are determined to drive you away from this Country and we will Stop you from emigrating here." I then told him we disturbed no man, and we always Kept to the laws of the land, and interfered with the rights or privileges of no man, he again observed that, "that is to no purpose. We will drive you from this place." I told him that certainly the laws would not Suffer him to commit Such a crime, he remarked, "that the old laws and Constitution are all worn out, and we are about to frame a new One." ... A few days after the foregoing, I attended meeting, where we had assembled to offer Prayer to the Almighty God for his assistance and protection, and in the midst of our prayers, two men made their appearance, who were Sent by the mob party, to inform us <about> what their intentions were, we all immediately went out to hear what they had to Say. One of them whose name was Masters, Said "Are you all ready to hear[?]" We answered, "Yes," Said he, "There is a great difficulty between us, and we are sent by the Authority, and a large body of men <are> already Collected together at Independence, and all are under arms, and now the proposals are these, If you will forsake your Mormon prophet religion, and become of Our Religion, we will become your brothers, and will fight for you, and we will protect you in any difficulties or troubles you may have, we will Stand by you and never forsake you, but if you will not, why we will fall upon you. Our men are now all under Arms, and it has been with great difficulty they have been Kept back, and now you have Some Knowledge of your Situations. We feel for, and beg of you to consider your Situation and Save yourselves, from the calamity which will Soon follow, Should you fail to comply with our request.

2. Young, "Autobiography," p. 106.

Forsake your Prophet Religion, for we will not suffer Mormonism amongst us."[3]

In March 1833, more than three hundred citizens of Jackson County assembled in Independence "to consult upon a plan, for the removal, or immediate destruction, of the church." On this instance, they [the citizens] "spent the day in a fruitless endeavor."[4] Despite such an overt demonstration of displeasure, church leaders and members continued on normally, even as tensions increased. William McLellin recalled, "The Church at first was taught and practiced the principle of non-resistance … Would not return evil for evil or railing for railing or smite when smitten."[5] Church members wished to claim the privileges of heaven without due consideration of the usual earthly cost of such privileges. They wanted both the privileges of aggressive beliefs and blessings of a Christlike demeanor.

The absence of a uniformly articulated church philosophy about self-defense left Smith's Missouri followers unprepared for the events of 1833, according to Mormon history researcher Graham St. John Stott. He further elaborates that it was not until after the outbreak of violence against church members in July 1833 that Smith finally codified the church's official position on self-defense via revelation (CofC D&C 95; LDS D&C 98). Smith pronounced a complex formula guiding his followers in the face of offense. "Following Christ's commandment to turn the other cheek (found in III Nephi 5:85 as well as the New Testament), the Saints were to suffer two provocations, and only respond after a third." At a later time, Smith elaborated further, "Be not the aggressor bear until they strike on the one cheek offer the other & they will be sure to strike that, then defend yourselves & God shall bear you off."[6] "As a group, the Saints were to meet each provocation with an offer of peace, and only if three such offers had been rejected were the Saints justified in responding in their own defense."

So, there was not a commonly held understanding about these matters within the colony of disciples in Missouri as nonmember hostility

---

3. Pettigrew, autobiography and diary, pp. 17–18.

4. "History of Joseph Smith," *Times and Seasons*, 5:754.

5. Larson and Passey, *William E. McLellin Papers*, 326.

6. Stott, "Just War, Holy War, and Joseph Smith, Jr.," 137–38, 139. Internal quotation from Ehat and Cook, *Words of Joseph Smith*, 11.

against the church began to peak. In July 1833, according to John H. Beadle, an 1870s researcher of Mormonism:

> A Mormon meeting was called in the yard in front of John Corril[l]'s home, where the Doctor [William E. McLellin] was called upon for remarks. He expounded from the scriptures, (this is his account,) that the Gentile world was in bad straits; that a general wind-up was at hand, and that the result would be blood and destruction to the unbelievers and a glorious triumph for the Saints. The Doctor was careful not to specify how this would be brought about, or to set any time, but the speaker who followed him prophesied that before five years all unbelievers in Jackson County would be destroyed. Upon this a few Missourians in the outskirts of the crowd signified an emphatic dissent and went down town. That evening an "indignation meeting" was called in the public square, where Russel [*sic*] Hicks, a lawyer, and Saml. C. Owens, county clerk, gave it as their opinion that the Mormonites intended to raise the slaves, join them and massacre the whites. This set the ball rolling and the next Tuesday three hundred armed men from the county were assembled in town.[7]

Meeting at the courthouse on Saturday, July 20, 1833, for the purpose of deciding what was to be done with the Mormons, the citizens drew up resolutions "to put a stop to their seditious boasts as to what they proposed to do, etc."[8]

---

7. John Hanson Beadle, "Jackson County: The Early History of the Saints and Their Enemies," *Salt Lake City Tribune*, October 6, 1875. Viewed online at Uncle Dale's Readings In Early Mormon History, Dale Broadhurst's website, accessed May 4, 2012, http://www.sidneyrigdon.com/dbroadhu/UT/tribune1.htm. McLellin himself in "Our Views Relative to the Legal Successor of Joseph Smith in the First Presidency," 61, confirmed this information:

> Having just returned from a long tour, it was announced that on the next Sunday I would preach at our usual place of meeting on the "Temple lot." A large number of the old citizens with whom I had been intimate, turned out to hear. I delivered a discourse of some two hours length on "the gathering of the last days." That same evening some of the principle [*sic*] men of the place, and of the regions round about, gathered themselves together and drew up the famous document in which they "pledged to each other, their property, their lives and their sacred honors, to drive all members of the Church of Christ, (whom they called Mormons,) from the county, peaceably if they could, but forcibly if they must."

8. Col. Thomas Pitcher interview, in Etzenhouser, *From Palmyra, New York*, 322–25.

John recorded in his history that, on July 20, 1833, "a committee was appointed at the foregoing meeting and waited upon us, viz. Partridge, Corrill, Phelps, etc. Cowdery &c. [also John Whitmer, Sidney Gilbert, and Isaac Morley] ... The committee ... required of us to shut up our printing office, store, mechanical shops &c. immediately and leave the County."[9] A circular, demanding the immediate removal of the Mormons, with "between 70 and 100 signatures to it" was handed to the church leaders.[10] According to Isaac Morley, "We told them that we should want a little time to consider upon the matter, they told us that we could have only fifteen Minutes, we replyed [*sic*] to them that we could not comply with their proposal with in that time, one of them observed and said then I am Sorry, I think it was Lewis Franklin Said he then, the work of destruction will then Commence immediately [*sic*], they went out and Repared [*sic*] to the Court house, in company I should think with 4 or 5 hundred men. We then returned home."[11]

At the courthouse, the citizens' committee reported to the larger group, which decided to demolish the printing establishment. They walked a short block south down Liberty Street to the printing establishment and completely razed the building. One of these citizens, Thomas Pitcher, was later asked if the Mormons made any resistance. "No they did not," he answered. "Some of them tried to argue the case, but it was of no avail.... Several were knocked down, but as a general thing the Mormons had sufficient discretion to keep out of the way."[12]

Men entered Phelps's living quarters above the print shop and threw much of the family's property into the yard and street.[13] But they were

9.   Whitmer, Book of John Whitmer, chap. 10, pp. 42–43. Isaac Morley, one of Partridge's counselors, testified under oath that the following men were members of the citizens' committee: Robert Johnson, Moses G. Willson [*sic*], James Camel, Joel F. Childs, Richard Fristoe, Abner Steeples, Jan [Gan] Johnson, Lewis Franklin, Russel M. Hicks, Samuel D. Lucas, Thomas Willson [*sic*], James W. Hunter, and Richard Simpson. Morley, affidavit, January 9, 1840, Johnson, *Mormon Redress Petitions*, 499.

10. [Oliver Cowdery], "The Mormons So Called," in Crawley, "Two Rare Missouri Documents," 507.

11. Morley, affidavit, 1.

12. Pitcher, in Etzenhouser, *From Palmyra, New York*, 322–25.

13. Barrett, *Joseph Smith and the Restoration*, 250.

mainly concerned with the press. The mob's leaders took a piece of timber up the outside steps and knocked open the door of the pressroom. Chapman Duncan, a church member, said, "I saw a man [John King] go up the stairs, burst open the door. Others followed."[14] The men pied the type and threw it into the street, where it could be found for years—a plaything for little boys.[15] Next, the press itself "was thrown from the upper story," along with the apparatus, bookwork, and paper, which was scattered through the streets.[16] In the ensuing legal action, Phelps described the items damaged or destroyed, as including, "other goods and Chattel viz: printing paper, printing ink, blank deeds, blank forms of various other things, unprinted manuscripts, and other unpublished works."[17] The press, broken in the fall, lay in the street until the following February.[18] Chapman related that, after the mob threw the type and press from the window, "they took a long tree and put it into a window, crossed the corner of the house into another window, and sprung the tree to throw out the corner of the house.... I did not stay to see it fall."[19]

Benton Pixley, a Baptist missionary in Independence, wrote that after the mob pulled down the building, they hauled its roof into the highway.[20] Sally Phelps gathered her children into a horse-drawn con-

14. Duncan, "Reminiscences about Experiences in Missouri," 6; Temple Lot Case, 250.

15. Temple Lot Case, 249–50. "Pied type" means the type was mixed together to render it unusable without hours of tedious sorting.

16. "A History, of the Persecution, of the Church of Jesus Christ, of Latter Day Saints in Missouri," 18.

17. William Phelps v. Lewis Franklin, filed December 22, 1833.

18. Jennings, "Factors in the Destruction of the Mormon Press in Missouri," 71. "The mob sold the materials, or rather gave 'Davis and Kelly' leave to take the Evening and Morning Star establishment, to Liberty, Clay County, where they commenced the publication of 'The Missouri Enquirer' a weekly paper. They also paid our lawyers, employed as counsel against the mob, three hundred dollars, on the one thousand dollar note," which church members had agreed on as a fee. "History of Joseph Smith," *Times and Seasons*, 6:961.

19. Duncan, autobiography, p. 33.

20. Pixley, cited in Mulder and Mortensen, *Among the Mormons*, 82. A defense brief submitted by attorneys representing the individuals whom Phelps sued for the destruction, argues that the noise, disturbance, forcing open doors, tearing off the roof, and pulling down the walls was justified because the participants were servants of Jones H. Flournoy and others who claimed to be lawful owners of the lot and dwelling.

veyance and drove away from their home with moments to spare. When she looked back from a safe distance, she thought the entire building was burning. Members of the family recalled, "After driving rapidly for some time, grandmother gazed back at her beloved home, and saw the house in flames. Outlined against the flames were the fiendish forms of the mobbers who were battering to pieces the press which had been purchased at such a sacrifice." Sally was mistaken. The building was not set afire, but flames from burning papers may have been mixed with swirling dust from the falling building.[21]

In 1848, William McLellin published a statement providing a partial chronology of the day's happenings: "On Saturday, the 20th of July, 1833, about five hundred men assembled in Independence, and deliberately tore down a two story brick building, in which was a printing press and fixtures, which were partly destroyed, and thence they proceeded to demolish the store of A. S. Gilbert, but he agreed to pack his goods and cease trade, which for the time prevented their destruction."[22]

During the destruction of the Independence printing press, John's volume of holograph Book of Commandments revelations was somehow preserved. Probably he, Phelps, or a printing office employee seized it as the vigilantes were assembling and spirited it away to a place of safety.

The "press then and there set up for use, and the type furniture and apparatus ... had been wrongfully and injuriously put and placed ... encumbering the same." See Chiles, [Russell?], Hicks, Wilson, Young, Reynolds, Burden [Bradin?], and J. H. Bunch [history has not preserved the first names of all of these individuals], attorneys for the defendant, W. W. Phelps v. Richard Simpson et al., December 22, 1833. See also Phelps, Grant, and Fiske, *Appleton's Cyclopedia of American Biography*, cited in *Phelps Family History in America and Kindred Family Histories*, cited in *Phelps Family History in America and Kindred Family Histories*, accessed January 4, 2007, http://www.phelps-familyhistory.com/bios/william_wines_phelps.asp.

21. W. W. Phelps, grandson of W. W. and Sally Phelps, letter dated 20 July 1938. This letter states that on July 20, citizens of Jackson County, "proceeded immediately to demolish the brick printing office and dwelling house of W. W. Phelps & Co., and destroyed or took possession of the press, type, books and property of the establishment; at the same time turning Mrs. Phelps and children out of doors." Pratt, *History of the Late Persecution Inflicted by the State of Missouri Upon the Mormons*, also available online at Book of Abraham Project, accessed May 4, 2012, http://www.boap.org/LDS/Early-Saints/PPratt-pers.html.

22. McLellin, "Our Views Relative to the Legal Successor," 61.

McLellin also said the old settlers "next assembled around my house"—a cabin on Main Street. "But seeing them coming, I stepped a little out of the way"—meaning that he wisely sought refuge in the woods—"but their rage caused them to search our premises thoroughly."[23] Meanwhile, other groups headed west of town in search of other church members.

As the demolition of the printing office continued, Bishop Partridge must have retreated to his home, beyond the west edge of town. His wife, Lydia, who was recovering from the birth of Edward Jr. three weeks earlier, recalled, "While the mob, were gathering together for the purpose of carrying out their threats many of the brethren were hiding from them, but my husband said he would not run from them, as he was innocent of crime."[24]

Emily Partridge remembered that her mother "sent me, with my sister Harriet, to the spring, a short distance from the house, when we looked back and saw about fifty of the mob surrounding the house. We stood and looked at them until they rode away, then we went up to the house again. The mob had taken father with them.... They took him to Independence Square."[25]

Hiram Rathbun, whose family was among Mormonism's early converts, recalled, "They caught some of the elders of the church here, and among them my father [Robert Rathbun] and brought them up to the square to tar and feather them."[26] Chapman Duncan remembered in 1852: "Bishop Partridge, Chas. Allen, Harvey Allen, and myself were taken by the mob into town. They tarred Bishop Partridge and Allen's Brother;

---

23. Ibid.
24. Lydia Partridge, quoted in Edward Partridge Jr., "Journal of Edward Partridge," 15. Despite the title, it is a compilation of documents made by Edward Partridge's son in 1878.
25. Young, "Autobiography," p. 106. The girls were probably at Forbis Spring. A large spring with reputed medicinal qualities, it was located near the Partridge home on what is today the northwest corner of the intersection of River and Maple Streets. Joanne Chiles Eakin, verbal statement to the author, ca. 1995. Eakin is a lifelong resident of Jackson County, Missouri.
26. Robert Rathbun, ordained a high priest in the church, operated a blacksmith shop in Independence, Missouri. Temple Lot Case, 217.

Harvey and myself passed out through the mob unobserved, as they were gazing intently on the usual proceedings."[27]

For Partridge, the tarring and feathering represented the most brutal experience of his life. He left at least three records of his experience, which I have harmonized into one account for the purposes of this narrative:

> On the 20th day of July A.D. 1833 George Simpson and two other mobbers entered my house (whilst I was sitting with my wife, who was then quite feeble my youngest child being about three weeks old), and compelled me to go with them, soon after leaving my house I was surrounded by about fifty mobbers who escorted me about half a mile to the court house on the public square [in Independence].[28]
>
> A few rods from the court house, surrounded by hundreds of the mob, I was stripped of my hat, coat and vest.[29]
>
> Russel Hicks Esqr. appeared to be the head man of the mob, he told me that his word was the law of the county, and that I must agree to leave the county or suffer the consequences. I answered that if I must suffer for my religion, it was no more than others had done before me. That I had lived in the county for two years and I was not conscious of having injured any one in the county, therefore I could not consent to leave it. Mr. Hicks then proceeded to strip off my clothes and was disposed to strip them all off—I strongly protested against being stripped naked in the street, when some more humane than the rest interfered and I was permitted to wear my shirt and pantaloons.[30]
>
> Before tarring and feathering me I was permitted to speak. I told them that the Saints had suffered persecution in all ages of the world; that I had done nothing which ought to offend anyone; that if they abused me, they would abuse an innocent person; that I was willing to suffer for the sake of Christ; but to leave the country, I was not then willing to consent to it. By this time the multitude made so much

---

27. Duncan, autobiography, p. 31. Duncan also mentions Harvey Olmstead, whose affidavit supports Duncan's statement: "They tared and fetherd Bishop Partridge and they took me prisner ~~and kept~~." Harvey Olmstead, affidavit, p. 1. See also Johnson, *Mormon Redress Petitions*, 509.

28. Partridge, affidavit, p. 1.

29. Partridge, "History of Joseph Smith," 6:818–19.

30. Partridge, affidavit, p. 1; see also Johnson, *Mormon Redress Petitions*, 512–13. A portion of Partridge's petition is quoted in *History of the LDS Church*, 1:390–91.

noise that I could not be heard; some were cursing and swearing, saying, "call upon your Jesus," etc.; others were equally noisy in trying to still the rest, that they might be enabled to hear what I was saying. Until after I had spoken, I knew not what they intended to do with me, whether to kill me, to whip me, or what else I knew not.[31]

Tar and feathers were then brought and a man by the name of ____ Davis [blank in original] with the help of an other [Robert Johnson], daubed me with tar from the crown of my head to my feet.[32]

Next they ripped open a pillow and shook the feathers out on him.[33] Many in the crowd began to whistle like a cock partridge, in derision.[34] They rolled him in the feathers, covering his body.

According to Lydia Partridge, they "intended to whip him, but in this they were not agreed, and when one raised the whip another held him back saying that they had done enough, the crowd then parted."[35] According to Edward's own account, they turned him loose but focused their fury on the clothes they had taken from him. According to his affidavit, they "with great force and violence, rent, tore and damaged the clothes and wearing apparel, to wit, one coat, one hat, one waistcoat, one pair of breeches, one coat, one shirt, and one pair of stockings":[36]

31. Partridge, "History of Joseph Smith," 6:818–19.

32. Partridge, affidavit, p. 1.

33. Partridge, petition, quoted in Richards, "Missouri Petitions for Redress," 533–34; *History of the LDS Church,* 1:391. Partridge tells his story in his 1839 redress petition; it is also documented in the court records of the suit against those who tarred and feathered him. *Edward Partridge v. Samuel D. Lucas et. al.* For removing the tar, see also Lightner, *The Life and Testimony of Mary Lightner.*

34. Majors, *Seventy Years on the Frontier,* 46; Martin Rice, an old settler from Lone Jack, Missouri, wrote, "Some of the heathen gentiles about Independence got together, pulled down their printing office, tarred and feathered their Elder Partridge, and whistled Bob White at him." Rice, *Rural Rhymes and Talks and Tales of Olden Times,* 31.

35. Lydia Partridge, quoted in Edward Partridge Jr., "Journal of Edward Partridge," 15.

36. "Edward Partridge complains of [damaged original—Samuel D. Lucas], Russell Hicks, Lewis Franklin, Richard Simpson, George W. Simpson, Leonidas K. Oldham, Thomas W. Wilson, James M. Hunter, Henry Chiles, Nathan K. Olmstead, Zachariah Waller, Samuel [Weston], William L. Irwin, Samuel C. Owens, Aaron Overton, [John Harris, Harmon] Gregg, Jones H. Flournoy, Moses G. Wilson, Robert Johnson, James Campbell, Joel F. Chiles, Richard Fristoe, Abner F. Staples [Steeples], William [Conor], John Smith, John Davis, Joseph C. Davis, Thomas Pitcher, Gan Johnson, James Reynolds,

For this abuse I have never received any satisfaction, although [in 1833] I commenced a suit against some of them for $50,000. damage, and paid my lawyers six hundred dollars to carry it on, I also paid near two hundred dollars to get a change of venue.—My lawyers after getting their pay of me, made a compromise with the defendants without my consent, and threw my case out of court without giving me any damages by their agreeing to pay the costs, which they have never paid that I know of. And I never could prevail upon my lawyers to collect them for me though they agreed so to do.[37]

During this ordeal, Partridge made no effort to resist but instead "I bore my abuse with so much resignation and meekness, that it appeared to

---

James Cockrell, Jonathan Shepherd, John W. Danewood, Tarlton Elledge, David A. Stayton, John Cornet, John Cook, Daniel King, Edwin F. Hicks, William Masters, Richard W. Cummins, James P. Hickman, Richard McCarty, Allen Chandler, Robert Rickman, William Brown, Samuel Johnson, William Pugh, John Lewis, James McGee, Roland Flournoy, John M. Walker, and Benjamin Majors of a plea of trespass for which the said defendants, to wit, on the 25th [20th] day of July, 1833, with force and armed at the County of Jackson aforesaid, assaulted the said Edward Partridge, and then and there took and carried the said Edward into a public place in the town of Independence, and then and there, in the presence of a large concourse of people, indignantly and abusively treated the said Edward, and the said defendants then and there with great force and violence, shook and pulled him about the said Edward and cast and threw him down to and upon the ground, and then and there violently kicked the said Edward, and gave and struck him a great many other blows and strokes, and also then and there, with great force and violence, put on the body of the said Edward Partridge, a large quantity of pitch, and tar and completely covered his body therewith, and then and there rolled him in feathers, so as to completely cover his body with feathers, and then and there in that situation, turned him the said Edward loose, among the said large concourse of people, and then and there, with great force and violence, rent, tore and damaged the clothes and wearing apparel, to wit, one coat, one hat, one waistcoat, one pair of breeches, one coat, one shirt, and one pair of stockings of the said Edward, of great value, to wit, of the value of fifty dollars, which he, the said Edward, then and there, wore and was clothed with.... [T]he said Edward, was then and there greatly hurt, bruised and wounded, and then and there from the indignity and public insult offered him, was greatly insulted and suffered in his reputation and standing in society—To wit at the County of Jackson aforesaid and other wrongs to the said Edward then and there did, contrary to the form of Statute in such case, and to the great damage of the said Edward Partridge of fifty thousand dollars, and therefore he brings his suit: Wood, Atchison, Wells, Doniphan & Rees, attorneys for plaintiff," *Edward Partridge v. Samuel D. Lucas et al.*, quoted in Parkin, "A History of the Latter-day Saints in Clay County," 304.

37. Partridge, affidavit.

astound the multitude, who permitted me to retire in silence, many looking very solemn, their sympathies having been touched, as I thought; and
as to myself, I was so filled with the Spirit and love of God, that I had no
hatred towards my persecutors or anyone else."[38]

Charles Allen, who was also tarred and feathered at the same time,
followed Partridge's example. Charles's daughter, Maria Allen Galland, recalled the event in the 1890s, saying he would have been whipped except
that he was a Freemason: "My Father Charles Allen saw a crowd of the
mob and went to see what they ware doin they got holt of him and wanted
him to say he would give up his faith or leave the country he said he was
a free man and he intended to live thare and die thare so they tard and
fethered him. When they ware goin to whip him he maid the mason sine
of distres the whip was jurked out of the mans hand and as father was the
first to bee whipped they did not whip Brother Partridge."[39]

After returning from the spring with her sister Harriet, Emily Partridge stayed in the house throughout her father's ordeal:

> I stood at the window looking in the direction they had gone, won-
> dering what the mob were doing with father, for we could hear their
> yells and shouts, when I saw two men coming toward the house. One I
> knew—a young man by the name of Albert Jackson—he was carrying
> in his hand a hat, coat and vest. The other I thought was an Indian, and
> as they seemed to be coming right to the house I was frightened and
> ran upstairs; but when they came in it was our dear father, who had
> been tarred and feathered.[40]

Six-year-old Caroline hid in terror under the bed.[41] Eliza recalled
that the children were "very frightened" at "how my Father looked," but
"the Brethren were very kind and assisted my Father to rid himself of the
tar, but the clothes he had on were spoiled."[42] They worked late into the

---

38. Partridge, quoted in *History of the LDS Church*, 1:391.

39. Maria Galland, statement.

40. Young, "Autobiography," p. 106.

41. Caroline Partridge Lyman, quoted in Albert R. Lyman, "Edward Partridge Family," 19.

42. Eliza Maria Partridge Lyman, "Life and Journal," 3: "The next spring we moved into a
     house that my Father rented of Lilburn W. Boggs where we lived until he (my Father)
     built a house on his own land, here we lived while we staid in that country. In July 1833
     a number of armed men came to our house in the afternoon and took my Father to the

night, "removing the tar, [a] little at a time from ... sore and tender flesh, and all the time they were in suspense lest they be attacked again.... These ruffians had put acid in that tar, and wherever it touched the flesh it began at once to eat with a hot fury which made it imperative that it be promptly removed or its effects would be fatal."[43] Lydia Partridge recalled that "the tar was thoroughly through his hair, and all over his body except his face and the inside of his hands."[44]

Mary Lightner, then a girl of fifteen, recalled that "a friend who had helped remove the tar 'said it came off as easy as dust.'" This account contradicts others, and is probably an exaggeration intended to show the folly of Partridge's attackers.[45]

Church member Elizabeth Holsclaw, age unknown, lived near the courthouse square and witnessed the destruction, apparently having ventured out on the street: "They also broke open a store and scattered the goods in the streets and I saw two men that they had tard [*sic*] and feathered, they also cut open a feather bed in the yard destroyed a barrel of flower stoned houses, broke in windows and chased me."[46] Elizabeth apparently ran to the home of Widow Corkins, a neighbor. Lucy Corkins reported:

> A mob arose and demolished a two story brick building belonging to our people occupied as a dwelling house and a Printing Office and they broke the Press and strewed the type and papers and Book works in the street and they came and surrounded my house and fastened

<hr>

public square where they administered to him a coat of tar and feathers and raised a whip with the intention of whipping him but a friend to humanity interfered and prevented it. I well remember how my Father looked; we (the children) were very much frightened, my Mother was very weak having a babe (a boy named for his Father) but three weeks old. The Brethren were very kind and assisted my Father to rid himself of the tar, but the clothes he had on were spoiled."

43. Lyman, "Edward Partridge Family," 19; see also Roberts, *A Comprehensive History of the Church*, 1:333. Tar was sticky and would melt or soften when heated. But unlike the petroleum-based tar of our day, wagon drivers kept buckets of tree tar (pitch) on hand to dress wagon brakes. Edward's daughter Emily and a later account in the *Millennial Star* 61:435, suggest that acidic pearl ash had also been added to the tar to damage Partridge's skin.

44. Lydia Partridge, quoted in Edward Partridge Jr., "Journal of Edward Partridge," 15.

45. Barrett, "Mary Elizabeth Rollins Lightner," 7.

46. Holsclaw, affidavit, p. 1.

me in with others and would not suffer us to pass out and afterwards one broke into my house. I was a widow and had none to protect me from their insults and I saw that they had tarred and feathered [church men] and we was compelled to leave the county.[47]

Elizabeth Holsclaw agrees: They "fastened our doors, surrounded our house and would not let us pass out, there was 200 of them. And there was none with in but widdow [*sic*] women and children. Afterwards they broke open the door and rushd [*sic*] in with a Dirk knife upon us."[48] Apparently satisfied with terrifying the women and children, the armed men left without injuring anyone. According to the *Evening and the Morning Star,* these groups of men were looking "for other leading elders, but found them not," a search they pursued "with horrid yells and the most blasphemous epithets." By then it was night, so "they adjourned until the 23d inst."[49]

William McLellin, who was then living in Independence, explained that the old settlers "felt much chagrined at not being able to catch and abuse myself and Oliver Cowdery, [so] they offered that if any man would catch us and deliver us up to them on the 23rd, they would pay $80 for either of us."[50] Tuesday, July 23, was the date set for a follow-up meeting. As the vigilantes dispersed, the church members, anxious about their friends, slowly emerged from "their hiding places around the town of Independence; in the brush, basements, roof tops, and any place they could find to hide like foxes in holes."[51]

McLellin, writing thirty-seven years later, recalled that on Monday, July 22:

I slipped down into the Whitmer's settlement, and there in the lonely woods I met with David Whitmer and Oliver Cowdery. I said to them, "brethren I never have seen an open vision in my life, is that book of Mormon true"? Cowdery looked at me with solemnity depicted in his face, and said, "Brother William, God sent his holy An-

---

47. Corkins, affidavit, p. 1.

48. Holsclaw, affidavit, p. 1.

49. "To His Excellency, Daniel Dunklin, Governor of the State of Missouri," 114.

50. McLellin, "Our Views Relative to the Legal Successor of Joseph Smith," 61.

51. Kleinman, "Life Story of James Clark Owens, Sr.," 3; see also Roberts, *Missouri Persecutions,* 86.

gel to declare the truth of the translation of it to us, and therefore we *know*. And though the mob kill us, yet we must die declaring its truth." David said, "Oliver has told you the solemn truth, for we could not be deceived. I most truly declare ~~declare~~ to you its truth!" Said I, boys I believe you. I can see no object for you to tell me falsehood now, when our lives are endangered.[52]

Apparently, David Whitmer's resolve was soon put to the test. Either in Kaw Township, or perhaps after having ventured to Independence to assist church leaders, David was seized by old settlers. Then, they attempted to force him to recant his testimony. He later proclaimed: "I had a mob of from four to five hundred surrounding me at one time, demanding that I should deny my published statement in the Book of Mormon; but the testimony I bore the mob made them tremble before me."[53] John Greene, Brigham Young's brother-in-law, recorded another instance of this story: "The commanding officer then called twelve of his men, and ordered them to cock their guns and present them at the prisoner's breasts, and to be ready to fire when he gave the word,—he addressed the prisoners, threatening them with instant death, unless they denied the book of Mormon and confessed it to be a fraud; at the same time adding, that if they did so, they might enjoy the privileges of citizens. David Whitmer, hereupon, lifted up his hands and bore witness that the Book of Mormon was the Word

---

52. McLellin, "W. E. McLellan's [*sic*] Book," January 4, 1871. This source consists of three tantalizing photographic images of McLellin manuscript material, copied onto glass plate negatives, probably by C. Ed. Miller, RLDS graphic arts bureau, ca. 1920–40. One negative contains a close-up detail of the title page reading: "W. E. McLellan's Book Jan. 4th 1871." The other two images reproduce, in McLellin's hand, portions of a narrative from the bottom and top of consecutive manuscript pages. The original glass negatives are housed in the CofC Pictorial Archives in a photographic envelope sleeve bearing the following descriptive inscription: "McLellan Mss, Bk of Sermons, contains testimony of Book of Mormon witnesses, Wm. O. Robertson—priest, born 1881, in possession of mss., H. W. Burwell, President, Louisville Branch, 3243 Virginia Ave., Louisville Ky. [n.d.]." A note with the negatives reads: "Copies of W. E. Mclellan Book of Sermons in his handwriting. Book at present [n.d.] in possession of a Bro. Robertson of Louisville, Kentucky. F. F. Wipper." The images were media-substituted onto safety film in the 1980s.

53. David Whitmer, interview by James H. Hart, 3, reprinted in Cook, *David Whitmer Interviews*, 95–96, 97–98.

of God."[54] Once again, a leading church member responded to threats and violence with steadfast courage and nonviolence.

Oliver Cowdery stressed the contrast between the Mormons and the old settlers in describing this second confrontation:

> Early in the day, the mob again assembled to the number of about 500, many of them armed with rifles, dirks, pistols, clubs and whips; one or two companies riding into town bearing the red flag, raising again the HORRID YELL—They proceeded to take some of the leading elders by force declaring it to be their intention to whip them from fifty to five hundred lashes apiece, to demolish their dwelling houses, and let their negroes lose [*sic*] to go through our plantations and lay open our fields for the destruction of our crops.[55]

John commented in his history: "Tuesday arrived and death and destruction stared us in the face. The whole county turned out and surrounded us came to WW Phelps, and my house and took us upon the publick Square as also Partridge, Corrill, Morley, and Gilbert and were determined to massacre us unless we agreed to leave[e] the county immediately."[56] A petition to the governor adds these details: "Whereupon John Corrill[l], John Whitmer, W. W. Phelps, A. S. Gilbert, Edward Partridge, and Isaac Morley, made no resistance, but offered themselves a ransom for the church, willing to be scourged or die, if that would appease their anger toward the church."[57]

The significance of this selfless gesture by six of Zion's high priests was lost upon their attackers. The non-Mormons had resolved to drive every disciple out of Jackson County. Angry citizens again selected a committee who again demanded that church leaders agree to leave. By the day's end, Edward Partridge, Isaac Morley, John Corrill, W. W. Phelps, Sidney Gilbert, and John Whitmer had, under duress, signed a pledge agreeing to "remove with their families out of this county on or before the first day of

---

54. Greene, appendix, *Facts Relative to the Expulsion of the Mormons*, 17; see also, Heman C. Smith, "Editor Herald," *Herald*, 31:442.

55. "To His Excellency, Daniel Dunklin, Governor of the State of Missouri," 114.

56. Whitmer, Book of John Whitmer, chap. 10, p. 43.

57. "To His Excellency, Daniel Dunklin, Governor of the State of Missouri," in *History of the LDS Church*, 1:412.

January next ... and ... [to] use all their influence to induce all the brethren now here to remove as soon as possible–One half, say, by the first of January next, and all by the first day of April next. To advise and try all means in their power to stop any more of their sect from moving to this county, and as to those now on the road, they will use their influence to prevent their settling permanently in the county."[58]

W. W. Phelps estimated the church's financial losses at almost $7,000, enumerating "my printing office, a brick building ... type[,] paper and Book of Commandments nearly printed."[59] Some printed signatures of the Book of Commandments forms were salvaged and later bound by hand. Seven laborers lost their jobs and "three families [were] left destitute of the means of subsistence."[60]

As a result of this violence, Phelps was never able to begin Emma's hymnal, the almanac, or the envisioned religious curriculum for church youth.[61]

By early August, Oliver Cowdery was on his way to Ohio to report these developments in Jackson County to Joseph. The *Star* was in such demand by the church that Cowdery, on behalf of the literary firm, planned to secure another press and continue its publication from Kirtland, Ohio. One source suggests that Cowdery also carried the precious Book of Commandments manuscript with him.[62] During his absence, Elizabeth Ann Cowdery found shelter with her parents in the Whitmer Settlement.

58. Ibid., 114–15; see also Whitmer, Book of John Whitmer, chap. 10, pp. 43–44.

59. Phelps, "A Short History of W. W. Phelps' Stay in Missouri," 7.

60. *History of the LDS Church*, 1:114.

61. For plans to print Emma's hymnal, see *History of the LDS Church*, 1:270.

62. William E. McLellin to John L. Traughber, 14 December 1878, in Larson and Passey, *William E. McLellin Papers*, 510.

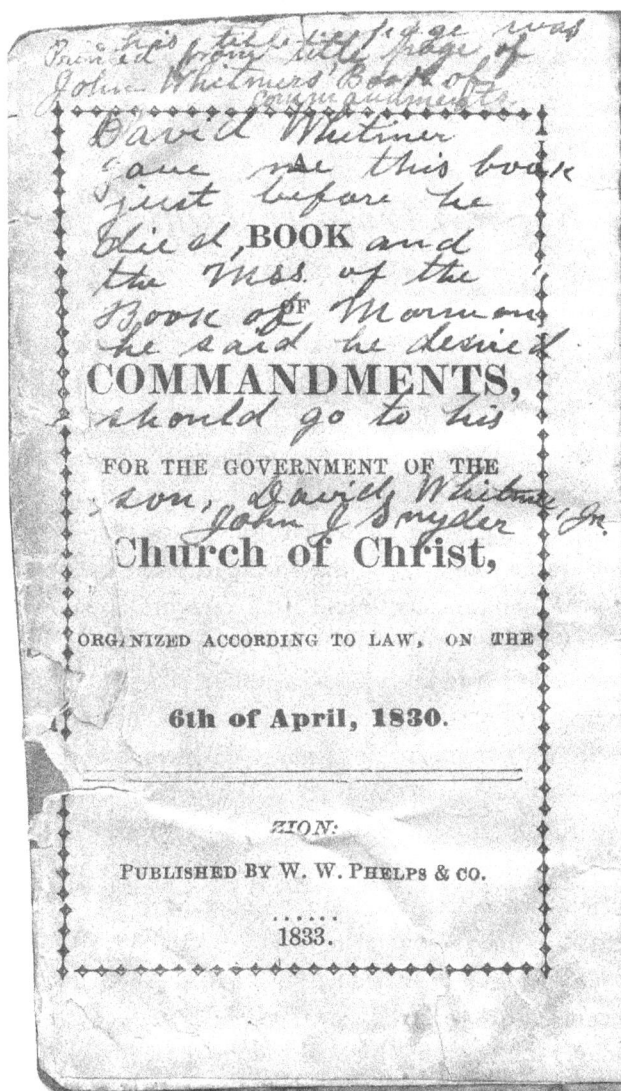

Title page of David Whitmer's copy of the Book of Commandments. The book was salvaged after the destruction of the church printing press operation in Independence, Missouri. Near his death, David gave his personal copy of the Book of Commandments to John Snyder, a member of the Whitmerite church. Courtesy of Community of Christ Archives.

CHAPTER FIFTEEN

Expulsion from Jackson County

HOSTILE CITIZEN RESISTANCE to the Mormon presence in July 1833 indelibly marked the future of the church. It was the beginning of the end of a short, young innocence for the organization. The early dreams of building the kingdom would never again be so sweet. It is not clear whether John, now jobless, and Sarah stayed in Independence, or whether they moved to the Whitmer Settlement to be nearer John's family. Sarah became pregnant in August, and the uncertainty about their future must have intensified John's anxiety to find a stable, secure situation.

Tension eased when the Mormons agreed to leave Jackson County. But as summer turned to fall, church members sought political and legal counsel, thinking that perhaps they might yet find a way to retain their homes and property. In inevitable response, a new round of violence flared up when Jackson County citizens perceived that church members were not actively preparing to move according to the forced agreement.

By early September, Oliver Cowdery reached Kirtland with the news of the violence inflicted on the Independence Saints on July 20 and 23. Joseph Smith convened a council and had Frederick G. Williams write to Jackson County church leaders advising them that "measures should be immediately taken to seek redress by the laws of [the] county."[1] Although technically proper, this counsel was already outpaced by events. Furthermore, this same letter continued with advice that was guaranteed to exacerbate tensions: "It has been manifested to Joseph, and communicated to me by him, that the brethren in Zion should not sell any of their inheritances, nor move out of the country, save those who signed the agreement to go."[2]

---

1.   Frederick G. Williams to Elders in Zion, 10 October 1833, *Times and Seasons*, April 15, 1845, 6:864.

2.   Ibid.

Church leaders in Missouri had not received this letter by September 28, 1833, when John Whitmer, Edward Partridge, Isaac Morley, John Corrill, William Phelps, Algernon Sidney Gilbert, and others—a total of 111 Mormon men—signed a petition forwarded to Governor David Dunklin. It asked the state to enforce the rights of church members and argued that the unusual civil unrest barred them from seeking legal redress through normal avenues.[3]

Upon receiving an encouraging response from Dunklin dated October 19, 1833, Missouri church members once again "began to labor as usual and build and set in order their houses, gardens, &c."[4] Writing from notes made in October 1833, John observed: "About these days we employed counselors to assist in prosecuting the law, which we had been advised by J. Smith Jr the seer to do. They employed Doniphan, Atchison, Rees, and Wood, of Liberty Clay County Mo. who engaged to carry on our Suits for $1,000.00 which was agreed to be paid by E. Partridge and W. W. Phelps which came from the church."[5]

During the preceding year, Joseph Smith had repeatedly reproved church leaders in Zion for various offenses. John was understandably a bit anxious about his own relationship with Joseph. Soon after Oliver left for Ohio, John wrote to Cowdery asking Oliver to "remember me to Joseph in a special manner, and enquire of him respecting my clerkship[;] you very well know what I mean & also my great desire of doing all things according to the mind of the Lord."[6] By "my clerkship," John was no doubt refer-

---

3. Partridge et. al., "To His Excellency Daniel Dunklin," *History of the LDS Church*, 1:410–15. A portion of this petition reads: "Influenced by the precepts of our beloved Savior when we have been smitten on the one cheek, we have turned the other also; when we have been sued at the law, and our coat been taken, we have given them our cloak also; when they have compelled us to go with them a mile, we have gone with them twain; we have borne the above outrages without murmuring; but we cannot patiently bear them any longer; according to the laws of God and man, we have borne enough." ... All this, knowing "that every officer, civil and military, with a very few exceptions, has pledged his life and honor to force us from the county, dead or alive; and believing that Civil process cannot be served without the aid of the executive" (415).

4. Governor Daniel Dunklin, reply to petition, 115. "History of Joseph Smith," *Times and Seasons*, 6:880.

5. Whitmer, Book of John Whitmer, chap. 10, p. 45.

6. John Whitmer to Oliver Cowdery, 29 July 1833.

ring to the interruption of his duties, both recording the official business of the church and his work in the printing office. There appears to be more to this story than we may ever know.

Meanwhile, in an attempt to get the literary firm back on its feet, Joseph sent Cowdery to New York with Newel K. Whitney, to purchase a press to replace the one the church had lost in Independence. Cowdery and Whitney returned with the press about December 1, 1833, and temporarily set it up in a large brick inn recently acquired by John Johnson, located on the corner in the Kirtland Flats diagonally from Whitney's store.[7] On December 18, Joseph dedicated the printing press "and all that pertained thereunto, to God."[8] The first issue of the *Evening and the Morning Star* printed in Kirtland was issued in December 1833.

On New Year's Day, Oliver wrote John, telling him that it was "the will of the Lord, or wisdom[,] that I should tarry here." He was naturally concerned about Elizabeth Ann: "I have not been able to ascertain where my wife was, though Brother Gilbert says she is well, and you say she is with Father and Mother. I suppose of course, you know, but it would be a satisfaction to me to know also. I want you to see her and hand her the following [ten dollars], and write me immediately."[9] At Oliver's request, John prepared and forwarded a list of former *Star* subscribers. Also, in January 1834, Oliver explained to his former colleagues in Missouri that they planned, in the spring, to move the press "on the hill near the Methodist meeting house" in Kirtland.[10]

Superseding even the construction of the House of the Lord, the firm quickly erected a temporary building to house the printing office. This multipurpose structure was available for use by February 1834, immediately west of the temple site. A council of Kirtland leaders met October 10, 1833, and decided "to discontinue the building of the Temple during the winter, for want of materials, and ... to recommence it early in the spring. It was also agreed that we should set the hands immediately to erect a house for

7.	Berrett, *Sacred Places: A Comprehensive Guide to Early LDS Historical Sites*, 3:17; On December 4, 1833, Cowdery and Whitney "commenced distributing the type." *History of the LDS Church*, 1:448.

8.	Ibid., 1:465.

9.	Oliver Cowdery to John Whitmer, 1 January 1834.

10.	Oliver Cowdery to William W. Phelps and John Whitmer, 21 January 1834.

the printing office, which is to be thirty by thirty-eight feet on the ground; the first story to be occupied for the School of the Prophets this winter, and the upper story for the printing press."[11] Designers also converted the building's attic or loft into meeting room space. Here, Joseph Smith temporarily set up his office. It also housed council meetings and priesthood activities.[12]

Meanwhile, circumstances had worsened in Jackson County. Nonmembers were unified in their desire to remove all Mormons from Jackson County. But despite rough talk, there was probably no initial intention to actually kill anyone. Interpersonal disputes were a kind of sport. There were frontier rules for conducting disputes; fist-fights, club-swinging, gouging, and knifings were common, but seldom was someone actually killed.[13]

During the fall, raiding parties began swooping down on Mormon settlements, wrenching log cabins apart, burning crops, and beating the men. Women and children were usually not mistreated. Despite the general nonresistance of the Mormons, their stubborn staying resulted in escalations of violence. Although the old-settler posses carried guns, they typically fired through houses or into the air, obviously with the intent of frightening the Mormons.

Church leaders were at a loss about how to respond. Although Cowdery was not present, he obviously formed his picture of events based on reports of participants and later, around February 1834, summarized the church's transition. "Having passed through the most aggravated insults and injuries, without making the least resistance, a general inquiry

11. Frederick Granger Williams to Dear Brethren [in Missouri], 10 October 1833. Reprinted in *History of the LDS Church,* 1:417.

12. Joseph's 1835–36 journal recorded on Thursday, 21 January 1835, "At about 3 o'clock P.M. I dismissed the [Hebrew] School. The Presidency retired to the loft of the printing office, where we attended to the ordinance of washing our bodies in pure water. We also perfumed our bodies and our heads in the name of the Lord." Faulring, *An American Prophet's Record,* 118.

13. "The philosophy of violence, combined with the accepted belief that a gentleman was above the law when it came to the defense of honor, set dangerous precedents." Steward, *Duels and the Roots of Violence in Missouri,* 4. Frontier men of status tended to settle serious personal differences by dueling, while "disputes between common men—the farmers and merchants—were settled with their fists." Kimmel and Aronson, "Guns," *Men and Masculinities,* 1:364.

prevailed at this time, throughout the Church, as to the propriety of self defense."[14] Lyman Wight, a New Yorker with frontier attitudes and no particular disposition toward meekness, had earned the respect of non-members because of his fighting skills and strongly advocated that church members act in their own defense.

Back in Ohio, Joseph Smith received a revelation on August 6, 1833 (CofC D&C 95; LDS D&C 98), that expressed the underlying Christian paradox of mercy versus justice. Smith's view of the gospel principle of Christian restraint included this interpretation: "If there was no threat to life, no matter what the number of provocations, it was better to spare an enemy and 'be rewarded for righteousness than to respond in kind.'"[15] Nevertheless, under certain circumstances, the Saints could have divine permission to fight back. Joseph's counsel provided members with a necessary rationale for a more aggressive response. Smith's revelatory guidelines instructed disciples to meet each provocation as a group with an offer of peace; if their overtures were rejected three times, then members could defend themselves with force (CofC D&C 95:6c–d; LDS D&C 98:34–36). The LDS *History of the Church* explains, "Soon after the arrival of Oliver Cowdery at Kirtland, arrangements were made to dispatch Elders Orson Hyde and John Gould to Jackson County, Missouri, with advice to the Saints in their unfortunate situation."[16] Elders Hyde and Gould would have most certainly carried a copy of Smith's revelation, advising church members to "renounce war and proclaim peace" (CofC D&C 95:3d; LDS D&C 98:16). Elders Hyde and Gould arrived in Jackson County around the end of September 1833.[17] John Whitmer would have been among key leaders who initially received Smith's instruction from Kirtland. Partridge had powerfully modeled the pacifistic approach during his public tarring and feathering. Smith's advice also seemed to support such continued nonviolence.

---

14. [Oliver Cowdery], "'The Mormons' So Called," *Evening and the Morning Star Extra*, February 1834; see also [Oliver Cowdery], *Star Extra,* February 1834, reproduced in Crawley, "Two Rare Missouri Documents," 502–15; and also in Flake, *A Mormon Bibliography, 1830–1930,* 226.

15. Stott, "Just War, Holy War, and Joseph Smith, Jr.," 138.

16. *History of the LDS Church,* 1:407.

17. Ibid., 1:410.

However, some members, such as Lyman Wight, favored being more assertive. Because of his frontier-style approach to conflict, Wight's non-member neighbors had already learned it was not easy to push him around. John Whitmer also knew about Wight's determined and courageous personality. Between February and April 1831, John and Lyman had served a successful mission in the Nelson, Portage County, Ohio, area where they "built a branch of the Church of Christ."[18] Many of Wight's converts who gathered to Jackson County continued to look personally to Wight for guidance. Wight had also been responsible for resettling a number of converts from Cincinnati, Ohio, into the Big Blue Settlement in Missouri. As the situation worsened for the Missouri colonists, members felt less assurance in Partridge's nonviolent example and were increasingly swayed by Lyman Wight's more militant urgings.

Hyde and Gould, during their brief stay in Jackson County, could see the condition of their fellow church members rapidly deteriorating. Hyde noted in his journal:

> We delivered our letters and documents, and were sometimes surrounded by the mob, who threatened to wring our heads off from our shoulders. Several little skirmishes took place while there, and some few were killed and wounded. Times began to be warm, and expulsion seemed inevitable. The Saints began to flee over the river to Clay County, and we, having done all we could, took a steamer for St. Louis on our return home. We arrived home in Kirtland in the month of November 1833.[19]

The most serious clash yet between the Mormon disciples and local citizens of Jackson County erupted at the Whitmer Settlement during the night of October 31–November 1, 1833. This would have directly impacted John's family. As part of the countywide conflict, about fifty nonmembers, many with firearms, raided the settlement. Ten or twelve houses belonging to church members were unroofed and partly demolished. The Missourians also "took two of the Mormonite men and beat them with stones and

---

18. D&C 42; Book of Commandments 44. See also Westergren, *From Historian to Dissident*, 55; Whitmer, Book of John Whitmer, chap. 6, p. 24. John Whitmer had returned to Kirtland briefly during this mission when he was called to be church historian on March 8, 1831.

19. Hyde, "History of Orson Hyde," 790.

clubs, leaving barely a breath of life in them."²⁰ George Beebe was the first victim of these brutal beatings, and John's brother-in-law, Hiram Page, was the second. The women and children, roused from sleep, ran into the woods in terror. Philo Dibble, a resident of Whitmer Settlement, later recalled that anxious night:

> About one hundred and fifty came upon us in the dead hour of night, tore down a number of our houses and whipped and abused several of our brethren. I was aroused from my sleep by the noise caused by the falling houses, and had barely time to escape to the woods with my wife and two children when they reached my house and proceeded to break in the door and tear the roof off. I was some distance away from where the whipping occurred, but I heard the blows of heavy ox goads upon the backs of my brethren distinctly.²¹

Hiram Page had tried to avoid a beating by subterfuge when his cabin was assaulted by forty men who simultaneously broke in all the windows and doors. He hurriedly dressed in Catherine's clothes, hoping that this disguise and the darkness would protect him. Catherine, five-year-old John, and two-year-old Elizabeth were lined up outside the cabin, guarded by men with rifles pointed at them. The men shouted that if Page did not come out, his family would be shot. Hiram emerged carrying their youngest son—Philander, who had been born a year before—in his arms. The disguise did not work. General Wilson, leader of the mob, told his men that the woman was "too d—d tall." At his command, they stripped Page and beat him mercilessly. Sixty or seventy times the hickory withes fell upon his back as Catherine and the children looked on in horror. So severe were his injuries they feared for his life.²² Hiram survived, but he

---

20. Orson Hyde to editors of *Booneville Herald*, 8 November 1833, 117. Hyde and Gould wrote their account after having learned details of the attack on the Whitmer Settlement secondhand while aboard a Missouri River steamboat en route back to Kirtland.

21. Dibble, *Early Scenes in Church History*, 82.

22. *History of the LDS Church*, 4:394–95; "The Outrage in Missouri," *Evening and the Morning Star*, December 1833, 119; quoted in Stewart, "Hiram Page," 43. A variety of implements were used to assail unfortunate recipients of this abusive treatment: Ox goads, withes, whips, clubs, and even gun breaches are mentioned in members' written accounts.

was scarred for life. William McLellin, who was then in Jackson County, Missouri, later reported this version of events:

> In 1833 some young men ran down Hiram Page in the woods one of the eight witnesses, and commenced beating and pounding him with whips and clubs. He begged, but there was no mercy. They said he was a damned Mormon, and they meant to beat him to death! But finally one [of] them said to him, if you will deny that damned book, we will let you go. Said he, how can I deny what I know to be true? Then they pounded him again. When they thought he was about to breathe his last they said to him Now what do you think of your God, when he dont save you?[23]

News of this devastating raid rapidly spread among church members. David Whitmer led an effort to secure a peace warrant against some of those known to be mob leaders. This effort met with passive resistance from local lawmen. On Sunday, November 3, 1833, church men Joshua Lewis, Parley P. Pratt, and Thomas B. Marsh, taking with them Hiram Page, who was well enough to travel but who was a walking visual aid of the brutal attack, traveled to Lexington, Missouri, forty miles from Independence. There they attempted to obtain a peace warrant from the circuit judge. But Judge Ryland "refused to issue any process against the mob, and advised that the Saints fight and kill the mob whenever the latter came upon them."[24] The night after (Monday, November 4, 1833), the mob again threatened different areas. Church leaders advised members in each branch to gather into bodies as best they could for their own preservation.[25]

That night of October 31–November 1 was pivotal in the life of the church. The church had announced bold doctrines and confrontational claims. Yet, despite the violence visited upon them, many church members individually continued to enact Christ's pronouncement to turn the other cheek. However, when attackers rejected their determined peacekeeping efforts and aggression against them escalated, the vulnerable Saints responded by steadily moving toward a decided defense of their own persons

---

23. McLellin, "W. E. McLellan's [*sic*] Book," January 4, 1871.

24. Pratt, "A History, of the Persecution," 37, quoted in *History of the LDS Church*, 1:429.

25. Corrill to Oliver Cowdery, December 1833, reproduced as "From Missouri," 124.

and property. Their untried religion presented a paradox they were unable to solve during a time of life-and-death testing.

In the end, members followed Lyman Wight's more militant stance rather than Partridge's example of meek suffering and resolute nonviolence. Once introduced, this militaristic reaction continued to intensify, setting off a spiraling reaction of accelerating hostilities. The result was the final expulsion of the church from Jackson County in November 1833. Ironically, the Mormons' resort to force would ultimately prove no more successful than nonviolence.

Additional attacks on church members followed at Independence and other settlements in late October and early November. Then, on Monday, November 4, 1833, a large party of Missourians gathered at Wilson's Store above the Blue River. Orrin Rockwell and his son, Orrin Porter Rockwell, who had both joined the church in New York within days of its organization, were running the ferry across the Blue. Disgruntled citizens took the boat, uttered additional threats, and, eventually, returned to Wilson's Store. However, the Mormons who had assembled the previous night at the Colesville Branch on the west side of the Blue, seeking safety in numbers, heard that the mob was doing damage on the east side of the Blue and that the brethren there needed help.[26] That was followed by "an affray between an organized mob of about eighty citizens and about eighteen Mormons."[27]

Two Mormon participants left excellent resources for reconstructing this battle. Henry Alanson Cleveland, a twenty-four-year-old convert from Kirtland, left a detailed description, and Levi Jackman, a resident of the Whitmer Settlement, later drew a map which detailed the settlement's center and battle details.[28]

The Colesville group sent out a small party, which included David Whitmer and Newel Knight, to scout out the mob's location and activities.[29] After going partway toward the Big Blue Settlement, they learned

---

26. Ibid.

27. David Whitmer, "Mormonism: Authentic Account," 198.

28. Henry Alanson Cleveland to LDS Church Historian, 1854, in Journal History, 4 November 1833, 7–8; Jackman, "Battle above Big Blue, November 24, 1833."

29. Cleveland to LDS Church Historian, in Journal History, 4 November 1833, 7–8.

that the body of men had returned to Wilson's Store and started to return to Colesville. But Wilson's son, who was driving the family milk cows in from grazing, saw the Mormon scouts and told his father.[30] According to Bishop Partridge's counselor, John Corrill, "a party of them, thirty or forty started on horse back with guns to fall upon our men; and after riding two or two and a half miles they overtook them."[31] Seeing the armed party, "We were obliged to scatter in every direction in order to save [our] lives," Cleveland wrote.[32]

Their pursuers continued on to the Whitmer Settlement, engrossed in the hunt. "They searched in the cornfield of Christian Whitmer, and fed their horses freely upon his corn. They also took Christian and pointed their guns at him, threatening to kill him if he did not tell them where the brethren were. They also got up on the top of his house, and threatened some women and children."[33]

Messengers rode hard to Colesville and raised a company to disperse the aggressors. David Whitmer and Caleb Baldwin were selected as leaders. David recalled: "At the time the alarm was given Philo Dibble and myself were standing as picket guards and we immediately started for the Timber Branch, but before arriving there we waited till the company came up, when we found that they had raised nearly 30 men with 18 or 20 guns and one pistol." Harkening back to his training with the Seneca Grenadiers, David Whitmer divided the company, Caleb Baldwin taking command of one unit while he led the other.[34]

According to Henry Cleveland, the attackers:

> About 60 <in> number, were first discovered about sunset tearing down Christian Whitmer's house. D. Whitmer's company, to which I was attached, marched down the street toward the house, while C. Baldwin's men took across the lots. When we arrived within gun shot, one of the mob captains, Brazeal, rallied his forces and shouted, "The Mormons are for a fight, give them hell." Two or three guns were then

30. Majors, *Seventy Years on the Frontier*, 46–47.

31. Corrill, "From Missouri," 124.

32. Cleveland to LDS Church Historian, 1854, in Journal History, 4 November 1833, 7–8.

33. Corrill, "From Missouri," 124.

34. Cleveland to LDS Church Historian, 1854, in Journal History, 4 November 1833, 7–8.

discharged, which we immediately answered by a general discharge. The mob fired again, when I received a ball in my left shoulder, which disabled me from action, but our company immediately rushed upon and dispersed the enemy, leaving their wounded and arms.[35]

David corroborated: The attackers "destroyed a number of our dwellings and fired upon the little party of Mormons, killing one young man and wounding several others. The Mormons returned the fire, killing the leader of the mob, a Campbellite preacher, named Lovett."[36]

Five of the Whitmer men had been involved in the skirmish. Christian Whitmer and his family were no doubt traumatized as violence erupted in their settlement. David played a central role commanding the Mormon defenders. Philo Dibble's partial list of other Mormons in the battle includes Peter Whitmer and Hiram Page, despite his beating less than a week before. Jacob Whitmer was shot in the wrist during the battle.[37] There is no documentation of John's activities—whether he was in Independence or at the Whitmer Settlement.

After Henry Cleveland was wounded, he was immediately taken to the nearest house—the Peter Whitmer Sr. home. The sixty-year-old Whitmer "refused to receive me into his dwelling, fearing that the mob would discover me and destroy his family. I was then removed to Nathan West's house."[38] Philo Dibble was shot in the abdomen with "an ounce ball and two buck shot, all entering my body just at the right side of my navel." Abdominal wounds usually resulted in an agonizing and lingering death from gangrene and infection in those pre-antibiotic days. But, apparently, Dibble was not incapacitated, for he continued the engagement:

> After the battle I took my gun and powder horn and started for home. When I got about half way I became faint and thirsty. I wanted to stop at Brother Whitmer's [Peter Sr.'s] to lay down. The house, however, was full of women and children, and they were so frightened that they objected to my entering, as the mob had threatened that wherever they found a wounded man they would kill men, women and children.

35. Ibid.

36. David Whitmer, "Mormonism: Authentic Account," 198.

37. Dibble, statement, 15 April 1861, in Journal History, 4 November 1833.

38. Cleveland to LDS Church Historian, 1854, Journal History, 4 November 1833.

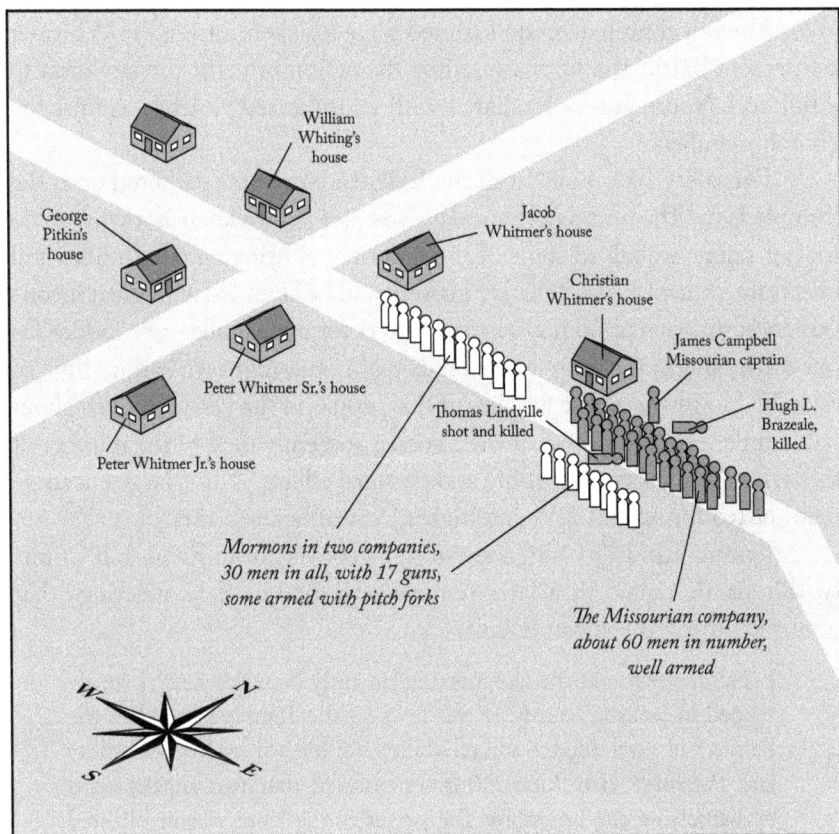

Fig. 15.1. Detail Map of the Whitmer Settlement battle, showing house locations. The "battle above the Big Blue" took place the evening of November 4, 1833. This map is based on a sketch of the battle by Levi Jackman.

I continued on and arrived home, or rather at a house in the field that the mob had not torn down, which was near my own home.... I bled inwardly until my body was filled with blood, and remained in this condition until the next day.... David Whitmer, however, sent me word that I should live and not die.... Brother Newel Knight came to see me ... He laid his right hand on my head ... and I knew immediately that I was going to be healed.[39]

Indeed, Dibble fully recovered.

39. Dibble, *Early Scenes in Church History*, 84–85.

Though church defenders routed their attackers during the Whitmer Settlement battle, the furor caused by the action brought the situation to a full boil. Nonmembers retaliated with an increased violence against the church members.

For safety, Mormons from the Independence area gathered onto the Temple Lot. "The next day, [Saturday, Nov. 2, 1833,] we knew not what to do for our safety; we talked some of the propriety of bringing our families and effects into one place; and this we knew would be attended with great inconvenience; for we had no houses nor shelters for our families, nor fodder for our cattle; and as the mob was upon us night after night we had no time to do it."[40] However, "all the families of this people, in the village, moved about half a mile west, with most of their goods; and embodied to the number of thirty, for the preservation of life and personal effects."[41] This large encampment lasted for several days and nights, November 2–9, 1833.

Jemima Lindsey Calif, a senior-aged convert from Randolph County, Illinois, described in a later reminiscence one of their meetings that occurred during the encampment:

> I shall never forget the last meeting [in early November 1833] we attended in Jackson county. It was held on the Temple Lot. After the Saints had assembled, some children were blessed by Brn. Cowdery and Partridge. Bro. John Whitmer testified that two angels stood by witnessing the ceremony. The power of the Lord was manifested through the gifts of the gospel, prophecy, tongues, interpretations, &c.; and in the trying days which followed, we often thought of that last meeting, it was a source of joy and consolation to our troubled hearts.[42]

The second evening "while we were gathered on the temple lot, the word came [by an express from the village after midnight] from the spies that the mob was destroying and stealing goods from the store in the town in the care of A. S. Gilbert.... [M]en volunteered to go into the town under the command of Elder Lyman Wight, this is the man the mob feared. There

---

40. Corrill, "From Missouri," 125.

41. [Oliver Cowdery], *Star Extra.*

42. Calif, letter to the editor, *Herald,* 28:208.

Church members began fleeing Jackson County, Missouri, en mass, around
November 13, 1833, seeking passage across the Missouri River to Clay County.
Courtesy of Community of Christ Archives.

was not one gun ordered to be fired."[43] "We immediately repared to the
Store and though[t] if posible to Save the property."[44] "As we drew near the
store of brother Gilbert, we saw a number of men sending stones and brick
bats against the same."[45] "The mob disbursed [dispersed] at our approach.
The church store kept on the public square we found had been sacked and
the goods were strewed over the street."[46]

Lyman Wight returned to the settlements around the Big Blue
River and recruited church men to come aid their Independence brethren. As Wight's force approached the town on the morning of Tuesday,
November 5, 1833, a hastily assembled body of Jackson County militiamen
commanded by Colonel Thomas Pitcher blocked their way. Outnumbered,
Wight's men and defenders already in Independence were subsequently
forced to surrender their arms. No longer able to defend themselves, "On

43. Duncan, insert from *Star Extra*.

44. Isaac Morley, affidavit.

45. Corrill, *Evening and the Morning Star*, 125.

46. Duncan, *Star Extra*.

Tuesday and Wednesday nights, the 5th and 6th of November, women and children fled in every direction before the merciless mob."[47] Jemima Calif reported her family was "forced by the mob to leave [the county] on the 9th of November 1833."[48]

Before abandoning the Whitmer Settlement, Hiram Page "prophesied ... that the stars would fall from heaven and frighten many people." David Whitmer was among those who took this prediction seriously, and later recorded: "I could give you many instances of true prophesies which came through the...named brethren: [John, Peter, Christian Whitmer, Ziba Peterson, Oliver Cowdery, Parley P. Pratt and Orson Pratt, and Hiram Page]."[49] Group cohesion disintegrated. Saints from some of the church settlements attempted to travel together, while individuals from others went in their own direction.

Julia Ann Whitmer was in the last stages of pregnancy, so she and David remained behind until the baby was born, apparently undetected by the old settlers. Their firstborn, David John, was born in a cold and empty Whitmer Settlement, November 27, 1833.[50]

The Clay County line was just across the Missouri River, less than two miles north of Independence. Clay County was more settled than Jackson, having been created in 1822, five years before Jackson. Clay County residents initially welcomed the refugees, a merciful response, since the weather took a turn for the worse, adding to the misery of the exodus.

Mormon refugees set up temporary camps along the Clay County side of the Missouri River in an effort to sustain life itself through the harsh conditions. Some with more opportunity and means pushed farther into the county, taking up residence in abandoned buildings or finding the best situations they could.

John's family—his parents, three brothers, and their families—went to the vicinity of Liberty, the seat of Clay County, where, on November 16, 1833, John was fortunately able to rent a house from a local citizen, Michael

---

47. "History of Joseph Smith," 6:897.

48. Calif, letter to the editor, *Herald*, 28:208.

49. David Whitmer, *Address to All Believers in Christ*, 32.

50. Wilcox, *Latter Day Saints on the Missouri Frontier*, 105. See also Blankmeyer, *David Whitmer, Witness for God*, 33.

Arthur. Their arrival nearly coincided with the memorable "night the stars fell."[51] The Saints received this spectacular meteor shower as a testimony that Jesus Christ's Second Coming was near—then all that they had suffered for his sake would be put right.

Because housing proved difficult to arrange, the larger Whitmer family scattered for a time. At first, John supported his family by taking odd jobs, such as pulling corn, making ax handles, butchering, and chopping wood for Arthur or fellow exiled church members. For a time he sublet a chamber of his home to Solomon Daniels.[52] Later, he and Sarah moved into the chamber themselves.

On December 19–20, John attended a court of inquiry at Liberty, called by the state, to investigate the actions of Colonel Thomas Pitcher who had commanded the Jackson County militia in its illegal role in disarming church members and hastening their 1833 expulsion from the county. On February 24, 1834, the court convened in Independence; but Missourian citizens "so intimidated the court that no trial was held."[53] John also attended various church council meetings and helped John Higbee build a home on March 1, 1834. Because of his role in the literary firm in Independence, John retained possession of some printed matter that survived the destruction of the printing office and exodus. His account book details sales of unbound copies of the Book of Commandments to

51. Whitmer, account book, 16 November 1833, p. 5. The annual Leonid Meteor Shower of November 13, 1833, was more spectacular than usual, producing one of the most memorable light shows ever seen over the eastern United States. During the early morning hours, the skies were lit by thousands of shooting stars every minute. Samuel Rogers, an itinerant minister in the East wrote, "I heard one of the children cry out, in a voice expressive of alarm: 'Come to the door, father, the world is surely coming to an end.' Another exclaimed: 'See! The whole heavens are on fire! All the stars are falling!' These cries brought us all into the open yard, to gaze upon the grandest and most beautiful scene my eyes have ever beheld. It did appear as if every star had left its moorings, and was drifting rapidly in a westerly direction, leaving behind a track of light which remained visible for several seconds. Some of those wandering stars seemed as large as the full moon, or nearly so." Samuel Rogers, "Toils and Struggles of the Olden Times," The Great Leonid Meteor Storm of 1833, Hill Freeburn, "Leonids 1833," accessed July 31, 2013, http://freepages.genealogy.rootsweb.ancestry.com/~wjohn55447/leonids%20 1833.htm.

52. Whitmer, account book, 10 December 1834, p. 5.

53. *History of the RLDS Church*, 1:407.

Saints—for instance, "Let Lyman Wight have Book of Commandments [$].25" on July 13, 1834.[54] John may have been selling the books as an agent for the literary firm or as compensation for his work as a member of the firm. Hyrum Smith had formerly sold copies of the Book of Mormon in Ohio on a similar basis.[55] Following the destruction of the Independence printing press, John apparently also retained custody of the holograph Book of Commandments and Revelations. He made updates through the summer of 1834, and eventually filled the bound volume.[56]

John briefly taught school in Liberty that spring, March 18–June 16, 1834.[57] On April 8, John noted in his account book that "Elizabeth" joined their household.[58] This Elizabeth may have been Elizabeth Schott Whitmer, Jacob's wife, or another Elizabeth from the extended church community. It seems more likely, however, that this woman was John's sister, Elizabeth Ann. Her husband, Oliver Cowdery, was still in Kirtland; and Sarah, now in the last stages of pregnancy, needed household help. Nancy Jane was born May 28; but just six days later on June 3, John was called home from school. He noted tersely: "infant died."[59] The next day, he was back at school teaching.

John devoted a significant portion of his manuscript history to describing this period. It was clearly compiled later, although it is not possible to determine the date of composition. The last half of chapter 10 through chapter 13 describes the church's expulsion from Jackson County. John played an integral role as scribe for extensive correspondence, as church leaders struggled to secure redress from state and local officials, and he integrated verbatim copies of letters to and from Governor Daniel Dunklin into his account. These chapters about the situation of the Missouri church are actually only a thinly veiled narrative of his family's experience as they labored on, daily hoping to return to their homes and property in Jackson County: "We had hard struggling to obtain a living as may well be under-

54. Whitmer, account book, 13 July 1834, p. 12.
55. Corbett, *Hyrum Smith, Patriarch*, 64.
56. Jensen, "From Manuscript to Printed Page," 39.
57. Whitmer, account book, 18 March–16 June 1834, pp. 8–11.
58. Ibid., p. 10.
59. Ibid.

stood, being driven having no money, or means to subsist upon, and being among strangers in a strange place; being despised, mocked at, and laughed to scorn by some, and pitied by others.... Thus we lived from Nov 1833 till May 1834, and but little prospect yet to return to our homes in Jackson Co. in safety—the mob rages, and the people's hearts are hardened, and the saints are few in number, and poor, afflicted, cast out, and smitten by their enemies."[60] One cannot help sympathizing with John as the Whitmers, and the Saints in general, endured this bleak period.

In the spring of 1834, Joseph Smith shepherded Zion's Camp to Missouri. He had organized this group of men with the hope of helping the dispossessed Saints return to their lands in Jackson County. John wrote that, as Zion's Camp neared Liberty in Clay County, they stopped initially "at Fishing River, where the enemy desired to head them [off] being led by Priests &c. But God interposed and sent a storm of Thunder lightening and rain at an astonishing rate. Which stopped our enemies in consequence of the flood of water which swelled the river and made it impassable."[61]

The day following the storm, June 22, 1834, John "went beyond fishing river to the Camp of Saints" to meet with these Kirtland supporters. The next day, Joseph "Recd. a revelation at the camp."[62] The revelation, since known as the "Fishing River revelation," indicated: "The first Elders were to receive their endowment at Kirtland Ohio in the house of the Lord built in that stake."[63] It specified that John, David, and thirteen other church leaders in Missouri were to return to Kirtland to receive their endowments. Heber C. Kimball, a thirty-three-year-old convert from New York, noted, "John Whitmer is called and chosen, and it is appointed to him to receive his endowment in Kirtland, with power from on high; and continue in his office."[64]

---

60. Whitmer, Book of John Whitmer, chap. 12, pp. 60–61.

61. Ibid., chap. 13, p. 67.

62. Whitmer, account book, 22–23 June 1834, p. 11.

63. CofC D&C 102; LDS D&C 105; Whitmer, Book of John Whitmer, chap. 13, p. 68.

64. Kimball, "Extracts from H. C. Kimball's Journal," 1105–6; see also Heber C. Kimball, Diary 1834–35, in Kimball, *On the Potter's Wheel,* appendix B, 194–95.

While camped at Fishing River, some members of the camp began showing symptoms of cholera. John returned home on June 24 while the camp moved to Burket's field on Rush Creek, about two miles east of Liberty. The epidemic moved with them, striking the camp with deadly force on June 26, with fresh cases occurring over the next four days.

John wrote, "Joseph the Seer had frequently exhorted the Saint[s] on their way up that if they would not heed his words the Lord would scourge them. The Cholera broke out in the camp an[d] several died with it to the grief and sorrow of the brethren—and lamentation of their wives and families. The Camp immediately scattered in the Counties of Ray and Clay. Some returned to Kirtland immediately, while others tarried."[65]

Joseph ordered Zion's Camp disbanded and directed the members to return home as best they could. Heber C. Kimball was among those stricken with the cholera. He found refuge in the home of Peter Whitmer Jr. in Liberty, "which place I reached with difficulty, being much afflicted myself with the disease that was among us. I stayed there until I started for home. I received great kindness from them and also from sister Vienna Jaques, who administered to my wants and also to my brethren—may the Lord reward them for their kindness."[66]

John noted further that because of the cholera, Joseph "Received a[nother] revelation that it was not wisdom to go to Jackson county at this time and that the armies of Israel should become very great and terrible first, and the Servants of the Lord [need to have] been <en>dowed with power from on high previous to the Redemption of Zion. Thus our fond hopes of being redeemed at this time were blasted at least for a season."[67]

Camp participants scattered from the site of the cholera attack seeking refuge in the various settlements of Saints across Clay County. Joseph went to a small settlement several miles west of Liberty for a few days. It was probably the Hulet Branch, where Peter Sr. and Mary Whitmer were living.

Before returning to Ohio, Joseph Smith convened a conference on July 3, 1834. The conference convened a short distance southwest of Liberty

---

65. Whitmer, Book of John Whitmer, chap. 13, p. 67.

66. Heber C. Kimball, diary, in Kimball, *On the Potter's Wheel*, 200.

67. Whitmer, Book of John Whitmer, chap. 13, pp. 67–68.

on the farm of nonmember friend, Michael Arthur, where John Whitmer, Lyman Wight, and other disciples had found refuge. During this
multiple-day event, Joseph organized the Missouri church. Despite former
administrative modifications, tensions over authority continued. Joseph
added another new church administrative layer—establishing a Missouri
presidency, complemented by a high council of twelve high priests. He
named David Whitmer as president of the church in Missouri, perhaps
as recognition of David's leadership gifts and staunch friendship and support. William McLellin, remembering the event some thirteen years later,
quoted Joseph as saying:

> Now, brethren, there has been an anxiety in the minds of many to
> know who, if I would be taken, would be the ONE to lead this Church
> "in my stead." I want now to put that matter to rest.["] Joseph then
> called David Whitmore [*sic*] forward, and said, "THIS IS THE MAN."
> He then with others laid his hands upon HIM, and ordained him to
> his station. "Now," said Joseph, "If I should be taken away, the Church
> need not be rent with schisms on this point. And I say to you, that,
> should I be taken, THE WORK will roll with more rapidity, and with
> more power than it ever has done."[68]

Whether or not this event occurred exactly as McLellin remembered
it, the ordination itself took place; later, David and many in his circle of
influence saw it, understandably, as conferring on him the right to succeed Smith as leader of the church. Using different titles, David recalled
more than fifty years later: "He [Joseph Smith] ordained me as successor
as 'Prophet Seer and Revelator' to the church. He did this of his own free
will and not at any solicitation whatever on my part. I did not know what
he was going to do until he laid his hands upon me and ordained me."[69]

John, who wrote chapter 14 of his history much closer to this event—
sometime around August 1834—briefly alluded to the organization of the
Missouri church. "Joseph the seer began to set in order the Church in this
country," by which he meant Joseph's ordaining David Whitmer as presi-

---

68. McLellin, "A Special Conference of the Church of Christ," 6.

69. David Whitmer, *Address to All Believers in Christ*, 55.

dent of the Missouri church.[70] Modestly, John declined mention of his own ordination, along with W. W. Phelps, as counselors to David. Joseph also "commenced to organize a high council according to the Patran [pattern] received in Kirtland Ohio. After which Joseph Smith Jr. F. G. Williams and others returned to Kirtland and the Saints remained in their places of abode to wait the due time of the Lord to be redeemed from wicked mobbers."[71]

At the time of the organization of the Missouri church, the twelve members of the Missouri high council were also selected (listed by ranking): Simeon Carter, Parley P. Pratt, William McLellin, Calvin Beebe, Levi Jackman, Solomon Hancock, Christian Whitmer, Newel Knight, Orson Pratt, Lyman Wight, Thomas B. Marsh, and John Murdoch/Murdock.[72] Under this arrangement, the bishopric was further constrained, becoming an appendage to the new regime.

The *History of the LDS Church*, without identifying its source, dates these ordinations as occurring on July 7, 1834, at the house of Lyman Wight on the Michael Arthur farm.[73] The best indication that John was also living on the Arthur farm appears in his account/day book, where he notes on [Tuesday], July 8: "At home, attended to the organization of high council."[74] Throughout the Zion's Camp episode, John's account/day book dating of events vary by one day from those adopted during the writing of Joseph's history.[75]

---

70. Minutes of this meeting report: "High Priest, Elders, Priests, Teachers, Deacons & members covenanted with hands uplifted to heaven, that they would uphold Brother David Whitmer as President, head and leader in Zion (in absence of br. Joseph Smith jr.) & John Whitmer & W.W. Phelps, as assistant Presidents and Counselors also covenanted to uphold him and one another at the throne of grace." Cannon and Cook, July 7 [8], 1834, *Far West Record*, 73.

71. Whitmer, Book of John Whitmer, chap. 14, p. 68.

72. "History of Joseph Smith," *Times and Seasons*, 6:1109–10.

73. This section of Joseph Smith's History was compiled by Willard Richards at Nauvoo, Illinois, between December 1842 and Joseph's death in 1844. See Jessee, "The Writing of Joseph Smith's History," 466.

74. Whitmer, account book, p. 12. John dates the high council's organization at July 8, rather than July 3, 1834, the date given in *History of the LDS Church*, 2:122–26.

75. John's notations about which day was the Sabbath agree with the 1834 calendar, so his dates are probably both contemporaneous and correct. Also, the Far West Record

During this same gathering on July 8, 1834, Peter Whitmer Sr. blessed his three sons, David, John, and Christian Whitmer, in the name of the Lord. Jacob's absence is puzzling. During the early months of the Mormon settlement in Clay County, beginning in November 1833, Jacob was living near his father in the Hulet Settlement, west of Liberty.[76] But he was apparently not in the neighborhood at the time of these blessings or was kept from attending those meetings by some unspecified event.

As the conference continued on July 8, W. W. Phelps proposed "that David Whitmer, the president of the church in Zion, should go to Kirtland, and assist in promoting the cause of Christ, as being one of the three witnesses.... After which it was decided ... that Br. David Whitmer go to the East and assist in the great work, of the gathering and be his own judge as to leaving his family or taking them with him. It was also decided that John Whitmer and Wm. E. McLellin go east, as soon as convenient" to help prepare for the dedication of the Kirtland Temple with its promised endowment experience. "To the East" meant "to Ohio." Frederick G. Williams, clerk of the conference, then reported how Joseph Smith spelled out the implications of this organizational move: "The high priests, elders, priests, teachers, deacons and members present, then covenanted with hands uplifted to heaven, that you would uphold Br. David Whitmer, as president in Zion, in my absence, and John Whitmer and W. W. Phelps as assistant presidents or councilors, and myself as first president of the church, and one another by faith and prayer."[77]

At this same meeting on July 8, Joseph dictated a proclamation, approved by the high council, intended as an appeal to Missouri state government officials. John devoted July 9, 1834, to copying this "proclamation

---

minutes of the July 3, 1834, meeting read, "Meeting adjourned to meet on monday, [Tuesday] the 8th inst." LDS historian Andrew Jenson later changed the date to read, "7th inst." Cannon and Cook, *Far West Record*, 70–71n5.

76. Gilbert, Petition to the President. The petition was signed consecutively in each settlement, providing what constitutes a loose pairing of members with settlements. Peter [Sr.], Jacob, David, and Christian Whitmer are grouped together. John Whitmer and Hiram Page appear to be grouped with residents of the town of Liberty or the Michael Arthur farm. Peter Whitmer Jr. did not sign the petition. Whitmer, account book, 29 October 1834, p. 16, notes on October 29, 1834: "Went to Jacobs and fathers &c."

77. "History of Joseph Smith," *Times and Seasons*, 6:1110.

of peace."[78] But immediate hopes for a return to Jackson County were put on hold.

Following the conference, Lyman Wight agreed to make one hundred thousand bricks and build a large brick home for Michael Arthur. Wight's biographer, Jermy Wight, observes that Wight's "title Colonel was more a title of honor rather than a military title," perhaps related to Wight's role in defense of the disciples during the expulsion from Jackson County.[79] Wilford Woodruff, Milton Holmes, Heman T. Hyde, and the Winchester brothers, Stephen and Benjamin, labored for Wight through the summer on the brick-making and house-building project. This concentration of Mormon men made the Arthur farm the unofficial church headquarters between the spring of 1834 and fall 1836 when the Mormons again moved on.

During this year and a half, John Whitmer wrote letters for the Saints as needed.[80] He often rode into Liberty to see his brother, Peter Jr., and paid frequent visits to his parents, who were probably living in the small Hulet Settlement about nine miles west of Liberty. In the late fall of 1834, John hauled back a load of turnips to supplement his and Sarah's winter food supply.[81] He also visited Sarah's parents who lived west of Liberty, perhaps in the same settlement as John's parents: "Went to Father Jacksons [*sic*] with my truck."[82] On August 22, 1834, John wrote a letter for Lyman Wight[83] and spent September 16 "writing Lyman Wight's history."[84] This history probably involved copying source notations into a single volume of Lyman Wight's account of the Mormon expulsion from Jackson County, incident to the church's legal efforts to obtain redress. However, John may have written the initial portion of the much sought, but no longer extant,

---

78. Whitmer, account book, p. 12.

79. Wight, *Wild Ram of the Mountain*, 99.

80. Whitmer, account book, 9 July 1834, p. 12.

81. Ibid., 21 November 1834, p. 16.

82. Whitmer, account book, 13 September and 8 October 1834, pp. 14, 15. John Jackson's affidavit reveals he is living in Van Buren County, Iowa, in 1840. Johnson, *Mormon Redress Petitions*, 248.

83. Whitmer, account book, 22 August 1834, p. 13.

84. Ibid., 16 September 1834, p. 14.

Lyman Wight journal.[85] Also, demonstrating what came down in the family as his reputation as a keen eye for a fine steed, John traded horses with Joseph Broadbuck on September 18, 1834.[86]

While Joseph Smith had returned to Kirtland in July 1834, it became Smith's prophetic preoccupation to restore his Missouri followers to their temporal properties and spiritual inheritance. By revelation, he announced two prerequisites for repossessing Jackson County. Church members must first build the House of the Lord in Kirtland, Ohio, and second, they must receive an endowment in that house.[87] Then the way would be opened for Zion's "redemption." Members in Missouri became aware of this complicated plan in August 1834 when Joseph wrote, urging them to be patient about the expected return to Jackson County: "In case the excitement continues to be allayed, and peace prevails, use every effort to prevail on the churches to gather in those regions, and situate themselves, to be in readiness to move into Jackson Co., in two years from the 11th of Sept. next, (1866) [*sic* 1836] which is the appointed time for the redemption of Zion. If verily I say unto you—if the church, with one united effort, perform their duties—if they do this, the work shall be complete."[88]

85. Ibid. RLDS church historian Heman C. Smith, whose parents had belonged to the Lyman Wight colony, had Lyman Wight's journal in his possession and quoted from it during the 1890s while he was writing the *History of the RLDS Church.*

86. Whitmer, account book, 18 September 1834, p. 14.

87. Fishing River revelation, see *History of the LDS Church,* 2:110, verse 33.

88. Edward Stevenson, 16 August 1834, 35–36, recorded in his journal, "On the 16th of August 1834, a very encouraging letter was written by the Prophet Joseph to the high council in Clay Co." Smith instructed the members: "If the citizens of Clay, Co. do not befriend us, to gather up the little army, and be set over immediately into Jackson County, and trust in God, and do the best we can in maintaining the ground.... But, in the case the excitement continues to be allayed, and peace prevails." The September 11, 1836, date harkens back to Smith's revelation of September 11, 1831, appointing Kirtland as a "stronghold" for the kingdom for five years.

CHAPTER SIXTEEN

Return to Ohio

A S PART OF Joseph Smith's plan to construct the House of the Lord, endow church leaders with power, and redeem Zion, he summoned David Whitmer and other Missouri leaders to Kirtland in August 1834. In preparation for David's departure, the extended Whitmer family gathered at Peter Jr.'s home in Liberty. John recalled that he and Sarah "stayed all night together with D. Whitmer & family E[lizabeth]. Cowdery & L. [Leonard] Rich who left Liberty Tuesday morning [August 26, 1834] for Kirtland." David remained at Kirtland, where, in February 1835, as one of the three witnesses to the Book of Mormon, he helped identify those called to create the newly constituted Quorum of Twelve Apostles.

Meanwhile, John Whitmer stayed in Missouri. Chapter 14 of his history chronicles additional efforts to redress Mormon losses in Jackson County between July 1834 and April 1835 when he left for Ohio.

Smith's method of accomplishing the liberation of Zion would prove both ambitious and expensive—and ultimately futile. The Fishing River revelation conveys the understanding that Zion's Camp would not achieve its initial purpose, but that Smith's intention to follow up with a second armed attempt would succeed in retaking Zion. In contrast to the overt drama of Zion's Camp, Smith planned, the second time around, to employ a more gradual "gathering" process that would build up his army in place under the very noses of their unsuspecting Missouri neighbors. Smith's missionaries began to encourage existing adherents and new converts to gather to Clay County, Missouri, which Joseph saw as the staging area for the projected second Jackson County campaign.[1] LDS historian Max Par-

---

1. Parkin, "Latter-day Saint Conflict in Clay County," in Garr and Johnson, *Regional Studies in Latter-day Saint Church History: Missouri*, 253. According to Parkin, after Joseph returned to Kirtland from the Zion's Camp expedition, he "developed plans

248

kin has described Joseph's strategy concisely, writing: "The Fishing River revelation instructed: 'Mine elders should wait for a little season for the redemption of Zion.'...The 'little season' was to give the Saints in Clay County time 'to gather up the strength of my [the Lord's] house' to that place. They were to gather and purchase land in Clay County and otherwise fortify their position until their 'army became very great.'"[2]

Upon Smith's departure for Ohio on July 9, 1834, he assigned Lyman Wight and Amasa Lyman the task of assessing the "strength"—meaning Mormon men capable of fighting—in Missouri. The newly ordained high council assembled on July 12, 1834, and appointed Amasa Lyman to serve as Wight's assistant.[3] Amasa Lyman circumspectly recorded, "In council held on the 12th [of July] I received a mission to go with brother Lyman Wight to visit the brethren who were driven out from their inheritances and learn the strength of the Lords house in this land and on Monday the 14th [of July 1834] began to make preparations for fulfilling the mission.... The 3d of August attended to the business of my mission agreeable to appointment in numbering the saints."[4]

Smith also urged the Missouri disciples to apply political pressure. In retrospect, counsel to build political and economic alliances would probably have been wiser; for the same forces were still at work, keeping the Mormons separate, different, and suspicious "others" where their Missouri neighbors were concerned. Mormon apostle Parley P. Pratt, who was then in Ohio, recalled:

> On the eleventh of August, 1834, he [Joseph] wrote to the brethren in Missouri [and] ... requested that another petition be written such as the High Council would approve, asking the Governor of Mis-

---

for the 'little season' of preparation. He instructed Partridge and Phelps to take the initiative in the West in encouraging the eastern Saints to gather to Clay County. The Prophet spoke of the two years which was provided for the 'little season' of preparation. The day he set for them to return to Jackson County was 11 September 1836—the appointed date for the 'redemption of Zion.'"

2. Ibid.; see also CofC D&C 102:3c–9a; LDS D&C 105:9–31.

3. *History of the LDS Church,* 2:136.

4. Lyman, journal, 14–15 July and 5 August 1834, pp. 12–13, also available in DVD format, "Selected Collection from the Archives," vol. 37; see also Cannon and Cook, *Far West Record,* 75.

souri to call on the President of the United States to furnish a guard to protect the saints to their homes in Jackson County (when they should be restored) from the insults and violence of the mob. Copies of this petition were to be placed in the hands of the elders going on missions through the United States, and every effort was to be made to get signers.[5]

John and Sarah remained on the Arthur farm until October 7, 1834, then moved in with Peter Jr. and Vashti in Liberty. John indicated in his account book that he "wrote Rev." for four days in a row between October 15 and 18, 1834. From this information, it is possible to deduce that John had the holograph Book of Commandments and Revelations in his possession and took the time to make copies of the Fishing River revelation, given June 22, 1834, for his brothers and others.

That autumn was unusually cold, and John spent much of his time chopping wood, for much of which he found a ready market. In his official capacity as a president and church historian, John attended the Clay County Court in Liberty on October 20–22, 1834, which was hearing the literary firm's suit (*Phelps v. Simpson*) being litigated by their attorneys, Alexander W. Doniphan and Amos Rees.[6] John also frequently visited W. W. Phelps, then living in the Burk Settlement, out westward toward the Missouri River, to confer about church matters. In David's absence, the high council continued to meet regularly and the two counselors shouldered the administrative burden.

John and W. W. Phelps knew they were expected to return to Ohio for their endowments soon and to help with the church's printing efforts. The literary firm acquired a second press in February 1835, and Oliver Cowdery began to issue a political paper, the *Northern Times,* in addition to a new periodical, the *Messenger and Advocate.* Instead of looking for work or land to farm as the spring of 1835 approached, John and Sarah began making travel plans. On March 15, 1835, Sally Phelps gave birth to her ninth child, Lydia. She would remain in Liberty, looking after the children, except for their eldest son, twelve-year-old Waterman. He would accom-

5.   Roberts, *Missouri Persecutions,* 165.
6.   Whitmer, account book, 7, 15–18, and 20–22 October 1834, p. 15–16.

pany William to Kirtland and learn his father's trade at the new printing office.[7]

In March 1835, in Liberty, Missouri, John helped Peter Jr. raise a new house. Then Sarah stayed with her parents while John, presumably with his brothers' help, built another log house for her.[8] On April 1, he "went to L. [Sarah's brother Lewis] Jacksons for to bring my wife home."[9] Obviously, John and William thought they would be returning to Missouri after spending perhaps a summer in Kirtland, but larger movements were under way. Peter Jr. also planned to accompany them to Ohio.

Church leaders in Ohio no doubt kept reminding John he was needed in Ohio. Oliver Cowdery, who was beginning preparations to print an expanded compilation of the Book of Commandments, this time under the title of the Doctrine and Covenants, may have reminded John to bring with him the bound holograph volume, Book of Commandments and Revelations.[10]

On April 4, 1835, John, Sarah, Peter Jr., and Vashti visited the Whitmer parents, asking for and receiving Peter Sr.'s blessings on their upcoming trip to Ohio.[11] No one knew how long it would be before they would be reunited. Furthermore, Christian was not well. He had never recovered from the stress and exposure suffered during the expulsion from Jackson County. During 1834–35, he was practically an invalid, unable to do more than grow a garden to help provide food for his family.[12] As for the fifth brother, Jacob, little is known about his activities during this period, whether he had recovered from his injury during the battle at the Whitmer Settlement in Jackson County, or how he was supporting his family.

7. William Waterman Phelps, the twelve-year-old son of W. W. and Sally Phelps, wrote to his mother following his arrival in Kirtland. William Waterman Phelps to Sally Phelps, [20?] July 1835, included in a four-part letter. One section is from John Corrill to his wife Margaret, two other sections are signed by W. W. Phelps, and the fourth section (unsigned and fragmented) was written by William Waterman Phelps.

8. Whitmer, account book, March 1835, p. 20.

9. Ibid., 1 April 1835, p. 20.

10. Jensen, "From Manuscript to Printed Page," 39.

11. Whitmer, account book, 4 April 1835, p. 20.

12. Pollard and Woods, *Whitmer Memoirs*, 19.

By this time, Hiram and Catherine Page were also apparently living in the vicinity of the Hulet Branch in Clay County. Apparently recovered from his beating the previous fall, Hiram was functioning as branch leader, even though no record exists of a formal ordination as presiding elder. On May 24, 1835, Hiram officiated in the marriage of Charles English to Lydia Whiting and, a year later on May 13, 1836, performed the marriage of Nathan West and Adaline Louise Follett.[13] These families had been associated with the Whitmer Settlement in Jackson County.

On April 17, 1835, John sold two horses to Father John Jackson for five dollars, gave a third horse to Sarah's brother Lewis, and crated up their furniture, preparing to ship it to Ohio.[14] Although John never commented on the Phelpses' marriage, he must have seen the strain of their lengthy and repeated separations; and he and Sarah had made a different decision about their marriage. In his baggage, John carefully packed his Book of Commandments and Revelations manuscript. Perhaps John also carried his history, known as "The Book of John Whitmer," and other documentary sources that he thought would be useful in Kirtland.

Peter Whitmer Jr. and his family delayed their departure for unknown reasons; but John, Sarah, W. W. Phelps, and Waterman Phelps started east in mid-April 1835. The quickest route was down the Missouri and up the Ohio River. They planned to take the steamboat *Cats of Siam* downriver, but the boat broke down about twelve miles below Liberty. On April 21, John and William rowed out to the stranded boat, arranged passage with the captain, and freighted their goods down to it on April 25. Repairs were completed the next day, and the combined Whitmer-Phelps party embarked for Ohio. John noted in his account book: "Left the Landing at 2 O'clock this afternoon and the feelings which passed my mind can easily be felt but not expressed; and this because of the ~~situation of the saints may the Lord preserve them and us till we meet again, Amen,~~ [strikethrough in the original]."[15]

The party arrived at Portsmouth, Ohio, on May 8, 1835, transferred to a canal boat, disembarked at Cleveland on May 15, and reached Kirtland

13. Clay County, Missouri, Marriage Records, Book A, Marriages no. 447, no. 478.

14. Whitmer, account book, 17–18 April 1835, p. 21.

15. Ibid., 26 April 1835, p. 21.

Near the bottom of page 21 of his account book, John Whitmer chronicled his departure from Clay County, Missouri, while he was en route to Kirtland, Ohio. John wrote: "Left the Landing at 2 O'clock this afternoon and the feelings which passed my mind can easily be felt but not expressed; and this because of the situation of the saints may the Lord preserve them and us till we meet again, Amen, [strikethrough in the original]." Courtesy of the LDS Church History Library.

the next day, where they were warmly greeted by the Kirtland Saints.[16] Phelps wrote to Sally two months later: "Our passage from Missouri to Kirtland was not as quick as it might have been, but I thank the Lord that we got here safe."[17] Phelps and Waterman began boarding with Joseph and Emma Smith.[18]

On May 17, 1835, John attended church services with the Saints and renewed acquaintances with many old friends.[19] It is not clear where John and Sarah found accommodations, since it was not until June 15 that they moved in with David and Julia Ann. David did not own a house and may, in fact, have been living with Jared Carter near the temple during this period.[20] To begin housekeeping in Kirtland, John and Sarah unpacked their furniture, then bought a table, a bedstead, and a

Sarah (Jackson) Whitmer, ca. 1830s. Portrait by Henry Inouye.

cow. John, a skilled woodsman, no doubt planned to build another log house for his family. It would be an easy task for him, and he was anxious to install Sarah, then a little more than three months pregnant, in

---

16. Ibid., 26 April–16 May 1835.

17. W. W. Phelps to Sally Phelps, 19–20 July 1835, p. 529, cited in Van Orden, "Writing to Zion," 554.

18. William Waterman Phelps to Sally Phelps, [20?] July 1835. See also Journal History, 20 July 1835, p. 2. In this section, addressed to Mother, Sisters, &c., twelve-year-old William Waterman says he has begun to live with Joseph and Emma Smith.

19. Ibid., 17 May 1835.

20. David and Julia Ann could have as easily been living with the Cowderys during this period, but Lucy Mack Smith indicates David was living with Jared Carter in 1837. Proctor and Proctor, *History of Joseph Smith by His Mother*, 336, 338. Luman Shurtliff's reminiscence suggests that David lived somewhere in Kirtland overlooking the flats. In August 1836, after visiting with David, the party "tired of sitting, [and] we walked out to where we could overlook the flats." Shurtliff, "Biographical Sketch of the Life of Luman Andros Shurtliff," 72.

comfortable surroundings. John quickly arranged for hired girls, who may have worked for room and board. The first was a young woman identified only as Adaline (possibly West) (June 15–July 21, 1835), then Mary Lyman, and then Eleanor Shaver, who "commenced work" September 14, 1835, and remained in their employ through March 1836.[21]

Joseph Smith was focused on achieving his twin objectives, building the House of the Lord at Kirtland and redeeming Zion. Both projects were expensive, and Smith began to deploy his missionary force to gather human and financial resources. Before John and Phelps reached Kirtland, Joseph had already launched two major solicitation campaigns. In February 1835, he had sent Hyrum Smith and Jared Carter south, soliciting money from members for the temple's construction.[22] In May 1835, the newly called were assigned their first mission: to visit local branches in New England and gather contributions for purchasing lands in Missouri.

21. Whitmer, account book, 17–18 April 1835, pp. 23, 24.
22. Hyrum Smith, record book, 24 February 1835–26 March 1844, p. 5, cited in O'Driscoll, *Hyrum Smith: A Life of Integrity*, 117.

CHAPTER SEVENTEEN

Editing the Messenger and Advocate

O NLY TWO DAYS after arriving in Kirtland, on May 18, 1835, John attended his first Kirtland High Council meeting and was startled to hear the announcement that Oliver Cowdery, who had been editing the *Messenger and Advocate*, published by F. G. Williams & Co., had been reassigned to work full-time preparing the Doctrine and Covenants for publication. In a rare entry that reports personal feelings, John recorded in his account book: "This day held a council and contrary to my feelings or expectations I was appointed to Edit the Messenger and Advocate."[1]

There is no question that John was qualified for this job. He was a member of the church's literary firm and had gained the necessary experience by helping both Phelps and Cowdery publish the *Evening and the Morning Star* in Independence. Furthermore, as a member of the extended presidency, John had the suitable stature for a prestigious responsibility. But in the end, John received this big responsibility primarily because others were needed elsewhere. And, because of his nature, John naturally felt inadequate to the task.

Pragmatically, John's assignment freed Oliver Cowdery to once again function as Joseph's chief scribe and also concentrate on bringing out an updated edition of Joseph's revelations. This new work, to be called the Doctrine and Covenants, would combine the Lectures on Faith (the "doctrine"), delivered in Kirtland during December 1834, with Joseph's revelations (the "covenants"), many of which had formerly appeared in the interrupted Book of Commandments, but with the addition of fifty-seven new revelatory documents.[2]

1. Whitmer, account book, 18 May 1835, p. 22.
2. Dahl and Tate, *Lectures on Faith in Historical Perspective*, 3–4. Noel Reynolds, an LDS religious studies scholar, observed, "Three independent authorship studies conducted

John made his Book of Commandments and Revelations (BCR) manuscript available to Cowdery and other compilers who were busily working on the Doctrine and Covenants. They used the BCR to supplement several other sources from which this new collection of church scripture was drawn.

To further free Oliver, Frederick G. Williams took over editorship of the *Northern Times,* a nonsectarian political newspaper that Cowdery had started in February 1835 in support of President Andrew Jackson and the Democratic Party. In addition to helping Cowdery with the Doctrine and Covenants, W. W. Phelps was assigned to print Emma Smith's hymnal and to write articles for the *Messenger and Advocate.*[3]

Oliver introduced the new editor to readers:

> [The *Messenger and Advocate*] will be conducted hereafter by Elder JOHN WHITMER, late from the State of Missouri. It is proper for me to say, that wherever Elder Whitmer is personally known, a commendation from me would be uncalled for and superfluous; and I hardly need to add, that those to whom he is unknown will find him to be a man of piety, uprightness and virtue, such as adorns the walk of the professor of the religion of the Lord Jesus, and one bearing testimony to the truth of the great work of God.[4]

Despite his anxiety, John hoped to fulfill this new responsibility in an acceptable fashion. He introduced himself in the next issue:

> The principles of my predecessor have been faithfully written and ably defended; and it is only necessary to add, that the patrons of this paper will find mine [my principles] to correspond with his.... If, in the performance of the duties which now devolve upon me, I so discharge them as to meet the approbation of the pure in heart, and still maintain the present respectability of this paper, and above all to have my work correspond with the principles of holiness, that at the great day

---

in recent decades, using different reputable techniques, all conclude that Sidney Rigdon was the primary author of the *Lectures.* According to these studies, not a single lecture can be confidently attributed to Joseph Smith." Reynolds, "The Case for Sidney Rigdon," 8.

3. *History of the LDS Church,* 2:227. Waterman Phelps worked with his father in the printing office as the printer's devil.

4. Cowdery, "Address to the Patrons," 120.

of the Lord Jesus, I may but receive the reward of the just and the approbation of the same, that a crown of righteousness may be placed upon my head, I shall be satisfied and give the praise and glory to the exalted name of the Most High.

John also solicited news from former correspondents and offered free subscriptions to anyone obtaining and forwarding new subscribers.[5]

Though his new duties came as a shock, John's editorial appointment provided ongoing financial support for his family. The "United [Kirtland-Zion] Firm" arrangement had ended on April 23, 1834. At that point, Cowdery and Williams were placed in control of the Kirtland printing operation's assets.[6] The literary firm functions were continued at Kirtland, providing support for key local church leaders. This financial mechanism eventually operated under the name of F. G. Williams and Co., the formal publisher of the *Messenger and Advocate*. The firm's "Cash Book," which spans October 1833–November 1835, lists business receipts and expenses related to church publications. The firm also managed any income generated by leaders, as well as recording their living and church-related travel expenses. John's new assignment meant that he became a joint partner in F. G. Williams and Co. Entries for John Whitmer's editorial work and family-related expenses appear in the cash book beginning May 22, 1835. For example, on June 20, 1835, John, obviously still setting up his new household, was reimbursed 37½ cents for bed cording.[7]

Six days after his initial assignment, John participated in a council meeting on May 26, 1835, during which Joseph Smith identified and assigned "inheritances" in Zion (Missouri). Whitmer recorded: "Soon after our arrival in this place [May 16, 1835] we held many counsels [*sic*] an[d] in particular I will here notice [one, held May 26, 1835,] in which were several selections, made for particular individuals according to the dictation of the

5.   Ibid.

6.   The revelation suggests that Phelps and John Whitmer would, at some unspecified date, renew literary firm functions in Missouri as the "united order of the city of Zion." CofC D&C 101:9b, 101:5c; LDS D&C 104.

7.   John's expenses are typically small (under $3.50), unidentified, and infrequent. Faulring, "Cash Book of the Firm of F. G. Williams, & Co."

spirit of the Lord through Joseph the Revelator, for inheritances in Zion."[8] In theory, these inheritances would be "redeemed" when the Mormons returned to Jackson County and were clearly intended to encourage members to contribute money with which to purchase land in Jackson County, a markedly over-optimistic view of future events, as matters turned out.

John recorded this list of sixty-two inheritance assignees in his history, an interesting glimpse into the relative status of leading church figures at that moment in time. Martin Harris is first, in recognition of his funding the Book of Mormon printing in New York and having made a major donation toward the purchase of the Independence temple lot. "J. Smith Jr." is listed second, for obvious reasons. Oliver Cowdery is third, in recognition of his early role as second elder. David Whitmer appears fourth, reflecting his important role as president of the Missouri church. Sidney Rigdon is fifth, as first counselor to the president of the church. Edward Partridge's position as sixth acknowledges the relative status of Zion's bishop. John Whitmer's inheritance is fourteenth, just after Peter Whitmer Jr. and two before W. W. Phelps's as the sixteenth.

On June 2, 1835, Phelps made a rough sketch of the city of Zion on the top right corner of a letter to his wife, Sally. He has written "ours" on lot number 16, near the center.[9] Phelps's sketch adds meaning to John's listing of the heirs' names by establishing a reference from which it is possible to locate some twenty or more of these anticipated inheritances. Obviously, hopes remained high for a forthcoming return to Zion.

Paralleling the high council that Smith established in Missouri in July 1834 was the Kirtland High Council, organized on February 17, 1834, with the following members, listed in order of seniority: Joseph Smith Sr.; John Smith; Joseph Coe; John Johnson; Martin Harris; John S. Carter;

---

8. Whitmer, Book of John Whitmer, chap. 15, p. 71. In his previous chapter, John indicated that their party arrived in Kirtland on May 17, but his account/daybook entry dates their arrival at 4 o'clock the evening of May 16, 1835. Whitmer, account book, 16 May 1835, p. 22. See also McKiernan and Launius, *An Early Latter Day Saint History*, 130–40. Interestingly, certain well-known names do not appear on this list of inheritances. Many of the lesser-known names are former Saints from Jackson County.

9. W. W. Phelps to Dear Wife and Children, 2 June 1835. For the illustration, see Romig, "Jackson County, 1831–33: A Look at the Development of Zion," 300. The sketch is accompanied by the admonition, "Keep such things to yourself."

Jared Carter; Oliver Cowdery; Samuel H. Smith; Orson Hyde; Sylvester Smith; and Luke Johnson.[10]

As one of David Whitmer's two counselors in the presidency of the church in Zion, John continued to be intimately involved in high council meetings at Kirtland. According to council minutes between June 7, 1835, and January 13, 1836, John attended eight of nineteen related meetings. The high council was not a policy-making body as much as a court system for arbitrating disputes. John and Oliver were conspicuous participants in efforts to resolve what were sometimes serious questions related to conduct and interpersonal difficulties.

On May 6–7, 1835, church leaders traveled to New Portage, Portage County, Ohio, about forty miles southwest of Kirtland, where they held a conference and contemplated establishing a stake. While leading the afternoon service, John provided "a short relation of the facts connected with the translation of the book of Mormon," declaring that he had "seen, hefted, and handled [the plates] with his own hands." Commenting on this talk, Oliver Cowdery asserted "no man possessed of common reason and common sense, can doubt, or will be so vain as to dispute" John's testimony.[11]

In June 1835, like almost everyone else in the church during this period, John loaned Joseph Smith money: twenty-six dollars in cash on June 2, 1835.[12] On June 6–7, 1835, church leaders returned again to New Portage for a conference. This gathering, really more of a function of the high council than a members' conference, adjudicated a number of local difficulties in Portage, Medina, and Richland Counties, Ohio.[13]

On Sunday, June 7, 1835, the council authorized Jacob Myers's ordination to the priesthood office of elder, a rite performed by John and Oliver. Myers was a millwright and mill operator from Richland County, Ohio, a hundred miles southwest of Kirtland. Missionaries had success-

10. Collier and Harwell, *Kirtland Council Minute Book*, 23.

11. [Oliver Cowdery], "New Portage Conference," 143.

12. Whitmer, account book, 2 June 1835, p. 23. There is no notation of repayment.

13. Collier and Harwell, *Kirtland Council Minute Book,* 118.

fully established three branches in Richland County. Myers was quite well off and frequently loaned money for church purposes.[14]

On Thursday, June 25, 1835, Joseph solicited subscriptions toward the temple's construction, and members pledged $6,232.50. John and several of the other eight presidents subscribed $500 each "all of which they paid within one hour, and the people were astonished."[15]

Throughout June, the staff of the printing office made splendid progress on the Doctrine and Covenants. The Book of Commandments manuscript was once again called into service, being employed in a limited way during the production of the Doctrine and Covenants. In 1834, when Oliver Cowdery started preparing to print the Doctrine and Covenants at Kirtland, Whitmer's volume of revelations was still in Missouri. In fact, much of the work on the Doctrine and Covenants was already complete and the book was offered for sale within a few months of Whitmer's arrival from Missouri. Thus, Oliver Cowdery and other compilers of the Doctrine and Covenants clearly worked from other manuscript and printed sources.

However, Cowdery, Williams, and Joseph Smith apparently used John's manuscript as a source while preparing sections 22–29. Evidence is the fact that internal numbers were added to John's Book of Commandments manuscript, which exactly corresponds to the sequence of these sections as printed in the Doctrine and Covenants. Also, the holograph manuscript shows that the compilers occasionally inserted Doctrine and Covenants section numbers near John's headings, as well as corresponding versification and punctuation. And, finally, a few words inserted into John's manuscript correspond with the 1835 edition. These insertions predominantly consist of last names at places in his manuscript where only forenames were used previously.

It appears that no further additions were made to John's manuscript—by John or anyone else—after the publication of the Doctrine and Covenants in early August.[16] After this point, John may have no longer retained the volume in his personal custody. It seems reasonable that it was

14. Ibid., 118.

15. *History of the LDS Church*, 2:234.

16. Robin Jensen observed, "The volume itself can be used to determine the chain of custody [of the BCR] through 1835, when Whitmer and others ceased writing in the volume." Jensen, "From Manuscript to Printed Page," 42.

probably consigned to a shelf in the church's printing and office building, which stood directly behind the temple, where it would have been stored alongside similar holograph bound volumes of church papers. Examples of similar ledgers, include John Whitmer's manuscript history, the Kirtland Revelation Book, and the Elder's Quorum Record Book, among others.

John was present in the printing office as work on the Doctrine and Covenants neared its end in June–August 1835. In June 1835, with W. W. Phelps's help, John also published his first issue of the monthly *Messenger and Advocate*. Phelps supplied news items, drafted articles, and wrote two new hymns, "Adam-ondi-Ahman" and "Sabbath Hymn."[17] Both hymns gained the disciples' immediate acceptance.

John's nine months as editor was a period of prolific writing for him. Much of his extant original writing dates from this time, revealing deep feelings, perhaps even at times emotionalism. Largely self-educated, John was clearly literate and of at least average intelligence. The most powerful force in his life was his strong religious convictions. They dominated and guided his thoughts.

In between editorial duties with the *Messenger and Advocate*, perhaps even as its type was being set, John wrote and arranged his history. He refined his narrative, drawing from earlier sources and drafts. Source documents and revelations are interspersed throughout his narrative history, suggesting that they were readily at hand. Typically providing brief transitional commentary linking the documents, he apparently intended that they speak for themselves. Revelations were usually inserted in their entirety, without interpretation. Citations from the 1835 Doctrine and Covenants confirm how Joseph's revelations influenced John's view of church events. To John, the life of the church was centered on revelation.

The early part of John's history manuscript covers December 1830–March 4, 1831 (pp. 1–21). It is written as if he had drafted it four years earlier, but he probably copied it into his 1835 manuscript from his notes or earlier sources. During this phase, John copied the revelations dating from these three months directly into his text. John could have written this part anytime from 1831 up to July 1835, when the Doctrine and Covenants received its final page arrangement; it seems unlikely that he wrote this section any later, or he could have simply cited the published text for these pages.

17. Phelps, "Adam-ondi-Ahman" and "Sabbath Hymn," 144.

The Book of John Whitmer that describes events of March 7 through June 1831 (comprising pp. 22–31 and covering through the end of chapter 8) was clearly written after the publication of the Doctrine and Covenants in August 1835. John could not have written this section before he had access to the 1835 Doctrine and Covenants texts, as he makes reference to the page numbers on which various sections appeared. Also, John's occasional marginal comments reveal a later perspective. Bruce Westergren, an editor of The Book of John Whitmer, observes:

> On page 28, when listing some of the names of those ordained to various priesthood office during an 1831 church conference, Whitmer lists the names of some who later left the church, specifically Ezra Booth, Harvey Whitlock, and Joseph Wakefield. These men did not leave the church until 1833. In the same entry he lists his own name among those who fell from the faith, although he was not excommunicated until 1838. He also lists the names of Joseph Smith, Jr., and Joseph Smith, Sr., which shows his feeling that Joseph Smith, Jr., had become a fallen prophet—feelings he did not entertain until 1838.[18]

The ledger version of John's holograph history is in a bound volume of white paper pages, 8" x 12 ½" in size, bound with paper sides and cloth binding.[19] The way some letters trail off at the end of a line suggests that the book was already bound when John wrote in it. The ledger also appears to be a manufactured item, probably readily available from a local stationer or supplier.[20] The pages are numbered by hand in the upper outside corners. That several priority printing projects came to fruition during this prolific period probably encouraged John to continue his own work on the history. Manuscript notations, such as, "The poor saints have suffered.... You will find in one of the Nos of the Star printed at Kirtland Ohio a piece headed

18. Westergren, *From Historian to Dissident*, xi.

19. Jenson, Book of John Whitmer, 1893, typescript. A note is attached to Jenson's typescript which reads: "March 14, '94, The enclosed is double Copy of John Whitmer's Record—Obtained by Andrew Jensen [*sic*], 1893. Duplicate copy with Andrew Jenson's Church Papers."

20. Whitmer's original bound volume is also in the CofC Archives. The end boards are covered with marbled paper. "Church History" is written in ink across the front. This is probably not the paper purchased for "history" in 1832 at Independence. He may have secured this bound volume especially to compile a finished copy while working in the Kirtland printing office.

the Mormons which will serve to illustrate (to be published.) Dated Feb. 1834," strongly suggest that John anticipated that he would soon see his narrative in print.[21]

The Doctrine and Covenants was printed in early August, and the books were sent to Cleveland for binding. Bound copies of the Doctrine and Covenants began to arrive in Kirtland the second week in September, retailing for one dollar. Phelps wrote jubilantly to Sally: "We got some of the Commandments from Cleveland last week; I shall try to send one hundred copies to the Saints this fall by Br. Wm Tippets. He starts next week. I know there will be one hundred Saints who will have their dollar ready, when he arrives.... I would not be without one for five dollars."[22] The price was set at one dollar per book in hopes that members of the literary firm could recoup revenue lost from the destruction of the Independence printing operation.

To mark the completion of the Doctrine and Covenants, Sidney Rigdon and Oliver Cowdery—members of the "committee to arrange the items of doctrine" on behalf of the presidency—convened a general priesthood assembly on August 17, 1835. Joseph Smith and Frederick G. Williams were absent on a mission to Michigan. The twelve were also away from Kirtland on various missions. Those attending were seated by quorums as was the order for a solemn assembly. John and W. W. Phelps headed the Missouri high council as representatives of the presidency of the church in Missouri.

The purpose of the gathering was "to hear the report of the compiling committee" of the Doctrine and Covenants, "and determine, by vote, whether they 'accepted and acknowledged it as the doctrine and covenants of their faith.'"[23] On behalf of the compiling committee, Cowdery introduced the "Book of doctrine and covenants of the church of the Latter Day Saints." Rigdon "explained the manner by which they intended to obtain the voice of the assembly for or against said book."[24] After these

21. Whitmer, Book of John Whitmer, chap. 11, p. 45.

22. W. W. Phelps to Sally Phelps, 16 September 1835, in Van Orden, "Writing to Zion," 566.

23. Robinson, "Items of Personal History," 88; see also *History of the LDS Church*, 2:243–53.

24. *History of the RLDS Church*, 1:573–74; see also Collier and Harwell, *Kirtland Council Minute Book*, 126–29.

reports, "several official members of the church, Presidents of quorums, arose, one after another, and testified to the truth of the book."[25]

John Whitmer and W. W. Phelps had previously served with Oliver on the 1833 committee that had prepared the Book of Commandments for publication. Now they testified to the correctness of the Doctrine and Covenants: "W. W. Phelps bore record that the book presented to the assembly, was true. President John Whitmer, also arose, and testified that it was true."[26]

Then, the quorums accepted and acknowledged it as the Doctrine and Covenants of their faith. Afterward, the question was put to the whole assembly and carried unanimously. The work was ratified as a whole and was accepted as "our belief, and ... the faith and principle of this society as a body" (1835 D&C, Preface, iv).[27] By this action, the work was instantly added to the church's canon of scripture, since the practice of having a general conference canonize new scripture would not be implemented during Joseph Smith's lifetime. Immediately thereafter, "David Whitmer and Samuel H. Smith were appointed general agents to the Literary firm[28] to take and sell Books among the extensive branches of the Church, &c."[29]

That same day, John Whitmer and W. W. Phelps ordained Morris Phelps (no known relation to W. W. Phelps) "to the High Priesthood of the Holy Order of God by the voice of the Presidency. Laying their hands upon him, they said: 'The Lord [will] instruct [thee] with all wisdom necessary to fill this important station according to the will of God. Thou shalt, if faithful, be sent to the nations of the Earth, and gather Sheaves from the East & West & from the North & South with all power necessary to accomplish thy mission.'"[30]

Joseph Smith and F. G. Williams were back in Kirtland by August 23, 1835. On August 31, the presidents of the Kirtland and Missouri church-

25. Robinson, "Items of Personal History," 88; see also *History of the LDS Church*, 2:243–53.

26. *History of the RLDS Church*, 1:573–74.

27. Robinson, "Items of Personal History," 88; *History of the LDS Church*, 2:243–53.

28. Collier and Harwell, *Kirtland Council Minute Book*, 126–27.

29. W. W. Phelps to Sally Phelps, 16 September 1835, in Van Orden, "Writing to Zion," 566.

30. Collier and Harwell, *Kirtland Council Minute Book*, 124. That same day Warren Parrish was ordained to the First Quorum of Seventy, Sherman Gilbert was ordained an elder and several others received blessings, 124–26.

es, (Joseph Smith, Oliver Cowdery, Sidney Rigdon, Frederick G. Williams, W. W. Phelps, and John Whitmer) except David Whitmer, prepared a letter to Zion in Missouri. The letter was addressed to Hezekiah Peck, a counselor in the Missouri bishopric and member of the Colesville Branch in Clay County, to be read publicly to the Missouri Saints. It harshly rebuked the disciples. By performing an ordination, Missouri church officials had risked drawing too much public attention to the activities of the church:

> The Presidency of Kirtland and Zion say that the Lord has manifested by revelation of His Spirit, that the High Priests, Teachers, Priests, and Deacons, or in other words, all the officers in the land of Clay County, Missouri, belonging to the Church, are more or less in transgression, because they have not enjoyed the Spirit of God sufficiently to be able to comprehend their duties respecting themselves and the welfare of Zion; thereby having been left to act in a manner that is detrimental to the interest, and also a hindrance to the redemption of Zion.... Now we say there is no need of ordaining in Zion.[31]

Joseph intricately linked the temple with the redemption of Zion. As an extension of this concept, beginning in September 1835, Joseph began giving patriarchal blessings, thus weaving into the theological and ecclesiastical fabric of early Mormonism several strands that had originated almost two years earlier. On December 18, 1833, Joseph Smith Jr. had pronounced some of what would later become known as patriarch's/evangelist's blessings. He blessed his father and other male members of the family; then, with the assistance of Oliver Cowdery, Sidney Rigdon, and Frederick G. Williams, Joseph ordained Joseph Sr. a president and patriarch. Joseph Smith Sr. thus became the church's first patriarch-evangelist. On February 19, 1834, Joseph Sr. pronounced blessings upon his sons, Joseph Jr. and Samuel. He began visiting families to give blessings in the summer of 1834.[32]

---

31. Joseph Smith, Jun., Oliver Cowdery, Sidney Rigdon, Frederick G. Williams, W. W. Phelps, and John Whitmer, portion of letter to Hezekiah Peck, 31 August 1835; retained copy inserted in Whitmer, Book of John Whitmer, chap. 16, pp. 77–78; also *History of the LDS Church*, 2:229–31.

32. Joseph Smith Jr., blessing for Joseph Smith Sr., 18 December 1833; *History of the LDS Church*, 2:32; see also Johnson, *My Life's Review*, 17.

On June 21, 1835, before the completion of the Doctrine and Covenants, Joseph had preached in Kirtland on the evangelical order.[33] In September 1835, Joseph Jr. again gave blessings to those who had been with the work from the beginning, including Oliver Cowdery, David Whitmer, and John Whitmer, in preparation for the promised empowerment associated with the dedication of the Kirtland Temple. Joseph Jr. blessed John Whitmer on September 22, 1835. John's blessing promised that he would "make a choice record of Israel unto the memory of his name.... [and] be blessed with abundance of the good things of this earth with houses and lands, in the fruit of the field, with horses and with asses and she asses, with gold and with silver, and with precious stones, even the things of the lasting mountains. He shall be made mighty in the hands of his God, in bring [*sic*] to pass the redemption of Zion."[34] Like John's blessing, the dedication of the temple in late March 1836 rang with strong overtones pertaining to the redemption of lost lands in Zion.

Expectation was building among members for some type of Pentecostal endowment experience as a prerequisite of the church's long-awaited return to Jackson County. Planning for the redemption of Zion was conducted at the highest levels of church government. Such plans kept high hopes alive for a forthcoming return to Zion. The intensity of this effort is reflected in an entry penned in Joseph's own hand in his 1835–36 sketch book, only two days after he had blessed John:

> September 24 1835 This day the High Council met at my house to take into consid[e]ration the redeem[p]tion of Zion. It was the voice of the spirit of the Lord that we petition to the Governor [of Missouri]. That is those who have been driven out /should/ ~~to~~ do so to be set back on their Lands next spring. We [should] go next season to live or dy [die] ~~to this end so the dy is cast~~ in Jackson County.
>
> We truly had a good time and Covena[n]ted to strug[g]le for this thing u[n]till death shall desolve [dissolve] this union. And if one falls that the rest be not discouraged but pe[r]sue this object untill it is ac[c]omplished. Which may God grant u[n]to us in the name of Christ our Lord.

33. Journal History, 21 June 1835.

34. John Whitmer, blessing, 22 September 1835, recorded 2 October 1835, in the handwriting of Oliver Cowdery, p. 14.

...This day drew up an Arti/c/le of inrollment for the redeem[p]
tion of Zion that we may obtain volunteers to go next spring /to
M[iss]o[uri]/. I ask God in the name of Jesus that we may obtain
Eight hundred men / or one thousand/ well armed [men] and that
they may ac[c]omplish this great work. Even so. Amen.[35]

The 1834 Zion's Camp expedition, which had approached the problem of restoring the Saints to their Jackson County property using a militaristic strategy, had been both a public relations and a legal failure, but
Joseph Smith apparently entertained continued hopes that a second armed
expedition would produce different results. Joseph believed that building
and dedicating the Kirtland Temple, would unleash an anticipated endowment-like conferral of power from heaven. Such an endowment would at
long last allow the church's triumphal return to Jackson County, Missouri.
Central to all of this was Smith's vision of a second Zion's Camp expedition in the spring of 1836, comprised of eight hundred young and middle-
aged church men.[36]

Smith's expectation regarding the redemption of Zion was further
manifested in a supper conversation on October 29, 1835, involving Joseph,
Emma, bishops Partridge and Whitney, and others. "We were called to
sup[p]er. After being seated around the table," wrote Joseph in his 1835–36
diary, "We were called to sup[p]er. After being seated around the table,"
wrote Joseph in his 1835–36 diary, "Bishop Whitney observed to Bishop
Partridge that /the/ thought had just occur[r]ed to his mind that perhaps
in about one yea[r] from this time they might be seated together around a
table in the land of Zion. ~~Sister Emma~~ /My wife/ observed that she hoped
it might be the case that not only they but the rest of the company present
might be seated around her table in the land of promise ... and my heart
responded 'Amen!' God grant it, I ask in the name of Jesus Christ."[37]

35. Faulring, *An American Prophet's Record*, 34–35.

36. Romig and Riggs, "Reassessing Joseph Smith's 'Appointed Time for the Redemption
     of Zion,'" 31–33.

37. Faulring, *An American Prophet's Record*, 42–43; *History of the LDS Church*, 2:294.

CHAPTER EIGHTEEN

Tension and Reconciliation

JOHN'S BROTHER PETER arrived in Kirtland on October 17, 1835.[1] Albert Brown, a traveling companion, left the following reminiscence of their trip and the conditions in Kirtland at the time of their arrival:

> I left Missouri in the 12th of September in company with Peter Whitmer and arrived in Kirtland Ohio the 17 of October we had a prosperous journey and found our relatives all in good health and the church in great prosperity here numbers increasing and the blessings of heaven poured out upon them and Many coming from all parts of the United States to Kirtland and to missionaries to obey the commandments of the Lord and to escape the calamity and judgments pronounced against this generation or those that obey not the fullness of the gospel of our Lord Jesus Christ thus the work of the Lord rolls on and the power of Godliness begins to be maid manifest and the great things of the kingdom revealed I will relate one incident that happened not long since in our favor by some men that had four Egyptian Mummies which they were carrying through the world to exhibit and also an ancient record that was found in their coffins this record containing some of the history of <Joseph> while in Egypt and also of Jacob and Many prophesies Delivered by them these records were bought by the church and also the Mummies and are now in Kirtland they bought the Mummies for the sake of the records and paid 2400 hundred Dollars for them. And we are very anxious to have them translated. Many of the Learned have been to Kirtland to examine the characters but none of them have been able to tell but very little about them and yet Joseph without any of the wisdom of this world can read them and know what they are.[2]

1.   Whitmer, account book, 17 October 1835, p. 23.

2.   Albert Brown to Dear Parents, 1 November 1835.

John Whitmer, in his capacity as church historian, noted, "Joseph the Seer saw these records and by the revelations of Jesus Christ could translate these words, which gave an account of our forefathers ~~even Abraham~~. Much of which was written by Joseph of Egypt who was sold by his brethren which when all translated will be a pleasing history and of great value to the Saints."[3]

Joseph Smith, Oliver Cowdery, and W. W. Phelps devoted much of July to studying the papyri. The history of the church that Phelps later wrote for this period (phrased as though Joseph was speaking) states, "The remainder of this month, I was continually engaged in translating an alphabet to the Book of Abraham, and arranging a grammar of the Egyptian language as practiced by the ancients."[4] Most of the Egyptian Alphabet and Grammar written during this period is in W. W. Phelps's handwriting.

Temple construction progressed; and in anticipation of its dedication in the spring of 1836, church leaders began studying

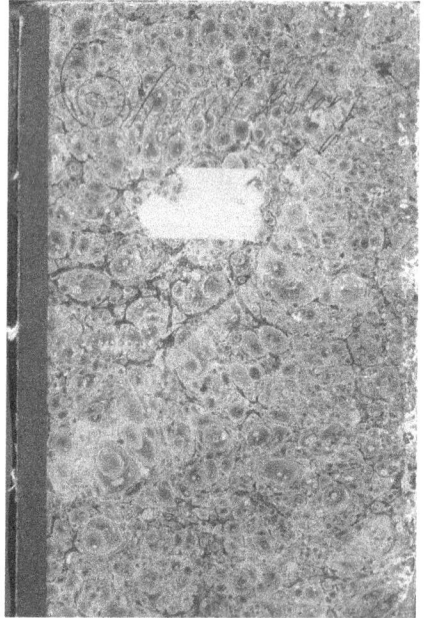

John Whitmer History, ledger book cover. Courtesy of Community of Christ Archives.

Hebrew. John Corrill recalled: "In the fall, and early part of the winter of 1835, the elders gathered in to Kirtland, to the number, I should think, of three or four hundred, who remained there through the winter. Schools were instituted for the use of the elders and others. Some studied grammar

---

3.   Whitmer, Book of John Whitmer, chap. 16, p. 76.

4.   *History of the LDS Church*, 2:238.

Church members used this copy of Seixas's Hebrew grammar during the winter of 1836–37 in the Kirtland Temple. Courtesy of Community of Christ Archives.

John Whitmer's signature from the back of an original copy of Seixas's Hebrew grammar, ca. 1836. Courtesy of Community of Christ Archives.

and other branches: they also employed the celebrated Hebrew teacher, Mr. Seixas, who gave them much insight, in a short time, into that language."[5]

Initially, John and Phelps were apparently too busy working on printing-related projects to attend the Hebrew class. W. W. Phelps wrote to his wife, Sally, in Liberty, Missouri, on November 14, 1835: "The Elders are coming in every day, almost; the school has commenced under the

5. Corrill, *Brief History of the Church of Christ*, 22–23.

272 *Eighth Witness: The Biography of John Whitmer*

charge of President Sidney Rigdon as teacher. I shall not be able to go much, if any.... My time and that of President John Whitmer is all taken up in the printing office."[6]

Joseph Smith was so enthused about studying Hebrew, that he began moving students from other classes into Seixas's class. Elisha Hurd Groves observed, "Went into An English grammer [*sic*] School for a few weeks. From there I was taken out by the Prophet Joseph and put into an Hebrew School."[7] Then on February 1, 1836, Joseph opened a second class of thirty additional Hebrew students.[8]

As excitement about the study of Hebrew spread throughout the church community, John and W. W. Phelps were invited to participate. Hebrew classes met each morning and afternoon. Many evenings, John, Oliver, and W. W. Phelps gathered in Smith's office in the attic of the temple to study their lessons.[9]

A special copy of Seixas's Hebrew grammar has survived as an artifact of this academic pursuit and is now housed in the Community of Christ Archives. John Whitmer inscribed his name in the back of this volume. Also, a Hebrew alphabet practice sheet bearing Peter Whitmer Jr.'s signature on the reverse is inserted in the back of the book.[10]

The burdens of debt, pressures to redeem Zion (meaning, reclaim Jackson County real estate), completion of the temple, and anxiety over their ability to accomplish the grand vision of Zion all weighed heavily upon church leaders during this time. In November, John joined leading brethren as they offered up a united prayer for petition and deliverance. Cowdery, the meeting's clerk, included the prayer in the minutes. As with one voice, the brethren requested the following blessings: "That the Lord will give us means sufficient to deliver us from all our afflictions and difficulties, wherein we are placed by means of our debts; that he will open the

6. W. W. Phelps to Sally Phelps, 14 November 1835, quoted in Van Orden, "Writing to Zion," 568.

7. Groves, "An Account of the Life of Elisha Hurd Groves," 3.

8. *History of the LDS Church*, 2:390.

9. Oliver Cowdery, diary, 11 February 1836, quoted in Arrington, "Oliver Cowdery's 'Sketch Book,'" 423.

10. Seixas, *A Manual Hebrew Grammar*.

way and deliver Zion in the appointed time and that without the shedding of blood."[11]

The first copies of the newly printed Doctrine and Covenants became available in September 1835. Book blanks were sent to a bindery in Cleveland, Ohio, although this approach proved expensive. In November 1835, Oliver Cowdery went to New York City to purchase equipment so that the church could bind its own published materials.[12]

John obtained one of these first editions. In the 1920s or 1930s, after John's death, M. Wilford Poulson, a mid-twentieth-century instructor at Brigham Young University, acquired the book from John's family at Mirabile, Missouri. This book is now housed in the L. Tom Perry Special Collections Library at Brigham Young University, Provo, Utah. John's Doctrine and Covenants contains probably one hundred handwritten marginal notations. All are typically short. In one example, John notes that others have the "Same gifts as Joseph."[13]

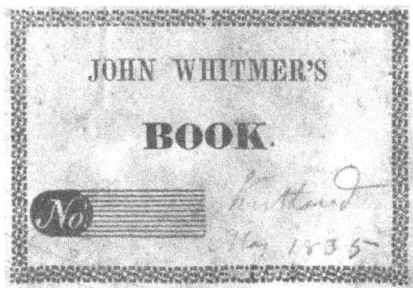

John Whitmer's Bible book plate, inscribed: "Kirtland May 1835." Courtesy of the LDS Church History Library.

John and Sarah's second child, a healthy son whom they named John Oliver Whitmer, was born November 30, 1835,[14] and John purchased a Bible in which to record vital events for his family. After John's death in 1878, his daughter, Sarah Elizabeth Whitmer Johnson, recorded the deaths of David Whitmer (1888) and David Whitmer Jr. (1895).[15] The book plate inside the front cover of John's Bible bears the inscription, written in John's hand, "Kirtland, May, 1835." John also marked passages

---

11. Smith, "Ohio Journal," in Jessee, *Papers of Joseph Smith,* 2:90–91.

12. W. W. Phelps to Sally Phelps, 14 November 1835, in Van Orden, "Writing to Zion," 568.

13. John Whitmer, Doctrine and Covenants (1835), John Whitmer's personal copy.

14. Barchers, "The Descendants and History of the Peter Whitmer Sr. Family," 42.

15. John Whitmer family Bible.

which were supportive of the Book of Mormon; for example, in the top margin above Romans 11:17–25, John wrote, "grafting in of branches."[16]

Historian Richard Bushman points out that August–December 1835 was a time of heightened strife in Kirtland. For Joseph Smith, especially, who, Bushman argues, espoused the "culture of honor," these months presented a grueling series of difficult interactions and angry responses within the church body, its leading quorums, and with his own extended family. This same sense of honor also fueled Smith's compulsion to resolve the movement's Missouri defeats. "Supported by militants like Lyman Wight, Joseph even showed a willingness to make the military gesture. He spoke of the armies of Israel and gave himself a military title."[17]

John was more specific about the emerging spirit of militarism in chapters 15–18 of his history, describing activities at Kirtland. He recorded: "On the twenty-fourth day of September, 1835, on which day we met in counsel at the house of J. Smith, Jr., the Seer, where we according to a previous commandment given, appointed David Whitmer, captain of the Lord's Host, and Presidents F. G. Williams and Sidney Rigdon his assistants; and President W. W. Phelps, myself and John Corrill, as an assistant quorum, and Joseph Smith, Jr., the Seer, to stand at the head and be assisted by Hyrum Smith and Oliver Cowdery. This much for the war department by revelation."[18] It is not clear what Joseph Smith had in mind as a "war department" nor what the duties of "captain of the Lord's Host" might be, but the language shows the rhetoric's appeal to Joseph.

Joseph Smith made it clear that he was the supreme head of the church; but at the same time, he instituted a confusing proliferation of new administrative officers. The organization Smith had set up in Missouri was obviously handicapped throughout 1835 because all three members of its presidency were in Kirtland. At this time, Joseph Smith, Sidney Rigdon, and Frederick G. Williams were presidents of the high priesthood as well as presidents of the Ohio church. On December 5, 1834, to further confuse matters, Oliver Cowdery had been appointed associate president, while Jo-

16. John Whitmer family Bible. See also "Rare Photos Donated to Church by John Whitmer's Descendants," *Church News*, November 29, 1958, 11.

17. Bushman, *Joseph Smith: Rough Stone Rolling*, 249; see also, pp. 235–39.

18. Whitmer, Book of John Whitmer, chap. 17, p. 81; McKiernan and Launius, *An Early Latter Day Saint History*, 151.

seph Smith Sr. and Hyrum Smith became assistant presidents.[19] By March 1836 there were a total of nine church "presidents."

Not surprisingly, signs of growing administrative and interpersonal tensions emerged within the leading quorums and between Smith and the Whitmer clan. However, Smith's inclusive administrative arrangement seemed to garner unwavering public loyalty. During their residence in Kirtland, both Oliver and John reflected this predisposition, intentionally countering anyone who challenged Joseph Smith or the leading authorities. As an example, the Kirtland High Council met on September 16, 1836, to hear a complaint "against brother Henry Green for accusing President Joseph Smith Junr. of rebuking brother Aldridge wrongfully & under the influence of an evil spirit." Oliver "arose and showed by a few very plain remarks, how Satan had sought from the beginning to destroy the Book of Mormon, and in order to do this, had been continually leveling his shafts against the servants of God who were called to bring it forth, and bear testimony of it to the world."[20] But the nature of their private conversations, at least in regard to Joseph, may have begun to change.

Joseph still needed to draw succor at times from the longstanding Smith-Whitmer family relationship. Capitalizing on David's repute as a spiritual healer, Joseph turned to him on October 10, 1835, when Joseph visited his father and found "him failing very fast." On October 11, Joseph wrote, "At evening Brother David Whitmer came in. We called on the Lord in mighty prayer in the name of Jesus Christ, and laid our hands on

---

19. *History of the LDS Church*, 2:176. For another explanation of this rather complicated organizational structure, see Van Orden, "William W. Phelps," 2. Van Orden wrote, "Early the next week [ca. May 25, 1835] Joseph Smith called a council of the 'presidents' of the Church who were in Kirtland. This council consisted first of Joseph Smith, Sidney Rigdon, and Frederick G. Williams of the First Presidency who also served simultaneously as the Ohio presidency. The Missouri presidency—David Whitmer, W. W. Phelps, and John Whitmer—would also now be part of this council. Finally, three other brethren who had been called as 'presidents' the previous December were, now, also members of the council. The first of these was Oliver Cowdery, who actually held the second highest position in the Church as Associate President. The other two were the Prophet's brother Hyrum Smith and his father Joseph Smith, Sr." See also Jessee, *Papers of Joseph Smith*, 20n1.

20. Collier and Harwell, *Kirtland Council Minute Book*, 132, 133–34. Another example appeared in a later case before the high council on September 19, 1835, 135–40.

him [Joseph Sr.], and rebuked the disease.... Our aged father arose and dressed himself, shouted, and praised the Lord."²¹

Peter Whitmer Jr.'s arrival at Kirtland coincided with John's and David's growing awareness that the church's rapid evolution was increasingly straining their relationship with Joseph. Hints may be seen of many small problems by the fall of 1835. On November 8, Joseph penned the following censure in his journal, though without recording the reason for his displeasure: "The word of the Lord cam[e] unto me, saying, that President Phelps & President J[ohn]. Whitmer are under condemnation before the Lord, for their errors <for which they made satisfaction the same day>."²²

Such a rebuke must have deeply troubled John. An added blow came when he, David, and Peter learned that their brother Christian had died in Missouri on November 27, 1835. In a letter to Sally, Phelps observed that Christian Whitmer's death "made a deep impression upon his relatives and the brethren."²³ The high council designated Peter Jr. to fill Christian's place on the high council of Zion in Missouri.²⁴ Christian's cause of death is not known, but he had suffered for many years with a sore on his leg that would not heal. Nevertheless, his death must have been a shock. Christian, the eldest son, either lived at the Michael Arthur farm or with Father and Mother Whitmer among the Saints of the Hulet Settlement, west of Liberty. He and his wife, Anne, had been among the first members of the church, baptized in Seneca Lake by Oliver Cowdery, April 11, 1830. Christian, who had supported his family as a shoemaker, was buried in a now-forgotten grave "on a farm about two miles from Liberty."²⁵ Soon thereafter, Anne married Sylvester Hulet.

21. Smith, "Ohio Journal," in Jessee, *Papers of Joseph Smith*, 2:51.

22. *History of the LDS Church*, 2:304. The insertion is W. W. Phelps's handwriting and was probably added during the Nauvoo period, while he was preparing Joseph's history for publication. Jessee, *Papers of Joseph Smith*, 2:68.

23. W. W. Phelps to Sally Phelps, 5 January 1836.

24. *History of the LDS Church*, 2:357.

25. Christian Whitmer was born January 18, 1798, at Harrisburg, Pennsylvania. Jenson, *LDS Biographical Encyclopedia*, 1:276–77. The Hulet Settlement was located about nine miles west of Liberty while the Arthur farm was about two miles southwest of Liberty on Whithers Road, section 25, range 32, township 50. The farm therefore better fits the description of the location of his grave.

Over the course of 1835, Kirtland's elected non-Mormon overseers had taken care to "warn out" many prominent Mormons who were considered potential burdens on the local economy. John Whitmer and other prominent Mormons were among those asked to leave.[26] Despite such gratuitous harassment, John's stay in Ohio eventually stretched to more than a year. As one of the church presidents and as editor of its newspaper, John remained at Kirtland through the dedication of the temple in March 1836, and played an important role in its dedication. Participants had come to anticipate that they would experience a significant spiritual empowerment during the temple's dedicatory events. To impart a heightened sense of significance to preparatory events, Smith turned to the use of ritual.

On January 21, 1836, in anticipation of the actual temple dedication, under the management of the first presidency, John took a leading role in administering the first ordinances, namely: a series of preparatory sessions transmitting blessings and privileges. W. W. Phelps informed his wife, "We are preparing to make ourselves clean, by first cleansing our hearts, forsaking our sins, forgiving every body, all we ever had against them; and by washing the body; putting on clean decent clothes, by anointing our heads, and by Keeping all the commandments. As we come nearer to God we see our imperfections and nothingness plainer and plainer."[27]

The Whitmer clan participated in the preliminary or initiatory ritual washings and anointings along with other key leaders. Oliver Cowdery recorded that "[we] washed our bodies with pure water before the Lord, preparatory to the anointing with the holy oil." He added, "After we were washed, our bodies were perfumed with a sweet smelling oderous wash."[28]

---

26. Kirtland Township, trustees minutes, 1835, quoted in Quinn, *Mormon Hierarchy: Origins of Power*, 90.

27. W. W. Phelps to Sally Phelps, [17] January 1836, in Van Orden, "Writing to Zion," 574. In the holograph of this letter, someone inserted "Jan 17 1836" on this page written in graphite, in Phelps, journal, p. 110.

28. Oliver Cowdery, diary, 1836, quoted in Arrington, "Oliver Cowdery's 'Sketch Book,'" 419. Washing and anointing were the prelude to a unique spiritual experience that lasted the night. Smith, "Ohio Journal," 21 January 1836, in Jessee, *Papers of Joseph Smith*, 2:145–48. W. W. Phelps's hymn "The Spirit of God," sung at the Kirtland Temple dedication, memorialized this sacred observance: "We'll wash, and be wash'd, and with oil be anointed, / withal not omitting the washing of feet," in Smith, *A Collection of Sacred Hymns*, 120–21.

Church leaders led a series of preparatory sessions in the Kirtland Temple in advance of the March 27, 1836, temple dedication. Courtesy of Henry Inouye.

The ancient origins of ritual purification and cleansing as an act of devotion are present in many religious traditions. Smith's adaptation may draw on Old Testament scriptural precedent by which priests of Israel were washed and anointed in association with temple functions (Ex. 29:4–7). Joseph knew that the strict observance of ritualized belief was likely to heighten the group spiritual experience. Consequently, he invested considerable energy and creativity in conveying a prescribed ritual to participants.

The use of alcohol for washing the body in this manner is consistent with Smith's earlier instruction known as the word of wisdom, which states: "Strong drinks are not for the belly, but for the washing of your bodies" (CofC D&C 86:1d; LDS D&C 89). Alcohol added to water was known to be superior to water alone for cleansing, in part, due to poor sanitary conditions and the prevalence of ground water contamination by fecal matter that was characteristic of the period. In fact, some believed that bathing in water alone was harmful to the body.[29] Smith may have selected cinna-

---

29. Smith's counsel was consistent with contemporary medical and emerging temperance understandings about the use of alcohol. Bush, "The Word of Wisdom in Early Nine-

mon to perfume their bodies because cinnamon was a common element in Judeo and Egyptian ceremonial practices. The Egyptians used cinnamon and cassia along with myrrh in embalming, perhaps because cinnamic acid (and also myrrh) has antibacterial effects. The Hebrews and others, used cinnamon and cassia in religious ceremonies.[30] In the Old Testament, God instructed Moses to make a holy anointing oil for use in the ritual ordination of the priesthood and for the consecration of the articles of the tabernacle. Holy anointing oil was to be composed of a mixture of cinnamon, cassia, olive oil, myrrh, and hemp (Ex. 30:22–25).[31] Oliver Cowdery said that participants preparing for the dedication of the Kirtland Temple "were annointed with the same kind of oil and in the man[ner] that were Moses and Aaron, and those who stood before the Lord in ancient days."[32] Richard Bushman, a Joseph Smith biographer, observed, "Exodus called for myrrh and calamus to be mixed with 'sweet cinnamon,' but cinnamon was all these poor Latter-day priests could manage."[33]

On Saturday evening, February 6, 1836, Smith "called the anointed together to receive the seal of all their blessings." Smith separated participants by quorums, thus grouping the men with familiar cohorts. He charged each group to engage in silent prayer. After a suitable period, a member of the presidency concluded the experience by offering a sealing prayer, and the group responded with the "hosanna shout." Those who had

---

teenth-Century Perspective," 165–67. "Many Americans felt about a bath as had their European forebears in the time of the plague; that to remove dirt from the pores was to open them to various kinds of ailments that were lurking in the breeze." Following this logic, in the late nineteenth century, the Boston city council passed a bill making baths illegal unless prescribed by a doctor. Burns, *The Smoke of the Gods: A Social History of Tobacco*, 154. My thanks to Mike Hoey for identifying sources about mixing water, whisky, and cinnamon.

30. "Cinnamon," *Spices, Exotic Flavors and Medicines*, History and Special Collections, Louise M. Darling Biomedical Library, UCLA, accessed December 20, 2010, http://unitproj.library.ucla.edu/biomed/spice/index.cfm?displayID=5.

31. Pure myrrh, 500 shekels, (about 6 kg); sweet Cinnamon, 250 shekels, (about 3 kg); Sweet Calamus, 250 shekels, (about 3 kg); Cassia, 500 shekels, (about 6 kg); and Olive oil, one hin, (about 5 quarts). "Holy Anointing Oil," *Wikipedia*, accessed December 20, 2010, http://en.wikipedia.org/wiki/Holy_anointing_oil#cite_note-4.

32. Arrington, "Oliver Cowdery's 'Sketch Book,'" Thursday, January 21, 1836, 419.

33. Bushman, *Joseph Smith: Rough Stone Rolling*, 312.

experienced a vision or received prophecy were encouraged to rise up and share their empowering experiences with the group.[34]

Many participants probably experienced these activities as being appropriate, even familiar. Quorums who followed Smith's instructions "enjoyed a great flow of the holy spirit.... Many arose & spok[e] testifying that they were filled with the holy spirit which was like fire in their bones so that they could not hold their peace."[35] Oliver Cowdery also recorded that "many saw visions, many prophesied, and many spoke in tongues."[36] But Smith was clearly exasperated because some groups did not get it right. Joseph wrote in his journal, "While I was in the east room with the Bishops Quorums [*sic*] I f[e]lt by the spirit that something was wrong in the quorem of Elders in the west room.... The quorem of elders had not observed the order which I had given them.... [S]ome of them replied that they had a teacher of their own.... [T]his caused the spirit of the Lord to withdraw ... & this quorem lost th[e]ir blessing in a great measure."[37]

Bushman suggests that these experiences elevated ritual within the movement as an adjunct method of revealing the mind and will of God—thus giving ceremony the same level of importance as "the visitations of angels, the voice of the Spirit speaking for God, the translations of historical texts, and the organization of church council by precedent and experience."[38]

Around January 1836, Phelps advised his wife, Sally: "Brother Whitmer's father and mother came [two words covered by tape] from Vermont in October and have both been [one word covered] baptized."[39] It is not known to whom Phelps referred. During the Kirtland period, David

34. Jessee, *Papers of Joseph Smith*, 2:169–70.

35. Ibid., 2:170–71.

36. February 6, 1836, in Arrington, "Oliver Cowdery's Kirtland, Ohio, 'Sketch Book,'" 422.

37. Jessee, *Papers of Joseph Smith*, 2:170.

38. Bushman, *Joseph Smith: Rough Stone Rolling*, 315.

39. W. W. Phelps to Sally Phelps, http://www.boap.org/LDS/Early-Saints/Phelps-letters.html, accessed November 2013. The Whitmer reference is apparently a typographical error. Probably this is a reference to Newel K. Whitney's parents, Samuel and Susanna (Kimball) Whitney, of Vermont. The senior Whitneys moved to Kirtland, Ohio, where they joined the church. See Phelps, letter, undated fragment, [ca. January] 1836, Phelps Papers, Journal, Perry Special Collections, p. 68. William Jolly "died at Parkman, Geauga County, Ohio." Jessee, *Papers of Joseph Smith*, 1:494.

Whitmer's in-laws, William and Elizabeth Jolly, apparently relocated to the Kirtland area.⁴⁰

However, the joy characterized by such family gathering was tempered by concern in February 1836 as Peter Whitmer Jr. experienced a serious health crisis. Although it was a time of general anticipation as the House of the Lord was completed, an entry from Oliver Cowdery's diary reveals the continual struggle against disease and illness that represented another aspect of the Kirtland community: "Saturday, [February] 27 [1836].... I was called to lay hands upon pres. T. B. Marsh, in company with pres. J. Smith, jr., and also [to lay hands upon] my brother-in-law, Peter Whitmer, jr., the latter was very sick of a Typhus fever, and was immediately healed and arose from his bed."⁴¹ Peter Jr.'s condition was grave indeed, and, having only recently been bereaved by Christian Whitmer's death, the family remained hopeful that Peter Jr. would be restored to good health.

A meeting on February 2, 1836, seemed to capture a wished-for spirit of friendship in the gospel with Smith. "Some other business was transacted in Union and fellowship," Joseph Smith recorded. "The best of feelings seemed to prevail among the brethren and our hearts were made glad on the occasion. There was joy in heaven."⁴²

Throughout the fall and winter of 1835–36, F. G. Williams & Co. worked furiously to complete the anticipated printing jobs in time for the temple dedication. Phelps reported in November 1835 that the print shop was then employing three apprentices and four journeymen but was still unable to meet its deadlines. Their persistence paid off, however, and by the spring of 1836, bound copies of the Doctrine and Covenants and Emma Smith's hymnal had been prepared.⁴³ The hymnal, appearing in March 1836, was one of the first books bound at Kirtland.⁴⁴

---

40. It is believed that William Jolly, born 1777 in Massachusetts, joined the church for a short time. He was living in Parkman, Geauga County, Ohio, at the time of his death in 1863. Elizabeth Jolly, born 1788, wife of William, died in 1843, also at Parkman, Geauga County, Ohio. Jessee, *Papers of Joseph Smith*, 1:494.

41. Cowdery, diary, in Arrington, "Oliver Cowdery's 'Sketch Book,'" 425.

42. Faulring, *An American Prophet's Record*, 96.

43. Crawley, *A Descriptive Bibliography*, 20.

44. The volume bears an 1835 date but was not completed until just before the temple dedication in late March 1836. Crawley, "A Bibliography of the Church of Jesus Christ

Finally, all was in readiness for the dedication of the Kirtland Temple. Before the service began on March 27, 1836, John and other church officials, including the temple doorkeepers, "dedicated the pulpits, and consecrated them to the Lord."[45] After the congregation was seated, the presidents of the church took their places in the Melchisedec pulpits at the west end of the house of worship. Frederick G. Williams, counselor in the first presidency, Joseph Smith Sr., associate president, and W. W. Phelps, counselor in the Missouri presidency seated themselves in the top row of pulpits. President Joseph Smith Jr., associate president Hyrum Smith, and Sidney Rigdon, counselor in the first presidency, occupied the second row from the top. David Whitmer, Missouri president, Oliver Cowdery, assistant president, and John Whitmer, counselor in the Missouri presidency filled the third.[46] David Whitmer testified that he saw angels in the building during the dedicatory service.[47]

On March 29, 1836, following the dedication, presidents of the Ohio church Joseph Smith, Frederick G. Williams, Sidney Rigdon, Hyrum Smith, and Oliver Cowdery met in the house (of the Lord) to receive further revelation about their "going to Zion."[48] Three hundred or so official members of the Kirtland Stake, in an all-night session, capped the extended endowment experience by gathering to seal blessings, prophesy, and pronounce curses upon their Jackson County enemies. After washing their faces, the presidents of the church also washed each other's feet. Hyrum Smith washed David Whitmer's feet, David washed W. W. Phelps's feet, and Phelps washed John Whitmer's feet. Then, the bishop and his counselors were washed.[49] The entire ceremony ended with a militant covenant: "If any more of our brethren are slain or driven from their lands in Missouri

---

of Latter-day Saints in New York, Ohio, and Missouri," 503–4.

45. *History of the LDS Church*, 2:410–11; also Faulring, *An American Prophet's Record*, 142.

46. *History of the LDS Church*, 2:410–11.

47. "During his prayer Presdt David Whitmer also saw angels in the house." Joseph Smith, diary, 27 March 1836, in Jessee, *Personal Writings of Joseph Smith*, 213.

48. Jessee, *Papers of Joseph Smith*, 2:203.

49. Faulring, *An American Prophet's Record*, 153.

by the mob ... we will give ourselves no rest until we are avenged of our enemies to the uttermost."[50]

This firm resolve was a natural outgrowth of the much-anticipated and emotionally satisfying empowerment accompanying the dedication of the Kirtland Temple, a high-water mark for the movement. Allusions to the redemption of lost lands in Missouri occurred frequently through the dedication.[51] The ceremony integrated both endowment elements dating from 1831 and the theme of Zion's longed-for redemption.[52]

At some point following the dedication of the Kirtland Temple, a series of portraits of church leaders and their wives was planned to adorn the walls of the temple. Extant portraits from this series appear to date around 1837. Documentary sources suggest that portraits were completed for Oliver and Elizabeth Ann Cowdery, David and Julia Ann Whitmer, and Frederick G. and Rebecca Williams.[53] All of these prominent church

50. Jessee, *Papers of Joseph Smith*, 2:206.

51. In a January 21, 1836, meeting of the first presidency and the twelve, several participants saw magnificent visions during purification rites of washing and anointing. Joseph, who experienced a vision of the celestial kingdom, wrote, "My scribe also received his anointing /with us/ and saw in a vision the armies of heaven protecting the Saints in their return to Zion." Faulring, *An American Prophet's Record*, 120.

52. In addition to the redemption of Zion, endowment elements included a gathering, preparatory ordinances, supernatural manifestations, and empowerment for mission. An earlier endowment experience had occurred June 4, 1831, at a Kirtland conference. Corrill, *Brief History of the Church of Christ*, 18. A second endowment-like event is associated with the opening of the School of the Prophets. Collier and Harwell, *Kirtland Council Minute Book*, 6. This third endowment experience took place in conjunction with the dedication of the Kirtland Temple. Faulring, *An American Prophet's Record*, 153–55. During this later event, little distinction was made between "First Elders" endowed earlier and those selected later. See also "History of Joseph Smith," *Times and Seasons*, 6:1104–5.

53. Ella E. Johnson of Far West, Missouri, a granddaughter of John Whitmer, donated portraits of William Cowdery, Oliver Cowdery, and Elizabeth Ann Whitmer Cowdery to the RLDS church in or about 1929. Ethel Johnson Lewellen, Ella Johnson's niece, of Kingston, Missouri, May 26, 1932, wrote in a letter to C. Edward Miller: "Oliver Cowdery and his wife had these portraits in their home at Richmond, Mo and Oliver Cowdery['s] wife died in 1892.... And Aunt Ella's mother was there at the time of her death or near then, and they gave her the portraits. So they had been in Aunt Ella's home until she donated them to the church." The Cowdery portraits were formally presented to the RLDS church at its 1930 conference. [RLDS] *Conference Daily, Herald, 1930*, 14, 50, 70. C. Edward Miller paid to have them restored by the Sarachek Art

individuals remained in Kirtland through early 1837. The artist of all six portraits was a Mr. Welber, identified by Vilate Kimball in a letter to her husband, Heber, then on a mission with other members of the twelve in England,[54] Because John and Phelps returned to Missouri in the fall of 1836, the completion of their portraits seems doubtful; however, more than one source suggests that John's portrait was also completed and transported to Far West.[55] A completed portrait of Sally Phelps seems least likely, since she remained in Missouri throughout this period. If Sally Phelps's portrait was completed, its whereabouts is unknown.

During his nine-month stint as editor of the *Messenger and Advocate*, John "provided the church with its official news, theological studies, and letters of missionaries in the field."[56] Under his tenure, circulation increased. Of his efforts, John observed in his farewell address to readers in the March 1836 issue:

> The great and responsible relation which a man sustains in occupying this station, to his fellow man, will have a tendency to humble, rather than exalt him in his own eyes; for he truly becomes a servant of all; and his words are left on record for present and future generations to scrutinize.... Though weak may have been my arguments and feeble my exertions, to persuade others to believe as myself, the few months I have labored in this department, I trust, I have been the means of doing some good to my fellow men. If I were not sensible that I have been doing the will of my heavenly father, I should regret, that I had

---

Galleries, Kansas City, Missouri. C. Edward Miller to Bishop J. A. Becker, 1 January 1930. The Auditorium Laurel (Service) Club paid for their framing. Portraits of David and Julia Ann are mentioned in George Q. Cannon, interview, February 27, 1884, Richmond, Missouri, in George Q. Cannon, journal, quoted in Cook, *David Whitmer Interviews*, 107. Nancy Clement Williams, a descendent of Frederick Granger Williams, commented in *Meet Dr. Frederick Granger Williams*, 128: "His [Frederick's] oil portrait [was] taken with the other two presidents to hang in the Kirtland temple when completed."

54. "Doctor Avard has gone to move his family to Missouri, he did not feel right to take the [your] Portrait with him as (Mr. Welber has not painted another for me) he said if he was able he would give it to me; he said he would rather keep it than to take twenty Dollars for it; but I should have it for ten." Vilate Kimball to Heber C. Kimball, 12 September 1837.

55. Hunt, "An Acknowledgment to John Whitmer," 131.

56. McKiernan and Launius, *An Early Latter Day Saint History*, 17.

John Whitmer's granddaughter, Ella E. Johnson, sitting in the yard of John Whitmer's house in Far West, Missouri, ca. 1930s. Courtesy of Community of Christ Archives.

ever suffered my name to become public; I could not endure the idea of having been the means of persuading men to detract from truth, and embrace error: it has been a principle in my heart to embrace truth, and reject error; and I trust it will remain in my heart forever.

In concluding his farewell, this quiet man once again bore testimony of the Book of Mormon in the strongest terms possible: "I have most assuredly seen the plates from whence the Book of Mormon is translated, and ... have handled these plates, and know of a surety that Joseph Smith, Jr., has translated the Book of Mormon by the gift and power of God."[57] Oliver Cowdery resumed the editor's chair for the April 1836 issue of the *Messenger and Advocate*.

During the April 2, 1836, meeting of the firm of F. G. Williams & Co., a "partial division" of stock (inventory) was agreed upon. John and Phelps were released from any further financial responsibility; and both, along with David Whitmer, were compensated for their labors with "five hundred books of Doctrine & Covenants when bound and five hundred hymn books together with the subscription list for the *Messenger & Ad-*

---

57. John Whitmer, "Address," March 1836, 285–86.

vocate and *Northern Times* now due the firm in Clay Co., Missouri."[58] Obviously, the plan was that they would sell the publications, keeping the proceeds as their wages.

Members of the Missouri presidency were now free to return to their Missouri homes. John did not record his feelings about the forthcoming move, but they must have been somewhat mixed. As missionaries brought additional converts into the movement, the church's ambiguous future in Missouri drew new members once again to Kirtland. In part, to accommodate the needs of this influx and in response to the opportunity it created, Joseph began building a magnificent city of "Saints." Kirtland became a place where religious beliefs dominated all phases of adherents' social, economic, and political lives. The twin institutions of sacred cities and the economic system of consecration were seen as vehicles of public salvation.[59] The abstraction of the kingdom of God began to evolve political dimensions. Priestly assignments assumed the embellishment of temporal government.

During the year John spent in Kirtland, he saw a great deal of community growth. The *Messenger and Advocate* for July 1836, with Oliver Cowdery at the helm, praised Kirtland's amenities:

> The house of the Lord is here, and a congregation of between 800 and 1000 assemble in it ... every Lord's day.... A very considerable branch of Chagrin river runs in a diagonal direction through the North part of this town, making ... good mill sites.... There are two saw mills, one gristmill, one fulling-mill, and one carding machine in the short distance of two miles. A steam saw-mill 35 by 60, designed for two saws is being erected in this place.... As you approach the place from the North you come to the brow of a hill.... Here the eye ... catches the Lord's House on a beautiful eminence or table land on the south side of the stream, at an altitude of from 80 to 100 feet from its bed.... The house of the Lord is here, and a congregation of between 800 and 1000 assemble in it ... every Lord's day.... We have one public inn or tavern, three stores of dry goods kept by our brethren, and two by other people, making five in all, and quite a number of mechanics of

58. *History of the LDS Church*, 2:433–34.
59. Cooper, *Promises Made to the Fathers*, 100–101, 132–49.

Overview of Kirtland, Ohio, as depicted in James Harrison Kennedy's book, Early days of Mormonism, Palmyra, Kirtland, and Nauvoo, *1888. Courtesy of Community of Christ Archives.*

different occupations.... Our village has been laid out in a regular plot, and calculated for streets to cross each other at right angles.[60]

As a result of Kirtland's Mormon development, some observed an increasing preoccupation with extensive temporal and financial matters. This engagement created a desire for a facility to handle church banking. On November 2, 1836, articles of agreement were prepared for the establishment of the "Kirtland Safety Society Bank." John Whitmer's history notes, "Leaders of the church at Kirtland Ohio Established a bank for the purpose of Speculation and the whole church partook of the same Spirit."[61] This disapproving tone, as borne out by history, was not misplaced. Despite legal barriers to such an endeavor, participants subscribed to stock and bound themselves to payment of notes issued by the institution. Many lots, with inflated values, were subscribed in exchange for stock. It was not long before the venture failed; and by February 1837, the bank was no longer redeeming its bank notes with specie.[62]

60. "To the Saints Abroad," July 1836, 349.

61. Whitmer, Book of John Whitmer, chap. 20, p. 86; McKiernan and Launius, *An Early Latter Day Saint History,* 161.

62. *Telegraph,* January 27, 1837, comments: "Joseph Smith publicly withdrew his support from the bank and transferred his stock to Granger and Carter." Kirtland Safety So-

William McLellin, who left the church primarily because of the bank's failure, later described the episode:

> Although the Lord had said to him [Joseph Smith], that, "In temporal labors thou shall not have strength, for this is not thy calling;" yet the Arch Deceiver of man made him believe, that he could accumulate riches of the world. The first great move for this purpose was the formation of a mercantile firm, composed of the Presidency of the Church. They went east and purchased thousands of dollars worth of goods; and that, too, upon credit—thus violating a plain principle of God's word: "Owe no man anything, but love one another." Kirtland was stocked with plenty of merchandize. Pride, folly, and riotous living soon took the uppermost seats in the hearts of the Latter Day Saints. Not content with merchandizing, they also speculated in a city plot, and they purchased many farms in the region round about. And one door of transgression will soon open another.—
>
> These leading men, among a numerous people, have an ambition to rise to the pinnacle of fame as great speculators, so that they might lay up much worldly treasure. Soon, therefore, it is determined that a KIRTLAND BANK must be established, to hold their treasures; and to aid them to get more. So eager were they, and so sanguine of success, that they did not even wait to get a charter from the State, but seemed to think that everything must bow at their nod—thus violating the laws of the land in which they live, which in the end brought upon them swift destruction. Their merchandizing, their city plot, and land speculations, together with their pretended banking system, brought ruin, inevitable ruin, upon thousands.[63]

McLellin was not alone in placing the blame for the bank's failure primarily on Smith, but the actual causes were much more complex.[64] And

---

ciety Ledger Book, p. 273, cited in Hill, Rooker, and Wimmer, *The Kirtland Economy Revisited: A Market Critique of Sectarian Economics*, 44.

63. McLellin, "A Special Conference of the Church of Christ," 7.

64. Regarding the Kirtland Safety Society, see Sampson and Wimmer, "Kirtland Safety Society: The Stock Ledger Book and the Bank Failure," 427–36; Partridge, "Failure of the Kirtland Safety Society," 437–54; Hill, Rooker, and Wimmer, "Kirtland Economy Revisited: A Market Critique of Sectarian Economics," 391–476; Staker, *Hearken, O Ye People*, 463–517.

something of a domino effect was taking place. With Smith's continuing emphasis on gathering to Missouri, pressure was building in Clay County. Smith became aware that one aspect of his grand plan for the redemption of Zion was working too well. Enthusiasts were embarking for Clay County, according to plan "to build up the strength of mine house." Before leaving their homes in the East, members loaned money to Joseph's church-appointed committee, anticipating that land would be purchased for them in Missouri.[65] But they arrived to find only confusion. No land had been purchased, and the Clay County Saints were unable to absorb all of the newcomers. Reed Peck, a member who broke with the church in 1838, claimed that much of the money remained in Kirtland, rather than reaching its intended destination in Missouri:

> While the Society [of church members] were making arrangements to remove from Clay county, [to northern Ray County, Missouri] [Joseph Smith[,]] H. Smith and O Cowdery borrowed some thousands of dollars of the church in Ohio giving the lenders orders on their agents in Missouri for land in payment, a part of which money was sent to Caldwell County and invested in land which was immediately sold at a small advance per acre to those holding the orders spoken of, but it was soon made apparent that the money sent to Missouri fell far short of the amount of Orders prescribed consequently many persons arriving in Caldwell county destitute of means were unable to purchase the homes they anticipated finding having as they supposed sent their money in advance to secure them one.[66]

Meanwhile, the path to Jackson County remained blocked by its citizens' absolute refusal to tolerate a Mormon return. Simultaneously, old settlers in Clay County who had willingly given refuge to the suffering Saints from Jackson County in 1834 were now, in 1836, increasingly anxious for them to move elsewhere. With pressure continuing to build in Missouri, it became critical that Smith find a solution. He realized that land must be obtained elsewhere. John Whitmer pinpoints March 11, 1836—

---

65. Tanner and Tanner, Reed Peck Manuscript, 4; Peck, born in New York, was the son of Hezekiah Peck and a member of the Colesville Branch. Reed drafted a lengthy narrative of his Missouri experiences after his 1839 excommunication. See Biographical Register in Jessee, *The Papers of Joseph Smith: Journal, 1832-1842*, 2:578.

66. Ibid., 14–15.

two weeks before the temple's dedication—as the point at which Joseph Smith decided to begin buying land outside Jackson or Clay Counties. John noted, "On the 11, March 1836, [Smith] Held a council [at Kirtland] in which Edward Partridge I. Morley, John Corrill and W. W. Phelps were appointed wise men and were sent to Mo. with some money [to] purchase land for the Saints—to seek a place for them &c."[67] To this point, money targeted for "the redemption of Zion" had meant buying out the old settlers in Jackson County. In consultation with key leaders—probably Frederick G. Williams, Sidney Rigdon, Hyrum Smith, and Oliver Cowdery—Smith designated the four "wise men" that John lists as agents, to use church money to buy land in what became Caldwell County, Missouri.[68] Phelps recalled in 1864: "There were four men appointed in a private meeting in the Temple at Kirtland as *'wise men'* to purchase all the land in Jackson County and in the regions round a bout for money &c I was ordained president of this new quorum, with Edward Partridge, John Whitmer and John Corril for my assistant *wise men.*"[69] Although Phelps is specific that Jackson County land was part of the shopping list, almost certainly, the church's immediate priority relative to the acquisition of land was shifting to Caldwell County, Missouri. But, church expectations in relation to the redemption of Jackson County continued to play a central role in the life of the church for the next several years. Smith would devise several more approaches in hopes of remediating the outcome.

---

67. Whitmer, Book of John Whitmer, 11 March 1836, chap. 17, p. 83. A more probable date for this meeting is March 13, 1836. Joseph Smith makes no mention of such a meeting on March 11 but wrote on the 13th: "Met with the presidency & some of the 12, and counseled with them upon the subject of removing to Zion this spring. We conversed freely upon the importance of her redemption and the necessity of the Presidency removing to that place, and that their influence might be more effectually used in gathering the Saints to the country. We finally come to the resolution to emigrate on or before the 15th of May next if kind providence Smiles upon us and opens the way before us." Jessee, *Papers of Joseph Smith,* 2:188.

68. Whitmer, Book of John Whitmer, 11 March 1836, chap. 17, p. 83; McKiernan and Launius, *An Early Latter Day Saint History,* 154. Whitmer includes Isaac Morley, while omitting himself as one of the four. Phelps, in contrast, includes John.

69. Phelps, "A Short History of W. W. Phelps' Stay in Missouri," 4. Phelps considered that they had succeeded: "We did the best we could, and I have the documents to claim some thousands of acres of this purchase from Uncle Sam yet."

Though Jackson County's time was over as a Mormon gathering place for the rest of the nineteenth century, Smith never relinquished his own hopes of reclaiming the sacred land. But, he continued to adjust his own expectations and those of church members. Richard Bushman points out that Joseph Smith realized he could turn "the Missouri experience into a usable past."[70] This recontextualization process enabled his movement to heal and move beyond immediate prophetic disconfirmations.

"Such accommodations over time wrought a change in Mormon perceptions that redefined the meaning of the redemption of Zion. A major shift in Mormon cosmology followed among believers regarding the nature and geographical boundaries of Zion."[71] The movement's recontextualization of Zion-oriented events and concepts would prove remarkably successful, helping transform Mormonism into an enduring movement.

70. Bushman, *Joseph Smith: Rough Stone Rolling,* 404.
71. Romig and Riggs, "Reassessing Smith's 'Appointed Time,'" 42–43.

CHAPTER NINETEEN

Return to Missouri: 1836

A LTHOUGH THE CHURCH in Missouri was expecting its leaders to come home any day, Smith's plans for the redemption of Zion required that David Whitmer remain in Ohio. A big part of the plan involved convincing as many members and converts as possible to gather to Clay County, Missouri. Oliver again took over as *Messenger and Advocate* editor, which freed John Whitmer to devote his attention to new duties.

Typically content to remain in the shadow of his younger brother David, John was again thrust to the forefront. With David and Oliver's return delayed for the foreseeable future, John prepared to return to Missouri with a heavy set of new responsibilities. The citizens of Clay County were growing weary of the Mormon presence in their midst. It was becoming apparent that church members could not remain there much longer.

Kirtland and Missouri presidents met on April 2, 1836, to transact business "which was to have bearing upon the redemption of Zion." After the meeting, Smith and Cowdery spent the remainder of the day raising funds for the redemption of Zion.[1] The "wise men" needed all that could be obtained with which to buy land in Missouri. A few days later, on April 9, the wise men left Kirtland, but John was not with them. It was Phelps, Partridge, Corrill, and Morley who set out first for Clay County, arriving there in early May.[2]

1.   Jessee, *Papers of Joseph Smith*, 2:208–9.
2.   William McLellin dates the departure of Partridge, Phelps, Corrill, and Morley from Kirtland as Saturday, April 9, 1836. Shipps and Welch, *Journals of William E. McLellin*, 213. Edward Partridge recorded: "Friday the 6th ... arrived at Clay Co. Liberty landing about 3 P.M. Arrived at my family about 5 P.M. and found them well." Partridge, "Journal of Bishop Edward Partridge," 46; see also Whitmer, Book of John Whitmer, chap. 19, p. 84; McKiernan and Launius, *An Early Latter Day Saint History*, 156.

Expecting that he would also soon be leaving, in May 1836, John arranged to send a wagonload of goods on ahead to Missouri with other returning members. Levi Jackman recalled, "Tuesday 17 [May 1836] On this day Brother Follett and I started in company with Brother McHenery [*sic*] and family. We had a wagon and horses belonging to Brothers David and John Whitmer to go home with, taking the most of the load for them."[3] When John left for his home in Missouri, he apparently retained custody of his manuscript history and possibly also his revelations manuscript.

Meanwhile, in Missouri, the initial sympathy of Clay County residents for the exiled Mormons in 1833 had been replaced by apprehension at their growing numbers. By the spring of 1836, the county's non-Mormon citizens were becoming openly hostile. In May 1836, they learned of Joseph Smith's plan for the Mormon reoccupation of Jackson County, by force if necessary. General irritation turned into a fear of violence at the hands of what they increasingly saw as "religious fanatics."

News of a pending Mormon invasion appeared in the Liberty newspaper, *Far West*, on May 3: "Information has been received from Kirkland, [*sic*] Ohio, through various channels of another movement among the Mormons to obtain possession of the 'promised land,' and to establish their Zion in Jackson county, the scene of their former disastrous defeat. They are said to be armed to the number of 1500 or 2000 and to be making way in [detached] parties to the 'debatable ground.'"[4]

On May 12, a letter written by well-known Jackson County fur trader Francois Chouteau shows that word of the threat had spread rapidly throughout the region, sending Jackson County Missourians into a state of alarm: "Apparently we are going to wage war here very soon with the Mormons. They have a force of 2000 men in Clay County who are organizing and making the arrangements necessary to attack us in Jackson County and we have to take measures in order to make serious resistance. It appears that they are disposed to retake possession of their land by force."[5]

John Whitmer astutely chronicled in his history the connection between the upswing in public animosity against the Mormons and the ar-

3. Jackman, "A Short Sketch of the Life of Levi Jackman."

4. "Another War Brewing," July 16, 1836.

5. Francois Chouteau to Pierre Menard Sr., 21 May 1836, in Marra and Boutros, *Cher Oncle, Cher Papa*, 154; see also Flagg, *The Far West*, 2:111.

rival in Missouri of the "wise men" Edward Partridge, Isaac Morley, John Corrill, and W. W. Phelps: "As soon as these men first arrived at home [in early May 1836] the Devil roared in this land and stired [*sic*] the old Jackson Co. Mob up to great anger, and [also] the People in Clay Co."[6]

David Pettigrew, a Mormon living in Clay County, also believed that the Jackson County citizens were responsible for stirring up tensions in Clay: "The old feelings and excitement of Jackson County now began to show itself in Clay. It was first started by the ministers of the gospel such as Elder John Edwards and Balden [probably Baldwin], Baptist ministers, and others soon followed. They soon had the people to arms and, I suppose, made the people believe they were doing God's service. I am satisfied that many of their leading men were from Jackson County."[7]

The four "wise" Mormons realized immediately that they urgently needed to buy undisputed land on which to settle the gathering Saints, if only temporarily. Member Emily Austin recalled an assembly of church members in Missouri "to make arrangements for purchasing farms. It was therefore put to vote in this assembly, and carried, that Newel Knight, I. Morley, and J. Carrel [Corrill], were elected to go to Caldwell County [northern Ray territory], Missouri, and look out [for] lands for the Mormon church."[8] Acting on the general terms of Smith's advice, they dispatched survey parties to the area north of Clay County, a nearly uninhabited portion of Ray County. Edward Partridge's daughter, Eliza, recalled that her father formed one of the party "to look for a location for the Saints as the people with whom we resided began to be somewhat uneasy about us."[9]

John Corrill, who also formed one of this party, provides a view of this critical time for Mormons: "In May 1836 ... we went on to Grand River Country, and on Shoal Creek, Ray County; prairie, some timber on the

6.   Whitmer, Book of John Whitmer, chap. 19, p. 84; McKiernan and Launius, *An Early Latter Day Saint History*, 156.

7.   Pettigrew, "History of David Pettigrew," 6. Henry Hill, a Clay County Baptist elder, recalled, "I was ordained to the Christian ministry by the well-known elders, William Thorp and John Edwards. [I] have been a member of the Fishing River Association ever since." Hodges and Woodruff, "Henry Hill," 19.

8.   Austin, *Mormonism; or, Life Among the Mormons*, 85.

9.   Lyman, "Life and Journal of E. M. P. L S.," 4.

streams, a large open country with a few settlers in the timber; bees abound and deer, turkeys and wild game in abundance. So we are preparing to leave our old neighbors."[10]

The decision was quickly made. On June 3, 1836, church representatives went to the land office in Lexington, Missouri, to complete the first land purchases. The selected locations were discrete and scattered. They entered a second round of purchases on June 22, 1836. On the heels of this exploration into Ray County, old settlers in Clay County made it known that they wished the Mormons to move out. Relations between the Saints and Missourians had disintegrated to the point that, by mid-June, Clay citizens had appointed a public meeting to discuss what should be done. In short order, the fear of a pending Mormon invasion and a general distaste for the Latter Day Saints translated into acts of violence against them. Clay County citizens began a campaign of surveillance over the county roads, attempting to prevent the immigration of Saints into the county.[11]

Perhaps, during Phelps's and Whitmer's last meeting with Smith in Ohio, Joseph had agreed that he could amass his Army of Israel elsewhere just as well as in Clay, County. Smith was also probably aware that the plan would be subject to adjustment because of Kirtland's mounting cash-flow crisis. Increasing pressures in Missouri made a mid-course correction necessary. Joseph hoped to buy out the Jackson County settlers, return the Mormons to that county, and fulfill his prophecy that September 11, 1836, would be the date set for redeeming Zion. But at the moment of greatest opportunity, the Mormons could not raise the needed cash. Because of Kirtland's debt, funds intended for Missouri were diverted for the Ohio emergencies.

John, Sarah, and baby John Oliver reached Clay County in June 1836, just as local non-Mormons were adopting a series of resolutions urging Latter Day Saint removal.[12] Another mass meeting was scheduled for June 29, 1836. On the evening of June 28, some Clay County citizens attacked

---

10. Corrill, quoted in Stevenson, *Stevenson Family History*, 1:16.

11. Andrew Wilson, letter, quoted in Parkin, "History of the Latter-day Saints in Clay County, Missouri," 255.

12. *History of the LDS Church*, 2:448–52. Clay countians offered to collect money to aid with the relocation of destitute Saints. Davis, *Story of the Church*, 262–63.

one of the Saints' settlements on Fishing River.[13] According to Drusilla Dorris Hendricks, regulators "harassed many and whipped one man nearly to death."[14]

At a meeting the next day, Clay citizens passed a resolution instructing the Mormons "to leave us, when their crops are gathered, their business settled, and they have made every suitable preparation to move."[15] The Mormons agreed. Because the situation was so volatile, local Missouri Mormon leaders had to start making tough decisions on their own.

On July 1, 1836, church representatives "resolved, for the sake of friendship and to be in a covenant of peace ... notwithstanding the necessary loss of property and expense we incur in moving, we comply with the requisitions of their resolutions in leaving the county of Clay, as explained by the preamble accompanying the same; and that we will use our exertions to have the church do the same; and that we will also exert ourselves to stop the tide of emigration of our people to this county."[16]

Anticipating this outcome, the Mormons had already made the two land purchases described above in northern Ray County.[17] Reed Peck corroborated that "to remove from Clay County was in accordance with their [the Mormons'] feelings, having for some time contemplated a settlement in some new and uninhabited place that they could enjoy their constitutional privileges as other societies, but they had feared opposition to their collecting in a body."[18] Two years later, Parley P. Pratt reflected much the same view of these events: "The committee in behalf of the citizens [of Clay County] requested that they (the Saints) should look themselves a new location.... However, a location had already been selected and about sixteen hundred acres of land purchased but a short time previous; and they were willing to go, and some of them were making preparations to move

13. Andrew Wilson, letter, quoted in Parkin, "History of the Latter-day Saints in Clay County," 255.

14. Hendricks, "Historical Sketch of James Hendricks and Drusilla Dorris Hendricks," quoted in ibid., 256.

15. *History of the LDS Church*, 2:448–52.

16. "Public Meeting," 359, 360.

17. LeSueur, "Missouri's Failed Compromise: The Creation of Caldwell County for the Mormons," 120.

18. Tanner and Tanner, *Reed Peck Manuscript*, 3.

there soon before the meeting of the committee. Wherefore the committee on the part of the church consented to the proposition made to them."[19]

John Murdock, then living on Crooked River, observed, "The High Council and the Presidents, W. W. Phelps and John Whitmer, and the Bishopric met in council in Clay County, and agreed on a removal of the Church to Shoal Creek. I proclaimed the same to the brethren in this vicinity and on the 30th, [August 1836] according to previous agreement."[20] Murdock next visited Ray County on about August 1 with John Corrill, "met the Ray County Committee, and laid our complaint before them, and desired of them that if we could not have a home with them that they would grant us the privilege of settling on Shoal Creek in the Territorial part of the state; and after calling in a meeting of the county, they granted the latter but would not let us live with them."[21] On December 29, 1836, the state legislature enacted legislation establishing Caldwell County in northern Missouri.[22]

When informed of the decision to move north by a letter that reached Kirtland in late July, the church leaders were supportive. In Smith's mind, buying land in Ray County territory in no way precluded the eventual redemption of Zion. On July 25, 1836, Joseph Smith, Sidney Rigdon, Oliver Cowdery, Frederick G. Williams, and Hyrum Smith wrote letters to Missouri church leaders and to Clay County representatives.[23] They advised followers to leave the county as fast as they could.[24]

By way of advice to their people, Kirtland's Mormon officials urged, "Be not the first aggressors. Give no occasion, and if the people will let you dispose of your property, settle your affairs, and go in peace, go.... Relative

19. Pratt, "A History, of the Persecution, of the Church of Jesus Christ, of Latter Day Saints in Missouri," 51.

20. Murdock, journal, p. 17.

21. Ibid., ca. August 1, 1836.

22. John Corrill may be credited, working with Alexander Doniphan at the state level, in securing this sanctuary for the church. Winn, "'Such Republicanism as This,'" 57–58; Doniphan's bill became law in December 1836. *Journal of the Missouri Legislature*, 188, 194, 200, 220.

23. Sidney Rigdon et. al., to John Thornton et. al., and Sidney Rigdon et. al., to Dear Brethren, 25 July 1836, 355–59.

24. Joseph Smith, quoted in *History of the RLDS Church*, 2:69–71.

of your going to Wisconsin, we cannot say; we should think if you could stop short [in Missouri?] in peace, you had better."[25] Later that same day, Joseph, Hyrum, Sidney, and Oliver started east for Salem, Massachusetts, in what became an unsuccessful search for additional funds.

Also that same day, in Missouri, a general assembly of the church met at President W. W. Phelps's house and authorized Phelps, John Whitmer, Edward Partridge, Isaac Morley, and John Corrill to "search out land for the Church to settle upon."[26]

Reed Peck later documented: "The excitement in Clay and the adjacent counties favored their design and through the intercession of John Corrill with the concurrence and active influence of lawyers D. R. Atchison A. W. Doniphan Amos Rees and a few other gentlemen, leave was granted the Mormons, by common consent of the surrounding counties to settle in a body a tract of land north of Ray County twenty four miles long and Eighteen miles wide."[27]

The Mormons' decision to leave Clay County exacerbated the church's delicate financial situation, since the exodus required additional funds. Saints in the East had their own financial problems. On July 25, 1836, Missouri Saints sent apostle Thomas B. Marsh to borrow "and collect money among the Churches in Mo., Illinois Indiana, Kentucky and Tennessee, and put the same into the hands of the Zion Presidency, for the upbuilding and benefit of 'Poor Bleeding Zion.'"[28] Marsh's success later proved a stumbling block for John and Phelps.

Around August 1, 1836, John and William guided a small vanguard of Saints directly to what would become Caldwell County, selected a site, negotiated with the few nonmember inhabitants in the vicinity, bought out their interests, and purchased other lands directly from the US govern-

25. Ibid., 2:73.

26. Cannon and Cook, *Far West Record*, 105.

27. Tanner and Tanner, *Reed Peck Manuscript*, 3. The dimensions he describes are of Caldwell County, created by the state legislature in December 1836.

28. Cannon and Cook, *Far West Record*, 105. Wilford Woodruff, on a mission in Tennessee, noted, "Thomas B. Marsh ... came in Company with Councellor Groves by order of the High Council of Zion to visit the Churches in the South to Borrow monies to purchase lands in Zion." Kenney, *Wilford Woodruff's Journal*, 1:88.

ment.[29] They secured their new homeland using money that the "wise men" had brought from Kirtland and perhaps some from their own pockets.

Murdock recorded that, on August 3, "I started for Shoal Creek, and on the 5th arrived in that Section of country, where the brethren W. W. Phelps, John Whitmer in company with the Bishopric, E. Partrige [*sic*], I. Morley and John Corrill, had looked out a location."[30]

On August 8, 1836, Whitmer and Phelps traveled to the federal land office at Lexington, Missouri, where they successfully entered bids for sections 10, 11, 14, and 15 in Mirabile Township (29 west, range 56 north), Caldwell County. The north half of the town site was entered by W. W. Phelps and the south half by John Whitmer.

Each of the principal Mormon settlements in Clay County also sent their own representatives to investigate options for mass removal. Emily Austin observed, "On returning, they brought a good report, that the site was far superior to any they had previously seen; a good grazing country, plenty of timber and good water, and few inhabitants."[31] Rank-and-file Mormons in Missouri were eager to take up land where they might live in peace and avoid further violence[32] and, consequently, seemed relieved at the decision to move north.

Reed Peck's account confirms this perception. "In the course of the fall of 1836 and succeeding winter nearly all the Mormons in the state had collected in Caldwell county and by persevering industry <soon> opened extensive farms and it seemed by magic that the wild prairies over a large tract were converted into cultivated fields."[33]

Simultaneously with this new beginning, the Whitmers experienced two psychological blows. First, the much-anticipated prophetic date of September 11, 1836, for redeeming Jackson County property passed unrealized, refocusing hopes for a long-term Mormon stronghold on Caldwell

---

29. John Murdock, journal, p. 17; quoted in Murdock, *John Murdock: His Life and His Legacy,* 142; Joseph Holbrook, autobiography, p. 38. List of lands purchased August 8, 1836, by John Whitmer (400 acres) and W. W. Phelps (560 acres) in Johnson and Romig, *An Index to Early Caldwell County, Missouri, Land Records,* 232.

30. Murdock, journal, p. 17.

31. Austin, *Mormonism; or, Life among the Mormons,* 85.

32. March, *History of Missouri,* 556.

33. Tanner and Tanner, *Reed Peck Manuscript,* 3.

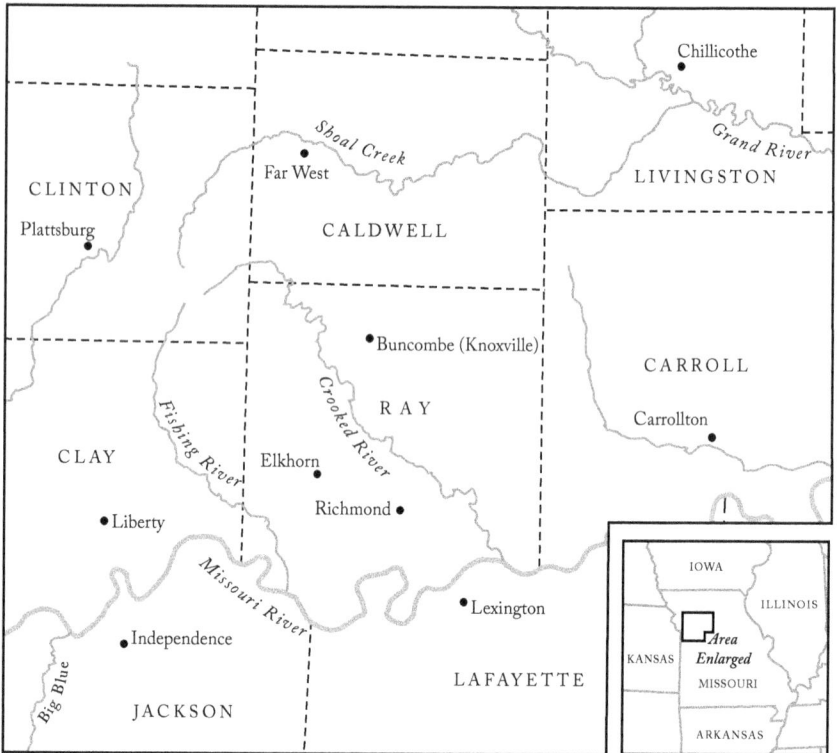

Fig. 19.1. Caldwell County was formed from a northern portion of Ray County in 1836.

County. Second, Peter Whitmer Jr., who had suffered from consumption for many years, suddenly took a turn for the worse and died on September 22, 1836, at Liberty. He was buried beside his brother Christian. Brother-in-law Oliver Cowdery commemorated the death of the two brothers in the *Messenger and Advocate:* "By many in this church, our brothers were personally known: they were the first to embrace the new covenant, on hearing it, and during a constant scene of persecution and perplexity, to their last moments, maintained its truth—they were both included in the list of the eight witnesses in the Book of Mormon, and through they have departed, it is with great satisfaction that we reflect, that they proclaimed to their last moments, the certainty of their former testimony."[34]

34. Cowdery, "The Closing Year," 426.

Surviving Peter Jr. were his wife, Vashti, and three daughters, one born after his death. Vashti continued to live with her Whitmer parents-in-law, now in their mid-sixties.[35]

Also at this critical juncture, pending lawsuits in Jackson County by Partridge and Phelps seemed to promise a sizeable cash settlement. A windfall of this type would have eased church debt and helped to underwrite the return to Jackson County. But it, too, failed. Rather than pushing these legal actions to their anticipated conclusion, attorneys representing the church settled in July 1836, which netted the church less than its legal costs.

David Pettigrew reflected the profound sense of loss the Mormons felt in leaving Clay County: "The land we had purchased we had to leave unsold, and we left behind us many graves of beloved fathers, mothers, brothers, sisters wives and husbands and children who had partly shared in our sufferings but now are gone to <their home where> there is neither strife, nor tribulation."[36]

The Saints made their new domain an unoccupied expanse measuring eighteen by twenty-four miles. According to Whitmer descendant Lorene Pollard: "The area was a waving vastness of rippling prairie, the bounty of which sometimes reached the height of a man's shoulders or more ... lush enough to promise abundant food for the horses, cattle and other livestock. Decorating this wonderland were also clusters of many different kinds of wild flowers and summer butterflies flitting to and fro."[37]

The land that John and Phelps had selected in the northwestern portion of this territory became the focus of a fast-growing community. At first called "the city at Shoal Creek," it was soon formally named Far West. By April 13, 1837, a town plat was recorded occupying the common corners of Phelps's and Whitmer's four sections. John served as a trustee of the municipal corporation, appraising and dividing the land, and supervising the sale of town lots.[38]

35. Pollard, quoted in Pollard and Woods, *Whitmer Memoirs*, 19.

36. Pettigrew, "History of David Pettigrew," 6.

37. Pollard, quoted in Pollard and Woods, *Whitmer Memoirs*, 21.

38. Evan Fry to Ella Turner, 25 January 1949. Ella Turner is Hiram Page's granddaughter.

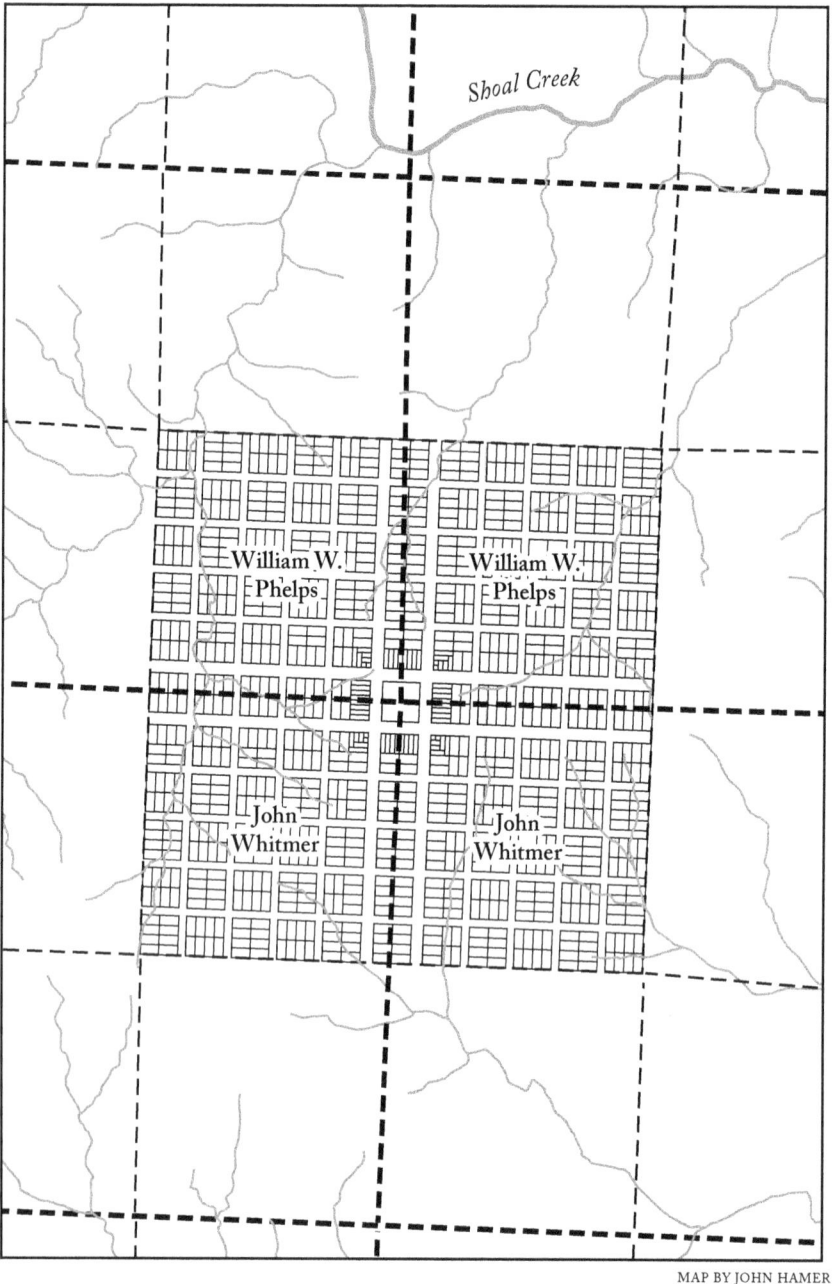

Fig. 19.2. The original 1 square mile plat of Far West comprised four quarter sections of land near Shoal Creek owned by John Whitmer and William W. Phelps.

For the next year or more, with Phelps's assistance, John played a prominent role directing colonization in this locale. But John needed more help to complete the many mundane tasks associated with founding a city. On February 7, 1837, Alonzo Winchester, a young nephew of Stephen Winchester, "commenced laboring for twelve dollars per month at 9 months."[39] Alonzo had been born September 27, 1814. Two Winchester brothers, Stephen and Daniel, and their families were living in Erie County, Pennsylvania, when they were attracted to Mormonism through the preaching of John Boynton and Evan Greene in the winter of 1832–33. Stephen (1795–1873) and Nancy Winchester, and their son Benjamin were the first in the family to be baptized on January 27, 1833. Stephen's older brother Daniel (1790–1878) and Paulina (Alonzo's stepmother) were baptized on February 19, 1833. Alonzo followed them on March 21, 1833. Stephen and Nancy immediately moved to Kirtland. In 1834, Alonzo signed up for Zion's Camp, joining his uncle's family in Ohio and marching to Missouri beside his cousin Benjamin. Benjamin's father, Stephen, was the captain of one of the Zion's Camp companies. When Stephen and his family moved to the Far West area in late 1837, twenty-four-year-old Alonzo accompanied them.[40]

Sawn boards and lumber, purchased in lower Ray County, facilitated the construction of frame houses.[41] John Whitmer built the second home in Far West, possibly that town's first frame structure. John hired as his carpenter Gilbert Miller, who labored eighteen-and-one-half days, from September through October 25, 1836. The total cost of construction was $155.75.[42] John's building was finished January 19, 1837.[43] Some sources refer to this building as "Whitmer's hotel," so it must have been of generous

39. Whitmer, account book, 7 February 1837, p. 29.

40. Stephen Winchester's family followed the church to Nauvoo, Illinois, then to Winter Quarters, and eventually to Salt Lake City. Daniel and Paulina Winchester lived out their lives in Erie County, Pennsylvania. It is not known if Daniel or Paulina had contact with Mormonism after 1833. Kiddle, et al., *The Family of Auer Winchester Proctor,* 327, 344, 619. My thanks to Winchester descendant John C. Hamer for this source.

41. Shoemaker, "Far West."

42. Whitmer, account book, September–25 October 1836, p. 27.

43. *History of Caldwell and Livingston Counties, Missouri,* 119; Fry to Turner, 25 January 1949.

proportions.[44] Whitmer descendants recall this hotel as standing directly south of the temple lot and east of the modern Community of Christ congregation building.[45] Local historian Pearl Wilcox postulated that John also built a log house during the initial Mormon occupation of Far West on a forty-acre farm a half-mile east of the Far West temple site. Wilcox claimed that the foundation stones for John's first log house could still be seen "out in the pasture" in 1959.[46]

Joseph Thorp, a resident of Clay County and later a county judge, recalled, "A city emerged with houses of every description, from a log cabin to a board shanty.... Far West was spread over a great deal of ground ... and had very shabby buildings for a city ... but the Mormons were industrious people and soon a great change was made in the appearance of the county."[47]

The extended Whitmer clan followed John to Far West. Extant federal land entries indicate John amassed 1,120 acres of land in Caldwell County during 1836–37. Jacob acquired 120 acres, while forty additional acres were purchased in David's name. This land lies about two miles directly east of the public square.[48] The brothers may initially have lived on

---

44. In 1837, Whitmer furnished a warranty deed to A. B. for "Lot 4, Block 4," Whitmer Account, [undated], reverse of title page. A portion of the hotel appears in George Edward Anderson's photograph of the Far West Temple area, 1907–8. Holzapfel, Cottle, and Stoddard, *Church History in Black and White*, 83. This location appears to agree with the legal description of the warranty deed. "The Whitmer hotel stood until about 1900 and was then used as a stable on a nearby farm." Booth, *A Short History of Caldwell County, Missouri*, 35.

45. Whitmer's daughter, Sarah Elizabeth, "was born in her father's hotel at Far West near where the [RLDS] church stands." Ethel Johnson Lewellen to C. Edward Miller, 26 May 1932. Lewellen is Ella Johnson's niece.

46. Wilcox, *Saints of the Reorganization in Missouri*, 90, describes Whitmer's first house as built of logs. Wilcox, "Saints in Northwest Missouri, Part III," 1009, describes Whitmer's house as located in the pasture south of his 1857 frame house on forty acres about one-half mile east of the Far West public square. Wilcox once owned John Whitmer's original land title for this forty-acre tract. Wilcox, *Latter Day Saints on the Missouri Frontier*, 168. This information suggests that John may have lived in a log house on his farm on the east side of the town while also operating his hotel nearer the public square.

47. Thorp, *Early Days in the West*, 82.

48. Johnson and Romig, *An Index to Early Caldwell County, Missouri, Land Records*, 232.

these properties, but a church census of March 25, 1838, indicates that the extended Whitmer clan, numbering twenty-nine, including the Pages and Hulets, lived in the southwest quarter of the town.[49] John probably arranged for family home sites south and west of the public square on some of the town lots he administered.

Church member Ethan Barrows recalled, "I went to the new country about the middle of September [1836]. There were then perhaps half a dozen families in and around Far West, but it populated very rapidly."[50]

John Whitmer's descendant Lorene Pollard described the emerging city in this way: "What a happy place the new city was growing to be, and such a busy site as well. Saws hummed and hammers pounded away, the work sounds clanging across the country side while horses and wagons lumbered along, up and down the roads. Always, it seemed, the many children could be heard laughing and playing through the throng."[51]

Craftsmen of various kinds, skilled mechanics, and artisans were among gathering church members.[52] Regional merchants were willing to furnish Mormon businessmen with a large stock of goods on credit; and in a short time, stores and businesses began to flourish. According to Reed Peck, "In 1837 there were six Mormon stores in Far West and all doing very good business."[53] An early approach to church funding favored the establishment either of firms, such as the literary firm or of church stewardship businesses, like those at Independence and Kirtland. It was anticipated that proceeds from firms would sustain leaders' families and also fund construction of the House of the Lord.

Among the first of the general stores erected in Far West was a large establishment known as the "Committee Store."[54] John Corrill was ap-

---

49. "A List of Names of the Church of Latter Day Saints Living in the S.W. Quarter of Far West."

50. Barrows, "Journal of Ethan Barrows," 42.

51. Pollard, quoted in Pollard and Woods, *Whitmer Memoirs*, 21.

52. *History of Caldwell and Livingston Counties, Missouri*, 119.

53. Tanner and Tanner, *Reed Peck Manuscript*, 4.

54. "Viator" [pseu.], "Far West: The Old Mormon Settlement in Missouri. How It Appeared Thirteen Years Ago and What It Is To-day. A Sketch of Its History," *Daily Morning Herald* (St. Joseph, MO), January 1, 1875.

pointed agent and "Keeper of the Lord's Storehouse" on May 22, 1837.[55] A church resolution on June 11, 1837, authorized John Corrill, Isaac Morley, and Calvin Beebe to open a mercantile business.[56] Traditionally, a depression in the ground behind the present Community of Christ chapel has been identified as the site of the old Far West store, perhaps the church store.[57]

Another resolution on June 11, 1837, authorized Lyman Wight, Simeon Carter, and Elias Higbee to operate a leather store.[58] Wight initially located his home about three miles from Far West; but on February 9, 1838, he moved his family to Adam-ondi-Ahman in neighboring Daviess County.[59] Hervey Green was one of the storekeepers on the public square of Far West, and his family lived in the store.[60] George M. Hinkle was also a merchant.[61] For a time, Cowdery was also a partner in Hinkle's store, in order "to get his fees for living."[62] Reed Peck was an entrepreneur (exact business not specified).[63] Lyman Littlefield and Calvin Graves opened a business in Far West, offering a stock of dry goods and family groceries. They also opened a branch in the Adam-ondi-Ahman area.[64] Before the end of 1837, Adam Lightner, another merchant, moved to Far West from Liberty, in Clay County, and built a log store. Lightner, a nonmember, was

55. Cannon and Cook, *Far West Record*, 112–13.

56. Ibid., 114.

57. Rounds, "Editorial Trail Beams," 2.

58. Cannon and Cook, *Far West Record*, 114.

59. Orange L. Wight, "Recollections of Orange L. Wight, Son of Lyman Wight," Book of Abraham Project, accessed November 30, 2007, http://www.boap.org/LDS/Early-Saints/OWight.html; "Testimony of Lyman Wight," *History of the LDS Church*, 3:441; see also Jermy Benton Wight, *The Wild Ram of the Mountain*, 122.

60. Sarah DeArmon Pea Rich (1814–93), autobiography, p. 41. Her sister-in-law, Jane Ann Rich Green, married Hervey Green in November 1837. Jenson, *Latter-day Saint Biographical Encyclopedia*, 3:208.

61. Cannon and Cook, *Far West Record*, 166–67, 268.

62. Ibid., 166–67.

63. Gentry, "A History of the Latter-day Saints in Northern Missouri from 1836 to 1839," 55; Gentry and Compton, *Fire and Sword: A History of the Latter-day Saints in Northern Missouri, 1836–39*, 54; Also, *History of the LDS Church*, 3:285.

64. Littlefield, *Reminiscences of Latter-day Saints*, 34.

married to Mary Elizabeth Rollins Lightner, a Mormon who had joined the church in Kirtland.[65] Samuel Musick operated a tavern at Far West that later came into Joseph Smith's hands.[66] Joseph Smith's parents ran the tavern after they reached Far West in the summer of 1838.

The community also had six blacksmiths, although not all are identified. Theodore Turley may have been one;[67] and Heber C. Kimball, who arrived in Far West from Kirtland in July 1838, was also trained as a blacksmith.[68]

A well at the north end of town stood in the middle of the principal highway in front of the blacksmith shop, "so that weary-worn travelers could stop to refresh themselves," water their stock, and refill their barrels.[69]

The community also attracted at least three herbal or Thompsonian doctors. According to Bertha Ellis Booth, Caldwell County historian in the 1930s, these doctors included William McLellin, Sampson Avard, and James Earl. Earl remained behind during the Mormon exodus from the state in 1838, continuing his practice in Caldwell County.[70] Frederick G. Williams, who had practiced medicine in Kirtland, continued his services after his move to Missouri in November 1837.[71] Burr Riggs was also a physician.[72]

Sometime in the late summer of 1837, John constructed a house for his parents. It may have been a frame house, since he records paying $6.75 for boards.[73]

65. Lightner, *Life and Testimony of Mary Lightner*, 9.

66. Cannon and Cook, *Far West Record*, 175, 189, 278.

67. In Nauvoo, Joseph Smith mentioned "Bro[ther] Turly['s] Blacksmith shop." Faulring, *An American Prophet's Record*, 399. Peck also operated a blacksmith shop at Nauvoo. Smith, *Journals of William Clayton*, 270.

68. Kimball, *Heber C. Kimball*, 56; Epperson, *Mormons and Jews*, 213.

69. Pollard and Woods, *Whitmer Memoirs*, 21.

70. Booth, *A Short History of Caldwell County*, 47.

71. Williams, *Meet Dr. Frederick Granger Williams*, 51. She states that Joseph traveled to Missouri with Frederick in Frederick's wagon, leaving Kirtland about September 28, 1837. They were in Far West, Missouri, by November 7, 1837. Smith returned to Ohio, and Williams stayed in Missouri where his family joined him.

72. Burr Riggs, biographical note, in Cook, *Revelations of the Prophet Joseph Smith*, 155.

73. Whitmer, account book, [late summer 1837], p. 139.

The Mormons successfully began to recontextualize the boundaries of their lost Zion. Their concept of Zion gradually became less geographically restricted to Jackson County, expanding to include the upper northwestern Missouri counties.[74] Despite the success of the new community and its zionic elements, members did not entirely forget their hopes for redeeming their first Zion in Jackson County. Elizabeth Gilbert, widow of former Jackson County leader Sidney Gilbert, expressed her hope for the redemption in a tangible form by giving John Whitmer fifty dollars to fund the building of homes in Jackson County. John noted this transaction in his account book: "Elizabeth Gilbert[—]to apply on the first house built in Jackson Co. Mo. $50.00."[75]

Meanwhile, at Kirtland, the Mormon spiritual kingdom continued to assume larger civic and governmental dimensions. John and David Whitmer were becoming more concerned by the increasing secular power and influence Smith was wielding. From their perspective, these incursions into arenas that were not traditional religious realms were inappropriate. While Smith tried to blend governmental and ecclesiastical power, the Whitmers remained strongly in favor of the separation of church and state affairs. Around them, within and outside of the church, they noticed that others were, also, growing wary of Smith's ambitions.

As the national financial depression negatively impacted the Kirtland economy, a clash of cultures inevitably developed. Smith had overutilized credit in the construction of the Kirtland Temple and in purchasing goods for Kirtland stores with which he was associated. The failure of the bank at Kirtland, followed almost immediately by plummeting land values, brought church leaders up short. The community was beset with calls for debt payment both locally and from creditors in the East. At first, Mormons rationalized such external activity as "persecution." But the situation continued to worsen. This growing tension set the stage for an extraordinary reaction within the close-knit community, and not the least effect was mushrooming mistrust between Smith and many leading members.[76]

74. Romig and Riggs, "Reassessing Joseph Smith's 'Appointed Time for the Redemption of Zion,'" 41.

75. Whitmer, account book, "Loaned Moneys," [ca. 1836], p. 28.

76. See Hill, Rooker, and Wimmer, "The Kirtland Economy Revisited," 389–475.

The fracturing community vented some of its rising exasperation on nonmembers whom they targeted as "persecutors." On November 7, 1836, in an effort at intimidation, general authorities and fifty-nine other Mormons warned Ariel Hanson, a non-Mormon justice of the peace, to leave Kirtland.[77] Although John Whitmer was already in Missouri, he alluded to the beginning of "secret combinations" at Kirtland late in 1836.[78]

According to historians of the banking fiasco, "in June 1837, Joseph Smith publicly withdrew his support from the bank and transferred his stock to [Oliver] Granger and [Jared] Carter."[79] Dismayed and facing serious financial consequences, many members called Joseph a "fallen Prophet." Up to this point, Joseph had been able to use the leverage of friendship to keep discontented members in line. Time and time again, men of standing had been cut off, only to return. Joseph always extended warm forgiveness to the repentant. But the magnitude of the bank failure seemed to surpass previous crises. The fabric of the church community frayed. Throughout their stay at Kirtland, for John, David, and Peter Whitmer, the church in Missouri remained central in their focus. Outwardly, David, who was still in Kirtland at least as late as May 29, 1837, remained supportive of Joseph, but his misgivings were also growing. Some, including Lucy Mack Smith, placed David Whitmer at the center, as resistance to church authorities began to heighten. Mother Smith was doubtless reading David Whitmer's ultimate break back into the events of this early summer of 1837, but his disaffection was probably a matter of timing and degree, not ultimate effect.

David, who remained in Kirtland for about a year after the temple dedication, had been fascinated by Joseph Smith's early use of seer stones as an aid to understanding the mind and will of God. This interest in the

77. Joseph Smith Jr., petition to Ariel Hanson.

78. Whitmer, Book of John Whitmer, chap. 20, p. 86. The October 18, 1837, Kirtland High Council minutes describe a discussion led by Samuel H. Smith during which the high council and presidents of the different quorums discussed "existing evils." The body "concluded that it was time to commence the work of reform … [by] pruning the vine of God in Kirtland, and to follow up the work night after night until it should be thought best to stay the hands." Collier and Harwell, *Kirtland Council Minute Book*, 196. As a result, a number of individuals were disfellowshipped.

79. Kirtland Safety Society ledger book, p. 273, quoted in Hill, Rooker, and Wimmer, *The Kirtland Economy Revisited*, 44.

prophetic function may have been heightened in 1834, when Joseph Smith set David apart as a seer and revelator as part of his ordination as president of the Missouri church. During his 1835–37 stay in Kirtland, perhaps wishing to better understand the appropriate use and function of seer stones, David obtained a seer stone of his own from Adeline Fuller, who was living with the Cowderys (or Whitmers) at Kirtland.[80] Lucy Mack Smith wrote,

> A young woman ... lived with David Whitmer and pretended to be able to discover hidden things and to prophesy by looking through a certain black stone which she had found.... Those persons who were disaffected towards Joseph began collecting together around this girl.... Dr. Williams ... wrote down the revelations that were given to this girl. Jared Carter ... lived in the same house with David Whitmer and soon invited the same spirit.... They still held their secret meetings at David Whitmer's ... They made a standing appointment for meetings to be held every Thursday, by the pure church in the house of the Lord. They also circulated a paper, in order to ascertain how many would follow them, and it was found that a great proportion of the church were decidedly in favor of the new party. In this spirit they went to Missouri, and contaminated the minds of many of the brethren against Joseph, in order to destroy his influence.[81]

Brigham Young also recalled, "On a certain occasion several of the Twelve, the witnesses to the Book of Mormon, and others of the authorities of the Church, held a council in the upper room of the temple. The question before them was to ascertain how the Prophet Joseph could be deposed and David Whitmer appointed the President of the church."[82]

Despite such associations, David always insisted he was not a party to such activities.[83] He may have even attempted to forestall further trou-

---

80. Traughber, "David Whitmer, 'The Last Witness,'" 24. "Adeline Fuller was born between 1810 and 1820 and apparently lived with the Cowdery family for several years, beginning in Kirtland, and moved with them to Far West and Tiffin, Ohio, where she married Lewis Bernard in 1845." Adeline may have been related to Oliver's mother, Rebecca Fuller. Morris, "Oliver Cowdery and His Critics," in Welch and Morris, *Oliver Cowdery: Scribe, Elder, Witness,* 313n10.

81. Proctor and Proctor, *History of Joseph Smith by His Mother,* 336, 338.

82. "History of Brigham Young," 1.

83. David Whitmer, to Dear Brethren, 90, one of four related letters; three are from David Whitmer and all appear to have been written December 9, 1886, in "Letters from Da-

ble. On January 17, 1837, David delivered a timely lecture on union and brotherly love to the seventies in the loft of the temple.[84]

In 1886, David wrote to Joseph Smith III, defending his view of events at Kirtland during this period:

> I do not believe that Lucy Smith wrote those things about me. Did not some man [Martha and Howard Cory] write that history for her? If she wrote those things about me, it occurred in this way; she *had been told these things* by some one, and believing them to be true, she wrote them. It is certain she knew none of these things *of her own personal knowledge.* We all know how easy it is to sometimes believe rumors and hearsay and it is easy for false reports to be started about one who is innocent. I will state, that the whole of these things from first to last are *entirely false*, and Satan is at the foundation of them all. I suppose the girl to whom reference is made, was Adaline Fuller. She was a meek, humble girl, who had but little to say to any one. She was a good, honest girl, of strong faith, and if there ever lived on this earth an humble follower of Christ, she was one. In those days several of us had this gift. I would call it the gift of discernment, or prophecy; but none of them pretended to dictate for the church, or for any member of the church. She, nor any of them, never did give a revelation to the church, or to any member of the church. I have no knowledge whatever of her ever receiving a revelation that I would fill Joseph's place when he died. This has been made up like many other things about me, after I left the Latter Day Saints. We never did hold any secret meetings at my house, or any other house; and this girl never did give any revelations at any of our meetings. As to her jumping out of her chair and dancing over the floor and boasting of her power, I say this is false in toto, and Satan has started this base falsehood about an humble follower of Christ.[85]

Rather than working against Joseph, David explained that the seed of his own (David's) downfall was in his attachment to his friend Joseph: "I loved your father; I upheld him as far as he taught the doctrine of Christ; yea, I loved him so much and had so much confidence in him, that I fol-

---

vid and John C. Whitmer," 89–90.

84. Journal History, 17 January 1837.

85. David Whitmer, to Dear Brethren, 90; emphasis his.

lowed him into many errors before I was aware that I was trusting too much in 'an arm of flesh,' instead of trusting in God only, and relying upon 'that which is written.'"[86]

David Whitmer participated in a high council meeting held in the Kirtland Temple on May 29, 1837, at which complaints were discussed against "Presidents F. G. Williams and David Whitmer and Elder Parley P. Pratt, Lyman Johnson & Warren Parrish."[87] However, the meeting broke up in confusion; and David, who had lived in Ohio for nearly three years, left the unraveling city. He was back in Missouri by July 1837. Some accused David of leaving Kirtland because of his dissenting views; but his 1886 letter to Joseph III claims that he left at Joseph's instigation:

> As to the spirit in which I left Kirtland to go to Missouri, I will tell you of a revelation received through Joseph at Kirtland which was the cause of my leaving Kirtland to come to Missouri. It was received in the presence of Hyrum Smith, Sidney Rigdon, Frederick G. Williams and others. It was not printed, as many others were never printed, so I give you a part of it from memory: "That my servant Sidney must go sooner or later to Pittsburgh; that I, Joseph, must remain here in Kirtland, for this is my appointed place; and the brethren must not keep my servant David here any longer, for he is needed in Missouri, for that is his appointed place." I parted from the brethren in Kirtland in the spirit of love.[88]

Despite David's optimism and hopes, the enthusiasm of the entire Whitmer clan for institutional Mormonism was wearing thin. Their founding friendship with Smith and the group dynamics of Mormonism that had successfully tempered their public dissent could no longer offset a developing pattern of alienation from Smith.

Meanwhile, in Far West, John and Sarah anticipated the birth of a third child. To ease the burden of housework on his wife, John hired a young woman, Ester Eggleston, to live in and help with the housework. On March 28, 1837, she "commenced labor," only to leave three weeks later. Ruby Brace replaced her and worked from May 1, 1837 to August 23, 1837.

86. Ibid., 89.

87. Collier and Harwell, *Kirtland Council Minute Book*, 181–83.

88. David Whitmer to Dear Brethren, 90.

She returned a month later on September 18, 1837.[89] On October 5, 1837, their daughter, Sarah Elizabeth, was born in one of the rooms of John's hotel.

89. Whitmer, account book, 28 March, 25 April, 23 August, and 18 September 1837, pp. 30, 33, 34.

CHAPTER TWENTY

A Gathering to Missouri: A Ragged Break

WHILE THE SPIRITUAL dimension of Mormonism buttressed David Whitmer's reliance on the Restoration gospel, his faith in Joseph Smith as a prophet continued to waiver. Most of his concerns stemmed from the increasing secular power and influence he saw the prophet wielding. From Whitmer's perspective, the incursions of Smith and the institutional church into nontraditional areas of his life was inappropriate. More comfortable with the pluralism of Jacksonian America, Whitmer did not fully support Smith's use of political and economic influence to advance the movement's religious aims.

His misgivings were not groundless. Throughout this era, Smith appeared determined to blend governmental and ecclesiastical power, a trend that would reach its climax in Nauvoo. Because of his position as president of the Missouri church, Whitmer was drawn into a greater exercise of the church's political power than he felt was desirable, but his philosophy remained strongly in favor of the separation of church and state affairs. He was not alone in this belief. The entire Whitmer clan shared David's orientation, including his brother John. Oliver Cowdery, a Whitmer in-law, wrote to his brother Lyman in 1834, revealing his own fear that the church's potential of usurping the role of government would thereby foster a spirit of intolerance that might transcend the justice and equality of individual liberties.[1]

Such political-like activities clearly highlighted a growing concern over what some intimated to be Smith's consolidation of power. Whitmer later expressed even more explicit dismay at the church hierarchy's

---

1.   Oliver Cowdery to Lyman Cowdery, 13 January 1834, p. 18.

meddling in secular concerns: "Poor Joseph! He was blinded and became ensnared by proud, ambitious men. I labored hard with him to get him to see it—from 1835—and God alone knows the grief and sorrow I have had over it.... The majority of the members—poor weak souls—thought that anything Bro Joseph would do must be all right."[2]

Meanwhile, a meeting of the Missouri presidency on November 15, 1836, sanctioned John and William Phelps's continued planning for the construction of a temple at the center of the town plat.[3] A meeting of the leading quorums on April 7, 1837, ratified this course by appointing the Missouri presidency (David and John Whitmer, and Phelps) "to superintend the building of the house of the Lord in this city Far West."[4]

David Whitmer may have reached Caldwell County in time to participate in a grand commemoration in Far West early in July 1837. The temple foundation excavation was begun on July 3, 1837. Accomplished in half a day, the cellar was dug to the depth of five feet by more than five hundred men using mattocks, spades, and wheelbarrows. The Saints also hauled a few loads of stone to the site from a nearby quarry.[5]

W. W. Phelps described the groundbreaking services for the Far West Temple and provided an overview of the prospects of the new community:

Far West, Missouri, July 7, 1837.

Monday, the 3d of July, was a great and glorious day in Far West. More than fifteen hundred saints assembled at this place, and at half past eight in the morning, after prayer, singing, and an address, proceeded to break the ground for the Lord's house. The day was beautiful; the Spirit of the Lord was with us. A cellar for this great edifice, one hundred and ten feet long by eighty feet broad, was nearly finished. On Tuesday, the 4th, we had a large meeting and several of the Missourians were baptized; our meetings, held in the open prairie, were larger than they were in Kirtland, when I was there. We had more or less to bless, confirm, and baptize, every Sabbath. This same

2.   "Letters from David and John C. Whitmer," 92–93.

3.   Cannon and Cook, *Far West Record*, 102.

4.   Ibid., 103–4.

5.   Joyce, "Mormons in Missouri," 838.

day our school section was sold at auction, and although entirely a prairie, it brought, on a year's credit, from $3.50 to $10.20 per acre, making our first school fund $5,070.00!! Land cannot be had round town now much less than ten dollars per acre. Our numbers increase daily, and notwithstanding the season has been cold and backward, no one has lacked a meal, or went hungry. Provisions have risen, but not as high as accounts say they are abroad.... Our town gains some; we have about one hundred buildings, eight of which are stores. If the brethren abroad are wise, and will come on with means, and help enter the land, and populate the county, and build the Lord's house, we shall soon have one of the most precious spots on the globe.... As ever, W. W. Phelps

   N. B.... a Post office has been established at Far West, Caldwell County, Missouri.[6]

David had arrived in Far West by July 29, 1837, and attended a high council meeting on that date. Perhaps the purpose of this trip was to arrange his family's return to northwestern Missouri,[7] but the record shows that David took vigorous steps to reassert his presidency of the Missouri church. During a general meeting of the church on August 1, 1837, the high council and quorums were reorganized. The acts approved by the high council during the absence of the presidents and bishopric, were declared "null and void." A subsequent high council meeting on August 5, 1837, considered issues about Far West lot sales and decided to proceed moderately with plans to "build a house [temple] unto the name of the lord in this

---

6.   "History of Joseph Smith," *Millennial Star*, 16:13, quoted in *History of the RLDS Church*, 2:113–14.

7.   Cook and Cannon, *Far West Record*, 118: The meeting at Far West "voted that the Committee [for the erection of the house of the Lord in Far West] stand ... until President David Whitmer goes to and returns from Kirtland." Samuel Miles's diary suggests that Whitmer was in Far West in early July 1837. "Father entered 80 acres of land at the land office being mostly prairie land with several acres of good timber situated 2½ miles south of Far West ... David Whitmer being in charge as President in Far West.... I attended the exercise [excavation of the temple, July 3, 1837] with my parents while on the way, I stepped on a scythe taken along to cut prairie grass for the team, and being bare-foot, was partly severed in two. Father took me to the house of David Whitmer, where my foot was attended to. A crutch improvised so that I went out and heard the Martial band, [and] attended the services at the Temple foundation." Samuel Miles, diary, [Miles wrote this reminiscence about 1904], p. 4.

place, as we have means."[8] Bishop Edward Partridge was designated as treasurer for temple donations and subscriptions.[9]

Missouri leaders also used the occasion to make a statement about the general church's economic philosophy. Having participated in the literary firm and united firm, designed to advance the printing concerns in Jackson County and Kirtland, they were now suspicious of the efficacy of such joint stewardship ventures. As a result, they determined that the Far West Temple would not be a joint stock project. On August 5, 1837, the council "voted that the building Committee of the house of the Lord have no store connected with the building of the house. But that every firm or individual that embarks in that business—have, own and claim such property as their own private individual property and stewardship."[10] This action reflects a growing philosophical separation that was beginning to develop between Smith and his former companions. David, who had been in Missouri for barely a month, headed back to Kirtland after this meeting to get his family.

Oliver Cowdery remained in Kirtland a little longer than David Whitmer. Cowdery had served as publisher and editor of the *Messenger and Advocate* through January 1837 when the business was transferred to Joseph Smith and Sidney Rigdon. He continued to act as clerk and recorder for the next nine months, and then left for Missouri. On September 17, 1837, an "assembly" of Saints in the Kirtland Temple, unanimously elected George W. Robinson "to act in that office as general clerk & recorder for the whole Church ... to fill the place of O. Cowdery who had lately removed to the West."[11]

Whitmer and Phelps were unable to give land purchasers clear titles to city lots, awaiting receipt of power of attorney from Smith. As a consequence, the development of Far West was somewhat hindered through 1837. John wrote to Oliver Cowdery and David Whitmer about the problem in a letter that was apparently written over several days, starting on August 29, 1837. The letter was postmarked September 3:

8.   Cannon and Cook, *Far West Record*, 116–18.

9.   Ibid., 118.

10. Ibid.

11. Collier and Harwell, *Kirtland Council Minute Book*, 189–90.

The brethren here, or some of them are becoming impatient, they want a title for their land which is to come from yourself and J. Smith Jr. I would urge the necessity of your sending your power of attorney—lest they should make unnecessary cost, which would be greatly lamented by many here. There are some who have declared that they would have a title soon if they must obtain it from the Sheriff—I tell them that the great pressure of business, is what delays the power, and that they must be patient, it will come in time, to secure them. I will do all that I can to prevent cost.[12]

Printing a Missouri church periodical remained another priority. Initially, the purpose of the church printing press was to reinstitute the *Evening and the Morning Star*, interrupted in 1833, and to publish a paper in Far West. In 1836, Phelps and John Whitmer had returned to Missouri with a supply of church publications and subscription lists. But events in Clay County also interrupted this plan.

At Kirtland in late 1837, church leaders terminated the *Messenger and Advocate*. Hoping "to make the official organ more appealing to its subscribers and bring its control into more congenial hands," officials launched the *Elders' Journal* under Joseph Smith's editorship. Oliver Cowdery transferred the print shop in Kirtland to Smith and Rigdon in February 1837 but retained control over one of the printing presses. In 1838, Rigdon testified that Cowdery "wished to get a press & some of the type which they granted him on conditions that he should give up the notes [he had against them].... [H]e then went into the office and took whatever he pleased & so completely stripped the office, as he (Rigdon) was informed by D. C. Smith, that there was scarcely enough left to print the 'Elders Journal,' whereas, before there was a sufficient quantity to print a weekly and monthly paper, the book of Covenants, Hymn Book, Book of Mormon &c. but the notes he did not give up."[13]

About the same time that Oliver acquired the press, church leaders in Missouri arranged for Elisha Hurd Groves to travel to Kirtland and bring the press to Missouri.[14] Meanwhile, as early as May, John Whitmer

12. John Whitmer to Oliver Cowdery and David Whitmer, 29 August 1837.

13. Cannon and Cook, *Far West Record*, 168.

14. Crawley, *A Descriptive Bibliography*, 1:1, 20, 72, 74; Packer, "Life History of Elisha Hurd Groves," chap. 5, p. 3.

and W. W. Phelps started fitting up a facility for the printing operation at Far West.[15] Notations in John Whitmer's account book suggest that they may have started preparing a new frame building. John's undated note reads, "Due to Hor [Herr?] and Marsh for hauling boards on Printing Office (whole amount $24.68)."[16] John hired another young church member, Chapman Duncan, to help with the construction and paid him five dollars for sawn lumber in September.[17] Duncan's autobiography suggests about six months' labor: "In the month of May [1837] I found myself in Far West.... Worked at whipsawing until fall, spent the fall, winter and spring clerking for Higbee and Morey in a store."[18] Circumstances intervened to prevent the Whitmer clan from placing Cowdery's press into operation at Far West.

David Whitmer and Oliver Cowdery were both still in Ohio at the beginning of September 1837. All this time, dissension was welling up throughout the church. Clearly, Joseph was growing increasingly concerned about the resistance he felt from the Missouri presidency, and he saw the Whitmers and Cowdery as a major part of the rising tide of opposition. Joseph seemed to interpret David's departure from Kirtland, although planned, as evidence that the Whitmers were conspirators. On September 4, 1837, Joseph informed the church that Oliver Cowdery, David Whitmer, John Whitmer, William W. Phelps and others were in transgression, and would lose their standing unless they humbled themselves and made satisfaction.[19]

15. Whitmer, account book, 18 September 1837, p. 139. See also W. W. Phelps to John Whitmer, 4 March 1840: "As to the debts we contracted, I have ever done and meant to do my part. My house and lot, and some small parcels around town, after paying Mr. Boyce the post office deficit, I want sold to apply on those concerns: The printing office and lot I will deed to you as soon as I can get to some place where I can tarry long enough to do the business."

16. Whitmer, account book, [January 1838?], p. 139. See also expense entries labeled "Printing Office," p. 135.

17. Ibid., 18 September 1837, p. 133.

18. Duncan, autobiography, p. 7, records that he was born in Bath, New Hampshire, July 1, 1812. He ventured out on his own and joined the church in Jackson County in 1832. After Zion's Camp, Chapman returned to Kirtland for the temple dedication, moved to Far West in 1837, and married Rebecca Rose on May 18, 1838. They then moved to Duncan's farm in Daviess County. He assisted in the defense of Far West.

19. Hill, *Joseph Smith: The First Mormon*, 112; *History of the LDS Church*, 2:511.

That same day, Joseph wrote to John Corrill, a member of the Missouri high council, and the "whole Church in Zion" warning of the transgression of David, Oliver Cowdery, and others. Smith advised John Corrill of recent actions in Kirtland, thus insuring that dissenters would have no place in the church, and suggesting that similar action might be needed in Zion.[20] He strongly hinted that his purpose was "that you, John Corrill, may know how to proceed to set in order and regulate the affairs of the Church in Zion whenever they become disorganized."[21] Of this period, John Whitmer noted, "The situation of the Church both here and in Kirtland is in an unpleasant situation in consequence of the reorganization of its authorities, which was not satisfactory to all concerned."[22]

If the church in Missouri hoped to get the press into production it was urgent that Oliver Cowdery return to northwest Missouri. In his August 29–September 3 letter, John Whitmer traded Cowdery "some timbered land" for "the press & Type,"[23] He added: "I hope that you [Oliver] will be in a situation to move to this place this fall—David will no doubt come this fall, we need him here very much. I think if we are prospered we shall be enabled to issue a paper by the first of Jan. next." John was also hoping to arrange for the acquisition of printing stones to be used once the Far West press was in operation. Cowdery wrote back, "I want you would urge Br. Orton about the Stones so as not to be disappointed. Send me a line whether he can send them or not—do so without fail. One No. 4 and 2 No. 3 Or some other good pattontee [?]. though 2 small ones. And one good size for myself."[24] Elisha Groves was back in Missouri by September 1837 and transported the press as far as Camden, Missouri.[25] Then, however, lack of funds to pay the freight stalled Cowdery's press. Along with other

20. Joseph Smith to John Corrill, and the Church in Zion, 4 September 1837, in Jessee, *Personal Writings of Joseph Smith*, 391–92.

21. *History of the LDS Church*, 2:508–11.

22. Whitmer, Book of John Whitmer, chap. 19, p. 85.

23. Crawley, *A Descriptive Bibliography*, 1:20, 74; John Whitmer to Oliver Cowdery and David Whitmer, 29 August 1837.

24. John Whitmer to Oliver Cowdery and David Whitmer, 29 August 1837. Cowdery may have meant "platen," or they may have been intended for lithographic use.

25. Whitmer, account book, November 20 [1837], p. 127. See also September 16, 1837, p. 134; September 18, 23, 1837, p. 135; December 15, 1837, p. 133.

goods, the press was put into storage at Camden until September 18, 1837, when John arranged to have the press redeemed and hauled to Far West.[26] John Whitmer paid Elisha Groves one hundred dollars on Cowdery's behalf for his expenses in freighting.[27]

Appending a last thought to his August 29, 1837, letter to Kirtland, John advised Oliver and David: "The law in this State permits any man to hold all the tools or utentials [sic] of any mercantile shop what ever free from execution."[28] The Whitmers were increasingly concerned that the impact of Smith's worsening Kirtland indebtedness might follow them to Missouri.

Amid this mixture of euphoria and mounting strife, on October 5, 1837, Sarah Elizabeth was born to John and Sarah in one of John Whitmer's hotel rooms.

On October 20, 1837, John jotted in his account book: "Oliver Cowdery arrived this day." Cowdery initially purchased land three miles south of Far West, but he and Elizabeth Ann first moved in with John and Sarah Whitmer.[29] Writing to his brother Warren in January 1838, Oliver reported: "My family are about as usual. We [are] a part of bro. J[ohn] W[hitmer]'s house and expect to be till spring."[30] At Far West, Cowdery served as clerk of the high council and as general church recorder.[31] Isaac Morley was appointed patriarch over the Missouri church and Oliver Cowdery was given the responsibility of recording blessings. The clerk of the council, the patriarch, and the church agent received one dollar and

26. "Sept 18 1837 Dr for halling [sic] part of press from Cambden 2½ days 7.50." Whitmer, account book, p. 135.

27. Whitmer, account book, 20 November 1837, p. 127: "E. H. Groves per O. Cowderys freight in his goods press &c. 100.00." See also 15 December 1837, "For freight & Carriage for goods Press & Type from Kirtland to Wellsville 125," and "For Storage press & type at Cambden 2.00." Whitmer, account book, 15 December 1837, p. 133.

28. John Whitmer to Oliver Cowdery and David Whitmer, 29 August 1837.

29. One hundred and sixty acres of land in sections 26 and 36, Mirabile Township, were entered in Cowdery's name in 1836. Johnson and Romig, *An Index to Early Caldwell County, Missouri, Land Records*, 30. A meeting "convened at the home of Oliver Cowdery [probably John Whitmer's] in Far West, Caldwell Co. Mo." Oliver Cowdery to Warren Cowdery, 30 January 1838, p. 85.

30. Oliver Cowdery to Warren Cowdery, 21 January 1838, pp. 80–82.

31. Jenson, "Oliver Cowdery," *Latter-day Saint Biographical Encyclopedia*, 1:247.

On page 34 of his account book (October 20, 1837), John Whitmer noted the arrival of Oliver Cowdery to Far West, Missouri. Courtesy of the LDS Church History Library.

Joseph and Hyrum Smith served together in the first presidency of the church for the first time in 1837. This depiction is attributed to David Rogers by W. Edwards, engraver, ca. 1842. Courtesy of Community of Christ Archives.

fifty cents per day for church-related work.[32] For a time, Cowdery tried his hand as a partner in Hinkle's store, in order "to get his fees for living."[33] Oliver also turned to the study of law.[34] He began to function in the community as a legal advocate.[35] While residing in northwestern Missouri, Oliver also helped select locations for the gathering of the Saints.

Meanwhile, in Kirtland, a number of the leading members of the church became concerned over the policies and financial practices of Joseph Smith and other Kirtland church leaders. Ebenezer Robinson, who worked in the printing office, observed that a "split occurred between a

32. Cannon and Cook, *Far West Record*, 127.

33. Ibid., 166–67.

34. After being "cut off for lying, counterfeiting and immorality," Oliver Cowdery, first witness of the Book of Mormon, turned his attention to law and real estate. Beadle, "Jackson County: The Early History of the Saints and Their Enemies," 4.

35. Cannon and Cook, *Far West Record*, 167.

number of the leading Elders of the church.... These all objected to the course being pursued by brother Joseph Jr. and the church."[36]

As dissent expanded among church members in Kirtland, the pace of gathering to Missouri increased. For the most part, the economy of Far West in northwestern Missouri was less seriously impacted, making it a haven for church members as conditions in the church in Kirtland deteriorated. Members who were uncomfortable with the direction of the church had been made to feel unwelcome in Kirtland and were blamed for the deteriorating situation.

Frederick G. Williams moved to Missouri between May and November 1837. While there, he was released as a counselor in the church presidency in Kirtland, another casualty of tension rippling throughout the church as a result of the Kirtland Safety Society Bank failure. Joseph Smith and Frederick remained good friends, but putting the focus of discontent on Williams provided Smith with desirable breathing room. A general church assembly on November 7, 1837, at Far West, replaced Williams with the unfailingly loyal Hyrum Smith.[37] Sometime between September 10, 1837, and April 1838, apostle Lyman E. Johnson (1811–59) moved his family to Far West where they lived for a time with David Patten's family.[38]

William McLellin and others who were no longer enthusiastic supporters of Joseph Smith also made their homes in Far West. McLellin had written a letter of withdrawal from the church in August 1836 in Kirtland but sought reconciliation with Joseph and retained his calling as one of the twelve. In Kirtland, on September 3, 1837, McLellin was again sustained as a member of the twelve. A couple of months later, on November 8, 1837, he was sustained to the twelve in a conference at Far West and commissioned as a captain in the Caldwell County Division of the Missouri State Militia. In late 1837 or early 1838, McLellin moved his family to Far

36. Robinson, "Items of Personal History," 116.

37. *History of the LDS Church*, 2:522–23.

38. Lyman Johnson was removed from the Quorum of the Twelve Apostles on September 3, 1837, then restored to his apostleship on September 10, 1837, at Kirtland, Ohio. Collier and Harwell, *Kirtland Council Minute Book*, 184–86, 188–89. On April 7, 1838, assistant-president pro tem David W. Marsh, spoke against Lyman Johnson and four other apostles. On April 13, 1838, along with others, Lyman E. Johnson was again expelled from the church. Lyman was in Far West at the time of his excommunication. Cannon and Cook, *Far West Record*, 160, 172–74.

West where his wife, Emeline, gave birth to their third child, James Martin McLellan [*sic*], on February 22, 1838. On May 11, 1838, McLellin was again called before a bishop's court in Far West. There is no official record of his excommunication, but it probably occurred on that day since McLellin admitted he had "no confidence in the heads of the Church, believing they had transgressed."[39]

Thomas B. Marsh, president of the twelve, came to play a central role in ensuring that many of Smith's camp would also gather to Missouri. Marsh's family had moved to Jackson County, endured the hardships of the Jackson and Clay county periods, and relocated his family in Far West. Marsh wrote, "I procured a lot immediately, built a house and moved into it. During the winter I made improvements on my lot; got up my firewood, attended councils and preached to the Saints." In response to difficulties in Ohio following the failure of the Kirtland bank, as president of the twelve, Marsh journeyed to Ohio. Marsh recalled, "About the month of June, 1837, I started for Kirtland in company with D. W. Patten and Wm. Smith, to try and reconcile some of the Twelve and others of high standing who had come out in opposition to the Prophet." In Kirtland, Marsh played a prominent role in trying to help Joseph patch things up with former supporters. "About this time a special meeting was appointed at Joseph's house, by himself, to which several of the brethren who were disaffected were invited. I was chosen moderator, and called upon the aggrieved parties to speak first. A reconciliation was effected between all parties."[40] In late September 1837, Thomas B. Marsh and Hyrum Smith left Kirtland for Far West.[41]

After David Whitmer's short visit to Kirtland in August 1837, he returned to Missouri for good in early November 1837—about the same time the Smith and Rigdon party was also journeying to Far West. Joseph and Sidney arrived in Far West about November 6, 1837, to tackle its ever-mounting internal stresses.

---

39. Porter, "Odyssey of William Earl McLellin," 322, 323, 368n178.
40. Marsh, "History of Thomas Baldwin Marsh [by himself]," 406.
41. Thomas B. Marsh to Wilford Woodruff, p. 36; O'Driscoll, *Hyrum Smith: A Life of Integrity*, 159–61.

CHAPTER TWENTY-ONE

Competing Visions

JOSEPH SMITH AND Sidney Rigdon traveled to Far West in November
1837 to reassert their control over the church in Missouri. Smith immediately convened the high council, and adjusted differences of opinion
over the purchase of land for the gathering of church members and the
management of the town plat. During a general assembly of the Missouri
church held November 7, 1837, some participants raised objections to the
presidency of Zion—to David Whitmer as president, and to his counselors, John Whitmer and W. W. Phelps. The exact objections were not
recorded in the minutes, but they no doubt had to do with questions about
David's loyalty to Joseph.

The meeting minutes, with the same lack of detail, record: "Pres't Joseph Smith jr. then nominated John Whitmer for an assistant President, who
was objected, and Elder Marsh spake in opposition to him, and read a list of
charges from a written document against him, and Pres't Phelps. Pres't. John
Whitmer then spake a few words by way of confession, and was followed
by Elder Isaac Morley. The vote was called and carried unanimously."[1] Thus,
in the end, both John and W. W. Phelps were re-sustained as counselors to
David in the Missouri presidency.[2] Joseph may have intended this exercise to
be a wake-up call to his Missouri friends, putting them and the entire Missouri church on notice that dissent would not be tolerated. Perhaps the most
telling outcome of this meeting was the selection of a new Missouri high
council composed of Smith loyalists. Jacob Whitmer, Thomas B. Marsh,

1.   Cannon and Cook, *Far West Record*, 123.
2.   Ibid.

Isaac Higbee, and David Patten were removed, and Newel Knight, Calvin Beebe, Solomon Hancock, and George Morey replaced them.[3]

The church needed to find additional land for future expansion. So many members were gathering to the West under the reconstituted leadership that the Missouri presidency could clearly envision the day the church would begin to spill out of Caldwell County. Resale of newly acquired real estate also promised to alleviate continuing cash flow problems in both church centers. At Kirtland, on September 17, 1837, a conference of elders approved the identification of additional stakes for gathering. Two months later, during his November 1837 visit to Far West, Joseph explained that the object of his mission there was to encourage the establishment of stakes in the upper-Missouri counties.[4] The Missouri church appointed David Whitmer, Oliver Cowdery, John Corrill, and Lyman Wight to explore Daviess County and they set out immediately to appraise unsettled lands north of Caldwell.[5]

The continued gathering to Far West was also sanctioned, but the city was filling up very fast. During Joseph Smith and Sidney Rigdon's 1837 visit, the council decided to adjust the city plat by narrowing the streets so that each block contained a full four acres of ground rather than 396 square feet as first designated.[6] A general meeting of ordained members also voted in favor of enlarging the size of the town plat. Bishop Edward Partridge and his counselors were appointed to assess the land adjacent to the one-mile plat, compensate landowners, and enlarge the plat to four full sections (four square miles).[7]

Through this trip, Smith succeeded in putting his own unique stamp of approval on all that the Missouri leaders had accomplished. Though challenged, the Missouri presidency was ultimately sustained for the short

3. The twelve high counselors were John Murdock, Solomon Hancock, Elias Higbee, Calvin Beebe, George Morey, Thomas Grover, Simeon Carter, Newel Knight, George M. Hinkle, Levi Jackman, Elisha H. Groves, and Lyman Wight. Cannon and Cook, *Far West Record*, 123.

4. Smith, "We Would Say to the Patrons of the Journal," 28.

5. Ibid., 27, 28.

6. Cannon and Cook, *Far West Record*, 119.

7. Thomas B. Marsh and John Corrill were selected to petition the court for the alteration of the town plat. Ibid., 125, 135.

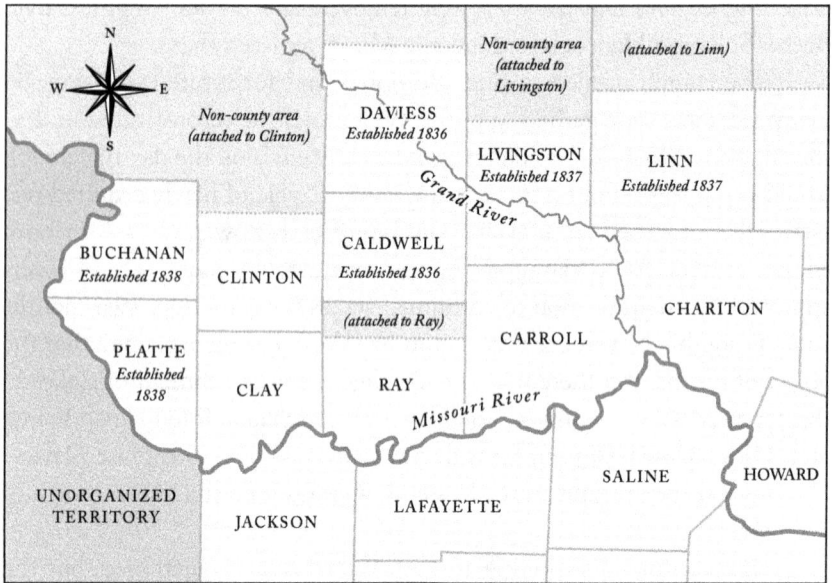

Fig. 21.1. Counties in northwestern Missouri, 1836–39.

term. But, just as apostle Thomas B. Marsh had helped patch up strained allegiances in Kirtland, he now emerged as the apparent leader of an increasingly strong loyalist movement in Missouri. During Joseph's fall 1837 visit, his concern about the leadership of the Missouri church came into sharper focus. According to John Whitmer's history, after July 1837, Joseph "seemed to be in doubt whereunto this thing [the Missouri presidency] would grow and began to upbraid D. Whitmer, and abuse him as his natural custom was to do with those whom he feared ... therefore, he harangued [*sic*] the conference and sought to destroy the confidence of the people present in D. Whitmer."[8]

Looking back on this time, David wrote in 1886: "The heads of the church went into one error after another. I followed them into many errors in doctrine, which the Lord has since shown me, and which errors I have confessed and repented of.... In the spring of 1838, the heads of the church and many of the members had gone deep into error and blindness.

8.   Whitmer, Book of John Whitmer, chap. 22, p. 95.

I had been striving with them for a long time to show them the errors unto which they were drifting, and for my labors I received only persecutions."[9]

David told Zenas Gurley about the collapse of events from 1837 to 1838: "I was appointed in charge of church affairs in Zion Missouri, but from my teachings disaffection grew, and Joseph and Sydney came out and visited the various branches of the Church, pledging them to themselves as against my teachings upon the word of wisdom and other matters, until for the establishment of their views they organized the Danites by which each member was sworn to sustain the Heads of the Church whether right or wrong—the penalty of refusing so to do being death, 'the throat cut.'"[10]

Joseph Smith and Sidney Rigdon's return to Kirtland in November 1837 did not end the growing crisis in Missouri. Soon after their departure, the presidency attempted another initiative. The Whitmers had never been comfortable with the law of consecration. To further differentiate the Missouri church's economic policy from the one followed in Ohio, David Whitmer encouraged the bishopric to "take into consideration and report upon the subject of raising a revinue [*sic*] to defray the expenses of the Church"—in essence, establishing procedures that would let church operations run more like a business. To ease the financial burden of supporting their families, key leaders would be compensated for performing administrative duties. John Whitmer was appointed clerk pro tem in Phelps's absence and Oliver was appointed to record patriarchal blessings in the Missouri church, perhaps foreshadowing the arrival of patriarch Joseph Smith Sr., from Kirtland in April 1838.[11]

On November 6, 1837, a number of members of the church of the Latter Day Saints met with Smith and Rigdon "to take into consideration some of the affairs of said Church." This gathering voted to postpone building the temple for which Joseph had helped break ground for on July 7, 1837. The project was not to proceed further "until the Lord shall reveal it to be his will to be commenced."[12] John later commented that "the heads of the Church," by whom he meant Smith and Rigdon, "dissolved ... that

9. "Letters from David and John C. Whitmer," 91, 92.

10. David Whitmer, interview by Zenas Gurley, January 14, 1885.

11. Cannon and Cook, *Far West Record*, 127.

12. Ibid., 120.

committee for building the house of worship ... and the subscription[s] [were] withdrawn and refunded by said committee."[13] John's brother Jacob had served on that committee with Elisha H. Groves, and George M. Hinkle, expending considerable time and energy in fundraising and assembling building materials.[14]

The Missouri high council and bishop's council met on December 6, 1837. Elias Higbee, Simeon Carter, and Elisha H. Groves submitted a report recommending "that the aforesaid officers [presidency, high council, and bishopric] together with the clerk of the council the Patriarch and also the agent of the Church (as also any other person who may be employed in the same or the like business) receive per day each one dollar and fifty cents."[15]

At the December 7, 1837, high council meeting, Bishop Partridge and his counselors recommended a new economic basis for financing Missouri church operations. The bishopric's plan combined elements of the law of consecration and tithing. They suggested soliciting an annual voluntary freewill offering from members and annually ask "a per centage on what a man is worth," as a more equal mode of raising funds than tithing "what a man raises [crops or cattle] or his income."[16] To accomplish this end, tithe payers would be expected to render an annual inventory to the bishop. The percentage that an individual would be required to pay would vary depending upon the church's projected budgetary needs for the coming year. Members would be asked to endorse their financial support via a subscription paper.[17]

On January 21, Cowdery enthused to Ohio leaders about the "great and precious country" seen by the survey committee, not knowing that they were en route to Missouri.[18] But as events progressed, Cowdery and

---

13. John Whitmer to Edward Partridge, 20 March 1840.

14. Cannon and Cook, *Far West Record*, 134. On December 23, 1837, Jacob Whitmer asked the high council of Zion to compensate him for the 120 days he had devoted to this project while he was serving on the high council. The council agreed to his request of one dollar a day.

15. Ibid.

16. Ibid., 129.

17. Ibid., 129–30.

18. Oliver Cowdery to Warren Cowdery, 21 January 1838.

other survey committee members began to view northern lands as "far more than a mere means of locating gathering sites."[19] Given their rapidly deteriorating relationship with Joseph, they came to see northern lands as a place of refuge. It became clear that the extended Whitmer family and others of like mind would break with Joseph. As the Whitmer clan began, in good conscience, to examine their alternatives, their reports to Joseph became infrequent.

Because of their involvement in the Missouri literary firm, John Whitmer and W. W. Phelps still controlled church printing, and modified or erected a building to house the press in Far West. John would have had access to any equipment and church materials that Cowdery had sent to Missouri. By February, 1838, it became apparent that the Whitmers and Cowdery planned to use the press to issue an opposition paper.[20]

John may have had his revelations manuscript in his care or had access to it. In either case, at some point, several pages of the Book of Commandment manuscript were removed from the bound ledger and apparently inserted between the pages of John's church history volume. When the RLDS church acquired John's history in 1903, along with the printer's copy of the Book of Mormon manuscript, four double-sided pages of the Book of Commandments manuscript were with it.

Today, we know that the original ledger book was disassembled at some point. The volume's original outer pasteboard covers are no longer extant. As discovered in 2008, the manuscript is wrapped in a single, heavy piece of cardstock paper. Notations on some of its pages refer to the publication of the 1835 Doctrine and Covenants; thus, the volume was not disassembled (and the pages removed) until after the printing of the Doctrine and Covenants at Kirtland was complete, between August and September 1835.[21] John could have removed these pages from the revelations manuscript before he returned to Missouri in 1836, or he could have inserted them into his history when Cowdery shipped church printing office materials to Far West in 1837 or 1838.

19. Thompson, "The Initial Survey Committee Selected to Appoint Lands for Gathering in Daviess County, Missouri," 309.

20. Oliver Cowdery to Warren Cowdery, 30 January 1838.

21. Jensen, "From Manuscript to Printed Page," 20, 39. See also Crawley, *A Descriptive Bibliography of the Mormon Church*, 1:54–57

Joseph Smith was preoccupied through late 1837 dealing with inter-quorum rivalries. Quorums at Kirtland sought to advance their own interests while the first presidency at Kirtland found itself increasingly at odds with the presidency of the Missouri church. John and his extended family came to symbolize the intensifying internal opposition to Joseph's leadership. Joseph's solution, instead of trying to mend the unraveling relationships, was to undo the very Missouri presidency he had created in 1834.

Religious, social, and legal circumstances in Kirtland quickly turned against Smith, and burgeoned completely out of his control. As the strain built up, Smith and his adherents set their sights on eliminating the "dissenting party." Joseph had applied pressure to Thomas Marsh and David Patten during their visit to Kirtland, expecting them to return to Far West and help rein in the Missouri presidency.[22] Now, looking to the future, Smith began envisioning another move—abandoning Kirtland, relocating to Missouri, and assuring a transition of power into his own hands. An organized dissenting party surfaced in Kirtland out of the growing difficulties associated with the bank failure. A number of members who followed the leadership of Warren W. Parrish were cut off by the Kirtland High Council, probably in December 1837. On New Year's Day, John Smith, Joseph's uncle and a counselor in the first presidency, wrote to his son, George A. Smith: "The Church has taken a high and mighty pruning, and we think she will soon rise in the greatest of her strength."[23] Church printing activities were suspended and dissenters jockeyed to take possession of the printing office. Joseph and Sidney permanently left Kirtland for

22. Particularly hopeful of reclaiming four wayward members of the twelve who were no longer functioning in their office, Smith voiced his expectations via revelation directed to Thomas B. Marsh, president of the twelve: "Exalt not yourselves; rebel not against my servant Joseph; for verily I say unto you, I am with him, and my hand shall be over him; and the keys which I have given unto him, and also to youward, shall not be taken from him till I come. Verily I say unto you, my servant Thomas, thou art the man whom I have chosen to hold the keys of my kingdom, as pertaining to the Twelve, abroad among all nations. That thou mayest be my servant to unlock the door of the kingdom in all places where my servant Joseph, and my servant Sidney, and my servant Hyrum, cannot come. For on them have I laid the burden of all the churches for a little season." Joseph Smith, revelation to Thomas B. Marsh, 23 July 1837.

23. John Smith to George A. Smith, 1 January 1838, p. 252.

Far West on the night of January 12, 1838. A few days later, an arsonist set fire to the print shop.[24] The opposition party also tried to seize the temple.

Before Joseph Smith and Sidney Rigdon fled from Kirtland, Joseph had enlisted apostles Thomas B. Marsh and David Patten, with the assistance of William Smith (who remained at Kirtland) to do his bidding.[25] Acting on their behalf, Thomas B. Marsh organized several "social gatherings," as Joseph and Sidney journeyed to Missouri. Marsh was then president of the Quorum of the Twelve Apostles and president of the high council in Missouri. These meetings crystallized zealous opposition to the Missouri presidency.

One of these social meetings convened at the Marsh home in Far West on January 20, 1838. "Being grieved at their [the Missouri presidency's] doings," this group "took into consideration the preceding of the Presidents in this place viz David Whitmer W. W. Phelps John Whitmer and Oliver Cowdery."[26]

This alleged "social" gathering discovered sinister rumors that the presidents had sold their lands in Jackson County, thus signaling that they did not expect to return. They were also convinced that the presidents were not keeping the word of wisdom as they ought. Censoriously, they appointed George M. Hinkle, Thomas Grover, and George Morey a committee to visit the presidents to "enquire into their feelings and determinations."[27]

Six days later, on January 26, 1838, the same group, now calling themselves vaguely but more grandly, "The Council," reconvened at the home of John Anderson, who was not, unlike the other participants, a member of the high council. The three-man committee reported:

> Respecting their selling their lands in Jackson County, they, the Presidents, declared they had not broken revelation or Law of God in so doing and further if they were deprived of that privilege they would

24. Crosby, "A Biographical Sketch of the Life of Jonathan Crosby written by himself," 18. The printing office was apparently destroyed by those loyal to Joseph in order to preclude the publication of anti-Joseph literature.

25. Cannon and Cook, *Far West Record*, 138; see also, Marsh, "History of Thomas Baldwin Marsh [by himself]," 406.

26. Ibid., 135. This group reconvened on January 26, 1838, moderated by John Murdock; Samuel Bent took minutes.

27. Ibid., 135–36.

sell their possessions in Far-West and move out of the place and W. W. Phelps said he would move out of the accursed place and further they declared they would not be controlled by an ecclesiastical power or revelation whatever in their temporal concerns. And respecting the word of wisdom, W. W. Phelps said he had not broken it but had kept it. O Cowdery said he had drank [*sic*] tea three times a day this winter on account of his ill health. David and John Whitmer said they did use tea and coffee but they did not consider them to come under the head of hot drinks.[28]

"The Council" expressed displeasure with these aggressive responses by agreeing to no longer recognize David, John, W. W., and Oliver as presidents. They also determined to lay "the case" before the church membership and began scheduling meetings in the various church settlements.

Four days later, on Tuesday, January 30, 1838, Frederick G. Williams, the three Whitmer brothers, W. W. Phelps, Lyman E. Johnson, and Oliver Cowdery met to consider their options. John, W. W. Phelps, and Lyman E. Johnson agreed to form "a committee to look for a place ... in which to settle where they may live in peace." That same day, Oliver wrote to his brother Warren explaining that the seven men had met:

> to take into consideration the state of said church and the manner in which some of the Authorities of the same have for a time past, and are still endeavoring to unite ecclesiastical and civil authority and force men under a pretence [*sic*] of incurring the displeasure of heaven to use their earthly substance contrary to their own interest and privilege; and also how said authorities are endeavoring to make it a rule of faith for said church to uphold a certain man or men right or wrong.... Oliver Cowdery, David Whitmer, Frederick G. Williams were appointed a committee to Draft a declaration and resolutions.... W. W. Phelps, John Whitmer and Lyman E. Johnson were appointed a committee to look for a place for the above named individuals in which to settle where they may live in peace.... As soon as our Declarations etc., are adopted we shall proclaim them publickly [*sic*], and send a copy to you.... We believe in enjoying equal rights and privileges and we believe it to be our duty to separate ourselves from <u>all</u> who are disposed to fulminate pretend revelation and uphold corruption by

28. Ibid., 136.

lying.... Judge Phelps says we shall have a Printing Press started before long.... We do not expect the great body of the church here to unite in our views—We do not ask—we want none but independent men—not the rag-muffins who believe in <u>man</u> more than God.[29]

On February 5, 1838, a "Committee of the Whole Church in Zion," moderated by Marsh, met to consider charges against the presidency of the church in Missouri: David Whitmer, John Whitmer, and W. W. Phelps. The three men were not present.

John Whitmer and Phelps were charged with selling their lands in Jackson County. Thomas B. Marsh began by reading a revelation by Smith, given in Kirtland on September 4, 1837, more than a year earlier, warning that John Whitmer and William W. Phelps "were in transgression," and that "if they repented not, they should be removed out of their places." Marsh "also, read a certain clause contained in the appeal, published in the old *Star*, under the 183rd page, as follows:—'And to sell our lands would amount to a denial of our faith, as that is the place where Zion of God shall stand according to our faith and belief in the revelations of God.'"[30]

George M. Hinkle reviewed the charges that the committee of inquiry had discussed with the presidency, "then read a written document containing a number of additional accusations against the three Presidents."[31]

John Corrill tackled the accusations on procedural grounds "and labored hard to show that the meeting was illegal, and the Presidency ought to be had before a proper tribunal, which he considered to be a Bishop and twelve High Priests."[32] Corrill's arguments failed to persuade the loyalists and "the vote against David Whitmer, John Whitmer, and William W. Phelps was unanimous, excepting eight or ten and this minority only wished them to continue in office a little longer, or untill [*sic*] Joseph Smith jr. came up."[33] Quickly consolidating this public feeling against the

29. Minutes of a meeting of members of the Church of the Latter Day Saints, F. G. Williams, chair, Oliver Cowdery, clerk, 30 January 1838, included in a letter from Oliver Cowdery to Warren and Lyman Cowdery, 4 February 1838, pp. 83–87.

30. Cannon and Cook, *Far West Record*, 137.

31. Ibid., 137–38.

32. Ibid., 139.

33. Ibid., 139–40.

presidency, Marsh and his supporters held meetings at "the S. Carter and Edmund Durfee Settlement, Nahum Curtis dwelling house, and Haun's Mill." These small groups unanimously rejected the presidents over the next four days.

On February 4, the day before this council met, Oliver Cowdery described the charges with considerable exasperation to his brothers Warren and Lyman, who were still in Kirtland:

> Messrs. W. W. Phelps J. Whitmer and myself had a partial claim to a few lots in Indipendence [*sic*], Mo. sold some time since on some of the Jackson suits costs [these lots has been property of the Literary Firm]. We [later] quit claimed our interest in and to, the same, for a small sum, (and glad to get that,) which has caused considerable stir. Not long since, Messrs. D. and J. Whitmer W. W. Phelps and myself were waited upon by (as they said,) a committee of the High council, who said the church were dissatisfied with our conduct, &c. in selling those lots and not Keeping the word of wisdom, and also, in not teaching the church to fulfil[l] the consecration law. I told them that if I had property, while I lived and was sane, I would not be dictated, influenced or controlled, by any man or set of men by no tribunal of ecclesiastical pretences whatever. And when I or my family were sick or any other time, I would eat and drink what I thought would do me the most good: this was about the substance of what the others told them. The next day the council met again and resolved not to have those men (the 3) to be their Presidents, and to call on the church to Know if they would concur in the same. They say they have no legal accusation against them, but dont want them to preside over the church any longer.[34]

Six days later on February 10, the high council and bishopric "moved, seconded & carried, that Oliver Cowdery, William W. Phelps and John Whitmer stand no longer as Chairman & Clerk, to sign and record [licenses]."[35]

Ironically, even while Marsh's loyalists were accusing the Whitmer clan of selling their lands in Jackson County, Jacob Whitmer was negotiating with Edward Partridge to acquire title to some land near their old

---

34. Oliver Cowdery to Warren and Lyman Cowdery, 4 February 1838.

35. Robinson, "Items of Personal History," 131; see also Cannon and Cook, *Far West Record*, 141.

home in the Whitmer Settlement in Jackson County. Edward and Lydia Partridge sold 19.3 acres of land to Jacob Whitmer on March 9, 1838.[36] No known documentation explains Jacob's motivations; but perhaps the Whitmers, foreseeing a move from Far West, may have been thinking of returning to Jackson County. Once they were no longer Mormons in good standing, they may have seen no reason to fear hostility from the Missourians who had driven them out of the county almost five years earlier.

On February 10, the high council selected Thomas B. Marsh and David W. Patten to serve as presidents pro tem. in Missouri, pending the arrival of Joseph Smith and Sidney Rigdon.[37] There matters stalled until March 10, when Marsh and Patten charged W. W. Phelps and John Whitmer "for persisting in unchristian-like conduct."[38]

Declining to be called to account economically or to personally appear before these ecclesiastical tribunals, John and David Whitmer, and W. W. Phelps wrote a joint letter back the same day: "Sir: It is contrary to the principles of the revelations of Jesus Christ, and his gospel, and the laws of the land, to try a person for an offence, by an illegal tribunal, or by men prejudiced against him or by authority that has given an opinion, or decision beforehand or in his absence. [Signed by] David Whitmer, W. W. Phelps and John Whitmer: Presidents of the Church of Christ in Mo."[39]

David later denied any knowledge of this letter and suggested, "If that letter was written by Brother John or Brother Phelps, one of them may have signed my name to it."[40] Whether David actually signed the letter or not, its existence clearly indicates that the Whitmers, Cowdery, and Phelps had taken a decided stand in opposition to the church's direction and Joseph's leadership.

---

36. South end of W ½ of NE ¼ of section 16, township 49, range 22, for $154.48. Jacob in turn transferred ownership of the land to his father, Peter Whitmer Sr., on August 20, 1838, for $150.00. Jackson County, Missouri Land Records, Recorder's Office, Courthouse, Independence, Book F, 110, 249.

37. Cannon and Cook, *Far West Record*, 141.

38. Ibid., 146.

39. Cannon and Cook, *Far West Record*, 146. See also, Anderson, *Investigating the Book of Mormon Witnesses*, 127.

40. David Whitmer, *An Address to Believers in the Book of Mormon*, 6.

The issue of accountability for lot sales proved to be a persistent problem. When the high council convened on the evening of March 10:

> A number of charges were sustained against those men; the principal of which, was, for claiming $2,000 Church funds which they had sub-scribed for the building an house to the Lord in this place, when they held in their possession the city Plot, and were sitting in the Presi-dential chair, which subscription they were intending to pay from the avails of the town lots; but when the town plot was transferred into the hands of the Bishop, for the benefit of the Church, it was agreed that the church should take this subscription from off the hands of W. W. Phelps & John Whitmer, but in the transactions of the business they bound the Bishop in a heavy mortgage, to pay them the above $2,000 in two years from the date thereof; a part of which they have already received, & claim the remainder.[41]

The evening's business concluded with the Missouri high council and Far West congregation officially excommunicating John Whitmer and W. W. Phelps, and announcing that they should "be given over to the buffetings of Satan, until they learn to blaspheme no more against the authorities of God, nor fleece the flock of Christ.... The vote was then put to the congregation which was carried unanimous."[42] No action was taken that night against David Whitmer or Oliver Cowdery, perhaps because the letter had again raised the question of jurisdiction that could not be resolved until Joseph Smith was present.

The charges against John seem largely related to differences over the proper approach to the conduct of church business and personal steward-ship. And for the time being, he remained in Far West. After his excom-munication, Whitmer penned a brief review of the Far West period in chapter 19 of his history. Believing that it would be his last entry, John wrote:

> Some temporal movements, have not proved satisfactory to all par-ties has also terminated in the expulsion of <many> members ~~among~~

---

41. Cannon and Cook, *Far West Record*, 148–49. On April 21, 1838, after replacing the Mis-souri presidency, the high council decided that Edward Partridge should not pay the mortgage held by John Whitmer and W. W. Phelps. Ibid., 182.

42. Ibid.

whom is W. W. Phelps and myself. ... Notwithstanding my present
situation, which I hope will soon be bettered and I find favor in the
eyes of God <, All men> and his Saints. Farewell.[43]

John believed he had completed his duties as church historian.

43. Whitmer, Book of John Whitmer, chap. 19, p. 85. Strikethroughs are in John's original.

CHAPTER TWENTY-TWO

Exclusion

MOUNTING DEBT, LEGAL challenges, and growing dissension in Ohio made it impossible for Joseph Smith and Sidney Rigdon to remain at Kirtland any longer. The church's financial problems were not only a heavy burden in and of themselves, but complicated the other two factors that were unraveling the movement's unity—the corporate indebtedness of the church and Smith's personal indebtedness. Both were intermingled in ways that were, themselves, problematic. At a council meeting on June 16, 1836, in Kirtland, president Frederick G. Williams had said, "The case before us is an important one. The Church [is] poor, Zion [is] to be built and we have not means to do it unless the rich assist & because the rich have not assisted, the heads of the Church have to suffer and are now suffering under severe embarrassments and are much in debt."[1] John Corrill's history summarized the situation in 1836:

> After finishing the house of the Lord ... the Church found itself something like fifteen or twenty thousand dollars in debt.... Notwithstanding they were deeply in debt, they had so managed as to keep up their credit, so they concluded to try mercantile business. Accordingly, they ran in debt in New York, and elsewhere, some thirty thousand dollars, for goods, and shortly after some fifty or sixty thousand more.... They also spent some thousands of dollars in building a steam mill, which never profited them anything. They also bought many farms at extravagant prices, and made part payments, which they afterwards lost, by not being able to meet the remaining payments. They also got up a bank, for which they could get no charter ... and, after struggling with it awhile, they broke down.[2]

1. Collier and Harwell, *Kirtland Council Minute Book*, 178.
2. Corrill, *Brief History of the Church of Christ*, 26–27.

Marvin Hill, C. Keith Rooker, and Larry T. Wimmer applied both historical and economic tools to the Kirtland situation and concluded that Smith was probably not overleveraged.[3] However, the sources they cite in their analysis suggest that they did not consider at least one significant aspect of Smith's debt problem. Contemporary sources strongly suggest that Joseph Smith's multi-layered plan for the redemption of Zion seriously overextended the young movement's available resources to underwrite an orderly and financially stable gathering. Smith could not extract enough funds from his followers to accomplish his entire prophetic agenda. Granville Hedrick, an early church member and eventual leader of one of Mormonism's various expressions, claimed in 1864:

> Joseph borrowed a large sum of money, through the security of his friends, at Kirtland, established a bank at Kirtland, and in the event, himself and family, together with many of the leading elders, soon went to excess in fine clothes, became involved, failed in business, but lived high upon a borrowed capital, until being sorely pressed by his creditors, he fled from Kirtland, as a bankrupt, by night, and went to Missouri.... At a place called Far West, he was known to be in debt for a large sum variously estimated at from 100,000 to 200,000 dollars.[4]

Unquestionably, a number of factors were responsible, some of them external to the Saints' community and others of them internal forces. In any case, Joseph Smith, who had been meditating a permanent move to Missouri since at least November 1837, abruptly felt in mid-January 1838 that his situation in Ohio had become untenable. On January 16, 1838, he and Sidney Rigdon fled under the cover of darkness on horseback. They found temporary refuge in the New Portage/Norton Township area sixty miles south of Kirtland.

Emma also had to leave everything behind. Traveling with Phoebe Rigdon and their children, they joined their husbands on the road thirty-six hours later. Four days after Joseph's sudden departure from Kirtland, the party of exiles was en route to Far West. Fearing pursuit by armed men, Joseph and Sidney often hid in the back of their wagons. Five-year-old Joseph III recalled walking to avoid the jerky movements of the pitching

3.   Hill, Rooker, and Wimmer, *Kirtland Economy Revisited*, 40, 69.
4.   Hedrick, "Review of the 'Herald,'" 69.

wagon over rough log corduroy roads.[5] Emma also climbed the longer hills on foot, braving the icy rain, snow, and wind, and waded through the mud-churned ruts of the road.[6] The family reached Quincy, Illinois, by February and crossed the frozen Mississippi River on dangerously thin ice. At Salt River, Missouri, Emma, then six months pregnant, had to walk across an unsteady canoe in order to reach solid ice from the shore.[7]

The Smiths arrived at Far West on March 14, four days after John's excommunication. The removal of David and John Whitmer, and their subsequent replacement with loyal supporters would, from Joseph's perspective, successfully domesticate what had become yet another semi-autonomous administrative misadventure in the life of the church.

After abandoning an enormous amount of corporate and private property eight hundred miles away in Ohio, Joseph and Sidney sought to regain spiritual and temporal control in Missouri. One of the first acts of the high council in Far West was to give Smith and Rigdon town lots. Although John, David, Oliver, and their associates had planned to publish a declaration of their intentions, organize an alternative church body, and/or finalize arrangements for a move north into Daviess County, time had run out.[8] About three weeks later, Thomas B. Marsh was appointed president pro tem of the church in Missouri, with David Patten and Brigham Young as counselors or assistant presidents.[9]

On April 6, 1838, the eighth anniversary of the church's organization, Joseph and Sidney Rigdon abruptly demanded that John surrender his history manuscript for the editing they felt his "incompetency [*sic*] as a historian" required.[10] Anticipating that they would be getting the church

5.   Howard, *Memoirs of President Joseph Smith III*, 2.

6.   Smith, "Biography of Patriarch Alexander H. Smith," 4.

7.   Newell and Avery, *Mormon Enigma*, 70.

8.   Oliver Cowdery to Lyman Cowdery, 30 January 1838, pp. 85–86.

9.   Cannon and Cook, *Far West Record*, 158. Also, Jenson, "The Three Witnesses: John Whitmer," 612–15.

10. "Mr. J. [John] Whitmer: Sir: We were desirous of honoring you by giving publicity to your notes on the history of the church of Latter Day Saints after making such corrections as we thought would be necessary, knowing your incompetency [*sic*] as a historian, that writings coming from your pen, could not be put to press without correcting them, or else the church must suffer reproach. Indeed, sir, we never supposed

printing press in operation soon, Smith planned to begin publishing the church's history. He and Sidney anticipated that John would refuse—which he did—and announced plans to begin writing the history themselves that very week. John Corrill and Elias Higbee were appointed as historians in John's place.[11] The two immediately began working on a replacement manuscript.

The situation in Far West became even more strained during the April 7, 1838, church conference. Knowing that the Whitmers and Oliver Cowdery had already been successfully targeted and removed, David Patten identified further opponents to Smith's policies by publicly voicing objection to the actions of William McLellin, Luke and Lyman Johnson, and John Boynton.[12] A few days later on April 12, formal charges were laid against David Whitmer.[13] The next day, David Whitmer simply withdrew from fellowship.[14]

Meanwhile, as part of a complicated arrangement, John Whitmer transferred his interest in the press to Thomas B. Marsh as publisher on behalf of the Far West High Council, noting in his account book: "[April 17, 1838[,] Sold to [T.] B. Marsh &c. Press Type & Fr[eight] to the amount of $504.95."[15] He also agreed to pay two outstanding notes amounting to about

---

you capable of writing a history but were willing to let it come out under your name, notwithstanding it would really not be yours but ours. We are still willing to honor you, if you can be made to know your own interest, and give up your notes, so that they can be corrected and made fit for the press; but if not, we have all the materials for another, which we shall commence this week to write." Your obedient servants, JOSEPH SMITH, jr. SIDNEY RIGDON Presid'ts of the whole ch'rch of Lat'-rd'y S'nts," printed in Robinson, "Items of Personal History," 133; also *History of the LDS Church,* 3:15–16.

11. Cannon and Cook, *Far West Record,* 158.

12. Porter, "Odyssey of William Earl McLellin," 323. John Boynton's nephew, Aroet Lucious Hale, described the cause of Boynton's separation from the church. At Kirtland, "The Prophet Joseph Smith called on him [John Boynton] for money. He had the money but refused. This was a turning point in his life. The Prophet wanted money to redeem land ... in Jackson County, Missouri, at the center stake of Zion." Hale, Diary of Aroet Lucious Hale, p. 3.

13. Cannon and Cook, *Far West Record,* 176–77.

14. Ibid., 177.

15. Crawley, *A Descriptive Bibliography,* provides the most comprehensive description available of the management and ownership of Mormon printing operations at Kirtland, Ohio, and Far West, Missouri, 19–20.

$500 that he, Phelps, and Cowdery owed related to the printing business.[16] In return, during a meeting of the high council on April 21, it transferred "the printing press, type and furniture" to Bishop Partridge, who was acting as the church's agent, and authorized him "to pay for the same out of the avails of the City lots or donations."[17]

This action was part of Joseph's expansive plans for the new headquarters city. A circular appeared around the end of April 1837 announcing that the *Elders' Journal* "would be revived at Far West on the same terms as before."[18] In May, the high council appointed Sidney Rigdon "to correct the matter for the 'Elder's Journal' (that is) the Orthography and Prosody of the different letters &c."[19] With the faction loyal to Joseph again in control of the press, Brigham Young asked Newel Knight for the use of his home to house the operation. Newel donated his house and moved his family into a new home.[20] Two issues of the *Elders' Journal*, dated July and August 1838,[21] appeared that summer with Joseph identified as editor and Thomas B. Marsh as the publisher-proprietor and typesetter; but Rigdon undoubtedly had a significant hand in the editorial work on these two issues, and the content evokes Rigdon's militant stand against those who opposed the leaders of the church. According to bibliographer Peter Crawley, "Both issues include articles by Alanson Ripley, who may have helped edit the paper."[22]

Ebenezer Robinson also worked at the printing office.[23] The press also produced miscellaneous materials, including a property deed form and

16. Whitmer, account book, page listing credits and income following indenture with "A.B.," 17 April 1838, p. 133.

17. Partridge arranged payment to John Whitmer for the printing press, type, and the print shop's furniture from city lot sales or donations. Cannon and Cook, *Far West Record*, 181–82; Crawley, *A Descriptive Bibliography*, 1:20, 74.

18. Crawley, *A Descriptive Bibliography*, 1:74.

19. Ibid.

20. Hartley, *A History of the Knight Family*, 121.

21. These two specific issues bear a slightly different name from previous issues: *Elders' Journal of the Church of Latter Day Saints* and *Elders' Journal of the Church of Jesus Christ of Latter Day Saints*.

22. Crawley, *A Descriptive Bibliography*, 1:74.

23. Robinson, "Items of Personal History," 170. See also "Robinson," obituary, 207.

Rigdon's Fourth of July oration as a pamphlet. According to Reed Peck, the print shop prepared "tickets" (listings of church-supported candidates) for the general election held on Monday, August 11, 1838.[24] In late 1838, there was some discussion of having Sidney Rigdon edit a weekly newspaper.[25]

At this point, the extended Whitmer family shared John's disaffection from Joseph Smith and expressed dismay over the direction the church was moving. Zenas Gurley reported that John told him "he [had] left the Church in ... 1838, because of tendencies he could not approve."[26] The wording suggests that the high council's excommunication of John merely formalized a break in the relationship that John had already made.

During the early months of 1838, Oliver Cowdery was writing regularly to his brothers in Ohio, and the letters provide perhaps the most detailed contemporary picture of the conflicted relationship. In February 1838, Oliver expressed dismay: "The radical principles taught when Messrs. Smith and Rigdon were here, have given loose to the enthusiastick [*sic*], and their [*sic*] seems to be a disposition prevalent to carry forward those damning doctrines to the subversion of the liberties of the whole church."[27]

In addition to very real administrative differences, Cowdery apparently knew or believed that Joseph had been guilty of adultery with Fanny Alger, a young woman who was a hired girl in the Smith household in 1834 in Kirtland—an affair abruptly terminated when Emma Smith learned

---

24. Tanner and Tanner, *Reed Peck Manuscript*, 14.

25. "August 6th 1838[.] This afternoon the Citizens of Far West assembled in the school house in the S[outh] W[est] qr [quarter] of the Town. The meeting was opened by Calling Judge Elias Higbee to the Chair and appointing Geo[rge] W. Robinson Secretary."

    "1st Whereupon it was unanimously agreed that the Citizens of the counties of Caldwell and Davis ought and [s]hould have a Weekly News paper published for their information upon the news of the day. Pres[iden]t Smith said the time had come when it was necessary that we should have som[e] thing of this nature to unite the people and aid in giving us the News of the day &c. Whereupon it was unanimously agreed that Pres[iden]t S[idney] Rigdon should Edit the same."

    "2nd That a petition be drawn up to remove the County seat to this place. Some remarks were made by Pres[iden]t Rigdon upon the subject showing the great necessity of so doing." Faulring, *An American Prophet's Record*, 200–201.

26. Gurley, "Synopsis of a Discourse Delivered at Lamoni, Iowa," 369–71.

27. Oliver Cowdery to Warren A. and Lyman Cowdery, 4 February 1838, pp. 83–86.

about it.[28] Oliver had confronted Joseph, which launched a protracted and heated discussion that came to the attention of other parties, including the high council.[29] The two supposedly resolved their differences during Joseph's fall 1837 visit to Far West.[30] Oliver was therefore shocked and dismayed to read in letters from his brothers that Joseph continued to make public statements suggesting that Oliver had slandered Joseph and intimating that you couldn't trust anything Oliver said. Around the end of January 1838, Oliver wrote to Joseph stating he had heard that Joseph had told others that "I [Oliver] confessed to you [Joseph] that I had willfully lied about you—this compels me to ask you to correct that statement, and give me an explanation—until which you and myself are two."[31] After copying out for his brother on January 21 the letter that Cowdery had written to Joseph, Oliver went into more detail:

> As God is to judge my soul at the last day, and as I hope for salvation in the world to come, I never confessed, intimated <or admitted> that I ever willfully lied about him. When he was here we had some conversation in which in every instance, I did not fail to affirm that what I had said was strictly true. A dirty, nasty, filthy affair of his and Fanny Alger's was talked over in which I strictly declared that I had never deviated from the truth in the matter, and as I supposed was admitted by himself. At any rate, just before leaving, he wanted to drop every past thing, in which had been a difficulty or difference—he

28. Fanny Alger was Levi Hancock's niece. Newell and Avery, *Mormon Enigma*, 319n44. Church member Benjamin F. Johnson remembered Alger from Kirtland, saying she was "A very nice & Comly young woman about my own age towards whom not only mySelf but every one Seemed *partial* for the ameability of her character and it was whispered eaven then that Joseph *Loved her.*" Zimmerman, *I Knew the Prophets*, 38. William McLellin interviewed Emma Bidamon at Nauvoo in 1847. McLellin related that he discussed the Alger affair with Emma and wrote about the details in a letter to Joseph III in 1872: "I told him I heard that one night she missed Joseph and Fanny Alger, she went to the barn and saw him and Fanny in the barn together alone. She looked through a crack and saw the transaction!!!! She told me this story too was verily true." William E. McLellin to Joseph Smith III, [31] July and 8 September 1872.

29. Warren Parrish, one of Joseph Smith's Kirtland-era clerks, alleged to Benjamin Johnson, "That He himself & Oliver Cowdery did know that Joseph had Fanny Alger as a wife for They were *spied upon* & found together." Zimmerman, *I Knew the Prophets*, 38.

30. Cannon and Cook, *Far West Record*, 166–68.

31. Oliver Cowdery to Warren A. Cowdery, 21 January 1838, 80–83. This letter contains a retained copy of the letter (same date) that Oliver had just written to Joseph Smith.

called witnesses to the fact, gave me his hand in their presence, and I might have supposed of an honest man, calculated to say nothing of former matters.[32]

Because of Joseph Smith's own forced flight from Kirtland during January 1838, he may have never received Oliver's letter. While Joseph and Sidney were still en route to Far West, Oliver further described his overall discontent in a letter to his brothers Warren and Lyman dated February 24, 1838: "There is a great stir here, and so far as I am able to learn, the names of all who refuse to confess those disorganizing doctrines lately introduced into the church to be correct, are denounced as wicked, devilish, and more than all with them, 'Not friendly to Joseph.' I am certainly sick of such perfect foolery—there is no God in it!"[33] Furthermore, Cowdery had come to believe that the only appropriate response was to resist. "I want to say, however, that if those who have taken a stand against those wicked doctrines heretofore taught, they may be instrumental in preserving the church of Christ on earth."[34]

Cowdery clearly anticipated that the arrival of Joseph and Sidney in Missouri would bring underlying communal and personal stresses to a boil. "I know not what will follow their arrival here, but I fear that a blast like that which has fallen on the devoted town of Kirtland will come after time sufficient to test the impropriety of those plans advocated by some in this church." Oliver did not foresee reconciliation. Instead, he wrote, "we shall eventually go from this place, I have no doubt. The county of Daviess,

---

32. Ibid. Oliver copied the letter he had written to Joseph Smith (same date) into his January 21, 1838, letter to Warren Cowdery, 80–83. Oliver Cowdery wrote, "Sir—I should have written you long since but for ill heath. I have anxiously waited to recover, that I might give you a full history of my excursion to the north according to my promise were it not for the recent intelligence from Kirtland, which gives me much surprise, should still defer you will be able to judge from the formation of my letter how weak and injured are my nerves.... I learn from Kirtland by the last letters that you have publicly said, when you were here, I confessed to you that I had lied about you. This compels me to ask you to correct that statement and give me an explanation–until which you and myself are two. Oliver Cowdery Mr. Joseph Smith." See also Gunn, *Oliver Cowdery*, 157–58.

33. Oliver Cowdery to Warren A. and Lyman Cowdery, 24 February 1838, 94–96.

34. Ibid.

north of this, offers many facilities to us."[35] His references to "we" and "us" communicate that he was acting in concert with the extended Whitmer family.

A fundamental issue of disagreement between Joseph and those who resisted his course was the appropriate rule of law. John Whitmer believed that the laws of the land were supreme.[36] But, according to John, Joseph and Rigdon had convinced rank-and-file Mormons that the kingdom of God should be governed by its own law.[37] During a meeting held around April 17, 1838, John recalled that Joseph declared "he did not intend in [the] future to have any process served on him, and the officer who attempted it should die; that any person who spoke or acted against the presidency of the church, should leave the country or die."[38]

35. Ibid.

36. *Document Containing the Correspondence, Orders, &c. in Relation to the Disturbances with the Mormons*, 139.

37. Ibid. John Whitmer stated to the court, "Some time in June, after Mr. Rigdon had preached his 'salt sermon,' I held conversations with several Mormons on the subject of that sermon, and the excitement produced by the course and conduct of the presidency. Among others, I conversed with Alanson Ripley. I spoke of the supremacy of the laws of the land, and the necessity of, at all times, being governed by them. He replied, that as to the technical niceties of the law of the land, he did not intend to regard them; that the kingdom spoken of by the prophet Daniel had been set up, and that it was neces-sary every kingdom should be governed by its own laws. I also conversed with George W. Robinson, on the same subject, who answered, (when I spoke of being governed by the laws and, their supremacy,) 'when God spoke he must be obeyed,' whether his word came in contact with the laws of the land or not; and that, as the kingdom spoken of by Daniel had been set up, its laws must be obeyed. I told him I thought it was contrary to the laws of the land to drive men from their homes; to which he replied, such things had been done of old, and that the gathering of the saints must continue, and that dis-senters could not live among them in peace. I also conversed with Mr. J. Smith, jr., on this subject. I told him I wished to allay the (then) excitement, as far as I could do it. He said the excitement was very high, and he did not know what would allay it; but remarked, he would give me his opinion, which was, that if I would put my property into the hands of the bishop and high council, to be disposed of according to the laws of the church, he thought that would allay it, and that the church after a while might have confidence in me. I replied to him I wished to control my own property. In telling Mr. Smith that I wished to be governed by the laws of the land, he answered, 'Now, you wish to pin me down to the law.'"

38. Ibid., 138.

Assuming John recalled Joseph's language accurately, even as hyperbole, it must have been disturbing. Over the years, the Whitmers had grown increasingly uncomfortable as Joseph displayed greater intolerance for differences of opinion, greater hostility in response to the aggressiveness of anti-Mormons, and greater willingness to describe such conflicts with polarized language of increasing militarism. The pacific Christian attitudes the Whitmers had experienced in the culture of their youth had been first challenged in Jackson County. Although the Saints had sought peace and accepted their exile without resistance, Joseph Smith's own answer had been to lead Zion's Camp—perhaps two hundred armed men—to Missouri. Although church members did not come to blows with their adversaries, subsequent events led to a continual escalation of and dependence upon force as a solution to church problems. Joseph's vision of the kingdom had finally proven inconsistent with that of the Whitmers.

When Joseph reached Far West on March 14, 1838, Cowdery's predictions of clashes between church leadership and dissenting members began to come true. Having already deposed the Missouri presidency, Smith's adherents began picking off others who were also considered to be unsupportive.

During the quarterly conference of the church held at Far West on April 7, 1838, David Patten spoke out against apostles William McLellin, Luke Johnson, Lyman Johnson, and John Boynton.[39] Oliver Cowdery was brought to trial before the high council and bishopric in Far West on April 12, 1838. This was followed by trials against Lyman Johnson and David Whitmer. Joseph preferred not to attend these high council trials, and let subordinates do this work for him.

William McLellin was brought to trial for "transgression" (not specified) before the bishop's court in Far West on May 11, 1838. Joseph Smith did attend McLellin's trial. Smith reported McLellin's response to the court: "He had no confidence in the heads of the Church, believing they had transgressed, and had got out of the way, consequently he quit praying and keeping the commandments of God."[40] McLellin, his wife Emeline, and their baby, James Martin McLellan, born February 22, 1838, in

39. Cannon and Cook, *Far West Record*, 160.

40. *History of the LDS Church*, 3:31.

Far West, immediately moved to Tinney's Grove, about twenty-five miles away in Ray County.[41]

W. W. Phelps also experienced increased pressure to leave the county. Testifying a few months later, at the Richmond hearing, in November 1838, he said: "For sometime in June, steps were taken to get myself and others out of the county of Caldwell, and efforts were made to get the post office from me (being postmaster), by demand for it. I explained the law, which seemed satisfactory, and it [the demand] was given up.... [A]n armed guard was kept in town and one of them at my house, during the night, as I supposed, to watch my person."[42]

Even beyond such intimidations, ecclesiastical trials, and lawful proceedings, Joseph's presence at Far West seemed to stir what had been largely administrative disagreements into open acts of violence and retribution focused against the dissenters. On June 17, 1838, Sidney Rigdon preached his notorious "Salt Sermon," which threatened that dissenters would be "cast out, and literally trodden under foot."[43] This public sermon served to legitimatize what had been occurring in private. A company of Smith loyalists, initially intent upon purging dissenters from the church, secretly banded together. Spurred on by a local Mormon named Sampson Avard, this group was known by various names: the Brother of Gideon, Daughters of Zion, Sons of Dan, the Big Fan, and eventually Danites. Soon after Rigdon's sermon was delivered, eighty-three Mormons signed a letter "warning out" the Whitmers. Signers did not include the church or Missouri church presidencies—the first name on the threatening letter was Avard's, followed by eighty-two rank-and-file Mormons:

FAR WEST, June, 1838.

To Oliver Cowdery, David Whitmer, John Whitmer, William W. Phelps, and Lyman E, Johnson, greeting:

---

41. Porter, "Odyssey of William Earl McLellin," 323–24. William McLellin spelled his name several ways throughout his lifetime. McLellin has become the standardized spelling throughout the literature of the Mormon movement. However, his son apparently preferred the more common spelling "McLellan."

42. W. W. Phelps, testimony, in *Senate Document 189*, 43–44.

43. Corrill, *Brief History of the Church of Christ*, 30.

Whereas the citizens of Caldwell county have borne with the abuse received from you at different times, and on different occasions, until it is no longer to be endured; neither will they endure it any longer, having exhausted all the patience they have, and conceive that to bear any longer a vice instead of a virtue. We have borne long, and suffered incredibly; but we will neither bear nor suffer any longer; and the decree has gone forth from our hearts, and shall not return to us void. Neither think, gentlemen, that, in so saying, we are trifling with either you or ourselves; for we are not. There are no threats from you— no fear of losing our lives by you, or by any thing you can say or do, will restrain us; for out of the county you shall go, and no power shall save you. And you shall have three days after you receive this communication *to you*, including twenty-four hours in each day, for you to depart with your families peaceably; which you may do undisturbed by any person; but in that time, if you do not depart, we will use the means in our power to cause you to depart; for go you shall. We will have no more promises to reform, as you have already done, and in every instance violated your promise, and regarded not the covenant which you made, but put both it and us at defiance. We have solemnly warned you, and that in the most determined manner, that if you do not cease that course of wanton abuse of the citizens of this county, that vengeance would overtake you sooner or later, and that when it did come it would be as furious as the mountain torrent, and as terrible as the beating tempest; but you have affected to dispise [*sic*] our warnings, and pass them off with a sneer, or a grin, or a threat, and pursued your former course; and vengeance sleepeth not, neither does it slumber; and unless you heed us this time, and attend to our request, it will overtake you at an hour when you do not expect, and at a day when you do not look for it; and for you there shall be no escape; for there is but one decree for you, which is depart, depart, or a more fatal calamity shall befall you.[44]

The Whitmers, as former founders of the community, appeared indisposed to fully withdraw from Far West. Furthermore, they were naturally reluctant to back down in the face of threats. But it was a turning

---

44. Quoted in *Document Containing the Correspondence, Orders, &c. in Relation to the Disturbances with the Mormons*, 103–7. The names of signers also appear in this source.

point. Once Joseph's trusted counselors, the Whitmers and Cowdery could no longer expect Joseph's support.

In later years, David tended to blame Sidney Rigdon more than Joseph for his loss of mutuality with Smith and the church. Forty years later, David's grandson by marriage, James Van Cleave, wrote to Joseph Smith III: "As far as I have been able to learn, (and I have been unbiased in my search for truth) he [David] stands today just where he stood in June 1838—40 years ago—when his life was sought, for his steadfast defense of truth, and because he would not second every word that came from Sidney Rigdon and others who carried the 'Church of Christ' into the abominations which ultimately caused the unconditional Banishment of the whole Church."[45]

Church leaders showed no disposition to seek a peaceful resolution but vigorously sought other means of forcing the Whitmers and Cowderys out. "Even before they [the Whitmers and Cowdery] left town," Richard S. Van Wagoner, Sidney Rigdon's biographer reports, "George Robinson swore out writs of attachment against them and took possession of 'all their personal property, clothing & furniture,' leaving their families homeless."[46] John Whitmer's history further explains:

> They commenced suing at the law of the land by attachment for debts which they knew were paid ... against David Whitmer, L. E. Johnson, O. Cowdery, F. G. Williams W. W. Phelps and myself ... [We] went to obtain legal counsel to prepare to overthrow these attachments which they had caused to be issued against us which we were abundantly able to do by good and substantial witnesses ... But to our great astonishment when we were on our way home from Liberty Clay Co. we met the families of O. Cowdery and L. E. Johnson whom they had driven from their homes and robed [*sic*] them of all their goods save clothing & bedding, &c. While we were gone ... their band of gadiantons [Danites] kept up a guard and watched our houses and abused our families and threatened ... our lives if they ever saw us in Far West.[47]

---

45. James R. B. Van Cleave to Joseph Smith III, 29 September 1878.

46. Van Wagoner, *Sidney Rigdon: A Portrait of Religious Excess*, 219. Van Wagoner is apparently quoting George W. Robinson, but furnishes no source for this internal quotation.

47. McKiernan and Launius, *An Early Latter Day Saint History*, 162–65.

The Whitmer brothers finally heeded this not-so-subtle warning and left in haste on June 19, 1838.[48] William McLellin wrote in 1847: "All things seemed to admonish them they only could have safety in flight, consequently near sunset, David, Oliver, John and Lyman [Johnson], bid farewell to their youthful wives, and their little children, their homes and firesides, and with heavy hearts, and solemn step they left that people who had been enlightened and brought together, to a great extent, by their labors and testimony."[49] John documented his departure in his account book with the brief note: "Left Far West June 19, 1838."[50]

David Whitmer wrote that as he fled from Far West on horseback, "The voice of God from heaven spake to me" and told him to "separate myself from among the Latter Day Saints, for as they sought to do unto me, so should it be done unto them."[51]

Church authorities alleged that stolen property had been found in the house of W. W. Phelps. These allegations also implicated John Whit-

48. George W. Robinson, whose journal forms the basis of Joseph Smith's *History of the LDS Church* for this period, wrote shortly after the expulsion of the dissenters from Far West: "I would mention or notice something about O. Cowdery, David Whitmer, Lyman E. Johnson, and John Whitmer, who being guilty of base iniquities and that to manifest in the ages of all men, and being often entreated would continue in their course seeking the lives of the First Presidency and to overthrow the kingdom of God which they once testified of. Prest Rigdon preached one Sabbath upon the salt that had lost its savour that it is henceforth good for nothing but to be cast out, and trodden under foot of men. And the wicked flee where no man pursueth. These men took warning, and soon they were seen bounding over the prairie like the scapegoat to carry off their own sins. We have not seen them since, their influence is gone, and they are in a miserable condition. So also it is with all who turn from the truth to lying, cheating, defrauding, and swindling." Robinson, "The Scriptory Book of Joseph Smith Jr.," July 1838. Terminal punctuation and initial capitals added.

49. McLellin, "A Special Conference of All the Ministerial Authorities," 9. An interesting story, true or not, is contained in an 1884 interview with David Whitmer: "The Mormon priesthood held a council at Far West and John Whitmer, brother of David, was the secretary of it. David was aware that he was being tried as an apostate, and had an understanding with his brother that, if the council decided favorably, he was to come outside and raise his hat, but if they decided against him, then he was to wipe his face with a handkerchief. John finally came forth, and wiping his face with his handkerchief, David knew that was a signal for him to leave, and, mounting his horse, he made his escape." David Whitmer, interview, mid-July 1884, Richmond, Missouri, pp. 150–51.

50. Whitmer, account book, 19 June 1838, note pinned to p. 36.

51. David Whitmer to Dear Brethren, 91.

June 19, 1838, must have been a sad day, indeed, as John Whitmer noted his departure from Far West, Missouri—the city he had helped found. Courtesy of the LDS Church History Library.

mer and Oliver Cowdery.[52] No details have been preserved about what they allegedly stole; but possibly Joseph Smith's adherents alluded to official church records. David later corroborated in an interview: "John, [having served] as clerk of the church, had its records, and Oliver Cowdery bore off the original translation [printer's manuscript of the Book of Mormon], and eventually transferred it to the keeping of David."[53]

The group of five—John, David, and Jacob Whitmer, Hiram Page, and Oliver Cowdery—found brief refuge with the McLellins at Tinney's Grove. In 1847, William McLellin gave a lurid account of the flight from Far West:

> The duty of driving these men from Caldwell Co., was assigned to the Danites, and they in secret conclave had fixed the night on which their blood should flow, if they did not flee. But an old friend of theirs, who happened to hear the time fixed by the Danites, came to some of them privately late in the afternoon, and told them, that nothing would be restrained from these Danites, which they had attempted to do—and that he would advise them to leave.... But alas! who had now fallen, and become their bitterest enemies, and high handed persecutors. After these men, the "witnesses of truth," and taken an affectionate leave of their innocent families, resigning them into the hands of "the Father of lights," they left "the city of their homes" and began to wend their way across those extensive prairies lying south of Far West.
>
> But the darkness of night soon coming on, and being comparative strangers to the way, they directly lost their path. Pensive, mourn-

---

52. *Senate Document 189*, 6–9.

53. David Whitmer, interview by the *Chicago Times*, August 7, 1875, 8. At a minimum, John took with him the Book of John Whitmer holograph, some Joseph Smith New Translation materials, and pages of the Book of Commandments manuscript. He probably retained other materials, such as a manuscript copy of a revelation to Thomas B. Marsh, a plat of the city of Far West, as well as personal possessions, such as his copy of the Book of Commandments. Cowdery retained the printer's copy of the Book of Mormon. Church leaders retained possession of the majority of the pages from the holograph Book of Commandments and Revelations that John had been keeping. When the church left Missouri, the Book of Commandments manuscript was apparently transported to Nauvoo, Illinois, and from there to Utah. Book of Commandments scholar Robin Scott Jensen reports, "There is possibly a reference to the volume in the 1846 inventory of church documents made previous to the exodus: 'Rough Book-Revelation History &c.; Church Historian's Office Inventory, 1846, LDS Church Library.'" Jensen, "From Manuscript to Printed Page," 42–43.

Ebenezer Robinson, who worked in the Kirtland printing office during the 1830s, published The Return, a paper in support of the claims of David Whitmer's Church of Christ, in the 1880s and 1890s. Courtesy of Community of Christ Library-Archives.

ful, and solemn, see them wander they know not where. All before them, behind them, and round about them, is a vast wilderness of prairie. Not a tree, not a stump, hedge, nor even a stone to guide their onward step....

But onward see those men wander, until the light of a new day broke in upon that part of the earth, and meeting a stranger, he points them to the road that will lead them to an old and tried friend's who lived about twenty-five miles from Far West. With joy, mixed with sorrow, he received them. Mrs. McLellin soon furnished them with a repast, while the family listened to their sad tale. W. E. McLellin had, in August, 1836, ceased to be an active Minister among that people, because he verily believed that the course pursued by their Leaders would sooner or later bring inevitable destruction upon them and their followers. Here they found a home from the "pitiless storm," and remained and refreshed themselves for some days, until their friends had succeeded in bringing to them their families. And when retrospecting his past life, there is no period he contemplates worth more pleasure, than when he fed those persecuted men, David, Oliver, and friends at his table.[54]

The refugees then moved on to Richmond, Missouri, where they established new homes. Here, they were not only safe against Mormon activity but also could draw on resources for a legal defense against the possible charges of theft.

George Schweich, David's grandson and Ebenezer Robinson's successor as editor of *The Return*, later chronicled David's circumstances:

After the dispersion at Far West he returned to Richmond, Mo., contemplating the ruin of his people and his personal losses, both spiritual and temporal, left without anything in the world but the light of God in him, and the resolve he had pledged to heaven to stand a witness to the truth. He at one time took a notion to leave this place, and while yet under the ban of poverty, his thumb was blown from his hand unexpectedly while kindling a fire on his hearthstone, when amid the blood and tears he took this as an omen of God that he should remain in silence in this place until the world should ask of him, where is he? And what is it? Although a man that never told his own miseries until they were asked of him here is a little story that shows his childlike faith and his God-like perseverance.

When he had not seen any money for two months and gained his daily bread with his crippled, bleeding hand in the winters snow, among the then lonely forests, weary with the days and the hardships, almost asleep in that chill that snow and winter brings to exposure, he stopped and bowed in the tracked furrow of his wagon and lifting his soul to heaven prayed the All-wise to give him death and rest, and as the blood from his wounded member stained the beautiful snow the fire-light of heaven came like an exhalation and David Whitmer there in the blood and the snow once again saw the light of God and renewed his covenant with Him who comes in the deepest trouble where man is powerless to save and He is all in all. Here came to him

54. McLellin, "A Special Conference of All the Ministerial Authorities," 9. Ebenezer Robinson, "Items of Personal History," 147, quotes part of McLellin's account of this same flight.

the resolve that marked his after steps in life. Here came his servant-
ship to God anew, and here came the promise once again that he
should not be forsaken or his seed begging for bread.[55]

The day after John Whitmer left his Far West hotel, Sidney Rigdon
took possession of it.[56] Far West boasted two hotels or taverns at this time.
Joseph Smith took over Samuel Musick's tavern, installing Joseph Sr. and
Lucy in it when they arrived in July 1838 as tavern keepers. Church leaders
arranged for the continued use of John's hotel and the location was remembered as John M. Burk's Tavern during the dark days of the Mormon
War.

According to a biographer of David Whitmer, the "banished men
were made to appear the vilest of characters, thus facilitating the ease with
which their removal was made possible." If the statements and charges
were true, "there would have been no reason for expelling them under
threats since the law would have taken care of them in a much more satisfactory manner; their subsequent lives would indicate there was very little
truth in these vilifying statements."[57]

Milton Backman, historian of the Kirtland period, described the
shock of intra-organizational strife upon that community. The trailing impact as Joseph Smith moved church headquarters to Missouri can only be
imagined: "Between November 1837 and June 1838, possibly two or three
hundred Kirtland Saints withdrew from the Church, representing 10 to 15
percent of the membership.... Many of the apostates had served in major
positions of responsibility. During a nine-month period, almost one-third
of the General Authorities were excommunicated, disfellowshipped, or removed from their Church callings."[58]

55. Schweich, "The Position of David Whitmer," 4. Ebenezer Robinson died in 1891, but
Schweich continued to publish *The Return*.

56. Marryat, *Travels and Adventures of Monsieur Violet*, 307.

57. Richardson, "David Whitmer," 75.

58. Backman, *Heavens Resound*, 328.

CHAPTER TWENTY-THREE

New Beginnings

T HOUGH THE WHITMERS were forced to flee from Far West, W. W. Phelps managed to remain in the community throughout 1838. The actions of the church increasingly drove a wedge between their respective worldviews. W. W. Phelps noted Smith's growing disdain for the law of the land, saying, "In the fore part of July [1838], I being one of the justices of the county court, was forbid by Joseph Smith, Jr., from issuing any process against him."[1]

The question of legal rights bore additional import for John. The practice of consecration had been largely abandoned by the church since the Jackson County exodus, and the Whitmers had never been strong advocates of consecration. But church debt and resources left behind at Kirtland sorely plagued church leadership. Smith and Rigdon seemed obsessed with regaining control over the temporal resources of the church. Thus, at Far West, on July 8, 1838, Joseph reinstituted a modified form of consecration. The authorizing revelation reads: "Verily, thus saith the Lord, I require all their surplus property to be put into the hands of the bishop of my church of Zion, for the building of mine house, and for the laying the foundation of Zion and for the priesthood, and for the debts of the presidency of my church; and that shall be the beginning of the tithing of my people."[2]

Rather than consecrating all possessions, this form of consecration required one's surplus, although without specifying how necessities were

---

1. *Document Containing the Correspondence, Orders, &c., in Relation to the Disturbances with the Mormons*, 122.

2. CofC D&C 106:1a, b; LDS D&C 119:1–3. Hedrick in "Review of the 'Herald,'" observed: "He [Joseph] desires a revelation to do it up to his own advantage; and behold, he gets one which requires the brethren to PAY ALL HIS DEBTS" (69).

to be differentiated from surplus. To insure success, provisions of the law were enforced by a secret organization of members loyal to the presidency. John now held considerable land in his own name. John returned to Far West and sought out Joseph to ask how he might allay growing hostility toward himself and his family. Joseph recommended putting his "property into the hands of the bishop and high council, to be disposed of according to the laws of the church" as a way of restoring the church's confidence. At this point, John clarified his own perspective, telling Smith, "that I wished to control my own property" and "that I wished to be governed by the laws of the land" Joseph Smith rejoined, "Now, you wish to pin me down to the law."[3] John's need to completely break philosophically with Joseph and the church was now clear.

Throughout the Clay and Caldwell Counties period, John had been one among many who had attempted to look after the best interests of Algernon Sidney Gilbert's widow, Elizabeth. After Gilbert's untimely death in Clay County, Elizabeth made her home with the Saints in Far West and was to some degree dependent upon the church and its members for her well being. In part due to the continuing troubled state of the church, her husband's estate remained unsettled. On July 14, 1838, John entered into a complex legal action intended to resolve this estate. Frederick G. Williams was the principal (administrator), and Jacob Shumaker and John Whitmer signed on in this legal undertaking as security. The three pledged themselves by a bond of $1,200 to "faithfully administer said Estate, account for, pay and deliver all money and property of said estate and perform all other things touching said administration required by law, or order of any Court having Jurisdiction, then the above bond to be void."[4] It is remarkable that John assumed the extra legal obligation of such a bond knowing his own financial situation was uncertain at best. This action must reflect a high sense of obligation to his dead friend's widow and children, as well as

3. *Document Containing the Correspondence, Orders, &c. in Relation to the Disturbances with the Mormons*, 139.

4. Gilbert, notice [about estate], *Western Star*, March 1839. Despite Whitmer's removal from Far West and the exodus of the Saints from Missouri, this legal proceeding continued several years before it was finally settled, which may explain why Elizabeth Gilbert continued to reside in Far West for an indefinite period before later joining the Saints in Illinois.

confidence that his own legal efforts to protect himself and his family and their holdings would prevail in Missouri courts of law.

By July 18, 1838, John had left Far West and moved his family to Richmond, Missouri, paying S. B. Stoddard six dollars to move their possessions. John rented a home from a Mr. Gudgel. But by the end of July 1838, the family moved into a rental from a Doctor King where Oliver and Elizabeth Ann were apparently also living.[5] John's brother David had owned only a single horse and wagon when he reached Richmond in June 1838. To support his family, he began hiring out his wagon and hauling goods to and from the Missouri River.

Even while living in Richmond, John was apparently buying land in Far West. On August 13, 1838, John purchased eighty acres from Burr Riggs. The property was located one mile south of Far West, on Goose Creek.[6]

Some of Sarah's family remained in the Far West area throughout the Mormon War. John's brother-in-law, John Zimmer, who was married to Sarah's sister, Eliza, lived just south of Far West in Rockford Township.[7] Sarah's mother, Martha Jackson, must have been living with John and Eliza. The whereabouts of Sarah's father, John Jackson, during this period are not known. A decade later, he was in Iowa.[8] Meanwhile, W. W. Phelps somehow continued his sojourn at Far West, apparently without serious molestation. On August 29, 1838, Phelps conveyed to John his interest in the mortgage that Edward Partridge gave for their interest in town lots.[9]

Joseph Smith may have privately continued to anticipate that John Whitmer and his associates would repent, seek his good graces, and return to the fold, as many others had done before. But Smith's subsequent writings suggest he was not making things easy. In a particularly bad-tempered moment, he wrote a letter to the church on December 16, 1838, from Liberty Jail. In it, he characterized David Whitmer as a "dumb beast to ride"

5. Whitmer, account book, 23 November 1838, p. 38.

6. Burr Riggs, indenture to John Whitmer, identifies "the West half of the North West Quarter of Section No. Twenty-Three township No. Fifty-Six Range No. Twenty-Nine Caldwell County, containing Eighty acres."

7. 1840 census, Rockford Township, Caldwell County, Missouri.

8. Andrew and Eliza Jackson to Sarah and John Whitmer, 2 May 1849.

9. Edward Partridge to W. W. Phelps and John Whitmer, 17 May 1837.

and "an ass to bray out cursings instead of blessings."[10] At this point, there was no going back; the gulf on both sides had finally grown too wide to bridge. Joseph believed that the dissenting brethren had betrayed their friends because they wished "to gain the friendship of the world." In his mind, "Mormon 'renegades'" were only capable of construing "the Saints' communitarian practice of consecration and dedication of property to the cause of 'Zion,' through the eyes of 'the world,' which increasingly honored only self-made men and which respected only private, secular, and competitive property ownership."[11] Ironically, on September 7, 1838, barely two months after John had been forced to leave, land patents were issued in John's name for two parcels of land at Far West—a total of two hundred acres.[12] These patents from the federal government certified that the land had been paid for in full.

Ten days later on September 17, John Whitmer traveled to the land office in Lexington, Missouri, and also purchased 160 acres of farmland near Richmond.[13] John was a farmer at heart and was no doubt anxious to resume this familiar way of life, by which he could provide a good living for his family. His pattern of acquisition of land shows that he must have been torn between making the Richmond area or Far West his permanent home, but of course, the season was too advanced for a move in either direction.

With the dissenters removed from Far West, the new regime's attention refocused on forestalling perceived attacks from beyond the fellowship.[14] Sidney Rigdon's Salt Sermon, so effective in galvanizing church support of Joseph Smith and driving out supposed dissenters, also captured the attention of nonmember neighbors. From the summer of 1838 on, hostility

---

10. *History of the LDS Church*, 3:228.

11. Epperson, "The Grand, Fundamental Principle," 89; See Faulring, *An American Prophet's Record*, 216, 220–21, 224.

12. The northwest quarter of section 14 in township 56, north of the baseline, of range 29 last of the fifth meridian, 160 acres, patent no. 8269, 19:303; and the northeast quarter of the southeast quarter of section 14, patent no. 5629, 40 acres, John Whitmer, land patents, 21:453.

13. Pollard and Woods, *Whitmer Memoirs*, 25.

14. Joseph's response to the crisis was the adoption of a Book of Mormon pattern described in Alma 28:14–19.

toward the church from those beyond its bounds dramatically increased. Smith's aggressive expansion of church territory beyond Caldwell into Daviess County to the north lit a fuse that eventually flared into an explosive clash of cultures in northern Missouri. This conflict became known as the 1838 Mormon War. The Danite society, with the church presidency's silent support of Sampson Avard's leadership, was transformed into a secret Mormon army. The Danites first functioned defensively but were ultimately deployed to consolidate and expand Mormon territory with preemptive raids on nonmember communities in Daviess County.

Ironically, the Whitmers, by being among the earliest to bear the brunt of the Danites' violent threats, were lucky in missing out on subsequent hardships experienced by those at Far West as the situation of the Saints rapidly spiraled downward into a contest of military force with the state of Missouri.

CHAPTER TWENTY-FOUR

The Mormon War in Missouri

TENSION OVER POLITICAL and geographic control of the region escalated, as Mormon immigrants secured land beyond Caldwell County—primarily in Daviess County, where in May 1838 they laid out the city of Adam-ondi-Ahman (Diahman).[1] Hostilities broke out on August 6, 1838, at the election for state officers held at Gallatin, the seat of Daviess County.[2] After winning the affray, in which there were many gashes, cuts, and bruises but no fatalities, the Mormons retreated to Adam-ondi-Ahman. Members from Caldwell County responded by sending almost 150 men under the church's paramilitary Danite leaders to their aid. While these church members viewed their actions as defensive, Daviess citizens were alarmed, as Missouri law prohibited bodies of armed men from crossing county lines without proper authorization.[3] Members in Daviess gathered their families to Diahman for protection under Lyman Wight's leadership.[4] As the violence escalated, church leaders resolved to defend the

1.   LeSueur, "Missouri's Failed Compromise," 137.

2.   John L. Butler, a large and powerfully built Mormon, bristled after a speech that advocated restricting Mormon suffrage. "The first thing that came to my mind was the covenants entered into by the Danites ... and I hollowed [sic] out to the top of my voice saying 'O yes, you Danites, here is a job for us.'" He waded into the fray, wielding an oak club from a nearby woodpile. "I never struck a man the second time, and while knocking them down, I really felt that they would soon embrace the gospel." Butler, Journal History, 6 August 1838.

3.   LeSueur, *The 1838 Mormon War in Missouri*, 67.

4.   "Impetuous, bold, and fiercely loyal to Joseph Smith, Wight personified the growing militant spirit in Mormonism," quoted in ibid., 68. But church men resisted trial by Daviess County citizens. Lyman Wight took the position that "he owed nothing to the laws—the laws had not protected him," quoted by Swartzell, *Mormonism Exposed*, 32. However, the first armed encounter occurred at DeWitt, in neighboring Carroll County, Missouri, where church families had been sent to establish a Mormon port on

church at any cost. Corrill later recalled that Joseph Smith stated publicly: "If the people would let us alone, we would preach the gospel to them in peace; but, if they came on us to molest us, we would establish our religion by the sword; and that he would become to this generation a second Mahomet."[5]

Parties of Mormon raiders were dispatched throughout Daviess and Clinton Counties. Capturing suspected enemies and driving others from their homes, they returned to Diahman with cattle, hogs, and property with which to support the church's army. The belief that they were chosen people, that they were helping to build the kingdom of God, and that they were justified in their retaliation spurred them to acts they would not normally commit.

Despite growing difficulties within the Mormon realm, Smith continued sending out missionaries to encourage converts to gather and to raise funds to assist northwestern Missouri Saints. His brother, Don Carlos Smith, and cousin, George A. Smith, set out on such a mission to Kentucky and Tennessee on September 26, 1838. Don Carlos reported an encounter in his journal en route with David Whitmer at Richmond, Mis-

---

the Missouri River to facilitate the transportation of goods in and out of their domain. Their makeshift town of tents and wagons overlooked the river. LeSueur, *The 1838 Mormon War in Missouri*, 102. Carroll County residents, set on removing the Mormons, prepared for an anticipated battle. The arrival of two hundred Saints from Canada in late September provoked an attack. George Hinkle, a Mormon who was also a colonel in the state militia "declared that he would rather die than be driven from the town." (102, 109) This caused a dilemma for many DeWitt Saints. He continued: "Some of the Mormons, having endured several months of abuse from the Carroll settlers, stood ready to fight eye-for-eye and tooth-for-tooth against the vigilantes. Other Mormons, especially those who had just arrived from Canada and who knew little about the long-developing conflict, were reluctant to turn so quickly to guns and violence" (104). Zadock Judd, autobiography, pp. 8–9, reflected the powerful feelings of some at DeWitt: "This state of affairs was very trying to some of our sober, serious Christians that had been taught that it was wicked to fight; it almost rocked their faith in the gospel; to take up arms and try to kill their fellow mortals was a new doctrine that some could hardly endure." See also Merkley, *Biography of Christopher Merkley*, 4. Joseph's arrival with additional troops fortified the Missourians' determination to force the church from their county. Though the Saints sought to end the crisis peacefully, repeated appeals to civil authorities were fruitless. Church leaders saw the hopelessness of their position and withdrew to Caldwell and Daviess Counties.

5. John Corrill, testimony, *Senate Document 189*, 12.

souri, "On the twenty-sixth of September, 1838, we took leave of our friends and started on our mission. ... When we got to the landing [Richmond] we found the river very low, and but one boat up, which was the 'Kansas.' Whilst waiting for the boat, we had an interview with David Whitmer.... He had become our enemy; yet he shook hands with us quite cordially, and wished us success."[6] The two Smiths were cordial in their turn, helping David load thiry-eight hundred pounds of freight into his wagon at Richmond landing. They also helped David across a soft patch of ground, "by lifting at the wheels." George A. Smith later recalled in a letter to David "Your little span of horses pulled it through nobley [*sic*]."[7]

George M. Hinkle wanted to call up the Caldwell militia when encroaching units of the state militia began probing the county's outer defenses. Instead, without legal authorization, the church deployed its own "Army of Israel." The Mormon attack on a group of legally constituted militia at Crooked River was seen as mob action against state forces, which sealed public fears and hostile opinion. Church members from surrounding settlements began flooding into Far West. As prospects worsened for the residents, the normal printing routine was suspended, pending resolution of these mounting hostilities. In preparation for siege or flight, the church's printing "press was taken down and the type hastily boxed and buried, in the night, and a haystack put over it to protect it."[8]

For reasons that seem insubstantial in retrospect, Joseph Smith, like Sidney Rigdon, seemed willing to engage in heated, militaristic rhetoric that only intensified the tensions. Burr Riggs reported, "Two or three days before the surrender of the Mormons to the militia at Far West, I heard Jos. Smith, jr. say that the sword was now unsheathed, and should not again be sheathed until he could go through these United States, and live

6.   Don C. Smith, journal, 26 September 1838, p. 11.

7.   George A. Smith, statement, Journal History, 22 February 1859.

8.   Robinson, "Items of Personal History," 170. Two additional accounts of protecting the press are in Crawley, *A Descriptive Bibliography*, 1:20: "During the night of October 30, 1838, while General Samuel D. Lucas and the Missouri militia were camped outside Far West, some of the [print] shop hands buried the press and type, including an inked form for the September issue of the Journal"; and Wilcox, "The Saints in Northwest Missouri, Part IV," 1004: "The old press was preserved from destruction by Brother William Miller who dug a hole on his property and put the press in it, covering it with poles and then stacking hay on top."

in any county he pleased, peaceably."[9] Cast in the role of peace seekers, Hinkle, John Corrill, Reed Peck, W. W. Phelps, John Cleminson, and others tried simultaneously to support church leaders while attempting, with little success, to redirect the church from its militaristic course.[10] Member Reed Peck wrote, "A few individuals of us were ever after this opposed to the rule of the presidency perceiving that all spiritual and temporal affairs were under their control."[11]

On October 27, 1838, Missouri governor Lilburn Boggs issued his infamous "Extermination Order," and state militia units moved toward Far West, intending to drive the Mormons out of Missouri or kill them. Acting even before they had received word of the order, during the late afternoon of October 30, 1838, anti-Mormon regulators in eastern Caldwell and Livingston Counties staged an attack upon the outlying Mormon settlement Haun's Mill, apparently in retaliation for the Mormon attack at Crooked River that occurred four days earlier.[12] The superior anti-Mormon force quickly overwhelmed unsuspecting defenders at Haun's Mill, and the

9. Burr Riggs, testimony, *Senate Document 189*, 29–30.

10. Joseph's 1838 diary reflects his perception of Corrill's peace-seeking proclivities during this period. Faulring, *An American Prophet's Record*, 209. Overcome by these manifestations of zeal gone astray, John Cleminson indicated he had little choice. "I went in the expedition to *Daviess* in which Gallatin was burnt, as I felt myself compelled to go from the regulations which had been made. It was generally understood that *every movement* made in *Daviess* was under the direction and supervision of the first presidency." Cleminson, testimony, *Senate Document 189*, 16. W. W. Phelps wrote, "Finding that I should *have* to go out, and not wishing to be put in front of the battle, I sought a situation, and went out with my wagon. This was the expedition in which Gallatin and Millport were burnt." Corrill, testimony, *Senate Document 189*, 45; LeSueur, in *The 1838 Mormon War in Missouri*, 251, observed, these dissidents were not cowards or apostates interested only in working at cross purposes with the majority church members. They accurately foresaw church policies resulting in disastrous consequences, but their warnings brought only condemnation from church leaders. Hinkle related, "I spoke to Mr. Smith, jun., in the house, and told him that this course of burning houses and plundering, by the Mormon troops, would ruin us; that it could not be kept hid, and would bring the force of the State upon us; that houses would be searched, and stolen property found. Smith replied to me, in a pretty rough manner to keep still; that I should say nothing about it; that it would discourage the men." Hinkle, testimony, *Senate Document 189*, 21–22.

11. Tanner and Tanner, *Reed Peck Manuscript*, 9.

12. Baugh, "Jacob Hawn and the Hawn's Mill Massacre," 1–25.

attack turned into a massacre. Fourteen Mormons were injured and eighteen Mormons lay dead, while only three Missourians were injured.[13] Also on October 30, 1838, Major General Samuel Lucas's troops arrived at Far West, closing off escape from the refugee-filled town.

David Whitmer was pressed into duty during the siege, an experience he recalled forty-eight years later in a letter to the *Herald*. Hypothesizing on the root of a rumor, published in an earlier *Herald* article, which accused him of aiding the Missourians against church members, Whitmer stated:

> [It] may have originated in this way: when I came to Richmond, General Parks, who was in command of the State Militia, was short of wagons and teams, as they were scarce here then; so he pressed me and my team into service and I was forced to go and drive a wagon load of baggage to Far West. I told them if I had to go I would take no gun. They said "all right;" and I took no gun.... God knows that I did not encourage the militia in the least to persecute the Saints. He knows I was praying for them and did not lay a straw in their way, instead of aiding in their persecutions. Our persecutions [persecution of the church] began five years before I left the body in 1838; now was I in any way the cause of that? Brethren, it is ridiculous; it is wrong; it is an injury to an innocent man; and an injury to the cause and to my testimony to the Book of Mormon! It is an abomination in the sight of God, and he will justly reward all those who have originated such falsehoods about me!! Now brethren—I want to repeat, in the fear of God, that my testimony will stand at the judgment day as the truth, concerning all of these matters. May this writer in the *Herald* some day see wherein he is in error, and may he find the truth as it is in Christ, is my prayer for him.[14]

As reported in the *Chicago Tribune* in 1885, while on duty at Far West, David Whitmer "was handed a musket by the soldiery and ordered to shoot Joseph Smith, but [he] threw the musket down, declaring he 'would not harm the Lord's anointed.'"[15]

13. Baugh, "A Call to Arms," 203–18.

14. "Letters from David and John C. Whitmer," 34:90.

15. David Whitmer, interview by the *Chicago Tribune*, December 17, 1885.

THE EXTERMINATION OF THE LATTER DAY SAINTS FROM THE STATE OF MISSOURI IN THE FALL OF 1838.

This engraving showing the situation of members during the surrender of Far West was produced by Samuel Brannan in New York and was sold through the church's New-York Messenger printing office in the mid–1840s. Courtesy of the Community of Christ Archives.

Besieged in Far West and struck by the news of the massacre at Haun's Mill, Joseph realized that the church could not win. Facing utter destruction, according to both Corrill and Peck, Joseph urged them to work out a compromise with the militia and, if necessary, "beg like a dog for peace."[16] Hinkle added that Joseph wished a treaty "on any terms short of a battle."[17]

Following a negotiated surrender, the terms of which have resulted in conflicting accounts, Joseph and Hyrum Smith, Sidney Rigdon, Parley P. Pratt, George W. Robinson, Amasa Lyman, and Lyman Wight were arrested and court martialed. Eventually, sixty or more Mormons were taken into custody and sent to Richmond, Missouri, to await a preliminary hearing and eventual trial.

With their leaders under arrest in northern Missouri, church defenders surrendered to the surrounding Missouri militia. The militia occu-

16. Corrill, *Brief History of the Church of Christ*, 41; Tanner and Tanner, *Reed Peck Manuscript*, 24.

17. George Hinkle to W. W. Phelps, 14 August 1844, p. 449.

pied Far West and took over John M. Burk's Tavern as headquarters. Burk wrote indignantly about this appropriation:

> I here by Certify that General John Clark and his aid at their arrival at far West in Caldwell Co Misorie [*sic*] came to my Tavern stand and without my Liave [*sic*] Pitched their Markees in my yard and did take my wood and hay to furnish the same and did bring their horses in also and without my Leave take hay for them and did take Posession [*sic*] of my house and use it for a council house and did place a strong guard around it so as to hinder any person from going in or out and I myself was not permitted to go in.[18]

After the Mormon men surrendered their weapons, they were kept overnight at Burk's under guard. Young Chapman Duncan, among those thus confined, recalled that in the morning, "Joseph the Prophet was brought up in a wagon with the balance near to us at the tavern. I went up to the wagon."[19] Five of the church leaders—Joseph and Hyrum Smith, Sidney Rigdon, Parley P. Pratt, and Lyman Wight—were transported to Independence, allegedly for trial but actually for the beginning of many moves, numerous legal maneuvers, and constant incarceration for the next six months. After their departure, General John B. Clark arrived, accompanied by sixteen hundred more militia troops. Seizing the public occasion, Clark delivered his famous speech from the doorstep of Burk's Tavern. Ebenezer Robinson wrote: "Several other brethren were brought and placed in our company, until they obtained near fifty. They marched us to a hotel [Burk's Tavern], before the door of which two columns of soldiers were stationed, extending out about forty feet from the door, facing each other, with their guns poised so their muzzles were about breast high, between which we marched into the hotel. After we had been taken to the hotel

---

18. Burk in Johnson, *Mormon Redress Petitions*, 148–49. Although the siege of Far West ended without a battle, some church members were apparently shot and wounded in connection with the city's surrender and occupation. Levi Richards testified, "I was called to extract led, dress the wounds, etc., for several persons (Saints) who were shot in the above siege, two of whom died." Levi Richards, affidavit, *History of the LDS Church*, 4:71.

19. Duncan, autobiography, p. 38.

Gen. Clark made the fallowing [*sic*] speech to the brethren on the public square:"[20]

> It now devolves upon you to fulfil [*sic*] the treaty that you have entered into, the leading items of which I will now lay before you. The *first* of these, you have already complied with, which is, that you deliver up your leading men, to be tried according to law. The *second* is, that you deliver up your arms: *this*, has been attended to: The *third* is, that you sign over your property to defray the expences [*sic*] of the war; *this* you have done. Another thing yet remains for you to comply with, that is, that you leave the State forth-with.... As for your *leaders*, do not once *think*—do not imagine for a moment—do not let it enter into your minds, that they will be delivered, or that you will see their faces again; for their fate is fix'd—their dye is cast—their doom is seal'd.[21]

Eventually, the Smiths, Rigdon, Pratt, and Wight were sent to Richmond, Missouri, for a preliminary hearing. Between fifty and sixty of the church men placed under custody in Far West were also transported to Richmond and incarcerated at three locations around town.

In Richmond, on November 12, 1838, Judge Austin A. King convened a preliminary hearing to ascertain whether the evidence was sufficient to hold the Mormon prisoners for trial. During this hearing, John Whitmer was called and testified as a state witness. John's testimony follows in full:

> John Whitmer, a witness for the State, produced, sworn and examined, deposeth and saith: About the 17th of April last, at a meeting of perhaps fifteen or twenty-five, in Far West, Joseph Smith, jr., spoke in reference to difficulties they had, and their persecutions, &c., in and out of the church. Mr. Smith said he did not intend in future to have any process served on him, and the officer who attempted it should die; that any person who spoke or acted against the presidency or the church should leave the country or die; that he would suffer no such to remain there; that they should lose their head. George W. Harris, who was there present, observed, "the head of their influence, I suppose." Smith replied, Yes, he would so modify it. Mr. Rigdon then got up, and spoke in connection with what Mr. Smith had been saying; and in speaking of the head of their influence, he said, that he meant that ball

20. Robinson, "Items of Personal History," 211.

21. Snow, "Eliza R. Snow: Letter From Missouri," 548.

on their shoulders, called the head, and that they should be followed to the ends of the earth. Mr. Rigdon further remarked, that he would suffer no process of law to be served on him hereafter.

Some time in June, after Mr. Rigdon had preached his "salt sermon," I held conversations with several Mormons on the subject of that sermon, and the excitement produced by the course and conduct of the presidency. Among others, I conversed with Alanson Ripley. I spoke of the supremacy of the laws of the land, and the necessity of, at all times, being governed by them. He replied, that as to the technical niceties of the law of the land, he did not intend to regard them; that the kingdom spoken of by the prophet Daniel had been set up, and that it was necessary every kingdom should be governed by its own laws. I also conversed with George W. Robinson, on the same subject, who answered, (when I spoke of being governed by the laws and, their supremacy,) "when God spoke he must be obeyed," whether his word came in contact with the laws of the land or not; and that, as the kingdom spoken of by Daniel had been set up, its laws must be obeyed. I told him I thought it was contrary to the laws of the land to drive men from their homes; to which he replied, such things had been done of old, and that the gathering of the saints must continue, and that dissenters could not live among them in peace.

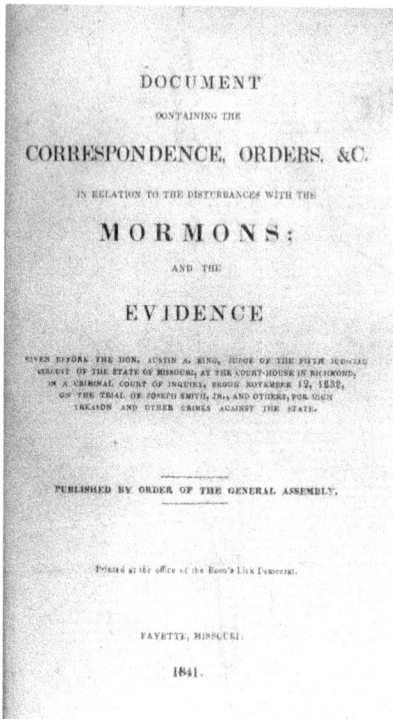

In 1841, the state of Missouri published the proceedings of the Richmond Preliminary Hearing. The publication was entitled Document Containing the Correspondence, Orders, &c. in Relation to the Disturbances with the Mormons and included John Whitmer's testimony as a state witness. Courtesy of Community of Christ Library–Archives.

I also conversed with Mr. J. Smith, jr., on this subject. I told him I wished to allay the (then) excitement, as far as i could do it. He said the excitement was very high, and he did not know what would allay it; but remarked, he would give me his opinion, which was, that if I would put my property into the hands of the bishop and high council, to be disposed of according to the laws of the church, he thought that would allay it, and that the church after a while might have confidence in me. I replied to him I wished to control my own property. In telling Mr. Smith that I wished to be governed by the laws of the land, he answered, "Now, you wish to pin me down to the law." And further this deponent saith not.

JOHN WHITMER.[22]

During this hearing, W. W. Phelps and other former members also testified for the state, including: Sampson Avard, John Cleminson, John Corrill, Addison F. Green, George M. Hinkle, Reed Peck, Morris Phelps, Burr Riggs, and Benjamin Slade.

The majority of Mormons were released. A group of six, including Parley P. Pratt was jailed in Richmond, while Joseph Smith and five companions—Hyrum Smith, Sidney Rigdon, Lyman Wight, Alexander McRae, and Caleb Baldwin[23]—were transported to Liberty Jail, in Clay County. Around February 1838, the general exodus of church members from the state began. Quincy, Illinois, was designated as a temporary place of refuge. Some members, however, were unable to leave Missouri until later in the spring, and the refugees straggled eastward from February through May 1839.

Although most members were anxious to leave the state, a few families simply remained in the Far West area, many of them because they had disaffiliated from Mormonism and had no interest in yet another grueling journey of about 175 miles in the winter. Deacon George Strope's family had arrived in the vicinity of Far West from New York, via Kirtland, in 1838, shortly before the Saints surrendered, but quietly stayed on their farm

---

22. *Document Containing the Correspondence, Orders, &c. in Relation to the Disturbances with the Mormons*, 138–39.

23. See Bray, "Caleb Baldwin: Prison Companion to Joseph Smith," 83–86.

on Plum Creek, two miles west of Mirabile. Elder William T. Bozarth also ignored the militia order to vacate his farm near what became Mirabile.[24]

In November 1838, the John Whitmer family moved from Doctor King's to S. Miller's house in Richmond near his brother David, paying four months' rent in advance.[25] At this point, it was clearly to the Whitmers' advantage to remain aloof from the drastically changed status of the Saints. Unlike many others who separated themselves from the church, David took firm action and established himself clearly as no longer affiliated with Smith; but he did not move in the opposite direction adopted by some as active and indignant adversaries. The firmness of his action provided a clear model for the rest of the extended family, including John. Both brothers had been loyal to Joseph for eight years, often sacrificing their own interests to show loyalty for positions they later repudiated. Unlike the perpetually vacillating Sidney Rigdon, however, when it became apparent that their core values no longer harmonized with the direction in which Joseph was taking the church, the family—especially David and John, who played the most public roles—invoked those values, took a principled stand, and demonstrated remarkable personal strength and determination which put their beliefs and church experiences in a larger perspective. Except for their intra-family support, they did not seek to draw away other followers, nor did they use their long experience with Joseph Smith to peddle information to those hostile to Smith. Although all of the brothers were now decisively excluded from the inner circle, none of them cultivated alliances with the outside world except those of shared citizenship and neighborliness. This stoic approach to banishment set a tone of dignity and manliness for the entire Whitmer clan.

During the winter of 1838–39, John reevaluated his options. It was clear from both civilians and militia alike that most Mormons had either left Far West or soon would, so John began to think about his farm and other property at Far West. A shrewd Kentucky trader, Oliver Craig, made the rounds of fleeing Saints, securing land entries for pennies on the dollar. New settlers coming in after the departure of the Saints employed Craig to provide defensible land titles while, according to a local historian, "oth-

---

24. Wilcox, *Saints of the Reorganization in Missouri*, 87; also Wilcox, "Saints in Northwest Missouri, Part III," 1008.

25. Whitmer, account book, 23 and 25 November 1838, p. 38.

ers forged land entries, holding the paper in smoke to give it the aged look of an original paper.... It took decades to clear the land titles."[26] Jeffery Walker, an editor with the legal and business series of the Joseph Smith Papers Project, builds a case that manipulation of land tenure laws by Missourians for gain was a significant underlying factor in the 1838 expulsion of the Mormons from Missouri:

> The "north countries" [Caldwell and Davies counties] had yet to be fully surveyed, which allowed the Saints to settle on the land and qualify for preemption rights that did not require payment until the surveys were completed. After the surveying was finished, these same rights were an impetus for non-Mormon land speculators to force Mormons out of Missouri. The imminent vesting of these property rights [in November 1838] further explains the frantic efforts to dislodge Mormons from their lands in Missouri altogether in late 1838.[27]

Their detention following the fall of Far West, prevented Mormons from traveling to Richmond, Missouri, to make preemption and land payments, while affording an opportunity for others to secure much of the Mormons' improved land. This timing and General Clark's forcing his Mormon prisoners to deed away their land assured a substantial transfer of Mormon lands into the hands of local non-Mormon residents.

Mormon sources accused some former church members of participating in this ethically questionable transfer of property. "During our trial William E. McLellin, accompanied by Burr Riggs and others, at times were busy in plundering and robbing the houses of Sidney Rigdon, George Morey, the widow Phebe Ann Patten, and others, under pretense or color of law, on an order from General Clark, as testified to by the members of the different families robbed."[28]

While John is usually not directly mentioned, he either owned or could claim an interest in a considerable amount of Far West land. Even though bishop Edward Partridge had left the state, John was also now the sole holder of a substantial note against Partridge for unsold Far West lots. John began to realize that he was also in a position to acquire the lands and

26. Wilcox, *Latter Day Saints on the Missouri Frontier*, 319.

27. Walker, "Mormon Land Rights," 4.

28. *History of the LDS Church*, 3:215.

lots of church members fleeing from the state. Thus, on February 1, 1839, John finalized his transaction with Burr Riggs for eighty-acres of land lying near his own holdings for $800.[29] Like John, Burr Riggs had become uncomfortable with church affairs during the last days of the Far West period. This transaction suggests some stronger link between John Whitmer and Burr Riggs. One wonders whether John and Burr shared their growing concern about the direction of the church with each other or whether these feelings developed independently.

Like some former stalwarts of the church, such as John Corrill, a counselor in the Missouri bishopric, Reed Peck, George M. Hinkle, and eventually even chief apostle Thomas B. Marsh, Riggs quietly withdrew from church involvement following the expulsion from Missouri. Though a loyalist during the Mormon War, supporting the church's activities and participating in Danite raids, Riggs was driven from the state in November 1838 and testified as a witness on behalf of the state during the Richmond hearings. Riggs went to Quincy, Illinois, where like some of the Whitmer family, he was excommunicated on March 17, 1839.[30]

Despite the major setback of separation from the church, The Whitmer family had found a home in Missouri. Their experiences document a strong pragmatic, even stubborn, family streak, which kept them together as a family and in Missouri. They had heavily invested in the westward movement of the church a decade earlier and now had nothing behind in New York or Ohio to which they might return. More than his brothers, as a founder of Far West, John seemed to have formed an enduring attachment to Caldwell County. Just as John had resisted being told to leave Far West by his former Mormon friends, for the same reason, if told to do so by Missourians, he would have also resisted leaving the state. However,

---

29. Burr and Lovina Riggs, indenture to John Whitmer.

30. Cook, *Revelations of the Prophet Joseph Smith*, 155. Burr Riggs was born April 17, 1811, at New Haven, Connecticut, to Gideon Riggs and Susan Pitcher Riggs and had a brother named Harpin. He married Lovina Williams. Burr, a physician, was one of the early Mormons to settle in Caldwell County (1836–38), acquiring about two hundred acres of land. In Quincy, when he swore an affidavit petitioning for redress, he listed his lost assets as his land, a town lot in Far West, and about forty acres of corn and other vegetables. Riggs remained in the Quincy area until his death on June 8, 1860. Johnson, *Mormon Redress Petitions*, 330. See also *Document Containing the Correspondence, Orders, &c. in Relation to the Disturbances with the Mormons*, 134–36.

because of his separation from the main church, his presence proved less objectionable to Missouri neighbors.

Peter and Mary Whitmer, David, and Jacob may have all found more benefit in living near a commercial center like Richmond, Missouri, but John's brother-in-law Hiram Page, sought out the isolation of farm life where he could provide for his family in relative peace. John also remained a country boy at heart.

It was becoming clear to John that the Missourians stood to gain a great deal in driving Mormons from improved lands throughout Caldwell and Daviess Counties. John was perfectly positioned to observe the unfolding of the tragedy of the Mormon expulsion. Moreover, the news, as he heard it, came to him through the filter of the nonmember perspective. John began to see a way forward for himself and his family. Considering his options, no situation looked as promising to him as the farm lands rapidly being vacated in Caldwell County. In fact, John perceived an opportunity that promised to help him regain some lost dignity.

CHAPTER TWENTY-FIVE

Reclaiming Far West

A S IT BECAME clear that the Latter Day Saints would soon be gone from Missouri, John and his family began preparations to move back to Far West.[1] On January 15, 1839, David Whitmer, accompanied by Lyman Cowdery, William McLellin, Burr Riggs, and others, met with Anson Call at W. W. Phelps's home. According to Call's biographers, Lyman Cowdery "hoped to get Anson to retract his testimony" for the state warrant against Oliver Cowdery and David Whitmer that had resulted in their arrest "for stealing my [Anson's] goods somewhere between Wellsville on the Ohio River and that place and that he [Lyman] had come to settle with me. He said he knew the cause of my taking them because Joe had told me to and I was not particularly to blame.... This has caused my brother and Mr. Whitmer much difficulty."[2] Call refused to recant and heard nothing more from them.

Peter Whitmer Sr. had suffered many financial reverses during his years with the Mormons; but at this point, the family had been in Richmond long enough to know they wanted to settle there. Perhaps in an attempt to generate some funds, on January 31, 1839, Peter and Mary Whitmer sold sixty acres of their Jackson County property in the former Whitmer Settlement to Michael Collins. This sale marked a definitive end to their hopes of returning to Jackson County—if they still harbored any—but generated $580 of desperately needed cash.[3] All of the Whitmers were renting from others through this period.

---

1. John Whitmer moved back to Far West from Ray County and settled on section 14, township 56, range 29. *History of Caldwell and Livingston Counties*, 120–21.

2. Call, Call, and Call, *Journal of Anson Call*, 18–19.

3. Part of SE ¼ of section 16, township 49, range 33 beginning 80 rods W of SE corner of section, N 160 rods, E 40, S 80, E 40, S 80 to the point of beginning. Peter and Mary

In late January 1839, Emma Smith made her final visit to Joseph in Liberty Jail. As she was leaving, sheriff Samuel Hadley, who was in charge of the jail, pulled her aside and said, "All the authorities are waiting for is for you to get out of the state ... [and] the prisoners will be let out."[4] The church's committee of removal, a group of seven, was working hard to help the most impoverished members leave the state and had decided to seek refuge to the east in Illinois.[5] Hoping their departure would speed the church leaders' release, the Smith clan began preparing to leave about February 1, 1839. William Smith was the first. He took his wife, Caroline, and their two daughters to Quincy, Illinois, and sent his wagon back for his parents. Lucy Mack Smith said, "We loaded the wagon with our goods but just before we were redy to start he word came that Sidney Rigdons family were ready to start and they must have the wagon. Thus we were compeled [sic] to remain a season longer until William sent again the waggon [sic]." Around February 6, 1839, they packed the wagon again, but "another messenger came saying that Emma my sons wife was ready and she must have the waggon [sic]."[6] So they again unloaded their goods, and Emma packed her possessions and the four children.[7] Before leaving Far West, Emma also retrieved Joseph Smith's manuscripts of the Bible revision from Ann Scott, to whom Joseph's scribe, James Mulholland, had entrusted them for safe keeping while the church headquarters city was occupied by state militia. Meanwhile, church member Joel Edmonds was at Theodore Turley's blacksmith shop in Far West "getting my horses shod to take sister Emma

Whitmer, indenture to Michael Collins, 31 January 1839, 250.

4. Newell and Avery, *Mormon Enigma*, 78.

5. Far West committee minutes, January–April 1839. The January 29, 1839, committee meeting, chaired by John Smith, approved the following motion from Brigham Young, "That we this day enter into a covenant to stand by and assist each other to the utmost of our abilities in removing from the state and that we will never desert the poor.... After an expression of sentiments by several who addressed the meeting on the propriety of taking effective measures to remove the poor from the state it was resolved that a committee of seven be appointed to superintend the business of our removal and to provide for those who have not the means of moving till the work shall be completed. The following were then appointed. Wm. Huntington, Charles Bird Alanson Ripley, Theodore Turley, Daniel Shearer Shadrack Roundy Jonathan H. Hale" (2–3).

6. Anderson, *Lucy's Book*, 680.

7. Ibid.

and her children out of the State."[8] It was bitterly cold on the morning of February 7, 1839, when "Emma and her children left Far West with a group headed by Stephen Markham."[9] Lucy and Joseph Smith Sr.'s departure was delayed until later that month:

> We after a long time succeeded in getting one waggon [*sic*] in which to convey beds and clothing for My own family and 2 of our sons in law and their families and this was our dependence for a place to ride and to convey all our baggage. Don Carlos my youngest son was in company with us he rode with his wife and children in a one horse buggy and the greatest part of their baggage was in our wagon. In consequence of our crowded situation we left a large stock of provision and most of our furniture ~~los~~ in boxes and barrels in the house.[10]

Even as the Smith family was leaving Far West, John and Sarah moved back into the town from Richmond, about a half-day's travel away. John proudly noted in his account book, "Feb. 10 1839 Arrived with my family from Richmond." John's mother-in-law, "M[artha]. F. Jackson came to live with us."[11] The weather was extremely cold that week, and normally, no one would attempt such a move during the inclement season. However, John knew that his former land and buildings would be vacant and wanted no disputes with incoming squatters. Thirteen days later, John took in his first boarder, a Dr. Lyons.[12] Sarah's brother, Andrew, also joined the household within the first few weeks since, on March 11, 1839, John bought a pair of pants for "A. Jackson … at Lyons['s store]," paying two dollars.[13] Whether Martha and Andrew had been with John and Sarah in Richmond is unclear.

In March and April, John took on other boarders—William Slade, Dr. Zebulon Metcalf, and M. Landon—and provided stabling for Land-

---

8.   Edmonds, quoted in "Conferences, Pacific Slope Mission," 351.

9.   Newell and Avery, *Mormon Enigma*, 79.

10.   Anderson, *Lucy's Book*, 680–81.

11.   Whitmer, account book, 10 February 1839, p. 38.

12.   Ibid., 24 February 1839, p. 36.

13.   Ibid., 11 March 1839, p. 36.

Image of Kirtland, Ohio, ca. 1880s, showing a portion of Oliver Cowdery's law office in the foreground. Courtesy of Community of Christ Archives.

on's horse. With these increased responsibilities, he hired Mark Brindle and Sally McPhearson as help.[14]

After a short stay in Richmond, Oliver and Elizabeth Ann Cowdery and their daughter, Maria Louise, moved back to Ohio where they settled first in Kirtland and then in Tiffin. In both towns, Oliver practiced law. Oliver and Elizabeth Ann eventually had six children, of whom only one lived to adulthood: Maria Louise was born August 21, 1835, at Kirtland, Ohio, and died January 11, 1892, at Southwest City, Missouri. (The other children were Elizabeth Ann, born November 14, 1836, at Kirtland, Ohio, died May 9, 1837, at Kirtland; Josephine Rebecca, born March 21, 1838, at Far West, Missouri, died October 21, 1844, at Tiffin, Ohio; Oliver Peter Jr., born August 8, 1840, at Tiffin, Ohio, died August 13, 1840, at Tiffin; Adeline Fuller, born September 29, 1844, at Tiffin, Ohio, died October 13, 1844, at Tiffin; and Julia Olive, born May 29, 1846, at Tiffin, Ohio, died July 3, 1846, at Tiffin).[15]

14. Ibid., 24 March, 1, 3, 23 April 1839, p. 37.

15. "Oliver Cowdery Family Group," *Vaughan/Gnarini Genealogy Project*, accessed May 6, 2012, http://www.ralphvaughan.com/vaughan/gp3012.htm. See also Gunn, *Oliver*

In March 1839, Frederick G. Williams was trying to conclude the legal steps necessary for settling Sidney Gilbert's estate. He published the required notice of the estate's settlement in the *Western Star,* Clay County's newspaper.[16] On May 21, 1839, he transferred title in Gilbert's share of one undivided fourth part of lots nos. 1–4, 105, 108, 109, and 51 in Independence, Missouri to Michael Arthur for $300.[17] This action freed John Whitmer from any further obligation in the matter. Elizabeth Gilbert continued to reside in Far West for several months.

In April 1839, a Mormon crew—Elias Smith, Hiram Clark, and some others—returned from Illinois, unearthed the press, and hauled it to Commerce, Illinois, soon to be named Nauvoo. Here, Don Carlos Smith and Ebenezer Robinson used it to publish a new church periodical, the *Times and Seasons.* Also in April 1839, five members of the twelve apostles returned to Far West in fulfillment of the revelation given the preceding July (LDS D&C 118). In the predawn darkness at the temple site, they officially laid a "cornerstone," inaugurated their mission to England, ordained Wilford Woodruff and George A. Smith as apostles to fill gaps in the quorum, and excommunicated Canadian convert Isaac Russell and others whom they perceived as dissenters.[18]

Cowdery, 219. Maria Louise Cowdery Johnson's headstone gives her birthdate as August 21, 1835. Dear, *Two Hundred-Thirty-eight Years of the Whitmer Family,* 48, corroborates these dates with a couple of minor exceptions.

16. "Now at this day came Frederick G. Williams, administrator of all and singular, the goods and chattels, rights and receipts, lands and tenements which were of Algernon S. Gilbert, deceased, and filed this petition, accounts lists and inventories, for the sale of the real estate belonging to said judgment—and here of it is ordered by the court here, that all persons interested in the said estate be notified thereof, and that unless the contrary be shewn on the first day of next May term of said Court as ordered will be made for the sale of the whole or so much of such real estate described in said petition, as will pay the debts of said deceased, and it is further ordered that this cause stands continued until the first Monday of May next. A true copy text, Abraham Shafer, Clerk, March 15 [, 1839]." Gilbert, "Notice," *Western Star,* March 1839.

17. Gilbert, estate papers, 1838–39, 21 May 1839.

18. Kenney, *Wilford Woodruff's Journal,* 1:326–27. Woodruff listed thirty people who were excommunicated at Far West by the twelve: a Sister Cavanaugh, William Dawson Sr. and wife, Freeborn Gardner, Simeon Gardner, Luman Gibbs, a Brother Griggs and wife, John Goodson and wife, Jotham Maynard, Nelson Maynard, George Miller, George Nelson, Joseph Nelson, his wife, and mother, Isaac Russell, Mary Russell, Ann Scott, Isaac Scott, Jacob Scott Sr. and wife, Jacob Scott Jr., George Walters, Robert

Sally Phelps was in Illinois, but W. W. Phelps and some of their children were still in Far West. On May 4, 1839, Phelps bought twenty-six-and-a-half pounds of flour from John.[19] That same day he shared his highly negative perspective on the return of the twelve to Caldwell County in a letter to Sally:

> On the morning of the 26th of April, in secret darkness about three O'clock in the Morning Probably seven shepherds and eight principal men, from Quincy Ill and else where assembled on the big house [temple] cellar, and laid one huge stone in addition to those already there, to fulfill the revelation given the 26th of April one year ago.... They cut off from their church all the Canadians here.... [T]hey gave no notice nor do [due] trial to the offending men, women and children.... I think the people of Caldwell on the 4th of next July will remove those untimely laid stones.... At the same meeting at the big house cellar, there not being a quorum of the old "Twelve" present, they had recourse to "shift" and ordained Wilford Woodruff and Geo. Smith as Apostles which, with H. C. Kimball Orson Pratt, Brigham Young (old ones) and John E. Page and John Taylor (new ones) made seven. They prayed (in vain) sung Adam ondi ahman and closed.[20]

Then he added a mournful description of Far West: "There is such a wide difference in the aspect and prospect of Far West, that I hardly know how to describe it to you. The inhabitants are going the sound of the hammer, and the bustle of business has ceased. The grass is growing in the streets or where they were. The fences have disappeared, and nothing but empty houses, and the moaning of the Spring breeze, tell what was in Zion (So with it My love of it has [gone?])." Despite this dismal picture, at least some of their former co-believers were still in the town, for Phelps

---

Walton, a Sister Walton (possibly Robert's wife), Ann Wanless, and William Warnock and wife.

19. Whitmer, account book, 4 May 1839, p. 39.

20. W. W. Phelps to Sally Phelps, 4 May 1839. Kenney, *Wilford Woodruff's Journal*, 1:327, recorded that, in addition to the apostle, an additional eighteen Latter Day Saints were also present—apparently all of those who were still residing in the area: William Barton, Darwin Chase, Hiram Clark, John W. Clark, William C. Clark, Alpheus Cutler, Artemesia Granger, Sarah Granger, Richard Howard, Stephen Markham, Hezekiah Peck, Martha Peck, Mary Ann Peck, Shadrach Roundy, Daniel Shearer, Norman Shearer, Elias Smith, and Theodore Turley.

reported: "[John] Cleminson [clerk of the Caldwell County court] is now preparing to move as soon as he can Reed Peck, and his folks, and [Jotham?] Maynard and his family, mean to leave this week. The people have been staying and trading here this winter part, now the Mormons have gone, show visible signs of discontent I think myself they are quite lonesome There is a mysterious hanging back about resettling Far West Some say it is account of John's Mortgage [from Bishop Partridge for Far West property that John placed in the bishop's hands]; some think one and some another."[21]

Elizabeth Van Benthusen Gilbert, Sidney Gilbert's widow, was still living in town at that point, hoping to begin a business with Rachel Kingsley of "supplying the Far West market, with Fresh fish in time of need." John Whitmer, who had moved back in February, "is enlarging his buildings, has bought and removed Henry Woods house just before his south door, for a Kitchen He seems to be preparing to stick in Far West a while."[22]

In his closing, Phelps reveals that Sally's parting had not been mutual. The strain of events over recent years had been too much for Sally. At her first opportunity in early spring, Sally had taken off on her own. Phelps ended his letter, "My next to you will be directed to 'Sally Waterman'"[23]

Theodore Turley, who was winding up church business in Far West, encountered John that spring and questioned him about his testimony of the Book of Mormon. Turley reminded John that he had "published to the world that an angel did present those plates to Joseph Smith." Whitmer willingly affirmed that the plates "were shown to me by a supernatural power" but reminded Turley that he could not vouch for the translation because he could not read the engravings on the plates.[24]

21. W. W. Phelps to Sally Phelps, 4 May 1839. Reed Peck was a state witness during the preliminary hearing in Richmond in November 1838. He was excommunicated at a church conference in Quincy, Illinois, March 17, 1839. In September 1839, Peck recorded his observations about the church in Missouri in a document commonly known as "The Reed Peck Manuscript."

22. W. W. Phelps to Sally Phelps, 4 May 1839.

23. Ibid.

24. *History of the LDS Church*, 3:307–8.

Lyman O. Littlefield, then a church member working in a newspaper office in Lexington, Missouri, visited Far West in the spring of 1839, and found it largely abandoned:

At Far West the principal buildings stood intact, but many of the private dwellings were not occupied by their owners and builders. Those of the inhabitants still there were preparing to go upon their forced exit, as the gubernatorial mob edict had fixed the time when they must depart.

I contemplated, with sadness, the change that had taken place in such a brief period of time. Those residences where I had passed happy hours and months, with the friends of my youthful prime, were deserted and desolate. My feet, as I stepped towards the thresholds where once I met with friendly greetings, awoke no responsive echoes. The voices of my young associates pronounced no word of tender recognition. The hand of affection was not there to grasp mine, as in the past. Those smiling faces that once beamed with gladness at my coming, while the eye sparkled with brightness and bosoms heaved with emotions of fidelity—alas, where were they all? My God! Why were they not there? The cruel truth full well I knew and my spirit was crushed! They were gone to hunt an asylum from oppression! Was not that the new city our parents had built? Had they not acquired lawful titles to the soil? Was not that their country and rightful place of abode? Yes, but they were what the world call "Mormons," and such, in the estimation of a cruel, wicked populace, had no rights that should be regarded.

That town site—Far West—and as far as the eye could extend over the rolling prairie towards the four points of the compass—was not marked by a single habitation for the abode of man, when our people halted their wagons and pitched their tents there in 1836. But within the short period of their residence, the scene had been transformed, as if by the hand of magic, and small towns, settlements and farm houses with their accompanying improvements, heightened the broad and dappled beauty of the undulating landscape, exhibiting evidences of the industry and skill of the hunted and ever-toiling Mormon people.

A short time previous I had looked over this romantic region with pride, hope and inspiring joy, but now with emotions of sadness, despondence and grief. Wherever I turned, loneliness and desolation were unbroken by any feature calculated to awaken cheerfulness or mollify the tendency to despondence. My people were not there! They had left their homes empty and desolate—all save a few, and they were struggling to prepare for the dreary journey. The houses, nearly all, were in the midst of stillness—save the sweet melody of birds, which fell upon my ear like a requiem dirge. No axmen were in the enclosures or groves; no curling smoke arose from the chimneys, indicative of bright firesides and tempting repasts; the voices of bleating lambs and lowing herds sent forth no echoes upon the ambient air. No, not even the barking of the faithful watchdog broke the monotonous silence.

At that time, what was missed more than all else were the voices of the loved ones which had saluted me in the past. Their cheerful music was hushed and the melody of their Sabbath orisons no more sent up anthems of praise into the ears of the God of Sabbaoth. Alas, where were they all? The forms of those early associates, those trustworthy young men, and the rosy-cheeked bevies of happy girls—once so vivacious and merry-hearted—indeed, where were they? Once we mingled there, in life's halcyon prime; but now I walked alone and the happy past lived but in memory. The aged, also, with gray heads and bent forms, the mother with the suckling babe and the father with his group of plodding boys—all, all had left, and at that hour were on the weary march, exiled and cast out from the homes their hands had built, and from the streets they had surveyed and converted into thoroughfares for enterprise and traffic. In the midst of those scenes, endeared by so many tender memories, I felt as a stranger, and almost as an intruder; for why should I be there, and they, the owners, ejected and driven away? That hour, though peculiar, was full of interest as the past and future were contemplated. To me, that was an interesting spot.[25]

Within the next few weeks, probably in July 1839, W. W. Phelps left Far West to rejoin his family, leaving John Whitmer, his virtual partner in many church-related endeavors in an awkward situation. Even though Phelps had been numbered among the dissenters during the March–April 1838 excommunications, he had somehow managed to remain in Far West, while the Whitmers and Cowdery were forced out with death threats.

25. Littlefield, *Reminiscences of Latter-Day Saints,* 97–102.

Phelps had grudgingly participated in the defense of Far West and had testified against the church during the November 1838 Richmond hearing. While the faithful Saints were evacuating Far West during the winter of 1838–39, Phelps had remained to wind up business affairs, but they proved inextricably tangled, some of them dating back to 1833 in Independence. Finally, he simply abandoned them, leaving many obligations unsatisfied. Apparently, he had maintained some kind of communication with John in the months after his departure, for in March 1840, he wrote John a semi-wheedling letter that partially excused his failures but expressed intentions of resolving matters. He authorized John to sell some of his (Phelps's) remaining Far West assets to help resolve matters for which they were jointly responsible:

> As to the debts we contracted, I have ever done and meant to do my part. My house and lot, and some small parcels around town, after paying Mr. Boyce the post office deficit, I want sold to apply on those concerns: The printing office and lot I will deed to you as soon as I can get to some place where I can tarry long enough to do the business. The whole matter shall be arranged as speedily as possible. It would have been arranged on my part last summer with Frye but sickness prevented, and I barely escaped to a healthier climate by the threads of life, which held soul and body together for the time being.[26]

When he wrote this letter, Phelps was living in Bellbrook, Ohio, but the next month, he was in Dayton, Ohio. There, Orson Hyde and John E. Page, en route to their mission in Europe and Palestine, encountered him, struggling to provide for his family. Phelps eventually resolved his difficulties. On June 29, 1840, William wrote to Joseph Smith, seeking to regain his former standing. He confessed: "I have seen the folly of my way.... I will repent and live, and ask my old brethren to forgive me, and though they chasten me to death, yet I will die with them, for their God is my God."[27]

Joseph warmly invited Phelps back into the fold, and Phelps moved his family to Nauvoo and immediately set to work preparing the manuscript history of the church, a project made necessary by John Whitmer's refusal to turn over his own manuscript history to Smith's control in 1838.

26. W. W. Phelps to John Whitmer, 4 March 1840.
27. Bowen, "The Versatile W. W. Phelps," 84–110.

John stayed in Far West and, by persistent effort, Whitmer eventually succeeded in untangling his business, legal, financial, and property affairs. In the process, he reclaimed much of his lost land. Actually, John's timing was perfect, positioning him to consolidate land claims from departing Saints. He eventually acquired the greater part of the town site of Far West, including the temple site.

Hints of a sour note on the domestic front show up in John's account book, which contains numerous notations through 1839–41 for items of clothing for his mother-in-law. Presumably, Martha was preoccupied with fashion, a difficult obsession in such a frontier environment. In July 1839, the patient John got a short reprieve from Martha's spending while she made a short visit to her other daughter Eliza Zimmer, but two days later, Martha was again buying a skirt, gloves, and sundries at Sublet's store, items that she charged to John's account. Eliza and John H. Zimmer were also living in the area in 1839–41 and may have been residents during the Mormon War. Apparently John's farming efforts during the 1838 season were only marginally successful, for it was not until November 1839—a year later—that John had a surplus. In that month, he sold J. H. Zimmer bacon, butter, meal, and flour. On December 29, 1839, John paid the rather substantial amount of $14.08 to Dr. Zebulon Metcalf for Martha's doctor bill, for an ailment not specified.[28]

On March 12, 1840, John arranged to buy a Far West city lot owned by George Walters for fifty dollars cash.[29] Accumulating such a sum again attests to John and Sarah's thrift.

On March 20, 1840, John Whitmer wrote from Far West to his former friend bishop Edward Partridge at Nauvoo, in an attempt to collect on a mortgage he had held from the church for former land holdings since 1838. John still keenly recalled as an injustice how church leaders had forced him and William Phelps to relinquish control of Far West lots to Bishop Partridge. John now intended to enforce the mortgage he held from Par-

---

28. Whitmer, account book, Zimmer—18, 28 November, p. 45; See also 20 January and 5 June 1840, pp. 46, 48, for similar transactions; M. F. Jackson—29 December 1839, 30 December 1840, pp. 46, 50.

29. George Walters, indenture to John Whitmer, 12 March 1840. The property was "lot number 3 in block number twenty nine" with the date for making the quit claim specified as "in the month of July next."

tridge on behalf of the church for some $900. Partridge had evidently deferred paying, excusing the church on the basis that John had subscribed a like amount for the building of the Far West Temple. John found this argument unpersuasive and bluntly rejoined, "You know that that committee for building the house of worship was dissolved by a meeting of the heads of the Church, and the subscription withdrawn and refunded by said committee. Now therefore you know that I have as good a right to withdraw my subscription as any man and <am> as much justified by law."[30]

In previous correspondence, which apparently no longer exists, John had evidently offered Partridge a compromise, which Partridge had declined. Although John no doubt still had friendlier feelings toward Partridge than toward many of the other church leaders, he had no intention of leaving the injustice unresolved: "[I] will say this much to you, I have no personal enmity against you, but am sorry that we cannot arrange the matter between us, ourselves but as it is it, [*sic*] is a matter [ink faint—of fairness?] if we cannot do it ourselves and must have help and then one or the other will be disappointed."[31]

John sincerely wished to avoid suing his old friend. But as he attempted to consolidate his former land holdings, he urgently needed to quiet all legal encumbrances on the tracts. Unsatisfied with Partridge's response, John continued firmly:

> You say that you can have no Justice in this state from the tribunals that exist you need not fear and the subject of the Mortgage I hold against you on that amount for Justice will give me the balance due me on that investment, but for your conscience I was willing to make a compromise with you, and for your sake only. I have no fears of obtaining judgment against you in that case. And to that end I am determined. Suit will be ... instituted immediately. I regret that so many of your society will meet a loss in consiquence [*sic*] of your evil advisors. You ... <say> that it will be no great loss to you—to sustain—if you loose [*sic*] all you have here, but remember that something is better than nothing. But be your own judge on these matters.[32]

30. John Whitmer to Edward Partridge, 20 March 1840.

31. Ibid.

32. Ibid.

John was also acutely aware that Joseph Smith and church leaders were even then petitioning national leaders for redress for their losses during the expulsion and the return of their lost lands in Jackson County, although their possibility of success on that score was even more remote. Should they succeed, even partially, John's superior claims to Far West lands would be jeopardized. But he had been with the movement on the other side long enough to predict the likely outcome of their efforts: "You say your case is before Congress and you have hopes of being redressed for all your wrongs, this is a pleasing idea no doubt to you, and is calculated to stimulate your drooping spirit—but don[']t indulge to much in banking upon the fruits of <u>air castles</u>, for if Mr. [Fair lain?] should not explode agreeable to Smiths predictions it might turn out like the Country milk maids imaginary happiness."[33]

Perhaps never recovering from his exertions during the expulsion of the church from Missouri, and without any forewarning as far as John was concerned, Partridge died on May 27, 1840. The forced settlement of Edward's estate worked greatly to John's advantage. Although fully settling this legal matter took several years, John tenaciously pursued his claim. A church member named William Jones was appointed executor of the Partridge estate, which could not be settled without also resolving John's claim. Jones hired John's brother-in-law, John Zimmer, as one of the appraisers to evaluate the lots and lands involved in Far West.[34] In February 1841, Jones placed a notice in the *Western Star*, published in Liberty, Missouri, announcing his intent to sell Partridge's real estate.[35] Several other individuals also filed for judgments against the Partridge estate. As the complicated case dragged on into 1843, Jones made two small payments to John on the outstanding balance and interest that Partridge owed him.[36] Finally, on

33. Ibid. The "milk maid" alludes to a traditional story about a prideful milkmaid carrying milk to market who begins to fancy how she will parley the cash into a small fortune which she will spend on rich clothing. Her dazzling future ends when, through inattention, she trips and spills the milk.

34. Edward Partridge, estate, October 1840.

35. William Jones payment to Rennie & Duncan, February 19, 1841. The payment was forty dollars for announcements about the upcoming sale of lots in Far West in six weeks.

36. Receipts from John Whitmer, October 6, 1841 and March 4, 1843.

December 8, 1846, John received a lump-sum payment of $456.85, settling his claim. Jones conveyed Partridge's "right title and interest" in more than 200 Far West lots in forty-some blocks to John Whitmer—all of Partridge's lots in the eastern portion of Far West.[37]

John's efforts to redeem Far West landholdings were certainly not confined to his action against Partridge. Even as the suit commenced, on May 21, 1840, John acquired title to lot 8 in block no. 86 in Far West, from Paris T. Judy, for fifty dollars.[38] On July 9, 1840, John "Moved to our farm [Whitmer's land at Far West],"[39] where he either built a new hand-hewn log house or reconstructed one out of abandoned materials. This structure was just east of the temple site. With his hotel directly south of the temple site, this gave John two buildings in the center of town.[40]

Only four days after the Judy transaction, John bought another two acres from Peter Burnett, one of the attorneys who had represented the church during legal difficulties associated with the Mormon War.[41]

Throughout this period, the physical remains of the town of old Far West were rapidly dismantled and carted away to surrounding communities. A later newspaper article noted disapprovingly, "Many who had obtained lawful possession of the buildings in the old town, moved them away. And, a large portion of these deserted habitations were simply car-

---

37. William Jones, indenture to John Whitmer, 8 December 1846; John Whitmer, receipt to William Jones, 8 December 1846.

38. Paris T. Judy, indenture to John Whitmer, 21 May 1840.

39. Whitmer, note inserted in account book, 9 July 1840, p. 48.

40. Lorene Elizabeth Burdick Pollard, a fourth-generation descendant of John and Sarah Whitmer, indicated that, upon their return, John's family built a log house near his former hotel, directly east of the temple site in Nauvoo. Pollard, talk, October 6, 2006, Richmond, Missouri. When John and Sarah built their two-story frame house one-half-mile east of the temple lot in 1857, David Whitmer's son, Jacob D. Whitmer, occupied the log house.

41. Burnett, indenture to John Whitmer, 13 July 1840, transferred about two acres on the southwest corner of the "South East Quarter of Section No. Eleven, Township No. Fifty-Six Range No. Twenty nine commencing at the Northwest corner of the West half of North East Quarter of Section No. 14 Township 56, Range 29, running thence due North bounded on the East line of the Town plat of Far West twenty rods—North by Joseph Knights [*sic*] Jr. about seventeen rods—East by a line running South about twenty rods—to John Whitmer's land & South about Thirteen rods to the place of beginning."

ried off piecemeal by parties who had no shadow of claim to their possession, or were wantonly destroyed by others."[42] Vacant city lots soon reverted
to farmland. John made his living by farming, raising stock, transporting
people, and hauling freight. He also reopened his hotel near the temple
lot to accommodate travelers. "His own table was constantly set for ten,"
recalled great-great-granddaughter Lorene Pollard, "always ready to welcome any wandering soul in to sup with the family."[43] Although Far West
was a bit lonely at times, it was home for John, Sarah, and their two growing children.

Around this same time, a visit from another old friend, William
McLellin, further reminded John of former days. McLellin stayed with
John from June 21 through July 3, 1840. McLellin may have still been living
nearby in Tinney's Grove, Ray County, where he had moved after distanc-
ing himself from the Far West church. McLellin wanted to take a tour of
the Crooked River battle site, just inside Ray County. John charged him
two dollars for a "one day ride" to the site.[44] What an interesting conversation the old friends must have had! Their discussions would have naturally turned to church matters—old hurts—and future hopes. It appears
McLellin was already formulating a plan to redeem the reputations of the
Whitmer clan, including Oliver Cowdery, and he must have speculated
about the role that John might be persuaded to play.

42. "Far West: The Old Mormon Settlement in Missouri."

43. Pollard and Woods, *Whitmer Memoirs*, 28.

44. Whitmer, account book, 21 June 1840, p. 48.

CHAPTER TWENTY-SIX

Life after the Mormons

JOHN AND SARAH had returned to Far West in time to be enumerated in the 1840 census. A few other former church members also remained, scattered around the area. Canadian convert, Isaac Russell who had also stayed behind, was branded a dissenter and excommunicated by the church in April 1839. But Missourians who thought he was still too much of a Mormon, arrested him sometime after May 1839, and jailed him in Richmond for an extended period, well after other church prisoners had managed to leave the state. For several years after Isaac's release, the Russell family remained in Richmond where Isaac died in 1844.[1]

Although some church members remained in the Far West area, most residents were new settlers, like the Kerrs, Stoners, and Johnsons. With this influx, the locale prospered for a time.

Among new residents settling in Caldwell County following the expulsion of the Mormons was the family of Eli Penney, grandfather of noted merchant and chain store executive J. C. Penney (1875–1971). Eli (1799–1871) and Mary "Polly" Burris (1802–75) were married in 1821 in Mercer County, Kentucky, and moved their family to Caldwell County, Missouri, around 1841. They settled near Goose Creek, a few miles south of Far West, where they established their farm. In addition to farming, Eli was also a minister.

---

1. According to Jacob Scott to Mary Warnock, 24 March 1842: "John Dawson & family & Russell & family & Wm Dawson & family, & Sarah Havenaugh, & Eliza and Ann Manless are all living near Richmond—But Mr. Walton & family, are living about a mile from Mr. Walter's about 3 miles from Far West." A branch of Russell's family later gathered to Utah. His son, Samuel, recalled, "The old log jail was still standing on the public square in Richmond when we left Missouri, and I never looked upon it, even in my childish days, without thinking of father, the Prophet Joseph, and others of God's servants. To me it stood as a monument to integrity and faith, and a reproach to their persecutions." See also Samuel Russell (son of Isaac Russell) to Dear Lucy Ettie Friends and Kindred, 3 November 1882.

Eli and Mary joined the Log Creek church in 1844. This church, affiliated with the Primitive Baptist movement, was located about a mile north of present Highway 116 on County Road T. Eli served as pastor for this group in 1847. The first child to join Eli and Mary's family after their move to Missouri was James Cash Penney Sr., born December 29, 1841.[2]

John and Sarah's fourth child, Alexander Peter Jackson Whitmer, was born February 7, 1841, at Far West.[3]

In mid-1841, John's brother-in-law, John Zimmer, moved to Davis County, Iowa. From that point on, John Whitmer's account book no longer mentions John and Eliza Zimmer, their four sons, or Sarah and Eliza's mother, Martha Jackson.[4] Thomas and James Jackson, Sarah and Eliza's brothers were apparently still in Missouri, since they borrowed seventy-five dollars from John Whitmer on April 22, 1845.[5]

James Williams, a new resident of Caldwell County, provided an interesting description of the Whitmer family and Far West as it appeared

2. James Cash Penney (1841–95) grew to manhood in the neighborhood and married Mary Frances Paxton (1842–1913) in 1862. The couple resided in Caldwell County where they farmed. James Cash Sr. also served as a pastor of the Log Creek church in 1874. Their son James Cash ("J. C.") Penney Jr. was born in 1875. Three years after J. C.'s birth, the family relocated from their 390-acre farm in the Far West-Mirabile area to nearby Hamilton, Missouri. "Church and Family History Research Assistance for Caldwell County, Missouri, Churches: Log Creek," *The Primitive Baptist Library of Carthage, Illinois*, accessed January 12, 2012, http://www.carthage.lib.il.us/community/churches/primbap/FamHist-CaldwellMO.html; "J. C. Penney Papers: A Guide to the Collection," *Texas Archival Resources Online*, accessed January 12, 2012, http://www.lib.utexas.edu/taro/smu/00012/smu-00012.html. See also: *Penney and Allied Families Genealogical and Biographical*, 21.

3. Barchers, "The Descendants and History of the Peter Whitmer Family," 44. Alexander Peter Jackson Whitmer's birth date is given in the John Whitmer family Bible.

4. Sherry Case, posting on "John H. Zimmer," *GenForum*, Genealogy.com, 1998, accessed May 10, 2012, http://genforum.genealogy.com/cgi-bin/pageload.cgi?Jackson::zimmer::72.html. John H. Zimmer "lived in MO, where his four sons were born. In 1841, John Zimmer moved to Davis Co, Iowa." In 1848 he moved to the Centerville area in Appanoose County, Iowa. Zimmer later served in the Civil War as a member of the Graybeard Regiment (Company F, 37th Iowa Infantry). John Zimmer died in Mount Pleasant, Iowa, in 1875.

5. Thomas and James Jackson, promissory note to John Whitmer, 1845. There is no record of repayment.

in 1842, although he may have confused brothers John and David Whitmer
in this reminiscence, recorded in 1911:

> In trying to tell how Far West, the old Mormon town looked, the first
> time I saw it in 1842, I regret that I have no daguerreotype or photo-
> graph to assist me in describing its lonely desolation. Its glory had
> departed with most of its, at one time, 3000 inhabitants.
>
> I think the first time I was in the old town was at a Fourth of July
> celebration in 1842, the first I was ever at, but I can remember it as well
> as if it had been yesterday, and how the principal managers looked and
> acted. The marshal's name was Branch and he wore a black broadcloth
> coat, which made a great impression on me. I was told that cloth was
> made in France and mother had been telling me about the Marquis
> De Lafayette, the great, good Frenchman. I think that was one reason
> I was so impressed with that black coat. Miles Bragg was his assistant
> and Volney Bragg, the first lawyer I ever saw, was the speaker, who
> read the Declaration of Independence very impressively. I don't re-
> member his speech. Of course, it was along patriotic lines.
>
> There was a long ditch and some slick looking niggers roast-
> ing the beef, which was very fine, I remember. At the head of the
> long table, which was a scaffold under a brush arbor, was seated a very
> old man, whose name was Benjamin Middaugh. I think this old man
> served in the War of 1812 and was the father or brother of old Timothy
> Middaugh, who lived many years about two miles east of Cameron
> and I think was the grandfather of the family of Middaugh brothers
> near Mirabile. The long table was located a short distance north and,
> I think, a little east of the old Temple excavation, which at that time,
> was nearly intact, and the great cornerstone lying in the bottom. I have
> been told by those who were on the ground that it took 14 yoke of oxen
> to haul it. I've not seen it for about 40 years, but am told that most of
> that big rock has been carried away for souvenirs by the faithful Saints.
> When I first saw Far West, many of the smaller frame houses had
> been moved away for farm buildings. A good many of the larger build-
> ings had been torn down and rebuilt after removal, hence, the houses
> left standing were dilapidated, old looking, unpainted structures, many
> of them two stories high.
>
> They were nearly all frames with poles flattened on two sides for
> studding, and split native timber for lathing and weather boarding[.]
> The boarding was usually 6 feet long, sap taken off, gauged and shaved,

which made a good, substantial building. The boarding usually was of big bottom burr oak, the best timber on Shoal and Log Creek. The town was situated on a divide between those two creeks, and had the Hannibal & St. Joseph Railway run up Shoal Creek (as was talked of), Far West today would be the biggest town between St. Joseph and Chillicothe instead of Cameron.

Not only that, there is but little doubt that in place of a desolate waste, the Temple lot would have had a magnificent temple, and Far West would be the "Mecca" of the pilgrim Saints, as Independence is today. The best church building in Independence today is the fine, brown stone [Community of Christ Stone Church on what is today Lexington Ave.] on the high ridge along the Kansas City Electric line. The only Mormon I ever heard preach was in that building a few years since and I am free to admit, I think was about as good a sermon as I ever listened to, with a few exceptions. If people will live up to the exhortations of that good man, I think it will matter little whether they think Smith, Rigdon, Pratt, Whitmer, Cowdry [*sic*], or anybody else were inspired, or the Book of Mormon a Revelation.

I knew David Whitmer quite well when I'd meet him in Cameron. He was an up-to-date farmer, and purchased the first two horse corn planter ever unloaded off the cars at Cameron. I think I, and some other by-standers, helped him put it in his wagon. I remember the wheels of that planter were wooden drums. Mr. Whitmer moved to Richmond some thirty years ago, and died there. I think the Whitmer family own the old Temple lot, which is now on the old Whitmer farm, as I am told.

I have never seen Oliver Cowdery, but have seen one of his daughters, who was pointed out to me at church many years ago. She was visiting in the vicinity of Far West. It was at old Plumb Creek school house I saw her. She was strikingly handsome. I do not know whether she is yet living. It is not the province of this article to discuss whether Latter Day Saints as a church organization is good or otherwise, but I'll say this, I've been familiar with and a neighbor to them for nearly seventy years, and from what I've seen of those in Missouri, I think they've hardly had a fair treatment, inasmuch as our laws allow every one to worship as he pleases, so long as he is law abiding.[6]

6. Williams, *Seventy-Five Years on the Border*, 142–44. I am indebted to Michael Riggs for this source.

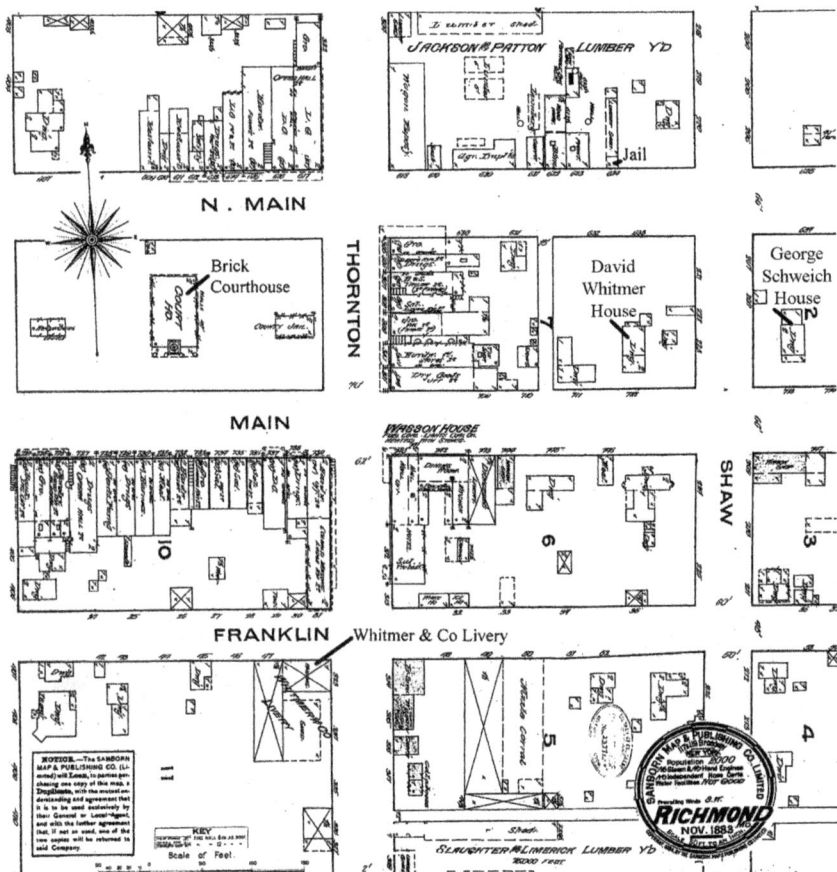

This 1883 insurance map from Sanborn Map and Publishing Company details Whitmer family and church history locations. Courtesy of the Library of Congress.

The county seat remained at Far West until 1843 when the court and courthouse records were moved to neighboring Kingston. The post office also moved to Kingston about the same time; David Hughes was the postmaster.[7] According to a county history, "The first house in Kingston after the town was laid off was removed from Far West by Walter A. Doak."[8]

7.   "Far West: The Old Mormon Settlement in Missouri."

8.   *History of Caldwell and Livingston Counties*, 122.

Members of the David Whitmer family shown at their house in Richmond, Missouri, ca. 1880s. David Whitmer and Josephine Schweich are shown standing in the yard and Julia Ann (Jolly) Whitmer is visible in the second story window. Courtesy of Community of Christ Archives.

Meanwhile, even as John was making a new life in Far West, David Whitmer began to prosper in Richmond, Missouri. David's successful hauling business along with increasing acceptance by the citizens of Richmond enabled him to open a livery stable, apparently on East Main Street. The location was convenient for transporting customers between the courthouse, local hotels, and the river.[9] Whitmer soon diversified his business, operating hacks and carriages for local travelers, selling grain and

9.   *North-West Conservator*, quoted in Richardson, "David Whitmer," 83. See also Burch, indenture to David Whitmer, lot 84, 20 February 1849: "that portion of said lot upon which old man Whitmer [Peter Whitmer Sr.] now lives and adjoining the stable lot of David Whitmer."

feed at the livery stable, and hauling freight and building materials. Local resident James Nading told an interviewer that the Whitmers "were clean livers and no drinkers. They were people who knew how to tend their own business and let other people do likewise."[10]

As early as April 1840, David took on a business partner, Alonzo Winchester, who had formerly helped with Whitmer family business activities in Far West. He was a nephew of Stephen Winchester who also relocated to Richmond during the Mormon exodus. Receipts for the business accounts of Whitmer and Winchester for this period reveal varied activities. They gathered and delivered corn, and hauled loads of wood, hay, planks, and weatherboarding. They let horses by the

David Whitmer established a solid reputation in Richmond, Missouri, while making a valuable contribution to the development of the community. Courtesy of Community of Christ Archives.

day and transported local residents about town. For example, they furnished one James Smith a ride to the races "on the [Richmond] bottoms." Another time, they helped a local resident move household belongings. The partners gained a reputation for providing good service and seemed well integrated in the community. One Sunday in 1841, as a result of hauling some freight, apparently meeting an emergency, David was found guilty of breaking the Sabbath and fined five dollars.[11]

By this time, David's finances allowed him and Julia Ann to build a home. In January 1842, David took possession of lot 80 in Richmond's

10. James Nading, interview by Ebbie Richardson, ca. 1952, in Richardson, "David Whitmer," 21.

11. D[avid A.] Queesenbe[r]ry, note to David Whitmer and Alonzo Winchester for hauling, 3 April 1840.

original plat in exchange for $300 worth of promissory notes to Sinclair K. Miller. He bound himself to make two payments of one hundred dollars in cash payments by January 1843 with another hundred dollars worth of hauling. Construction began on their substantial new house at 216 East Main Street in Richmond, described as "a pleasant two-story white frame residence near the center of town."[12] Though a house of simple lines, it boasted seven rooms and a summer kitchen. A regional periodical suggests that, in addition to his livery business, he and Julia Ann also accepted boarders: "In this house, Whitmer received all such as came to him for food and rest. In Richmond he conducted a post station, and travelers passing over the old State road, stopped to enjoy the hospitality of his home."[13] In 1844, having completed his purchase agreement, David received a clear title from Miller.

During 1843–45, David also began acquiring additional land in northeast Richmond, reinforcing the probability that his livery stable was located in the vicinity. In 1843, Whitmer purchased from David Ewing a piece of land located just outside the then-platted portion of Richmond, directly east of the Peter Whitmer Sr. home (lot 84).[14] In 1845, he paid a hundred dollars for lots 55 and 56 from Joseph and Maria Shoop.[15] As David's business partner, Alonzo Winchester, also acquired lot 54 in this vicinity, the additional land was probably associated with their livery business. However, Winchester died unexpectedly in Richmond around 1845.

12. David Whitmer, "David Whitmer: The Only Living Witness to the Authenticity of the Book of Mormon," 156.

13. "Mormon Landmark Passing, Home of David Whitmer at Richmond Being Torn Down," *Kansas City Post*, January 10, 1920.

14. David Whitmer, indenture from David Ewing, 26 May 1843, p. 79. David's acquisition is identified as lot 42 on the Richmond plat in *An Illustrated Historical Atlas of Ray County, Missouri*, 21. The Peter Whitmer Sr. family was living in Richmond in a house on lot 84, which they rented from Celenary Burch, widow of Thomas C. Burch. Thomas Burch was born in Tennessee, ca. 1805. His family moved to Howard County, Missouri, when he was a child. He studied law at Jefferson City, began his practice at Richmond in 1831, and married Celenary Jacobs in 1834. Burch was appointed judge of the Eleventh Judicial Circuit, 1838. He was also the state's attorney in 1838 during the arraignment of Mormon prisoners in the Richmond Court House. Thomas died that same year at Keytesville, Chariton County, Missouri. Bay, *Reminiscences of the Bench and Bar of Missouri*, 487–88.

15. Joseph and Maria Shoop, indenture to David Whitmer, 1 January 1845, p. 241.

David's business records indicate that in 1846, he took on "Free Jim," a free African American, as a livery partner.[16] His business records show that David hired out servants through his livery-related businesses to residents who were seeking day laborers. The status of these individuals is not always clear, but David owned at least two slaves. One was Carter Thornton, to whom David loaned money in April 1844 and whom he freed on September 4, 1849, more than ten years before the Emancipation Proclamation.[17]

Although details about the relationship between David and John are sparse, they were evidently close, despite the distance in miles that separated Far West from Richmond. John took an active interest in family affairs and, according to David, "came to Richmond very often."[18] Sarah and the children frequently accompanied him for gatherings of the extended family. In addition to Father and Mother Whitmer, Jacob, Elizabeth, and their seven children also lived in the Richmond area. Family members made welcome return visits to Far West, especially Hiram Page's son Philander, who turned thirteen in 1844.[19]

In early 1844, John, still in Far West, wrote to W. W. Phelps in Nauvoo, Illinois. Although his letter has not survived, he evidently asked about Phelps's prospects among the Saints and mentioned church records, apparently an allusion to John's manuscript history. Willard Richards answered this letter on February 23, 1844. Formerly Joseph Smith's private secretary and an apostle since 1840, Richards had risen through Mormon ranks to the office of "Recorder and Historian for the <whole> church of Jesus Christ of Latter Day Saints." Writing as historian, Richards reopened an old wound: "As you mention something about the church records it becomes necessary to reply. We have already compiled about 800 pages of church history ... closely written one page. probably, contains about 4 times

16. David Whitmer, livery business record, 13 June 1846–5 February 1849.

17. Carter Thornton and Fanny Thornton to David Whitmer, 12 April 1844; Carter Thornton, deed of manumission, 4 September 1849, pp. 166–67.

18. David Whitmer, *An Address to Believers in the Book of Mormon*, 1.

19. Philander Page was the eldest living son of Hiram and Catharine Page. He was named after an uncle, Philander Higley, brother of Peter Whitmer Jr.'s wife, Vashti Higley. "Philander" was formerly a literary term for a lover, from the Greek word *philandros*. Philander Page was later an elder in David Whitmer's church. In 1888, his home was located two miles south of Richmond.

the amount of matter of 1 [the one] which you ~~kept~~, wrote … which covers all the ground of which you took notes, therefore any thing which you have in the shape of church history would be of little or no consequence to the church at Large."[20] There is no record of John's reply, but it seems doubtful that he would have responded to this brusque dismissal.

On a happier note, Sarah and John welcomed their fifth child, Jacob David Jefferson Whitmer, on May 26, 1843, in Far West. John was forty-two, Sarah was thirty-five, John Oliver was eight and a half, daughter Sarah was six, and Alexander Peter was two.[21] The next year Joseph and Hyrum Smith were assassinated in Illinois; but John's thoughts at the time and how he learned the news is not recorded. Like John, the entire extended Whitmer family remained aloof from institutional Mormonism.

Although John apparently did little writing, late entries in his manuscript indicate he continued to maintain his history of the church long after his excommunication. He remained well apprised of subsequent church activity through friends and contacts still in the church and read newspaper reports on the continually newsworthy Mormon doings in Illinois. He probably wrote the final three chapters of his history, which cover the Whitmers' excommunication, the Missouri War, and Nauvoo, on his farm at Far West, surrounded by the reminders of an interrupted dream. John must have awaited with interest the outcome of the succession crisis as various candidates contested each other's claims. Members of the twelve ultimately succeeded in asserting their leadership over those who remained in Nauvoo; but John could not have failed to notice that a peaceful resolution had not yet been achieved.

20. Willard Richards to John Whitmer, 23 February 1844.

21. Pollard and Woods, *Whitmer Memoirs*, 25; Barchers, "The Descendants and History of the Peter Whitmer Family," 44. Jacob D. Whitmer's birthday is given in the John Whitmer family Bible.

CHAPTER TWENTY-SEVEN

Succession Questions

AROUND 1846, THE worsening clash of cultures in western Illinois forced members of the early Mormon church out of Nauvoo. As followers of the Quorum of the Twelve Apostles crossed the Mississippi River into Iowa by wagon trains, isolated individuals and families searched for other solutions. Among the roiling claims and counterclaims was that of James J. Strang. He positioned himself as Joseph Smith's successor and enjoyed considerable success during this period.

Launching his campaign in August 1844, Strang attracted a number of disaffected Book of Mormon witnesses and their families into his movement. In January 1846, James Strang circulated an epistle which proclaimed himself to be Joseph Smith's successor. As authority for the calling, Strang claimed both a letter from Joseph Smith written before his assassination, and a visit from an angelic messenger.[1] According to Strang:

> Immediately I received a letter from Hiram Page, one of the witnesses of the Book of Mormon, and a neighbor and friend to the Whitmers', informing me that he had received that [my] tract and read it with joy and gladness, and went on to tell at length of reading it to the two Whitmers' [*sic*; David and Jacob] who lived near him, and that they rejoiced with exceeding joy *that* GOD HAD RAISED UP ONE *to* STAND *in* PLACE *of* JOSEPH, and was so much overjoyed that they could not rest till they had gone and communicated the glad news to

---

1. Strang, "An Epistle," 1–4. Historian D. Michael Quinn writes, "James J. Strang had been baptized into the Church on 25 February 1844, and had left Nauvoo shortly thereafter to explore a possible location for the Mormons in Wisconsin. He claimed that while there he received a revelation in a letter from Joseph Smith dated 18 June 1844, which appointed him Joseph's successor." "In addition to the letter, Strang also claimed he had been ordained successor by an angel." Quinn, "The Mormon Succession Crisis of 1844," 193, 194.

their brother [John] who lived at some distance. He [Hiram Page] goes on to say that all the witnesses of the Book of Mormon living in that region received the news with gladness, and finally that they held a council in which David and John Whitmer and this Hiram Page were the principal actors; and being at a loss what they ought to do about coming to Voree, sent up to me as a Prophet of God to tell them what to do.

If Strang's account is accurate, John and others of the extended Whitmer clan briefly considered Strang as Smith's legitimate successor. Strang reinforced this point by suggesting in a published epistle that the Whitmers were willing to turn over the valuable early church records in their possession, a move that would naturally bolster Strang's cause. Strang continued:

This letter I answered shortly after receiving it, and last April (1847) I received another letter from the same Hiram Page, acknowledging the receipt of mine and of many papers from me, and giving me the acts of another council of himself and the Whitmers', in which, among other things, they invite me to come to their residence in Missouri and receive from them, David and John Whitmer, church records, and manuscript revelations, which they had kept in their possession from the time that they were active members of the church. These documents they speak of as of great importance to the church, and offer them to me as the true shepherd who has a right to them, and were anxious that I should come and receive them in person because they were [of] too much importance to be trusted in the mails. It is very true that these letters were not written by David Whitmer, but they were written by Hiram Page as the common epistle of himself and the Whitmers.[2]

Chapter 21 of John Whitmer's manuscript history, written about this time, provides some circumstantial support for Strang's description of their intentions. Sometime after Joseph Smith's assassination on June 27, 1844, John wrote:

God, knowing all things prepared a man whom he visited by an angel of God and showed him where there were some ancient Record hid, and also put in his heart to desire of Smith to Grant him power to

establish a stake to Zion in Wisconsin Territory, whose name is James
J. Strang. Now at first Smith was unfavorably disposed to grant him
this request but being troubled in spirit and knowing from the things
that were staring him in the face that his days must soon be closed
therefore he enquired of the Lord and behold the Lord said Appoint
James J. Strang a Prophet, Seer <&> Revelator unto my church for
thou shalt shurly do a mistry [sic] thy cup is bitter &c[.] Shortly after
the appointment of Strang the mob gathered and took by Stratagem
Joseph and Hyrum Smith and conveyed them to Carthage.[3]

Although John does not say that his extended family either accepted
Strang's claims or made declarations of support, the fact that he recorded
Strang's own version of his claim to succession demonstrates access to
Strang's epistle. It also establishes that, at least through 1846, John con-
tinued to see himself as a historian of the larger movement. However, he
subsequently crossed out this entry, instead inserting an argument favoring
David Whitmer as Joseph Smith's rightful successor (discussed below).

Strang endeavored to surround himself with as many movement notables as possible to bolster his claim as successor, attracting former leaders
and members with a range of inducements, then using their support to extend his influence still further. Naturally, the family would have also been a
great prize, but the pattern revealed by his interactions with Smith family
members suggest that James's parallel account of the Whitmers' support
is not fully persuasive. For example, Strang first wrote Emma Smith on
February 11, 1846: "Now Sister ... if you intend to remain in Nauvoo, you
cannot well imagine how much I should rejoice in your full and hearty cooperation in my efforts for the regulation and salvation of the city." Emma
offered no such cooperation. Strang also offered William Smith, who had
been dropped as apostle and church patriarch, followed by excommunication, "a coveted position as patriarch" in Strang's organization "if William
brought with him his mother, with the mummies and papyrus, together
with the bodies of Joseph and Hyrum."[4] William was energetically seeking
an alterative movement to that headed by the twelve and eagerly followed
up. Strang's periodical published a letter from William Smith that concludes: "This is to certify that the Smith families do believe in the appoint-

3. Whitmer, Book of John Whitmer, chap. 21, pp. 93–94. Strikethrough in original.

4. Newell and Avery, *Mormon Enigma*, 232.

ment of J. J. Strang."⁵ It was signed "William Smith, Patriarch, Lucy Smith, Mother in Israel, Arthur R. Milliken, Nancy [*sic*] Milliken, W. J. Salisbury, Catherine Salisbury, Sophronia McLerie." In addition to the name variations, unusual even for the nineteenth century ("Nancy" should have been "Lucy," the youngest of Mother Smith's daughters), Katherine Salisbury published a letter in the *Herald* in 1899 denying that she had ever signed such a document and also expressing doubt that her sisters and mother had signed such a letter. She further asserted that her husband, Jenkins Salisbury, also "looked forward to Joseph Smith [III] taking his father's place."⁶ Strang named William as church patriarch, but within months William had been excommunicated for adultery.

Even assuming that Strang accurately expressed the Whitmer clan's interest in his claims, that interest quickly died. John and his extended family remained aloof from all claimants. Unfortunately, two pages later (dealing with David as Joseph's successor), John's manuscript history ends in mid-sentence at the bottom of page 96. The next four numbered pages are missing, and are followed by additional blank numbered pages.

Almost at the same time, John and Sarah experienced the heart-wrenching loss of their son John Oliver, who was not quite eleven. On October 25, 1846, he died of pneumonia.⁷ Rather than interring their child at the long-unused Far West burial ground, the grief-stricken parents purchased a family plot in the new cemetery at Kingston, now the county seat.

The departure of a body of Mormons from Nauvoo, Illinois, with Brigham Young left many Saints unresolved about the important question of presidential succession, including some in northern Missouri. An unsigned letter from "a near friend of David Whitmer," in Caldwell County, Missouri, dated December 24, 1847, appears in Strang's *Gospel Herald*: "Mr. Strang ... I want you to still continue sending me the Gospel Herald, until I do know beyond a doubt whom we are to receive as Prophet, Seer and Revelator.... I am satisfied myself that it belongs either to yourself or David Whitmer, and I do not know which.... I am a looker on, and have been for

5. William B. Smith to James J. Strang, 1 March 1846.
6. Salisbury, "Testimony of Katharine Salisbury," 261.
7. Barchers, "The Descendants and History of the Peter Whitmer Family," 42.

years, and calculate to be until I am convinced which is wrong."[8] Doubtless many others who had rejected Brigham Young shared the uncertainty of this letter writer.

It is significant that this individual considered David Whitmer to be a probable successor. When Joseph Smith ordained David as president of the Missouri church in 1834, he identified David as "a leader, or a prophet to this Church."[9] During an extended period of religious uncertainty beginning in 1847, first William McLellin attempted to persuade David Whitmer to present himself as such a successor. Such persuasions, of course, may have also come from the extended Whitmer family.

In September 1847, McLellin traveled from Kirtland to Far West[10] for a meeting that reflected upon days of former glory as well as considered possibilities for the future. At that point, Oliver and Elizabeth Ann Cowdery were in Ohio, leaving David, though not the eldest son, indubitably the head of the extended Whitmer family. The clan in Missouri then consisted of: father, Peter Whitmer Sr. (age seventy-three); mother, Mary Whitmer (age sixty-nine); Jacob Whitmer (age forty-seven), Jacob's wife Elizabeth (age forty-four) and their six children; John Whitmer (age forty-five), John's wife Sarah (age thirty-seven) and three living children; David Whitmer (age forty-two), wife Julia Ann (age thirty-two) and their two children; and brother-in-law, Hiram Page (age forty-six), Hiram's wife Catherine Whitmer (age forty), and their eight children.[11]

McLellin later reflected on this visit in his periodical, *Ensign of Liberty of the Church of Jesus Christ of Latter Day Saints*, which was published in Kirtland. The article was written with the editorial "we":

> We reached there [Richmond, Missouri] on Saturday, the 4th of Sept. [1847], and put up with our old friend D. Whitmer. One o'clock at night still found us communing in close conversation. On Monday, the 6th, David and Jacob Whitmer and Hiram Page, accompanied

8. "Mr. Strang," *Gospel Herald*, 2:206.

9. The Far West Record reports minutes of a meeting in which Joseph Smith Jr. "gave a history of the ordination of David Whitmer, which took place in July 1834, to be a leader, or a prophet to this Church, which (ordination) was on conditions that he (J. Smith jr) did not live to God himself." Cannon and Cook, *Far West Record*, 151.

10. Hiram Page to William McLellin, 4 March 1848.

11. Curtis, "Whitmer Family," 7–11.

me to Far West to visit with their brother, and our old friend John Whitmer. We remained with him two days and nights, and never did men since this world began have a more pleasant time. Union of feeling, and harmony of action, governed our every movement. Brethren and friends, let me say to you, "All is right, all is well," with those witnesses.[12]

John and Sarah Whitmer hosted this 1847 gathering. Nearly ten years had passed since they had been forced from Far West by former associates. John and Sarah's home was small, but three other buildings were available for their use: the Whitmer hotel, the old Far West school, or the former courthouse on the public square.

Gathered at Far West, the five men engaged in a series of religiously significant rituals. McLellin biographer Larry Porter wrote, "McLellin reported to them a revelation received in Kirtland on February 10, 1847, relative to the rebaptism and the reordination of all adherents to the [reorganized] Church of Christ. The revelation was read, approved, and acted upon."[13] On September 6, the day of their arrival, David, John, Jacob, and Hiram Page baptized one another, probably in nearby Shoal Creek. McLellin had probably already been rebaptized at Kirtland, but was now "ordained a President to build up the church of Christ in Kirtland."[14] McLellin assisted the others in ordaining David as "Prophet, Seer, and Revelator, and Translator." The term "seer" may be indicative of David and his brothers having access to seer stones from earlier days. A Whitmer associate, John Logan Traughber, later reported that David had obtained his stone in Kirtland.[15] RLDS apostle T. W. Smith reported secondhand information: "I was since informed that David Whitmer had seen divers wonderful things through a 'seer stone.'"[16]

McLellin did not linger. "On Saturday, the 11th, I bid farewell to those faithful witnesses of that sacred record, called the book of Mormon."[17]

12. McLellin, "Our Apology—and Our Tours," 34–35.

13. Porter, "Odyssey of William Earl McLellin," 343.

14. Hiram Page to Leonard Rich, 24 September 1847.

15. Traughber, "David Whitmer, 'The Last Witness' of the Book of Mormon."

16. Smith, "Urim and Thummim," 67.

17. McLellin, "Our Apology—and Our Tours," 34–35.

Even before McLellin left, David wrote to Oliver Cowdery, stating: "It is the will of God that you should be one of my councilors in the presidency of the Church ... to stand in relation to me as you stood to Joseph &c. &c. Now you behold that THE TIME HAS COME, to clear away old rubbish, and build again those principles which constitute the church of Christ."[18] Oliver's response is not known, but almost as soon as McLellin departed, David had second thoughts.

Of the original eight witnesses to the Book of Mormon, three were dead. All five of the survivors, members of the extended Whitmer family, were briefly associated with the newly reaffirmed Church of Christ. In January 1848, McLellin claimed that this reorganized Church of Christ numbered forty-two at Kirtland.[19] However, McLellin's successive contacts and claims were met largely with silence. David declined direct communication, leaving his brother-in-law Hiram Page to respond to McLellin's letters. No correspondence or other papers are extant from John during this period, and Hiram Page seems to have served as the family spokesperson. John's location in Far West may have also discouraged more active involvement. Extant letters from Page to McLellin written during the winter of 1847–48 suggest increasing demands from McLellin and intensifying resistance from the Whitmers. On February 12, 1848, in a letter to the Whitmers which has not survived, William McLellin apparently asked David to appoint a bishop to serve the reaffirmed Church of Christ. In his reply, February [March] 2, 1848, Page reports: "We held a council on the 13 it was Solm [sic] and the powers of darkness were dispersed and the Subject of your letter was fairly investigated." Page chastised McLellin for trying to set the church in order contrary to David Whitmer's understanding of divinely given principles: "As I am Situated I can not help you pull, but I can keep an eye out and see if you are likely to run into a mudhole and tell you how to Shun it, or if you draw to[o] near the mount which is insurmountable I will caution you."[20]

18. David Whitmer to Oliver Cowdery, 8 September 1847.

19. McLellin, "Things in Kirtland," 53.

20. Hiram Page to William E. McLellin, 2 February [March?] 1848, p. 1. The text mentions receiving a letter from McLellin on February 12, 1848.

McLellin had asked David to appoint an agent to oversee the Kirtland Temple. On David's behalf, Hiram Page further informed McLellin that it would be inappropriate for David Whitmer to appoint such an agent; rather, the church as a whole should select its own officers. Page wrote:

> We have learned for certainty that those who are called to labor in the word are not to labor in church property, he who is at the head of the spiritual affairs in the church has no right to apoint agents; or any bishops or any one to act in the temporal afairs of the church at the presant but the church is to apoint her own officers if she neads any and let not the ministry be burthened therewith and if bro. David should apoint an agent to act in temporal maters in kirtland it would be medling with other mens buisaness [prerogatives?] [and] would prove his ruin.[21]

Additionally, Page cautioned against repeating what the Whitmers perceived to be one of the principal errors of Joseph Smith's church organization—the establishment of the high priesthood. "We find that many false principles were introduced into the church, which brought distraction, one of its great evils was the introduction of the high priesthood into the church of Christ."[22]

Page also informed McLellin, David was uncomfortable with McLellin's apparent description of David as a prophet (meaning prophet, seer, and revelator), because David did not possess the interpreters:

> He who has these things (the interpreters [or spectacles]) is called Seer; if it requires the possession of these means to constitute a Seer then David can not be said to be a Seer at this time, no more than Joseph [Smith] could from the [time] of receiving power till he had the means because[e] the Specticles are reserved to go with the plates and we expect the one will come with the other and david [*sic*] is the man whom the Lord has appointed to fill this office; that is; to be the head of the church in all Spiritual matters as a man posessed of all the necessary gifts for the church of Christ at this time.[23]

21. Ibid., 4.

22. Ibid., 5.

23. Ibid., 6. The Whitmers apparently differentiated between spectacles and seer stones, and anticipated that Book of Mormon plates and spectacles would be manifested to

Then on March 4, 1848, Page intimated that McLellin had misunderstood some important gospel principles. Page reminded William of their experience together at Far West in 1847: "In one of those precepts rece[i]ved at far west [*sic*] Sept. 7th, it was Said of his Servant Wm, I inspired his heart to discern the true principles of my kingdom that he may build up my church as at the beginning (See cov not with high priests but with elders) therefore I have inspired him to build it up according to my law."[24]

Referring to McLellin, Page counseled, "Our hearts is pained and our bowels yearn for those who will not receve truth and true wisdom[,] who want to be led by revelation instead of taking the bible book of mormon and the church covinants as the man of their council." McLellin was apparently anxious to reinstitute many ecclesiastical features of Smith's church in their fledgling movement. As a further check to McLellin's plans, Hiram rejected the proposed reinstatement of the School of the Prophets, writing, "Then we [say] that the idea of having a School of the prophets to endow men by the wisdom of this world to do that which the Lord has reserved to do himself is but chaff and the wind will blow it until it lodges amonghst [*sic*] the hay; wood and Stubble.... It is contrary to the mind and will of heaven that there should be a school of the prophets in Kirtland."[25]

The distance between Missouri and Kirtland, along with McLellin's procedural impetuousness, eventually proved too big an obstacle for McLellin's reestablishment of the Church of Christ. By March 1848, the Whitmers had apparently begun to perceive McLellin as overreaching his authority as one of David Whitmer's counselors in the Church of Christ. Page observed, "It was said [during their Far West meetings] that Wm. was to build up the church as it was in the beginning; not with high priests but with elders who <are> to take the lead of all meetings when assembled with the church; then we See that you [William McLellin] are to establish and build up the church of Christ as it was in the beginning; being assisted by him [David Whitmer] who Stands at the head; and you are to continue this Same order as the only Shure [*sic*] rule."[26]

David before he could function as prophet, seer, and revelator.

24. Hiram Page to William E. McLellin, 4 March 1848, p. 3.

25. Ibid., 3, 9.

26. Ibid., 7.

Page also expressed misgivings about McLellin's use of the Whitmers' names to promote his initiatives: "If your publications are in accordance there with [the gospel and its true principles] we bid you gods Spead; but if they are not we do not want our name used to Support any other principle."[27] And finally, Hiram rebuffed McLellin's suggestion that David move to Kirtland. "David is in the Lords hands and if he wants him to go he will send him."[28] It was clear that David and the extended Whitmer family were beginning to see McLellin's goals as no longer compatible with their own. Following this lead over the next two years, the Whitmer clan separated themselves completely from McLellin's Kirtland endeavors.

Nevertheless, throughout this period, McLellin continued to advocate David's role as Joseph Smith's successor through the pages of his *Ensign of Liberty*. One of his contributions was the important, though typically ignored, perspective that John, the other Whitmers, and Oliver Cowdery, had been victimized by an intentional smear campaign that Joseph Smith had allowed and even encouraged during his lifetime and which followers of Brigham Young continued. It is an example of the maxim, "History is written by the victors." However, McLellin's interpretation presents a valid alternative to traditional, institutional Mormon historical accounts from which to examine the events of John's life. McLellin narrated turning points in the story of the Restoration that made Joseph Smith distrustful of the Missouri leaders and others. Geographical separation and differences in doctrinal interpretation expanded over the Kirtland/Missouri period, leading to alienation, perhaps exacerbated by jealousy, hurt feelings, and misunderstandings. Joseph Smith's leadership style moved inexorably in the direction of demanding obedience so that the only method of achieving reconciliation was for someone who dissented from his decisions to recant, submit, and ask for forgiveness. Those who refused to follow this approach moved with accelerated speed toward intensified separation and, ultimately, a conscious decision made by those loyal to Smith to excommunicate the dissenters.

McLellin persuasively argued for an alternative view of history. Expressing this thesis in the inaugural issue of the *Ensign of Liberty*, McLel-

27. Ibid., 8–9.
28. Ibid., 9.

lin wrote: "For years past, I have had one continued and abiding desire in my heart, concerning the THREE WITNESSES of the book of Mormon, viz. Oliver Cowdery, David Whitmore [*sic*], and Martin Harris; who some years since received pre-meditated, willful, and outrageous abuse at the hands of the Church, which had assumed the name of 'Latter Day Saints.' An embodiment of those foul slanders, intended to be fastened upon the characters of those worthy men—especially O. Cowdery, and D. Whitmore [*sic*]—may be found in an official document of the State of Missouri. Two thousand copies of which were published, by a joint resolution of the Senate–the House of Representatives."[29]

Joseph successfully used friendship as a means to control and manipulate those around him. Further, a common pattern is that former friends, once fallen from favor, were made the subject of public abuse. McLellin observed that the Latter Day Saints expressed "no repentance for the abuse they had wantonly heaped upon 'the witnesses,' whom they had driven from their midst."[30] This pattern is certainly visible in John and David Whitmer's lives; but regrettably, no documentation exists of John's personal thoughts on the subject.

The period of 1846–48 provided John with a second grand opportunity to consolidate his land holdings. The hasty departures of so many Latter Day Saints from Caldwell County, complicated by the fact that those present at the surrender of Far West had been forced by the terms of surrender to deed their property to the state, had left a cloud over the titles of many farms and town lots. Missouri's tax laws gave former residents up to 1845 to pay delinquent taxes on vacated lands. In 1846, Caldwell County published its first listing of delinquent taxes and extended the payment deadline to 1848. After the 1848 deadline, probably the first Monday in December, property with overdue taxes was subject to a sheriff's sale on the county courthouse steps.[31]

---

29. McLellin, "A Special Conference of All the Ministerial Authorities," 1.

30. Ibid., 10.

31. The delinquent tax list does not mention the date of the sale. However, the Caldwell County, Missouri Back Tax List, dated November 4, 1872, and published as a supplement to the *Sentinel*, indicates that the 1872 sale was to occur on the first Monday of December. "Back Tax List," ca. November 4, 1872.

David Whitmer owned forty acres northwest of Far West that the county sold for back taxes in 1848.[32] The county also sold thirty-eight acres belonging to Jacob Whitmer for unpaid taxes plus an additional forty acres of Jacob's land in the northwest quarter of the southwest quarter of section 34, township 57 (township 11 of Caldwell County), range 29.[33] John saw some advantage in consolidating his holdings and therefore allowed one of his noncontiguous plots to be sold at the 1848 sheriff's sale.[34] Contiguous to his major holdings at Far West was an additional plot of seventy-three acres[35] that he also allowed to be sold, possibly so that he could purchase it himself for less than back taxes with the added advantage of also clearing the title.[36]

Of course, most Mormons, who were either in Nauvoo or on the move again, probably never knew their property was being auctioned for back taxes. However, the delinquent tax listing provided an excellent summary for John about what lands were available, and he no doubt took advantage of this opportunity to pick up land at bargain prices and receive a clear title.

Meanwhile, before Joseph Smith's death in 1844, Oliver Cowdery had begun to correspond with Phineas Young, a former friend, exploring the possibility of reuniting with the institutional church. Scott Faulring's study of Oliver Cowdery, notes: "In October 1847, Hiram Page ... advised Oliver not to commit to any Mormon reaffiliation until they (i.e., Page, the Whitmers, and Cowdery) could counsel together. Probably because Cowdery could afford neither the time nor the expense in traveling to Missouri for a meeting, he did not respond to Page's invitation. What-

32. "List of Lands [in Caldwell County, Missouri] Sold for the State in 1848 for Arrears of Taxes, &c., for Taxes of 1844." This plot was in the southeast quarter of the southwest quarter of township section 7, township 56 (township 8 in Caldwell County), range 28.

33. Ibid. Jacob's property lay in the southwest quarter of the northwest quarter of section 3, township 56 (township 11 of Caldwell County), range 29.

34. This piece was forty-five acres of part of the west half of the southeast quarter of section 15, township 56 (township 11 of Caldwell County), range 29.

35. This plot, the west half of the northeast quarter of section 5, township 56 (township 11 of Caldwell County), range 29, also was sold.

36. Ibid. See also "List of Lands Sold to the State in 1846 for Arrear[s] of Taxes, &c., for taxes of 1844 [Caldwell County, Missouri], delinquent tax list, 1845"; "List of Lands Forfeited to the State in 1848 for taxes of 1847."

ever his reasons for not replying, within six months Oliver wrote to David Whitmer encouraging him to meet at Council Bluffs so they could settle their differences with the Latter-day Saint church led by Brigham Young."[37] David remained aloof despite Oliver's coaxing. Over the next several months, Oliver sold his property in Wisconsin[38] and went to Council Bluffs in November 1848 for a face-to-face meeting with LDS leaders. As a result of this meeting, Cowdery asked for and accepted rebaptism into the body of the church that had previously shunned him.[39]

What Elizabeth Ann thought of these plans is not known, including Oliver's commitment to gather with the Saints in the Salt Lake Valley in the spring of 1849. She was doubtless pleased (and it may have been at her urging) that the Cowderys decided to visit Elizabeth Ann's parents in Richmond, Missouri, rather than spend the winter at Council Bluffs. "By early January 1849,"[40] according to Faulring, they arrived in Richmond, where they probably moved in with Peter Sr. and Mary Whitmer, who were still living a block east of David and Julia Ann's home near the east edge of Richmond on land owned by Celenary Burch.

In 1887, David Whitmer claimed that Oliver Cowdery had second thoughts about his recommitment to the LDS church: "In 1849, the Lord saw fit to manifest unto John Whitmer, Oliver Cowdery and myself nearly all the remaining errors in doctrine into which we had been led by the heads of the old church. We were shown that the Book of Doctrine and Covenants contained many doctrines of error, and that it must be laid aside."[41] Whether Oliver experienced second thoughts or not, their visit

---

37. Reference to Oliver Cowdery to Phineas Young, 16 April 1848, in Faulring, "The Return of Oliver Cowdery," p. 337.

38. Oliver left Tiffin, Ohio, in April 1847 and moved his family to Elkhorn, Wisconsin, where he practiced law with his brother Lyman. Faulring, "The Return of Oliver Cowdery," 335.

39. George A. Smith to Orson Pratt, 31 Oct 1848, p. 14. "Oliver Cowdery, His Life, Character and Testimony," Book of Abraham Project, accessed May 6, 2012, http://www.boap.org/LDS/Early-Saints/OCowd-his.html.

40. Ibid.

41. David Whitmer, *An Address to Believers in the Book of Mormon*, 1. David later wrote to Joseph Smith Jr.'s son, Joseph III, regarding doctrinal errors in the early movement: "I loved your father; I upheld him as far as he taught the doctrine of Christ; yea I loved him so much and had so much confidence in him, that I followed him into many errors

lengthened into an extended stay. In 1849, Oliver applied to and was accepted as a member of the Richmond Bar.[42] In December 1849, John furnished Oliver's family with 387 pounds of pork for $7.74.[43]

Meanwhile, on behalf of the family, in January 1849, David had acquired title to "the lot upon which old man Whitmer [Peter Sr.] now lives, for $81.00." This transaction also mentions "the stable lot of David Whitmer" next door.[44] That same year, David also bought two larger irregular lots, just north of his father's house and east of his other holdings, all contiguous to the eastern edge of the Richmond town plat.[45] In 1851 David made another purchase: the old brickyard on lots 57 and 58, lying directly in the middle of his land holdings.[46] This pattern of land acquisition additionally reinforces the probability that Whitmer's first livery was located on East Main Street near his father's house. David's larger surrounding

before I was aware that I was trusting too much in 'an arm of flesh,' instead of trusting in God only, and relying upon 'that which is written.'" David Whitmer to Dear Brethren, 89.

42. Members of the bar and officers of the court adopted the following resolutions: "To Wit: 1. Resolved, By the members of the bar and officers of the court, that in the death of our friend and brother, Oliver Cowdery, his profession has lost an accomplished member, and the community a valuable and worthy citizen. 2nd. Resolved, That we deeply sympathize with his afflicted widow and daughter in this their heaviest bereavement and do offer them our most sincere condolence. 3. Resolved, That in respect for our deceased brother and friend we will wear the usual badge of mourning for thirty days. 4. That the Clerk of this court furnish the widow of our deceased friend and brother with a copy of the foregoing resolutions. And hereupon it is further ordered that the court adjourn at three o'clock P. M. today to attend the funeral of said deceased." "Oliver Cowdery, His Life, Character and Testimony," Book of Abraham Project, accessed May 6, 2012, http://www.boap.org/LDS/Early-Saints/OCowd-his.html.

43. Whitmer, account book, 20 December 1849, p. 72.

44. Burch, indenture to David Whitmer, describes lot 84: "that portion of said lot upon which old man Whitmer now lives and adjoining the stable [?] lot of David Whitmer" (333). This suggests that the livery was on one side or the other of Peter Whitmer Sr.'s home.

45. James F. McCoun, indenture to David Whitmer, 19 September 1849, for lots 1 and 2, Richmond, Missouri, "bounded on the north by lot 3 purchased by George J. Wasson on the west by the eastern boundary line of the town, the south by the street which runs along the north side of the public square, on the east by the ravine which runs along the western boundary of Mary McCoun's dower land."

46. George J. Wasson and Angeline B. Wasson, indenture to David Whitmer, 1 May 1851.

parcels, all quite close to the center of the city, could provide convenient pasturage for his livery stable's livestock.

The weeks and months flew quickly by for David, filled with the usual activities of providing for and raising a family, and dealing with the joys and sorrows of daily life. John, like David in Richmond, continued to supplement his income by breeding horses and mules, chopping and delivering wood, splitting rails, running his hotel, hauling people and goods, and selling farm produce. Sarah had not heard from her family for some time when she received a welcome letter dated May 2, 1849, from Sarah's father, John Jackson, her brother Andrew, and either her sister-in-law Eliza Jackson, or sister Eliza Jackson Zimmer. They were then living in Centerville, Appanoose County, Iowa. Ap-

AN ADDRESS

TO

ALL BELIEVERS IN CHRIST.

BY

A Witness to the Divine Authenticity of The Book of Mormon.

DAVID WHITMER.
RICHMOND, MISSOURI.
1887.

David Whitmer's An Address to All Believers in Christ *and* An Address to Believers in the Book of Mormon *advocate the (Whitmerite) Church of Christ and represents the views of many members of the Whitmer family. Courtesy of Community of Christ Libary-Archives.*

parently Sarah's mother, Martha, was no longer with them, and the letter provides no news of her; but they reported the death of a brother, James Jackson, the birth of a nephew, John, born to Sarah's brother, Andrew Jackson, and the expedition of another brother, Thomas, to the gold fields of

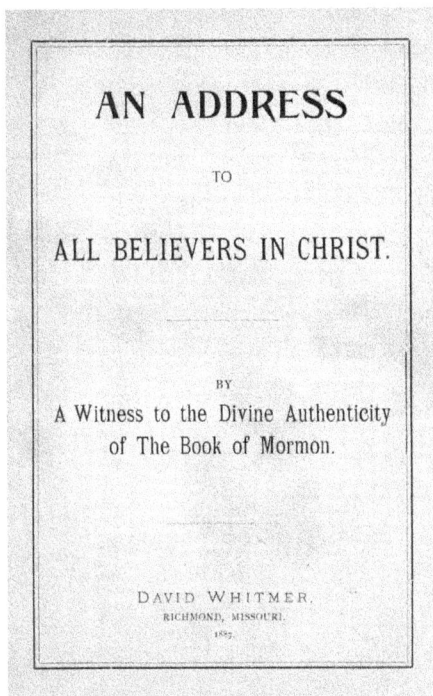

California.[47] In 1850, Sarah's sister, Eliza Jackson Zimmer, then residing in Appanoose County, Iowa, died.[48]

It is a virtual certainty that Oliver Cowdery participated in a reconsideration and restatement of the Whitmer clan's core beliefs in the wake of William McLellin's attempts to regenerate a version of Mormonism. But the extent and exact contributions of Cowdery's participation is not possible to sort out, given the lack of documentation. It seems equally certain, but equally impossible to document, that David and John Whitmer, and Hiram Page influenced Oliver in reconsidering his allegiance to Brigham Young.

The extent to which John participated, given his location at Far West, is not clear either. Around the first of October 1848, McLellin sent John a letter which has not survived, but which Hiram Page answered on October 8, 1848.[49] He alludes, in passing, to the contents of McLellin's letter and writes disapprovingly about McLellin's attempted organization: "We have seen the folly.... and we renounce it and come back in principle to the organization

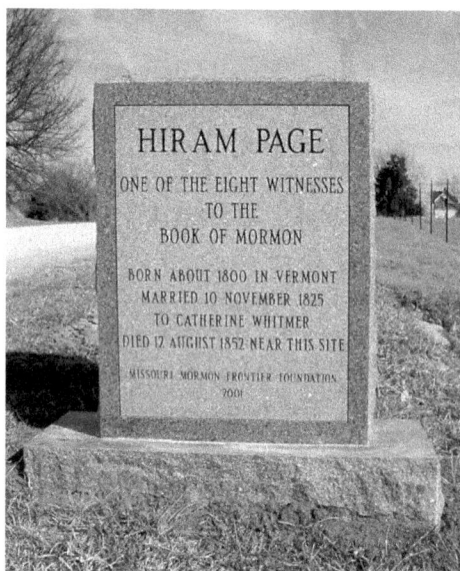

Commemorative marker on Hiram Page's grave, Excelsior Springs, Missouri, 2002. Courtesy of the Missouri Mormon Frontier Foundation.

Signature of Hiram Page. Courtesy of Community of Christ Archives.

47. John Jackson, Andrew Jackson, and Eliza Jackson to Sarah and John Whitmer, 2 May 2, 1849.

48. Taylor, *Past and Present of Appanoose County, Iowa*, 2:118–19.

49. Hiram Page to William E. McLellin, 8 October 1848.

of 1830 which is in accordance with the church established by the apostles [indecipherable word]; and we say to brother Wm and to all in like circumstances, go thou and do likewise."[50]

It is known that John wrote directly to William McLellin on January 18, 1849, no doubt also on a religious topic.[51] Unfortunately, again, neither this letter nor McLellin's answer, if any, has survived. However, it seems reasonable to assume that John's beliefs were not distant from David's, as expressed in his *Address to All Believers in Christ* and *Address to Believers in the Book of Mormon*, or from the views Hiram Page presented in his letters to McLellin.[52]

On June 24, 1849, Hiram Page sent a letter to Kirtland, Ohio, addressed to "Alfred Bonny, Isaac N. Aldrich, and M. C. Ishem," describing, apparently at their request, the Whitmer clan's religious history and current beliefs:

> Since we were driven from far west by the Mormons, (at which time we were obliged to go into an adjoining country where we could get the protection of the civil law,) we have been laying dormant, while fifty odd persons have been appointed to rule and govern the church by Joseph Smith, and there were divisions and sub-divisions, until the true order of the church of Christ was entirely neglected. In 1847 brother William [E. McLellin] commenced vindicating our charcters [*sic*] as honest men; in that he done well. In September 1848 he made us a visit and professed to have been moved upon by the same spirit of God that led him to do us justice by vindicating our characters, moved upon him to come here and have us organize ourselves in a church capacity; but it must come through him, which would give a sanction to all that he had done, which would give a more speedy rise to the cause than any thing else could; and by our hoding [holding] him up, he could build up the church according to its true order, which

50. Ibid.

51. Whitmer, account book, 18 January 1849, p. 70.

52. Hiram Page also took an active role in the founding of Far West. In 1838, he moved to a farm north of Excelsior Springs, near the boundary of Ray and Clay Counties. His son, Philander, described his father as "true and faithful to his testimony of the divinity of the Book of Mormon until the very last." Hiram died August 12, 1852, and is buried on his farm. Jenson, "The Eight Witnesses: Hiram Page," 614; Hiram Page to William E. McLellin, 2 February [March] and 4 March 1848. See also "Hiram Page Grave," 1.

would be a source of consolation to us. But we had not as yet come to an understanding, but consented to the organization after *three days successive intreaties.*[53]

Page's remembrance of their meeting presents some questions, since the Whitmer brothers' rebaptisms apparently occurred soon after McLellin's arrival at Far West on September 8, 1847, but in this letter, Page suggests organization of the new body was deferred three days, taking place closer to the time of McLellin's departure on September 11. Page may be remembering less unanimity among participants regarding the 1847 organization than McLellin perceived. More than this, Page decisively disassociated the Whitmer family from McLellin's efforts: "We acknowledge that the [McLellin] organization *was not in accordance* with the order of the Gospel Church."[54] This letter, then, was prompted by the Whitmers' need to differentiate their own beliefs from those of McLellin. The 1849 proto-Whitmerite church, as described by Page, believed:

> When a man receives authority of God by ordination, his authority remains with him until death or translation, unless he denies the faith or defiles the priesthood.... That any Elder of the church who has not lost his authority upon the principles of injustice, according to the order set forth in the Holy Scriptures, has a perfect right to organize and build up according to that order, laid down by the Apostles at Jerusalem, the order among the Nephites upon this land, and the order of the church as established on the 6th of April, 1830, and he can ordain others.[55]

The Whitmers no longer recognized the office of Melchisedec High Priest or seer. Further, "the gathering dispensation has not come" since "spiritual authorities ... have no right to interfere with the temporal matters, except being stewards of their own." And "the manner of the teaching to the world should be to teach the plain, simple doctrine of the gospel of salvation." Teachings pertaining to stewardship and the gathering were

---

53. Hiram Page to Alfred Bonny, Isaac N. Aldrich, and M. C. Ishem, 24 June 1849, pp. 27–28.

54. Ibid., 28; emphasis Page's.

55. Ibid., 29.

Brothers David and John Whitmer. ca. 1870. Courtesy of Community of Christ Archives.

also problematic.[56] Commenting about organizational attempts, Page declared, "It is evident that the way is not opened for us to organize as we would; but when the way is opened, we shall organize according to the Apostolic order."[57]

The extended Whitmer clan had experienced a great deal of change as the Mormon movement transitioned from a loosely organized group of co-equals voluntarily held together by Smith's charismatic personality into a complex religious system. In a relatively short time frame, the church developed a complex organizational structure with increasingly sophisticated beliefs and lines of authority. Based on Page's reporting of their views, it seems clear that the extended Whitmer family longed for the days of a minimal organizational structure and the practices associated with the founding of the early Church of Christ.

56. Ibid., 28.
57. Ibid.

CHAPTER TWENTY-EIGHT

Building a Legacy

Although Oliver Cowdery's reasons for delaying his plans to travel to Utah in the spring of 1849 are unknown, his ongoing battle with tuberculosis intensified, and he died on March 5, 1850, in the Peter Whitmer Sr. home. Present at his deathbed were his wife, Elizabeth Ann, their only surviving child, Maria Louise, brothers-in-law David Whitmer and Hiram Page, his half-sister Lucy and her husband, Phineas Young, and others of the extended Whitmer family.[1]

In the mid-1840s, Richmond city officials authorized the establishment of a "Public Burial Ground" by Richmond resident John C. Richardson. This burial ground, the (Richmond) City Cemetery, is located six blocks north of the Richmond Square on the corner of North Thornton and Crispin Streets.[2] Known today as the (Richmond) Pioneer Cemetery, this area served as Richmond's main public burial ground from 1864 to 1875. Oliver Cowdery's survivors secured one of Richardson's lots, and Oliver was lovingly laid to rest. The family honored Oliver's request to be buried in an unmarked grave.[3]

1. Faulring, "The Return of Oliver Cowdery," 351.

2. Thanks to Linda Emley, local historian in Ray County, Missouri, for this information. Emley, "If Postcards Could Talk," 8. Linda explains, "John Richardson bought the land from John Thornton in 1845 to be used as a family cemetery. On August 13, 1846, Richardson deeded it to the town of Richmond as a public burial ground. On March 3, 1850, Oliver Cowdery was buried there." See also Ray County, Missouri, land records, cited in Black, "Pioneer Cemetery in Richmond, Missouri," 181, 189n1. This burial ground was located in the northwest corner of lot A, of lot 1, in the subdivision of the southwest quarter of section 30, township 52, range 27, in Ray County.

3. According to Wilhelm Poulson, David Whitmer said, "On his deathbed he [Oliver Cowdery] requested to be buried without any display or large attendance, and he wanted no gravestone to be erected over his ashes." Poulson, "Correspondence: Interview with David Whitmer," 13, reprinted in Cook, *David Whitmer Interviews*, 20.

Richmond City Cemetery, now known as Pioneer Cemetery. Photo by George Edward Anderson, ca. 1907. Courtesy of the LDS Church History Library.

The home of Peter Sr. and Mary (Musselman) Whitmer in Richmond, Missouri. Elizabeth Ann Cowdery and her daughter lived in a room in this house for several years after Oliver's death in 1850. Photo by George Edward Anderson, ca. 1907. Courtesy of the LDS Church History Library.

Elizabeth Ann and Maria Louise remained in Richmond, living in a room in the Peter Sr. and Mary Whitmer home.[4] The bereaved widow and daughter must have provided care for and received comfort from the Whitmer parents. The 1850 US census, taken soon after Oliver's death, gives a snapshot of the extended family. Elizabeth Ann and Maria Louise Cowdery are enumerated as part of Peter Sr. and Mary Whitmer's household. The seventy-seven-year-old Peter is identified as a "farmer." Mary was seventy-three, Elizabeth Ann thirty-five, and Maria Louise fourteen.[5]

The enumerator identified David Whitmer, age forty-five, as a "Livery Keeper." Julia Ann was thirty-five, and their two children were living at home: sixteen-year-old David John and fourteen-year-old Julia Ann (later Schweich).

Jacob Whitmer's family is also included in the census. Jacob, a "shoemaker," was fifty. His wife, Elizabeth Schott Whitmer, was forty-seven, and five children were living at home: David Peter, age twenty-one; Sarah Elizabeth ("Sally"), age nineteen; Anna, age seventeen; John Christian, age fifteen; and Daniel E. age three. Also listed with the family is twenty-three-year-old David T. Tanner, Anna's future husband. A neighboring census district enumerates the entire Hiram Page family: parents—Hiram, age fifty, a "farmer," and Catharine, age forty-two. Eight children were in the household: John David, age twenty-two; Mary Elizabeth, age nineteen; Phylander [Philander] Alma, age eighteen; Mary May, age fifteen; twelve-year-old Peter Christian; ten-year-old Nancy L. (later Johnson); seven-year-old Hiram Jr.; and five-year-old Oliver.[6]

Many of Oliver's valuable historical manuscripts and artifacts were distributed among the Whitmers. Oliver had entrusted the holograph printer's copy of the Book of Mormon to David's care before his death. In

4. David and Julia Ann Whitmer, indenture to Dr. Charles Johnson, 31 January 1855: "all of town lot 84 except that part heretofore conveyed to Elizabeth Cowdery." After Elizabeth Ann's daughter, Maria Louise, married Charles Johnson, a young medical doctor, Elizabeth Ann joined them in Colorado. A few years later, the family moved to Southwest City, Missouri, where Charles continued his medical practice. Elizabeth Ann and Maria Louise died within days of each other and are buried in side-by-side plots in the Southwest City Cemetery.

5. 1850 census, Richmond, Ray County, Missouri.

6. Ibid., district 71 and district 75.

1878, John Whitmer had in his possession a copy of the Book of Mormon "Caractors" [*sic*] from the plates.[7]

In his 1887 autobiography/doctrinal argument, David Whitmer claimed that Joseph Smith gave Oliver Cowdery a brown stone that he had used in translating the Book of Mormon, reportedly saying that "he was through with it, and he did not use the stone any more."[8] After Oliver's death, this seer stone passed into Phineas Young's possession. Oliver's daughter, Maria Louise, recalled that Phineas:

> Came in to Grandfathers House while my Father lay dead—and asked my Mother to let him see this stone—she got it—& let him take it when he kept it she felt so bad and troubled at the time did not think what we were about—My Mother says she cant remember whether he asked her to give it to him or not—I do not remember that he asked to keep it—but do not think he did only to see it—and then kept it. I remember his coming in and asking to see this stone—as well as though it were only yesterday—but do not recollect that my Mother gave it to him [to] keep.[9]

7. "John Whitmer was in possession of copies from the plates, with the translation below, and showed that to me." Poulson, "Correspondence: Death of John Whitmer," 2, cited in Vogel, *Early Mormon Documents*, 5:247–49. The Caractors manuscript (without the translation portion) is housed in the CofC Archives. It is approximately one-fourth of a sheet of typing paper containing handwritten copies of the characters. It was previously believed to be in the hand of Joseph Smith or John Whitmer, but as it contains only a little text in English it is difficult to make a definitive comparison. See MacKay, Dirkmaat, and Jensen, "The 'Caractors' Document: New Light on an Early Transcription on the Book of Mormon Characters;" also, MacKay, et al, *Joseph Smith Papers Documents*, Vol. 1, July 1828–June 1831. New research suggests it may actually be the hand of Christian Whitmer. See Metcalfe and Metcalfe, "Who Wrote the Book of Mormon 'Caractors.'" For further discussion on the Caractors, see appendix Y. It is believed this document accompanied the Book of Mormon printer's manuscript when it was transferred to Joseph Smith III and the RLDS church in 1903 from the heirs of David Whitmer. Some have claimed that it is the Anthon Transcript, and that was David Whitmer's belief. There is no documentation to confirm or refute this claim. This manuscript seems to be the source of most reproductions of the characters appearing in printed sources over the years. No other original copy of the characters is currently known. Stevenson, interview with David Whitmer, January 2, 1887, in Cook, *David Whitmer Interviews*, 211–14. See also Kimball, "The Anthon Transcript: People, Primary Sources, and Problems," 325–52.

8. David Whitmer, *An Address to All Believers in Christ*, 32.

9. Maria L[ouise Cowdery] Johnson to David Whitmer, [14?] January 1887.

Phineas was Brigham Young's brother, and a resident of Utah. Maria Louise was naturally concerned. This incident could easily (and perhaps accurately) be interpreted as taking advantage of a distraught widow and also acting with a politicized agenda, given ongoing disputes about succession.

David further consolidated his land holdings in his immediate neighborhood in May 1851, buying lots 57 and 58 from George J. Wasson for $150. Not only was David good at amassing land, but he was also diligent about keeping current with his property taxes.[10]

Throughout this period, Brigham Young and James Strang continued to attract former church members. But a few scattered Restorationists still looked to David Whitmer as a possible successor to Joseph Smith Jr. Although the Whitmers had distanced themselves from McLellin's ambitions, they continued to debate their anticipations about the reappearance of the Church of Christ. Remnant movements within the church in the Midwest, such as the Reorganization, which began to coalesce in 1851, proved unappealing to the Whitmers.

Like David in Richmond, John, whenever possible, augmented his homestead landholdings. On May 10, 1852, John purchased one acre from William N. DeHawn for fifty dollars.[11]

A blow to the family occurred in August 1852. Hiram Page was fatally injured when his wagon rolled over. He died August 12, and was buried on his farm near Excelsior Springs, Missouri, about twenty miles from Richmond. A spokesperson for the Whitmers was again silenced, and his eight children were left fatherless. Catharine and her oldest son still at

10. George J. Wasson and Angeline B. Wasson, indenture to David Whitmer, 1 May 1851. David paid $150 for lots 57 and 58. David acquired an additional lot, no. 60, lying kitty-corner across the intersection from his own house lot, from George J. and Angelina B. Wasson in 1857. David's annual tax receipts may be found in the Whitmer Papers, CofC Archives.

11. William N. DeHawn, indenture to John Whitmer, 10 May 1852. John purchased "one acre in a square opposite to Lot No. Eight on Block Eighty-five in the town of Far West allowing room for a street between said block and land to be on the West half of South East corner of Section 11, Township 56, Range 29, also Two acres out of the West half of South East Quarter of the same Section at the North East corner of Lot No. One Block Eighty-five in the town of Far West beginning at Benjamin Slade Stable and running East Twenty-nine rods and Eleven feet thence South Twelve rods thence West Twenty-nine and Eleven feet to the place of beginning, containing two acres."

home, Philander, sold the farm and moved closer to Richmond to an area known as Grape Grove.[12] Early church-related artifacts apparently passed into the care of Hiram Page's descendants at that point. For example, in 1880, RLDS apostle T. W. Smith, wrote, "When I was in Ray county, Mo., a few years ago I was told of a certain 'peepstone' that was owned by members of the Hiram Page family."[13]

Because Peter Sr. and Mary Whitmer's first-born child, Christian, had died in 1835 in Clay County, Missouri, Jacob, their second child (born January 27, 1800, in Harrisburg, Pennsylvania), functioned as a leader of the extended family during early years in Richmond. Jacob and Elizabeth Schott Whitmer remained close to the Whitmer patriarchs throughout life, moving with them through each chapter of their various experiences. By 1843, however, Jacob was virtually an invalid, and had exhausted his limited means. He acquired two-and-a-half acres of land in the southern portion of Richmond from George and Nancy Woodward for $87.50, on August 30, 1843.[14] Jacob erected a shoe shop in 1845. As health permitted, he farmed during the summer and worked as a shoemaker during the winter.[15] Through industry, he acquired additional land.[16] He also acquired an additional 13.52 acres of what had been Woodward land on October 21, 1853.[17] In all, Jacob and Elizabeth owned about sixteen acres on the northeast corner of Wellington and South Streets. Jacob also secured a family plot near Oliver Cowdery's grave in the city burial ground.

Peter Whitmer Sr., the family patriarch, died August 13, 1854, and was buried near Oliver. According to tradition, Peter Sr.'s grave is located near the southeast corner of the sixteen-by-sixty-foot Whitmer family lot.[18] In January 1856, less than two years after her husband's death, Mary Musselman Whitmer also passed from this life.

12. 1860 census, Grape Grove, Ray County, Missouri.

13. Smith, "Urim and Thummim," 67.

14. George and Nancy Woodward, indenture to Jacob Whitmer, 30 August 1843.

15. *History of Ray County, Missouri*, 530.

16. Barchers, "The Descendants & History of the Peter Whitmer Family," 38.

17. [George Woodward to] David P. Whitmer, indenture to Jacob Whitmer, 21 October 1853, p. 4.

18. Black, "Pioneer Cemetery in Richmond, Missouri," 181.

Daguerreotype image of Jacob and Elizabeth (Schott) Whitmer, ca. 1850. Courtesy of Community of Christ Archives.

Then, in April 1856, Jacob Whitmer died.[19] P. Wilhelm Poulson noted in August 1878: "His grave is only [a] short distance from Cowdery's. On Jacob's grave is erected a fine marble stone. On the top of the stone appears his name and next we discover the cut of the Book of Mormon laid open, with a blooming rose resting on the divide, and the book resting upon the closed up Bible."[20] Father, mother, and son were thus buried close together. By the time of Jacob's death, he had acquired additional land just south of his earlier land purchases. Anticipating his death, Jacob arranged for this land to pass to his wife, Elizabeth Schott Whitmer. When Elizabeth died

19. Jacob's son, John Christian Whitmer, reported, "My father, Jacob Whitmer, was always faithful and true to his testimony to the Book of Mormon, and confirmed it on his death bed." Jenson, Stevenson, and Black, "Historical Landmarks," 7.

20. Poulson, "Correspondence: Interview with David Whitmer," 13.

in Richmond nearly twenty years later, on April 11, 1876, she owned about 116 acres of land.[21] The town paper reported Elizabeth's passing:

> Another Mother in Israel has folded her hands and passed through the portals of eternity. Wednesday last Mrs. Elizabeth Whitmer was borne to her silent resting place, and placed with in the bosom of our common mother, accompanied thither by sorrowing relatives and sympathizing friends. The lilies of seventy-seven summers had nestled in her hair, for years she had been listening for the call that would summon her home, and when it came found her ready, having been a consistent member of the church of Christ, and folding her hands she peacefully passed away, confident in her trust in Him who doeth all things well, and firm in her belief in the promise of her Savior. She was among the early settlers in Ray county, having removed here in 1837, and her death will be mourned by many who loved her for her many acts of kindness and Christian virtues.[22]

Descendants believe Elizabeth lies buried next to Jacob in the old city cemetery. Eventually twelve or more family members were lovingly secured in the cemetery near one another.[23]

After Jacob's death in 1856, John was the sole survivor of the original eight witnesses to the Book of Mormon. He prospered as a farmer, providing a good livelihood for his family. During the remainder of his relatively long life, he found many opportunities to affirm his testimony of the book and beliefs in primitive Mormonism. Among the many who traveled to Missouri to visit the Whitmers were representatives of the fledgling New Organization (to become the Reorganized church), who were prompted

---

21. "Eighty acres [being the] East half of Northwest Quarter of Section 6, Township 51, Range 27, containing 80 acres, [purchased on] October 21, 1853." Also, "Twenty acres, [being] all that part of North half of West half of the Northwest Quarter of Section 6, Township 51, Range 27, which lies east of the east side of the middle of [the] main branch of [the] water course." "She also owned the original sixteen acres where they [first] lived on the Northeast corner of Wellington and South Street." Barchers, "The Descendants & History of the Peter Whitmer Family," 38.

22. "Another Mother in Israel," *Richmond Conservator,* 23:3.

23. Black, "Pioneer Cemetery in Richmond, Missouri," 191–96. Only Jacob Whitmer's stone survives today in the Pioneer Cemetery. The burial ground was not used after 1875, following the establishment of the new Richmond Cemetery west of town. For photographs of the burial ground, see Holzapfel, Cottle, and Stoddard, *Church History in Black and White,* 68, 69.

to go into the mission field by the excitement of their June 1852 conference held at the Newark Branch, Rock County, Wisconsin. It is not known whether David Powell and John Harrington visited John specifically; but in his *History of the Reorganization*, Jason Briggs recalled, "Brn. David Powell and John Harrington took a mission south ... through Illinois and Missouri, calling upon the Whitmers, and into Arkansas."[24]

It has been said that John never plowed the Far West temple lot because of the meaning he attached to it. The family prospered and began building a larger frame house on their farm east of the temple site in 1856. A relative wrote: They "star[t]ed it in 1856 and completed it in 1857."[25] John noted the precise date of moving into their new house in his account book: November 16, 1857.[26] Like his father before him, John developed a reputation among local residents as an honest and trustworthy neighbor. "Mr. Whitmer is regarded by all who Know him as an estimable Citizen," reported a newspaper article in 1875, "and a living evidence of the fact that among those who professed the strange faith were occasionally to be found men of sterling integrity and unblemished Character."[27]

James Cash Penney Sr. and family were the Whitmer's near neighbors. John Whitmer knew the Penneys and had business dealings with them. John's daybook records several sales of farm produce, such as wheat, oats, and lard, to Eli and James Penney during 1855–56. In April and May 1857, John bred several of his mules with Penney's mules and horse.[28]

In addition to on-going labor on his farm, John also planted a garden of beautiful perennial flowers west of the new house. Though it involved quite a bit of labor to keep up, the garden probably reminded him of his mother's flower and herb garden in Fayette, New York, when he was a boy. A family story suggests that John's mother had maintained plantings of their lilac bushes ever since they left Fayette. Perhaps John continued such a tradition next to his home. Sarah also helped tend this flower garden,

24. Briggs, "History of the Reorganization of the Church of Jesus Christ of Latter Day Saints, Chapter 5," 17.

25. Ethel Johnson Lewellen to C. Edward Miller, 26 May 1932.

26. Whitmer, account book, 16 November 1857, p. 90.

27. "Far West: The Old Mormon Settlement in Missouri."

28. Whitmer, account book, 2 August 1855, 4 April 1856, 8 April–26 May, and 15 June 1857, pp. 84, 85, 87, 88.

spending much of her time there. The family probably maintained a convenient kitchen garden or potager near the house, supplying the family with a ready supply of vegetables. In a significant act of beautification, John set out "a quarter mile long row of Locust trees" lining the lane between the temple site and his home.[29]

John dug a commodious cistern at the northeast corner of the new house. His great-great-granddaughter Lorene Pollard wrote:

> [Water for the cistern] was collected by runoff from the tip of the house though the eaves troughs. This water was then piped to the cistern.... The cistern pump was distinctly different from any others I'd known. There was a long chain filled with small, square metal cups attached every few inches to collect the water and bring it up. As water came to the top, the cups would empty into a bucket. There was a handle attached to the chain, so that by turning it round and round you would eventually get the container full of water. This cistern water was considered most valuable. When the ladies used it to shampoo their hair, it made it extra shiny and glossy.[30]

Of course John also constructed the necessary complement of barns and outbuildings. A barn was as essential to farming as haying. Lorene Pollard observed:

> With all the mules and horses, such as John Whitmer chose to have, several big, big stacks of hay had to be amassed for the winter.... It took quite a crew of men to get this job accomplished ... It was a hot and dirty job which took many days of mowing, raking, gathering it onto the wagons and pitching it onto the stacks. As it got higher and higher, the job became more difficult to get each pitchfork of hay at the exact right place so that the rain could not penetrate the mass. There was another haying process in which they used a hay fork to move the hay through the top barn door under the roof for storage.[31]

Around 1856, a young man named James Edward Johnson located in the Whitmer neighborhood. James, born in 1830, came from New York to Missouri and worked as a surveyor for a proposed railroad anticipated

29. Pollard and Woods, *Whitmer Memoirs*, 45.

30. Ibid., 51.

31. Ibid., 63.

to run through Caldwell County. It was logical for him to board with the Whitmers in their hotel. From this association, a courtship with John and Sarah's daughter, Sarah Elizabeth, blossomed, and the two were "married in the Whitmer home on April 3, 1856, by Eli Penney, father of the renowned J. C. Penny."[32] The newlyweds remained with the Whitmers for a time. Johnson initially assisted with John's efforts to obtain clear title to the Far West lands formerly held by W. W. Phelps. John and Sarah must have been overjoyed when their first grandchild, Ella Edith, was born on March 23, 1857, at Far West. Ella was born in a building sounding remarkably like the old George M. Hinkle house into which Joseph and Emma Smith had moved in March 1838. "The house she [Ella] was born in was ... a two room house with large fireplace."[33]

One of Sarah Elizabeth's cousins, Jacob's son, John Christian Whitmer, also married in 1856. His bride was Mary Gant of Ray County.[34]

32. Ibid., 29, 43; see also Dear, *Two Hundred Thirty-Eight Years of the Whitmer Family*, 40.

33. Ethel Johnson Lewellen to C. Edward Miller, 26 May 1932.

34. Notice of John Whitmer's death, "John C. Whitmer Dead," *Herald*, 41:582. See also, George W. Schweich to Joseph Smith III, 30 October 1894, also published as "John C. Whitmer Dead," *Herald*, 41:741.

CHAPTER TWENTY-NINE

Consolidating the John Whitmer Farm

W. W. PHELPS, John's former associate in founding Far West, was now securely reintegrated among his former church associates. In fact, when the Mormons who followed Brigham Young left Nauvoo, Illinois, for the West, Phelps traveled with them to Utah. William wrote to John from Salt Lake City on October 12, 1859. During the exodus from Nauvoo, Emma Smith had retained the manuscripts of Joseph Smith's Bible revisions. Recalling that John had produced many copies of Joseph Smith's biblical literary efforts, Phelps asked for a "full copy": "When you lived along with me, you had a few of the first chapters of Genesis as translated by brother Joseph Smith; and if you still have them, I would like that you send me by mail, a full copy of all you have as I have lost some of mine—and I will try to accommodate in a way that will afford you as much Satisfaction. Be not afraid to respond John, it will redound for your good."[1]

Phelps continued to contribute to the life of the movement in Utah. He filled his role as printer, publishing the first of a series of annual Deseret almanacs in 1851. He served in the state legislature, was a regent of the University of Deseret, and became a charter member of the Deseret Theological Institute, organized in 1855.[2] Phelps knew that, while in England, Franklin D. Richards had printed portions of Joseph's revisions in the Pearl of Great Price.[3] This publication's contents sparked considerable debate in Utah about the nature of scripture in the movement, and no doubt

1. W. W. Phelps to John Whitmer, 12 October 1859.

2. Jenson, *Latter-day Saint Biographical Encyclopedia*, 3:696–97.

3. These sections are the Book of Abraham and "Joseph Smith—Matthew" (Matt. 23:39–Matt. 24) in the LDS edition of the Pearl of Great Price. Orson Pratt prepared the first American edition in 1878, and it was canonized in 1880. Millet, "Pearl of Great Price," in Garr, Cannon, and Cowan, *Encyclopedia of Latter-day Saint History*, 900.

members of the Theological Institute also discussed the topic. Furthermore, Phelps was in a good position to know that Richards's publication represented only a small part of Joseph's intended larger work.

Interestingly, Phelps is also credited with the publication of the Deseret Alphabet in 1859.[4] No doubt because he had enjoyed success in his many printing efforts, Phelps confidently approached John about obtaining copies of Joseph's translation manuscripts. Perhaps he was remembering his calling to publish Joseph's New Translation of the Bible during the Jackson County era. Or perhaps he was simply looking for his next potentially viable professional project.

John wanted no part of Phelps's plans. If he responded, his letter has not survived; and he did not send Phelps the desired copy. As a result, much of the content of Joseph's New Translation remained unavailable to the Utah-based Latter-day Saints.[5]

By the time the 1860 census was enumerated, fifty-seven-year-old John, despite his varied business enterprises, described his occupation as that of a farmer. Sarah was fifty. Living at home were eighteen-year-old Alexander Peter and sixteen-year-old Jacob David. Also a member of the household was Malinda Vance, age fifteen, and almost certainly a hired girl helping with the housework and the hotel.[6] John's farm almost always required seasonal laborers. He recorded in his account book on March 1: "Samuel Dillon commenced work for five months, first month at $16.00 per month."[7] Dillon was still there when the census was enumerated.[8] Nearby were James Edward Johnson, age thirty, twenty-two-year-old Sarah Elizabeth (Whitmer), and their three-year-old daughter, Ella Edith.[9]

<hr>

4. "William Wines Phelps, Judge, Mormon, Publisher and Writer," *Phelps Family History in America and Kindred Family Histories*, accessed May 6, 2012, http://www.phelpsfamilyhistory.com/bios/william_wines_phelps.asp#source4.

5. Faulring, Jackson, and Matthews, *Joseph Smith's New Translation of the Bible*, 12. The current (1979) LDS edition of the King James Bible has extensive footnotes quoting Joseph Smith's "New Translation" and contains an appendix of "Excerpts Too Lengthy for Inclusion in Footnotes," 797–813.

6. 1860 census, Rockford, Caldwell County, Missouri.

7. Whitmer, account book, 1 March 1870, p. 105.

8. Ibid.

9. 1860 census, Mirabile, Rockford, Caldwell County, Missouri.

A view of John Whitmer's farm lands which encompassed a large portion of the southeast portion of what had once been John's beloved city of Far West, Missouri. John Whitmer's house and farm outbuildings are visible in the background. Courtesy of the LDS Church History Library.

By 1860, the town that John had helped found had essentially vanished from the landscape, its buildings principally dismantled and moved to other locations. The Kingston courthouse suffered a fire that destroyed most of Caldwell County's early land records. Consequently, details about the physical layout of Far West are now obscure. What is known comes from only a handful of scattered sources. In the 1930s, Bertha Booth, a devoted local historian, hand copied a document presumed to be a plat of Far West.[10] When historians Donald Q. Cannon and Lyndon W. Cook published a volume of minutes of Latter Day Saint meetings in 1983, known as the Far West Record, they included an expanded and revised re-creation of a plat by Jack Wood, based on the Booth plat.[11] A local resident, J. B. West, during the 1980s, possessed a plat drawn on sheepskin that was similar to Booth's. He said that his ancestors had obtained the plat from George M. Hinkle's home at Far West. Mr. West is now deceased and the location of

10. Bertha Booth's plat is reproduced in Johnson and Romig, *An Index to Early Caldwell County, Missouri Land Records*, xii.

11. Cannon and Cook, *Far West Record*, 121.

the sheepskin plat is unknown.[12] Variations among extant plats of Far West have fostered confusion about their authenticity, but a deed has survived, dated May 10, 1852, conveying land from William N. DeHawn to John Whitmer (for fifty dollars) which confirms the correctness of the Booth plat.[13]

A decade after John's death, on July 22, 1881, John's nephew, David Peter Whitmer, a lawyer at Richmond, wrote an intriguing letter to surviving members of the family that provides some information about the town's layout:

> My Dear Cousins
>
> Jeff Davis atty at Kingston has been here about the 5th inst and said he wanted to use the Phelps Mortgage in a trial of a case involving part of the old town tract of Farwest—and said he would have supoened [*sic?*] for me or you to bring the same to court to use in the trial referred to.
>
> I told him that I would forward the cause to you by Mail. He thinks that with the Mortgage and Uncle David's Deposition on file ... that he can make a case But if they are not careful they will get mixed up when they undertake to make up a plat. I need explain no further— I presume they know nothing about the copy of Plat and as it covers so much of your land—I hope you will not be requested to show any thing of that kind to stir up the Inquisitions.... D. P. Whitmer[14]

12. J. B. West, plat of Far West, attributed to George M. Hinkle, sheepskin, ca. 1836, photograph, ca. 1975, Pictorial Archives, CofC Archives.

13. William N. DeHawn, indenture to John Whitmer, 10 May 1852: "One acre in a square opposite to Lot no. Eight on Block Eighty-five in the town of Far West allowing room for a street between said block and land to be on the West half of S.E. Corner of Section 11 Town 56, Range 29 also Two acres out of the West half of S.E. Quarter of the same section at the North East corner of Lot No. one Block Eighty-five in the town of Far West beginning at Benjamin Slade Stable and running East Twenty-nine rods and Eleven feet thence South Twelve rods thence West Twenty-nine and Eleven feet to the place of beginning containing Two acres." Fortunately, this deed provides a description of Slade's lot as lying just inside the early one-mile-square plat, as well as, a lot lying just beyond in the area of the expanded city plan. This confirms block 85 as lying on the east edge of the initial plat, demonstrating that this legal description perfectly conforms to the Booth plat. An alternate drawing of the plat of Far West, apparently related to the settlement of Bishop Partridge's estate, located in the M. Wilford Poulsen Collection of John E. Page documents, also confirms Booth's description. See also Edward Partridge estate settlement.

14. David Peter Whitmer to My Dear Cousins, 22 July 1881; terminal punctuation added.

David P.'s letter suggests three interesting items: 1) John's family possessed a plat of Far West. 2) Title to some of the lands John had acquired within the plat of Far West apparently remained clouded, a particularly problematic point if the plat detailed the names of former lot owners. 3) The larger Whitmer family apparently regarded this legal effort unenthusiastically and wished to keep the details of the Far West plat obscure in order to protect their consolidated lands.

Having helped lay out Far West and sell lots, John would have been in an ideal position to have retained a populated plat. Scholars can hope that this plat still exists and will one day become available for research.

As John prospered in Far West, the remaining family was also becoming financially well established in Richmond. The 1860 federal census lists David's occupation as "Livery Keeper," valued his real estate holdings at $3,000, and estimated his personal property at $2,200. David and Julia Ann were fifty-five and forty-five-years-old, respectively. Their son David John was twenty-six, and their daughter Julia Ann was twenty-four. Julia Ann had married Julius Schweich, on November 24, 1852, but almost no details about him have survived except that he was of Jewish descent. The census records Julia Ann's married name as "Swash," an important phonetic clue about its pronunciation, but Julius was not living with the family at that point. Julia Ann had two children: seven-year-old George Washington Schweich and five-year-old Josephine Helen Schweich (later Van Cleave). A twenty-three-year-old "livery hand," James Soister, who had been born in Maryland, rounded out the household.[15]

Julia Ann (Whitmer) Schweich, daughter of David and Julia Ann (Jolly) Whitmer, ca. 1850s. Courtesy of Community of Christ Archives.

15. 1860 census, Richmond, Ray County, Missouri. George Washington Leopold Schweich's birth is recorded as George "Schwash," April 19, 1853. See Julia Ann Whitmer Schweich family Bible.

Many landholders in the Richmond area were wealthier than David, but his persistent hard work was paying off, and his standing in the community continued to improve. Following Jacob Whitmer's death on April 21, 1856, his family had become less cohesive. Some members stayed on Jacob's farm on Richmond's southeastern edge. His son, John Christian Whitmer, appears to have acquired land south of Richmond where his descendants resided for many years. Hiram Page's widow and her children had moved away from Excelsior after his death in 1852 and were living south of Richmond.

Julius Schweich, son-in-law of David and Julia Ann (Jolly) Whitmer, ca. 1850s. Courtesy of Community of Christ Archives.

Within the year, the Civil War inflicted more suffering on the resilient family. On July 26, 1861, John, David, and perhaps members of their families, gathered at Far West. They, no doubt, saw the specter of civil strife—only five months away—as signaling the fulfillment of God's warning to the unrighteous, previously articulated through Joseph Smith. During this season of anxiety and renewal, someone, probably David, received a revelation that affirmed many of their anticipations. It began by warning that "the inhabitants of the Earth are well nigh ripe for destruction" and "that destruction shall come unto the inhabitants of the Earth" as foretold by "the Bible and the Book of Mormon, and the Sacred Revelations." God's "word should be fulfilled concerning the wicked and rebellious. And behold and lo. They will not repent. For this cause I let fall the sword of my indignation upon the land of your inheritance. And it shall continue from time to time, and from day to day, until the most wicked shall be subdued."

But this somber revelation also contained comfort and reassurance: "I the Lord will preserve all those that seek righteousness." The revelation, enunciating a third familiar theme, promised the long-anticipated redemption of Zion: "And then I say if my disciples will be wise and humble, then shall the time commence, for the redemption of you my Servants and all those that will come unto the Ensign, that I have caused to be raised,

by my servants in these last days. And then shall the arm of the Lord be revealed unto you, from time to time, and the Lord your God shall commence the redemption of Zion."

Furthermore, succeeding generations of Whitmers could look forward to safety and security during Christ's millennial reign: "Christ ... shall ... reign on Earth. And so shall you. And your children, and childrens [*sic*] children, and all the saints, and all the faithful now on Earth, live and reign with him forever and ever."[16]

No doubt, the Whitmers found reassurance in this revelation even as turmoil thickened around them. To further complicate the worrisome situation, John was expected to serve in the Missouri militia along with other eligible men of Caldwell County. David may have been facing the same situation in Ray County. On July 22, 1862, Missouri's governor, Hamilton Rowan Gamble (1798–1864), "issued an order directing.... every able bodied man in the state to report immediately to the nearest military outpost to enroll and be sworn into the new militia organization." The Enrolled Missouri Militia was the state of Missouri's solution to the need for additional soldiers, creating a force of part-time citizen-soldiers subject to call-up in times of emergency that would be paid only for days of active service. "On the average, most men in the Enrolled Missouri Militia served only a few weeks of active duty over the course of the next two and a half years." John Whitmer's certificate of enrollment records: "John Whitmer of Caldwell County, Missouri, over 45 years of age is enrolled loyal at Kingston this 23 oct [*sic*] 1862, John T. Rass, Capt., Enrolling officer."[17]

16. Pollard and Woods, *Whitmer Memoirs,* 30–33. This revelation is in John Whitmer's handwriting. In her *Whitmer Memoirs,* Pollard suggests that this is a revelation to and through John. However, by this time, the family had begun to focus on David's role as Joseph's successor, so John's more probable involvement with this revelation was that of David's scribe. See appendix L.

17. John Whitmer, certificate of enrollment, October 23, 1862. For information about the Enrolled Missouri Militia, see Ross Kirby, "Federal Militia in Missouri," accessed January 25, 2011, http://www.civilwarstlouis.com/militia/federalmilitia.htm#4.%20Enrolled%20Missouri%20Militia. The Enrolled Missouri Militia Act forced many fence sitters and men who would not otherwise have been qualified for service to declare their loyalties during the war. The Enrolled Missouri Militia was a precursor of the stringent Missouri Loyalty Oath of 1865—an extreme attempt to exclude any but the staunchest Unionist from public life in Missouri after the war.

A traveler who passed through Far West in 1862 or 1863 recorded the wartime atmosphere in Caldwell County:

> We had occasion to travel by private conveyance from Cameron in Clinton, to Mirable [*sic*], a small village in Caldwell county. Our journey was rather a monotonous one, unrelieved by any incident worthy of note, for the only persons we encountered were a small party of Federal soldiers and a solitary traveler wending his way northward, and who returned our greeting with the cold glance of suspicion peculiar to those perilous days, for we were in the midst of the rebellion.
>
> After journeying some seven or eight miles through prairie and red brush, occasionally relieved by patches of scrub oak and graceful belts of young timber that fringed the winding course of a bold stream which we were sometimes under the necessity of crossing, about seven or eight miles from Cameron, in a southeasterly direction, we suddenly emerged upon a plain which had the appearance of a long deserted settlement.
>
> It was in the month of July, and the surface of the ground was literally matted with clusters of dewberry vines, laden with tempting fruit. But a single human habitation appeared to relieve the monotony of the landscape, and the utter solitude of the locality was only rendered the more pronounced by the presence of innumerable wells, whose boxes and windlasses had long since disappeared, leaving nothing but the gloomy pits to tell the tale of thronging life that once existed there, and afford us a theme for moralizing on the mutability of all human affairs.
>
> As we gazed with surprise and wonder on the strange and melancholy scene, our taciturn guide, the driver of the vehicle, broke his long silence with the remark: "We are now in the Mormon city of 'Far West,' and just across the hollow is the foundation of the temple."
>
> So, indeed, we were, and how many, like ourselves, had lived for years within forty miles of this interesting locality, scarcely conscious of its existence!
>
> But the matter of surprise was, that with the solitary exception before referred to, and with the occasional debris of a long-fallen chimney, scarce a vestige of the several hundred habitations that, some thirty years before, clustered in compact mass upon this beautiful prairie, remained to tell the tale of sudden rise and correspondingly prompt disappearance of a community which once counted its num-

bers by thousands. It seemed as though the vengeance of heaven had employed in its wrath the most uncompromising of Vandal means to wipe from the fair face of nature and the memory of men a foul and disgusting blot upon the body politic.[18]

One casualty of the Civil War was John and Sarah's son, Alexander Peter Jackson Whitmer, who turned twenty-one in 1862. At Cameron, Missouri, July 28, 1862, Alexander was enrolled in the 33rd Regiment of the Enrolled Missouri Militia. Such participation would have likely exempted Alexander from further service. However, on August 9, 1864, Alexander, then age twenty-three, volunteered for a one-year term of duty at Kingston, Missouri, as a federal soldier. He was mustered into the 44th Infantry as Alexander P. "Whitmore" on August 30, 1864, at St. Joseph, Missouri, as a private in the company of a Captain Hopkins. Alexander's enlistment record indicates he had "blue eyes, light hair, fair complexion, and is five feet eleven inches high." By November 30, 1864, Alexander's unit participated in a battle at Franklin, Tennessee, where he was reported missing in action. His status was later upgraded to killed in action.[19]

By 1864, John was discharged from military service due to an unspecified disability.[20] And it appears that neither John nor his other son, Jacob David, who turned twenty in 1864, was directly involved in the Civil War. As the grip of the war lessened, the economy improved, and Caldwell County began to look hopefully toward the future.

Sarah Elizabeth and James Johnson moved to Hamilton in northwest Missouri for a time, then to St. Louis, Missouri, in association with James's work. Their second child, John, was born November 26, 1863, surely a season of joy for the grandparents.[21] But trouble loomed ahead for the

---

18. "Far West: The Old Mormon Settlement in Missouri."

19. 1860 census, Mirabile, Rockford, Caldwell County, Missouri; Dear, *Two Hundred Thirty-Eight Years of the Whitmer Family,* 41; Alexander Whitmer, July 28, 1862, Enrolled Missouri Militia Record; Alexander P. Whitmore [Whitmer], "Volunteer Enlistment."

20. John Whitmer, certificate of exemption from service, 1864.

21. Pollard and Woods, *Whitmer Memoirs,* 29; Jacob David Whitmer family record, original in the possession of Gerd W. Buttgen, Independence, Missouri, photocopy in my possession. According to this record, Sarah Elizabeth Whitmer Johnson Kerr died June 15, 1922, at Far West, Missouri. Her second husband, Christopher F. Kerr, died in

little family. By 1870, James had abandoned his family, and Sarah Elizabeth brought thirteen-year-old Ella and seven-year-old John back to live with their grandparents on the Far West farm.

William McLellin visited upper Missouri again in about May 1869. During this trip, on June 5, 1869, McLellin affiliated with Granville Hedrick's movement, organized at Hedrick's home in Washburn, Illinois, in 1852. This organization consolidated several unaffiliated remnant branches of the Latter Day Saints in Illinois.[22] The sixty-three-year-old McLellin planned to sell his properties in Kirtland, Ohio, and move to Independence, Missouri, where he hoped to reconnect with his early Mormon roots. En route to Independence, McLellin visited sixty-four-year-old David Whitmer and paid him a second visit in July. Hospitably, the extended Whitmer family gathered for a visit. McLellin recalled:

> I reached Richmond [in May] and called on my old friend and brother David Whitmer. I found him [David] just recovering from a hard fall—pretty much well. In the first place he is wealthy, in the next place he is a perfect gentleman, in dress, manners, &c. Jacob Whitmer's and O. Cowdery's widows live there. Their children are grown and married. Jacob's oldest son [David Peter] married his cousin, Vashti, W.'s youngest daughter He [David Peter] is very popular, and wealthy. He is ... a lawyer and judge, of two courts. David's wife had but two children. They are widow & widower, and both live at home. David Jun [not Junior] is also quite wealthy. Oliver's wife had but one child—a daughter, married well to a Doctor, and the widow lives with them.[23]

McLellin's chief agenda was religious:

1925. When John Johnson grew to manhood, he married Stella E. Smith of Bonanza, Caldwell County, Missouri. When she died in 1895, John returned to the family farm bringing his three motherless children.

22. Representatives of at least three branches were present at this organizational event: Eagle Creek, Bloomington, and Half Moon Prairie. From 1852 to 1860, this group of Saints called themselves the Crow Creek Branch of the Church of Jesus Christ (of Latter day Saints). In 1860, they decided to revert to the original (1830) name of the church, i.e.: Church of Christ. My thanks to R. Jean Addams for this information.: E-mail to author, January 12, 2011. The date of McLellin's baptism into Hedrick's movement is given in Porter, "Odyssey of William Earl McLellin," 351.

23. William E. McLellin, letter fragment to [unknown], Monday, 24th [ca. May 1869].

But n[ow] as to my visit with David. I staid with him two nights and one day—talked a great deal. I found him a man of God, with clear, clean, unfeigned faith in God. He most firmly believes the great truths of the Latter Day work. He still firmly holds to his appointment under the hands of Joseph Smith. He thinks the time soon at hand when he must be <u>Active</u>. On Wednesday we retired to an upper chamber of his great two story white house, and there had a long talk together alone. We bowed and prayed together, and then he laid his hands upon me, and reordained or confirmed upon me all the Authority which I ever held legally in the "church of Christ."[24]

This action is somewhat surprising, given David's years of aloofness from McLellin's religious activities; but McLellin clearly interpreted this action as David's approval of McLellin's plans to gather to Jackson County and affiliate with Hedrick. "David was perfectly satisfied with my course," McLellin assured unnamed correspondents in Brownville, Texas, in July, "and even justified it. I tell you I feel as though I was in my element, only I want to be among my brethren and sisters in Zion. If prospered I'll soon be there."[25]

This July letter mentions that John had not been present during McLellin's first visit, although "John Whitmer visited David between the times that I was there, and they had familiar talks all about it."[26] Because "a Bro. [George] Frisby [a member of the Hedrickite Church] came home [to Brownsville, Salt Pond Township, Saline County, Missouri] with me, and he had great anxiety to see David so we again came by to see him. It's only about two miles out of the way, only we have to cross the river twice. We had remarkably pleasant visits with David & family, and while there we received a revelation through him. I tell you my soul rejoiced in God!"[27]

This revelation apparently dealt with the gathering to Zion. Though the gathering of the Saints to Jackson County had been suspended since

24. Ibid. See also William McLellin to Davis H. Bays, 23 November 1869, pp. 290–91.

25. William E. McLellin to Our Very Dear Friends, 12 July 1869.

26. Ibid.

27. Ibid. George Frisby was a prominent member of Hedrick's congregation in Independence, Missouri. This group is now known as Church of Christ Temple Lot. McLellin purchased land and settled in Saline County, Missouri, in 1867. Porter, "Odyssey of William Earl McLellin," 349.

1834, the Whitmers had also apparently come to believe that it was time to renew the effort. The end of the Civil War apparently signaled that the time of cleansing had ended, as alluded to in Whitmer's 1861 revelation. Others throughout the larger Mormon movement apparently had similar interpretations. In 1867, Granville Hedrick initiated the gathering of his followers to Jackson County, no doubt influencing McLellin's own mounting interest in gathering. Enthusiastically, but perhaps not accurately, he reported, "John [Whitmer] declared that he was going to sell out and move to Zion. That will stir up the balance of them."[28] However, John never acted on this intention if, in fact, it represented his feelings.

In February 1870, William McLellin paid a third visit to David Whitmer, only to find him less supportive. Somewhat disappointed, McLellin wrote to a correspondent: "David says the Lord tells him, 'When I want you I will call You.'"

William E. McLellin, ca. 1875. Courtesy of the LDS Church History Library.

28. Ibid.

CHAPTER THIRTY

A Passing Generation

D URING THE EARLY 1870s, John's beloved wife, Sarah M. Jackson Whitmer, grew ill and was gradually confined to bed. In March 1871, a letter from John to his "Dear Children" thanks their daughter Sarah Elizabeth and their son-in-law James Johnson, for a recent letter, accompanied in each case by "a Valentine which were gratefully received." He confessed, "Mother would be glad to answer your Letters, but does not feel able to [wright] <write> with pen and Ink as yet. Therefore you will have to be contented with the foregoing Scriblings [sic] of your old Fathers for I am a poor hand to write on family matters." He added some details: "Our health [s are] <is> slowly improving, I have not been bedfast. Mother is so that she sets up some her complaint, Inflamation [sic] of the Urether of the Bladder."[1] In those days before antibiotics or more than basic surgical procedures, such "inflammation" was probably age-related and, hence, was not likely to improve.

John and Sarah's children lived in Missouri much of their lives, and most of that time was spent at Far West.[2] The farm of John and Sarah's son,

---

1. John Whitmer to Dear Children [Sarah Elizabeth and James Johnson], 1 March 1871.

2. Black, *LDS Membership of the Church of Jesus Christ of Latter-day Saints*, 45:3, lists the five children as Nancy Jane Whitmer (died shortly after birth), John Oliver Whitmer (died at age ten), Sarah Elizabeth Whitmer, Jacob David Jackson [sic, Jefferson]Whitmer, and Alexander Peter Jefferson [sic, Jackson] Whitmer (killed during the Civil War). Jenson, *LDS Biographical Encyclopedia*, 1:252, notes that Sarah Johnson lived in Far West on the old Whitmer homestead, a short distance east of Jacob D. Whitmer's residence. Ethel Johnson Lewellen, a niece of Ella Johnson, wrote to C. Edward Miller, on May 26, 1932: "Sarah Elizabeth Whitmer was born in her father's hotel at far west near where the [RLDS] church stands…. [Her daughter] Ella E. Johnson was born March 23, 1857, and departed this life February 25, 1932. She was the daughter of James Edward [Johnson] and Sarah Elizabeth Whitmer Johnson. She had one brother John Edward Johnson. She was born in far west Mo. The house she was born in was torn

Jacob David Jefferson, usually referred to as Jacob D., or Jake, included the temple site.

Sarah Elizabeth had been born at Far West in the family hotel in 1836. She lived there most of her young life, except for a brief period spent in Richmond after Joseph Smith loyalists had forced the dissenting Whitmers out. Her marriage to the intriguing Maryland surveyor, James Edward Johnson, had produced a son and a daughter; but he proved unreliable. At some point that has not been preserved in the record, James abandoned his family—going off to Arkansas, Oklahoma, and elsewhere. Sarah Elizabeth initiated divorce proceedings and, in 1870, moved back to her parents' home in Far West with her two children.[3] Sarah's daughter, Ella, turned thirteen that year, and her younger son, John, was seven.

Sarah Elizabeth's divorce from James Edward Johnson was finalized in 1871.[4] Among the family papers are three letters from Johnson to John Whitmer, trying to establish contact with Sarah Elizabeth and their children. John wrote back only once and obviously offered no encouragement about an ongoing relationship. The first letter that has survived is from J. Edward Johnson to John Whitmer, written from St. Louis, on November 27, 1872:

> Sir I received a letter from you about the 1st of September which I answered a short time after enclosing contract between Whitman & Law and myself have not heard from you since I think it a matter of sufficient importance to acknowledge receipt of I would also like to have you write me the state of the heath of my children from time to time I cannot send them any money this year But will as soon as I can obtain it—I have not made any money for three years that I have collected—I expect to engage in business here next month—my address for the present is 923 Salisbury Street, St Louis—Tell my children I send my love to them and that I am not very well having had several of my old spells yesterday and for a week back Respectfully J. Edward Johnson

---

down several years ago. It was a two-room house with large fireplace. The larger house she lived in was built be [by] her grandfather John Whitmer. He star[t]ed it in 1856 and completed it in 1857. John Whitmer and his wife both died there."

3.   Pollard and Woods, *Whitmer Memoirs*, 29, 35.

4.   Ethel Johnson Lewellen to C. Edward Miller, 26 May 1932.

Sarah Maria (Jackson) Whitmer, 1809–73, ca. 1870. Courtesy of Lorene Pollard.

Sarah Elizabeth (Whitmer) Johnson Kerr at Far West, Missouri, ca. 1910s. Courtesy of the LDS Church History Library.

P.S. I would like to have Elly correspond with me that would save any one else the trouble—I have written her several letters in the last year but never received a line in response and only one letter from any of you for 15 months I think she should keep up a correspondence with me as she is my nearest relative able to write and it might be to her further interest to do so—[5]

Johnson's next letter, only a month later on December 20, 1872, suggests that he saw himself as having a fairly positive relationship with his father-in-law. In it, James again asks John to encourage Sarah Elizabeth to write.

Dr Sir Yours of the 15th inst. come to hand this morning and contents noted—I am more than pleased to think to know that you saw sufficient to answer my letter of the 26th ult.—so far as to let me know

5.   James Edward Johnson to John Whitmer, 27 November 1872.

my children were well and going to school and in proving [*sic*] in their studies—But I would like Ella to write me.... Although divorced—my children's & my wifes interest to me are the same as if I ever had been Give my love to my children & all enquiring of me—I shall be at Far West as soon as my business give me ready money to provide for those I love best. J. Edw. Johnson[6]

In 1873, Johnson tried in two successive letters, to persuade John to bring the children to visit him in St. Louis and also offered to help John consolidate his Far West land holdings.[7] John did not encourage James on either proposition, even though James appeared to know a great deal about John's business activities.

The next important family event was the marriage of John and Sarah's only surviving son, Jacob D. Whitmer, who married Celia Ann Tattershall on April 27, 1871.[8] Their wedding occurred on the "sly," as Jake confided to his sister, Sarah Elizabeth. Celia Ann had been born in Hornellsville, New York, and the Tattershall family had moved to Far West in 1868.

Meanwhile, Sarah's health grew steadily worse. Perhaps Sarah Whitmer's last great joys were having her daughter's care during her final illness, being able to have her grandchildren with her, and the marriage of her last surviving son. Sarah died October 15, 1873, in their frame home at Far West.[9] She was sixty-four years old.

Lorene Pollard wrote of her great-grandmother Sarah Elizabeth: "With her two children, she felt she must find a way to raise enough funds to care for them on her own. After consulting with her parents, she decided to raise chickens. Sarah excelled at this venture, ultimately raising very

6. Ibid., 20 December 1872.

7. Ibid., 16 May and 1 August 1873: "It might be for your interest to write to me as I hold the patents for the land bought by you from Garner—I send you the one which I consider belongs to you herewith—I have had some business transactions lately which if you will write to me will enable you to obtain the Patents on all the land which you now have not got.... I am not well.... I want to settle my business in Caldwell therefore write you. If you will write me in the right spirit it will greatly be to your advantage as by so doing you can through me get the Patent to the balance of your Phelps land in Sec 10 & 11."

8. Barchers, "The Descendants and History of the Peter Whitmer Family," 44. Jacob D. Whitmer added a postscript to John Whitmer to Dear Children, 1 March 1871.

9. Ethel Johnson Lewellen to C. Edward Miller, 26 May 1932.

beautiful and selective breeds of chickens.... They shipped eggs to people by mail. Others would come from miles around by horse and buggy to buy fertile eggs for hatching."[10]

For almost five years, John Whitmer continued to live on the old homestead comforted by the presence of his daughter, her children, and his son and his wife, who had no children at that point. Although John had a retiring disposition and did not seek the public eye, he remained steadfast in his testimony of the Book of Mormon. Though he participated in relatively few interviews, especially compared to David, he left a clear documentary record of his position relative to the book.

In 1873, old-time Saint Zenas H. Gurley, who was now affiliated with the Reorganization, visited John at Far West. Gurley recalled: "[John] Whitmer, at the time of the visit was receiving many letters from strangers, far and near. His characteristic answer to one of them was, 'My testimony was true, is true, and will remain forever.'"[11]

John Whitmer during the last decade of his life, ca. 1870. Courtesy of Lorene Pollard.

John was a man of relatively few words throughout his life. Only a handful of his writings provide insight into his thoughts and beliefs. His sparse writings in the *Messenger and Advocate* suggest anxiety over one's ability to recognize God's church from all others. John seems to struggle with this question again and again throughout his life. His letters from late in life are, like his manuscript history, typically short and concise. They portray a resolute, yet reserved individual, wishing to avoid notoriety,

10. Pollard and Woods, *Whitmer Memoirs*, 35.

11. Zenas H. Gurley's 1872 visit to the Whitmers is related in his "Synopsis of a Discourse, Delivered at Lamoni, Iowa," 371.

but also willing to speak out when the situation required. John appears to have agreed with his brother David about the need to return to primitive Mormonism and reclaim the church's earliest name, the Church of Christ. John's subsequent participation in attempts to refashion what he had so sadly lost in 1838 suggests the unresolved yearnings of a lonely man.

Whatever his spiritual longings, however, it must have given him great satisfaction to contemplate the transformation of the once-abandoned site of Far West under his careful husbandry. A visitor from nearby Cameron, Missouri, writing under the pen name Viator, described the differences he saw in Far West between the early 1860s and 1875:

> It was in this glorious season of the year, on the third day of last October, that, in company with Major A. T. Baubie, one of the first founders, and today, a leading citizen of the enterprising and flourishing young city of Cameron, we [he is using the editorial "we"] started on a tour of exploration to the deserted town of Far West in Caldwell county. Directing our course southward over a fair prairie road, we were struck with the beauty and excellence of the improvements that had developed in the past few years: well appearing and substantial residences, long rows of well kept and squarely cut hedges; young orchards, with the unmistakable promise of abundant fruit, all attested the thrift, enterprise and good taste of the settlers that had thus improved a territory which but a few years ago, was prairie and red brush.
>
> Drawing up to the door of the first farm house, we inquired: "How far are we from Far West?" "You are right in the middle of the public square," was the reply that greeted our astonished ears, "And where is the Mormon Temple?" "About two hundred yards ahead in a corn-field by the side of the road." So indeed we were. But what a change in the past twelve or thirteen years! Where all was solitude and melancholy evidence of complete and absolute desertion, were now well-improved farms, roads and fences. How many metamorphoses has the once stirring but now almost forgotten site of historic Far West undergone in the past thirty years!
>
> Advancing about a quarter of a mile we arrived at the pleasant residence of J. W. [*sic*] Whitmer, the pioneer settler of the locality, on whose farm is located the foundation of the Temple before referred to. Mr. Whitmer, by whom we were hospitably entertained, is an old

gentleman of fine intelligence and possessed of a fund of information in reference to Far West, for which we would vainly seek elsewhere.[12]

John's financial status, as reflected by his 1875 tax assessment, also provides evidence of his industry and thrift:

6 horses $235, 1 Mule or Ass, $20.45 Cattle $646, sheep 190 $213, hogs 5 $12 total $1126 Money, notes bonds and other credits $295 All other personal property $145 total valuation $1566

I John Whitmer do solemnly swear that the foregoing list contains a true and correct list of all the personal Property made Taxable.[13]

Joshua Davis of Provo, Utah, passing through upper Missouri in March 1875, visited John and stayed with him "one night and part of two days." John informed him that the winter of 1874–75 "has been the coldest known in that region within the memory of the oldest inhabitants.... [O]wing to drouth [*sic*] and the ravages of the cinch bug the last two seasons many of the people are bordering on starvation; the farmers in numerous instances are also without seed grain and potatoes, and teams, having lost their stock through the intense cold."[14] John did not express personal concerns, and the two men "spent most of their time in conversing about Mormonism." John affirmed his testimony of the Book of Mormon with uplifted hand. "I, with my own eyes, saw the plates from which the Book of Mormon was translated, and I also saw an angel who witnessed to the truth of the Book of Mormon." Davis also reported that John was interested in the activities of Mormons in Utah, especially their missionary work among Native Americans. "He was agreeably surprised to hear that Martin Harris, another of the three witnesses to the Book of Mormon, was living in Cache county, Utah, at the advanced age of ninety years." "Mr. Whitmer inquired if the Prophet Joseph Smith ever gave a revelation on the subject of celestial marriage, and, on receiving an answer in the affirmative, requested ... a copy of it." Davis concluded: "John Whitmer has become an

12. "Far West: The Old Mormon Settlement in Missouri."
13. John Whitmer, personal property assessment list, 1875.
14. Davis, "A Visit to John Whitmer," 655.

extensive landed proprietor, and now resides upon his property in the City of Far West."[15]

Only four months later, Martin Harris died on July 10, 1875, in Clarkson, Cache County, Utah. His death advanced John's standing in the shrinking circle of Book of Mormon witnesses, which now consisted only of him and his brother, David.

David Whitmer had also prospered during this period. On July 19, 1873, the *Richmond Conservator* reported: "Whitmer & Son have been adding to their livery stock, and have now some of the best rigs in this section, and it gives them pleasure to furnish a stylish turnout to parties that know what a good horse is. We have tried the 'Old Reliable,' for a number of years and have always

Martin Harris remained in the vicinity of Kirtland, Ohio, until 1870, and then moved to Utah. Harris died on July 10, 1875, in Clarkson, Cache County, Utah. Courtesy of the LDS Church History Library.

found Uncle Davy with a team that never fails to give satisfaction."[16] At this point, David was sharing business responsibilities with his son, David John Whitmer, who handled the day-to-day management of the livery operation.[17] The livery's weekly advertisement in the Richmond newspaper reads:

> Livery and Feed Stable, Richmond, MO.
> Whitmer & Son, are prepared at any and all times to accommodate the public with Hacks, Buggies and Saddle Horses.
> We convey passengers to any point desired at a moment's notice.
> Horses boarded by the day, week or month.

15. Ibid.
16. "Whitmer & Son Have Been Adding to Their Livery Stock," *Richmond Conservator*, July 19, 1873.
17. "An Old Citizen Passes Away," *Richmond Conservator*, January 26, 1888, reprinted in Cook, *David Whitmer Interviews*, 225.

One of the frequent advertisements for Dave Whitmer & Co. which appeared in the Richmond Conservator *during the 1870s and 1880s. Courtesy of the Richmond, Missouri, public library.*

Constructed around 1879, David Whitmer's livery stable was located on the southwest corner of Franklin and Thornton Streets, near the public square in Richmond, Missouri. Photo by Pearl Wilcox, ca. 1950s. Courtesy of Community of Christ Archives.

Hearse and Carriages for Funerals.
Customers may rely on promptness, good turnouts, safe horses
and moderate charges.
Stable near the Shaw House.[18]

The Whitmer Livery provided transportation around Richmond when needed as well as to and from the nearby railroad junction at Henrietta, Missouri. In 1874, David and David John saw an opportunity to expand their business by instituting two daily trips to the station:

> Whitmer & Son, and Thos. L. Shaw, have placed their hacks on the road, and will hereafter run a line of hacks between this city and R. & L. Junction, and will make connections with all trains on the N.M. Road, at the latter place, east and west, both morning and evening. For a safe comfortable ride to the Junction and back commend us to Whitmer & Son, or Tom Shaw.[19]

David also enjoyed a local reputation as a successful horse breeder and trotter horse racer.

> Dave Whitmer [is taking his mare Nellie] to the St. Joseph Exposition, which begins on September 7th [1874] and continues for one week, and will leave with her on Monday next for St. Joseph. Nellie is a magnificent animal, a rich chestnut sorrel, 16 hands high, long back, short coupling, well muscled, and is a perfect picture of a trotting animal, and we predict that she will throw dust in somebody's eyes at the Exposition, as she is hard to head on the trot, and is a regular rattler. We wish Dave success.[20]

David's daughter Julia Ann Whitmer had married Julius Schweich October 24, 1852, and returned to her parents' house about 1860 after Julius deserted his family. Julia Ann made her home with her parents through the 1870s, an arrangement that was doubtless congenial for David, who turned seventy in 1875, and his wife, Julia Ann, who turned sixty that same year. Josephine ("Josie") Helen Schweich was Julia Ann's daughter and David's and Julia Ann's granddaughter. The local paper took note of her activities

---

18. "Livery and Feed Stable," 4.
19. "Whitmer and Son," 3.
20. "Dave Whitmer," 3.

David Whitmer's granddaughter, Josephine "Josie" Helen Schweich, taught school in the southern part of Richmond, Missouri, in the Richmond High School. The high school was held in the former Richmond College building. Courtesy of the Richmond, Missouri, public library.

David Whitmer's granddaughter, Josephine "Josie" Helen Schweich, 1856–1937, daughter of Julius and Julia Ann Whitmer Schweich. Courtesy of Community of Christ Archives.

twice during this period. In 1874 the *Richmond Conservator* reported, "Miss Josie Schweich, who has been visiting friends in Atchison, Kansas, for the past three weeks, has returned home, highly delighted with her visit, we welcome her back, as does [*sic*] hosts of other friends."[21] Two years later the *Richmond Conservator* again noted:

> We are pleased to learn that Miss Josie Schweich, has accepted a position in our college, as one of Prof. Huffaker's corps of teachers. Miss Josie is one of the graduates of the college; a young lady of rare literary attainment, and will prove a valuable acquisition to the school, as she is thoroughly acquainted with the duties of the position. It is more in the right direction for the Board to fill vacancies occasioned by resignation, by the appointment of graduates from the school.[22]

Josie later married James R. B. Van Cleave, a newspaper reporter and, subsequently, a politician in Illinois.

Julia Alice Page Floyd, David Whitmer's grandniece and granddaughter of Hiram Page, recalled that David "would spend hours at the livery whittling. He would have neighborhood boys bring him blocks of sugar maple, a very hard wood, and he would cut items from this wood for his friends—butter paddles, spoons, etc."[23]

Although his advancing age brought with it more leisure time than he had known for many years, David still hoped to once again see the church reestablished as he had known it during his early years with the Mormon movement. As he sensed the inevitable end of life for him and his brother John, he felt an increased urgency about his calling and, in the fall of 1875, took steps to establish what he called the Church of Christ,

21. "Miss Josie Schweich," 3.
22. "We Are Pleased to Learn That Miss Josie Schweich," 3. The institution of learning mentioned in this notice is Richmond College, founded in 1851, located on a prominent hill in the southern portion of Richmond. But the building had become the public high school by the time Josie Schweich was a student. She graduated from high school in 1874 and began teaching there as a primary teacher during the 1876–77 school year. My thanks to Linda Emley, local Ray County historian, for information about Richmond College. Emley, "If Postcards Could Talk," 8; see also *History of Ray County, Missouri*, 356, 357.
23. Julia A. Page, interview by Ebbie Richardson, ca. 1952, in Richardson, "David Whitmer," 22.

based on his cherished religious principles. He now claimed his right as Smith's successor by virtue of his 1834 ordination; and the small congregation, which consisted largely of family members, began meeting just south of Richmond in the King school-house.

In 1875, David ordained his forty-year-old nephew, John Christian Whitmer, the son of Jacob Whitmer and Elizabeth Schott Whitmer, to serve as the movement's first elder.[24] John L. Traughber, a member of the RLDS church and collector of historical memorabilia, was considering compiling a biography of William McLellin. Traughber's family farm was not far from Richmond, Missouri, allowing him access to the Whitmers while gathering material about McLellin. Traughber recorded:

John C. Whitmer, 1876–94, son of Jacob Whitmer and first elder of the Whitmerite church, in Richmond, Missouri. Courtesy of Community of Christ Archives.

> In 1874, or 1875, he [David] claimed that God had again commanded him to act, and he took his nephew, John Christian Whitmer, who was a member of the Disciples church, and baptized and ordained him, and told him to go ahead and baptize and ordain others, and thus rebuild the church. Of course, so great a thing must have something of the miraculous in it to give it coloring; hence, John claims that he was inspirationally led to go to David to seek baptism, while David was in the same way prepared to be ready for him, having told his son that John would be there that day.[25]

---

24. Izora Dear (daughter of John C. Whitmer), statement to Ebbie Richardson, cited in ibid., 134.

25. Traughber, "David Whitmer: 'The Last Witness,'" 24.

According to LDS members, Andrew Jenson, Edward Stevenson, and Joseph S. Black, who visited John Christian Whitmer in 1888, John C. told them:

> He was baptized by his uncle, David Whitmer, September 15th, 1875, and by him also ordained an Elder January 28th, 1876, receiving instructions to go forth and preach the Gospel as it had been taught by Joseph the Prophet and organize a new church according to the original pattern, in which he [John C.] was to be the first Elder. In obedience to this he immediately commenced his labours and succeeded in baptizing the first three individuals on the following February 17th, [1876]. Others followed and soon the new church commenced to hold meetings and completed their organization as far as their members would permit them.[26]

In 1882, David Whitmer reflected on this initiative to a correspondent: "A few years ago I was moved upon to ordain Elders for the purpose of being prepared to administer in all the Holy ordinances of the house of God which I did."[27] However, the movement never attracted more than a small group of Whitmer's associates in Richmond, Missouri, and a few believers in the Kirtland, Ohio, area.

Old-time Saints and curiosity seekers regularly approached John at his home in Far West. E. C. Brand, an elder in the Reorganization, left the following account of his visit to John Whitmer on February 18, 1875, at Far West: "He also bore his tes-

David Whitmer initiated a restoration of the Church of Christ, commonly known as the Whitmerite church, ca. 1870s. Courtesy of Community of Christ Archives.

---

26. Jenson, Stevenson, and Black, "Historical Landmarks," 7, excerpt quoted as "Sayings of John C. Whitmer," 651.

27. David Whitmer to J. B. Price, 9 July 1882.

timony to me concerning the truth, and declared that his testimony, as found in the 'Testimony of Eight Witnesses,' in the Book of Mormon, is strictly true. He showed me a facsimile of the characters of the plates, copied from the plates in the handwriting of Joseph Smith. Both of these men (David and John) are respectable, and looked up to as truthful, honorable men, in the vicinity where they live."[28]

In the fall of 1875, John H. Beadle, a Mormon critic, visited northwestern Missouri and took special pains to inquire about former Mormon notables. Remarking sarcastically that "it seems as good as a life insurance to have been engaged in the Mormon war on either side," Beadle noted: "John Whitmer, brother of David and one of the 'eight witnesses,' lives near old Far West and is [one of] the wealthiest men in that vicinity, owning 700 acres of land in one body, cattle upon a thousand hills, and ready money in abundance. Evidently the 'curse' has missed him on a fair point blank range. But the 'Lord' may snatch him bald-headed yet, before 1890 and the return of the Saints. So it won't do to count too much on his case."[29]

In March 1876, Mark H. Forscutt, a member of the Reorganized church and friend of its president, Joseph Smith III, wrote to John asking for information about Oliver Cowdery and the whereabouts of his widow, Elizabeth Ann. In June 1887, RLDS leaders obtained a questionable title to the Temple Lot in Independence from Oliver and Elizabeth Ann's daugh-

28. The piece of paper containing the Caractors mentioned by Brand is in the CofC Archives. Some scholars believe that Joseph Smith drew the characters, but only the word Caractors is in English, so there is little to compare with Smith's handwriting. There are also others who believe it is in the handwriting of John Whitmer. See MacKay, Dirkmaat, and Jensen, "The 'Caractors' Document: New Light on an Early Transcription on the Book of Mormon Characters;" also, MacKay, et al, *Joseph Smith Papers Documents, Vol. 1, July 1828–June 1831*. However, new research suggests it may actually be in the hand of Christian Whitmer. Metcalfe and Metcalfe, "Who Wrote the Book of Mormon 'Caractor.'" For further discussion of the Caractors, see appendix Y. Brand, statement regarding visit to John Whitmer, 18 February 1875; see also John Whitmer to Heman C. Smith, 11 December 1876: "Your letter came to hand, and your requests considered. First. As for giving all particulars that I know of the Book of Mormon, could not be written on one sheet of paper; therefore, permit me to be brief. Second. From what you have written, I conclude you have read the Book of Mormon, together with the testimonies that are thereto attached; in which testimonies you read my name subscribed as one of the Eight witnesses to said Book. That testimony was, is, and will be true henceforth and forever. Respectfully yours. John Whitmer."

29. Beadle, "Jackson County: The Early History of the Saints and Their Enemies," 4.

ter Maria Louise and her husband, John Johnson. Forscutt's letter may have been prompted by the desire to check into the title's provenance as an early stage of anticipated legal action.[30]

John answered Forscutt with characteristic brevity and a certain amount of strategic vagueness that was doubtless based on a desire to shield Elizabeth Ann from what must have been frequent inquiries: "I hasten to answer according to best of my information at hand. Mrs. Cowdery Resides some place in Colorado. The address is mislaid, or I would give it." In point of fact, Elizabeth Ann was living with Maria Louise and her husband in Colorado, and John would certainly have been able to find her address if he had wished.

Forscutt had apparently asked about Oliver Cowdery's testimony of the Book of Mormon, for John replied:

> I think I am able to answer your enquiries to your satisfaction. Oliver Cowdery lived in Richmond, Mo., some 40 miles from here at the time of his death. I went to see him and I was with him for some days previous to his demise.
>
> I have never heard him deny the truth of his testimony of the Book of Mormon under any circumstances what ever.
>
> I have no knowledge that there was any effort made to force him to deny the Book of Mormon. Neither do I believe that he would have denied at the peril of his life, so firm was he that he could not be moved to deny what he has affirmed to be a divine revelation from God.

John then generalized his response, affirming the faithfulness of all of the Book of Mormon witnesses: "I desire to do good when it is in my power. I have never heard that anyone of the three or eight witnesses ever denied the testimony that they have borne to the book as published in the first edition of the Book of Mormon." With mingled sadness and pride, John added: "There are only two of the witnesses to that book now living

---

30. Maria Johnson's quit claim deed was only a small piece of a potentially much larger legal puzzle. The Church of Christ Temple Lot's claim to the Temple Lot was based on a similar quit claim deed obtained from Lydia Partridge, widow of early church bishop Edward Partridge, in the 1840s upon Brigham Young's advice. Lydia used the money she obtained in exchange for the quit claim to move her family to Utah. The Church of Christ Temple Lot averred that the RLDS church's case was based upon a fake title obtained from Cowdery's descendants.

to wit. David Whitmer one of the three and John Whitmer one of the eight."[31]

In December 1877, William Lewis, an RLDS member from Stewartsville, DeKalb County, Missouri, interviewed John and sent a letter describing the visit to the *Saints' Herald.* Asked if he still believed in the gathering, John answered, "Yes; and all that God has promised will be fulfilled. Jackson County, Missouri, is the place, and will be the final home of the saints." Lewis then asked whether John thought he would yet be among the Saints to return to Jackson County. This inquiry deeply moved John, who replied "with tears running down his cheeks, and he could hardly speak from crying. At last he did say, wiping the tears off, that the day would come when we would see eye to eye. I can say this for Father Whitmer; that he manifested a good spirit, and did not try to discourage us, but to encourage." Lewis concluded: "Father Whitmer is seventy-four years old and is quite smart," a term that, in the nineteenth century, meant "lively and alert."[32]

In 1878, another RLDS member, writing under the pseudonym of I. C. Funn, reported to a local newspaper that he had attended a service, held Sunday at 11:00 a.m. at the Far West schoolhouse, where John "delivered the discourse.... Mr. Whitmer is considered a truthful, honest and law-abiding citizen by this community, and consequentially, his appointment drew out a large audience. Mr. Whitmer stated that he had often handled the identical golden plates which Mr. Smith received from the hand of the angel, he said it was of pure gold, part of the book was sealed up solid, the other part was open and it was this part which was translated, and is termed today the Mormon Bible. This is the first time Mr. Whitmer has attempted to preach for a good many years; and time, who waits for no one, has written many a furrow upon his brow. He is upwards of sixty years [actually seventy-five years] old, and gave some good advice to both old and young."[33]

In 1877, the local paper noted that David's other grandchild, George Schweich, had assumed David's duties at the livery stable. "George Sch-

31. John Whitmer to M[ark H]. Forest [Forscutt], 5 March 1876.

32. Lewis, "Correspondence," *Herald,* 24:381–82.

33. I. C. Funn [pseud.] to *Kingston Sentinel,* as quoted in "Editors," *Salt Lake Herald,* January 12, 1878, and reprinted in *Herald,* 25:57.

Damage from a tornado that ravaged Richmond, Missouri, in June 1878. Courtesy of the Ray County Historical Society, Richmond, Missouri.

weich now holds forth at Whitmers' Old Reliable Livery Stable, he having taken charge of his Uncle [*sic*] Dave's interest in that establishment, and will be pleased to see his friends when they want a stylish rig or a good riding horse."[34]

In June 1878, a tornado ravaged Richmond, destroying the Whitmer livery. A new livery building was constructed on the southwest corner of Franklin and Thornton near the square in Richmond. "The livery stable of Messrs. Whitmer & Co. is one of the most complete in the upper country, having been recently rebuilt and enlarged."[35]

The establishment continued running weekly advertisements in the Richmond paper, with a slight adjustment to the company name. By now, it was doing business as Dave Whitmer & Co. The *Richmond Conservator* reported:

> D. Whitmer, G. W. L. Schweich, The Old Reliable, Livery and Feed Stable.

34. "George Schweich," 3.
35. "The Livery Stable of Messrs. Whitmer & Co.," 3.

Dave Whitmer & Co., Proprietors, Richmond, MO. are prepared at any and all times to accommodate the public with Hacks, Buggies and Saddle Horses! Will convey passengers to any point desired at a moment's notice. Horses boarded by the day, week or month, on reasonable term. Customers may rely on promptness, good turnouts, and safe horses and moderate charges. Stable near the Shaw House.[36]

In April 1878, both John and David were interviewed by Peter Wilhelm Poulson, a physician who was traveling cross country. Of David, Poulson observed, "In company with a son and grandson, Mr. Whitmer keeps a livery and feed stable at Richmond, Mo., the old grandfather is principally relieved from business, but he makes his regular trips down to the stables, and [arrives] to the minute as in olden times."[37] The grandson Poulson mentioned was George Schweich, the son of Julia Ann Whitmer Schweich.

In addition to Poulson's medical background, he was interested in psychoanalysis and spiritualism. Interviewing David and John Whitmer would have been an intriguing exercise for someone drawing upon the insights of these particular scholarly disciplines. His interests in spiritualism prompted him to probe John's and David's perceptions of their experiences as Book of Mormon witnesses with the evident goal of determining whether it had been a natural or supernatural experience. In his interview with John, Poulson asked:

Did you handle the plates with your hands?

He-I did so!

I-Then they were a material substance?

He-Yes, as material as anything can be.[38]

At the time of this interview, John was fully feeling his age and confided to Poulson "that he should not live and see the coming of Christ nor the restoration of Zion in Jackson County, Mo." But John did not appear sorrowful about this limitation, telling Poulson that Joseph Smith once gave him a blessing that he would "'live to a good old age, and ... walk over

---

36. "Dave Whitmer & Co.," 4.

37. Poulson, "Correspondence: Death of John Whitmer," 2.

38. Ibid.

the ashes of all thy enemies. Then you shall sleep with your fathers, and meet the Lord, when he cometh in the clouds.' Now, said John Whitmer, with evident satisfaction, 'I have lived to a good old age, and I have walked over the ashes of every single one of my enemies.'"[39] For nearly thirty years, John had, indeed, walked over and worked the ground of Far West, a literal reclamation of the former habitation of his adversaries.

As John approached the end of his life he must have been acutely aware that many of his religious hopes and dreams would not come to fruition during his lifetime. But as a community builder who had also been involved in the founding of two religious movements, the best he had to pass on to his son, Jacob David Whitmer, were his religious principles and his farm, which included the Far West Temple lot. About three decades after John's death, in 1909, Jacob D. sold the temple site and the surrounding property to the LDS church.[40]

39. Ibid.

40. Lorene Pollard, "Notes of a Talk and Subsequent Conversation with Ronald E. Romig," printout in my possession; Jacob D. moved with his son Harry to Kansas circa 1915 and then to Smithton, Pettis, Missouri, by 1919. Jacob is listed in the 1920 census with Harry and his family in Smithton. Jacob's wife died in 1912 and he died in 1921. Thanks to Erin Jennings Metcalfe for providing this information about Jacob D.'s later life. Erin Jennings Metcalfe, e-mail to author, March 22, 2013.

CHAPTER THIRTY-ONE

Death of the Eighth Witness

D AVID AND JULIA ANN finished raising their family in their Richmond home and were now growing old. Oliver Cowdery had entrusted David with the printer's manuscript of the Book of Mormon when
he died in 1850. David kept it in an old stagecoach trunk under his bed in
a room at the back of the house.[1]

In June 1878, a tornado roared through the southeastern portion of
Richmond. Mrs. Izora Dear claimed the wind was so severe that a ring
blown off the finger of George Schweich was embedded into a wall of the
livery stable. He found it there sometime after the disaster.[2] The tornado
destroyed nearly all of David and Julia Ann's home, except for part of the
back bedroom where the printer's manuscript was kept.

The *Richmond Conservator* reported the impact of the cyclone upon
Richmond:

> A Cyclone struck our city yesterday, at 4:05 p.m.; and in the short
> space of five minutes totally destroyed one third of the place.... Being
> nearly three squares wide ... [the tornado traveled] for over a mile in
> the city.... We noticed its approach from our office balcony, our atten-
> tion being attracted by its peculiar shape, that of a funnel, the small
> end down, the color of steam. At times it would break, emitting vol-
> umes of what appeared to be black smoke, then gather together again
> and assume its funnel like proportions, the wind all the while being
> attracted towards it. It came on slowly, not much faster than a man

1. Two extant trunks belonging to David Whitmer are candidates for the mentioned
   stagecoach trunk. One, covered in horse hair and bearing the initials D. W. on the lid, is
   housed at the LDS Museum of Church History in Salt Lake City, Utah, and the other,
   a leather trunk, is at the Community of Christ Museum in Independence, Missouri.

2. Izora Dear, interview by Ebbie Richardson, in Richardson, "David Whitmer," 19.

could walk, destroying everything by its infernal whirl, producing a sound like the roar of Niagara, creating a panic.... [Along with many other buildings] the Presbyterian and Baptist churches are a complete wreck, as well as the Shaw House, Whitmer's Livery Stable and the stone Calaboose.[3]

David Whitmer's home was among seventy-five or more residences also destroyed. The *Richmond Conservator* provided a list of those killed and injured. Among those on this list we find: "[David Whitmer relatives, (injured)] George Schweich, wife and baby .... and David Whitmer, seriously injured." An estimate of losses includes the "estate of Jacob Whitmer, house and outbuildings, loss $12.50.... George W. Schweich, house and furniture destroyed, $2000.... Whitmer & Co., livery stable, damage $1500.... David Whitmer, house and furniture destroyed, damage $1500."[4]

Another local paper, *Ray Chronicle*, described the widespread damage: "Language is too poor to adequately describe the desolation and ruin of Richmond. Within a few moments, a third of the town was made desolate. Five hundred persons made homeless with many of them left penniless. Richmond is in grief and mourning. We have buried twelve bodies of our good citizens." Speaking of the David Whitmer home, the paper reported: "The buildings all around it were torn to atoms, [but] it is an interesting fact that the room in which the original manuscript of the Book of Mormon was kept was uninjured, although the building itself was damaged."[5]

LDS member Edwin Gordon Woolley traveled to Richmond in 1882 where Mr. Hughes, a local banker, introduced him to David Whitmer. David was:

> Confined to his bed, having been severely injured in a cyclone that passed over his home a short time previously, doing considerable damage to that building and others of the neighborhood. The wind had struck the main portion of the home, but had not done any real damage to a small side room that contained the original "Printer's" copy of the translated portion of the Book of Mormon. In addition to that

---

3.   "Terrific Cyclone," in Curtis, "A Hometown Perspective on the 1878 Richmond Tornado," 7, 8.

4.   Ibid, 2.

5.   *Ray Chronicle*, June 3, 1878, quoted in Richardson, "David Whitmer," 19.

manuscript, the room contained a large number of books, including early editions of the Book of Mormon, some manuscripts and other relics of the early days of the church. The "printer's" manuscript was shown to us. It was written in a plain, but clear, small hand, on paper about like foolscap. We were also shown a piece of paper and we were told that the paper had been taken by Martin Harris and shown to Professor Anthon.[6]

Woolley added some details about David's injuries: "David himself was in an outhouse at the time and was found senseless."[7]

Another account of the tornado comes from Utah Mormon James H. Hart, who reported in 1883 that "the Whitmer house was all destroyed, except for the small room in which the said documents were kept, in which not a window was broken."[8] Hart added that David Whitmer's son, David J., had met an unbelieving scoffer in the street a few minutes after the catastrophe who asked, "'Well Dave, how about those records?' and I told him they were all right, although I had not then had an opportunity to look after them. My father was hurt by the flying timber, for the house on the west side of the road was blown through ours ... but when matters had subsided a little and we had examined the room and the box where the manuscript was kept we found it to our satisfaction as we had left it."[9]

John's daughter, Sarah Elizabeth, visited Richmond soon after the tornado to check on the family's situation. After John's death in July 1878, she wrote to P. Wilhelm Poulson and, in addition to the news of her father's death, included some details about the tornado: "I visited Richmond directly after the storm, and it was [a] sad-looking sight to behold." According to Sarah, by the end of July 1878, "Uncle David has about recovered from his injuries, and is out once more on the street."[10]

6. Woolley, autobiography, quoted in Cook, *David Whitmer Interviews*, 80–81. Woolley's description of his visit with David Whitmer is not dated, but Woolly indicated it occurred in 1882.

7. Ibid., 82.

8. David Whitmer, interview by James H. Hart, August 23, 1883, "David H. [*sic*] Whitmer, Etc.," 3, in Cook, *David Whitmer Interviews*, 97–99.

9. David Whitmer, interview by James H. Hart, August 23, 1883, 3.

10. Sarah Elizabeth Whitmer Johnson Kerr, quoted in Poulson, "Correspondence: Death of John Whitmer," 2.

David Whitmer corroborated the undamaged condition of the early records: "While I was camping around here in a tent, all my effects exposed to the weather, everything in my trunk became moldy, but the manuscript was preserved, not even being discolored."[11]

The tornado episode also provides important clues about the location of David Whitmer's livery stable. According to the local newspaper: "The Presbyterian and Baptist churches are a complete wreck, as well as the Shaw House, Whitmer's Livery Stable."[12] These buildings were obviously in close proximity. Julia Page, Hiram Page's granddaughter added that Philander Page, her father, "was caught in the 'big wind' in the street in front of the livery stable. He couldn't move forward at all so dropped on his knees and prayed for protection. All kinds of debris was blown on top of him so that when the storm was over, David, though injured, was obliged to dig him [Philander] out. He was uninjured; not a scratch upon him."[13]

Orson Pratt and Joseph F. Smith visited northwestern Missouri in September 1878 as part of a business trip to the East. They first called at Richmond where they visited David Whitmer. A newspaper clipping from the *St. Louis Times* reports: "The object of the elders' visit was to secure the [Book of Mormon printers] manuscript for deposit in the archives of the Mormon Church, but Whitmer declined to surrender it. It has been in his

---

11. David Whitmer, quoted in Wilcox, *Latter Day Saints on the Missouri Frontier*, 350. Many of the contents of David Whitmer's old stagecoach trunk, including the historic printer's manuscript and other valuable writings and mementos, were placed in the care of the Reorganized Church of Jesus Christ of Latter Day Saints on April 18, 1903, at Independence, Missouri. For acquisition information on Book of Commandments fragments, other manuscript revelations, the Book of Mormon printer's manuscript, John Whitmer's manuscript history, the Book of Mormon Caractors, and possibly the Thomas B. Marsh revelation, see Walter W. Smith to Samuel A. Burgess, 15 April 1926; Walter W. Smith to First Presidency, 14 September 1925; Frederick M. Smith to Oscar W. Newton, 20 June 1907. In 1953, the Blankmeyer family donated to the RLDS church additional historical materials and a trunk that belonged to David Whitmer. As noted above, another trunk, possibly the stagecoach trunk, covered with horsehair hide and bearing the initials D. W., is at the LDS Church History Museum in Salt Lake City.

12. "Terrific Cyclone," in Curtis, "A Hometown Perspective on the 1878 Richmond Tornado," 8.

13. Julia A. Page Hicks, quoted in Richardson, "David Whitmer," 19, 21.

custody nearly fifty [thirty] years, and he declared his intention of holding it until the proper time arrived for its surrender to those entitled to receive it."[14] However, according to the *Richmond Conservator*:

Last Saturday Elders Orson Pratt and J. F. Smith, two of the leading members of the Church of the Latter day Saints paid a visit to our city, and after taking in the ruin of the devastated district, inquired for David Whitmer, Esq., the only living witness of the translation of the Book of Mormon and custodian of the original manuscript [printers manuscript of the Book of Mormon], as taken down by Oliver Cowd[e]ry, and after repairing to his residence, at their request the manuscript was produced and Elder Pratt, who was familiar with the handwriting of Mr. Cowd[e]ry, at once pronounced the manuscript, as spread out on the table, the original [printer's] copy, and made an earnest request of Mr. Whitmer to surrender it to him, as he had been appointed to take charge of the archives of the church, and that should he do so that he [David Whitmer] would be rewarded for his care of it to any amount that he would name. But Mr. Whitmer, who had held it for near half a century, *the proper custodian*, refused to part with it on any terms, and after a pleasant conversation of about an hour they left with the request that he keep it safe.... The work is in a splendid state of preservation, the ink as bright as if written yesterday, and it is inscribed on large paper, unruled, in a small hand, clearly written, close to the edges, top and bottom, making over 500 pages.... Messrs. Pratt and Smith left Monday morning for Far West, Caldwell county, to look at the foundation of the temple that was started there before these peculiar people moved west ward."[15]

A clipping from a Kansas newspaper that David kept in his personal copy of the Book of Mormon suggests a possible motivation for the family's reluctance to sell the manuscript to the Mormon church. The Whitmers were strongly antipolygamous in their beliefs and saw the holograph as incontrovertible proof that Mormon doctrine had changed after they withdrew from the movement. The article observes: "One reason why the Mormon Church was so anxious about this document is shown in the ac-

14. "The Original [Copy of the] Book of Mormon," *St. Louis Times*, September 29, 1878.

15. "Valuable Manuscript," reprinted in Curtis, "A Hometown Perspective on the 1878 Richmond Tornado," 22.

companying facsimile reproduction of a portion of one of its pages ... taken from the second [*sic*] book of Jacob, sixth chapter.... [text omitted] The language of the first portion of this paragraph is so strong against the vice of polygamy that it would not bear reproduction here, but that which we have given proves that this doctrine is at direct variance with the teaching of the 'Divine Revelation [Book of Mormon].'"[16]

An article in the *St. Louis Republican* on the same date also speculated on Whitmer's motivation: "It was doubtless for fear that something might be done to the original record, either to interpolate it or strike out such passages as the above, that has caused him to watch with a jealous eye every move made by the elders of the Utah church. As to the custody of the book, he thinks it should be held by him and his descendants until the coming of the Saviour .... So far there has been no interpolation of the original book printed from these pages at Palmyra, New York, nor will there be while David Whitmer holds them in his possession."[17]

During their visit, Pratt and Smith also learned about the official founding of the Whitmerite Church of Christ. They reported it was composed of "six elders and two priests.... David and John were two of these six." After the pattern of the first organization, they had also ordained four others: John C. Whitmer, W. W. Warner, Philander Page, and (Edward) John Short.[18] William Warner was married to Philander Page's daughter,

16. "The Book of Mormon," *Daily Globe* (Atchison, KS) [September 1879].

17. "The Book of Mormon—More about It," *St. Louis Republican*, September 29, 1878.

18. John Whitmer had recently died at the time of this visit. Joseph F. Smith recorded in his journal, "It appears that David ordained four Elders, with himself and brother John, making six, and two Priests, and set them to preaching the 'Bible and the Book of Mormon, and nothing else.' We are told their church, or branch, numbers some 30 souls in and about Richmond .... James Morgan and Peter Page [son of Hiram Page] (1837–1924) are Priests.... I learned that Hiram Page, one of the Eight Witnesses, had three sons, Philander, Peter and John. The latter was killed in the way by 'bushwhakers' [*sic*]. The other two are members of the Whitmer organization called the 'Church of Christ,' the first being one of six Elders (now only 5 by the death." David and John Whitmer were two of the six Elders, four others, viz. John C. Whitmer, W. W. Warner, Philander Page, and John Short, were ordained by David and John. Smith, *Life of Joseph F. Smith, Sixth President of the Church of Jesus Christ of Latter-day Saints*, 246–48. Pratt and Smith, "Report of Interview with David Whitmer," 774. James Morgan was married to Elizabeth Gant Morgan, half-sister to John C.'s wife, Mary. Barchers, "The Descendants and History of the Peter Whitmer Family," 40a, 117. See also Pratt and

Lillian. Edward John Short was married first to John C.'s niece, Sally Bisbee, and second to her sister, Lutie Bisbee. Many of Jacob Whitmer and Elizabeth Schott Whitmer's descendants, including their daughter Mariann Whitmer Bisbee and her husband, Iram Packard Bisbee, lived a mile or so south of Richmond. Mariann Whitmer was born July 17, 1827, at Fayette, Seneca County, New York. Iram Bisbee was born in McDonough County, New York, in 1816. Mariann married Iram Bisbee October 14, 1847.[19]

Descendants of John Page, Hiram and Catherine Page's firstborn son, also lived about a mile south of Richmond. Because of this cluster of relatives, the Church of Christ held worship services on the third Sunday of the month in the nearby King schoolhouse, with John Christian Whitmer serving as the group's presiding elder.

John Whitmer and his family seldom came all the way from Far West, a distance of about thirty-five miles, which would have taken a day in a horse and buggy, to attend these services near Richmond. Between 1875 and his death in 1878, John Whitmer probably led regular devotional Sunday services with local family members in Far West. Then, in early July 1878, John's health failed rapidly. Family members reversed the usual flow, traveling from Richmond to Far West. John's two nephews, John C. Whitmer and Philander Page, spent about a week "with John Whitmer during his last sickness."[20]

Orson Pratt and Joseph F. Smith had hoped to also visit John Whitmer. They were apparently interested in purchasing John's manuscript history of the church. But they were too late. John died shortly before their arrival, on July 11, 1878, at age seventy-five. Inquiring about overnight accommodations at the Whitmer hotel, they received a rather cold reception from John's children, Sarah Elizabeth Johnson and Jacob David Whitmer. Pratt and Smith asked about John's papers and were informed that the manuscript had been sent to Richmond. Evidently, so had the paper bear-

---

Smith, "Report of Interview with David Whitmer," 2, reprinted in Cook, *David Whitmer Interviews*, 45.

19. Barchers, "The Descendants and History of the Peter Whitmer Family," 40a.

20. Jenson, Stevenson, and Black, "Historical Landmarks," 7; see Page, "Reminiscence, 1907," p. 28, quoted in Holzapfel, Cottle, and Stoddard, *Church History in Black and White*, 70; both quotations are also reproduced in Vogel, *Early Mormon Documents*, 5:251.

ing the transcription of the Book of Mormon Caractors. Pratt and Smith traveled on toward Illinois.

Like his wife, John died in their frame home at Far West.[21] His obituary stated:

> Mr. John Whitmer died at Far West on the 11th, aged 77 years. He came to Caldwell in 1836, to look out a home for the Mormons, who had been driven out of Jackson county. He selected Far West, which selection was confirmed by Joe Smith in a vision, and Far West soon became a flourishing town of over two thousand people. When they were driven from Missouri by the State militia in 1838–9, Mr. Whitmer remained at Far West and has since been a highly respected and law abiding citizen. Mr. Whitmer was one of the eight witnesses to the Book of Mormon or Mormon Bible, but like many other families of the sect he "kicked" against polygamy.[22]

John had been anticipating a second visit from Wilhelm Poulson, so on July 31, 1878, Sarah Elizabeth wrote the news of her father's death: "I seat myself to a painful task, this morning to inform you of the death of my dear father, who departed earthlife, the 11th day of this month [July]. Father's disease was congestion of the lungs, heart and stomach. He died very easily. I have the great consolation in knowing that he was prepared to meet his God. He asked only a few days before his death when I thought you would come. He always felt so very anxious to see you again."[23] Perhaps John had hoped that Poulson's medical experience would enable him to suggest a course of treatment that would relieve his symptoms. From Sarah Elizabeth's description, however, it appears that John was suffering from congestive heart disease, which could not be adequately treated in the nineteenth century. John's interest in Poulson's return no doubt heightened as his health rapidly deteriorated. Poulson also tried to treat David Hyrum Smith, Joseph Smith III's brother, who was confined to a mental asylum during this period.[24]

---

21. Ethel Johnson Lewellen to C. Edward Miller, 26 May 1932.

22. John Whitmer obituary, as quoted in *Richmond Conservator*, 25:2.

23. Poulson, "Correspondence: Death of John Whitmer," 2.

24. Joseph Smith III to Dr. E. A. Kilbourne, 11 March 1879.

The graves of John and Sarah Whitmer are located in the community cemetery at Kingston, Missouri. Sarah's stone stood in front of the Whitmer family marker for many years. An interpretive marker was erected at the John Whitmer gravesite in 1997 by the John Whitmer Historical Association and the Missouri Mormon Frontier Foundation. Courtesy of Community of Christ Archives.

Members of the extended Whitmer family standing in front of the John Whitmer house in Far West, Missouri, ca. 1915. From left to right: John E. Johnson, Sarah E. Johnson Kerr, Ella E. Johnson, Ethel Johnson Lewellen, Nathan Johnson, Christopher Kerr. Courtesy of the LDS Church History Library.

John was buried beside his wife Sarah in the Kingston Cemetery. With a pencil, Sarah Elizabeth outlined John chapter 14 in her father's Bible and noted: "Chapter read at Mothers & father's funerals, S."[25] In this text, the witness, whom Christ loved, reflects upon the sorrow of separation following Christ's death, as well as finding comfort by faith in Christ.[26]

Family survivors marked John and Sarah's graves with an unusual and impressive white marble gravestone.[27] Notice of John's passing appeared in the *Deseret News* in Utah, but there was no mention in the RLDS *Saints' Herald*.[28]

John's estate included 625 acres of farmland at Far West, considerable livestock and farm machinery, and his well-built and comfortable home.[29]

25. John Whitmer family Bible.
26. Eiselen, Lewis, and Downey, *Abingdon Bible Commentary*, 1084.
27. On September 25, 1999, the John Whitmer Historical Association and Missouri Mormon Frontier Foundation placed an interpretive marker at John Whitmer's gravesite to complement this gravestone and to provide additional information about John's historic life.
28. Poulson, "Correspondence: Death of John Whitmer," 2.
29. Anderson, "Five Who Handled the Plates," 44.

His son Jacob D. inherited the north half of the farm and Sarah Elizabeth the south half, including the home.[30] A few years later, on September 6, 1882, Sarah Elizabeth married Christopher Kerr, the son of a prosperous farming family at Far West whom she had known for more than ten years.[31] The two lived in Christopher's residence, but Christopher operated both farms.[32]

Much has been written about the steadfastness of the Book of Mormon witnesses to their dying day. John C. Whitmer, who was the son of the seventh of the eleven witnesses and the nephew to six of them, testified:

> I [John C. Whitmer] was closely connected with Hiram Page in business transactions and other matters, he being married to my aunt. I knew him at all times and under all circumstances to be true to his testimony concerning the divinity of the Book of Mormon. I was also at the deathbed of Oliver Cowdery in 1850, and I heard him speak to my Uncle David [Whitmer] and say: 'Brother David, be faithful to your testimony to the Book of Mormon, for we know that it is of God and that it is verily true.' He then closed his eyes in death. My father, Jacob Whitmer, was always faithful and true to his testimony to the Book of Mormon, and confirmed it on his deathbed. Of my Uncle John [Whitmer] I will say that I was with him a short time before he died at Far West, Missouri, when he confirmed to me what he had done so many times previously that he knew the Book of Mormon was true. I was also with Uncle David [Whitmer], who died here in January last, and heard him bear his last testimony in the presence of many witnesses whom he had called together for the occasion. He solemnly declared that the record of the Nephites, as he always called the Book of Mormon, was of God, and his testimony concerning it true.[33]

Following John Whitmer's death, his brother David received the valuable early movement manuscript materials John had preserved and protected throughout his life. They included John's holograph Book of

30. Pollard and Woods, *Whitmer Memoirs*, 37.

31. "Kerr," *History of Caldwell and Livingston Counties, Missouri*, 329–30.

32. Ibid.

33. John C. Whitmer, quoted in Jenson, Stevenson, and Black, "Historical Landmarks," 155–56.

John Whitmer, which contained the early history of the church, the Book of Mormon Caractors manuscript, and the manuscript copies that John had made of Joseph's revision of the Bible.[34] David Whitmer now became the caretaker of both John and Oliver's church historical artifacts.

Perhaps an awareness of John's recent passing and the knowledge that the voices of the Book of Mormon witnesses were now nearly silent prompted Joseph Smith III to invite David Whitmer to attend an RLDS conference at Galland's Grove, Shelby County, Iowa, on September 24, 1879. Galland's Grove, about 250 miles from Richmond, was a popular place of gathering for RLDS members living in southwestern Iowa and northwestern Missouri. Joseph III wrote cordially: "There are many who will be glad to meet you, and see one who has so long and faithfully testified to the Book of Mormon, and for this object to give you respect.... This invitation is not for the purpose of controversy, nor for the purpose of asking you to compromise yourself in any wise; but for the purpose of having the surviving witness with us for a season, without reference to any difference that may be between us, feeling that on the divinity of the Book we are one, and this shall be the token of our good will."[35] Clearly, Joseph III was explicit in his explanation that he was not attempting to align David with the Reorganization; but David apparently declined the invitation. It had, in fact, been years since he had left Richmond, even though he lived for another nine years.

John's descendants continued to make Caldwell County their permanent home. During the 1880s, John's son, Jacob D., owned one of the best farms in that part of the country. He had inherited the temple lot from his father; but following John's example, Jacob D. "never plowed the

---

34. Pratt and Smith, "Report of Interview with David Whitmer," 785–86: "Orson Pratt—Your father was once the historian of the Church, and I am the present historian; we are anxious to preserve all the items of history we can, we would therefore like to see the MS. your father kept, and if possible, to make satisfactory arrangements with you, to purchase the same, provided there is anything in the MS. which we have not already published. I suppose you are aware that the history of the Church has already been published. J. W.—We've got no history here, all father's papers have gone to Richmond long ago." See also Arthur Deming, statement citing Van Cleave, *Naked Truths about Mormonism*, appendix S.

35. Joseph Smith III to David Whitmer, 2 September 1879.

temple site, leaving about two acres untouched by plow or otherwise, since the cruel exodus."[36]

Samuel Russell, whose father, Isaac Russell, had been a Saint in Far West during the 1830s, passed through Far West in 1882 en route to his LDS mission field. Samuel recorded a wonderful portrait of Far West four years after John's death:

> By the Mirabile road—through a lane leading directly north—you enter far west Near the South West corner—the \<road\> leading on across Shoal Creek—which is spanned by an iron bridge. A half mile or less—above the old Henshaw Mill Seat—As you enter—on your left in a pasture is still to be seen a part of 2 chimneys—the remains of the old David Hughes—(or Joseph Smith) place— (The Hughes family [about half of a page seems to be missing] ... Passing the Hughes place a short distance—on your right a lane opens up to the east—facing that direction—a half mile distant stands the old John Whitmer place (occupied by his daughter Sarah—first married to a man by name Johnson whom she had left & lately married to another by [the] name [of] Kerr).... Then [I visited] the place where Sis was born North from Whitmers—a heavy piece of Corn stood on it but the old place where the house stood & the well was [discoverable].[37]

Another investigator followed in 1885. Arthur Buel Deming was a zealous anti-Mormon whose father, Miner R. Deming, had been sheriff of Hancock County, Illinois, during the Mormon period. Seeking to expose the movement's dark side, Deming collected some fifty affidavits from individuals "personally acquainted with the early history of Mormonism." Among his interviewees was James Van Cleave, then a newspaper reporter in Chicago, who was married to David Whitmer's granddaughter, Josephine. Intrigued by the family's experience, Van Cleave hoped to one day write a history of Mormonism from the Whitmers' perspective and had acquired some of John Whitmer's papers in preparation. He deposited

---

36. J. M. Terry to the editor, *Zion's Ensign*, 8:3. See also appendix J of this work, *History of Caldwell and Livingston Counties*.

37. Samuel Russell to Dear Lucy Ettie, Friends, and Kindred, 3 November 1882. Isaac Russell was excommunicated from the church following the expulsion from Missouri. He died September 25, 1844, near Richmond, Missouri. See Curtis, "Isaac Russell," 3.

them in a bank vault in Richmond, Missouri, for safekeeping until he was ready to begin. Deming explains:

> In looking through Tullege's [*sic*] life of the Mormon prophet, Joseph Smith, I saw the name of J. R. H. Van Cleve [*sic*], of Chicago, Ill. I called on Mr. Van Cleve, who at that time, July, 1885, was private secretary to U. S. Collector Spaulding of Chicago.... I told him that there had been much written about the Mormons that was erroneous, and that I was collecting facts for a true account of its origin and early history. He said that David Whitmer had the original manuscript from which the "Book of Mormon" was printed and would not sell it....
>
> He [Van Cleave] said that John Whitmer, David's brother, was the church historian by appointment and that after his death he spent several days looking over his manuscripts and papers, and that he found five volumes of manuscript history, also the revelation about celestial marriage, or polygamy, dated July 12, 1843, in Joseph Smith's own hand-writing (which he knew) the same as printed in the Doctrines [*sic*] and Covenants of the Utah Mormons....
>
> Mr. Van Cleve said he obtained consent of John Whitmer's daughters [*sic*] to remove the papers he had selected ... and brought them to Richmond, Mo. He said he purchased a safe in Chicago and sent it to Richmond and it was placed in the bank and contained the original manuscript of the "Book of Mormon," five volumes of manuscript Mormon history, the revelation about polygamy in Joseph Smith's handwriting, and other papers on Mormonism, he had been collecting ... which he intended to use in his proposed book.[38]

Although Van Cleave never completed his envisioned book on Mormonism, Arthur Deming published portions of his own research, including many affidavits from eyewitnesses of the early Mormon experience.[39]

---

38. Deming, "The Polygamy Revelation—Joseph Smith's Handwriting Still in Existence!," *Naked Truths about Mormonism* 1, no. 2 (April, 1888): 1. Deming published two issues of *Naked Truths*. See also Vogel, *Early Mormon Documents*, 2:185–86.

39. Ibid.

CHAPTER THIRTY-TWO

The Last Witness

BY THE 1880S a new generation of the Whitmer clan was well established while the influence of the former generation of Whitmers was quickly fading. Of the children of Peter Whitmer Sr. and Mary Musselman Whitmer, only David and Catherine were still alive.

Seventy-five-year-old David was no longer able to work actively in his livery business and spent most of his time visiting with family and friends, either in his livery office or at home. A constant string of interviewers made their way to Richmond to meet with the last living witness of the Book of Mormon.

Catherine was still living south of Richmond with her widowed son, Peter Page, age forty-two. The 1880 census lists Catherine's age as seventy-three and indicates her occupation as "keeping house." Catherine's place of birth is listed as Pennsylvania. The 1880 census also began recording the place of birth of an individual's father and mother. Catherine told the census enumerator that her father was born in Pennsylvania and her mother in Germany. Another son, Philander Page, was living nearby. Philander was forty-nine and his wife, Sarah, the third woman by that name in the family, was forty. Eight children were living at home: Marion, nineteen; Louisa, sixteen; Alonzo, twelve; David, ten; Julia, eight; Sarah, seven; Mary, four; and Cora, nine months.[1]

The spiritual leadership of the movement birthed by the Whitmer clan in and near Richmond had passed to the next generation. Jacob's son, John Christian Whitmer, continued to serve as presiding elder. In 1880, he turned forty-five and his wife, Mary F., was forty-four. They had seven children at home: Virginia (Jennie) Frances, seventeen; Nora Bell, fifteen; John Gant, twelve; Charles William, ten; Izora Beulah, six; David Alma,

---

1.   1880 census, Richmond Township, Ray County, Missouri.

three; and Mary [*sic*] Mayme Janetta, one.[2] The King schoolhouse near John C. and Mary's home, about a mile south of Richmond, continued to host their monthly worship services. At this point, the Whitmer Church of Christ reported about a hundred members. A few lived in Independence, while others were scattered throughout Iowa, Kansas, Illinois, Tennessee, California, and other states.[3]

The Whitmers' relationship with other Book of Mormon believers in the region was not always smooth. The Reorganization was then led by two of Joseph Smith's sons. Joseph Smith III was president, and Alexander Hale Smith was his first counselor. Later, Alexander also served as church patriarch. RLDS leaders at times viewed the Whitmers as competition for former members of the early church. Indeed, the Whitmer movement claimed some of the Reorganization's able believers. Ebenezer Robinson, former printer at Kirtland and Far West, affiliated with the RLDS church but, toward the end of his life, became an advocate for the Whitmerite movement. Despite such "defections," the Reorganization's basic attitude toward the Whitmers was positive and sympathetic.

In November 1886, Joseph III and Alexander H. Smith visited David Whitmer in Richmond. Their purpose was to compare the textual readings of the Reorganized church's editions of the Book of Mormon against the printer's manuscript then in David Whitmer's care. David graciously allowed them to undertake this exacting work in his home over a period of several days. On October 13, 1914, by then aged and blind, Joseph III dictated his memories of this episode to his son, Israel A. Smith, in notes that became the basis for Joseph's memoirs:

> The [RLDS] Conference of 1884 decided that it was advisable that the church should secure an examination of the manuscript of the Book of Mormon at that time in the possession of David Whitmer of Richmond, Ray County, Missouri, for the purpose of comparing with the editions published by the church and to correct by the manuscript any errors or descriptions that may have been made by transcription and publication. To this end the committee consisting of my brother Alexander H. Smith, W. H. Kelley and Thomas W. Smith were appointed to make an arrangement with Elder David Whitmer [to see]

2. Ibid.
3. Jenson, Stevenson, and Black, "Historical Landmarks," 651.

if it could be done by which such examination and comparison could be accomplished. By correspondence with David Whitmer he consented to such examination by the committee provided that I would be present with them during the time that the examination was made. He seemed willing to trust me with the temporary custody of the manuscript but did not seem willing that the others should examine it without my being present. I knew as a matter of course that there would be perfect safety to the manuscript in the hands of the committee and that the rights of Elder Whitmer would not be disregarded in any way or any advantage be taken of the permission granted by him. However, I was pleased with the confidence he seemed willing to place in me, and made arrangements to go with the committee and sit with them at Richmond so long as the examination might require. We reached Richmond on the 8th of July [1886] and secured quarters for the committee at Dales Boarding House and visited until ten o'clock p.m., and found that besides the four constituting the committee there was to be on the part of Elder Whitmer one or two of his relatives also present during the examination, the Elder himself feeling unable to undertake the carefulness of supervision with us alone. Accordingly for the most part of the time Philander Page, a relative of Elder Whitmer by marriage, and John C. Whitmer, were assigned duty with us, Mr. Page spending the greater part of the time with us. We repaired to the house of Elder Whitmer after dinner and together in his presence implored the divine sanction and aid of the Spirit to be with us to direct and confirm the duty we were striving to accomplish. It was agreed that one of our number was to hold and read the manuscript copy while others held respectively the Palmyra edition, the Nauvoo edition and the edition published by the Reorganization, taking turns in the reading of the manuscript as was found desirable. The committee continued the examination of the manuscript until Friday, the 11th, when a recess was called and on Saturday we visited Independence returning to Richmond to continue the work of examination, working each day from 7:00 a.m. to 6:00 at night with an omission for lunch until the 17th on which day we finished the examination. Elder T. W. Smith kept a daily record [of the examination], Alexander H. Smith also keeping note of the work as it was done. The committee subsequently reported the result of their examination in the Herald of August 23, 1884, signed by the committee as appointed by the conference.

In reflection upon this work, it must be conceded that the examination was timely, as so much had been said and so much speculation had as to the differences said to exist between the different editions of the Book of Mormon and the original manuscript. The result of the examination shows clearly that there had been no fatal divergence in the text and descriptions, the supposed errors being chiefly in verbiage, by none of which was the sense of the text changed. The list of errors showed differences in spelling and except in one instance the committee were at entire unity in the understanding of the manuscript as we found it. In one place in the published Book of Mormon occurred the words, "arrest the scripture," and in other places under similar circumstances in the construction of the sentence the work "arrest" is "wrest," twisted or changed out of place. In one place in the manuscript we found the word written in such a way as seemingly to warrant the conclusion the word was "arrest" at least so thought the majority of the committee. From this decision I disagreed believing that it was the same word meaning the same thing as the word "wrest" did in the other places of the book. My remembrance is that the time spent at the house of David Whitmer engaged in this examination and consideration was one of the pleasantest episodes of the period affording an association with the aged patriarch and communion in the reading and discussion of the manuscript in comparing it with the editions of the Book of Mormon which we held respectively.

At the close of our examination those who had sat with us from time to time, J. C. Whitmer and his relative Philander Page, expressed their satisfaction and approval of the fairness of the committee and of their courtesy in treating with Father Whitmer. There was during the sessions of the committee one or two visits by citizens and strangers to see Elder David Whitmer and passing the time of day with him. Upon one of these occasions a Colonel, a resident of the place, Colonel Jiles, came in with a stranger by the name of Captain Fall. The interview with Elder Whitmer was followed by there being brought into the room where the committee were at work and were introduced to us and permitted to see the manuscript. The Colonel in an affable and friendly manner discussed with Elder Whitmer the evidence which he had borne, and suggestively asked the question if it had not been possible that Elder Whitmer had been mistaken and had been moved by some kind of mental disturbance or hallucination in which he was deceived when he stated he had seen the personage and the angel to which he referred, the plates, the Urim and Thummim, and Sword of Laban. I remember very distinctly the manner in which Elder Whitmer rising to his full height, a little over six feet, said solemnly and impressively, "No sir, I was not under any hallucination nor was I deceived. I saw with these eyes, I heard with these ears, I know whereof I speak." The persons present including the Colonel and friend stood under the impressive silence as in the presence of an angel himself. I went out of the room with Colonel Jiles and Captain Fall and the Colonel said to me, "It is somewhat difficult, Elder Smith, for us every day men to believe the statement made by Mr. Whitmer, but one thing is certain, that no man could hear him make his affirmation as he did to us in there and doubt the honesty and sincerity of the man himself. He fully believes he saw and heard as he stated he did." We were wonderfully blessed at being permitted to hear this testimony of Elder Whitmer. Elder Whitmer himself at the close of our work and upon bidding us goodbye expressed his gratitude to God for the preservation of the manuscript and his thankfulness for the visit of the committee and the completion of the examination which had taken place. It will set to rest much controversy which indeed it has done.[4]

Upon leaving for the final time, Alexander said to Julia Ann, David's wife, "Before mother [Emma Smith Bidamon] died, she told us to visit the Whitmers, that they were good people and when we saw David Whitmer we would see an honest man."[5]

Near the end of David Whitmer's life, LDS leaders Andrew Jenson and Edward Stevenson also visited the Richmond area. Part of their journey took them through Far West. Jenson recorded in his journal:

[September 1887:] Took an early start and a two mile walk brought us to Mirabile, a neat little village containing several fine stores 2 churches and mills, situated near Goose Creek. Walked 2½ miles and crossed Goose Creek, then up hill to Far West 1½ miles further, Eat a melon at the first house <which formerly belonged to Joseph Smith, the Proph-

4. Joseph Smith III, notes for memoirs, 13 October [1914].
5. Julia Ann Whitmer, December 9, 1886, quoted in John C. Whitmer, "Letters from David and John C. Whitmer," 89. Emma's last testimony, reads, "Question. What do you think of David Whitmer? Answer. David Whitmer I believe to be an honest and truthful man. I think what he states may be relied on." Joseph Smith III, "Last Testimony of Sister Emma," 289–90.

Junius Wells (not shown) coordinated efforts by the LDS church to erect a monument to commemorate the three witnesses to the Book of Mormon. The marker is located on Oliver Cowdery's grave in Richmond, Missouri. Photograph by George Edward Anderson, November 22, 1911. Courtesy of the LDS Church History Library.

et> Brother Stevenson, who was here as a boy, knew the place again. We arrived at the Temple Lot at 11:30 a.m. Took dinner with Jacob D. Whitmer, a son of the late John Whitmer, who lives a little east of the Temple Lot, which he also owns. After dinner we went on the Temple Block and wrote in our journals.[6]

As years passed, physical evidence of the old town of Far West faded. One by one, the former landmarks faded from existence. As the former courthouse, schoolhouse, and multipurpose community building on the public square became dilapidated, "J. D. Whitmer, saw it tore down because [he was] afraid it would fall on the stock [his cattle]."[7] The family eventually closed the old Whitmer hotel, and only a portion of it was still standing on the hill south of the temple site when Mormon photographer George Edward Anderson visited Far West in 1907.[8]

In 1911, George E. Anderson visited northern Missouri to photograph the new Three Witnesses Monument at Richmond. As part of this

6.   Jenson, journal, 16 September 1888, pp. 107–9.

7.   Holzapfel, Cottle, and Stoddard, *Church History in Black and White*, 80.

8.   These photographs may be seen in ibid.

trip, he visited the John Whitmer clan at Far West and captured additional Whitmer-related images. Later, upon returning to Utah, Anderson forwarded copies of photos to John E. Johnson: 1) Sarah Elizabeth's son, John E. Johnson, posed at a table with a scarf that had belonged to Oliver Cowdery and a stone from the foundation of the Far West Temple, 2) Julia Ann Whitmer Schweich and her son, George Schweich, and 3) the Whitmer burial plot in the old Richmond (Pioneer) Cemetery.[9] As late as 2008, John Whitmer's great-great-granddaughter Lorene E. Pollard, of Clinton County, Missouri, still had a copy of the John E. Johnson photograph hanging on the wall of her home.[10]

In Richmond, throughout the remainder of his life, David declined all offers to purchase the Book of Mormon manuscript that had been entrusted to his care in 1850 by Oliver Cowdery. David, likewise, safeguarded his brother John's history of the church and handwritten copies of church scriptures. In 1878, David told Orson Pratt and Joseph F. Smith, "Joseph said my father's house should keep the records. I consider these things sacred, and would not part with nor barter them for money."[11]

A 1920s article in the *Kansas City Post*, although marred by historical errors, still relates an interesting story. It may be apocryphal but definitely speaks to the Whitmers' careful stewardship of the Book of Mormon manuscript:

> One evening there came a man [to David Whitmer's home] who asked for food and lodging. When all were seated at the table and David Whitmer was about to say grace, those present were surprised at his silence. Looking up, they saw him looking steadily at the stranger and pointing at him with his finger. "You have come to kill me. But you will not do it, will you?" he said, addressing the stranger. The man afterwards confessed that he was a Danite, and had come from Salt Lake City to murder Whitmer and obtain the manuscript."[12]

9. George Edward Anderson to John E. Johnson, 11 March 1912.

10. Ron Romig, visit to Pollard home, 2008.

11. Pratt and Smith, "Report of Interview with David Whitmer, September 7, 1878," 2.

12. "Mormon Landmark Passing, Home of David Whitmer at Richmond Being Torn Down," *Kansas City Post*, January 10, 1920.

The article continues, "After this occurrence, Whitmer placed the manuscript in the vault of the Ray County Savings bank, where it was kept until long after his death."[13]

Well after John Whitmer's passing, David put his religious thoughts into print. This 1887 pamphlet, *Address to All Believers in Christ*, was written to vindicate the Whitmer family and to promulgate the Whitmerite Church of Christ. David's pamphlet strongly condemned the practice of polygamy and may have been intended as his last formal testimony of his witness of the Book of Mormon.

David had been slowing down for some time. His last months were spent close to his bed. Much of his *Address* was prepared during his last illness, while he was nearly bedfast.[14] Soon after its 1887 publication date, David Whitmer died at his home, on January 25, 1888, a few days past his eighty-third birthday. The last Book of Mormon witness was finally silent.

Grave marker of David Whitmer in the new Richmond Cemetery, Richmond, Missouri, ca. 1900s. Courtesy of Community of Christ Archives.

Newspapers around the country carried the news of David Whitmer's death. The January 26, 1888, *Missouri Daily Republican* reported:

> [Special.]—David Whitmer, the last witness to the divinity of the Book of Mormon, died at his home in Richmond, at 5 O'clock this evening, surrounded by his family [son David J. Whitmer, daugh-

---

13. Ibid.

14. One of the two last members of Whitmer's Church of Christ shared this information with Jerald Tanner during a 1957 interview. The last two members were Izora Beulah Whitmer Dear (1873–1955) and Mayme Janetta Whitmer Koontz (1879–1961), both granddaughters of Jacob Whitmer. Since Izora Dear was dead, Jerald Tanner probably interviewed Mayme Koontz during his 1957 visit to Richmond, Missouri, quoted in Ronald V. Huggins, "Jerald Tanner's Quest for Truth," 3.

ter Julia Ann Whitmer Schweich, grandson George W. Schweich, and granddaughter Josephine Schweich (Mrs. James Van Cleave) of Chicago, all of whom were at his bedside during his last hours, and witnessed his peaceful and quiet death] and a few of his immediate friends.... Recently, and during his illness, he claimed to have received many manifestations as to the divinity of the Book of Mormon, and took great pleasure in so stating the fact to his many friends who were assembled at his bed side. And although in his 83rd year, with a feeble constitution and a frame bent with old age, his mind was as bright and active, and his conceptions as clear as the noonday sun.[15]

David's funeral was held the next day, January 27, 1888, in the family residence, at 10:30 a.m. He was buried immediately after the funeral in the new Richmond Cemetery west of town.[16] His grave is marked by a simple marble column with two books sculpted on its top, representing the Bible and Book of Mormon. David Whitmer's burial plot is one of the most prominent points in the entire cemetery, overlooking the city he had come to know and serve so well.

A tribute to David Whitmer that speaks to his character and conviction later appeared in *The Return*, a newspaper issued in support of Whitmer's Church of Christ:

> There were many opportunities for him to adopt the Phariseeism position, both with the believer and unbelievers in the Book of Mormon, but he preferred to be one of the people in very fact, isolated yet among all classes, a fellow mortal burdened with the guardianship of the sacred manuscript of the Record of the Nephites, a servant of God as an Elder in the Church of Christ, and the witness-ship to the voice of God and the vision of a just man made perfect before the shekina of the Holy Presence of the Lord God Almighty.... That there was not anything in this world that caused him so much temporal vexation as his position, but it was a life work and he had put his shoulder to the plow and would never turn back for he knew that his Redeemer liveth, and that his burden was for the relief of the nations.[17]

15. "The Last Witness Gone," reprinted from "An Old Citizen Passes Away," *Richmond Conservator*, January 26, 1888.

16. Ibid.

17. Schweich, "The Position of David Whitmer," 4–5.

CHAPTER THIRTY-THREE

The Whitmer Documents and Artifacts

I N S E P T E M B E R 1888, nine months after David Whitmer's death, Andrew Jenson, Edward Stevenson, and Joseph S. Black passed through Richmond to pay their respects to the Whitmers. The three elders from Utah forwarded their impressions to the *Deseret News*:

> We visited the new cemetery, situated a short distance west of town, where the mortal remains of the last witness of the Book of Mormon now slumber in the dust. We also visited the old cemetery about half a mile north of Richmond Center, where rest the remains of the senior Peter Whitmer (in whose house the church was organized [*sic*]) and his wife [Mary] together with their son Jacob (one of the eight witness) and Oliver Cowdery. A fine marble tombstone designates the resting place of Jacob Whitmer, but the grave of Oliver was entirely hid among and overgrown with weeds. While we found the new cemetery in a first class condition we found the old one entirely neglected and marble monuments, head stones and fences scattered promiscuously on the ground as the cyclone left it ten years ago. Standing over the graves of Oliver and Jacob we instinctively uncovered our heads, uttered a silent prayer and passed on with heavy hearts. How we should have appreciated a short interview with him who was blessed with the ministration of angels, the Savior, Moses, Elijah, the prophet and other holy beings![1]

Many of the second generation of Whitmers no longer lived in Richmond but, instead, in the township a mile or more south of town. Jacob Whitmer's descendants acquired fine farms and even opened a family cemetery where perhaps fifty or more individuals were interred.

---

1.   Jenson, Stevenson, and Black, "Historical Landmarks," 7, excerpt quoted as "Sayings of John C. Whitmer," 651.

Following David Whitmer's decease, the spiritual dimension of his life's work passed to his nephew, John Christian Whitmer. However, the tangible Mormon artifacts in his care passed into the stewardship of his immediate family—specifically, his children and grandchildren living at Richmond. Even though David's wife, Julia Ann Jolly, was ten years younger than David, she passed away about a year after his death and was buried beside him in the new Richmond Cemetery.

Assistant LDS church historian Andrew Jenson had made several attempts to locate John Whitmer's manuscript history of the church in order to acquire it or copy its contents. In early September 1893, Jenson traveled by train to Chicago, Illinois, to attend the World's Fair and Congress of Religions. On his way there, on September 5, 1893, Jenson stopped in Richmond, Missouri, where David's son, David John Whitmer, and grandson, George Schweich, showed him John's history book. Jenson wrote, "After perusing its pages most of the day, I visited David Whitmer's grave in the Richmond cemetery." The next day, Jenson proceeded to Chicago.

On the return leg of his trip from Chicago, September 24, 1893, Jenson again returned to Richmond, Missouri. This time, George Schweich allowed him to make a handwritten copy of the holograph history. Jenson recorded in his journal:

> I went to work immediately copying John Whitmer's old record, in the store of Geo. Schweich, who assisted me some in reading proof. Mr. Schweich did not think that the little old book with faded writing was the very book that I had been hunting for, but as I perused it, I came to the conclusion, without telling him so, that it contained all that John Whitmer ever wrote on Church history; hence I was anxious to copy every word contained in it. Mr. Schweich reluctantly allowed me to take it to my hotel where I spent all night copying, and in the morning returned the original to him. I was very pleased indeed to obtain a copy of this old Whitmer record ... [although] we discovered that it contained only a little of historical value. Yet John Whitmer recorded events which are not recorded elsewhere.[2]

Jenson remained in Richmond through September 27, 1893, while Schweich, who was associated with the Whitmerite church, assisted Jen-

---

2. Jenson, *Autobiography of Andrew Jenson*, 208, 209.

son in proofing his copy against the original manuscript. Upon his return to Utah, Jenson produced at least two typescript copies from his holograph copy.

David's son, David John Whitmer, died in a tragic accident on June 14, 1895. As he worked alone preparing to haul a load of sand, the sandbank around him collapsed, smothering him. Because David and Julia Ann's daughter, Julia Ann Whitmer Schweich, also lived in her parents' home except for the few years of her marriage, David's precious historical documents passed into the care of David's grandson (Julia Ann's son), George W. Schweich. Schweich took his stewardship seriously, keeping the Book of Mormon printer's manuscript in a Richmond bank vault during most of the years from 1888 to around 1902. John Whitmer's manuscript history of the early church also passed into Schweich's keeping.

During this time, a rumor, perhaps perpetuated by Schweich himself, persisted among local citizens that the gold plates of the Book of Mormon were also stored in the bank. In 1916, the *Wichita Beacon* reinforced this perception. "Schweisch [Schweich], in spite of his appearance, is the guardion [*sic*] of the golden tablets of the book of Mormon." The article quotes Schweich's description of the artifacts supposedly in his possession: "I don't want to make a statement as to where they are, but I will say what they are. They consist of the golden plates, the copper plates that are the record of the Jewish Sanhedrin, or great council, and the sword of Laban.... Then there are other minor articles, but I want to repeat that the searchers will never find them, and they need not bother my daughter [Katherine Schweich], after I am dead."[3]

Schweich had started out as a young stable hand in his grandfather's livery stable and, eventually, after the deaths of his grandfather David and his uncle David John, assumed management of the operation. On April 19, 1877, he married Sarah Keener, a local Richmond girl, at Richmond's Methodist Episcopal parsonage, with the ceremony being performed jointly "by Elder David Whitmer the maternal grandsire of the groom and

---

3. "Mormon Landmark Passing, Home of David Whitmer at Richmond Being Torn Down." See also, "Has This Missourian the Gold Plates of the Mormon Church?," *Kansas City Star*, March 12, 1915. This article states that George's daughter Katherine would eventually inherit the records of the church that were still in his possession.

Rev. George U. Keener the father of the bride."⁴ The marriage united two of Richmond's noted religious families.

After the turn of the century, George sold the livery and became a traveling salesman of steel fence posts. Later still, he worked as a banker and stockbroker. During a time of relative prosperity, George built a large house on a northeast corner lot (lot 81), east and across the street from David Whitmer's home site. As of 2011, this home was still standing at 510 South Shaw and East Main Streets in Richmond. Occasionally, Schweich made some of the documents under his stewardship available to researchers. I. Woodbridge Riley, author of *The Founder of Mormonism* (1902), claimed that the Book of Mormon printer's manuscript was in New York City in the possession of William Evarts Benjamin. Benjamin evidently gave Riley access to the manuscript while Riley was researching his biography of Joseph Smith. Riley illustrated his book with a photographic facsimile of the holograph manuscript showing the book of Jacob (RLDS 2:28; LDS 2:21).⁵

After Jonn's and David Whitmer's death, some of John's papers, taken to Richmond by James Van Cleave, also came into George Schweich's possession. Apparently among them was a paper in Christian Whitmer's handwriting containing hand-drawn Caractors, allegedly reproducing symbols from the Book of Mormon plates. Thought not the Anthon Transcript, it is clear that David Whitmer believed this to be the document Martin Harris carried to New York when Harris sought consultation with scholars Charles Anthon and Samuel Mitchill.

A *Philadelphia Press* reporter who had visited the aged David in Richmond on October 9, 1887, had been allowed to examine the docu-

---

4. Julia Ann Whitmer Schweich family Bible.

5. Riley, *The Founder of Mormonism*, figure between pages 102 and 103. This is a reproduction of the famous antipolygamy passage from the printer's manuscript of the Book of Mormon (RLDS Jacob 2:28; LDS Jacob 2:21); see printer's manuscript, p. 67. William Evarts Benjamin (1859–1940) was a prominent publisher and collector in Boston whose best-known work was the 1894 publication of Edmund Clarence Stedman's *A Library of American Literature from the Earliest Settlement to the Present Time.* "William E. Benjamin," *Wikipedia*, accessed May 6, 2012. The printer's copy of the Book of Mormon manuscript nearly became part of Benjamin's extensive collection of documents relating to significant American literature. The reason for its return to Schweich in 1902 would be an interesting story. George W. Schweich to O. R. Beardsley, 17 January 1900.

ment bearing the hand-drawn Caractors and recorded David's words: "It took Joseph Smith a whole week to copy [the characters], so particular was he that the characters should be perfectly reproduced, and that the 'reformed Egyptian' language should be shown up in all its native simplicity.... Martin Harris ... was despatched [*sic*] to New York with this copy of the gold plate, which he presented to Professor Anthon, with a request for the learned linguist to read it."[6]

Despite David's conviction, the documentation is not sufficient to support this claim. In 1903, the Community of Christ purchased from George Schweich the printer's copy of the Book of Mormon manuscript as well as this manuscript.[7] This holograph is the source of many of the reproductions of the Book of Mor-

George Washington L. Schweich, standing beside the printer's copy of the Book of Mormon, ca. 1902. The manuscript came into Schweich's possession after the death of David John Whitmer. Courtesy of Community of Christ Archives.

mon Caractors that have appeared in printed sources over the years. (See appendix Y: "Published Reproductions of Book of Mormon Caractors.")

6. Facsimile of the Caractors with David Whitmer's statement, in Lamb, *The Golden Bible*, 342.

7. Caractors photograph of Book of Mormon Caractors facsimile reproduction as a supplement to the *Herald*, September 29, 1909. See also Kimball, "The Anthon Transcript: People, Primary Sources, and Problems," 325–52; David Whitmer, interview by Edward Stevenson, January 2, 1887, in Cook, *David Whitmer Interviews*, 211–14.

Adherents of the Whitmerite Church of Christ continued to meet at Richmond, Missouri, for many years after the deaths of John and David Whitmer. In August 1894, John Christian Whitmer, Jacob's son and the presiding elder of the struggling Whitmer religious movement, died. When Joseph Smith III wrote to George Schweich to clarify who had been the Whitmerite presiding elder after David Whitmer's death, George Schweich replied: "Bro. Joseph Smith: Your letter of inquiry duly here; without consultation and not authoritatively, will give only my opinion. My grandfather was indefinitely first elder or presiding elder, then John [Christian] Whitmer; Now I cannot say if P[hilander]. A. Page occupies that office or not."[8]

Remaining leaders in the Whitmer religious movement decided to publish their own edition of the Book of Mormon. Perhaps reflecting the long-held fear that future editions of the Book of Mormon might change or omit the strong prohibitions of plural marriage contained in the manuscript itself, the Whitmerite edition was seen as a permanent witness to stand in the place of the now deceased Book of Mormon witnesses. This work appeared in 1899.

With the contents of the printer's manuscript securely in print, George Schweich, as its steward, felt freer to ascertain its monetary value. Some have suggested he needed money. George forwarded the manuscript and other early church documents (including John Whitmer's priesthood license) to William E. Benjamin, a Boston professional document collector and dealer, with instructions to secure a buyer.[9] During 1901, Benjamin corresponded with Samuel Russell, an LDS member and missionary, and perhaps others. Russell wrote to Joseph F. Smith to ascertain the LDS church's interest in the manuscript. Joseph F. had formed his own estimate of the manuscript's value during his previous visits to David Whitmer and disdainfully asserted:

> The Manuscript in the hands of Mr. Benjamin possesses no value whatever. It has been repeatedly offered to us, and numerous false re-

8. George Schweich to Joseph Smith III, 30 October 1894, published as "John C. Whitmer Dead," *Herald*, 41:741. See also "John C. Whitmer Dead," *Herald*, 41:582.

9. Jensen, Joseph Smith Papers Project, conversation, May 26, 2007. Even though the printer's manuscript was returned, John Whitmer's elder's license ended up in the Mormon Collection, Beinecke Library, Yale University, New Haven, Connecticut.

ports have been put in circulation with regard to our desire to obtain possession of it, but we have at no time regarded it as of any value, neither have we ever offered any money to procure it, all the stories to the contrary notwithstanding, for we have always known it was not the original, as aforesaid, and as many editions of the Book of Mormon have been printed and tens of thousands of copies of it circulate throughout the world you can readily perceive that this manuscript really is of no value to anyone. There is no principle involved in its possession, there could be nothing lost if it were utterly destroyed; it can neither add to nor diminish aught from the word of God as contained in the printed work which had already gone to the world and been translated into many languages. Indeed, it is not worth the time and paper I am using to convey these thoughts to you.[10]

Benjamin returned the manuscript to Schweich when he was unable to find a buyer. Schweich was no doubt severely disappointed that the treasured document that the Whitmer family had so long esteemed was regarded so scornfully. The next year, however, he approached the RLDS church and found greater interest. An agreement was reached for the church to buy the items for $2,450.[11] On April 18, 1903, George Schweich transferred the John Whitmer manuscript history, parts of the Inspired Version (New Translation) manuscript, handwritten copies of revelations intended for the Book of Commandments, and the document containing Book of Mormon Caractors to Joseph Smith III at Independence. The transaction took place in the Ensign building, in the presence of Frederick M. Smith (Joseph III's son), bishop E. L. Kelley, R. S. Salyards, Roderick May, and Walter Wayne Smith, a future RLDS church historian.[12] Walter W. Smith described the event:

> It was my good fortune, by the kindness of Brother Roderick May, to be present when Geo. Schweich, the grandson of David Whitmer, turned over to the church the manuscripts and papers that had been

10. Joseph F. Smith to Samuel Russell, 19 March 1901.

11. Israel A. Smith, "A 'Sealed' Book," 262–63; Walter W. Smith to Samuel A. Burgess, 15 April 1926; [RLDS] "General Conference Minutes," 1904, 689.

12. *Zion's Ensign* was an RLDS-oriented periodical published in the interests of the church by RLDS businessmen but was not considered to be an official RLDS publication. Walter Wayne Smith served as RLDS church historian from 1919 to 1923.

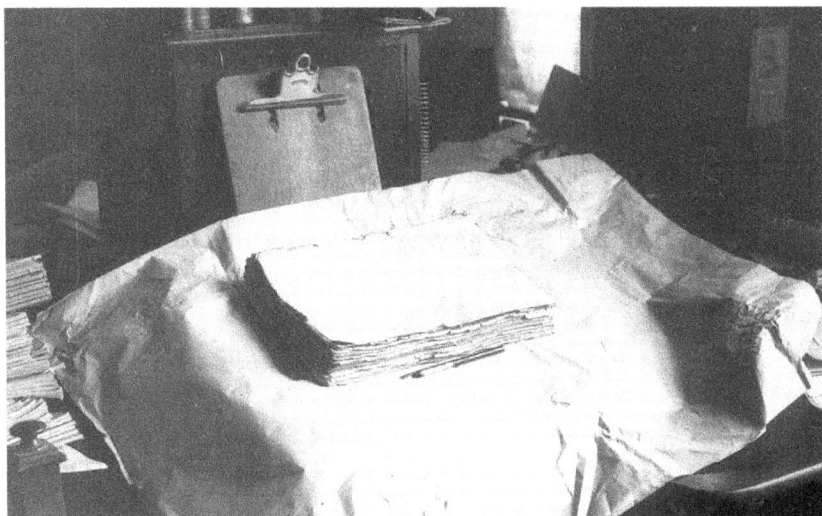

The printer's manuscript of the Book of Mormon was transferred to the care and keeping of the RLDS church in 1903. Courtesy of the Community of Christ Archives.

kept by David Whitmer one of the three witnesses. These he said had come into his possession at the death of David Whitmer.

There was in the lot, the manuscript of the Book of Mormon, a part of the book of Genesis from the Inspired Translation, of the Holy Scripture. The manuscript book of church history written by John Whitmer, the transcript of characters which Joseph Smith made, from the plates, and some pages of manuscript containing several revelations to the early church.[13]

In exchange for $2,450, the RLDS church had obtained a body of documents whose value, in the eyes of John and David Whitmer, could not be quantified.

The gift of seership also continued through the generations, and seer stones in possession of the family became part of the collection of historical artifacts. J. L. Traughber, who lived close enough to Richmond to frequently visit the Whitmers, wrote: "John C. Whitmer has a stone, the one which his son uses, and states that it belonged to his father, Jacob Whitmer." Jacob Whitmer's grandson, John Gant Whitmer, was also a seer who, "through his peepstone, sees caves in which are vast stores of

13. Walter W. Smith to Samuel A. Burgess, 15 April 1926.

records; cave in succession to cave, all filled with treasures of golden plates and sacred records."[14]

It certainly does appear that David, John, and Jacob each had seer stones in their possession after being separated from the main body of Joseph Smith's church. Two stones associated with the Whitmer movement eventually found their way into the Community of Christ Museum collection, in Independence, Missouri. Mormon memorabilia collector Mark Ashurst-McGee provides a further description of the Whitmer stones. "The [three] seer stones that were passed down through the Whitmer family are Native American artifacts of a class known as gorgets, perforated stones shaped and tooled by early indigenous Americans. Such stones, found in association with Native American burials, were no doubt perceived by their nineteenth-century discoverers to have been associated with ritual or religious uses."[15]

A seer stone known to have been in David Whitmer's possession (Stone 1) is now in the care of Rachel Killebrew, church archivist, at the Community of Christ Archives, as is a second stone, also believed to be a Whitmer family seer stone. Accession records, however, do little to clarify when or from whom either stone was acquired. The David Whitmer stone, or Stone 1, is a hand-formed stone object about three inches by five inches by one-half inch thick, with convex edges somewhat in elliptical form, pierced by two round holes. Stone 1 is slightly variegated, light gray or greenish in color. The existence of a photographic image of Stone 1 at the Community of Christ Archives, signed by David Whitmer's grandson, George Schweich, suggests that Stone 1 came into Schweich's possession after David's death. The RLDS church purchased a collection of Whitmer artifacts from George Schweich in 1903. However, Stone 1 is not listed

14. Traughber, "David Whitmer: 'The Last Witness' of the Book of Mormon," 24. Also cited in Smith, *Life of Joseph F. Smith,* 239. Jacob Whitmer's son, John C. Whitmer, had the following sons: Edwin Franklin, John Gant, Charles William, and David Alma. George Schweich and his wife, Sarah ("Sally") Elizabeth Keener, lived in Richmond, Missouri, and had seven children: Van Cleave Whitmer Schweich, born 1878; Helen Schweich Crowley, born September 9, 1879; Julia Clare Schweich, died as an infant, September 1881; Paul Schweich, born June 11, 1882; George Schweich, died as an infant, August 1885; Ruby Schweich Twelves, born February 18, 1886; and Katherine Louise Schweich, born February 19, 1891. Barchers, "The Descendants and History of the Peter Whitmer Family," 78.

15. Mark Ashurst-McGee, "A Pathway to Prophethood," 164–69.

among the items purchased from Schweich at that time, although it may have been. All that can be said is that it came into the possession of the Community of Christ between 1903 and 1940. The earliest documentation locating Stone 1 in the RLDS historian's office appears in an early 1940s letter by Fawn Brodie after she conducted research there, associated with the church library, while gathering sources for her Joseph Smith biography. Brodie incorrectly assumed, or was incorrectly informed, that it could be tied to Hiram Page. Brodie reported, the "Page [*sic*] stone, which seems originally to have been an Indian relic, is now in the library of the Reorganized Church [Community of Christ]."[16]

In 1948, Samuel Burgess showed Stone 1 to Mormonism scholar Dale Morgan during a research visit Morgan made to Independence.[17] In 1949, Burgess again mentioned it in correspondence with RLDS president Israel A. Smith.[18]

In 1953, Helen Farwell Blankmeyer, David Whitmer's great-granddaughter through David's daughter Julia Ann Whitmer Schweich, donated a leather trunk to the RLDS church. The trunk contained a number of Whitmer family artifacts and heirlooms, including photographs of the David Whitmer family and home, the David Whitmer family Bible,

16. Fawn Brodie, *No Man Knows My History*, 92. David Whitmer's stone was incorrectly identified as the Hiram Page stone by RLDS church historian Samuel A. Burgess during the 1940s. My thanks to Jared Tamez, author of "The Hiram Page Stone: Tracing a Mormon Artifact," for locating this reference. Subsequent researchers also misidentified another seer stone (Stone 3), with a provenance connected to Jacob Whitmer, as the Hiram Page stone. Before the 1960s, scholars throughout the movement remained cautious about saying Joseph used a seer stone. Historically associating seer stones to Hiram Page, rather than to Joseph Smith or other key leaders like the Whitmers, allowed writers to sidestep potentially troublesome questions about how the Book of Mormon was translated. From the 1940s (or earlier) and until the 1960s, RLDS historians had tangible proof in their hands that the Book of Mormon probably was translated by use of a stone but chose not to make this deduction explicit for church members. Given the intellectual climate at the time, RLDS church historian Burgess may have intentionally sidestepped questions about Joseph's use of the stone by consciously or unconsciously connecting it with Page. Joseph Smith Jr. clearly did not approve Page's use of the stone and omitting the rest of the story suggested that Joseph and the church disapproved in general of the use of seer stones.

17. Dale L. Morgan to Fawn Brodie, 25 February 1948, in Walker, *Dale Morgan on Early Mormonism: Correspondence and a New History*, 153.

18. Samuel A. Burgess to Israel A. Smith, 6 October 1949.

a Hiram Page letter, a copy of David Whitmer's *Address to All Believers in Christ*, and early newspaper clippings.[19] The trunk also included a photograph of the David Whitmer seer stone (Stone 1).

In the mid-1950s, the RLDS church acquired what is believed to be a second Whitmer seer stone, herein described as Stone 2. There is no mention of a stone being among the contents of the Blankmeyer trunk in 1953, so it apparently came to the church by another route. Records in the church archives provide little information to help clarify the provenance of this second stone.

Stone 2 is also an indigenous Native American artifact, approximately three inches by four inches by one-half inch in size. Although thin from the front or back, it appears somewhat egg shaped and is pierced by three round holes. It is light gray or chocolate in color. Since the first stone was clearly in the possession of David Whitmer, this second stone may have been John Whitmer's seer stone.

In the 1960s and 1970s, another Whitmer family stone (Stone 3) was reportedly in the possession of Jacob Whitmer descendants then living in Richmond, Missouri. Sometime between 1954 and 1958, Jacob Whitmer's granddaughter, Mayme Koontz, showed Stone 3 to LDS mission president and future apostle Alvin R. Dyer. Dyer described it as "a light-gray, highly polished stone about five inches by three inches, by one-half inch thick with two round holes in it."[20] Stone 3 is rather rectangular with convex sides and greenish in color. Subsequent research strongly suggests that it was Jacob Whitmer's seer stone. Like Stone 1 a half-century before, Stone 3 has frequently been misidentified as Hiram Page's seer stone.

John Whitmer's history manuscript, also among the Whitmer items purchased from George Schweich in 1903, remained unpublished until the twentieth century. Heman C. Smith, RLDS church historian, published John's history for the first time in 1908. John's history appeared serially in the *Journal of History*, a periodical devoted to RLDS church history, but with chapters 20–22 omitted. In these final chapters of his manuscript, John comments on the activities of secret bands, which he terms Gideonites (later known as Danites), and the introduction of polygamy in Nauvoo.

---

19. Israel A. Smith, "Whitmer Heirlooms," 245–46, 257.

20. Dyer, *Refiner's Fire*, 263.

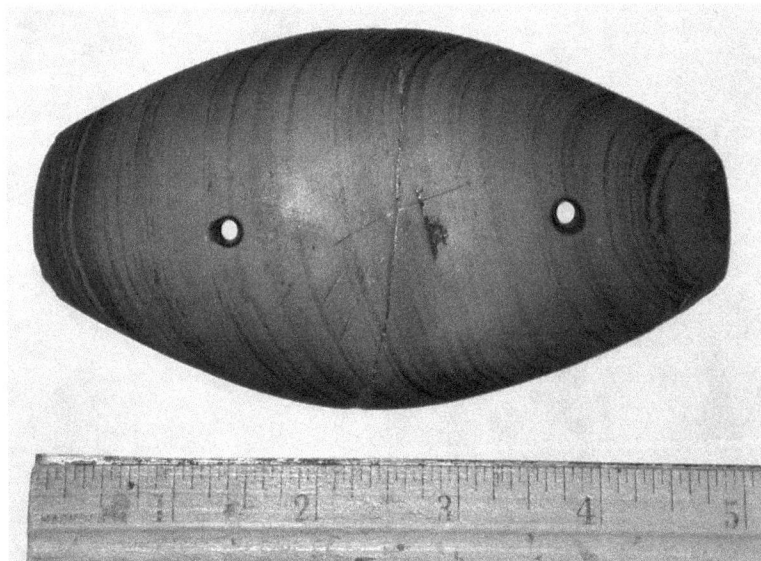

This seer stone (Stone 1) was in David Whitmer's possession. Stone 1 became part of the RLDS church's museum holdings sometime before 1940. Courtesy of Community of Christ Archives.

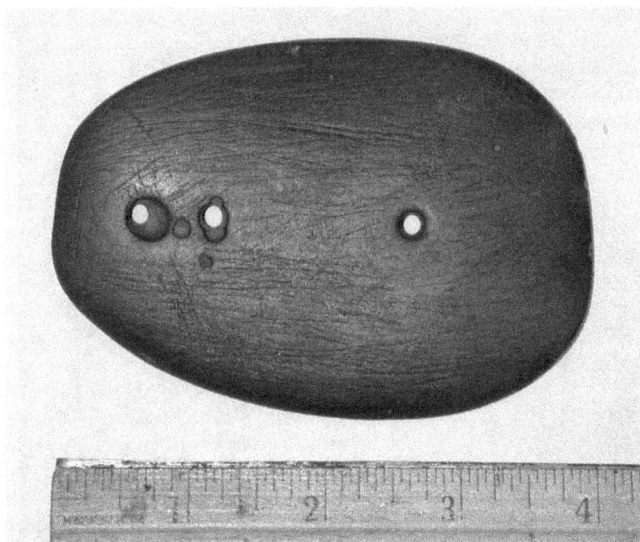

A seer stone (Stone 2) associated with the Whitmer family. This stone became part of the RLDS church's museum holdings sometime around 1950. Courtesy of Community of Christ Archives.

Jacob and Elizabeth (Schott) Whitmer descendants, Mayme (Whitmer) Koontz, Lillian Merle (Koontz) Barchers, and Lillian's husband Henry Barchers, exhibit the Jacob Whitmer artifacts in Richmond, Missouri, ca. 1950s. Courtesy of Community of Christ Archives.

Lillian Merle (Koontz) Barchers holds the Jacob Whitmer seer stone (Stone 3), in Richmond, Missouri, ca. 1950s. Photographs by Darrell Bolt, Independence, Missouri, courtesy of Community of Christ Archives.

Heman Smith omitted these concluding chapters, feeling that they might be inaccurate and therefore embarrassing to the RLDS church. While John was not a firsthand witness of all the events noted in his history, he kept in touch with some former friends and perused press accounts. Although Heman Smith found John's observations of the church's final days in Missouri and its sojourn in Illinois unpersuasive, John's observations are now known to be quite consistent with the findings of later scholarship.

Over the years, the contents of John's early church history have been available in the Community of Christ Archives in Independence and in facsimile formats at the LDS Church History Library in Salt Lake City.[21] The RLDS church also furnished a typescript of the manuscript to Clarence Wheaton of the Church of Christ Temple Lot in the 1920s as part of a period of "working harmony" between the two movements.[22]

One Sunday afternoon in 1922, C. J. Hunt and two other RLDS elders visited the Far West farmhouse where John and Sarah had lived. John's daughter, Sarah Elizabeth Whitmer Johnson Kerr, showed them the room where John died in 1878. "During this short interesting interview," wrote Hunt, "the aged daughter spoke feelingly of her noble parent." Wiping tears from her face, she said, "My father was an honest, truth-loving man."[23] In an adjacent room, they saw a large portrait of John. Although they did not describe this portrait, it seems likely it was a large charcoal portrait copied during the 1890s from an earlier photograph. This charcoal portrait came into the RLDS church's possession, probably in the 1930s.[24] In 1958, two of John's descendants presented photographs of John and Sarah and their family Bible to the LDS Church History Library "to

21. Whitmer's history has been published at least four times: Heman C. Smith, "Church History," 1908; Tanner and Tanner, *John Whitmer's History* (1966); McKiernan and Launius, *An Early Latter Day Saint History* (1980); and Westergren, *From Historian to Dissident: The Book of John Whitmer* (1995).

22. Samuel A. Burgess to Elbert A. Smith, 27 January 1926. This arrangement continued until 1925.

23. Hunt, "An Acknowledgement to John Whitmer, One of the Eight Witnesses of the Book of Mormon," 131.

24. The style of the frame matches three other family portraits that once hung in the John Whitmer homestead. Three oval photographs of later Whitmer generations, framed in the same style and material, hung in the home of Lorene Pollard.

David Whitmer's trunk. Courtesy of Community of Christ Archives.

Israel A. Smith, president of the RLDS church, with David Whitmer's trunk. The trunk was donated to the church by the Blankmeyer family in 1953. Courtesy of Community of Christ Archives.

preserve the memory of their ancestor."[25] The photograph of John is undated but was apparently that from which the charcoal portrait was copied
in the 1890s.

Oil portraits of Oliver Cowdery and Elizabeth Ann Whitmer
Cowdery that passed into John's daughter Sarah's hands after Elizabeth
Ann's death were still hanging in John Whitmer's farmhouse through the
1920s. The RLDS church acquired these treasured paintings in 1929 and
displayed them prominently as part of the RLDS church's centennial celebration conference in April 1930.[26] The Community of Christ Museum in
the Community of Christ Temple, Independence, Missouri, often displays
Oliver's and Elizabeth Ann's portraits.

Other important Whitmer family articles are two trunks. As noted
above, Helen Farwell Blankmeyer, David Whitmer's great-granddaughter,
donated the first David Whitmer trunk to the RLDS church in 1953.[27] The
second trunk, which also belonged to David Whitmer, is currently housed
at the LDS Church History Museum in Salt Lake City. Its acquisition was
reported at a conference of the Seattle Washington Stake on March 3, 1957,
by a LDS visitor, Donald Lee, who wrote this account:

> Brother Nelson Snow had a boy six years old who had a neighbor boy
> playmate the same age, and during the time they were together the

25. Mrs. Ethel Lewellen of Kidder, Missouri, and Mrs. Constance E. Johnson Burdick of Polo, Missouri, are "both extremely active in their Protestant community churches" and "are proud of the part their noted ancestor played in the early history of the Church," as noted in "Rare Photos Donated to Church by John Whitmer's Descendents," 11.

26. About 1929, Ella E. Johnson, John Whitmer's granddaughter, of Far West, donated portraits of William Cowdery, Oliver Cowdery, and Elizabeth Ann Whitmer Cowdery. The presentation was made formally at the 1930 conference. *Conference Daily, Herald* (April 1930): 14, 50, 70. C. Edward Miller paid to have them restored by the Sarachek Art Galleries. C. Ed. Miller to Bishop J. A. Becker, 1 January 1930. An RLDS church service group, Laurel Club, paid for their reframing. The portraits were probably paint-ed by a Mr. Welber of the Kirtland, Ohio, area. Vilate Murray Kimball to Heber C. Kimball, 12 September 1837.

27. Helen Farwell Van Cleave Blankmeyer is David Whitmer's great-granddaughter through the line of David's daughter, Julia Ann Whitmer Schweich. David's grand-daughter, Josephine Helen Schweich Van Cleave, married James R. B. Van Cleave. Their daughter, Helen Farwell Van Cleave, born November 19, 1908, married Dr. Charles Harrison Blankmeyer. Dear, *Two-Hundred-Thirty-Eight Years of the Whitmer Family*, 43.

Snow boy who was of an LDS family and attended Primary regularly, invited the neighbor boy whose family name was Twelve. When his mother found out he was going to a church organization, she asked the boy what Church it was. The boy said L. D. S.

The Twelve lady said, tell your father to come over to my place this evening; we might have something he would be interested in. When Brother Snow came home, his son gave him the message from Mrs. Twelve. After supper he went to the Twelve house. Mrs. Twelve went in another room and came out with a small chest, shaped like an old fashioned trunk about 20 inches long, 14 inches wide and perhaps 16 inches deep. Covered with cowhide, the hair side out, badly worn, the covering broken[,] some of it worn off and the initials D. W. on the side made by round headed tacks.

Mr. Twelve said, for many years they had moved the chest from place to place with them they didn't know why but supposed it was because it was an heirloom which was handed down until it finally come into their possession. On one occasion Mr. Twelve said a house was entirely destroyed by fire except the room where the chest was.

The chest was opened by Brother Snow and Mr. Twelve and they found several books and some papers among them a book of Mormon with Oliver Cowdery's name written on the fly leaf in his own hand-writing. There were other books—all church books. There was also a letter written by Mrs. Martin Harris telling that because Martin spent so much time away from home with the Prophet Joseph Smith she became vexed and begged Martin to bring home the manuscript of 116 pages and that during the night she burned them in their stove. Mr. Twelve said that the original book of Mormon manuscript was also in the chest but had been sold sometime before. Mr. Twelve said I don't know a thing about your church to my knowledge I or my wife have never been at one of your services, but we can testify that everything in the chest is true because it's always been in our family and you are welcome to all of it.... David Whitmer on his death bed asked for the chest and opened it, took the Book of Mormon from it and said, "Before God and angels I swear the book is true, that it is the word of God, and I did see and handle the plates from which it was translated by Joseph Smith."[28]

---

28. Donald Lee, untitled statement, 3 March 1957. Lee's hometown is identified as Springville, Utah.

This trunk is also associated with having held the Book of Mormon printer's manuscript. The Twelves are David Whitmer descendants through his grandson George Schweich's line.[29]

After the passing of John's daughter, Sarah Elizabeth Johnson Kerr, her daughter, Ella Johnson, continued living in the Whitmer homestead into the 1930s.[30] The LDS church acquired the property in 1974.[31] The building was razed before the decade's end.

In 1972, church history advocates honored John Whitmer by founding and naming a church-oriented historical association for him. The John Whitmer Historical Association is an independent scholarly society composed of individuals of various religious faiths who share a lively interest in the history of the Restoration movement.[32]

To sum up the life and significance of John Whitmer, eighth witness, it is appropriate to note that despite limited educational and economic opportunities, and at times a deep personal reluctance, John Whitmer proved to be a remarkably persistent participant in the unique religious events of his lifetime. Although he stood apart for forty years from the church he helped establish, his involvement in the beginnings of Mormonism continues to fuel a long-lived legacy of controversy and success.

Although Mormonism's earthly forms failed him, John found life-long meaning in the essence of its story. Despite separation from the church and alienation from former neighbors, he continually upheld the trust given to him by the friends of his youth.[33] John's seventy-plus years of life offers a testimony of faith in spite of disagreement. It transcends a

29. George and Sarah ("Sally") Schweich's daughter, Ruby Schweich Twelves, married Mr. Twelves. Dear, *Two Hundred Thirty-Eight Years of the Whitmer Family*, 41.

30. Ella Johnson died February 25, 1932. Ibid., 40.

31. On February 2, 1974, John P. Jones, Marjorie P. Jones, John E. Burdick, and Betty A. Burdick sold 361.5 acres in section 14, township 56, range 29 to the LDS church. The transaction was recorded March 4, 1974. Caldwell County Land Records, Book 151, 82. My thanks to Alexander L. Baugh for providing this source. Alex Baugh, e-mail to author, March 25, 2008.

32. On September 18, 1972, fourteen people met in RLDS historian Richard Howard's home in Independence, Missouri, and organized the John Whitmer Historical Association. During a debate on the name for the new group, Warren Jennings suggested that of John Whitmer, the first historian of the Latter Day Saint movement.

33. Roberts, "John Whitmer," *New Witnesses for God II*, 324.

record, though honorable in itself, of a man's simple devotion to family and work. The last of the eight witnesses to die, John was a fierce protector of church memories both tangible and intangible. His life story continues to intrigue and inspire.

APPENDIX A

Provenance of The Book of John Whitmer

ALTHOUGH DAVID WHITMER came into possession of a number of historical Mormon artifacts following the death of Oliver Cowdery in 1850, John Whitmer also apparently had in his possession, significant early Mormon documents throughout his lifetime.

One such artifact was an early copy of the Book of Mormon characters. Reorganization elder Edmund C. Brand, left the following account of a visit with John Whitmer at Far West, in 1875:

> I visited Mr. John Whitmer at his residence at Far West, Caldwell County, Missouri, on the 18th of February, 1875. He also bore his testimony to me concerning the truth, and declared that his testimony, as found in the "Testimony of Eight Witnesses," in the Book of Mormon, is strictly true. He showed me a facsimile of the characters of the plates, copied from the plates in the handwriting of Joseph Smith.[1]

John also had copies of the manuscripts of Joseph Smith's New Translation of the Bible and manuscript revelations from which the Book of Commandments were printed in Independence, Missouri, in 1833.[2]

Between 1831 and 1838, his period of service as church historian, John produced a ninety-six-page manuscript history of the church, known as "The Book of John Whitmer." The manuscript was written on the pages of an ordinary-looking, ledger-style book of about three hundred bound pag-

---

1. Brand, statement regarding his visit to John Whitmer on February 18, 1875. See also John Whitmer to Heman C. Smith, 11 December 1876.

2. One manuscript copy of Joseph Smith's Old Testament revisions was included with materials turned over by George Schweich to the RLDS church in 1903 with the printer's manuscript of the Book of Mormon. A second manuscript of Joseph's Bible revision remained in the hands of John Whitmer's descendant Lorene E. Pollard until 2006. Six fragments of the Book of Commandments manuscript were included with the materials furnished by Schweich. Walter Wayne Smith to First Presidency, 14 September 1925.

es with pasteboard covers. John left more than two hundred of these pages blank. This ledger is similar to other church record books from 1835–36. Records such as the Kirtland Revelation Book, Joseph Smith's 1835–36 diary, the 1836 Elders' Quorum Record, etc., are all recorded in similar-sized pasteboard-covered ledger books.

Church leaders asked John to relinquish his history in 1838, but Whitmer refused, and the manuscript history remained in John Whitmer's personal possession until near the time of his death in 1878. On a couple of occasions, John added additional entries after his separation from the church. Believing it would be his last entry, John inscribed,

> some temporal movements have not proved satisfactory to all parties has also terminated in the expulsion of many members, ~~among whom is W.E.~~ [*sic*] ~~Phepls and myself. . . . Notwithstanding my present situation, which I hope will soon be bettered and I find favor in the eyes of God and all men his saints . . . . Farewell.~~[3]

Again, sometime after Joseph Smith Jr.'s June 27, 1844, death, John added the following entry about prophetic succession:

> [Events] Brought Joseph Smith & his brother Hiram to an untimely end a[nd?] also the Scattering of the Church and the twelve who assumed the authority of leading the Church were Scattered from Nauvoo and suffered great afflictions. As also James J. Strang who also professes to be appointed by a letter received from Joseph as being appointed Seer Revelator Prophit [*sic*] & Successor of him Joseph, also Sidney Rigdon he drew a portion after him.
>
> Now it came to pass that the twelve of whom Brigham Young is leader. . . .[4]

John's manuscript ends here abruptly at the bottom of page 96 with an incomplete sentence. He must have experienced some kind of interruption this last time he worked on it.

Apparently, sometime before John's death, his manuscript history was forwarded to Richmond, Missouri. Evidence is that, shortly after John died in 1878, Orson Pratt and Joseph F. Smith visited Far West, Missouri, in hopes of obtaining The Book of John Whitmer. John's son, Jacob D.

3.   Whitmer, Book of John Whitmer, chapter 19, p. 85.
4.   Ibid., chapter 22, p. 96.

Whitmer, told them, "We've got no history here, all father's papers have gone to Richmond long ago."[5] From their account, Jacob was not overly cordial, so it is possible that he told them about the transfer to his uncle, David Whitmer in Richmond, and then, afterward, took steps to put the papers into David's possession. At some point, John's papers were apparently placed in the care of James R. B. Van Cleave, a Chicago newspaper reporter.[6] In October 1881, Van Cleave conducted a significant interview with David Whitmer that appeared in the October 17, 1881, *Chicago Times*. Van Cleave married David Whitmer's granddaughter, Josephine Helen Schweich, on November 12, 1882, at Richmond, Missouri, at the residence of David Whitmer.[7] As James became acquainted with the family experience, he became interested in one day writing a history of Mormonism from the Whitmers' perspective. After John's death, James Van Cleave spent several days looking over John's manuscripts and papers. In preparation for writing this history, James "obtained consent of John Whitmer's daughters [*sic*] to remove the papers he had selected … and brought them to Richmond, Mo."[8]

James located John's papers in Richmond, where they had been deposited in a bank vault. Since he was unable to complete his book on the history of Mormonism, the manuscript passed into the possession of Van Cleave's brother-in-law George Schweich, who was also David Whitmer's grandson.

Assistant LDS church historian Andrew Jenson was very interested in obtaining a copy of The Book of John Whitmer. His efforts proved fruitless until 1893 when he visited Richmond, on September 24–27, 1893, and obtained permission from George Schweich to make a handwritten copy of it. Schweich, who was associated with the Whitmerite church, as-

5. "Report of Elders Orson Pratt and Joseph F. Smith," *Latter-Day Saints Millennial Star* 40, no. 50 (December 16, 1878): 785–86.

6. "James R. B. Vancleave [*sic*], (a fine looking, intelligent young newspaper man of Chicago, who is paying his addresses to Miss Josephine Schweich grand-daughter of David Whitmer)." Pratt and Smith, "Interview with David Whitmer, September 7–8, 1878."

7. David Whitmer family Bible.

8. Deming, "The Polygamy Revelation," 1.

sisted Jenson in the proofing of his copy against the original manuscript. Jenson noted:

> I went to work immediately copying John Whitmer's old record, in the store of Geo. Schweich, who assisted me some in reading proof. Mr. Schweich did not think that the little old book with faded writing was the very book that I had been hunting for, but as I perused it, I came to the conclusion, without telling him so, that it contained all that John Whitmer ever wrote on Church History; hence I was anxious to copy every word contained in it. Mr. Schweich reluctantly allowed me to take it to my hotel where I spent all night copying, and in the morning returned the original to him….and now when found, we discovered that it contained only a little of historical value. Yet John Whitmer recorded events which are not recorded elsewhere.[9]

He described the manuscript as a bound volume of white paper pages, eight inches by twelve and one-half inches in size, "bound very plain, with paper sides and cloth back."[10]

Jenson carried his handwritten copy of the history to Salt Lake City and produced a typewritten copy. He then placed a copy of his typescript on file in the LDS church historian's office and made a second copy available to the Reorganized Church of Jesus Christ of Latter Day Saints, headquartered, at the time, in Lamoni, Iowa.[11]

Additionally, RLDS member Richard J. Lambert, of Lamoni, produced a certified typescript of the manuscript in 1918.[12]

When George Schweich sold the printer's manuscript of the Book of Mormon to the RLDS church in 1903, John's manuscript history, the

---

9. Jenson, *Autobiography of Andrew Jenson*, 209.

10. Jenson, Introduction to the 1893 typescript of The Book of John Whitmer.

11. Photocopy of Andrew Jenson's typescript of The Book of John Whitmer and accompanying note, which reads: "March 14–[18]'94, The enclosed is ~~double~~ Copy of John Whitmer's Record—Obtained by Andrew Jensen [*sic*], 1893."

12. "This is to certify that I have this day completed a comparison of the history written by the hand of John Whitmer, with the copy here presented and to which this certificate is affixed; having made such corrections as I found to be necessary to make them agree in word, punctuation, spelling and any other way which might possibly effect the sense in any degree." Lambert, certificate affixed to the The Book of John Whitmer Kept by Commandment.

Caractors, and fragments of the Book of Commandments manuscript were also transferred.[13]

Whitmer's history has appeared in print several times. In 1908, RLDS church historian Heman C. Smith published it as "Church History," in the RLDS history periodical, *Journal of History* 1, no. 1, 2, 3 (January, April, July, 1908): 45–63, 135–50, 292–305.

Historical enquirer and former RLDS member, Pauline Hancock, produced a typescript of John's history around 1960. The preface to Pauline's mimeographed copy reads:

> The manuscript up to page 85 was published by the [RLDS church in 1908]….This includes entries made up to March 1838, but the last three chapters have never been published. The entire manuscript of John Whitmer's History is in the Reorganized Church of Jesus Christ of Latter Day Saints' Library in Independence, Mo.
>
> A microfilm containing the complete history can be seen in the Genealogical Library of the Latter Day Saints in Salt Lake City, Utah, also a bound copy of the entire history is in the Utah State Historical Library in Salt Lake City.
>
> We found that the Latter Day Saints Historian's office in Salt Lake City has the microfilm of John Whitmer's History, but they emphatically refused to show it to us when we visited their Library, September 21, 1960.
>
> We have now obtained the microfilm of John Whitmer's complete history and have had it printed from the microfilm and bound into a book so that others may also read these items of history that have been held back by the churches that have the original history.[14]

In 1966, Jerald and Sandra Tanner of Modern Microfilm in Salt Lake City, Utah, published a version of the history. And, in 1980, the RLDS church's Herald Publishing House produced a new version edited by F. Mark McKiernan and Roger D. Launius. The McKiernan and Launius edition was subject to some editorial oversights and differs in places from both John Whitmer's manuscript and Jenson's typescript.

LDS scholar Bruce Westergren, authored an annotated edition of John's history entitled *From Historian to Dissident: The Book of John Whit-*

13. Walter Wayne Smith to First Presidency, 14 September 1925.

14. Hancock, preface to the "The Book of John Whitmer Kept by Commandment."

mer. Westergren produced a solid transcription of John's history. But, the work did little to help readers understand the life of John Whitmer, the man who compiled the text. This current attempt at a biography of John is an outgrowth of that perception.

The location of the manuscript is uncertain from 1903 until around 1930. It was probably in the possession of Heman C. Smith, RLDS church historian, from the date of its acquisition until the end of his tenure in 1919. The historian's office and church library were housed in the Herald Publishing House offices at Lamoni, Iowa.

In 1907, a devastating fire destroyed the Herald publishing operations along with the historian's office and library. The church historian had been busy collecting documents and historical materials dealing with the early church and with the period of the Reorganization. These valuable archives, as well as some "important books belonging to the church library, were kept in the office of church historian Heman C. Smith."[15]

About twenty-eight hundred volumes, as well as documentary materials relating to the rise of the Restoration and the Reorganization, were lost. Heman Hale Smith succeeded in rescuing fifty-two volumes from the library.[16] Several manuscripts, along with church membership records, were housed in the Herald House vault during this period. The fire occurred about 7:40 a.m. on January 5, 1907. Because the vault had not yet been opened for the business day, the materials within were preserved. Among these were the Book of Mormon printer's manuscript, and probably John Whitmer's history and the Inspired Version manuscript materials.

In 1918, the RLDS church furnished a copy of the manuscript to Clarence Wheaton of the Church of Christ (Temple Lot), during a time of cooperative harmony between the two religious bodies.[17]

---

15. Pement and Edwards, *A Herald to the Saints*, 108.

16. Goodyear, "A History of the General Church Library of the Reorganized Church of Jesus Christ of Latter Day Saints," 19.

17. In 1918, after a decade or more of negotiation, the Church of Christ Temple Lot and the RLDS church approved "Articles of Working Harmony," which recognized reciprocal priesthood authority and membership, CofC Archives. This arrangement continued until 1925. For the provision of a copy of John Whitmer's manuscript history to the Church of Christ Temple Lot, see Samuel A. Burgess to Elbert A. Smith, 27 January 1926.

The manuscript subsequently passed into the care of the next RLDS church historian, Walter Wayne Smith, whose tenure was from 1919 to 1923. Church headquarters moved from Lamoni, Iowa, to Independence, Missouri, in 1920; so the manuscript may have been moved to Independence during this period. Samuel A. Burgess became church historian in 1923 and served until 1942. However, the manuscript apparently remained in Walter W. Smith's possession until 1925. Walter Smith's following letter reveals that he transferred the history manuscript in 1925 into the care of the RLDS first presidency:

> I am returning Brother Burgess's letters and the following data.-
>
> The John Whitmer Manuscript History was written by John Whitmer, brother of David Whitmer, in accordance with revelation commanding him to write. It was left at the death of John Whitmer in the custody of David Whitmer at Richmond, Mo. At the death of David Whitmer in 1887, it was left in the custody of his grandson George Schweich who kept it until he turned it over to the Reorganized Church. The 11 pages of Manuscript containing the early revelations and a copy of the first six chapters of Genesis supplied and corrected by Joseph Smith the same as is published in the Inspired Version was with the book and had been received by David Whitmer from Oliver Cowdery at his death in 1850 at least that was the history of this Mss. given by David Whitmer's folks when interviewed at Richmond. This was substantially what Schweisch said when he turned over the Book of Mormon Mss. and the Whitmer History the Mss. of the Revelations, etc., in the old Ensign building. Some of the men who participated in this memorable event are still living. I was present with Roderick May, Joseph Smith and E. L. Kelley were there, R. S. Salyards, Heman C. Smith, and R. C. Evans, and I believe Pres. F. M. Smith was there.
>
> I made a careful search of these Mss. while I was Historian, the Whitmer History the Mss. of the Revelations which were apparently being set in the office of the Evening and the Morning Star at Independence as the Book of Commandments and the copy of the six chapters of Genesis were all together as they came from Whitmers, they all came from the same source to us.
>
> It is apparent that these pages are from the copies made in Ohio for publication in the Star and the Book of Commandments, the para-

graph marks indicate that this is true[;] no other place are the numbers as they are in the Mss. except in the Book of Commandments.[18]

During Samuel A. Burgess's tenure as church historian, the RLDS church constructed a spacious auditorium/headquarters building in Independence. Intended as a fire proof building, the Auditorium provided space for the historian's office and library. The manuscript was probably stored in this area, located along the central north wall of the Auditorium, in a space originally constructed to house a radio broadcasting studio. The historian's office and later, library-archives, were located in this area until 1992. During the summer of 1992, the library-archives moved into the temple complex adjacent to the Auditorium. The Book of John Whitmer manuscript now reposes at the archives, in the Independence Community of Christ Temple.

In 1974, in a historic agreement, RLDS historian Richard P. Howard and Earl E. Olson of the LDS church history department arranged an exchange of microfilmed historical materials between the RLDS and LDS churches. A microfilm of the John Whitmer manuscript was included among the microfilmed materials made available for scholarly use through the LDS church history department.[19]

The Whitmer manuscript is presently in the best state of preservation that it has enjoyed for many decades. Around 1970, RLDS church historian Richard P. Howard made arrangements for the manuscript's long-term preservation. The ninety-six pages containing John's history were removed from the ledger, laminated with a protective covering designed to minimize any harmful effects from future scholarly use, and bound in a modern binding. This format proved easier for scholars to use, but made it harder to read some portions of John's handwriting.

The institution that has provided stewardship and care for the manuscript for more than one hundred years, the Reorganized Church of Jesus Christ of Latter Day Saints, officially became Community of Christ on April 6, 2001.

18. Walter Smith to First Presidency, 14 September 1925.

19. "Microfilm of Historical Documents Will Benefit Saints Church Library," *Examiner* (November 23, 1974): 10; also "Churches Exchange Copies of Historic Documents," *Herald*, 122:90–91.

In 2005, visiting scholars associated with the Joseph Smith Papers Project were unable to read several obscure passages from this manuscript. Sharalyn Duffin, assistant editor on the project, proposed the initiation of a new round of joint conservation designed to provide better access to the manuscript's obscured handwriting and restore it to its original form. Fortunately, advances in conservation methods and materials made it possible to reverse the 1970s lamination process.

In late 2005, the Whitmer manuscript was released to LDS conservator, Chris McAfee, for transport to Salt Lake City where conservation work was provided courtesy of The Church of Jesus Christ of Latter-day Saints Family and Church Historical Department (now LDS Church History Library). This conservation work was similar to that earlier conducted by the churches on the Inspired Version/Joseph Smith New Translation manuscript materials, in 1996, and the Book of Mormon printer's manuscript, in 1998. During this year-long project, the pages of the delicate Whitmer history manuscript were carefully delaminated, cleaned, washed, deacidified, stabilized, repaired, and reassembled back into their original ledger book covers.[20] The manuscript was returned to the Community of Christ Archives on March 15, 2006, by Mark Lyman Staker. Visiting scholars may again experience the John Whitmer manuscript history as John knew it.

According to a 2008 agreement, the content of John Whitmer's history, which has long been available to scholars of the movement, is included as part of the extensive Joseph Smith Papers Project. In light of the improved access to the content, as a result of recent restoration efforts, this appearance should be the most accurate transcription yet available.

---

20. Following the recent conservation, Sharalyn Duffin observed, I "was exceptionally pleased with the results of conservation, and found that most of the once obscure passages (due to the lamination) are quite legible now." Sharalyn Duffin e-mail to author, March 20, 2006.

John Whitmer's First and Last Editorials

John Whitmer, "To the Patrons of the Latter Day Saints' Messenger and Advocate," *Latter Day Saints' Messenger and Advocate* 1, no. 9 (June 1835): 135–37.

To the Patrons of the Latter Day Saints' Messenger and Advocate.

On assuming the editorship of this paper, its patrons, no doubt, will expect me to give them an outline of the course I intend to pursue while conducting its columns in future.

The labors of this station, to those acquainted with them, are known to be many and complicated; the responsibility resting upon an individual who steps forward in our religious country, at this day, and assumes to teach others the gospel of the Lord Jesus, and point the path to holiness, is fraught with so many reflections of importance, that one would scarce venture forward without faltering, were it not for the fact, that good may be done, the field being wide, the harvest great and the laborers few. Not that all men are pursuing the right way, and are walking before God according to his holy commandments, do I say religious world—far from this. Were I sensible that all *religions* were *one* religion, and that *one* the true, it would be foreign from [to] my heart to think that my feeble exertions could benefit mankind: for if it were thus, my labors would be uncalled for. But while we discover so many, one is led to enquire, which is right? Has the Lord ordained so many ways for the salvation of his people? Does this, almost numberless train of professions, comport with the scriptures? Does it show one Lord and one faith? And amid so many professed gospels, where is the one which is correct, and where is that order of things which the Lord approbates and acknowledges his? If *all* are not *one*, and if these, or a part are incorrect, to convince men of the *correct* one, needs labor—and that mine may bear the strict scrutiny of my Master, in the great day approaching, I shall endeavor to have it correspond with the strictest principles of virtue and holiness.

Yet, another reflection, that one is destined to labor for some thousands, and suit matter for all, would be a sufficient excuse to urge on my own part, to my friend and brother,—who has conducted this paper since its commencement with so much talent and ability, for him to select another person, were it not that every man is to be rewarded for his diligence and perseverance in attempting to do good, by one who knows the thoughts and intents of the hearts of all.

In this introduction, then, I take the occasion to say, that I shall not labor to please men, any farther than a relation of sacred principles will be satisfactory. The applause of this world may be courted by whom it may, and enjoyed, (if enjoyment it can be called) by whoever possesses it, but with me it will be regarded as worthless as the idle wind or the vainly attempted allurements of fabled vision. So with the frowns and scoffs of men their worthlessness alike shall be considered as a parallel of the beating waves against the rocks in the distant ocean, and the rushing tornado in the trackless wilderness—one may foam its anger in perpetual solitude, and the other discharge its fury and its wrath without injury—they lose their force and spend their violence in fruitless attempts to harm in vain.

There is a way of salvation,—a path to heaven—a crown for the pure in heart, and principles teaching men how to escape the evil and enjoy the good. One way, and only one has the Lord pointed out for me to pursue in order to obtain eternal life, and it shall be my duty to set forth such facts as are calculated to inform the mind on those principles. That they are plainly written will not be doubted by those who have made themselves acquainted with *all* the revelations extant, notwithstanding a majority of the professing inhabitants of our country, doubt there being any other than the one given to the Jews, and a few churches among the Gentiles, by a part of the apostles.

The last item is one that has been, and still is a matter of much controversy. Such as profess to be in the right way and enjoy the true light, are disturbed, while those who fear for the safety and profits of their craft, are trembling lest the world will be dissuaded from following them.

No man, possessing his common faculties of understanding, unconnected with, or influenced by sectarian prejudice, will hesitate to say that something is wrong; and how is the evil to be remedied? Men act for themselves, choose for themselves, and if saved are saved for themselves, and not for another—they cannot be driven into salvation, as compulsion would at once destroy their agency; and if that is taken away, why was it ever spoken "Whosoever will may take of the water of life freely?" Correct reasoning, plain facts, and undeniable assertions, on the plan of redemption, when presented to the mind, will, if any thing, call up that serious enquiry which is requisite in all. How often do we see men of first moral characters, bountiful to the poor, and filled with compassion toward the afflicted, enquiring for the "old paths" wherein Israel used to walk, standing with deep anxiety and concern for their souls, and say, "If I could but see the consistent order of which the revelations of the Lord teach, how gladly would I embrace it." How frequently do we also hear those whose names are registered with a church, say they are dissatisfied? and only continue because they have been made to believe it important that they should belong to some church?

The great point at issue, is, whether the Lord ever promised to bring back an order, in the last days, like the one in former times, and set free those who are in bondage to the systems and crafts of men; and from this another would necessarily arise, whether the situation of the world in this day requires it? And if so, has it been ushered in? These cannot be considered any other than items of deep moment to the human family, and worthy the careful investigation of all. If our opinion is based upon the rock, it is worth believing, and if it is a fable, it is unworthy the notice of the intelligent and the concern of the sure; but till these facts are settled, it may be well to investigate.

The principles of my predecessor have been faithfully written and ably defended; and it is only necessary to add, that the patrons of this paper will find mine to correspond with his.

The former correspondents of the Messenger and Advocate, are respectfully solicited to continue to write for its columns; and the elders abroad and travelling brethren, earnestly desired to give us accounts of their prosperity and travels.

With its former, and increasing correspondents, it is hoped that this paper will continue to be worthy of patronage; and as it continues to circulate and receive accounts of the increase and spread of truth, to be interesting to every family wherever it may appear.

The Elders and brethren generally are requested to obtain and forward subscribers, who will be entitled to their numbers gratis according to the conditions on the last page.

One reflection more, and only one—If, in the performance of the duties which now devolve upon me, I so discharge them as to meet the approbation of the pure in heart, and still maintain the present respectability of this paper, and above all to have my work correspond with the principles of holiness, that at the great day of the Lord Jesus, I may but receive the reward of the just and the approbation of the same, that a crown of righteousness may be placed upon my head, I shall be satisfied and give the praise and glory to the exalted name of the Most High.

JOHN WHITMER.

John Whitmer, "Address," *Latter Day Saints' Messenger and Advocate* 2, no. 6 (March 1836): 285–88; partially reproduced in Vogel, *Early Mormon Documents*, 5:239.

It may not be amiss in this place, to give a statement to the world concerning the work of the Lord,

It becomes my duty to inform you, that in consequence of other business, and other duties which call my immediate attention, my labors in the editorial department of this paper must cease for the present; and as this is the case, I must beg leave to make some remarks, as I am about being freed from this great responsibility. I will here say that for the increase of patronage for nine months past, so gratuitously bestowed upon unmerited talents, you have necessarily obliged me to tender you my deepest heart-felt gratitude. I still indulge a hope, notwithstanding the Advocate is about being transferred into other hands, that it will continue to receive its present support, and a rapid increase to its present subscription list, insomuch as the prospect are flourishing, and the future editor's talents are deserving of patronage; I indulge a hope, that great good may be done by this means: and more especially in these last days, while "Darkness covers the earth and gross darkness the people."

Almost six years have passed, since the church of Christ has been established: many and various are the scenes, that have passed before my eyes, since its commencement, during which time, we have been favored with the privilege, of making known to the world our belief in regard to salvation.

I take occasion here to add, that I rejoice exceedingly that this Herald of truth is in being, and ı enjoy the privilege of resigning it into so good and able hands as Pres. O. Cowdery whose character and standing in society need no commendation from me where he is personally known: for he is known to be a man of piety, of candor, of truth, of integrity, of feeling for the welfare of the human family, and in short, he is a man of God: God acknowledge[d] him as such in his revealed will: and should we not do so too?

While I reflect on leaving the editorial department, such a complicated mass of ideas burst upon my mind, that it is not possible to communicate them all. The great and responsible relation which a man sustains in occupying this station, to his fellow man, will have a tendency to humble, rather than exalt him in his own eyes; for he truly becomes a servant of all; and his words are left on record for present and future generations to scrutinize.

However there is consolation attached to these responsibilities, that gladdens the heart of an honest and humble saint, even a servant of servants: For after that in the wisdom of God [t]he world by Wisdom knew not God, it pleased God by the foolishness of preaching to save them that believe.—It is those things, which the world by their wisdom count foolishness, which converts the soul, and will prepare it to dwell in the presence of God, in the day of the Lord Jesus. "God has chosen the foolish things of the world to confound the things which are mighty; and base things of the world, and things which are despised, hath God chosen, yea; and things which are not, to bring to nought things that are."

While I reflect on the above sayings of the holy writer, it gladdens my heart, that I enjoy the privilege of living in this age of the world, when God in his kind providence, has began to work for the good of his long dispersed covenant people; when he has again made manifest his will, and has called servants by his own voice out of the heavens, and by the ministering of angels, and by his Holy Spirit; and has chosen the weak and simple to confound the wisdom of the wise: and to raise up and bring the church of the Lamb up out of the wilderness of wickedness, fair as the sun and clear as the moon. Which church took its rise April 6, 1830; and has thus far come up through much persecution and great tribulation.

It may not be amiss in this place, to give a statement to the world concerning the work of the Lord, as ı have been a member of this church of Latter Day Saints from its beginning; to say that the book of Mormon is a revelation from God, I have no hesitancy; but with all confidence have signed my name to it as such; and I hope, that my patrons will indulge me in speaking freely on this subject, as I am about leaving the editorial department—Therefore I desire to testify to all that will come to the knowledge of this address; that I have most assuredly seen the plates from whence the book of Mormon is translated, and that I have handled these plates, and know of a surety that Joseph Smith, jr. has translated the book of Mormon by the gift and power of God, and in this thing the wisdom of the wise most assuredly has perished: therefore, know ye, O ye inhabitants of the earth, wherever this address may come, that I have in this thing freed my garments of your blood, whether you believe or disbelieve the statements of your unworthy friend and well-wishes.

It is no trifling matter to sport with the souls of men, and make merchandise of them; I can say, with a clear conscience before God and man, that I have sought no man's goods, houses or lands, gold or silver; but had in view for my chief object, the welfare of the children of men, because I know that I have been called of God, to assist in bringing forth his work in these last days, and to help to establish it, and as many souls as would believe, and obey the truth, might be saved in his kingdom; and also assist in bringing about the restoration of the house of Israel, that they might magnify his name, for what he has done and is doing for the fulfillment of the prophecies of all the holy prophets that have written on this great and important subject, since the days of Adam, to this present time; and while I have been in the editorial department, I have endeavored to write, obtain and select such matter as was calculated to promote the cause of God, as far as my judgment was capable of discerning; and wherein I may have erred, I am conscientious and innocent; but do cheerfully and humbly ask pardon of those whose feelings in any wise I may have injured; by digressing in the least, from the strictest path of rectitude.

I would do injustice to my own feelings, if I did not here notice, still further the work of the Lord in these last days; the revelations and commandments given to us, are, in my estimation, equally true with the book of Mormon, and equally necessary for salvation, it is necessary to live by every word that proceedeth from the mouth of God; and I know that the Bible, book of Mormon and book of Doctrine and Covenants of the church of Christ of Latter Day Saints, contains the revealed will of heaven. I further know that God will continue to reveal himself to his church and people, until he has gathered his elect into his fold, and prepared them to dwell in his presence.

Men at times depend upon the say of others, and are influenced by their persuasions to embrace different systems. This is correct, inasmuch as the principle is a just one: God always commissioned certain men, to proclaim his precepts to the remainder of the generation in which they lived; and if they heeded not their sayings, they were under condemnation. Though weak may have been my arguments and feeble my exertions, to persuade others to believe as myself, the few months I have labored in this department, I trust, I have been the means of doing some good to my fellow men. If I were not sensible that I have been doing the will of my heavenly Father, I should regret, that I had ever suffered my name to become public; I could not endure the idea of having been the means of persuading men to detract from truth, and embrace error: it has been a principle in my heart to embrace truth, and reject error; and I trust it will remain in my heart forever.

I feel it my duty to say, to the Elders who have been laboring in the cause of our blessed Reedeemer [*sic*], and have taken the trouble, to procure subscribers for the Messenger and Advocate, the have my sincere thanks, and shall ever occupy a conspicuous portion of my gratitude. There are others who have been somewhat negligent in this thing, which is owing perhaps, in part, for want of proper instruction upon this point; not realizing that this periodical is opening and preparing many places, for such as are traveling to proclaim the gospel of our blessed Redeemer; whereas, if it has not been for this means, would have been closed and impenetrable. I desire therefore, that the Elders of the church of Latter Day Saints will avail themselves of every opportunity that presents itself of procuring subscribers for this paper, not for pecuniary interests, but for the welfare of the children of men. I hope that the Elders will do all the good in their power, as this is a day of "Warning and not of many words." Therefore, I trust you will have the spirit of God in your hearts to guide you into all truth, until the knowledge of God shall cover the earth as the waters cover the great deep, and the saints of God are gathered together, and Zion becomes the joy of the whole earth.

JOHN WHITMER.

APPENDIX C

John Whitmer's Patriarchal Blessing

Typescript, M. Wilford Poulson Papers, Perry Special Collections.
September 22, 1835 [given by Joseph Smith Jr.]

Blessed of the Lord is brother John: he shall live to a good old age, and his generation after him shall be blessed. He shall live to a good old age, and wax more and more steadfast in the work of the Lord, and he shall make a choice record of Israel unto the memory of his name. He shall truly be chastened wherein he steps aside, yet he shall escape the hand of the destroyer, and shall never fall by the hands of his enemies: and he shall be avenged of the wrongs he has sustained by them. He shall be blessed and a means of bringing many blessings upon his fathers [*sic*] family.

He shall be blessed with abundance of the good things of this earth with houses and lands, in the fruit of the field, with horses and with asses and she asses, with gold and with silver, and with precious stones, even the things of the lasting mountains. He shall be made mighty in the hands of his God, in bring [*sic*] to pass the redemption of Zion. The Lord shall be on his right hand and on his left; and shall go before his face and shall be his rearward, and shall turn aside all the shafts of his enemies. And he shall go down in honor and gray hairs, to the grave, and shall be caught up in the land to meet the Lord, and shall ever be with him; even so. Amen.

John Whitmer's Missouri Mormon War Trial Testimony

Document Containing the Correspondence, Orders, &c. *in Relation to the Disturbances with the Mormons; and the* Evidence *Given before the Hon. Austin A. King, Judge of the Fifth Judicial Circuit of the State of Missouri, at the Court-house in Richmond, in a Criminal Court of Inquiry, Begun November 12, 1838, on the Trial of Joseph Smith, Jr., and Others, for High Treason and Other Crimes Against the State,* 138–39.

John Whitmer, a witness for the State, produced, sworn and examined, deposeth and saith: About the 17th of April last, at a meeting of perhaps fifteen or twenty-five, in Far West, Joseph Smith, jr., spoke in reference to difficulties they had, and their persecutions, &c., in and out of the church. Mr. Smith said he did not intend in future to have any process served on him, and the officer who attempted it should die; that any person who spoke or acted against the presidency or the church should leave the country or die; that he would suffer no such to remain there; that they should lose their head. George W. Harris, who was there present, observed, "the head of their influence, I suppose." Smith replied, Yes, he would so modify it. Mr. Rigdon then got up, and spoke in connection with what Mr. Smith had been saying; and in speaking of the head of their influence, he said, that he meant that ball on their shoulders, called the head, and that they should be followed to the ends of the earth. Mr. Rigdon further remarked, that he would suffer no process of law to be served on him hereafter.

 Some time in June, after Mr. Rigdon had preached his "salt sermon," I held conversations with several Mormons on the subject of that sermon, and the excitement produced by the course and conduct of the presidency. Among others, I conversed with Alanson Ripley. I spoke of the supremacy of the laws of the land, and the necessity of, at all times, being governed by them. He replied, that as to the technical niceties of the law of the land, he did not intend to regard them; that the kingdom spoken of by the prophet Daniel had been set up, and that it was necessary every kingdom should be governed by its own laws. I also conversed with George W. Robinson, on the same subject, who answered, (when I spoke of being governed by the laws and, their supremacy,) ["]when God spoke he must be obeyed," whether his word came in contact with the laws of the land or not; and that, as the kingdom spoken of by Daniel had been set up, its laws must be obeyed. I told him I thought it was contrary to the laws of the land to drive men from their homes; to which he replied, such things had been done of old, and that the gathering of the saints must continue, and that dissenters could not live among them in peace.

I also conversed with Mr. J. Smith, jr., on this subject. I told him I wished to allay the (then) excitement, as far as I could do it. He said the excitement was very high, and he did not know what would allay it; but remarked, he would give me his opinion, which was, that if I would put my property into the hands of the bishop and high council, to be disposed of according to the laws of the church, he thought that would allay it, and that the church after a while might have confidence in me. I replied to him I wished to control my own property. In telling Mr. Smith that I wished to be governed by the laws of the land, he answered, "Now, you wish to pin me down to the law." And further this deponent saith not. JOHN WHITMER.

John Whitmer and David Whitmer, Interviews by P. Wilhelm Poulson, 1878

John Whitmer, Interview by P. Wilhelm Poulson, *Deseret News* 27, no. 28 (August 14, 1878): 2. Also in Vogel, *Early Mormon Documents*, 5:247–49.

P. Wilhelm Poulson reported the following interview with John Whitmer, April 1878:

> I—I am aware that your name is affixed to the testimony in the Book of Mormon that you saw the plates?
>
> He—It is so, and that testimony is true.
>
> I—Did you handle the plates with your hands?
>
> He—I did so!
>
> I—Then they were a material substance?
>
> He—Yes, as material as anything can be.
>
> I——Were they heavy to lift?
>
> He—Yes, and as you know gold is a heavy metal: they were very heavy.
>
> I—How big were the leaves?
>
> He—So far as I recollect, 8 by 6 or seven inches.
>
> I—Were the leaves thick?
>
> He—Yes, just so thick, that characters could be en graven on both sides.
>
> I—How were the leaves joined together?
>
> He—In three rings, each one in the shape of a D with the straight line towards the center.
>
> I—In what place did you see the plates?

He—In Joseph Smith's house; he had them there.

I—Did you see them covered with a cloth?

He—No. He handed them uncovered into our hands, and we turned the leaves sufficient to satisfy us.

David Whitmer, interview by P. Wilhelm Poulson, in "Correspondence," *Deseret News* 27, no. 29 (August 21, 1878): 13, reprinted in Cook, *David Whitmer Interviews: A Restoration Witness*, 22.

Poulson also recorded David Whitmer's understanding of the experience of the eight witnesses, n.d.:

I—Did the eight witnesses not handle the plates as a material substance?

He—We did not, but they did, because the faith of Joseph became so great that the angel, the guardian of the plates, gave the plates up to Joseph for a time, that those eight witnesses could see and handle them.

William E. McLellin: Our Tour West in 1847

William E. McLellin, "Our Tour West in [September] 1847," *Ensign of Liberty of the Church of Christ* 1, no. 7 (August 1849): 99–105.

When I published the third number of this paper, I did not then deem it wisdom to publish the particulars of the conference held in Far West, on the 7th and 8th days of Sept., with some of the original "witnesses" of the book of Mormon. But as circumstances have transpired since, and as matters now stand, we believe it to be our duty to present to our readers a history of that important conference. But let us premise a little here. It will be remembered that in Dec. 1846, I wrote a long letter to President David Whitmer. And in March and April following, I published the first and second numbers of this paper, and immediately sent them to him and his friends. When I parted with O. Cowdery the last of July, in Wisconsin, he immediately wrote to David and acquainted him with the fact that I was on my way to make him a visit. This letter he had received some days before I arrived.—Hence the whole matter of the stand we had taken in Kirtland was well [page 99, col. 2] known and well understood by those men, many weeks and months before I visited them. I have made the above remarks because I have been charged with waking up the Prophet in his duty, and because some have thought that those men acted without mature deliberation.

On the 4th of Sept., about sunset, I arrived in Richmond, Ray Co., Mo., at the residence of David Whitmer. We spent until midnight's hour in familiar converse relative to his gifts and callings from God, and concerning the great work of the last days. Not a jar appeared in our sentiments or feelings, and we retired. On the 5th, he had an engagement but in the evening he, his bro. Jacob, and myself, retired to a lonely place, and there under the cover of the night, and in the forest, David gave me a succinct history of the dealings of the Lord with him back until the year 1839, when I had last seen him. At the close of this interesting interview we bowed together in the stillness of a late hour at night, in the shady grove, and each vocally called upon God, the one after the other, while his Holy Spirit distilled upon our hearts as the morning dew.

On the 6th, David and Jacob Whitmer, and Hiram Page, accompanied me to Far West, to visit their brother John Whitmer. On the 7th, in the morning, we bowed in family prayer—David being mouth. But in the midst of his prayer his own weakness, and the greatness of the work of the Lord pressed in full view before him; he shrunk and cried aloud for mercy. His head as it were, was a fountain of tears, and his eyes streams of water; his whole frame trembled and shook under the power of God, and his natural strength began to give way, and he cried out, "Brethren lay hands upon me that I may have strength to do my duty." We arose and ministered to him; and [page 100, col. 1] if ever deep and powerful feeling filled my whole heart, that was the time. He received strength and concluded his prayer.

After breakfasting, we retired to a pleasant inner room, and dedicated ourselves to God, in a council capacity; and then held a lengthy consultation about the first rise and progress of the work from the year 1827 up to 1834, and onward to the present time. We conversed freely, and particularly about the re-organization of the same church by us in Kirtland, in Feb. 1847. I was particular to relate to them all the great and important principles made known to us, and upon which we had acted. The following revelation which we had received on the 10th of Feb. preceding, which was the cause of the re-organization, was read and approved:

[Revelation given to William E. McLellin, on February 10, 1847, at Kirtland, Ohio]

Verily I the Lord say unto those who are now present, who have bowed before me and unitedly asked in the name of Jesus, to know my will, I am not angry with you, but the Angels rejoice over you when they behold your faith in me; and your willingness to receive light and truth at my hand. And if you will continue to be united in my name, and keep the covenant which you have now made that you will always obey my voice, and always seek unto me when you lack wisdom; verily I the Lord, will lift you up, and no power of evil shall ever prevail against you: but I will bless you and lead you, and I will be your Ruler in time, and in eternity you shall dwell with me in peace. It is my will that in as much as you have taken upon you my name that you should now be freed from all your dead works, from all evil spirits, and from all unrighteousness, by being born into the church by obedience to the ordinances of baptism and confirmation, that I may build up unto myself a holy people, zealous of good works; who [page 100, col. 2] will walk with me by faith, and be prepared when the face of the covering shall be taken off of all flesh, and heaven be revealed unto men. Come then unto me and I will own you. Let my servant William [E. McLellin], who has separated himself unto me, to obey the voice of my spirit, though all manner of evil be spoken against him therefore, repent and turn away henceforth from all blindness of mind, and harshness of spirit, and fear of evil doers; and let him trust in me continually for deliverance, and I the Lord will hold him in mine own hands, and fulfill all my promises to him.

And now in as much as you desire to know my will and how you shall go forward to please me, as you have taken upon you the name of Christ, mine Anointed, then it will be pleasing unto me that you should also take upon you mine ordinances of baptism and confirmation, and then re-ordination—or rather a confirmation of the holy authority of the Priesthood which you have received in my church. Yea, let my servant William [E. McLellin] baptize and confirm, and then re-ordain my servnat [servant] Martin [Harris]. And thus shall he confirm his authority upon him by the laying on of hands and saying, Brother Martin I lay my hands upon you in the name of Jesus Christ, and I re-ordain you, and confirm upon you the office of high priest in the church of Christ, after the holy order of the Son of God. And I pray God in the name of Jesus, his son, to give unto you in your calling, all the gifts and blessings and powers thereof, and keep you faithful unto the end, amen. And then let my servant Martin [Harris] administer unto my servant William [E. McLellin] in the same manner, according to the same pattern. And then let my servant Leonard [Rich] likewise receive the same ministration.

Yea, let my servants William [E. McLellin] and Martin [Harris] and Leonard [Rich], do as the spirit [page 101, col. 1] of truth now directs them, and in which they feel a clearness, and I the Lord will open the way before you as seemeth to me good, and no power shall stay my hand, but I will accomplish my work and that speedily. For gainsayers shall be confounded, but my people who know my voice and follow me shall rejoice and continue to rejoice; and the glory shall be ascribed unto me, instead of unto man.

And now concerning the authority of my servant David [Whitmer], I would say unto you that no man being directed by my spirit will ever condemn what my spirit now teaches you. Go forward then, that my designs in the work of the last days may prosper in your hands. And now I say unto you, to always trust in me, and you shall never be confounded, worlds without end, amen."

Every part and principle of the above was scanned, and as I supposed well understood by all those present. We then agreed to call upon the Lord to know his mind and will concerning those who were present. And we agreed or covenanted to implicitly obey what the Lord might reveal to us. I took my seat at a table prepared to write; David took his seat near to me, and he requested the others to gather near around him.—Then after a few moments of solemn secret prayer, the following was delivered solely through and by David Whitmer, as the Revelator, and written by me as scribe, viz:

[Revelations given to David Whitmer, on September 7–8, 1847, at Far West, Missouri]
[No. 1] [p. 101]

Verily, verily thus saith the Lord unto you my servants David [Whitmer], and John [Whitmer], and William [E. McLellin], and Jacob [Whitmer], and Hiram [Page], it is for my name's sake saith the Lord God of hosts, that your sins are now forgiven, and that you shall have my word concerning you. Therefore marvel ye not that I the Lord your God have dealt with you on this wise, concerning you on this land. Behold I have looked upon [page 101, col. 2] you from the beginning, and have seen that in your hearts dwelt truth, and righteousness. And now I reveal unto you my friends, through my beloved son, your Savior. And for the cause of my church it must needs have been that ye were cast out from among those who had polluted themselves and the holy authority of their priesthood, that I the Lord could preserve my holy priesthood on earth, even on this land on which I the Lord have said Zion should dwell.

Now marvel not that I have preserved you and kept you on this land. It was for my purpose, yea even for a wise purpose, that the world and my church should not know, speaking after your manner of language; for my church for a time did not dwell on earth, —speaking of the righteousness of the church of Christ. For verily, verily saith the Lord, even Jesus, your Redeemer, they have polluted my name, and have done continually wickedness in my sight, therefore shall they be led whithersoever I will and but few shall remain to receive their inheritances. Therefore I say unto you my son David [Whitmer], fear not, for I am your Lord and your God; and I have held you in my own hands. You shall continue your inheritance on this my holy land; and it is for a wise purpose in me, which purpose shall be revealed hereafter.

It is even for the testimony that all those who are present have borne and remain honest therein, that the covenants that I the Lord have given you should be kept sacred on this land, and were it not so, you could not now receive wisdom at my hand. For I the Lord had decreed that my people, who had taken upon them my holy name, should not pollute the land by the holy authority of their priesthood. Now I say unto you that my church may again arise, she must acknowledge before me that they all [page 102, col. 1] have turned away from me and built up themselves. Even in the pride of their own hearts have they done wickedness in my name, even all manner of abominations, even such that the people of the world never was guilty of.

Therefore I the Lord have dealt so marvelously with my servant William [E. McLellin]. Therefore I have poured out my spirit upon him from time to time, that the "man of sin" might be revealed through him. To him I have given my Holy Spirit. I have inspired his heart to discern the true principles of my kingdom, that he may again build up my church as from the beginning. Therefore I have inspired him to build it up according to my law. Therefore he shall continue to do all things according to the pattern that I have shown to him. Now I say unto you my servant William [E. McLellin], that you may not err, be meek and humble before me, and you shall always know by my spirit the correct principles of my kingdom. Therefore I the Lord command you to instruct all the honest in heart, and to break down all those false theories and principles of all those who claim to hold authority from my church.—And the work that thou shalt do in my kingdom shall be to preach and to gather out those who are honest in heart, whithersoever thou canst find them. And after this mission thou shalt return towards thy home and preach wherever my spirit commands thee. For I have a work for thee to do in the land where thy family resides. For there shalt thy work commence.

Thou shalt build up my church even in the land of Kirtland, and set forth all things pertaining to my kingdom. Thou shalt write concerning the downfall of those who once composed my church, and set forth to the world by the light and power of my spirit, why I the Lord did not prosper [page 102, col. 2] them. For verily, verily thus saith the Lord unto you, thine heart have I prepared to do this work. It must needs be, in as much as they have all wandered and been led astray in many instances, that they must now be proven and tried, so that they may learn to keep my law, and do my will, saith the Lord your God. And if they prove themselves holy before me, then they shall have my word and my law from Zion. Therefore have I the Lord said that "the meek shall inherit the earth," even so, amen.

One thing in the foregoing revelation came in direct contact with one of my previous opinions. I had supposed that Kirtland would become the residence of David, the Lord's Prophet. But while I was marveling in my mind how the work could go on and he remain in Missouri, and also freely speaking to John Whitmer some of my thoughts and feelings on the subject, brother David came and seated himself near me again, and said, brother William, the Lord has something more for us, and you may write again. And the word of the Lord came as follows:

[No. 2]

Behold I the Lord, say unto you my friends, in as much as you have covenanted to be my friends, and to keep all my commandments, I will reveal unto you this mystery, which you have sought for; that in as much as it was expedient in me to preserve my church or a remnant thereof, agreeable to the covenants which I have made with all the holy saints from the beginning of the world.—Therefore as I had built up my kingdom according to my holy order, and placed you upon this land, and consecrated you to the holy order of my priesthood, therefore my servant David [Whitmer] if thou should'st leave this land, and those of thy brethren who have [page 103, col. 1] remained with thee, then you shall forfeit your right and make the word of God of none effect. For I have said unto you in days past and gone, that but few should remain to receive their inheritances. Therefore a commandment I give unto you my servant David [Whitmer], and also my servants John [Whitmer], and Hiram [Page], and Jacob [Whitmer], that you must remain until I command you, and then you shall only be permitted to visit the faithful in my kingdom. For now ye do hold the right of this, the consecrated land of Zion, that in the fullness of time your brethren may claim by right of the covenant which ye have kept, inheritances in the land of Zion. Now I say unto you all, that from time to time ye shall see and know by my Spirit all things pertaining to these words which I have now given you. Now I say no more unto you concerning this matter, even so, amen.

With the above I was perfectly satisfied. Cause and effect were both set forth, and we felt to acquiesce.— But then I saw what a great responsibility would rest on me, especially when I should return to Kirtland. I then saw and in some measure realized, that we should see each other but seldom. Near a thousand miles would separate us and our fields of labor,—for a season at least. And I said in my heart, O Lord, if thou hast a word of intelligence more for me, reveal it, O reveal it now to me! I expressed my anxiety to my brethren present, and the enquiry being made, the Lord through his servant David, made known, while I wrote the following:

[No. 3]

Verily, verily thus saith the Lord your God, unto my servant William [E. McLellin], as I have shown unto you at many a time by the power of my spirit, that I have called you to my work. Therefore I admonish you to [page 103, col. 2] be meek and lowly in heart, that you may have my spirit always to be with you. For it must needs be that you must have my spirit, even the spirit of discernment. For thou shalt discern between the righteous and the wicked, for there will be many spirits which shall manifest themselves in the church of Christ. And it must needs be that my servants who teach my people must discern all these things. Therefore I have given you the pattern, and the power, and the wisdom, and the understanding, to build up my church in Kirtland, to be a standard and a light to the inhabitants of the earth, that they may know that the church of Christ is established here on earth. And I the Lord will that you should teach my servants at Kirtland, and else-where, to adhere to the order of my church as it is written in the holy scriptures; that all who have not obeyed the gospel in my church may be taught the principles of my church in the light of truth and righteousness, in all holiness and meekness before me, saith your God. For it is wisdom in me saith the Lord, that my people who name my name should observe harmony and good order, that the truth of God may prevail among the children of men.

But here David said a vision opened before him, and the spirit which was upon him bid him stop and talk to me concerning it. He said that in the bright light before him he saw a small chest or box of very curious and fine workmanship, which seemed to be locked, but he was told that it contained precious things, and that if I remained faithful to God, I should obtain the chest and its contents. I marveled at this relation from the fact that on the 29th day of April 1844, while in vision, I saw the same or a similar chest, and received a similar promise from the Spirit which [page 104, col. 1] talked with me. I was told that it contained "the treasures of wisdom, and knowledge from God."

At this point we counseled particularly relative to the authority by which the church was reorganized in Kirtland, and the reasons why the Lord required us to be re-baptized, confirmed, ordained. They said the principles and reason which had actuated us were correct, and that they were ready. They felt it, they said, to be their duty to do as we had done. But it was late in the afternoon, and was raining, therefore we deemed it wisdom to wait until morning. Here objectors could not reasonably find fault and say that these men were over-persuaded, or that they acted in haste in this important matter.—but morning came, and a beautiful bright day it was too. We repaired to the water about a mile distant, and there on the bank of a beautiful stream, we dedicated ourselves to God in the united solemn prayer of faith. I then led those four men into the water and ministered to them in the name of the Lord Jesus. But as we returned again to our council room, brother David and I turned aside, and called upon the Lord, and received direct instruction how we should further proceed. And we all partook of bread and wine in remembrance of the Lord Jesus. I then confirmed those who were now born into the church of Christ, anew.—And then (as directed) I ordained H. Page to the office of High Priest, in the holy priesthood which is after the order of the Son of God. And we two ordained Jacob Whitmer to the same office. Then we all laid hands on John Whitmer and re-ordained him to the priesthood, and to be counselor to David in the first presidency of the church. And then with the most solemn feelings which I ever experienced, we stepped forward and all laid hands upon David and re-or- [page 104, col. 2] dained him to all the gifts and callings to which he had been appointed through Joseph Smith, in the general assembly of the inhabitants of Zion, in July 1834. The above being accomplished,

David said to me we will now inquire of God, and finish the revelation to you, commenced on yesterday; and we received the following, viz:

[No. 4]

Now again I the Lord say unto you my servant William [E. McLellin], that you must be contented with what you have received concerning Zion. Thou shalt again return to the land of Kirtland, and there thou shalt teach and expound, and write all things concerning my kingdom. For to thee have I given power, and in as much as you ask wisdom concerning those matters relative to my church, thou shalt in no wise stumble. For I the Lord willeth that my people should know the great preparation that must be brought about in establishing this last kingdom. Therefore I command thee to do all things in wisdom; and set forth no points concerning the redemption of Zion, for that matter remaineth with me, and I shall see to it as seemeth me good, that I may have all the glory thereof. Therefore it must needs be that you instruct all my servants concerning these matters, and this for my cause's sake.—And thou shalt teach them to instruct all men that they are only called to preach the gospel, and build up the church of Christ here on earth, according to that which is written.—Now I say unto you, my servant William [E. McLellin], to thee have I given wisdom and light, therefore teach them in spirit and in truth, and thou shalt be blessed in thy calling. And now you know your calling, therefore see to it, and I will bless you forever; Amen.

At this point we closed our conference. W. E. McLELLIN, Secretary.

[p. 105, col. 1] Remarks on the Above.

By reading the foregoing revelations and narrative attentively, our friends can see plainly what the Lord requires of David Whitmer. And can also see the duty of W. E. McLellin. And can assuredly see what is and will be the fate of that people who rose up in Danite fury, hurled defiance at all civil law, and cast out from among them the Lord's chosen witnesses. "But few of them will remain to receive their inheritances." That people called the LATTER-DAY SAINTS, have polluted themselves, polluted the name of the church, and also polluted the holy authority of their priesthood. And lest they should pollute the land of Zion, the Lord suffered them to be driven out from it. Now to suppose that any party of L. D. Saints will ever really prosper, is to suppose that the Lord has spoken falsely in the above revelations through his servant David. It matters not to me whether it is the Twelveites in the wilderness, the Wightites in Texas, the Strangites in Wisconsin, the Brewsterites scattered up and down, or the Wm. Smithites of Covington, Ky. All, yes, all of them, as parties, are doomed to disappointment and wo. But few of them will ever come into the true fold of Christ and be saved. They seem wedded to their idols. They appear to love their heresies, their false principles and their false doctrines, and still yet they love their abominable practices more. Notwithstanding there are many among them whom we once loved in the truth, yet because of their principles and their practices, we are bound by the duty that we owe God, to ourselves and to our race to speak thus plainly concerning them. O that they had walked in the commandments of their God, then at this day they would have been the most lovely people on the face of the whole earth. —EDITOR.

Far West

"Far West: The Old Mormon Settlement in Missouri. How It Appeared Thirteen Years Ago and What It is To-day. A Sketch of Its History," *Daily Morning Herald*, January 1, 1875.

Some twelve or thirteen years ago we had occasion to travel by private conveyance from Cameron in Clinton, to Mirable [*sic*], a small village in Caldwell county.

Our journey was rather a monotonous one, unrelieved by any incident worthy of note, for the only persons we encountered were a small party of Federal soldiers and a solitary traveler wending his way northward, and who returned our greeting with the cold glance of suspicion peculiar to those perilous days, for we were in the midst of the rebellion.

After journeying some seven or eight miles through prairie and red brush, occasionally relieved by patches of scrub oak and graceful belts of young timber that fringed the winding course of a bold stream which we were sometimes, under the necessity of crossing, about seven or eight miles from Cameron, in a southeasterly direction, we suddenly emerged upon a plain which had the appearance of a long deserted settlement.

It was in the month of July, and the surface of the ground was literally matted with clusters of dewberry vines, laden with tempting fruit. But a single human habitation appeared to relieve the monotony of the landscape, and the utter solitude of the locality was only rendered the more pronounced by the presence of innumerable wells, whose boxes and windlasses had long since disappeared, leaving nothing but the gloomy pits to tell the tale of thronging life that once existed there, and afford us a theme for moralizing on the mutability of all human affairs.

As we gazed with surprise and wonder on the strange and melancholy scene, our taciturn guide, the driver of the vehicle, broke his long silence with the remark: "We are now in the Mormon city of 'Far West,' and just across the hollow is the foundation of the temple."

So, indeed, we were, and how many, like ourselves, had lived for years within forty miles of this interesting locality, scarcely conscious of its existence!

But the matter of surprise was, that with the solitary exception before referred to, and with the occasional debris of a long-fallen chimney, scarce a vestige of the several hundred habitations that, some thirty years before, clustered in compact mass upon this beautiful prairie, remained to tell the tale of sudden rise and correspondingly prompt disappearance of a community which once counted its numbers by thousands. It seemed as though the vengeance of heaven had employed in its wrath the most uncompromising of Vandal means to wipe from the fair face of nature and the memory of men a foul and disgusting blot upon the body politic.

Such was our impression of the place, twelve or thirteen years ago.

What is it to-day? The delightful air of our autumn months and the gorgeous variation of foliage presented in the appearance of our native woods at that season of the year, are characteristics of our clime that never fail to evoke the enthusiastic admiration of the intelligent and contemplative traveller who visits our land at that pleasant period. Familiar as the regular recurrence of seasons has rendered these natural attractions to our senses, we ourselves experience a new sentiment of delight as we gaze in each succeeding fall, at the glorious tintings of our native woods, and are less disposed to wonder at what we might otherwise be induced to regard as the unduly extravagant admiration of the stranger who looks upon them for the first time through the charming atmosphere of novelty.

It was in this glorious season of the year, on the third day of last October, that, in company with Major A. T. Baubie, one of the first founders, and today, a leading citizen of the enterprising and flourishing young city of Cameron, we started on a tour of exploration to the deserted town of Far West in Caldwell county. Directing our course southward over a fair prairie road, we were struck with the beauty and excellence of the improvements that had developed in the past few years: well appearing and substantial residences, long rows of well kept and squarely cut hedges; young orchards, with the unmistakable promise of abundant fruit, all attested the thrift, enterprise and good taste of the settlers that had thus improved a territory which but a few years ago, was prairie and red brush.

Progressing about four miles in a southerly direction, we struck the hazel brush and timber in the vicinity of Shoal Creek, and bent our course to the southeast for about three or four miles, scarcely, however, being out of sight of a human habitation of some kind; for a large portion of this brush has been cleared, and well improved farms and excellent residences occasionally appear, even in the comparatively wild district. Crossing Shoal Creek, we ascended an eminence from which we enjoyed a magnificent prospect of diversified scenery for many miles in circuit; while far to the background of the October sky, appeared in bold relief, the lofty and spacious structure of Kidder College, on the Hannibal and St. Joseph Railroad, with the roofs of the village buildings reflecting the glorious sunlight, and calling to mind the well-known lines of Rogers:

"Tis distance lends enchantment to the view,
And robes the cottage in a silver hue."

Drawing up to the door of the first farm house, we inquired: "How far are we from Far West?" "You are right in the middle of the public square," was the reply that greeted our astonished ears, "And where is the Mormon Temple?" "About two hundred yards ahead in a corn-field by the side of the road." So indeed we were. But what a change in the past twelve or thirteen years! Where all was solitude and melancholy evidence of complete and absolute desertion, were now well-improved farms, roads and fences. How many metamorphoses has the once stirring but now almost forgotten site of historic Far West undergone in the past thirty years!

Advancing about a quarter of a mile we arrived at the pleasant residence of J. W. Whitmer, the pioneer settler of the locality, on whose farm is located the foundation of the Temple before referred to. Mr. Whitmer, by whom we were hospitably entertained, is an old gentleman of fine intelligence and possessed of a fund of information in reference to Far West, for which we would vainly seek elsewhere; and we hold ourselves deeply indebted to his courteous communicativeness for a large proportion of whatever of interest we may offer our readers in this article.

Before entering upon the history of the settlement we would briefly refer to the few prominent landmarks which to-day recall the site of this interesting locality. The most prominent feature of the landscape is the spacious residence of this gentleman with its extensive yard shaded by a grove of lofty locust and other forest trees, beautiful and well kept blue grass lawn, and other surroundings, which bespeak the refined taste of the proprietor. A few hundred yards west of his residence is the foundation, or rather cellar, of the Temple which, in nine cases out of ten would escape the observation of the casual traveller who might happen to pass its site—for it is nothing more nor less than a more than a half filled rectangular excavation, 120 X 80 feet in extent, the corners of which are marked by four rude and ponderous corner stones which, though considerably sunk by the settling of the earth, are still distinctly and prominently visible.

The third feature of interest, perhaps the most attractive on the spot, is the former residence of Joseph Smith, the Mormon prophet, and founder of the Church of Jesus Christ of Latter Day Saints. Above we present a faithful cut of its appearance to-day. This is a rude, old fashioned, one story, frame building, with two rooms, situated about a quarter of a mile southwest of the temple site, on the n e qr of sec. 15, T. 56, R. 29. A small ell room which was afterwards added, was subsequently moved away. An unusually large and clumsy stone chimney at the north end of the building is its distinguishing characteristic. Otherwise the structure is an exceedingly ordinary and commonplace building, suggestive of anything rather than the residence of the founder of a mighty sect whose rise and progress constitute an era in the history of our Republic.

The location of the house, however, is strikingly beautiful; a blue grass pasture of emerald green slopes on all sides from its site, and a towering grove of locust and cottonwood trees embower the interesting relic. The house is at present occupied as a residence by N. Howard. The farm on which it stands was once the property of J. Hughes, but now belongs to Col. Calvin F. Burnes, of Saint Joseph.

It is a remarkable fact that many writers of respectable authority who have chronicled under various heads, the rise and progress of Mormonism in our land, have been content with the baldest and most cursory glance at the episode of Far West, which really constitutes one of the most important features of our State history; while others who have published abridgements of the same fail to refer in any way to the remarkable events which transpired in that locality, and speak of the Mormons as emigrating from Jackson county to Nauvoo, Ill., altogether ignoring the existence of such a place as Far West, which once boasted a Mormon population variously estimated from two to three thousand souls.

It is not our purpose to write a history of Mormonism, the outlines of which are sufficiently familiar to every general reader; but we propose in this brief sketch to fill a much neglected void in the history of our State, and preserve from utter oblivion one of the most stirring events in the story of its early settlement.

In the autumn of the year 1836, a band of Mormons from Clay county made their appearance in the neighborhood of the locality afterwards known as Far West, and requested of the few settlers who then inhabited that sparsely peopled district permission to settle among them.

Unsuspicious of any evil intent, the hospitable pioneers unhesitatingly consented, and the Mormon immigration immediately began.

This country, soon after erected into the county of Caldwell, then constituted a portion of Ray county. The Mormons, though openly expressing the dogma that "The earth is the Lord's and the fullness thereof, and we are his servants," did not seem disposed to run any unwarrantable risks on the first advent; they entered a large tract of land, paying for the same according to law.

We are informed, on reliable authority, that the poorest Mormon who desired to enter land had no difficulty in procuring from his brethren the necessary means, so powerful and practical was the bond which united this peculiar people. Almost immediately on their arrival they laid out the site of their future city of Far West. The town site was one mile square, including the northeast quarter of section 14, the northeast quarter of section 15, the southwest quarter of section 10, and the northwest quarter of section 11, in township 56, range 29, of what is now Caldwell county, about eight miles southwest of Hamilton, and about the same distance southeast of Cameron.

Among those who came on an exploring tour and afterwards selected the above described locality was John Whitmer, before mentioned, who owns the beautiful farm on which the site of the Temple is located. Mr. Whitmer is regarded by all who know him as an estimable citizen, and a living evidence of the fact that among those who professed the strange faith were occasionally to be found men of sterling integrity and unblemished character.

In the spring of 1836 there were not more than fifteen or sixteen houses in the county, but before the leaves had fallen from the trees in the succeeding autumn, a wonderful change appeared, and a young city had sprung on the late uninhabited waste, as by the stroke of the enchanter's wand.

The first house within the limits of the town site was built in August 1836 by a man by the name of Dombsby [Ormsby or Wamsley], and a very short time after John Whitmer built the second. This building was long used as a hotel, and afterwards served the purpose of a stable. Four years ago it was a complete ruin.

The town was laid out in blocks twenty-four rods square, and the streets were on a grand scale. The four principal avenues were each eight rods wide, and all the others five rods wide. These diverged at right angles from a public square in the centre designed as the site of a grand Temple, which, however, was never built. In 1837 the cellar under the prospective building was dug. We are informed that the excavation, 120 X 80 feet in area, and 4 or 5 feet deep, was accomplished in about one-half of a day, more than 500 men being employed in the work, with no other means of removing the earth than hand barrows.

It is generally believed that on the 4th of July following, which was duly observed as a national holiday, the corner stone of the Temple was laid. This, however, is a mistake. In the fall of 1838 and spring of 1839, the Mormons were expelled [from] the country.

But a short time after, in the same spring, a small band including some of the twelve Apostles, had the temerity to return, and at the dead hour of midnight, with no witnesses but the silent stars and the All-seeing Eye, amid hymns of solemn rejoicing and the exercise of such other rites as their peculiar faith demanded, deposited in the northeast corner of the Temple site a copy of the Bible and a copy of the Book of Mormon, which they claim to be a revealed interpretation of the mysteries of Holy Writ. They then lowered upon those evidences of their faith the rude and ponderous corner stone which, with the three others at their several corners, remain to this day, an unpretending but enduring monument of the bold and fearless zeal of these determined fanatics. The Temple was designed to be one of the most elegant and stately structures in the United States, and but for the extravagant assumption of despotic authority, and high-handed acts of lawlessness on the part of fanatical and unscrupulous leaders of these misguided people, which aroused the just indignation and determined resistance of the "Gentiles," as they designated all who were not Mormon, the fair proportions of a stately structure would soon have remained to this day, a monument of invincible enterprise, and a proud landmark on the beautiful plains of Caldwell county.

About half a mile west of town is the Old Burying Ground of the Mormons.

It is now included within the limits of a farm owned by Mr. Boulton. Here are some two or three hundred graves, all more or less obliterated, with scarcely an occasional rude headstone to mark the presence of a once sacredly guarded, but long forsaken and forgotten village of the dead.

But to return to the early history of the colony.

By December of the year 1836, the Mormons in vast numbers had flocked from Clay and Jackson counties, from which latter place they had been driven for their acts of lawlessness by the incensed citizens, and taken up their abode in their new home of Far West.

In an incredibly short space of time, from two hundred and fifty to three hundred buildings were erected, with workshops, stores, school houses, etc., and Far West began to assume the air and proportions of a thriving and prosperous village. On the 26th of December, 1836, the limits of the county of Caldwell were defined, its territory including a portion of what had been Ray county, and in the spring of 1837, the same was established by the Legislature. About this time a printing press for the colony arrived at Liberty Landing. This, however, never reached Far West. An election of county officers was forthwith ordered, which resulted in the choice of Frank Maguire, W. W. Phelps and Ramsey, recommended by the Governor, as County Judges. With W. W. Phelps as President of the Board; John Cleminson, County and Circuit Clerk; John Skidmore, Sheriff; and Squires, County Surveyor. Austin A. King, afterwards Governor of the State, was elected Circuit Judge, and the first court was held in Far West, then the only town in the county, in 1837. The first building used for a courthouse here was originally built for a school house. It was also used as a town hall and served various public purposes.

During Mormon rule, it stood in the southeast part of the town, but was afterwards moved to the centre of the square. In the winter of 1836–7 a saw and grist mill was built on Shoal creek, about one mile north of the town. In after years it was known as Fugitt's Mill. The mill building has long since been swept away by spring freshets; and in common with most of the old land marks, all traces of the mill dam have disappeared. In 1837, before internal dissentions began seriously to disturb the peace of the community, Far West enjoyed its palmiest days. Some five or six large general stores existed in the place, among which was the large establishment known as the "Committee Store." This was during the early days of Far West, when its name was a watchword to thousands who embraced the new faith, on either side of the Atlantic, just as Great Salt Lake City is to day.

The bulk of the population of the county was Mormons. The leading spirits among the latter at this period were Joseph Smith, the Prophet, Hyrum Smith, John Carroll, Sidney Rigdon, Edward Partridge, W. W. Phelps, Philo Dibble, Elias Higbee, Oliver Cowdery, John Clemmison, John Daley, John and David Whitmer, and the Bozarths. Orson Hyde and Heber Kimball were in England, spreading through the length and breadth of the land the doctrines of their bold and unscrupulous sect. Brigham Young, in the land of steady habits, was bending all the energy of his powerful intellect in the same cause, and astonishing the staid people of New England by the enthusiasm with which he defended its claims. Missionaries swarmed in every state of continental Europe, defying with a constancy worthy of a better cause the ridicule and contumely which they often encountered in the propagation of their strange doctrines, and meeting with the triumphant success rarely denied even though exercised in the wildest and most extravagant cause. In the appeals of these bold fanatics the name of Far West was heralded as the central point of the Promised Land, from whose borders the "saints" were to go forth and possess the earth and the fullness thereof.

Far West continued to improve rapidly in growth and prosperity. This condition of things induced many good and industrious citizens to settle within the limits of the growing young city, and its rapidly developing neighborhood, while the same attractions drew thither many desperadoes and thieves, who soon succeeded in obtaining almost unbounded sway in the Mormon councils. They boldly declared that "the Lord had given the earth and the fullness thereof to his people," and that they consequently had the right to take whatever they pleased from the Gentiles.

In pursuance of this declaration of right, bands of the most desperate and lawless characters strolled openly about the country taking forcible possession of whatever they pleased. Those among the sect whose sense of honor and justice revolted at these acts of villainy, were soon compelled, at least, to preserve a discreet silence in regard to their unpopular views of such conduct.

We would observe here, parenthetically, that though many conflicting opinions have been uttered in reference to the matter, we are prepared to state, on reliable authority, that the difficulty in Caldwell county was originated by the Mormons carrying the election of Representative to the State Legislature in August, 1839 [*sic*], the Mormons being anti-slaveholders, or Free Soilers. The other version, (frequently stated and accepted by many), is that the first occasion of the difficulty was that, at a mass convention, the Mormons passed a resolution to the effect that the soil belonged to the "Lord's chosen people" and that they were the only ones entitled to this heritage.

A band of miscreants known as Destroying Angels, were ever on the alert to detect the slightest defection on the part of those who presumed to call in question any set of lawlessness authorized by their leaders, and visit summary vengeance on their heads.

In the dissentions that naturally resulted from this condition of affairs, several of their leading men apostatized and accused Smith of gross crimes and frauds. On the 25th of October, 1838, Thomas B. March [Marsh], corroborated by Hyde, said: "They have among them a company, consisting of all that are considered true Mormons, called the Danites, who have taken an oath to support the heads of the church in all things that they say or do, whether right or wrong. The plan of said Smith is to take this State, and he professes to his people to intend taking the whole United States, and ultimately the whole world. This is the belief of the church, and my own opinion of the Prophet's plan and designs. The Prophet inculcates the idea, and it is believed by every true Mormon that the prophecies of Smith are superior to the law of the land. I have heard the Prophet say that he would yet tread down his enemies and walk over their dead bodies; that if he was not let alone he would be a second Mahomet to this generation, and that he would make it one gore of blood from the Rocky Mountains to the Pacific ocean."

Peaceful and law abiding citizens who had sustained repeated wrongs and outraged at the hands of these people, were not disposed to accept quietly this defiant and menacing tone of the Mormon leaders, and these harangues contributed to no small degree to add fuel to the flame of excitement enkindled against these blatant outlaws. Rigdon, in a sermon preached at Far West July 4th, 1838, said: "We take

God and all the holy angels to witness this day that we warn all men, in the name of Jesus Christ, to come on us no more forever. The man, or set of men, who attempts it, do it at the expense of their lives; and that mob that comes on us to disturb us, it shall be between them and us a war of extermination, for we will follow them till the last drop of their blood is spilled, or else they will have to exterminate us. For we will carry the seat of war to their own houses and to their own families, and one party or the other shall be utterly destroyed."

As the followers of Smith largely out numbered the Gentiles, and as the county officers were mostly Mormons, they were enabled to act with impunity until their overbearing lawlessness excited the furious indignation of the other settlers, who not being able to obtain justice by lawful means, also resorted to mob violence and retaliation in kind, and many a deed of revolting atrocity was perpetrated on both sides, to the regret of all good men and the disgrace of civilization. In 1839 [*sic*] this discord had assumed such a fiendish character that Governor Boggs issued a proclamation ordering Major General David R. Atchison to call out the militia of his division to quell the insurgents and enforce the laws. He called out a part of the first brigade of the Missouri State militia, under command of General Alex. W. Doniphan, who proceeded at once to the scene of disturbance. The militia were placed under the command of General John B. Clark. The Mormon forces, an undisciplined rabble, were led by G. W [M]. Hinkle. Far West, Haughn's [Haun's or Hawn's] Mills, and other points in the vicinity were fortified by the Mormons in a rude and unskillful manner that moved the derision and contempt of their comparatively well appointed and drilled adversaries. They intrenched [*sic*] themselves behind barricades of hastily collected logs, dilapidated wagons, old buggies, and literally anything and everything which presented itself in the terrible emergency which retributive justice had called down upon their heads.

The first skirmish took place at Crooked River, in the southwestern part of the county. It is a popularly accepted opinion that the principal engagement was fought at Haughn's Mill, about five miles south of the present site of the flourishing town of Breckenridge, on the Hannibal and St. Joseph railroad. We learn, on reliable authority, however, that the latter was not worthy of being dignified by the name of a skirmish, for the insurgents fled on the first approach of the militia. In the first fight, one man was killed on each side. The Mormon, in this instance, whose name we fail to recall, was one of the twelve Apostles.

We learn from one who was present on the scene of conflict, shortly after the fight, that the shooting, in this engagement, to use his own expression, "was of the wildest character," more damage being done to the upper branches of the trees in the neighborhood, than to the enemy. There were present in what is known as the Haughn's Mill fight 125 militia, one of whom it is claimed by some was killed. Some sixteen or eighteen Mormons who had taken refuge in a blacksmith shop within their rude intrenchments [*sic*], were ruthlessly shot down while in the act of surrender, and their bodies thrown into a neighboring well. That so revolting an atrocity should be perpetrated by men who claimed the character of enlightened and law-abiding citizens, is matter of astonishment to all unacquainted with the previous history of the insurrection; but when we call to mind the terrible threats and denunciations of Smith, Rigdon, and other Mormon leaders, and the deeds of high-handed robbery and cold-blooded assassination perpetrated by their minions, we are not disposed to be surprised that such outrages should have begotten a kindred spirit of retaliation.

The well into which the bodies of the slaughtered Mormons were thrown is on a farm owned at that time by Haughn. This land is now the property of James C. McCreary, [McCray] Esq., of Kingston, to whom it was sold for a St. Louis party, by Nathan Cope, Esq., of Kingston. It is about fifteen and a half miles east of Far West on S. E. Qtr. of Sec. 8, T. 56, R. 26. The bloody and sepulchral well was filled up by Charles Ross, Esq., now a resident of Kingston, who arrived on the spot just ten days after the tragic occurrence. Mr. Ross is one of the oldest settlers and most respected citizens of Caldwell county. His residence at that time, was but a short distance from the spot where the slaughtering occurred. We state, on his authority, that there were, in this affair, about forty Mormons under the command of one Capt. Evans; and that there were two companies of Missouri militia, of which Col. Jennings commanded one, and Capt. Comstock the other. Capt. C., who was a frequent guest at the house of Mr. Ross, admitted to the latter that he was the officer at whose command the Mormons were shot down and thrown into the well.

When the militia appeared at Far West, where the strength of the Mormon forces were concentrated, Joseph Smith surrendered to Gen. Doniphan, on the following terms, viz: That they should deliver up their arms, surrender their prominent leaders for trial, and that the remainder of the Mormons, should, with their families, leave the State. The leaders charged with murder, treason and felony, were taken before Austin A. King, presiding. He remanded them to Daviess county, to await the action of the grand jury, on the above charges.

The Daviess' county jail, however, being deemed insecure, they were confined at Liberty in Clay County.

Indictments were found against Joseph Smith, Hyrum Smith, Sidney Rigdon, Lyman Wight, Col. Hinkle, Baldwin and Lyman. Rigdon was soon released on a writ of habeas corpus.

It has been asserted and is still believed, by some, that Smith and his fellow-prisoners made their escape from the Liberty jail. Such, however, was not the case. At their request, change of venue was granted, and Judge King sent their cases to Boone county for trial. On their way to Columbia under military guard, Joseph Smith and his fellow-prisoners succeeded in effecting their escape.

That eight or nine men should have accomplished this end without the connivance of the strong force by which they were escorted, is simply absurd; and the prevalent belief in that day, was that the guard was bribed.

Thus did the leaders in a desperate career of iniquity temporarily escape the penalty of enormities which cried loud against them for justice, while many of their misguided followers, unable to get away in the general exodus which, in obedience to the terms of the surrender immediately followed, suffered at the hands of miscreants to whom such convulsions are ever a godsend, outrages and enormities almost as cruel and disgraceful as those perpetrated at the instigation of Smith and Rigdon against the Gentiles.

Disposing of their property.

Many of these Mormons who were poor, had invested all the little property they once possessed in these lands from which they were now driven.

Valuable farms were, at this time traded for an old wagon, a horse, or a yoke of oxen—anything which afforded the means of transportation from the Promised Land where they once lived in the firm faith of establishing a last home and final resting place on earth. Conveyances of lands were not unfrequently demanded and enforced from these wretchedly deluded victims of a fierce fanaticism, at the muzzle of the pistol or point of the dagger.

At the period of the general exodus which occurred immediately on the surrender, there were in the county of Caldwell about 5,000 inhabitants, fully four thousand of whom were Mormons. Most of these, with a blind faith in the leaders whose acts had entailed such terrible calamities on their followers, emigrated to Nauvoo, Ill., only to experience, at a future and not distant day, the same inevitable consequences of lawless and criminal assumption of despotic authority that has ever characterized the leaders of this strange fanaticism in Missouri.

The following extract from the message of the Governor of Missouri in 1840, giving a brief review of the character of the events to which we have just referred we deem not inappropriate to this article. In referring to the expulsion of the Mormons, he says: "These people had violated the laws of the land by open and avowed resistance to them; they had undertaken, without the aid of the civil authority, to redress their real or fancied grievances; they had instituted among themselves a government of their own, independent of and in opposition to the government of the State; they had, at an inclement season of the year, driven the inhabitants of an entire county from their homes, ravaged their crops, and destroyed their dwellings. Under these circumstances, it became the imperious duty of the Executive to interfere and exercise the powers with which he was invested, to protect the lives and property of our citizens, to restore order and tranquility to the country, and maintain the supremacy of our laws."

About the period of the final expulsion of the Mormons an association was instituted which might be termed a Vigilance Committee. These made it their business to compel the removal of all persons who were suspected of being in sympathy with these obnoxious fanatics, and for many months during the winter of 1839–40, mob law was supreme in Caldwell county. Emigrants from all parts of the Union flocked into the county with bitter hatred in their hearts towards Mormonism and every thing pertaining to it. The very name of Far West was an abominable sound in the ears of settlers; and after holding courts for about two and a half years longer, in the place, the county seat was removed to a locality called in honor of Austin A. King, Kingston, and which remains to-day the capital of Caldwell county. In the same year, the Post Office, the first ever established in the limit of the county, which had been held by David Hughes for three years, was removed from Far West to the new county seat. Many who had obtained lawful possession of the buildings in the old town, moved them away, but a large portion of these deserted habitations were carried off piecemeal by parties who had no shadow of claim to their possession, or were wantonly destroyed by others with whom the vandal spirit of destruction was paramount to every just claim; and in a very few years from the period of the expulsion of the Mormons scarcely a vestige remained of the once populous and flourishing town of Far West.

It will doubtless be a matter of interest to many to know that among the Mormon residents at Far West was the widow of Morgan, the so-called exposer of the mysteries of masonry, whose sudden disappearance from his home in New York, in the year 1826 created the suspicion of his having been abducted and murdered by certain zealous members of the craft. The excitement in that day, in reference to this matter, was of sufficiently grave and extensive character to result in the inauguration of a short lived party in National politics, the leading characteristic of which was its opposition to Masonry. But for this identification of the circumstance with the political history of the country, the occurrence, like the episode of Far West, would probably long since have passed from the memory of men for we live in an age of stirring events and rushing progress. An occurrence which fixed the attention of a nation yesterday, is forgotten in the pressing interests of to-day, just as the great claims of to-day will yield to the crowding incidents of to-morrow. Every throb in the great heart of National existence is but another stride in this feverish rush of constant change and unceasing progress. Few, even among the prominent actors in this mighty and over-shifting drama, pause long enough to review their own personal parts, far less the great events of which they have merely been spectators.

How necessary and important then becomes the office of the biographer and the historian; and what a weight of responsibility rests upon him who assumes to chronicle events which are to live as monuments of warning or example to future generations!

The story of Far West, trivial and unimportant as it may sound, compared with the mighty events that have since transpired in this government, is not without its thrilling interest, its voice of warning, and deep philosophy. That the revolutionary schemes of Smith and his desperate and determined followers signally failed of accomplishment in Missouri, and afterwards in Illinois, as they had previously in Ohio, does not render the alarming boldness of these unprincipled fanatics the less worthy of being chronicled, especially when we reflect that, thrice and four times defeated and expelled, they ultimately succeeded in building up a hierarchy on the distant plains of a farther West, which lives and flourishes to-day, in defiance of the accepted principles of social and moral rectitude, the wonder and astonishment of the civilized world.

With these reflections we close our sketch of Far West. The various written authorities which we have consulted in reference to the matter, all more or less meager in their details, often conflict in their several statements.

We have depended for our information more upon the statements of reliable parties who were eye-witnesses of the scenes and incidents we have attempted to describe. For assistance in securing information thus derived we hold ourself [ourselves] under special obligations to Nathan Cope, Esq., a prominent citizen of Caldwell county, and resident of the town of Kingston. It may not be improper here to add that, about the period of the first settlement of Far West, a band of Mormons numbering some three hundred, made their way to Daviess county, and built cabins in different parts of the county. On the east bluff of Grand river, about three miles above Gallatin, they build a small town which they called Adimondiamon [Adam-ondi-Ahman], and which in the Mormon jargon, is said to mean "The Grave of Adam," they claiming to have found that interesting locality on the site of their future village.

The lawless element among these people soon gained for the entire settlement the ill-will of the Gentiles, who heartily co-operated in driving them from the county, in 1838–9. They surrendered without resistance to the military, and made a partial restitution of the property they had stolen. Before this surrender, among other acts of lawlessness, they burned the town of Gallatin and many houses throughout the county. Adimondiamon, at the time of the expulsion, is said to have included a population of nearly five hundred Mormons, who nearly all emigrated to Nauvoo. Viator

APPENDIX H

William Lewis, 1877

William Lewis, "Correspondence," *Herald* 24, no. 24 (December 15, 1877): 381–82. For a partial excerpt, see also Vogel, *Early Mormon Documents*, 5:250–51.

STEWARTSVILLE, De Kalb Co., Missouri, November 29th, 1877.

Dear Herald:.—In company with Brn. Temme Hinderks and Charles Faul, I attended a meeting at Far West branch; and as we returned home, we called to see Father John Whitmer, one of the eight witnesses to the Book of Mormon. He informed us that he is the only one of the eight living; and David, his brother, one of the three, is the only one; so they are the only two out of the eleven witnesses that now live; and their testimonies are still the same as that recorded in the Book of Mormon. Father Whitmer says that he hopes that God will give him strength to stand firm to the testimony.

We asked many questions; among them the following:

1. Had he ever made it a subject of prayer to try and find out who was the proper one to lead the Church, as there were so many claims made? He replied that he did not think it to be his duty to make such inquiry; that the Lord would reveal it when he saw proper. We insisted on his making it a subject of prayer.

2. Did he believe in the gathering? He answered, Yes; and all that God has promised will be fulfilled. Jackson county, Missouri, is the place, and will be the final home of the saints.

3. Were not the Saints commanded to settle in this neighborhood of the Far West, and to build a temple? To this he said, "Well, there was, I believe, some talk of that kind; and they did gather here in a large body, and lay the corner stone of the Temple, which stone is there; some are taken off."

4. Do you not think that when the Saints return to Jackson county, and to the regions from which they have been driven, that you will fall into the ranks? To this he replied, with tears running down

553

his cheeks, and he could hardly speak from crying. At last he did say, wiping the tears off, that the day would come when we would all see eye to eye.

He had been living in that locality since 1831; forty six years. Was that when the Saints were mobbed and driven out? He also said that men you could not get near even fifteen years ago, are now anxious to learn and get all the information they can about Mormonism, and are friendly to the doctrine.

I can say this for father Whitmer; that he manifested a good spirit, and did not try to discourage us, but to encourage. I believe that if the Saints in his neighborhood will flock around him, and invite him to their testimony meetings, and go up after him, that good will be done. I don't (page 382) believe in forcing any man, but I do think we should try every legal way to bring back the strayed sheep. We should remember the parables of the lost sheep and prodigal son. Father Whitmer is seventy-four years old and is quite smart.

We could only stay a few hours, so we bade them good day, and went on our way rejoicing, remarking one to another, that now we could say that we had seen and talked with one of the eight witnesses to the Book of Mormon, in hopes to see his brother David, one of the three. We saw part of the house where the martyred prophet lived, and the spot where the temple was to be built, and also the place where a battle was fought with the mob. But now we are invited to come in and buy up farms; and some are sorry that the Saints ever were driven out of Missouri.

Said some of the leading men, "See what the Mormons have done in spite of all the persecution; they have built large cities, and what would this country be now had they not been driven out and had kept the law of God."

The set time has come for the Saints to gather, as the way opens for them to sell their property; for if ever a people could be suited in buying farms it is now; for I might say that all the land in the adjoining county to Jackson is for sale on terms to suit the poor and the rich. Land can be bought at from $8 to $15 per acre, and improved farms from $15 to $30. Truly as the Lord says in the Book of Covenants, "Gather into the regions around about, and I will bless you with favor in the eyes of the world," that time is now.

I am happy to say that there is more of a spirit of oneness in this part than there has been; and I think it will continue....

Orson Pratt and Joseph F. Smith, Visit to Far West, 1878

"Report of Elders Orson Pratt and Joseph F. Smith [Visit to Far West, Missouri, 1878]," *Latter-Day Saints Millennial Star* 40, no. 50 (December 16, 1878): 785–86.

> New York City, Sept. 17, 1878. President John Taylor and Council of the Twelve:
>
> On Monday, Sept. 9th, we visited Far West. To Convey a proper idea of our visit here, we think we cannot do much better than to give a few extracts from Bro. Smith's Journal: "We halted at the late residence of Mr. John Whitmer, deceased. I got out of the carriage and went to the house, where I met a man of whom I enquired if Mrs. Johnson was at home, and was informed that she was. I again asked if I could see her, when this individual stepped to the stair door, and called–"Sarah [Elizabeth (Whitmer) Johnson], there is a gentleman here who wants to see you." While waiting for her I said to the person before mentioned, "Is your name Whitmer?" "Yes sir, my name is [Jacob D.] Whitmer" [son of John Whitmer]." I replied, "and my name is Smith: I am a native of this place as I suppose, and I have come here with a friend to take a look at the place of my birth, as I never saw it before to the best of my recollection. Can you provide lodgings for us over night?" Mr. W.–"I don't know; my sister can tell you when she comes downstairs." Just then Mrs. Johnson came down. Mr. Whitmer introduced me as Mr. Smith. I asked her about the same as above written. She seemed to hesitate a little, and then said, "Yes sir, I think we can." Noting her hesitancy, I remarked, "We will go on to Illinois in the morning." Mrs. J.–"Do you live in Illinois?" I answered, "No ma'am, I live in Utah." At this, she and her brother looked strangely at each other, and then at me. I continued, "The gentleman that is with me, is Mr. Orson Pratt." Some more bewildered looks back and forth, but nothing was said for a moment; but presently Mr. Whitmer said to his sister, "You have heard of Mr. Pratt?" "Yes," she replied, "I heard

father speak of him." Another pause—then she continued, addressing her brother, "I do not know whether we can keep them or not; if those other gentlemen come, we shall be rather crowded." Here I remarked, "We should not like to discommode you too much, but we would be pleased to stop with you, if you have room." To this she paid no attention, but suggested to her brother, that "Mr. Edwards and Mr. Somebody else always kept strangers when they came along." Whereupon Mr. Whitmer said, "Yes," then turning to me, said, "You can get lodgings at Mr. Edwards' about a mile back on the road." I made some further enquiry about directions to Mr. Edwards, to which he rather gruffly replied. Said I, "I was in hopes, Mr. Whitmer, you could have shown us about the place a little, as we are strangers." To which he replied, "Well I haven't time." Said I, "Will you go to the carriage and see Mr. Pratt?" Without answering he started toward the carriage and I followed. On reaching which, I introduced him to Bro. Pratt, who tried to get in to conversation with him; but he was insolently gruff and abrupt. Said Bro. Pratt kindly, "[Jacob Whitmer,] I was well acquainted with your father [John]." [Jacob said,] "I suppose you was." [Previous two sentences were edited for clarity]. O. P.–Mr. Smith was born here, and would like you to point out the site of the old town, and if you know his father's house, or the spot where it stood. J. W.–don't know anything about it; that is, I know where the town was, and where the Temple site is; but I don't know where any person lived. He then pointed down in the field, northward, and continued, "There was a place over there that some said was the Smith place; there was another place over there, (a little further west,) that some said was the Smith place, but Joe Smith lived over there, beyond that locust grove, just this side of where you see the tops of those tall cottonwoods, near them stacks, there's where Joe Smith lived, and the Temple site is just at the corner of that orchard, just over the fence."

I pleasantly remarked, "Have you not enough respect for Joseph Smith to call him by his proper name?" J.W.–I have no particular respect or disrespect for him; Joe Smith is the name he goes by here. I retorted, "I generally respect all men enough, to call them by their proper names." O.P.–We were in hopes you could show us around a little, and point out those places to us. J.W.–Well, I have not time; anybody here can tell you as much as I can. O.P.–Your father was once the historian of the Church, and I am the present historian; we are anxious to preserve all the items of history we can, we would therefore like to see the MS. your father kept, and if possible, to make satisfactory arrangements with you, to purchase the same, provided there is anything in the MS. which we have not already published. I suppose you are aware that the history of the Church has already been published. J.W.–We've got no history here, all father's papers have gone to Richmond long ago. O.P.–We had a very pleasant interview with your uncle David, at Richmond. We arrived there last Friday, and remained two days, he showed us the MS. of the Book of Mormon, but said nothing about having any other papers. J.W.–We have got no papers here.

Convinced that there was no use of making any further efforts where the spirit of bigotry and opposition was so intense, we turned away, satisfied that all will come out right. After viewing the Temple ground at Far West, we concluded, as it was not yet very late in the evening, to drive on ten miles further to the town of Cameron, the nearest point to the railroad, where we arrived before dark, making the day's journey of about 48 miles by team.

APPENDIX J

Sketches of Christopher F. Kerr and Jacob D. Whitmer

Published in *History of Caldwell and Livingston Counties, Missouri, Written and Compiled from the Most Authentic Official and Private Sources*, 329–30, 340. These items are also reproduced in *Missouri Mormon Frontier Foundation Newsletter* nos. 21/22 (August 1999): 17–18.

CHRISTOPHER F. KERR
(Farmer and Stock-raiser, Section 14, Post-office, Kingston).

Of Kentucky nativity Mr. Kerr, from the date of his birth, October 28, 1838, has resided either in Kentucky or this county. His youth and early manhood, however, were passed in the State of his birth, and there he attended the schools which favored him with a good Education. His father was James Kerr, who married after growing up Miss Catharine Simpson. Christopher is the youngest of four children now living who were born of this union. The others are Mary J. McBeath, Nancy W. Morris, and Elizabeth I. Allen, of Texas. From the very time of his settlement here Mr. Kerr has applied steadfastly to agricultural pursuits, and with what success may be inferred when the fact is mentioned that he is now the proprietor of one of the best improved half-sections of land in this portion of the country. (He also married well, a daughter of John Whitmer, living on the home place.) Upon his 320 acres are to be seen a large number of cattle and hogs, stock raising receiving a considerable share of his attention. In the various affairs of the county and township he exerts an influence which all feel. For two terms he has held the position of township collector, discharging his official duties in a most satisfactory manner. Mr. Kerr's wife was formerly married to a Mr. Johnson, and they had two children, Ellen [Ella] E. and John E. Her maiden name was Sarah E. Whitmer and her marriage to Mr. K. occurred September 6, 1872 [September 6, 1882]. She was the daughter of John and Sarah M. Whitmer who were among the earliest and most respected citizens of the county. She claims Caldwell county as the place of her birth. Mrs. Kerr is a believer in the doctrine of Mormonism as taught by Joseph Smith, but has no support for the infamous practice of polygamy introduced by Brigham Young. In her possession is an original copy of the Mormon Bible printed by Joseph Smith, Jr., at Palmyra, N. Y., in 1830.

JACOB D. WHITMER
(Farmer and Stock-raiser, Section 11, Post-office, Kingston).

The career of Mr. Whitmer is one which has been passed without any especial departure from the pursuit of farming; and as far as his acquaintance with this county is concerned, perhaps no one is more familiar with it, for it is his birthplace. Born here on the 26th of May, 1844, he was educated at the common schools of this vicinity, and from his very birth has been closely associated with the county's growth and identified with its interests. His parents were John and Sarah M. Whitmer, nee Jackson, both from Ohio, in which State Mrs. W. was born and brought up, though her husband was a native of New York. After their marriage in Ohio they came to this county in 1833, being among the very first families to locate in the community. This continued to be their home for many years and during the time of their residence, the agricultural affairs of Caldwell County were worthily represented by Mr. [John] Whitmer and his noble companion. The father died in 1878, the mother in 1872. The son, Jacob Whitmer, now occupies [part of] the farm which they had improved. On the south-west corner of this place there can be seen at this writing (1886) the excavation and some of the rock intended for the old Mormon Temple, to be known as Far West. This estate embraces 216 acres of choice land, with superior improvements. The dwelling is a tasteful one, surrounded with flowers and beautifully arranged lawn, plainly indicating the home of enterprise and culture. Perhaps this is not to be wondered at when we consider Mr. Whitmer's natural characteristics. He is of German origin, his grandfather, John Whitmer, having come to America with his parents at an early day in the settlement of the Mauch Chunk Valley. Representatives of the family have since settled in various places. Mr. W. was married April 27, 1871, to Miss Celia Tatarshall, who was born in Homellsville, N. Y., but accompanied her parents to this county in 1868. One son, Harry, has been born of this union.

APPENDIX K

James Williams: Far West Seventy-Five Years Ago, Written in 1911

Excerpted from James Williams, *Seventy-Five Years on The Border*, 142–44; written December 21, 1911.

In trying to tell how Far West, the old Mormon town looked, the first time I saw it in 1842, I regret that I have no daguerreotype or photograph to assist me in describing its lonely desolation. Its glory had departed with most of its [*sic*], at one time, 3000 inhabitants.

I think the first time I was in the old town was at a Fourth of July celebration in 1842, the first I was ever at, but I can remember it as well as if it had been yesterday, and how the principal managers looked and acted. The marshal's name was Branch and he wore a black broadcloth coat, which made a great impression on me. I was told that cloth was made in France and mother had been telling me about the Marquis De Lafayette, the great, good Frenchman. I think that was one reason I was so impressed with that black coat. Miles Bragg was his assistant and Volney Bragg, the first lawyer I ever saw, was the speaker, who read the Declaration of Independence very impressively. I don't remember his speech. Of course, it was along patriotic lines. There was a long ditch and some slick looking niggers roasting the beef, which was very fine, I remember. At the head of the long table, which was a scaffold under a brush arbor, was seated a very old man, whose name was Benjamin Middaugh. I think this old man served in the War of 1812 and was the father or brother of old Timothy Middaugh, who lived many years about two miles east of Cameron and I think was the grandfather of the family of Middaugh brothers near Mirabile. The long table was located a short distance north and, I think, a little east of the old Temple excavation, which at that time, was nearly intact, and the great cornerstone lying in the bottom. I have been told by those who were on the ground that it took 14 yoke of oxen to haul it. I've not seen it for about 40 years, but am told that most of that big rock has been carried away for souvenirs by the faithful Saints.

When I first saw Far West, many of the smaller frame houses had been moved away for farm buildings. A good many of the larger buildings had been torn down and rebuilt after removal, hence, the houses left standing were dilapidated, old looking, unpainted structures, many of them two stories high.

They were nearly all frames with poles flattened on two sides for studding, and split native timber for lathing and weather boarding[.] The boarding was usually 6 feet long, sap taken off, gauged and shaved, which made a good, substantial building. The boarding usually was of big bottom burr oak, the best timber on Shoal and Log Creek. The town was situated on a divide between those two creeks, and had the Hannibal & St. Joseph Railway run up Shoal Creek (as was talked of), Far West today would be the biggest town between St. Joseph and Chillicothe instead of Cameron.

Not only that, there is but little doubt that in place of a desolate waste, the Temple lot would have had a magnificent temple, and Far West would be the "Mecca" of the pilgrim Saints, as Independence is today. The best church building in Independence today is the fine, brown stone [Community of Christ Stone Church on what is today Lexington Ave.] on the high ridge along the Kansas City Electric line. The only Mormon I ever heard preach was in that building a few years since and I am free to admit, I think was about as good a sermon as I ever listened to, with a few exceptions. If people will live up to the exhortations of that good man, I think it will matter little whether they think Smith, Rigdon, Pratt, Whitmer, Cowd[e]ry, or anybody else were inspired, or the Book of Mormon a Revelation.

I knew David Whitmer quite well when I'd meet him in Cameron. He was an up-to-date farmer, and purchased the first two horse corn planter ever unloaded off the cars at Cameron. I think I, and some other by-standers, helped him put it in his wagon. I remember the wheels of that planter were wooden drums. Mr. Whitmer moved to Richmond some thirty years ago, and died there. I think the Whitmer family own the old Temple lot, which is now on the old Whitmer farm, as I am told.

I have never seen Oliver Cowd[e]ry, but have seen one of his daughters, who was pointed out to me at church many years ago. She was visiting in the vicinity of Far West. It was at old Plumb Creek school house I saw her. She was strikingly handsome. I do not know whether she is yet living. It is not the province of this article to discuss whether Latter Day Saints as a church organization is good or otherwise, but I'll say this, I've been familiar with and a neighbor to them for nearly seventy years, and from what I've seen of those in Missouri, I think they've hardly had a fair treatment, inasmuch as our laws allow every one to worship as he pleases, so long as he is law abiding.

A Revelation Received at Far West, July 26, 1861

A Revelation given through [David Whitmer], July 26, 1861, published in Lorene E. Pollard and Rebecca Woods, *Whitmer Memoirs*, 30–33. The location of the holograph is in private possession.

Hear O Heavens, and give ear O Earth, for the Lord is God and besides him there is none else. And it behooveth me that I should fulfill that which I have spoken, by the mouth of all the Holy Prophets, concerning that which should come to pass upon the earth, in the latter days. For the inhabitants of the Earth are well nigh ripe for destruction. And as I have manifested to you, from time to time, that I am God. And the word that I have spoken, unto you from time to time, that all things pertaining to the Bible and the Book of Mormon, and the Sacred Revelations, that I have caused to be given by my holy prophets, and Apostles, that they truly testify unto you, that destruction shall come unto the inhabitants of the Earth. And behold and Lo I say unto you, that now is the beginning of sorrow. And wo shall continue until the inhabitants of the Earth <are Chastised> for their wickedness, and abominations. I have looked upon them, and I have sought that they might repent. But they would not. I have given unto them laws, that they might enjoy equal rights, and all the blessings that God could bestow upon the inhabitants of this Earth. And behold I say unto you, as a nation they have abused all there [*sic*] blessings, That I the Lord could bestow upon a people. Therefore have I the Lord called upon my servants in the last days, that they should go forth, and proclaim unto the children of men, the fullness of my Gospel. And of all the prophecies that were given by my holy prophets, that the time was drawing nigh. And that my [page 2 of document] word should be fulfilled concerning the wicked and rebellious. And behold and lo. They will not repent. For this cause I let fall the sword of my indignation upon the land of your inheritance. And it shall continue from time to time, and from day to day, until the most wicked shall be subdued. And if so be, that the inhabitants of this land will continue to enforce the laws that I the Lord your God have caused to be established by your Fathers. For unto them I have given a law to govern this land. And now I say unto you, if the children of men, will seek to uphold the law, I the Lord your God will sustain and uphold them by my Almighty power. And that the most wicked and rebellious shall be driven out, and cut off from this my holy land.

Now I say unto you that I the Lord will preserve all those that seek righteousness. And uphold the laws which are right and just according to the Constitution of your fathers. And behold and lo I say unto you. These are the desires [designs?] of this land. And when this be established, then I say unto you. That there shall be those in authority that will acknowledge equal rights. And then I say if my disciples will be wise and humble, Then shall the time commence, for the redemption of you my Servants and all those that will come unto the Ensign, that I have caused to be raised, by my servants in these last days. And then shall the arm of the Lord be revealed unto you, from time to time, and the Lord your God shall commence the redemption of Zion [page 3 of document].

And the Host of Heaven shall be revealed, for the redemption of my people. And my elect O house of Israel. Now I say unto you, that I the Lord am God. That my arm is not shortened that I cannot save. Nor is my ear deff [deaf] that I cannot hear the cries of my people. For this is according to the designs of your father which is in heaven. And as the lord your God, and your Redeemer even Jesus Christ liveth and reigneth in Heaven, so shall he also reign on Earth. And so shall you. And your children, and childrens [*sic*] children, and all the saints, and all the faithful now on Earth, live and reign with him forever and ever.

These word[s] are unto you and your children, for your special benefit, because you have asked of me.

Now I say unto you, that wo shall befall the inhabitants of the Earth if they will not repent, even until the Earth shall be cleansed from all her abominations, if they will not come unto me. But if they will seek my face, and observe my laws, and obey my everlasting covenant, I say unto you they shall rejoice upon this land. If they will heed not they shall be scourged from time to time ~~until~~ till they acknowledge my love, and my mercy, and my judgments, and know that I am God, even in life or in death.

Now concerning the wicked and the ungodly, you can see them. You have them before you. And I have told you by the mouths of all my holy prophets, what should be their end. And behold their end draweth nigh and they shall not escape [page 4 of document]. Now I say unto you, fear not, ever trusting in me, for the Lord is your God, even Jesus Christ your Redeemer, Has given these words unto you. Even so, Amen.

John Whitmer to Dear Children, 1 March 1871

John Whitmer to Dear Children, 1 March 1871, Perry Special Collections.

Far West March 1st 1871

Dear Children

We received several letters from you lately informing us of your health &c. together with each a Valentine which were gratefully received, with the expressions of kindness

Our healths are] <is> slowly improving, I have not been bedfast. Mother is so that she sets up some her complaint, Inflamation [*sic*] of the Urether of the Bladder.

We should be glad if it <you> could come and see us Soon. But I supose [*sic*] we shall have to be contented until the Lord in his wisdom shall se[e] fit to open the way. Jacob was at Kingston the other day, he saw Wm. Smith he informed him that Edward had gone to New York on business.

[page 2] We were some what surprised at the News of the letting of the Contract of the Tech and Nash R. R. as far as Cameron. I hope that the dark days are past and gone so far as the Road is concerned in its future progress.

John E. is well and hearty, and is gathering the Eggs every night he does not let Lynda cook them he wants to Sell them

We have got along, beyond my most sanguine expectations during us [our] Sickness. Malinda has improved so much in the art of Housewifery that you would not know her if you would see her in the Kitchen making Bread, Buisket [biscuits], Pies and Cakes, that are [not] hard to eat.

Mother would be glad to answer your Letters, but does not feel able to wright <write> with pen and Ink as yet.

[page3] Therefore you will have to be contented with the foregoing Scriblings [*sic*] of your old Fathers for I am a poor hand to write on family matters. Write soon &c.

Respectfully yours as ever John Whitmer

Dear Sister Father has left a few lines for me to fill out but I don't know what to Write. I have not got any thing of import Every body is in good spirits about the RR I have not bin up to see the olde lady this Winter I have bin up to Cameron twice in the Last few weeks I had the Jeweler send two [*sic*] Chichago [*sic*] fore my Engagement and W. R. the weding [*sic*] Ring is a fine chased ring I would like to see you [page 4] very mutch I am not going to have any weding [*sic*] or infare [*sic*] if I did I would send for you and famly [*sic*] but it is a going too [*sic*] come of the sly it will bee [*sic*] fore a few Wee[ks] the Day is not set yet but I have asked hur Mother and got hur Consent and the Rest of all F and Mother are Willin[g] more by and by, [Signed] Jake W. [Jacob D. Whitmer]

C. J. Hunt, "An Acknowledgement to John Whitmer"

C. J. Hunt, "An Acknowledgement to John Whitmer, One of the Eight Witnesses of the Book of Mormon," *Herald* 97, no. 6 (February 6, 1950): 131. (References to the Doctrine and Covenants in this quote are CofC D&C.)

JOHN WHITMER, a younger brother of David Whitmer [*sic*—David was younger than John], was born August 27, 1802, and baptized in June, 1829. Together with seven other selected men, he saw and handled the golden plates in 1829, from which the Book of Mormon was translated by use of the Urim and Thummim. The Prophet Joseph Smith showed the plates to the Eight Witnesses, and they gave their signed testimonies for publication to the world as recorded in the first pages of the Book of Mormon.

We are creditably informed that John Whitmer assisted the Prophet Joseph and Oliver Cowdery as scribe in the final preparation of the Book of Mormon manuscript for publication. In June, 1829, he was called by revelation to do missionary work. (See Doctrine and Covenants section 13.)

This talented servant was designated by the Lord in March, 1831, to be historian of the church and served in that capacity several years, devoting time while preaching and traveling from place to place, "copying, selecting, and obtaining all things which shall be for the good of the church, and for the rising generations that shall grow up on the land of Zion to possess it from generation to generation, for ever and ever" (Doctrine and Covenants section 69). In April of 1903, historical writings made by him were presented by the Whitmer relatives to President Joseph Smith of the Reorganized Church.

At a very sacred and special council of church officials held in Independence, Missouri, in May, 1832, it was deemed advisable that a Book of Commandments (forerunner of the Book of Doctrine and Covenants) containing revelations to the church by Joseph Smith be printed. The important work of selecting the revelations for this new book was entrusted to Elders William W. Phelps, Oliver Cowdery, and John Whitmer.

It was during 1833 that John Whitmer and five other faithful brethren, while trying to establish permanent homes for the Saints in Jackson County, Missouri, met strong opposition from prejudiced, unyielding enemies. The principal trouble was that the Saints did not believe in slavery. Rather than lose their homes and other possessions, John Whitmer and the five church leaders offered themselves a ransom for the church, being willing even to die if that would appease the anger of the mobs. However, the infuriated enemies dispossessed the Saints of their rightful holdings, and drove them from Jackson County, after which John Whitmer returned to Kirtland, Ohio (*History of the RLDS Church*, 1:316–17.)

As one of the capable, trusted servants of the church, John Whitmer was appointed assistant president of a high council in Clay County, Missouri, on July 3, 1834. Two years later, at Kirtland, Ohio, he held a like position. In May 1835, he was entrusted with the editorship of the *Messenger and Advocate* for the church.

Concluding his years of service as editor of this publication (3:287), he said: "I would do injustice to my own feelings if I did not here notice still further the work of the Lord in these last days. The revelations and commandments given to us are, in my estimation, equally true with the Book of Mormon, and equally necessary for salvation. It is necessary to live by every word that proceedeth from the mouth of God; and I know that the Bible, Book of Mormon, and the Book of Doctrine and Covenants of the Church of Jesus Christ of Latter Day Saints, contain the revealed will of heaven. I further know that God will continue to reveal himself to his church and people until he has gathered his elect into his fold and prepared them to dwell in his presence."—*History of the RLDS Church*, 1:581, 582.

Near the close of 1837, John Whitmer returned to Missouri to make his home. One Sunday afternoon in April, 1922, two other elders and I visited the farm home of the late Elder John Whitmer. The residence, built in 1857, was a half mile from the Temple Lot in Caldwell County, Missouri. At the time of our visit, his widowed daughter Mrs. Johnson and her daughter lived in the home. After a short testimonial service held in the room where John Whitmer died in 1878, Sister Johnson invited us into an adjacent room where a large painting of her father was hung above the century-old walnut dresser. While viewing the portrait, I said: "His face is that of an honest man." Before his death he had said that his "testimony recorded in the Book of Mormon was, is, and will be true henceforth and forever." During this short interesting interview, the aged daughter spoke feelingly of her noble parent. Wiping tears from her face, she said, "My father was an honest, truth loving man."

APPENDIX O

Ethel Johnson Lewellen to C. Edward Miller, 1932

Ethel Johnson Lewellen to C. Edward Miller, 26 May 1932, CofC Archives.

Kingston, Mo, May 26, 1932

Mr. C. Edward Miller
Independence, Mo

Dear Mr. Miller:

Your letter received and I am sending you a little sketch of Aunt Ellas [*sic*] history. I hope it will be a help to you. I could probably tell you more in talking. The old home place sure is lonesome without her. I live in [the] same place ¼ mile east. My brother lives in big house. I will see about that picture of David Whitmer see what the rest say about it, what could you offer for it.

Ella E. Johnson was born March 23, 1857 and departed this life February 25, 1932. She was the daughter of James Edwin [*sic*] and Sarah Elizabeth Whitmer Johnson. She had one brother John Edward Johnson. She was born in far west Mo. The house she was born in was torn down several years ago. it was a two room house with large fireplace. The larger house she lived in was built be [*sic*] her grandfather John Whitmer He star[t]ed it in 1856 and completed it in 1857. John Whitmer and his wife both died there. Aunt Ella had lived there all her life.

Her mother Sarah Elizabeth Whitmer was born in her father's hotel at far west near where the [Community of Christ] church stands. Her mother married James Edward Johnson of New York. To this union were born the two children John and Ella. As the years went by Aunt Ellas [*sic*] father and mother were divorced. And she married a man by [the] name of Christopher Kerr.

Oliver Cowdery married Elizabeth Whitmer and she was a daughter of Peter Whitmer brother to John Whitmer. Oliver Cowdery and wife had several children but they all died in infancy but Maria, and she married Dr. Charles Johnson, who was no kin to us.

Now Oliver Cowdery and his wife had these portraits in their home at Richmond, Mo and Oliver Cowdery['s] wife died in 1892 and so her husband hired on a housekeeper to stay with him. And Aunt Ella's mother was there at the time of her death or near then, and they gave her the portraits. So they had been in Aunt Ella's home until she donated them to the church. Aunt Ella's father had no brothers or sisters, her brother was my father and I have one brother and one sister, that is all there is left of [the] Johnson family.

[unsigned]

Evan A. Fry to Ella Turner, 1949

Evan A. Fry to Ella Turner, granddaughter of Hiram Page, 25 January 1949, CofC Archives.[21]

Dear Mrs. Turner:

I hope I am not too late in furnishing you the information which your daughter [Bessie Turner] requested. Peter Whitmer Sr. was born 14 April 1773, and his wife, Mary Musselman, was born 27 August 1778. I did not find the date of their marriage. Their children, in the order of their birth, are as follows:

Christian, January 18, 1798
Jacob, January 27, 1800
John, August 27, 1802
David, January 7, 1805
Catherine, April 22, 1807
Peter Jr., September 27, 1809
Nancy, December 24, 1812, died April 19, 1813
Elizabeth Ann, January 22, 1815

Peter Whitmer is characterized as a devout and God-fearing man, and a staunch Presbyterian. Joseph Smith and his wife, Emma, stayed with Father Whitmer during much of the time when the Book of Mormon was being translated, and it was in his home [some believe] that the new church was organized on April 6, 1830. He and several of the children were baptized on April 11, 1830.

Christian Whitmer was crippled partially from birth, and learned the trade of shoemaker. He married Anne Schott on February 22, 1825, went through the Mormon expulsion in Independence [Jackson County] in 1833, and died Nov 27, 1835. During his lifetime he served for a time on the High Council of the [Missouri] Church, being ordained a High Priest Aug 21, 1833, and to the [Missouri] High Council, July 3, 1834.

21. Fry's source material was probably Andrew Jenson, the *LDS Biographical Encyclopedia.*

Jacob Whitmer was married to Elizabeth Schott on Sept. 29, 1825. He and his wife were baptized together on April 11, 1830, a few days after the organization of the church. Jacob served on the building committee for the Temple which was barely begun at Far West, in Caldwell County, Missouri.

John Whitmer was probably the most active of all the Whitmer brothers in church work. In March on 1831 he was designated as church historian, and wrote several chapters of church history. He was for a short time editor of a church paper called The Messenger and Advocate, ending his tenure somewhere during the second volume on March 1836. In the troubles leading up to the expulsion of the Saints from Jackson County in 1833, he with several others offered himself to the mob as a hostage for the safety of his brethren. He explored Caldwell County and helped in selecting the site for the city of Far West. On Aug. 8, 1836 the south half of that town site was entered in his name. W. W. Phelps entered the north half. John's was one of the first houses built in Far West (There had been some log cabins before, but his was a frame dwelling). It was mentioned as "completed" on January 19, 1837. He was commissioned to appraise and divide and sell the town lots for the city of Far West. He was excommunicated from the church at the same time as David (1838) after a trial the legality of which has been seriously questioned by historians. He had three sons and one daughter. (Names not available).

There is almost endless material about David Whitmer, having to do with his activities in the church, his expulsion from it in 1838, his testimony of the Book of Mormon which he maintained to the end of his long and honorable life, etc. He was born January 7, 1805 near Harrisburg, Pa., but spent most of his early life in New York with the family. He married Julia Ann Jolly on January 9, 1831, and the following spring moved to Kirtland, Ohio and soon after to Independence. 1833 found him located in the "Whitmer Settlement" near the Big Blue west of Independence. I do not know how many children he had, but I found mention of at least one son, David J. After his excommunication from the church in 1838 he settled near Richmond, where he lived until his death on January 25, 1888. During his early years in Clay and Caldwell counties, he was ordained "President of the church in Zion" (July 3, 1834).

Catherine Whitmer married Hiram Page, November 10, 1825. (For her children, see account of Hiram Page, below.)

Peter Whitmer, Jr. was one of the eight witnesses of the Book of Mormon. He was born in 1809, and died Sept. 22, 1836.

Nancy Whitmer died in infancy, as noted.

Elizabeth Ann Whitmer married Oliver Cowdery, but I did not encounter the date. She was one of the group baptized April 11, 1830.

Hiram (occasionally I find this spelled Hyrum) Page was born in Vermont in the year 1800—the date—and month do not seem to be known. His wife, as noted above, was Catherine Whitmer. They were married November 10, 1825, and had nine children. Page studied medicine in his early years, and practiced some in Canada as well as in the U. S., but seems to have dropped that practice after joining the church. He moved with the church in Kirtland, Ohio in 1831 and from there to Independence in 1832. In 1833 he is mentioned as one of a committee which went from Independence to Lexington, Mo., to appear before and appeal to circuit court Judge Ryland, in an attempt to halt the mob violence in Independence. He severed his connection with the church in 1838—Was baptized April 11, 1830. Died on property near the present site of Excelsior Springs August 12, 1852.

I find that two different sources mention Peter Whitmer Sr. as a veteran of the Revolutionary War, but this seems unlikely in view of his birth in 1773.

This is the material I was able to gather in rather a superficial examination of such books as were immediately available. I suppose that much more might be found by an exhaustive perusal of every possible source, but hope that this will give you most of what you want. If there is any other point which you particularly wish to be informed about, please let me know and I shall be happy to try to find it for you. Looking this up has been great fun, and has added to my knowledge of church history considerably.

Sincerely,
[unsigned]
[Evan Fry, Radio Minister]

Samuel Russell, Correspondence, 1882

Samuel Russell, Family Correspondence, 3 November 1882, LDS Family History Library.

> Dear Lucy Ettie Friends and Kindred.... I went on to Far West took in the [?] Site Stayed all night with Mr. Sheldon Jones & wife. Had quite a talk with them. Then on Thursday Morning rode down Shoal Creek past the old Mill Site, Encircled the old town again packing my pockets full of Hazel nuts as I rode. then at 11 a.m. Started on the Back track arrived at Hines. Took diner with Nete at 2 p.m. got in a few words with her while eating dinner then bid them goodbye & resumed my Journey getting back to Alex (by way of Millville) about 7 p.m. Stayed all night & came over here to Ellen Sharps.... [page 4] By the Mirabile road—through a lane leading directly north—you enter far west Near the South West corner—the <road> leading on across Shoal Creek—which is spanned by an iron bridge. A half mile or less—above the old Henshaw Mill Seat—As you enter—on your left in a pasture is still to be seen a part of 2 chimneys—the remains of the old David Hughes—(or Joseph Smith) place—The Hughes family [about half of a page seems to be missing] ... Passing the Hughes place a short distance—on your right a lane opens up to the east—facing that direction—a half mile distant stands the old John Whitmer place (occupied by his daughter Sarah—first married to a man by name Johnson whom she had left & lately married to another by [the] name [of] Kerr) While still facing east—immediately on your right is the old shell of the Holman Store. (Where Bogart killed Alex Bates [Batu?] a nephew of Wesley Hines John Hines father) While a little farther on & more to the right in the field Still stands (& and is occupied) the old Wamsley place—while in the corner of the field close to your left is the Temple foundation & Lot and a little farther east & adjoining the east end of the Lot is a house built & occupied by Jake—John Whitmers Son—Whose wife (whose name was Tatershall) is said to be a regular vicious female devil against anything akin to Salt Lake Mormonism.

While Jake is not much better—facing again to the North and passing on toward Shoal Creek—half a mile with the places—where the
Hughes Baxter Store—Aunt Waltons—Phelps—& Kimball Houses
once stood—here a lane opens up to the west—passing by the old
grave yard. Thither I occupied [*sic*]—finding a field of corn on half
of it and the part that had not been plowed up so thick with prairie
grass—that I could not identify Robert Walton or James Dawsons
graves Nor could I tell whether they were on the part now in corn or
on the part now in the tall grass. Returning—on passing a house not
far from the grave yard I stopped to ask the man—some questions
He told me the man who had plowed up the grave yard was one John
Bolton & that he himself had counted some 45 graves—the stones of
which this "fiend" had knocked down and Plowed over—Which so
incised [*sic*] the neighborhood that the man was indicted by the grand
jury—but when the case came up the prosecuting attorney either from
being bought—or otherwise did not know anything [not even having
the No.s of the lot] so the case was thrown out of <court> [page 4]
it was said there was some 200 graves in all in that place I was now
asked to put up my horse & stay all night—which I accepted—He
then accompanied me around over the old land marks—we visited
the old stone Quarry—the Brush & woods around it—and up towards the town being thicker than ever—we found the well sight [*sic*]
& place where Anne Waltons [*sic*] house had stood—the foundation
where Ann Jane fell in the water & Mary & Sarah Dawson pulled her
out—where the old spot on which we were mobbed so long [ago]—
then the Foster place—& well from which we carried the water to
try to put out the burning hay stack. Then the place where Sis was
born North from Whitmers—a heavy piece of Corn stood on it but
the old place where the house stood & the well was [page 5] Then we
returned to the place again—here where the children were ordered
out to be shot Here where the mob so many times paid their nightly
visits here where they shot Alf Waltons dog—King—on the porch--
where they cut the tail off of Elijahs Cow & stuck it in the crack of
the door—here where they tore off part of the roof of the house &
smashed the windows in with rocks and rocking the roof when they
could no nothing else here where they aavused [abused or chased?] the
family so often from their beds and from here where they Marched
our father down the long hollow to the north & east of us to whip him
to death if he would not agree to leave—and finally from here they

sent him to the Richmond Jail confining him in the dark dungeon along with the prisoner White [Wight] [page 6] under sentence of death for murder—& finally from here: he was dragged to the Temple Square—and there sold on the Block—all on account of his religion. Next we went up on the hill just north where the old Stable used to stand—here when they shaved the manes & tails of Uncle John horses Doll & Charley Here where they shot the fine heifer of ours and here where father dug the hole in front of the stable—rolled her into it & covered her up—& yonder to the east of us a mile or more the field where they cut off the tail & ears & flesh so brutally of the Foster Horse—because he dared to defend a Mormon—next we passed over the hollow where they run Uncle Johns [*sic*] wagon & cut it to pieces [7] And lastly again we made our way to the Temple Lot—The Corner each have the stones still in there place—a cottonwood tree is growing in the foundation near the north side—at the N. E. Corner Stone—North & South of it and east of it for some 12 or 15 feet there had been considerable digging—this mine host informed me was the result of a nightdig for hidden treasure which had been kept up for several nights—And it was current over the neighborhood that while they were digging on the holes at night that balls of fire would come up out of the ground and roll all over & around in the holes—The Whitmers old John & family were in this job—but tried to hide it up But Murder would out—The sum of it was this—An all Seeing Nigger of Jackson County had told one Jim Howard of the money Jars. ... Sheldon Jones—guide—Wife is the daughter of Walter A. Doak they are Josephites—She remembered the terror which accompanied the scene [of my father being sold on the square]—that she never could forget it. Their house stood near the Walmsley house—and She could see our house—and saw the scene from the bringing of him out of his own house—up to the square and the sale—the mob surrounding him & getting like as many wolves. That her father could tell me much more than her. As he too witnessed it all. She remembered the name of Tatman distinctly and the Hughes outfit. Whose names she gave me—She remembered the name of Mary Russell—and the Walton Girls and told me the very place the Walton place stood & how it was told the girls used to stick pins in the mobbers and asked me if we didn't have a relation by the name of Kavanaugh I told her we did, but that the pin sticking was by the Dawson girls or Eliza in Stead of the Walton girls. She also recollected the name of Kellar—

Tell Sis to mail a news—now & than for a while to Sheldon Jones—& if she can get a copy of the Juvenile containing her piece—on the far west affair to send it to Mrs. Sheldon Jones as she requests me to send it to her Their address is Mirabile Caldwell Co Mo with this I will bid Far West good night Sincerely Samuel Russell

William B. Smith, 1879 Invitation to Gather at Far West

William B. Smith, "Mass Meeting at Far West, Mo., March 30, 1879," *Herald* 26, no. 23 (December 1, 1879): 355–56.

MASS MEETING AT FAR WEST, MO.,
March 30, 1879

Joseph [Smith III] and Henry [A. Stebbins, Secretary]:—

Meeting held at Far West on the Temple lot.... March 30th, at 11 o'clock met on the temple ground; a fair representation of the Saints from the vicinity of the place where, over forty years ago, a corner stone was laid for the purpose of rearing a temple unto the name of the Most High God. Previous notice having been given of this meeting, by the presiding Elder of the Far West branch in sufficient time for outsiders as well as for the Church in the vicinity to have due notice of the services, brethren were in attendance from the Delano branch, and from all parts of the adjacent country, to be on the ground at the beginning of the service. Notice was also given that William B. Smith, a brother of the Martyred Prophet would speak to the people, standing upon the corner stone that was laid upon the temple lot. This notice, and appointment brought in a large percentage of the outside world, to witness what might be said by the prophet's brother, upon so conspicuous an occasion. I [William B. Smith] am happy to state that those citizens present, who do not claim a kindred fellowship with us in the Church, seemed to take a deep interest in the meeting, and listened with attention to the preached word, and at the closing up of the meeting voted with the Saints in the adoption of certain resolutions, which were read at the closing of the services; a copy of which I herewith send to the Herald.

At 11 o'clock I took my stand upon the corner stone, after singing, and a prayer by Bro. Thomas J. Franklin. I read from 1 Cor. 15:29. "Else what shall they do which are baptized for the dead, if the dead rise not at all? Why are they then baptized for the dead?"

RLDS church members gather on the Temple Lot in Far West, Missouri, ca. 1880. A raised excavation area is visible in the background. Courtesy of Community of Christ Archives.

In connection with this statement made by Paul on the subject of baptism for the dead, I called the attention of the congregation to Paul's testimony, to his Ephesian brethren, on the dispensation of the fullness of times, Eph. 1:10. Showing that the doctrine of baptizing for the dead must have been at some previous time in the history of the ancient Church of Christ, an ordinance in the church. But, as by some means this subject of baptism for the dead had been lost from the knowledge of the world, it might be expected that in the dispensation when all things, both in heaven and upon earth, should be gathered in one, that this ordinance would again be restored to the Church. It was for this reason also, that these Saints of latter days build temples, in order to prepare a place for the administration of ordinances that belong in the order of the holy priesthood. And it was for this object also, that this corner stone was planted in this town of Far West, under the direction and superintendency of Joseph, the Martyr, in 1836–37 [1838]. Here still lies this corner stone upon this sacred spot of earth, once dedicated to God by solemn prayer. And still the Lord's dwelling place is here, as in all the congregations of the Saints; and the time will come when God's name will be honored here and upon this sacred spot of earth, in a temple reared up by human hands in honor to his name. For God's purposes ripen fast, and all his words must and will be fulfilled. In his own due time will all these things be accomplished.

In conclusion of my remarks in the forenoon session, I read from Book of Covenants, page three hundred and twenty-six, to the closing paragraph of Joseph Smith's letter written on the subject of baptism for the dead, and the welding together of the links of the present and past dispensations; holding the keys of power in the knowledge to be revealed concerning our dead; and the means by which salvation might reach them, that they with us might be made perfect and saved with us in the kingdom of God.

Meeting was dismissed by singing and prayer for intermission of one hour for lunch.

At two o'clock preaching again assisted by Bro. Bozarth, Elder Terry and Elder Gomer Griffiths. Elder Bozarth opened meeting by prayer; after which Elder Terry from the Delano Branch, preached a most interesting discourse from James 1:22, 23. He was followed by Elder Gomer Griffiths. After them I made some concluding remarks concerning Zion and the promised land, as pointed out by the prophets, and given by God as portrayed in the blessing of Jacob upon his son Joseph, many thousand years ago. And further, in token that the mob spirit had so far disappeared from the State of Missouri as to offer an asylum of peace for the Church in this land of Far West; and to give a fuller expression of the feeling and sentiment of the Church at Far West and of the people generally, the following preamble and resolutions were read to the people assembled, and placed before them for acceptance, or to be rejected, as the case might be. Liberty was given for remarks. Elder W. T. Bozarth rose and said, that the subject matter set forth in the resolutions offered by Bro. William B. Smith, met his hearty approval, and that so far as he understood the sentiments and feelings of the Church, the preamble and resolutions correspond to the teachings and doctrine taught by the leaders and heads of the Church, and therefore he would move that the preamble and resolutions be adopted by this meeting. The motion being duly seconded, it was put to vote and carried unanimously, the outside world taking part in the voting. The assembly adjourned to meet again at some future time at the same place, as the good Lord in his providence might direct. "Give us room that we may dwell" was sung, making the air resound with the music of one of the glorious songs of Zion. Brother Bozarth offered the closing prayer. The following is a copy of the preamble and resolutions passed at a mass meeting, held at Far West, by the Church, and the people of Caldwell county, Missouri, Sunday, March 30th, 1879:

Whereas, the Church of Jesus Christ of Latter Day Saints was expelled from the State of Missouri in 1838–39, by executive authority under mob rule; and whereas, the Church of the Saints having entered many thousand acres of land for which they paid their money in silver and gold, in this county of Caldwell; and, whereas, the Saints after having expended hundreds of thousands of dollars in the purchase of lands, making improvements, building houses, and devoting much labor in opening new farms among strangers, and in a strange land; and, whereas, according to the sacred order of our Church government, we, the Church of Jesus Christ of Latter Day Saints, assembled here to-day, en masse, do most sincerely regret our losses, and the great sacrifice of life and property, that fell to the lot of the Church that we are here to-day to represent; and, whereas, we, the Church of Jesus Christ of Latter Day Saints, esteem this spot of earth sacred; this Temple Lot where lies this corner-stone, that was laid with honors due to the sacredness of those Church rights and ordinances, wherein the worship and name of God are revered; not only in temples built with human hands, but honored and revered in the hearts of all men who are true believers in the gospel of Jesus Christ; and, whereas, this corner stone was laid here on this Temple Lot, over forty years ago, and consecrated to God by solemn prayer; and at a time when the blood of the Saints was made to drench this Missouri soil, in a land of boasted freedom, and yet by mob rule the Church of Christ was driven to seek an asylum in a more congenial clime; and, whereas, the principal causes that led to this expulsion of the Saints from this county of Caldwell and State of Missouri, have ceased to exist, since the emancipation of slaves, from the State; and, whereas, a more civilized spirit has taken possession of the masses of the people of the State of Missouri; therefore,

Resolved, that this meeting of the citizens of Caldwell county and Church of Jesus Christ, invite our brethren in the east and elsewhere, to emigrate to this land and secure their inheritances in Zion, by purchase; and, further,

Resolved, that we, the Church of Jesus Christ of Latter Day Saints, are a separate and distinct class of worshippers from that body of Mormons located in Utah, known as the Polygamic Mormons; and, further,

Resolved, that we, as the true Church of Jesus Christ of Latter Day Saints, deem it proper that we embody in these resolutions, for the benefit of our neighbors, and the world of mankind generally, the fact, that we, as a Church, have no fellowship whatever for that class of people, as we regard them as apostates from the faith; and therefore not worthy the confidence of any people. And further,

Resolved, that these resolutions and the minutes of this meeting be sent to the Herald Office, at Plano, Illinois, with the request that they be published in the *Herald* for the benefit of the Saints abroad; as there is now a good time for those who wish to locate near the temple ground, on easy and cheap terms for obtaining farms. There are also splendid locations near the City of Far West that are now for sale, that have not been moved by the plow for many years. And for timber there is plenty of it; and water. Come then, ye Saints of latter days, and possess the goodly land by purchase, and none to molest or make you afraid.

These facts I know. Amen. –Wm. B. Smith.

Arthur B. Deming, 1888

Arthur B. Deming, "The Polygamy Revelation—Joseph Smith's Handwriting Still in Existence!," *Naked Truths about Mormonism* 1, no. 2 (April, 1888): 1.

In looking through Tulle[d]ge's life of the Mormon prophet, Joseph Smith, I saw the name of J. R. H. Van Cleve [*sic*], of Chicago, Ill. I called on Mr. Van Cleve, who at that time, July, 1885, was private secretary to U. S. Collector Spaulding of Chicago. I introduced myself by showing him the extract from the *Deseret News* referring to my father. He read it and seemed much pleased. He received me cordially and said his father had been a Mormon, if I am not mistaken—though he was not—and that he married the granddaughter of David Whitmer. I told him that there had been much written about the Mormons that was erroneous, and that I was collecting facts for a true account of its origin and early history. He said that David Whitmer had the original manuscript from which the "Book of Mormon" was printed and would not sell it, although Orson Pratt and other Utah Mormons had requested him to name his price. He said the Utah Mormons sent two men to Missouri to steal it and other manuscript Mormon history. One of the men was captured in the attempt and sent to the penitentiary for two years. He said that John Whitmer, David's brother, was the church historian by appointment and that after his death he spent several days looking over his manuscripts and papers, and that he found five volumes of manuscript history, also the revelation about celestial marriage, or polygamy, dated July 12, 1843, in Joseph Smith's own hand-writing (which he knew) the same as printed in the Doctrines and Covenants of the Utah Mormons. I told him there was in the Chicago Historical Society a letter of Joseph Smith's, written to Emma, his wife, from Lancaster, Penn., which was presented to the society by his son. I requested Mr. Van Cleve to write to his relatives and have them send it to him so we could compare it with the letter in the historical rooms. He said it was not necessary for he had seen other writing of the prophet, Joseph Smith, and knew that the revelation was written by him. To please me he wrote and received a copy of another revelation by Joseph. He said there was so much opposition by Mormons to Joseph's revelation on polygamy that he obtained another confirming the first to appease the opposition. I told him I did not care to see it but did wish to see the one of July 12, 1843. He said when his successor was appointed he intended to go to Richmond, Mo., and write a history of Mormonism from David Whitmer's standpoint. He said Whitmer did not recognize the Reorganized Mormon Church led by the prophet's son, but claimed that he, David Whitmer, was the rightful successor of the church as its head. He said the Whitmers and Oliver Cowdery, whose wife was David's sister, left the Mormons in Missouri on account of Joseph and Rigdon's polygamy.

He promised me that if I would come to Richmond, Mo., when he was there he would show it to me and I could compare it with the revelation of July 12, 1843, printed in the Utah Doctrines and Covenants. I had twenty or more interviews with Mr. Van Cleve and obtained from him much information of great value on Mormonism. Mr. Van Cleve said he obtained consent of John Whitmer's daughters to remove the papers he had selected and that he placed them under some apples in the wagon, when the men were away, and brought them to Richmond, Mo. He said he purchased a safe in Chicago and sent it to Richmond and it was placed in the bank and contained the original manuscript of the "Book of Mormon," five volumes of manuscript Mormon history, the revelation about polygamy in Joseph Smith's handwriting, and other papers on Mormonism, he had been collecting. He had a good likeness of Rigdon taken about 1835, which cost him considerable, also of other Mormon leaders, which he intended to use in his proposed book.

APPENDIX T

George W. Schweich to O. R. Beardsley, 1900

George W. Schweich to O. R. Beardsley, 17 January 1900, Perry Special Collections.

> W.C. Paton, President Geo. W. Schweich, Secretary
> The Richmond Building and Loan Association
> "The Richmond" Hotel Building
> Richmond, Missouri, Jany 17, 1900
> Rev. O. R. Beardsley
> Dear Sir
>
> Your letter of 15th just received Yes I am the owner of the Original M.S of the Book of Mor. It is now in New York City with W. E. Benjamin #22 W. 33rd St. Op. Waldorf Astoria—I have not a[t] present time to answer all your questions but may some time soon—I send you my grandfather David Whitmers pamphlet which may answer some of your inquiries—
>
> I consider the M.S. an important document for the American people I also have M.S. History of the Church for some unpublished periods also—In combating the errors of Mormonism I think heretofore the wrong premises have been taken—I am fair and hope you have a least taken another track than has been used so long—you may give me some specific questions if you like and I will endeavor to answer them—I should also like to know your plan of procedure in the premises—Very Truly Geo. W. Schweich

Edmund C. Brand to Joseph Smith III, 1875

Edmund C. Brand to Joseph Smith III, *Herald* 22, no. 6 (March 15, 1875): 183.

KNOXVILLE, Ray Co., Mo.,
Feb. 17th, 1874.

Br. Joseph:—I have preached, in company with Br. Styles, since last writing, at Lees Summit, in the Christian Church, and at a place near Independence. Have visited the Whitmer family at Richmond; preached in John Whitmer's school-house six times. Br. David Whitmer showed me the original manuscript of the Book of Mormon, partly in Oliver Cowdery's, Martin Harris' and your mother's handwriting, it is in good preservation, clean and legible. I think that any member of the Whitmer family would suffer death rather than deny the divinity of that Book. They are respected here and all through the County as honorable, honest men; they treated me with the greatest of kindness; may God abundantly bless them.

I preach here, at Br. Cravin's, to-night, and go with him to-morrow to Far West, and shall visit John Whitmer; thence to Stewartsville and St. Joseph, and meet Br. Styles at Oregon, on the first of March.

Yours in bonds,
E. C. BRAND.

Joseph F. Smith to Samuel Russell, 1901

Joseph F. Smith to Samuel Russell, 19 March 1901, LDS Church History Library.

> With regard to the manuscript of the blessing supposed to have been given by the Prophet Joseph to David Whitmer, it is one of many similar blessings.... There is but one thing in the latter career of David Whitmer which will wholly commend him to the sympathies of the saints and the confidence of the people of God and to the favor of the Lord, and that is he was true to the last to the great testimony which he received of the divine authenticity of the Book of Mormon in which he did not falter in the least.... With regard to the letter of William E. Benjamin to you, respecting the manuscript of the Book of Mormon in his possession, I need only say to you that it is not the original manuscript, but is the copy made from the originals which was used in the printing of the first edition of the Book of Mormon, which was proof read by Oliver Cowdery and retained by him until the time of his death at David Whitmer's in Richmond, Missouri when it fell into David's hands. The original manuscript was retained by the Prophet Joseph Smith and kept in his own possession until it was placed by him in a stone box in the southeast corner of the Nauvoo house where it remained until Mr. Bidamon tore down that part of the building and removed the box, soon after which all that remained of the original manuscript fell into my own hands and into the hands of Franklin D. Richards, all of which are here with us at this time. The Manuscript in the hands of Mr. Benjamin possesses no value whatever. It has been repeatedly offered to us, and numerous false reports have been put in circulation with regard to our desire to obtain possession of it, but we have at no time regarded it as of any value, neither have we ever offered any money to procure it, all the stories to the contrary notwithstanding, for we have always known it was not the original, as aforesaid, and as many editions of the Book of Mormon have been printed and tens of thousands of copies of it circulate

throughout the world you can readily perceive that this manuscript really is of no value to anyone. There is no principle involved in its possession, there could be nothing lost if it were utterly destroyed; it can neither add to nor diminish aught from the word of God as contained in the printed work which had already gone to the world and been translated into many languages. Indeed, it is not worth the time and paper I am using to convey these thoughts to you.

Referring again to the blessing by the Prophet upon the head of David Whitmer is it not a little singular that the relatives of David Whitmer should attach any importance to it since they are and have been long agreed that Joseph Smith was a fallen prophet?

Your description of your visit to your grandfather's grave at Richmond, and also that of Father David Whitmer, one of the three witnesses, was very interesting to me, as also the kindness in which the memory of your father is held by the old residents of that neighborhood and also the kindness with which you were received while on your visit there. It is an evidence of the great change which has come over the minds of the people regarding the Later-day Saints. The recollection of my own visit in company with Elder Orson Pratt in 1878 to Father Whitmer, and the friends that were gathered around him are very similar to your own. I remember Mr. George Schweich on the occasion of our visit there and I have very pleasant recollections of Mr. R. B. Van Cleave who married the granddaughter of Father Whitmer sometime after our visit and while there, in the presence of Brother Pratt and a dozen others, I had the temerity to call the attention of Father Whitmer to the fact that the manuscript in his possession was but the copy of the original, and proved it to him by this circumstance: I asked him if he and the other witnesses each signed their own name to their testimony, and he unhesitatingly replied yes, we each signed our own names. Then I said, calling his attention to the names of the witnesses as inscribed in the manuscript. "How is it that these names are written by one man." He eagerly grasped the manuscript containing the testimony and glanced over the names, "Well he said, I don't know how this is, Oliver must have copied them." Still he persisted it was the original manuscript and not wishing to have an argument with him over the matter I let it drop.... I have reason for supposing that this blessing [and others] ... are all recorded.

Last House in Far West Destroyed, 1913

"Last House in Far West Is Destroyed," *Deseret News* 6, no. 40 (March 20, 1913): 1.

> Kingston, Mo., March 15.—The destruction of a cabin five miles north of here yesterday removed the last building from the site of Far West once a flourishing little city, which, before the Mormons established themselves in Utah, was chosen as the site for the headquarters of their church. Filed away among the records of the Mormon church at Salt Lake City are the original plans of Far West. The plans show that a great city was contemplated. Preparations were made for the building of a temple in the center of the town. The work on the temple was actually begun a short time before the Mormons of Missouri decided to go to Utah.
>
> When the foregoing Associated Press dispatch was read to Andrew, Jensen [*sic*], Church Historian, Mr. Jensen said that the cabin referred to was the former home of John Whitmer, one of the three witnesses to the authenticity of the Book of Mormon and himself a close associate of the Prophet Joseph Smith in the early days of Mormonism.
>
> Mr. Jensen added that when he visited Far West several years ago the Whitmer home was the only remaining structure in the old town of Far West. Regarding the work on the temple Mr. Jensen says that the cornerstone was laid in 1837, but later the Mormons were driven out of Missouri and went to Illinois. They never returned to Far West and the plan to build the temple was abandoned.

Ronald E. Romig, Review of From Historian to Dissident by Bruce N. Westergren

Ronald E. Romig, Review of *From Historian to Dissident: The Book of John Whitmer*, *John Whitmer Historical Association Journal* 17 (1997): 144–46.

The content of John Whitmer's history has been available to scholars for many years. Andrew Jenson's 1893 transcription of the original is known to interested students in a variety of formats. Researchers recognize that Jenson's work contains some inaccuracies—though none of very great importance. And the original manuscript continues to be accessible at the RLDS Archives in Independence, Missouri, for those wishing to pursue serious scholarly comparisons.

So why another edition of John Whitmer's history? In truth, it is useful to again have an edition of Whitmer's history readily available in print as a dependable standard resource for the bookshelf. As such, Bruce N. Westergren's 1995 publication, *From Historian to Dissident: The Book of John Whitmer*, is a success. This edition makes available a reasonably careful rediscovery of the original wordings of the "Book of John Whitmer." And each new generation of scholars is benefited in making the effort to reclaim and reinterpret such standard works, as with new eyes.

Given that, this new "Book of John Whitmer" is somewhat disappointing. It seems an opportunity was missed. Republication could have provided an occasion for a thoughtful reevaluation of the person of John Whitmer and his Mormon experience. Apparently this was not the author's purpose. Thus far there has been no truly novel effort to explore the life of John Whitmer. Treatment of the "essential Whitmer" is sketchy at best. In this vein, this book provides little more than a dull glaze as context for Whitmer's life. Despite evidence of meticulous work, I sense that the author never really got to know John Whitmer, nor those he chronicled. Annotations draw heavily from other published reference works. One might also expect to see more revealed of the process by which the history was originally created.

Westergren offers a novel observation in his introduction by suggesting that the manuscript for the "Book of John Whitmer" is a later copy made from a now non-extant earlier document. This is certainly a possibility. The existence of various early church documents in Whitmer's handwriting indicates that he did a lot of copy work. I believe the author's assertion is reasonable when considering the likelihood that the document is a continuously written manuscript drafted over an extended period of time. Westergren contends that the wording in a list of individuals ordained by Lyman Wight in 1831 (on page 28 of the manuscript) reveals that this continuously written passage could not have been penned until after John's own separation from the church. Westergren writes, "In the same entry he lists his own name among those who fell from the faith, although he was not excommunicated until 1838." In my opinion, the words "denied the faith" after the names of Ezra Booth and Harvey Whitlock were not meant to imply that all the names in the list which follow also denied the faith. Lyndon Cook suggests that the last of these, Whitlock, was disfellowshipped in 1835 and excommunicated in 1838. [Lyndon W. Cook, *The Revelations of the Prophet Joseph Smith,* (Provo, Utah: Seventy's Mission Bookstore, 1981): 81]. That this may have been written as late as 1835 does not prove that Whitmer penned it after 1838. Writing after the event in this instance, I believe that in his utilitarian, sometimes unsophisticated way, Whitmer's primary purpose was to list the names of individuals ordained by Lyman Wight on that occasion. Though imprecise at times, I think Whitmer succeeds in communicating his observations surprisingly well. In my opinion the "Book of John Whitmer" is an early original document.

From Historian to Dissident attempts to emphasize Whitmer's perceived rebellious nature. As such, it seeks to capitalize on what has become a somewhat popular theme in recent years. The book strives to create a somber mood. The selection of title, the colors and illustration for the cover, the manufacture and insertion of chapter headings in the text, and choice of excerpts displayed on the back cover, all reinforce this theme. Whether this was the author's or the publisher's intent is unclear. For inside the covers, the book contains little to support this view. The effort to cast Whitmer's writings as a dissenting work appears more a reflection of what might be politely described as bias.

Except for the presence of occasional comments to this effect within the author's annotations, an outside reader, not knowing the orthodox LDS view, might very likely conclude that rather than Whitmer leaving the church, the church left Whitmer. This bias implies that Whitmer both initiated and proved to be the ultimate cause of this unfortunate split. I believe the judgment of history remains open as to whether Whitmer chose a dissenting role or whether it was forced upon him and his family.

I am glad for Westergren's gracious acknowledgment of the LDS and RLDS archives in the introduction of the book. But that really doesn't tell the entire story. This book could have been enhanced through better collaboration between the author, publisher, and the involved repositories. I am certain that the RLDS Archives could have proven a more effective partner had it been given an opportunity. The same is probably true of the LDS Archives. Access to original manuscript materials was apparently received from the RLDS Archives a number of years ago. Since then, the staff has completely changed. In fairness, Westergren may have spent weeks, days, or even months at the facility working closely with the manuscript materials. I simply don't know. To my knowledge, after obtaining copies of the original manuscript, there was no further contact with the author until the book was ready for print. At this point he wrote to request materials and information with which to supplement the history. I responded affirmatively but attempted to clarify the nature of his permissions. I've never heard from him again. Neither the author nor the publisher involved the RLDS Archives any further in the process of publication. I would like to see repositories included in publishing agreements which substantively involve their holdings. I believe the larger church historical community will benefit when publishing efforts reflect a better consideration of the valuable contributions of all participants in the process.

Congratulations are in order to Westergren and Signature Books on the successful realization of what must have been a long and demanding project. Unfortunately, from my perspective as RLDS Church archivist, the publication of this book is not one of the church historical community's better success stories.

Published Reproductions of Book of Mormon Caractors

Facsimiles of the characters appear to stem from two sources. During the Nauvoo era, a facsimile of three lines of the characters was printed on a broadside sheet with gold lettering on black stock. As the copy associated with the Whitmers was unavailable to Nauvoo church leaders in the 1840s, this facsimile may be based on a copy of the characters in the possession of Hyrum Smith. The description of the broadside reads: "The Stick of Joseph … a correct copy of the Characters taken from the plates the Book of Mormon was translated from. The same that was taken to professor Anthon of New York, by Martin Harris, in the year 1827 [*sic*] in fulfillment of Isaiah 29:11, 12." The following note appears on the reverse of a copy at the LDS Church History Library, in Thomas Bullock's hand: "1844 placard Stick of Joseph. This was formerly owned by Hyrum Smith and sent to the Historian's Office March 22, 1860, by his son, Joseph Fielding Smith."[22] (Stick of Joseph, broadside, LDS Church History Library, cited in Danel W. Bachman, "Sealed in a Book: Preliminary Observations on the Newly Found 'Anthon Transcript,'" 324). However, this is incorrect since the broadside wasn't printed until December 1844. It was more likely a copy that Mary Fielding previously owned. This image is reproduced in Joseph Fielding Smith, *Essentials in Church History*, page 63. However, typesetters unintentionally printed the cut with the last series of characters in the last part of the last line flipped upside down and backward. An engraving based on this facsimile also appeared in the *Prophet* (a New York LDS newspaper) 2, no. 31 (December 21, 1844), but corrected the mistake previously printed in the broadside. J. H. Beadle, *Life in Utah* (1870), reproduced the cut from the *Prophet* facing page 30. The same image appears in M. T. Lamb, *The*

---

22. Joseph Fielding Smith, the son of Hyrum Smith, is usually known as Joseph F. Smith to prevent confusion with his own son, also named Joseph Fielding Smith. Both men were ordained LDS apostles (1866 and 1910, respectively) and both also served as LDS church presidents: Joseph F. from 1901 to 1918, and Joseph Fielding from 1970 to 1972.

Golden Bible, facing page 260, and in William Alexander Linn, *The Story of the Mormons*, facing page 46. Sometime in the 1870s, the F. C. Warnky Art Studio, in Independence, printed a handwritten *carte-de-visite* format photograph based on the defective image on the broadside. (Buddy Youngreen, "And Yet Another Copy of the Anthon Manuscript," 346.)

The source of the other line of facsimile reproductions may be traced from John Whitmer, to James Van Cleave, to David Whitmer, and finally to George Schweich. An early facsimile copy of this manuscript appears in M. T. Lamb, *The Golden Bible* (1887), page 342. After David Whitmer's death in 1888, the document passed into George Schweich's hands and, in 1903, to the RLDS church, which printed a large facsimile reproduction as a supplement to the *Herald*, September 29, 1909. In 1910, Charles A. Shook, *Cumorah Revisited*, page 522, published a slightly modified copy of the facsimile. It also appears in Vida E. Smith, *Young People's History*, facing page 14, and Robert C. Webb, *The Case against Mormonism*, page 22.

Community of Christ currently offers a high-quality facsimile for sale at its mercantile store at the Kirtland Temple Visitor and Spiritual Formation Center, 7809 Joseph Street, Kirtland, Ohio 44094.

BIBLIOGRAPHY

Short Citations

CofC Archives. Community of Christ Library-Archives, Independence, MO.

LDS Family History Library. Family History Library of The Church of Jesus Christ of Latter-day Saints, Salt Lake City, UT.

History of the LDS Church. Joseph Smith Jr. et al. *History of the Church of Jesus Christ of Latter-day Saints.* Edited by B. H. Roberts. 6 vols. 1902–12. Vol. 7. 1932. Reprint, Salt Lake City: Deseret Book, 1980.

History of the RLDS Church. Joseph Smith III and Heman Hale Smith. *History of the Church of Jesus Christ of Latter Day Saints, 1805–1890.* 4 vols. Continued by F. Henry Edwards as *The History of the Church of Jesus Christ of Latter Day Saints.* Vols. 5–8. Independence, MO: Herald House, 1897–1903, 1967.

Huntington Library. Henry E. Huntington Library and Art Gallery, San Marino, CA.

Journal History. Journal History of The Church of Jesus Christ of Latter-day Saints. Chronological scrapbook of typed entries and newspaper clippings, 1830–present. LDS Church Archives. Not to be confused with *Journal of History,* a periodical of the RLDS church.

Journal of Discourses. 26 vols. London and Liverpool: LDS Booksellers Depot, 1855–86.

JSLB. Joseph Smith III. Letterbooks, 1876–1896. 10 vols.

LDS Church History Library. Library of the History Department, Church of Jesus Christ of Latter-day Saints, Salt Lake City.

Marriott Library. Special Collections. Willard Marriott Library, University of Utah, Salt Lake City.

OCLB. Oliver Cowdery Letterbook. Henry E. Huntington Library and Art Gallery, San Marino, CA. Facsimile. P19, f6. Typescripts, P19, f5. CofC Archives.

Perry Special Collections. L. Tom Perry Special Collections and Manuscripts. Harold B. Lee Library, Brigham Young University, Provo, UT.

Temple Lot Case. *Complaint's Abstract of Pleading and Evidence in the Circuit Court of the United States, Western Division at Kansas City—The Reorganized Church of Jesus Christ of Latter day Saints vs. The Church of Christ at Independence.* Lamoni, IA: Herald Publishing House and Bindery, 1893.

Works Cited

Anderson, George Edward. Letter to John E. Johnson. 11 March 1912. Holograph. MS 6378. 10. LDS Church History Library.

Anderson, Lavina Fielding, ed. *Lucy's Book: A Critical Edition of Lucy Mack Smith's Family Memoir.* Salt Lake City: Signature Books, 2001.

Anderson, Richard Lloyd. "Attempts to Redefine the Experience of the Eight Witnesses." *Journal of Book of Mormon Studies* 14, no. 1 (2005): 18–31. This journal is a publication of the Foundation for Ancient Research and Mormon Studies, Provo, UT.

———. "Five Who Handled the Plates." *Improvement Era* 72, no 7 (July 1969): 38–40, 42, 44–47.

———. "The House Where the Church Was Organized." *Improvement Era* 73, no 4 (April 1970): 16–19, 21–25.

———. *Investigating the Book of Mormon Witnesses.* Salt Lake City: Deseret Book, 1981.

———. "Review of David Whitmer Interviews: A Restoration Witness." *Journal of Mormon History* 20, no. 1 (Spring 1994): 186–193.

———. "Who Were the Six Who Organized the Church on 6 April 1830?." *Ensign* (June 1980): 44–45.

Anderson, Rodger I. *Joseph Smith's New York Reputation Reexamined.* Salt Lake City: Signature Books, 1990.

"[An Anti-Polygamy] Do[cument]." *Daily Globe* (Atchison, KS) undated, [page not known], clipping in Book of Mormon Witnesses file. CofC Archives.

"[An Anti-Polygamy] Do[cument]." *Des Moines Daily News*, October 16, 1886, 20.

Arrington, Leonard J., ed. "Oliver Cowdery's Kirtland, Ohio, 'Sketch-book.'" *BYU Studies* 12, no. 4 (Summer 1972): 410–26.

Arrington, Leonard J., Feramorz Y. Fox, and Dean L. May. *Building the City of God: Community and Cooperation among the Mormons.* Salt Lake City: Deseret Book, 1976.

"Articles of the Church." *The Evening and the Morning Star* 1, no. 1 (June 1832).

"The Articles Covenants and Law of the Church of Christ Independence Jackson County Missorie [*sic*] January 12th 1832 Copied by J. Whitmer for Zebidee Coltrin Harvey Whitlock Sum [*sic*] Elders of the Church of Christ." MS 1443. Fd. 831, item 1. LDS Church History Library.

Ashurst-McGee, Mark. "A Pathway to Prophethood: Joseph Smith Junior as Rodsman, Village Seer, and Judeo-Christian Prophet." Masters thesis, Utah State University, 2000.

Austin, Emily M. *Mormonism; or Life among the Mormons.* Madison, WI: M. J. Cantwell Book and Job Printer, 1882.

Bachman, Danel W. "Sealed in a Book: Preliminary Observations on the Newly Found 'Anthon Transcript.'" *BYU Studies* 20, no. 4 (Spring 1980): 321–45; facsimile of Caractors, 321.

Backman, Milton R., Jr. *Eyewitness Accounts of the Restoration.* Orem, UT: Grandin Book Company, 1983.

Backman, Milton V. *The Heavens Resound: A History of the Latter-day Saints in Ohio, 1830–1838.* Salt Lake City: Deseret Book, 1983.

"Back Tax List." *Supplement to Sentinel.* Ca. November 4, 1872, no date or page number, copy in [John] Whitmer History subject folder. CofC Archives.

Barben, A. H. "Cayuga and Seneca Canal, 1813–1963." Four-page pamphlet distributed by A. H. Barben, Seneca Falls, NY. Cited in Porter, "A Study of the Origins of the Church," 316.

Barchers, Harold D. "The Descendants and History of the Peter Whitmer Family." Typescript, 1999. CofC Archives.

———. Untitled presentation at Whitmer Family Celebration, Richmond, MO, October 6, 2006. Notes by Ronald Romig in Whitmer History Folder. CofC Archives.

Barrett, Elsie E. "Mary Elizabeth Rollins Lightner: Came to Utah in 1863." MS 3538. LDS Church History Library.

Barrett, Ivan J. *Joseph Smith and the Restoration.* Provo, UT: Brigham Young University Press, 1973.

Berrett, LaMar C., ed. *Sacred Places: A Comprehensive Guide to Early LDS Historical Sites.* 6 vols. Salt Lake City: Deseret Book, 1999–2007.

Barrows, Ethan. "Journal of Ethan Barrows." *Journal of History*: 15, no. 1 (January 1922): 34–79, 15; no. 2 (April 1922): 180–214. 15; no. 3 (July 1922): 315–35. 15; no. 4 (October 1922): 430–53.

Bauder, Peter. *The Kingdom and Gospel of Jesus Christ: Contrasted with That of Anti-Christ. A Brief Review of Some of the Most Interesting Circumstances, Which Have Transpired Since the Institution of the Gospel of Christ, from the Days of the Apostles.* Canajoharie, NY: A. H. Calhoun, 1834.

Baugh, Alexander L. "A Call to Arms: The 1838 Mormon Defense of Northern Missouri." PhD diss., Brigham Young University.

———. "A Community Abandoned: W. W. Phelps' 1839 Letter to Sally Waterman Phelps from Far West, Missouri." *Nauvoo Journal* 10, no. 2 (Fall 1998): 19–32.

———. "Jacob Hawn and the Hawn's Mill Massacre: Missouri Millwright and Oregon Pioneer." *Mormon Historical Studies* 11, no. 1 (Spring 2010): 1–25.

Bay, W. V. N. *Reminiscences of the Bench and Bar of Missouri.* St. Louis, MO: F. H. Thomas and Company, 1878.

The Bay of San Francisco: The Metropolis of the Pacific Coast and Its Suburban Cities. 2 vols. Chicago: Lewis Publishing, 1892, 2:91–93.

Beadle, John Hanson. "Jackson County: The Early History of the Saints and Their Enemies." Written September 28, 1875. *Salt Lake City Tribune*, October 6, 1875, [page not known]. Uncle Dale's [Dale Broadhurst] Readings in Early Mormon History: http://www.sidneyrigdon.com/dbroadhu/UT/tribune1. htm. Accessed July 17, 2007.

Becker, John E., comp. *A History of The Village of Waterloo, New York, and Thesaurus of Related Facts.* Waterloo, NY: Waterloo Library and Historical Society, 1949.

Behrens, Richard K. "Dreams, Visions and Visitations: The Genesis of Mormonism." *John Whitmer Historical Association Journal* 27 (2007): 179.

Berge, Dale L. "Archaeology at the Peter Whitmer Farm, Seneca County, New York." *BYU Studies* 31, no. 2 (Winter 1973): 200–201.

Best, Jane Evans. "Martin Kendig's Swiss Relatives." *Pennsylvania Mennonite Heritage* 15, no. 1 (January 1992): 2–18.

Bidamon, Emma Hale Smith. *See* Smith, Emma Hale.

Black, Susan Easton, ed. *Membership of the Church of Jesus Christ of Latter-day Saints, 1830–1848.* 50 vols. Provo, UT: Brigham Young University Religious Studies Center, 1984–88.

———. "Pioneer Cemetery in Richmond, Missouri." *Mormon Historical Studies* 2, no. 2 (Fall 2001): 181–96.

———. "The Unheralded Role of Martin Harris in Missouri." Paper presented at From Conflict to Understanding: The Mormon Experience in Missouri, Columbia, MO, September 8–9, 2006.

Blair, W. W. "Editors Herald." 22 May 1879, Sandwich, IL. *Herald* 26, no. 12 (June 15, 1879): 190–91.

Blankmeyer, Helen Van Cleave. *David Whitmer, Witness for God: Written for His Descendants.* [Springfield, IL]: privately printed, 1955.

Blessing for Joseph Smith Sr. by Joseph Jr. December 18, 1833. Patriarchal Blessing Book 1. LDS Church History Library.

Blessing for John Whitmer. September 22, 1835, recorded October 2, 1835. Patriarchal Blessing Book 1, p. 14. Handwriting of Oliver Cowdery. LDS Church History Library.

Bolton, Andrew. "Pentecost and All Things Common." Paper presented at the annual meeting of the John Whitmer Historical Association, Kirtland, OH, September 2007. Photocopy in my possession.

Bond, Myron. Letter to Henry Stebbins. 2 August 1878. Cadillac, MI. "I Do Think Tithing." *Herald* 25, no. 16 (August 15, 1878): 253.

Book of Commandments. *A Book of Commandments for the Government of the Church of Christ Organized According to Law, on the 6th of April 1830.* Zion [Independence, Jackson County, MO.]: W. W. Phelps and Company, 1833.

Book of Commandments. Manuscript fragments. Vault. CofC Archives.

The Book of Mormon. Palmyra, NY: The Author, 1830.

Book of Mormon. Printer's manuscript. 1830. Holograph. Vault. CofC Archives.

Book of Mormon. Printer's manuscript. Photograph. D1738.9. Pictorial Archives. CofC Archives.

"The Book of Mormon." *Daily Globe* (Atchison, KS). Clipping in Book of Mormon Witnesses subject folder. CofC Archives.

"The Book of Mormon." *Telegraph* (Painesville, OH) 2, no. 24 (November 30, 1830): 3.

"The Book of Mormon-More about It." *St. Louis Republican.* Sunday, September 29, 1878. Clipping in Book of Mormon Witnesses subject folder. CofC Archives.

Booth, Bertha [Ellis]. Plat of Far West, Caldwell County, Missouri. Reprinted in Johnson and Romig, *An Index to Early Caldwell County, Missouri, Land Records.*

Booth, Bertha Ellis. *A Short History of Caldwell County, [Missouri].* 1936. Reprinted Independence, MO: Missouri Mormon Frontier Foundation, 1998.

Booth, Ezra. Letter No. 4, to Reverend Ira Eddy, 31 October 1831. "Mormonism No. 4." *Telegraph* (Painesville, OH) 3, no. 22 (November 15, 1831): 3.

———. Letter No. 6 to Reverend Ira Eddy, 14 November 1831. *Telegraph* (Painesville, OH) 3, no. 24 (November 29, 1831): 2.

———. Letter No. 7, to Reverend Ira Eddy. November 21, 1831. Contains Letter to Edward Partridge. September 20, 1831. *Ohio Star* 2, no. 47 (November 24, 1831). Also in *Telegraph* (Painesville, OH) 3, no. 25 (December 6, 1831): 1–2.

———. Letter No. 8, to Reverend Ira Eddy. 29 November 1831. *Telegraph* (Painesville, OH) 3, no. 27 (December 20, 1831): 2–3.

———. Letter No. 9, to Reverend Ira Eddy. 6 December 1831. *Telegraph* (Painesville, OH) 3 (December 27, 1831): 2–3.

Bowen, Walter D. "The Versatile W. W. Phelps." Masters thesis, Brigham Young University, 1958.

Brackbill, Martin H. "Family Data in Pennsylvania Land Patents." *National Genealogical Society Quarterly* 68, no. 2 (June 1980): 94.

Bracken, James B. Statement. November 6, 1881. LDS Church History Library.

The Braden and Kelley Debate: Public Discussion of the Issues between the Reorganized Church of Jesus Christ of Latter Day Saints and the Church of Christ [Disciples]. Lamoni, IA: Herald Publishing House, 1913.

Brand, Edmund C. Letter to Joseph Smith III. *Herald* 22, no. 6 (March 15, 1875): 183.

———. Statement regarding visit to John Whitmer. February 18, 1875. Whitmer Papers. P10, f 9. CofC Archives.

Bray, Justin R. "Caleb Baldwin: Prison Companion to Joseph Smith." *Mormon Historical Studies* 11, no. 2 (Fall 2010): 73–91.

Brechbill, Laban T. *History of the Old Order River Brethren.* Edited by Myron S. Dietz. N.p.: Brechbill & Strickler, 1972.

Briggs, Jason W., ed. "History of the Reorganization of the Church of Jesus Christ of Latter Day Saints, Chapter 5." *Messenger* 2, no. 5 (March 1876): 17–18.

Bringhurst Newell G., and John C. Hamer, eds. *Scattering of the Saints: Schism within Mormonism.* Independence, MO: John Whitmer Books, 2007.

Brooke, John L. *The Refiner's Fire: The Making of Mormon Cosmology, 1644–1844.* New York: Cambridge University Press, 1994.

Brown, Albert. Letter to Dear Parents, November 1, 1835. Amos L. Underwood Collection. MS 2427. LDS Church History Library.

Brunson, Lewis. Statement, 1861. Photocopy of holograph. MSS SC 1477. Perry Special Collections.

Bullock, Thomas. "1864 Listing of Members." Holograph. LDS Church History Library.

Burch, Celenary. Indenture to David Whitmer. Lot 84. 20 February 1849. Deed Record Book F, p. 333. Ray County Land Records. Ray County Recorders' Office, Richmond, MO. Also in Whitmer Papers. P10, f2, item 26. CofC Archives.

[Burgess, Samuel A.] Letter to Elbert A. Smith. January 27, 1926. Whitmer Papers. P10, f19, item 25. CofChrist Archives.

Burgess, Samuel A. Letter to Israel A. Smith. 6 October 1949. P22, f18. CofC Archives.

Burnett, Peter. Indenture to John Whitmer. 13 July 1840. John Whitmer Papers. MS 6378. LDS Church History Library.

Burns, Eric. *The Smoke of the Gods: A Social History of Tobacco.* Philadelphia, PA: Temple University Press, 2007.

Bush, Lester E. "The Word of Wisdom in Early Nineteenth-Century Perspective." In *The Word of God: Essays on Mormon Scripture.* Edited by Dan Vogel. Salt Lake City: Signature Books, 1990, 161–85.

Bushman, Richard Lyman. *Joseph Smith: Rough Stone Rolling, a Cultural Biography of Mormonism's Founder.* New York: Alfred A. Knopf, 2005.

Butler, John L. Statement. 6 August 1838. Journal History.

Cahoon, Reynolds. Journal. Quoted in Journal History, 13 August 1831.

Caine MSS Petitions. Mormon Affidavits and Petitions Relating to the Missouri Persecutions Comprised of Materials from the National Archives as cataloged in the Caine Manuscript Collection. Merrill Library Special Collections. Utah State University, Logan, UT. Copy of collection, P69 2. CofC Archives.

Calif, Jemima. Letter to the editor, 30 May 1881. Locust Hill, MO. *Herald* 28, no, 13 (July 1, 1881): 208.

Caldwell County, Missouri. List of Lands Sold to the State in 1846 for Arrear[s] of taxes, &c., for taxes of 1844. 631.112 C127 1846. Vault collection. Perry Special Collections.

[Caldwell County, Missouri]. List of lands forfeited to the State in 1848 for taxes of 1847, and List of Lands Sold to the State in 1846 for Arrear[s] of Taxes, &c., for Taxes of 1844. 631.112 C127 1846. Vault collection. Perry Special Collections.

[Caldwell County, Missouri]. List of Lands Forfeited to the State in 1848 for Taxes of 1847, 631.112 C127, 1846, 1848. Vault collection. Perry Special Collections.

[Caldwell County, Missouri]. List of lands Sold for the State in 1848 for Arrears of Taxes, &c., for Taxes of 1844. 631.112 C127 1846. Vault collection. Perry Special Collections.

Call, Anson, Ethan L. Call, and Christine Shaffer Call, eds. *Journal of Anson Call.* Afton, WY: Shann L. Call [distributor], 1986.

Campbell, Alexander, ed. *The Sacred Writing of the Apostles and Evangelists of Jesus Christ, Commonly Styled The New Testament. Translated from the Original Greek, by George Campbell, James MacKnight, and Philip Doddridge, Doctors of the Church of Scotland. With Prefaces to the Historical and Epistolary Books; and an Appendix, Containing Critical Notes and Various Translations of Difficult Passages.* Buffaloe, VA: Alexander Campbell, 1826.

Cannon, Donald Q., and Lyndon W. Cook, eds. *Far West Record: Minutes of the Church of Jesus Christ of Latter-day Saints, 1830-1844.* Salt Lake City: Deseret Book, 1983. The holograph, "The Conference Minutes and Record Book of Christ's Church of Latter-day Saints, Belonging to the High Council of Said Church or Their Successors in Office, of Caldwell County, Missouri, Far West; April 6, 1838," is at the LDS Church History Library.

Caractors. Photograph of Book of Mormon Characters. D1738.9. Vault. Pictorial Archives. D1738.9. CofC Archives. Facsimile reproduction as a supplement to the *Herald* (September 29, 1909). Inserted into the issue, not paginated.

Carter, Jared. "Manuscript History of the Great Lakes Mission, Ohio, July 1831." LDS Church History Library.

Carter, Simeon. Statement during conference. Minutes of a General Conference, Orange, Cuyahoga County, Ohio. Reprinted in Cannon and Cook, *Far West Record*, 22.

Case, Sherry. John H. Zimmer post. 1998. Genealogy.com, http://genforum.genealogy.com/cgi-bin/pageload.cgi?Jackson::zimmer::72.html. Accessed February 3, 2007.

Cheville, Roy. *They Made a Difference.* Independence, MO: Herald Publishing House, 1970.

Church of Christ Temple Lot and the RLDS Church. Articles of Working Harmony. Church of Christ Temple Lot subject folder. CofC Archives.

Cinnamon. "Spices." History and Special Collections. Louise M. Darling Biomedical Library. UCLA. http://unitproj.library.ucla.edu/biomed/spice/index.cfm?displayID=5. Accessed December 20, 2010.

Clay County, Missouri. Marriage Records. Book A. 1822–1882. Typescript. Clay County Archives, Liberty, MO.

Cleveland, Henry Alanson. Letter to Church Historian. 1854. Quoted in Journal History, 4 November 1833, pp 7–8.

Cole, Abner. "Gold Bible, No. 6." *Reflector* (Palmyra, NY), 2, no. 16 (March 9, 1831).

Collier, Fred C., ed. *Unpublished Revelations of the Prophets and Presidents of the Church of Jesus Christ of Latter Day Saints, Vol. 1.* Salt Lake City: Collier Publishing, 1981.

Collier, Fred C., and William S. Harwell, eds. *Kirtland Council Minute Book.* Salt Lake City: Collier Publishing, 1996.

[RLDS] Conference Daily, Herald, 1930, 14, 50, 70. Reference to Cowdery portraits.

Cook, Lyndon W. *Joseph Smith and the Law of Consecration.* Provo, UT: Grandin Book, 1985.

———, ed. *David Whitmer Interviews: A Restoration Witness.* Orem, UT: Grandin Book, 1991.

———, ed. *The Revelations of the Prophet Joseph Smith.* Provo, UT: Seventy's Mission Bookstore, 1981.

Cooper, Rex. *Promises Made to the Fathers: Mormon Covenant Organization.* Publications in Mormon Studies, No. 5. Salt Lake City: University of Utah Press, 1990.

"Copies of Revelations to Joseph Smith in the Handwriting of Frederick G. Williams, Orson Hyde, Joseph Smith, Oliver Cowdery, and Others, Kirtland Revelations Book." Quoted in Collier, *Unpublished Revelations of the Prophets and Presidents,* 60–61.

Corbett, Pearson H. *Hyrum Smith, Patriarch.* Salt Lake City: Deseret Book, 1963.

Corkins, Lucy. Congressional Affidavit. January 6, 1840. Photocopy of holograph. Mormon Affidavits and Petitions. P69, box 3, f29. CofC Archives.

Corrill, John. *A Brief History of the Church of Christ of Latter Day Saints (Commonly Called Mormons, Including an Account of Their Doctrine and Discipline, with the Reasons of the Author for Leaving the Church).* St. Louis, MO: n.p., 1839. Photomechanical reprint. Salt Lake City: Modern Microfilm.

———. "From Missouri." Letter to Oliver Cowdery. December 1833. Liberty, MO. Reprinted in *Evening and the Morning Star* 2, no. 16 (January 1834): 124.

"Covenants of the Lamanite Missionaries." Saints Without Halos website, http://www.saintswithouthalos.com/w/1830_covs_laman.phtml. Accessed February 18, 2007.

Cowdery, Oliver. "Address to the Patrons of the Latter Day Saints' Messenger & Advocate." *Messenger and Advocate* 1, no. 8 (May 1835): 120–22.

———. "The Closing Year." *Messenger and Advocate* 3, no. 3 (December 1836): 425–29.

———. *Defense in a Rehearsal of My Grounds for Separating Myself from the Latter Day Saints*. Norton, OH: Pressley's Job Office, 1839. Reprinted as "Original Articles: Oliver Cowdery Defense, A Review by Heman C. Smith," *Herald* 54, no. 12 (March 20, 1907): 229–30.

———. Letter to Dear Brother John, 1 January 1834. Oliver Cowdery Letter Book Typescripts. Pp. 14–16. Huntington Library.

———. Letter to Lyman Cowdery. January 1834. Oliver Cowdery Letter Book Typescripts. Pp. 18–22. Huntington Library. P19, f5. CofC Archives.

———. Letter to Warren Cowdery. January 1838. Oliver Cowdery Letter Book. Fd. 5, pp. 80–83. Huntington Library. Retained copy of a letter sent to Joseph Smith Jr. Facsimile. P19, f6. CofC Archives.

———. Letter to Warren and Lyman Cowdery. 4 February 1838. Oliver Cowdery Letter Book, pp. 83–87. Huntington Library. Includes Minutes of a Meeting, 30 January 1838 [*sic*]. Meeting of Members of the Church of Latter Day Saints. Facsimile. P19, f6. CofC Archives.

———. Family Group. Vaughan/Gnarini Genealogy Project. http://www.ralph-vaughan.com/vaughan/gp10433.htm. Accessed July 28, 2010.

———. Letter to Warren A. and Lyman Cowdery. 24 February 1838. Far West, MO. Oliver Cowdery Letter Book. Pp. 94–96. Huntington Library.

———. Letter to Ambrose Palmer. 30 October 1833. New Portage, Medina County, OH. Oliver Cowdery Letter Book. Pp. 8–9. Huntington Library.

———. Letter to William W. Phelps and John Whitmer. 21 January 1834, Independence, MO. Oliver Cowdery Letter Book. Huntington Library.

———. Letter to W. W. Phelps. 7 September 1834. *Messenger and Advocate* 1, no. 1 (October 1834): 13–16.

———. Letter to Joseph Smith. 28 January 1832. Independence, MO. Joseph Smith Collection. LDS Church History Library. Reprinted in Cannon and Cook, *Far West Record*, appendix A, 238.

———. Letter to John Whitmer. 1 January 1834. Oliver Cowdery Letter Book. Huntington Library.

Cowdery, Oliver, Clerk. F. G. Williams, Chair. Minutes. January 1838. Oliver Cowdery Letter Book. Huntington Library. Facsimile, P19, f6. CofC Archives.

[Cowdery, Oliver]. "The Mormons So Called." *Evening and the Morning Star, Extra*. February 1834, Kirtland, Ohio. Reprinted in Crawley, "Two Rare Missouri Documents," 506. Also in Flake, *A Mormon Bibliography, 1830–1930*, 226.

[Cowdery, Oliver]. "New Portage Conference." *Messenger and Advocate* 1, no. 9 (June 1835): 142–44.

Cowdery, Warren A., ed. "It Is a Well Known and Established Fact." *Latter Day Saint Messenger and Advocate* 2, no. 7 (July 1837): 535–43.

Cowdery Portraits. William Cowdery, Oliver Cowdery, and Elizabeth Ann Whitmer Cowdery. Originals housed at the Community of Christ Museum. Reference Ethel Johnson Lewellen (Ella Johnson's niece) to C. Edward Miller. 26 May 1932. Kingston, MO. Accretion Papers. P68, f80. CofC Archives.

Crawley, Peter L. "A Bibliography of the Church of Jesus Christ of Latter-day Saints in New York, Ohio, and Missouri." *BYU Studies* 12 (Summer 1972): 465–537.

———. *A Descriptive Bibliography of the Mormon Church: Vol. 1, 1830–1847*. 2 vols. Provo, UT: BYU Religious Studies Center, 1997.

Crawley, Peter. "Two Rare Missouri Documents," *BYU Studies* 4, no. 4 (Summer 1974): 502–15.

Crawley, Peter, and Chad J. Flake. *A Mormon Fifty: An Exhibition in the Harold B. Lee Library in Conjunction with the Annual Conference of the 1984 Mormon History Association.* Provo, UT: Friends of the Brigham Young University Library, 1984. http://relarchive.byu.edu/19th/descriptions/hymns.html. Accessed September 17, 2006.

Crosby, Jonathan. "A Biographical Sketch of the Life of Jonathan Crosby written by himself" (1807–92). MSS 2343. Fd. 1. Tom Perry Special Collections. Photocopy of Jonathan and Caroline Crosby Papers. Utah State Historical Society, Salt Lake City.

Cross, Whitney R. *The Burned-Over District: The Social and Intellectual History of Enthusiastic Religion in Western New York, 1800-1850*. Ithaca, NY: Cornell University, 1950.

Curry, Kate S. "Frederick Schott of Derry Township, Lancaster County, Pennsylvania, and Descendants." Washington, DC: n.p., 1933.

Curtis, Annette W. "A Hometown Perspective on the 1878 Richmond Tornado." *Missouri Mormon Frontier Foundation Newsletter* 43 (June–December 2008): 2–8.

———. "Isaac Russell." *Missouri Mormon Frontier Foundation Newsletter* 45 (2010): 3.

————. "Whitmer Family." *Missouri Mormon Frontier Foundation Newsletter* 21–22 (August 1999): 7–20.

Dahl, Larry E., and Charles D. Tate Jr., eds. *The Lectures on Faith in Historical Perspective.* Provo, UT: Brigham Young University Religious Studies Center, 1990.

Dauphin County, Pennsylvania. http://en.wikipedia.org/wiki/Dauphin_County,_Pennsylvania. Accessed September 15, 2007.

"Dave Whitmer." *Richmond Conservator* 21, no. 22 (August 29, 1874): 3. Microfilm. Ray County Library, Richmond, MO.

"Dave Whitmer & Co." *Richmond Conservator* 25, nos. 24 and 27 (September 6, 28, 1878): 4. Microfilm. Ray County Library, Richmond, MO.

"David Whitmer Interviewed." *Herald* 28, no. 22 (November 15, 1881): 347. Reprint of interview by the *Chicago Times.*

"David Whitmer on His Death Bed." *Herald* 33, no. 2 (January 2, 1886): 12–13. Reprint of Interview by Correspondent. December 15, 1885. *Chicago Tribune.* December 17, 1885.

Davis, Inez Smith. *Story of the Church.* Independence, MO: Herald Publishing, 1983.

Davis, Joshua. "A Visit to John Whitmer." *Herald* 22, no. 21 (November 1, 1875): 655. Reprint from *Deseret Evening News* 24, no. 11 (April 14, 1875): 13.

Davis, Richard W. *Emigrants, Refugees, and Prisoners.* 3 vols. Provo, UT: privately printed, 1997.

Day, Orville Cox. Letter to Mary Hulet Coburn. 17 February 1947. Special Collections. Merrill-Cazier Library. Utah State University, Logan, UT.

Dear, Mary Cleora. *Two Hundred Thirty-Eight Years of the Whitmer Family, 1737–1976.* Richmond, MO: Beck Printing Company, 1976.

DeHawn, William N. to John Whitmer. 10 May 1852. Holograph. MS 6378. LDS Church History Library.

Demill, Freeborn. Itinerary. [June] 21st 1831. MS 101. LDS Church History Library.

Deming, Arthur B. Statement. Citing James Van Cleave. *Naked Truths about Mormonism* 1, no. 2 (April 1888): Appendix S.

Deshler, John. Deed Record. Deed Books W, p. 318 and X, p. 25. Seneca County Courthouse, Waterloo, NY. Cited in Porter, "A Study of the Origins of the Church," 312.

Dibble, Philo. *Early Scenes in Church History: 8th Book of the Faith Promoting Series.* Appendix S.

————. Land Holdings. Geauga County [Ohio] Records. Deed Books 12:369–705, 792, 13:159, 352, 15:133, 17:48. Chardon, OH.

————. "Philo Dibble's Narrative." *Early Scenes in Church History: Eighth Book of the Faith Promoting Series.* Salt Lake City: Juvenile Instructor Office, 1882, 74–96.

Doctrine and Covenants [LDS edition] of The Church of Jesus Christ of Latter-day Saints. Salt Lake City: Church of Jesus Christ of Latter-day Saints, 1981.

Doctrine and Covenants [RLDS edition] Book of Doctrine and Covenants: Carefully Selected from the Revelations of God, and Given in the Order of their Dates. Independence, MO: Herald Publishing House, 1962.

Document Containing the Correspondence, Orders, &c. in Relation to the Disturbances with the Mormons; and the Evidence Given before the Hon. Austin A. King, Judge of the Fifth Judicial Circuit of the State of Missouri, at the Court-house in Richmond, in a Criminal Court of Inquiry, Begun November 12, 1838, on the Trial of Joseph Smith, Jr., and Others, for High Treason and Other Crimes against the State. Fayette, MO: Boon's Lick Democrat, 1841.

Duncan, Chapman. Autobiography. Ca. 1874. Holograph. MS 6936. LDS Church History Library.

————. "Reminiscences about Experiences in Missouri." Microfilm. MS 11333. LDS Church History Library.

Dunklin, Daniel. Reply to petition. 19 October 1833. *Evening and the Morning Star* 2 no. 15 (December 1833): 115.

Dyer, Alvin R. *The Refiner's Fire: The Significance of Events Transpiring in Missouri.* 4th ed. Salt Lake City: Deseret Book, 1980.

Eakin, Joanne Chiles. Verbal Statement to Ronald E. Romig. Ca. 1995. Independence, MO.

Edmonds, Joel. Elders' report. "Conferences, Pacific Slope Mission." *Herald* 26, no. 22 (November 15, 1879): 351.

Eiselen, Frederick, Edwin Lewis, and David Downey, eds. *The Abingdon Bible Commentary.* New York: Abingdon Press, 1929.

"Elder Myron H. Bond Passes Away." *Zion's Ensign* 31, no. 31 (July 29, 1920): 564.

Emley, Linda. "If Postcards Could Talk (Richmond College)." *Richmond News,* September 2, 2010, 8.

————. "If Postcards Could Talk (Pioneer Cemetery)." *Richmond News,* September 30, 2010, 8.

Epperson, Steven. "'The Grand, Fundamental Principle': Joseph Smith and the Virtue of Friendship." *Journal of Mormon History* 23, no. 2 (Fall 1997): 77–105.

———. *Mormons and Jews: Early Mormon Theologies of Israel.* Salt Lake City: Signature Books, 1992.

Etzenhouser, Rudolph. *From Palmyra, New York, 1830 to Independence: 1894.* Independence, MO: Ensign Publishing House, 1894.

Ewing, David. Indenture to David Whitmer. 26 May 1843. Deed Record Book E, p. 79. Ray County Land Records. Ray County Recorders' Office, Richmond, MO.

Far West Committee. Minutes. January–April, 1839. MS 2564. LDS Church History Library.

"Another War Brewing." (Liberty, MO). Reprinted in *The World As It Is, and General Advertiser* (Rochester, NY), 1. Uncle Dale's [Dale Broadhurst] Readings in Early Mormon History. http://www.sidneyrigdon.com/dbroadhu/ NY/miscNYSd.htm. Accessed December 12, 2007.

"Far West: The Old Mormon Settlement in Missouri." *Daily Morning Herald* (St. Joseph, Missouri). January 1, 1875. Clipping in CofC Newspaper Collection.

Faulring, Scott H., ed. *An American Prophet's Record: The Diaries and Journals of Joseph Smith.* Salt Lake City: Signature Books in association with Smith Research Associates, 1987.

———. "The Book of Mormon: A Blueprint for Organizing the Church." *Journal of Book of Mormon Studies* 7, no. 1 (1998): 60–69.

———, ed. "Cash Book of the Firm of F. G. Williams, & Co." Holograph. MS 3493. Item 1. Typescript copy by Foundation for Ancient Research and Mormon Studies. MS 3408. Fd. 2. LDS Church History Library.

———. "An Examination of the 1829 'Articles of the Church of Christ' in Relation to Section 20 of the D&C." *BYU Studies* 43, no. 4 (2004): 57–91.

———. "The Return of Oliver Cowdery." In *Oliver Cowdery: Scribe, Elder, Witness.* Edited by John W. Welch and Larry E. Morris. Provo, UT: Neal A. Maxwell Institute for Religious Scholarship, Brigham Young University, 2006, 321–62.

Faulring, Scott H., Kent P. Jackson, and Robert J. Matthews, eds. *Joseph Smith's New Translation of the Bible: Original Manuscripts, Table of Pages.* Provo, UT: Brigham Young University Religious Studies Center, 2004.

"Fayette Township Record." Waterloo Library and Historical Society, Waterloo, NY.

"The First Half Century of Mormonism." Clipping from an unidentified and undated publication. In Charles L. Woodward, comp. Scrapbook, p. 195. New York Public Library.

Flagg, Edmund. *The Far West; or, A Tour beyond the Mountains.* 2 vols. New York: Harper and Brothers, 1838.

Flake, Chad J., comp. *A Mormon Bibliography, 1830–1930: Books, Pamphlets, Periodicals, and Broadsides Relating to the First Century of Mormonism.* Salt Lake City: University of Utah Press, 1978.

Flake, Lawrence R. "A Shaker View of a Mormon Mission." *BYU Studies* 20 (Fall 1979): 94–99.

Fogel, Edward Miller. *Beliefs and Superstitions of the Pennsylvania Germans.* Philadelphia, PA: American Germanica Press, 1915, 18.

Fry, Evan. Letter to Ella Turner. 25 January 1949. Typescript. Copies in John Whitmer Biographical Folder and Hiram Page Biographical Folder. CofC Archives.

Funn, I. C. [pseud.]. Letter in *Kingston Sentinel.* Quoted in, "Editors," *Salt Lake Herald,* January 12, 1878. Reported in *Herald* 25, no. 4 (February 15, 1878): 57.

Gaddis, John Lewis. *The Landscape of History.* New York: Oxford University Press, 2002.

Galland, Maria. Statement. P68, f4. CofC Archives.

Garr, Arnold K., and Clark V. Johnson, eds. *Regional Studies in Latter-day Saint Church History: Missouri.* Provo, UT: Brigham Young University Department of Church History and Doctrine, 1994.

Garr, Arnold K., Donald Q. Cannon, and Richard O. Cowan, eds. *Encyclopedia of Latter-day Saint History.* Salt Lake City: Deseret Book, 2000.

Gaskill, Jacob, clerk. *Minutes of the Mahoning Baptist Association, Warren, Ohio, August 29, 1828.* Bethany, VA, 1829. Typescript in my possession.

Geauga [Ohio] County Records. Philo Dibble land holdings. Deed Books, pp. 12:369–705, 792, 13:159, 352, 15:133, 17:48. Chardon, Ohio.

Geddes, Joseph A. *The United Order among the Mormons (Missouri Phase): An Unfinished Experiment in Economic Organization.* Salt Lake City: Deseret News Press, 1924.

Gentry, Leland H. "A History of the Latter-day Saints in Northern Missouri from 1836 to 1839." PhD diss., Brigham Young University, 1965.

Gentry. Leland H. and Todd M. Compton. *Fire and Sword: A History of the Latter-day Saints in Northern Missouri, 1836–39* (Salt Lake City: Greg Kofford Books, 2011).

"George Schweich." *Richmond Conservator* 23, no. 46 (February 9, 1877): 3. Microfilm. Ray County Library, Richmond, MO.

"Gift of the Holy Ghost." *Times and Seasons* 3, no. 16 (June 15, 1842): 823–86.

Gibson, John, ed. *Biographical History of York County, Pennsylvania.* Baltimore: Centennial Publishing, 1975.

Gilbert, Algernon Sidney. Letters of Administration. May 21, 1839. Estate Papers, 1838–39. Clay County Court, MO. MS 3205. Item 6. LDS Church History Library.

Gilbert, Algernon S. Notice [about estate]. Clay County Court. *Western Star.* March 1839. MS 3205. Item 2. LDS Church History Library.

Gilbert, Algernon S., and William W. Phelps. Letters mentioned in January 13, 1833, Kirtland Council Minutes. In Collier and Harwell, *Kirtland Council Minute Book*, 5.

[Gilbert, Algernon S., handwriting]. Petition to the President. December 12, 1833. Signed by 111 Members of the Church. MS 143. Box 49, fd. 19. Marriott Library.

Gilbert, John H. Memorandum. September 8, 1892, Palmyra, NY. In Wilford C. Wood. *Joseph Smith Begins His Work.* Vol. 1. Introductory pages. Salt Lake City: Deseret News Press, 1958.

Gladden, Sanford C. "An Early Printing Press Used in Colorado." Typescript. LDS Church History Library.

Godfrey, Kenneth W. "The Shaping of Latter-day Saint History." Stephen D. Ricks, Donald W. Parry, and Andrew H. Hedges, eds. *The Disciple as Witness: Hedges.* Provo, UT: The Foundation for Ancient Research and Mormon Studies at Brigham Young University, 2000, 223–56.

"The Golden Bible." *Telegraph* (Painesville, OH) 2, no. 22 (November 16, 1830): 3.

Graffam, Merle, ed. *Salt Lake School of the Prophets: Minute Book, 1883.* Salt Lake City: Pioneer Press, 1992, 71. Quoted in Quinn, *The Mormon Hierarchy: Origins of Power*, 12n58.

Grant, Carter E. "Peter Whitmer's Log House." *Improvement Era*, May 1959, 349, 365–66, 369.

Greaves, Alexander. *The Gospel of God's Anointed, the Glory of Israel, and the Light of Revelation for the Gentiles: or, the Glad Tidings of the Service, Sacrifice, and Triumph of our Lord and Saviour Jesus Christ, the Only Begotten Son of God; and of the Gracious and Mightily Operative Powers of the Holy Spirit, Which Were the First-Fruits of That Labour of Divine Love: Being a Recent Version, in Two Parts, of the Christian Greek Scriptures (commonly called the New Tes-*

tament) in Which Is Plainly Set Forth the New Covenant Promised by God through Moses and the Prophets. London: A. Macintosh, 1828.

Greene, John P. *Facts Relative to the Expulsion of the Mormons from the State of Missouri.* Cincinnati, OH: R. P. Brooks, 1839.

Gregg, Josiah. *The Commerce of the Prairies.* Reprint. Lincoln, NE: Bison Book, 1967.

Groves, Elisha Hurd. Autobiography, written between 1861 and 1866. Holograph. MS 2050. Fds. 11, 13, item #1. LDS Church History Library.

———. "An Account of the Life of Elisha Hurd Groves." Photocopy of holograph, 1868. MSS SC 334. Perry Special Collections.

Grunder, Rick. "Treasures Past." October 12, 2006. Rick Grunder Books website, http://www.rickgrunder.com/HistoricalArchive/whitmerstone.htm. Accessed April 9, 2007.

Guide to the Willers Family Papers, 1820–1908. Collection Number 652. Division of Rare and Manuscript Collections. Cornell University Library, Ithaca, NY: *Guide to the Willers Family Papers, 1820–1908.* http://rmc.library.cornell.edu/EAD/htmldocs/RMM00652.html. Accessed October 9, 2007.

Gunn, Stanley R. *Oliver Cowdery: Second Elder and Scribe.* Salt Lake City: Bookcraft, 1962.

Gurley, Zenas H. "Synopsis of a Discourse Delivered at Lamoni, Iowa." *Herald* 26, no. 24 (December 15, 1879): 369–71.

Hadley, Jonathan A. Letter, 11 August 1829. *Palmyra Freeman* [no longer extant]. Reprinted as "Golden Bible," *Palmyra Freeman.* Reprinted as "Golden Bible," *Niagara Courier* (Lockport, NY) 2, no. 18 (August 27, 1829): 18.

Hale, Aroet Lucious. 1835. Diary of Aroet Luscious Hale, 1828–1849. Typescript, 22 pages. Perry Special Collections.

Hancock, Levi Ward. Journal. 1803–36. Holograph. MS 1395. LDS Church History Library.

———. Autobiography. Ca. 1854. Microfilm of holograph. MS 5072. LDS Church History Library.

Hancock, Pauline. Preface to the "The Book of John Whitmer Kept by Commandment. Typescript. CofC Archives.

Harper, Steven C. "Historical Headnotes and the Index of Contents in the Book of Commandments and Revelations." *BYU Studies* 48, no. 3 (2009): 53–66.

Harris, Emer. Letter, 7 May 1833. http://www.geocities.com/Heartland/Bluffs/2806/aqwg121.htm. Accessed November 11, 2007.

————. Statement. April 6, 1856. In Utah Stake, General Minutes. Local Record 9629. Series 11. Vol. 10 (1855–60): 6. LDS Church History Library.

Harris, Martin. Sermon—Salt Lake City—September 4, 1870. Quoted in Andrew Jenson, "The Three Witnesses," *Historical Record* 6, nos. 3–5 (May 1887): 216.

Hart, James H. Interview with David Whitmer. March 18, 1884. "About the Book of Mormon." *Deseret News,* April 9, 1884, 14.

Hartley, William G. "Letters and Mail Between Kirtland and Independence: A Mormon Postal History, 1831–33." *Journal of Mormon History* 35, no. 3 (Summer 2009): 163–89.

————. *"Stand by My Servant Joseph": The Story of the Joseph Knight Family and the Restoration.* Salt Lake City: Deseret Book, 2003.

————. *"They Are My Friends": A History of the Knight Family, 1825–1850.* Provo, UT: Grandin Book, 1986.

Hartmann, Thom. *Screwed: The Undeclared War against the Middle Class—And What We Can Do about It.* San Francisco: Berrett-Koehler Publishers, 2006.

Haskell, Ivan Y., comp. "Solomon Hancock." Extracted from C. E. Hancock, Autobiography. http://foremothers.homestead.com/files/Solomon_Hancock. htm. Accessed January 1, 2008.

Hatch, Nathan O. *The Democratization of American Christianity.* New Haven, CT: Yale University Press, 1989.

Hayden, Amos Sutton. *Early History of the Disciples in the Western Reserve, Ohio: With Biographical Sketches of the Principal Agents in Their Religious Movement.* Cincinnati: Ohio: Chase and Hall, 1875.

Hedrick, Granville. "Review of the 'Herald.'" *The Truth-Teller* 1, no. 5 (November 1864): 65–79.

Higbee, Elias, John Taylor, and Elias Smith. "To the Honorable the Senate and House of Representatives." In "The Second Memorial," *Mormon Redress Petitions,* 395.

Hinkle, George. Letter to W. W. Phelps. 14 August 1844. *Journal of History* 13 (October 1920): 448–53.

————. Plat of Far West, on sheepskin. Photograph. CofC Archives.

Hill, Donna. *Joseph Smith: The First Mormon.* Garden City, NY: Doubleday, 1966.

Hill, Marvin S. *Quest for Refuge: The Mormon Flight from American Pluralism.* Salt Lake City: Signature Books, 1989.

Hill, Marvin, S., C. Keith Rooker, and Larry T. Wimmer. *The Kirtland Economy Revisited: A Market Critique of Sectarian Economics.* Provo, UT: Brigham Young University Press, 1977.

―――. "The Kirtland Economy Revisited: A Market Critique of Sectarian Economics." *BYU Studies* 17, no. 4 (Summer 1977): 391–76.

"Hiram Page Grave." *Missouri Mormon Frontier Foundation Newsletter* 25 (August 2000–January 2001): 1.

"Historical Sketch of Far West," *Morning Daily Herald* (St. Joseph, MO), January 1, 1875.

History of Caldwell and Livingston Counties, Missouri: Written and Compiled from the Most Authentic Official and Private Sources. St. Louis, MO: National Historical Company, 1886.

History of Geauga and Lake Counties. Philadelphia, PA: n.p., 1878.

History of Ray County, Missouri. St. Louis: Missouri Historical Company, 1881.

History of the LDS Church. See complete citation under "Short Citations."

History of the Organization of the Seventies. Salt Lake City: Deseret News Steam Printing Establishment, 1878.

"A History, of the Persecution, of the Church of Jesus Christ, of Latter Day Saints in Missouri." *Times and Seasons* 1, no. 2 (December 1839): 17–20. 1, no. 4 (February 1840): 49–51.

History of the RLDS Church. See complete citation under "Short Citations."

"History of Thomas Baldwin Marsh [by himself]." In "The History of Brigham Young." *Millennial Star*: 26, no. 23 (June 4, 1864): 359–60. 26, no. 24 (June 11, 1864): 375–76. 26, no. 25 (June 18, 1863): 390–92. 26, no. 26 (June 25, 1863): 406.

"History of Joseph Smith." *Millennial Star*: 16, no 1 (January 7, 1884): 9–14.

"History of Joseph Smith." *Times and Seasons*: 3, no. 20 (August 15, 1842): 884–85. 4, no. 19 (August 15, 1843): 289–90. 5, no. 24 (January 1, 1845): 752–55. 6, no 4 (March 1, 1845): 818–19. 6, no. 13 (July 15, 1845): 960–63. 6, no. 22 (February 1, 1846): 1104–5.

"History of Brigham Young." *Deseret News* 6, no. 19 (February 10, 1858): 1.

Hitchcock, Elizabeth G. "Houses along the East Branch." *The Historical Society Quarterly, Lake County, Ohio* 18 (February 1979): 2–3. Photocopy in Kirtland Ohio subject folder. CofC Archives.

Hodges, N., and Audrey L. Woodruff. "Henry Hill." *Missouri Pioneers of Clay County*. Bowling Green, MO: InfoTech Publications, 1992.

Holbert, William. Obituary. *Evening and Morning Star* (Kirtland, OH), 2, no. 15 (December 1833): 117.

Holbrook, Joseph. Autobiography. Written between 1864 and 1871. Typescript. MS 1624. LDS Church History Library.

Holsclaw, Elizabeth. Congressional Affidavit. January 6, 1840. Photocopy of holograph. Mormon Petitions. Caine Manuscripts. P69–2, box 3, f28. CofC Archives.

Holzapfel, Richard Neitzel, T. Jeffery Cottle, and Ted D. Stoddard, eds. *Church History in Black and White: George Edward Anderson's Photographic Mission to Latter-day Saint Historical Sites.* Provo, UT: Brigham Young University Religious Studies Center, 1995.

"Holy Anointing Oil." *Wikipedia.* http://en.wikipedia.org/wiki/Holy_anointing_oil#cite_note-4. Accessed December 20, 2010.

"How the Prophet's Followers Left Jackson County and Settled in Caldwell–The Beginning of Trouble." *Herald* 34, no. 51 (October 22, 1887): 838.

Howard, Richard P. "The Knight Family and the Early Restoration." *Herald* 127, no. 9 (May 1, 1980): 240.

———, ed. *The Memoirs of President Joseph Smith III (1832–1914).* Independence, MO: Herald Publishing House, 1979.

———. *Restoration Scriptures: A Study of Their Textual Development.* 2d. ed. Independence, MO: Herald Publishing House, 1995.

Howe, E. D. *Mormonism Unvailed, or, A Faithful Account of That Singular Imposition and Delusion, from Its Rise to the Present Time.* Painesville, OH: privately printed 1834.

———. "The Book of Mormon." *Telegraph* (Painesville, OH) 2, no. 24 (November 30, 1830): 3.

———. "The Gold Bible Fever." *Telegraph* (Painesville, OH) 2, no. 41 (March 29, 1831): 2.

———. "Secret Bye Laws of the Mormonites." *Telegraph* (Painesville, OH) 3, no. 13 (September 13, 1831): 1.

———. "We Mentioned Two Weeks Since." *Telegraph* (Painesville, OH) 3, no. 2 (June 28, 1831): 3.

Huggins, Ronald V. "Jerald Tanner's Quest for Truth." *Salt Lake City Messenger*, No. 108 (May 2007): 3.

Hulet, Anne (Schott) Whitmer. Obituary. *Seneca Falls Reveille* (November 23, 1866).

Hunt, C. J. "An Acknowledgment to John Whitmer, One of the Eight Witnesses of the Book of Mormon." *Herald* 97, no. 6 (February 6, 1950): 131. Reprinted in "RLDS Archives Sources," *Missouri Mormon Frontier Foundation Newsletter* 21–22 (August 1999): 15.

Huntington, Oliver B. "History of the Life of Oliver B. Huntington, Written by Himself 1878–1990." Typescript. Perry Special Collections.

Hyde, Orson. Letter to editors of *Booneville Herald*. "History of Orson Hyde." *The Latter-day Saints' Millennial Star* 26 (1864): 742–44, 760–61, 774–76, 790–92.

Hyde, Orson. Letter to the *Booneville Herald*. November 8, 1833. Reprinted in *The Evening and the Morning Star* 2, no. 15 (December 1833): 117.

An Illustrated Historical Atlas of Ray County, Missouri. Philadelphia, PA: Edwards Brothers of Missouri, 1877.

Jackson, Andrew, John Jackson, Andrew Jackson, and Eliza Jackson. Letter to Sarah and John Whitmer. 2 May 1849. Centerville, IA. MSS 1214. Perry Special Collections.

Jackman, Levi. "Battle above Big Blue, November 24, 1833. Map, Furnished to the Church Historian's office, March 25, 1871." Holograph. MS 4153. LDS Church History Library.

———. Consecration and Inheritance Form. Photocopy of holograph. P26-3. CofC Archives.

———. Record Book. 1832–33. Transcription of original handwritten manuscript, MS 5940. LDS Church History Library.

———. "A Short Sketch of the Life of Levi Jackman." Ca. 1851. Typescript. MS 1583. LDS Church History Library. Holograph. Utah Historical Society, Salt Lake City.

Jackson, Kent P., and Peter M. Jasinski. "The Process of Inspired Translation: Two Passages Translated Twice in the Joseph Smith Translation of the Bible." *BYU Studies* 42, no. 2 (2003): 35–74.

Jackson, Thomas, and James. Promissory note to John Whitmer. 1845. MSS 242. Vault. Perry Special Collections.

Jackson County, Missouri. Land Records. 1827. Jackson County Recorder's Office, Independence, MO.

Jackson County, Missouri. Marriage Records. Book A, 1827–1881. Microfilm. County Clerk's Office, Jackson County, MO.

Jennings, Erin B. "The Whitmer Family and the Church of Christ." Paper presented at the annual meeting of the John Whitmer Historical Association, Independence, MO. Photocopy in my possession.

———. "Restoring the Root(s) of Jesse [Gause]." *Journal of Mormon History* 34, no. 1 (Spring 2008): 182–227.

————. "Whitmer Family Beliefs and Their Church of Christ." In *Scattering of the Saints: Schism within Mormonism.* Edited by Newell G. Bringhurst and John C. Hamer. Independence: John Whitmer Books, 2007, 25–45.

Jennings, Warren. "The City in the Garden: Social Conflict in Jackson County, Missouri." *The Restoration Movement: Essays in Mormon History.* Edited by F. Mark McKiernan, Alma Blair, and Paul M. Edwards. Lawrence, KS: Coronado Press, 1973, 99–119.

Jennings, Warren A. "Factors in the Destruction of the Mormon Press in Missouri, 1833." *Utah Historical Quarterly* 35, no. 1 (Winter 1967): 56–76.

Jensen, Marlin K. "The Joseph Smith Papers: The Manuscript Revelation Books." *Ensign,* July 2009, 46–51.

Jensen, Robin Scott. Smith Papers Project Editor. Conversation. May 26, 2007. Notes in my possession.

————. "From Manuscript to Printed Page: An Analysis of the History of the Book of Commandments and Revelations." Paper presented at the annual meeting of the Mormon History Association, Kansas City, MO, May 2009. Copy in Book of Commandments subject folder. CofC Archives. Published under the same title in *BYU Studies* 48, no. 3 (2009): 19–52.

Jensen, Robin Scott, Robert J. Woodford, and Steven C. Harper, eds. *Revelations and Translations: Manuscript Revelation Books.* Facsimile edition. Vol. 2. In THE JOSEPH SMITH PAPERS. General editors, Dean C. Jessee, Ronald K. Esplin, and Richard Lyman Bushman. Salt Lake City: The Church Historian's Press, 2009.

Jenson, Andrew. *Autobiography of Andrew Jenson.* Salt Lake City: Deseret News Press, 1938.

————. "The Eight Witnesses: Hiram Page." *Historical Record* 7, nos. 8–10 (October 1888): 614.

————. *Latter-day Saint Biographical Encyclopedia: A Compilation of Biographical Sketches of Prominent Men and Women in the Church of Jesus Christ of Latter-day Saints.* 4 vols. Salt Lake City: Andrew Jenson History Company, 1901–30.

————. Manuscript History of the Church in Missouri, 1864. Holograph. LDS Church History Library.

————. "A Partial Listing of Those Driven from Jackson County, Missouri, 1864." In Manuscript History of the Church. Holograph. MS 6019. LDS Church History Library.

————. "The Three Witnesses: John Whitmer." *Historical Record* 7, nos. 8–10 (October 1888): 612–15.

———. *History of the Scandinavian Mission.* Salt Lake City: Deseret News Press, 1927.

———. Introduction to 1893 typescript of *The Book of John Whitmer.* LDS Church History Library.

———. "John Whitmer." *Historical Record* 7, nos. 8–10 (October 1888): 612–13.

———. "Joseph Smith, the Prophet." *Historical Record* 7, nos. 1–3 (January 1888): 435–44.

———. Journal. Sunday, 16 September 1888. Book E, pp. 107–9. Holograph. MS 1230. Box 1, fd 3. LDS Church History Library.

———. "The Three Witnesses. Fd. 3. LDS Church History Library.

———. *Latter-day Saint Biographical Encyclopedia: A Compilation of Biographical Sketches of Prominent Men and Women in the Church of Jesus Christ of Latter-day Saints." Historical Record* 6, nos. 3–5 (May 1887): 212–19.

Jenson, Andrew, Edward Stevenson, and Joseph S. Black. "Historical Landmarks." September 13, 1888. In *Deseret News,* September 26, 1888, 7. Excerpt reprinted in "Sayings of John C. Whitmer," *Herald* 35, no. 41 (October 13, 1888): 651.

Jessee, Dean C., ed. "Joseph Knight's [Sr.] Recollection of Early Mormon History." *BYU Studies* 17 (Autumn 1976): 29–39.

———. "The Original Book of Mormon Manuscript." *BYU Studies* 10, no. 3 (Spring 1970): 259–78.

———, ed. *Papers of Joseph Smith. Vol. 1: Autobiographical and Historical Writings.* Salt Lake City: Deseret Book, 1989.

———, ed. *The Papers of Joseph Smith, Vol. 2: Journal 1832–1842.* Salt Lake City: Deseret Book, 1992.

———, ed. *The Personal Writings of Joseph Smith.* Rev. ed., Salt Lake City: Deseret Book, 2002.

"John C. Whitmer Dead." *Herald* 41, no. 37 (September 12, 1894): 582.

Johnson, Benjamin Franklin. *My Life's Review.* Independence, MO: Zion's Printing and Publishing Company, 1947.

Johnson, Clark, ed. *Mormon Redress Petitions: Documents of the 1833–1838 Missouri Conflict.* Provo, UT: BYU Religious Studies Center, 1992.

Johnson, Clark V., and Ronald E. Romig. *An Index to Early Caldwell County, Missouri, Land Records.* Independence, MO: Missouri Mormon Frontier Foundation, 2002.

Johnson, Irene. "Ziba Peterson, the Other Missionary." Paper presented at the annual meeting of the Mormon History Association, Claremont, CA, May 1991. Photocopy in my possession.

———. Letter to John Whitmer. 27 November 1872. St. Louis, MO. Holograph. MS 6378. Fd. 1, item 3. LDS Church History Library.

———. Letter to John Whitmer. 20 December 20, 1872. St. Louis, MO. Holograph. MS 6378. Fd. 1, item 4. LDS Church History Library.

———. Letter to John Whitmer. 16 May 1873 and 1 August 1873. St. Louis, MO. Holograph. MS 6378. Item 7. LDS Church History Library.

Johnson, Eldred A. "The Life History of Charles Hulet and His Wives Anna Taylor, Margaret Noah, and Mary Lawson Kirkman." N.p.: privately printed, 1991. Copy in my possession.

Johnson, Luke. "History of Luke Johnson." *Deseret News* 8, no. 11 (May 19, 1858): 1.

Johnson, Maria L[ouise Cowdery]. South West City, Missouri. Letter to David Whitmer. Richmond, Missouri. 14 January 1887. Whitmer Papers. P10, f16. CofC Archives.

Johnson, Mary Coffin. *The Higleys and Their Ancestry: An Old Colonial Family.* New York: D. Appleton and Company, 1841.

Jones, William. Indenture to John Whitmer. 8 December 1846. MS 6378. Fd. 2, item 6. LDS Church History Library.

———. Payment to Rennie & Duncan. February 19, 1841. Liberty, MO. MS 7062. Fd. 5, item 13. LDS Church History Library.

Journal of the Missouri Legislature: House of Representatives, 1st Session, 9th General Assembly, 1836–1837. Bowling Green, MO: Office of the Salt River Journal, 1837.

Joyce, Burr. Writer for the *St. Louis Globe Democrat.* October 6, 1887. Reprinted as "How the Prophet's Followers Left Jackson County and Settled in Caldwell–The Beginning of Trouble," *Herald* 34, no. 51 (October 22, 1887): 836–39.

Judd, Zadock Knapp. Autobiography. Typescript. Man A462. Utah State Historical Society, Salt Lake City.

Judy, Parris T. Indenture to John Whitmer. 21 May 1840. John Whitmer Papers. MS 6378. LDS Church History Library.

Kenney, Scott G., ed. *Wilford Woodruff's Journal, 1833–1898.* Typescript. 9 vols. Midvale, UT: Signature Books, 1983–85.

Kerr, C. W. "C. W. Kerr." In *History of Caldwell and Livingston Counties, Missouri,* 329–30.

Kiddle, Elizabeth Proctor, et al., eds. *The Family of Auer Winchester Proctor, Vol. II: Winchester.* Provo, UT: J. Grant Stevenson, 1978.

Kimball, Heber C. "Extracts from H. C. Kimball's Journal." *Times and Seasons* 6, no. 3 (February 15, 1845): 1105–6.

Kimball, Stanley B. "The Anthon Transcript: People, Primary Sources, and Problems." *BYU Studies* 10 (Spring 1970): 325–52.

———. *Heber C. Kimball: Mormon Patriarch and Pioneer.* Urbana: University of Illinois Press, 1986.

———. "Missouri Mormon Manuscripts: Sources in Selected Societies." *BYU Studies* 14, no. 4 (Summer 1974): 458–87.

———, ed. *On the Potter's Wheel: The Diaries of Heber C. Kimball.* Salt Lake City: Signature Books in Association with Smith Research Associates, 1987.

Kimball, Vilate Murray. Letter to Heber C. Kimball, 12 September 1837. Holograph. MS 12476. LDS Church History Library.

Kimmel, Michael S., and Amy Aronson. "Guns." *Men and Masculinities: A Social, Cultural, and Historical Encyclopedia, Vol. 1.* Santa Barbara, CA: ABC-CLIO, 2003, 364.

Kitchell, Ashbel. "A Mormon Interview: Account copied from Brother Ashbel Kitchell's Pocket Journal." By Elisha D. Blakeman. August 1856. Shaker Museum, Old Chatham, NY. Also, Photocopy. Small Manuscripts Collection. Perry Special Collections.

Kleinman, Horesa Lillywhite. "The Life Story of James Clark Owens, Sr., ca. 1979." Microfilm of typescript. MS 2735, 377. 3. LDS Church History Library.

Knecht, Stephen R. *The Story of Joseph Smith's Bible Translation: A Documented History.* N.p.: Associated Research Consultants Publication, 1977.

———. *The Story of Joseph Smith's Bible Translation, Newly Revised.* Rev. ed. N.p.: privately printed 1984.

Knight, Joseph, Jr. "Joseph Knight's Incidents of History from 1827–1844." Compiled August 16, 1862. Holograph. MS 286. Fd. 564, item 24. LDS Church History Library.

———. Deed of Consecration. October 12, 1832. Holograph. MS 5589. LDS Church History Library.

Knight, Joseph, Sr. "Reminiscences." 1832. Holograph. MS 3470. LDS Church History Library.

———. "Joseph Knight's Recollection of Early Mormon History." *BYU Studies* 17 no. 1 (1976): 29–39. The original undated and unsigned holographic account was written sometime between 1833 and 1847, and is housed at the LDS Church History Library.

Knight, Newel. [Between 5–10] August 1830. Journal History.

———. "Newel Knight's Journal." *Scraps of Biography: Tenth Book of the Faith Promoting Series, Designed for the Instruction and Encouragement of Young Latter-day Saints.* Salt Lake City: Juvenile Instructor Office, 1883. Reprinted in *Classic Experiences and Adventures*, Salt Lake City: Bookcraft, 1969, 46–104.

Jessee, Dean C. "The Writing of Joseph Smith's History." *BYU Studies* 11, no. 4 (Summer 1971): 439–73.

Lamb, M. T. *The Golden Bible.* New York: Ward & Drumwood, 1887.

Lancaster, James E. "By the Gift and Power of God." *Herald* 109, no. 22 (November 15, 1962): 798–806, 817.

Larson, Stan, and Samuel J. Passey, eds. *The William E. McLellin Papers 1854–1880.* Salt Lake City, Utah: Signature Books, 2007.

"Last House in Far West Is Destroyed." *Deseret News* 6, no. 40 (March 20, 1913): 1.

"The Last Witness Dead." *Herald* 35, no. 6 (February 11, 1888): 94–95.

"The Last Witness Gone." *Missouri Daily Republican* 80, no. 21,056, January 26, 1888.

"An Old Citizen Passes Away." *Missouri Daily Republican* 80 (January 26, 1888). Reprint of "An Old Citizen Passes Away," *Richmond Conservator*, January 26, 1888.

Lake Erie Steam-Boat Line. Advertisement. Buffalo to Detroit, with stops at Cleveland. *Telegraph and Geauga Free Press* (Painesville, OH) 2, no. 1 (June 22, 1830): 4.

Lee, Donald. Untitled Statement. March 3, 1957. MS 7165. LDS Church History Library.

LeSueur, Stephen C. *The 1838 Mormon War in Missouri.* Columbia: University of Missouri Press, 1987.

———. "Missouri's Failed Compromise: The Creation of Caldwell County for the Mormons." *Journal of Mormon History* 31, no. 3 (Fall 2005): 113–44.

"Letters from David and John C. Whitmer." 9 December 1886. *Herald* 34, no. 6 (February 5, 1887): 89–93.

[Unsigned] Letter to the editor, *Reflector* (Palmyra, NY) 2, no. 12 (February 1, 1831): 89–90. Uncle Dale's [Dale Broadhurst] Readings in Early Mormon History: http://www.sidneyrigdon.com/dbroadhu/NY/wayn1830.htm#020131. Accessed October 28, 2007.

Lewellen, Ethel Johnson. Letter to C. Edwards Miller. 26 May 1932. Kingston, MO. Holograph. Accretion Papers. P68, f80. CofC Archives.

Lewis, William. "Correspondence." Stewartsville, DeKalb County, MO. November 29, 1877. Printed in *Herald* 24 (December 15, 1877): 381–82.

Lightner, Mary [Elizabeth Rollins]. "Mary Elizabeth Rollins Lightner." *Utah Genealogical and Historical Magazine* 17 (July 1926): 193–205, 250.

———. *The Life and Testimony of Mary Lightner: M. Lightner's Testimony as Delivered at Brigham Young University.* Salt Lake City: Kraut's Pioneer Press, n.d.

Lindquist, Evan. "Recipes for Old Writing and Drawing Inks." http://evanlindquist.com/othermedia/oldinkrecipes. Accessed May 3, 2012.

Linn, William Alexander. *The Story of the Mormons.* New York: MacMillan, 1902.

"List of Lands [in Caldwell County, MO] Forfeited to the State in 1848 for Taxes of 1847." AC 901.A1a no. 1341. Vault. Perry Special Collections.

"List of Lands [in Caldwell County, MO] Sold for the State in 1848 for Arrears of Taxes, &c., for Taxes of 1844." 631 112 C127 1846. Vault. Perry Special Collections.

"List of Lands Sold to the State in 1846 for Arrear[s] of Taxes, &c., for taxes of 1844 [Caldwell County, Missouri], Delinquent Tax List, 1845." 631 112 C127, 1846, 848. Vault. Perry Special Collections.

"A List of Names of the Church of Latter Day Saints living in the S.W. quarter of Far West." Teachers' Quorum Minute Book. December 1834–December 1845. MS 3428. LDS Church History Library.

Littlefield, Lyman Omer. *Reminiscences of Latter-day Saints: Giving an Account of Much Individual Suffering Endured for Religious Conscience.* Logan, UT: Utah Journal Co., 1888.

"Livery and Feed Stable." *Richmond Conservator* 20, no. 19 (August 9, 1873): 4. Microfilm. Ray County Library, Richmond, MO.

"The Livery Stable of Messrs. Whitmer & Co." *Richmond Conservator* 25, no. 33 (November 8, 28, 1878): 3. Microfilm. Ray County Library, Richmond, MO.

"Local and Other Matters: "Old Times." *Deseret News.* December 21, 1881, 1.

Lyman, Albert R. "Edward Partridge Family." 1954. Typescript. MS 8336. Fd. 155, item 6, p. 19. LDS Church History Library.

Lyman, Amasa. Journal. 12 July–5 August 1834. Amasa Lyman Collection. MS 829. Box 1, vol. 2. January 1, 1834–December 21, 1834. Pps. 12–13. LDS Church History Library.

Lyman, Eliza Partridge Smith. Life and Journal of E. M. P. L. S., n.d., between 1820–1886. Holograph. MS 872. Item 3. LDS Church History Library.

Lyman, Eliza Partridge. Autobiography and Diary of Eliza Marie Partridge (Smith) Lyman. n.d. MS 9546. Microfilm of typescript copied by Brigham Young University Library. Perry Special Collections.

MacKay, Michael, et al., eds., *Joseph Smith Papers Documents*, Vol. 1, July 1828–June 1831. Salt Lake City: Deseret Book, 2013.

MacKay, Michael Hubbard, Gerrit J. Dirkmaat, and Robin Scott Jensen. "The 'Caractors' Document: New Light on an Early Transcription on the Book of Mormon Characters." *Mormon Historical Studies* 14, no. 1 (Spring 2013): 131–52.

Majors, Alexander. *Seventy Years on the Frontier.* Chicago: Rand, McNally and Company, 1893.

Manual of the Churches of Seneca County with Sketches of Their Pastors. Seneca Falls, NY: Courier Printing Co., 1896.

March, David D. *The History of Missouri.* New York: Lewis Historical Publishing Company, 1967.

Marks, Mariella, ed. *Memoirs of the Life of David Marks: Minister of the Gospel.* Dove, NY: Free-Will Baptist Printing, 1846.

Marquardt, H. Michael. "An Appraisal of Manchester as Location for the Organization of the Church." *Sunstone* 16, no. 1 (February 1992): 49–57.

Marra, Dorothy Brandt, and David Boutros, eds. *Cher Oncle, Cher Papa: The Letters of Francois and Berenice Chouteau.* Kansas City, MO: Western Historical Manuscript Collection-Kansas City, 2001.

Marsh, Thomas B. "History of Thomas Baldwin Marsh." MS 621. Item 3. LDS Church History Library.

———. "History of Thomas Baldwin Marsh [by Himself]." *Millennial Star* 26, no. 23–26 (June 4–25, 1864): 359–60, 375–76, 390–92, 406.

———. Letter to Wilford Woodruff, "Sir, your letter of the 9th of March." *Elders' Journal* 3, no. 1 (March 1838): 36.

———. Letter to Wilford Woodruff, n.d. *Elders' Journal* 1, no. 3 (July 1838): 36–38.

Marryat, Captain. *Travels and Adventures of Monsieur Violet: In California, Sonora, and Western Texas.* London, England: George Routledge and Sons, 1843.

Mather, Frederick G. "Early Days of Mormonism." *Lippincotts Magazine of Popular Literature and Science* 26, no. 152 (August 1880): 198–211.

Matthews, Robert J. "Joseph Smith Translation of the Bible." *Encyclopedia of Mormonism.* 4 vols. New York: Macmillan Publishing Company, 1992, 2:763–69.

———. *"A Plainer Translation": Joseph Smith's Translation of the Bible: A History and Commentary.* Provo, Utah: Brigham Young University Press, 1975.

McConkie, Mark L., ed. *Remembering Joseph: Personal Recollections of Those Who Know the Prophet Joseph Smith.* Salt Lake City: Deseret Books, 2003. Extracts posted on LDS Living. Deseretbook.com. May 23, 2005. http://deseretbook.com/mormon-life/news/story?story_id=6299. Accessed November 15, 2007.

McCoun James F. Indenture to David Whitmer. Deed Record Book G, p. 142. Ray County Land Records. Ray County Recorder's Office, Richmond, MO.

McElveen, Floyd C. *The Mormon Illusion.* Ventura, CA: Regal Books, 1977.

McKellar, Madge Hale. *Shellenbarger Family.* Compiled by Edythe R. Whitley. Nashville, TN: privately printed, 1946.

McKiernan, F. Mark. *The Voice of One Crying in the Wilderness: Sidney Rigdon, Religious Reformer, 1793–1876.* Lawrence, KS: Coronado Press, 1971.

McKiernan, F. Mark, and Roger D. Launius, eds. *An Early Latter Day Saint History: The Book of John Whitmer Kept by Commandment.* Independence, MO: Herald House, 1980.

McLellin, William E. Letter to unspecified addressee. Monday 24th, [ca. May 1869]. Holograph fragment. Miscellaneous Letters and Papers. P13, f2287. CofC Archives.

———. Letter to Davis H. Bays. 23 November 1869. Printed as "Letter and Reply," *Herald* 17, no. 10 (May 15, 1870): 290–91.

———. Letter to Samuel McLellin. 4 August 1832. Independence, MO. Holograph. P13, f6. CofC Archives.

———. Letter to Beloved Relatives. 4 August 1832. Independence, MO. Holograph. Miscellaneous Letters and Papers. P13, f6. CofC Archives.

———. Letter to My Dear Friends. February 1870. Independence, MO. Holograph, fragment. Miscellaneous Letters and Papers. P13, f191. CofC Archives. This letter contains a copy of an affidavit by Elizabeth Ann Whitmer Cowdery, February 15, 1870.

———. Letter to Our Very Dear Friends. 12 July 1869. Brownsville, MO. Holograph. Miscellaneous Letters and Papers. P13, f185. CofC Archives.

———. Letters to Joseph Smith III, [31?] July and 8 September 1872. Holograph. Miscellaneous Letters and Papers. P13, f213. CofC Archives.

———. "Our Apology—and Our Tours." *Ensign of Liberty of the Church of Christ* 1, no. 3 (December 1847): 34–35.

———. "Our Views Relative to the Legal Successor of Joseph Smith in the First Presidency." *Ensign of Liberty of the Church of Christ* 1, no. 4 (January 1848): 60–61.

———. "A Special Conference of All the Ministerial Authorities of the Church of Christ, in Kirtland, Ohio, Assembled." *Ensign of Liberty of the Church of Christ*, 1, no. 1 (March 1847): 1–13.

———. "W. E. McLellan's [*sic*] Book." January 4, 1871. Photograph of textual fragment. Pictorial Archives. D1334.2. CofC Archives.

McCune, George M. *Personalities in the Doctrine and Covenants*. Salt Lake City: Hawks Publishing, 1991.

Meader, Robert F. "The Shakers and the Mormons." *Shaker Quarterly* 2 (Fall 1962): 83–96.

Mennosearch.com: http://www.mennosearch.com. Accessed September 15, 2007.

Merkley, Christopher. *Biography [Autobiography] of Christopher Merkley*. Salt Lake City: J. H. Parry & Company, 1887.

Merriam-Webster's Collegiate Dictionary. 11th ed. Springfield, MA: Merriam-Webster, 2003.

Merrill, Ira. "Pioneer Stages." *Telegraph* (Painesville, OH) 3, no. 8 (August 1, 1828): 3.

Metcalfe, Erin B. Jennings, and Brent Lee Metcalfe. "Who Wrote the Book of Mormon 'Caractors.'" Paper presented at the annual meeting of the John Whitmer Historical Association, Council Bluffs, IA, September 2013.

Miller, C. Edward. Letter to Bishop J. A. Becker. 1 January 1930. Photocopy in Oliver Cowdery Biographical Folder. CofC Archives.

Miles, Samuel. Journal. 1826–81. MS 5096. LDS Church History Library.

Mills, Elvira Pamela. Autograph album. Gift from Marietta Streeter, May 1, 1832, upon departure from Nelson, Portage County, Ohio, to Jackson County, Missouri. Cited in Simmonds, "John Noah and the Hulets: A Study in Charisma in the Early Church."

"Miss Josie Schweich." *Richmond Conservator* 21, no. 29 (October 17, 1874): 3. Microfilm. Ray County Library, Richmond, MO.

"Missionary Covenant." *BYU Studies* 36, no. 2 (1996–97): 226.

Missouri Land Claims. MS 2703. F17. LDS Church History Library.

Morgan, Dale L., Letter to Fawn Brodie. February 25, 1948. Fort Leavenworth, KS. John Phillip Walker, ed. *Dale Morgan on Early Mormonism: Correspondence and a New History*. Salt Lake City: Signature Books, 1986, 153.

Morley, Isaac. Congressional Affidavit, Petition, January 8, 1840. Photocopy of holograph. Mormon Petitions. Caine Manuscripts. P69–2, box 2, f40. CofC Archives. See also Johnson, *Mormon Redress Petitions*, 449–501.

"Mormon Emigration." *Wayne Sentinel* (Palmyra, NY), 8 (May 27, 1831): 38.

"Mormon Landmark Passing, Home of David Whitmer at Richmond Being Torn Down." *Kansas City Post*. January 10, 1920. Clipping in Whitmer Papers. P1, f19. CofC Archives.

"Mormonism." *Telegraph* (Painesville, OH) 2, no. 31 (January 18, 1831): 3.

"Mormonism." *Telegraph* (Painesville, OH) 2, no. 35 (February 15, 1835): [page not known]. Uncle Dale's [Dale Broadhurst] Readings in Early Mormon History: http://www.sidneyrigdon.com/dbroadhu/NY/wayn1830.htm#020131. Accessed October 28, 2007.

"Mormonism." *Reflector* (Palmyra, NY) 2, no. 15 (March 9, 1831): [page not known]. Uncle Dale's [Dale Broadhurst] Readings in Early Mormon History: http://www.sidneyrigdon.com/dbroadhu/NY/wayn1830.htm#020131. Accessed October 28, 2007.

"Mr. Strang." Dated Caldwell County, December 24, 1847. *Gospel Herald* 2, no. 44 (January 20, 1848): 206. Uncle Dale's [Dale Broadhurst] Readings in Early Mormon History. http://www.sidneyrigdon.com/dbroadhu/NY/wayn1830.htm#020131. Accessed October 28, 2007.

M.S.C. [Matthew S. Clapp]. "Mormonism." *Telegraph* (Painesville, OH) 2, no. 35 (February 15, 1831): 1–2.

Mulder, William, and Russell Mortensen, eds. *Among the Mormons: Historic Accounts by Contemporary Observers.* New York: Alfred A. Knopf, 1958.

Mullin, Eri B. Letter to Dear Brethren. 15 January 15 1880. Taftsville, MO. *Herald* 27, no. 5 (March 1, 1880): 76.

Murdock, John. Journal. 1830–1859. Typescript. Manuscript Collection 1130. MSS SC 997. Perry Special Collections.

Murdock, S. Reed. *John Murdock: His Life and His Legacy.* Layton, UT: Summerwood Publishers, 2000.

Nauvoo Court. Affidavit. MS 4828. LDS Church History Library.

"New Bible." *Fredonia [New York] Censor* 10, no. 10 (June 2, 1830). Reprinting from the *Wayne County Republican.* http://www.sidneyrigdon.com/dbroadhu/NY/miscNYS1.htm#020131. Accessed September 11, 2006.

Newell, Linda King, and Valeen Tippetts Avery. *Mormon Enigma: Emma Hale Smith, Prophet's Wife, "Elect Lady," Polygamy's Foe.* 1984. Reprint. Urbana: University of Illinois Press, 1994.

Noble, Joseph Bates. Autobiography. Ca. 1890. Typescript. MSS 968. Perry Special Collections.

Nolt, Steven M. E-mail to Andrew Bolton. February 5, 2002.

O'Driscoll, Jeffrey S. *Hyrum Smith: A Life of Integrity*. Salt Lake City: Deseret Book, 2003.

"An Old Citizen Passes Away." *Richmond Conservator*, Thursday, January 26, 1888. Reprinted in Cook, *David Whitmer Interviews*, 225.

Olmstead, Harvey. Congressional Affidavit. January 4, 1840. Caine Manuscripts. Photocopy of holograph. P69–2, box 3, f21. p. 1. CofC Archives.

"Oliver B. Huntington: The Prophet's Physical Appearance While Translating." In *Remembering Joseph: Personal Recollections of Those Who Knew the Prophet Joseph Smith*. Edited by Mark L. McConkie. Extract posted on LDS Living, Deseretbook.com. May 23, 2005. http://deseretbook.com/mormon-life/news/story?story_id=6299. Accessed March 6, 2007.

"The Original [copy of the] Book of Mormon." *St. Louis Times*. September 29, 1878. Clipping. Book of Mormon Witnesses subject folder. CofC Archives.

Packer, Murland Ray. "Life History of Elisha Hurd Groves." 1990. Typescript. MS 20881. LDS Church Library.

Page, Hiram. Letter to Alfred Bonny, Isaac N. Aldrich, and M. C. Ishem. 24 June 1849. Published as "To All the Saints Scattered Abroad." In *The Olive Branch, or Herald of Peace and Truth to all Saints* 2, no. 2 (August 1849): 27–28.

———. Letter to William E. McLellin. 30 May 30 1847. Ray County, MO. *Ensign of Liberty* 1, no. 4 (January 1848): 63.

———. Letter to William McLellin. 2 February [March], 1848. Fishing River, Ray County, MO. Photocopy of holograph. Accretion Papers. P68, f15. CofC Archives.

———. Letter to William McLellin. 4 March 1848. Photocopy of holograph. Accretion Papers. P68, f16. CofC Archives.

———. Letter to William E. McLellin. 8 October 1848. Accretion Papers. P68, f15. CofC Archives.

———. Letter to Leonard Rich. 24 September 1847. Reprinted in *The Ensign of Liberty* 1, no. 6 (May 1848): 93.

Page, Philander. "Reminiscence, 1907." Diary. P. 28. Daughters of Utah Pioneers Museum, Salt Lake City, UT.

Palfrey, John Gorham. *The New Testament in the Common Version, Conformed to Griesbach's Standard Greek Text*. 3rd ed. Boston: Gray & Bowen, 1828, 1830.

Palmer, Grant H. *An Insider's View of Mormon Origins.* Salt Lake City: Signature Books, 2002.

Parkin, Max H. "Conflict at Kirtland: The Nature and Cause of Internal and External Conflict of the Mormons in Ohio between 1830 and 1838." Masters thesis, Brigham Young University, 1966.

———. "A History of the Latter-day Saints in Clay County, Missouri, from 1833 to 1837." PhD diss., Brigham Young University, 1976.

———. "Latter-day Saint Conflict in Clay County." In Garr and Johnson, *Regional Studies in Latter-day Saint Church History: Missouri*, 241–60.

Partridge, Edward. Affidavit. 1839. Photocopy of holograph. Caine Manuscripts. Utah State University. Photocopy. P69–2, box 1, f37. CofC Archives.

———. Edward Partridge v. Samuel D. Lucas et al., December 22, 1833. Missouri 5th Circuit Court. Photocopy of holograph. MS 899. Fd. 3. LDS Church History Library.

———. Estate. Receipt to John H. Zimmer, appraiser. Far West, October 1840. MS 7062. Fd. 5, item 16. LDS Church History Library.

———. "History of Joseph Smith." *Times and Seasons* 6, no. 4 (March 1, 1845): 818–19.

———. Note to W. W. Phelps and John Whitmer. 17 May 1837. MS 6378. F3, 1837, item 1. LDS Church History Library.

———. Petition. MSS 942.9. Perry Special Collections.

———. Petition. May 15, 1839. Caine Manuscripts. Photocopy of holograph. P69–2, box 1, f7, p. 1. CofC Archives.

Partridge, Edward, Jr. "The Journal of Bishop Edward Partridge, 1818, 1835–1836." 1975. Typescript by Lyman De Platt. 921.73, P258p. LDS Family History Library, Salt Lake City.

Partridge, Scott H. "The Failure of the Kirtland Safety Society." *BYU Studies* 12, no. 4 (Summer 1972): 437–54.

Pearson, Russell "Historic Press of the First Newspaper in Independence." *Restoration Trail Forum* 10, no. 1 (February 1984): 3.

Peterson, J. W. "The Urim and Thummim." Edited by Louise Palfrey Sheldon. *The Rod of Iron* 1, no. 3 (February 1924): 6–7.

Pettigrew, David. Autobiography and Diary. 1840–61. Photocopy of holograph. MSS 473. Perry Special Collections.

———. "History of David Pettigrew." Written between 1861 and 1885. Typescript of holograph. MS 2282, fd. 2. LDS Church History Library.

————. Missouri Land Claims. MS 2703. F 23. LDS Church History Library.

————. Pettigrew Collection, 1836–83. Compact disk. Electronic scan of original. MS 22278. LDS Church History Library.

Phelps Family History in America and Kindred Family Histories. http://family.phelpsinc.com/bios/william_wines_phelps.html. Accessed January 4, 2007.

Phelps, William W. Journal. January–June 1835. MS 3450. LDS Church History Library.

Phelps, William. William Phelps v. Lewis Franklin. Suit. Jackson County, Missouri. 5th Circuit Court. Filed December 22, 1833. MS 899. Fd. 4. LDS Church History Library.

————. W. W. Phelps v. Richard Simpson et al. See Phelps, W. W. Wilson, James Grant, and John Fiske, eds. *Appleton's Cyclopedia of American Biography.* 6 vols. New York: D. Appleton and Company, 1887-89. Cited in *Phelps Family History in America.*

Phelps, William Waterman. Letter to Sally Phelps. [20?] July 1835. Included in a four-part letter by W. W. Phelps (signed two sections), William Waterman Phelps (unsigned fragment), and John Corrill to wife Margaret. William Wines Phelps Papers. Photocopy. Vault MSS 819. Perry Special Collections.

Phelps, William Wines. Prospectus. *Evening and the Morning Star.* Quoted in *History of the LDS Church*, 1;259. Vault. MSS 810. Perry Special Collections.

————. "To Agents and the Public." *The Evening and the Morning Star*, 1, no. 1 (June 1832): 6.

————. "Common Schools." *The Evening and the Morning Star* 1, no. 1 (June 1832): not paginated.

————. "Elders Stationed in Zion to the Churches Abroad." *The Evening and the Morning Star* 2, no. 14 (July 1833): 111.

————. "The Gathering." *The Evening and the Morning Star* 1, no. 6 (November 1832): 5.

————. "Rise and Progress of the Church of Christ." *The Evening and the Morning Star* 1, no. 11 (April 1833): [4].

————. *Star Extra.* February 1834. Broadsheet. Reproduced in Crawley, "Two Rare Missouri Documents," 502–15; and also in Flake, *A Mormon Bibliography, 1830–1930,* 226.

————. "Adam-ondi-Ahman" and "Sabbath Hymn." *Messenger and Advocate* 1, no. 9 (June 1835): 144.

————. Letter to Sally Phelps. January 1836. In Van Orden. "Writing to Zion: The W. W. Phelps Kirtland Letters (1835–1836)," 574.

———. Letter to Sally Phelps. 14 August [1835]. Kirtland Mills, OH. In "Letters." *Utah Genealogical and Historical Quarterly* 31 (January 1940): 27–28.

———. Letter to Sally Phelps. 5 January 1836. Holograph. LDS Church History Library.

———. Letter to Sally Phelps. [17] January 1836. Reprinted in Van Orden, "Writing to Zion," 542–91.

———. Letter to Sally Phelps (Dear Wife and Children). 2 June 1835. Far West, MO. Joseph Smith Collection. MS 155. Box 6, fd. 2. LDS Church History Library.

———. Letter to Sally Phelps. 19–20 July 1835. In Leah Y. Phelps. "Letters of Faith from Kirtland." *Improvement Era* 45 (August 1942): 529.

———. Letter to Sally Phelps. 16 September 1835. Liberty, Clay County, Missouri. Reprinted in Van Orden, "Writing to Zion," 566.

———. Letter to Sally Phelps. 14 November 1835, Reprinted in Van Orden, "Writing to Zion," 568.

———. Letter to Sally Phelps. 1835. Far West, Missouri. Reprinted in Van Orden, "Writing to Zion," 568.

———. Letter to John Whitmer. 4 March 1840. Bellbrooke, Ohio. MS 667. LDS Church History Library. Typescript. BX 8608.Ala, #1616. Perry Special Collections.

———. Letter to John Whitmer. 12 October 1859. John Whitmer Family Papers 1837–1912. MS 6378. LDS Church History Library.

———. "A Short History of W. W. Phelps' Stay in Missouri." Salt Lake City. April 21, 1864. MS d 6019. Fd. 7. LDS Church History Library.

Phelps, W. W. (grandson of W. W. and Sally Phelps). Letter. 20 July 1938. Microfilm of typescript. Holographic signature. Christine Ellen Phelps Slagowski Collection. MS 20970. Frame 98–99.

Phinney, H. & E. *The Holy Bible, Containing the Old and New Testaments: Together with the Apocrypha.* Stereotype edition. Cooperstown, NY. "Marked Bible." CofC Archives.

Pitcher, Thomas. Interview. In Etzenhouser. *From Palmyra, New York,* 322–25.

Pixley, Benton. "New Jerusalem: Letter from Independence." In Mulder and Mortensen, *Among the Mormons,* 75.

"Plain Truth" [pseud.]. Letter to the Editor. *Telegraph* (Painesville, OH) 2, no. 33 (February 1, 1831): [page not known]. Uncle Dale's [Dale Broadhurst] Readings in Early Mormon History: http://www.sidneyrigdon.com/dbroadhu/ NY/wayn1830.htm#020131. Accessed October 28, 2007.

Pollard, Lorene E. Notes of a talk and subsequent conversation with Ronald E. Romig. Whitmer Family Celebration, October 6, 2006, Richmond, MO. Whitmer History subject folder. CofC Archives.

Pollard, Lorene E., and Rebecca Woods. *Whitmer Memoirs, 1793–2003.* N.p.: privately printed, 2003.

Porter, Larry C. "The Colesville Branch in Kaw Township, Jackson County, Missouri, 1831 to 1833." Garr and Johnson, *Regional Studies in Latter-Day Saint Church History: Missouri*, 281–311. Paper originally presented at the Missouri Symposium, Brigham Young University, March 1991.

———. "The Odyssey of William Earl McLellin: Man of Diversity, 1806–1883." In Shipps and Welch, *The Journals of William E. McLellin*, 291–378.

———. "A Study of the Origins of the Church of Jesus Christ of Latter-day Saints in the States of New York and Pennsylvania, 1816–1831." PhD diss., Brigham Young University, 1971. Published as *A Study of the Origins of the Church of Jesus Christ of Latter-day Saints in the States of New York and Pennsylvania, 1816–1831.* Provo, UT: Joseph Fielding Smith Institute for Latter-day Saint History and BYU Studies, Dissertations in LDS History Series, 2000. I use the published version.

———. Untitled presentation. Whitmer Family Celebration, Farris Theater, October 6, 2006, Richmond, MO. Notes by Ronald Romig. In Whitmer History subject folder. CofC Archives.

Porter, Nathan T. Journal. Entry written before March 21, 1878. Photocopy of holograph. MS 1842. Fd. 1. Notes by Ronald Romig. In Whitmer History subject folder. CofC Archives.

Porter, Nathan Tanner (1820–97). Reminiscences. Ca. 1879. Photocopy of holograph. MS 1842. Fd. 1, pp. 64, 65. LDS Church History Library.

Poulson, P. Wilhelm. "Correspondence: Interview with David Whitmer." 13 August 1878. *Deseret News.* August 21, 1878, 13. Reprinted in Cook, *David Whitmer Interviews.*

———. "Correspondence: Death of John Whitmer." 31 July 1878. Ovid, ID. *Deseret News*, August 14, 1878, 2. Reprinted in Vogel, *Early Mormon Documents*, 5:247–49.

Pratt, Orson. Statement. Reported in "Minutes of the School of the Prophets." January 14, 1871. Holograph. LDS Church History Library. Quoted in Matthews, *A Plainer Translation*, 40.

Pratt, Orson, and Joseph F. Smith. "Report of Interview with David Whitmer, September 7–8, 1878, Richmond, Missouri." *Deseret News* 27, September 7,

1878. *Millennial Star* 40, no. 49 (December 9, 1878): 2. And in Cook, *David Whitmer Interviews*, 45.

Pratt, Parley P. "A History, of the Persecution, of the Church of Jesus Christ of Latter Day Saints in Missouri." *Times and Seasons* 1, no. 2 (December 1839): 17–20. 1, no. 3 (January 1840): 3. 33–36. 1, no. 4 (February 1840): 49–51. 1, no. 5 (March 1804): 5: 65–66. 1, no. 6 (April 1840): 81–82. 1, no. 7 (May 1840): 97–99. 1, no. 8 (June 1840): 113–16. 1, no 9 (July 1840): 129–31. 1, no. 10 (August 1840): 145–50. 1, no. 11 (September 1840): 161–65. 1, no. 12 (October 1840): 177.

Pratt, Parley P., Jr., ed. *The Autobiography of Parley Parker Pratt, One of the Twelve Apostles of the Church of Jesus Christ of Latter-day Saints, Embracing His Life, Ministry and Travels, with Extracts, in Prose and Verse, from His Miscellaneous Writings*. 1874. Reprint. Salt Lake City: Deseret Book, 1980.

A Presbyterian. Letter. "The Mormon Delusion." 22 February 1831. Chester, Geauga County, OH. *New-Hampshire Patriot & State Gazette* 3 (May [16?], 1831). Reprint. History, http://www.sidneyrigdon.com/dbroadhu/NE/miscne01.htm. Accessed November 1, 2007. Reprinted in the *Independent Messenger*, May 1831, 96. Newspaper Collection. CofC Archives Archives.

Prince, Gregory A. *Having Authority: The Origins and Development of Priesthood during the Ministry of Joseph Smith*. Independence, MO: John Whitmer Historical Association Monograph Series, 1993.

———. *Power from On High: Development of Mormon Priesthood*. Salt Lake City: Signature Books, 1992.

Proctor, Scot Facer, and Maurine Ward Proctor, eds. *The Revised and Enhanced History of Joseph Smith by His Mother*. Salt Lake City: Bookcraft, 1996.

"Public Meeting." *Messenger and Advocate* 2, no. 11 (August 1836): 359, 360.

Quinn, D. Michael. *Early Mormonism and the Magic World View*. Salt Lake City: Signature Books, 1987.

———, trans. "The First Months of Mormonism: A Contemporary View by Rev. Diedrich Willers." *New York History* 54 (July 1973): 317–33.

———. *The Mormon Hierarchy: Origins of Power*. Salt Lake City: Signature Books, 1994.

———. "The Mormon Succession Crisis of 1844." *BYU Studies* 16, no. 2 (Winter 1976): 187–233.

Queesenberry, David A. Note to David Whitmer and Alonzo Winchester for hauling. April 3, 1840. Whitmer Papers. P10, f2, item 2. CofC Archives.

"Rare Photos Donated to Church by John Whitmer's Descendents. *[LDS] Church News*, November 29, 1958, 11. In John Whitmer biographical folder. CofC Archives.

Ray County, Missouri. Deed Record Book F, p. 120. Ray County Land Records. Ray County Recorders' Office, Richmond, MO. Cited in Black, "Pioneer Cemetery in Richmond, Missouri," 181, 189n1.

Ray County, Missouri. Probate Records. 1839. LDS Family History Library.

Reynolds, Noel B. "The Case for Sidney Rigdon as Author of the Lectures on Faith." *Journal of Mormon History* 31, no. 3 (Fall 2005): 1–41.

"Revelations." *Evening and the Morning Star* 1 (May 1833): 89.

Rice, Martin. *Rural Rhymes and Talks and Tales of Olden Times.* 2nd ed., enl. and improved. Kansas City, MO: Ramsey, Millett and Hudson, 1882.

Rich, Sarah DeArmon Pea (1814–93). Autobiography. Holograph. MS 1543. Fd. 1, item 1. LDS Church History Library. Typescript. Perry Special Collections.

Richards, Paul C. "Missouri Petitions for Redress." *BYU Studies* 13, no. 4 (Summer 1973): 520–43.

Richards, Willard. Letter to John Whitmer. 23 February 1844. Willard Richards Papers, 1821–54. MS 1490. Box 3, fd. 2. In Richard E. Turley, ed. *Selected Collections from the Archives of the Church of Jesus Christ of Latter-day Saints.* 2 vols. DVD (Provo, UT: Brigham Young University Press, [Dec. 2002], 1:38.

Richardson, Ebbie L. V. "David Whitmer: A Witness to the Divine Authenticity of the Book of Mormon." Masters thesis, Brigham Young University, 1952.

Rigdon, Sidney. Letter to the Brethren in Ohio. January 1831. Reprinted in Howe, *Mormonism Unvailed,* 110.

Rigdon, Sidney, et al. Letter to John Thornton, et al. Letter to Dear Brethren. 25 July 1836. *Messenger and Advocate* 2, no. 10 (July 1836): 355–359.

Riggs, Burr. Grandpa Bill's General Authorities Pages website. http://personal.atl. bellsouth.net/w/o/wol3/riggsbr.htm. Accessed January 6, 2007.

———. Biographical Note. Lyndon Cook. *The Revelations of the Prophet Joseph Smith.* Provo, UT: Seventy's Mission Bookstore, 1981, 155.

———. Indenture to John Whitmer. 13 August 1839. Indenture to John Whitmer. 1 February 1839. John Whitmer Papers. MS 6378. LDS Church History Library.

Riley, I. Woodbridge. *The Founder of Mormonism.* New York: Dodd, Mead & Company, 1902.

"RLDS Archives Sources." *Missouri Mormon Frontier Foundation Newsletter* 21–22 (August 1999).

[RLDS] "General Conference Minutes." 1904, 689. CofC Archives.

[RLDS] Conference Daily. *Herald* (1930): Pertaining to Cowdery portraits 14, 50, 70.

Roberts, Brigham Henry. *The Missouri Persecutions.* Salt Lake City: George Q. Cannon & Sons, 1900.

Roberts, Brigham H. "John Whitmer." *New Witnesses For God II: The Book of Mormon.* Salt Lake City: Deseret Book, 1950.

Roberts, Forest. "The History and Development of the Stewardship Idea, [RLDS Church]." Senior Religio Study Outline, 1923. Unpublished Collection. UP R542. CofC Library.

Robinson, George W. "The Scriptory Book of Joseph Smith Jr., President of the Church of Jesus Christ of Latter-day Saints in All the World." July 1838. Holograph. LDS Church History Library.

Robinson, Ebenezer. "Items of Personal History of the Editor." *The Return.* This brief periodical was published in Davis City, Iowa, by the Church of Christ. 1, no. 6 (June 1889): 88–91. 1, no. 8 (August 1889): 115–21. 1, no. 9 (September 1889): 131–37. 1, no. 10 (October 1889): 145–51. 1, no. 11 (November 1889): 169–74. 2, no. 2 (March 1890): 209–12.

———. "Robinson." Obituary. *Herald* 38, no. 13 (March 28, 1891): 207.

Rogers, Samuel. *Toils and Struggles of the Olden Times.* Standard Publishing Company, 1880. http://science.nasa.gov/newhome/headlines/ast22jun99_2.htm. Accessed April 22, 2007.

Romig, Ronald E. "Jackson County, 1831–33: A Look at the Development of Zion." *Restoration Studies* 3 (1986): 286–304.

———. "Perceptions of Discipleship within the Early Restoration Movement, 1830s." Paper presented to an internal RLDS/Community of Christ committee exploring discipleship, August 5, 2000.

———. Review of Bruce N. Westergren, *From Historian to Dissident: The Book of John Whitmer. John Whitmer Historical Association Journal* 17 (1997): 114–46.

Romig, Ronald E., and Michael S. Riggs. "The LDS Church and Its Army of Israel: The 9/11 Prophecy Crisis of 1836 in Clay County, Missouri." Paper presented at the Missouri Mormon Experience: From Conflict to Understanding, Jefferson City, MO, September 2006.

———. "Reassessing Joseph Smith's 'Appointed Time for the Redemption of Zion.'" In *The Missouri Mormon Experience.* Edited by Thomas M. Spencer. Columbia: University of Missouri Press, 2010, 27–49.

Rounds, William J. "Editorial Trail Beams." *Restoration Trail Forum* 9, no. 4 (November 1983): 2.

Rupp, I. Daniel. *A Collection of Upwards of Thirty Thousand Names of German, Swiss, Dutch, French and Other Immigrants in Pennsylvania from 1727–1776: With a Statement of the Names of Ships, Whence They Sailed, and the Date of Their Arrival at Philadelphia, Chronologically Arranged, Together with the Necessary Historical and Other Notes, also, an Appendix Containing Lists of More than One Thousand German and French Names in New York Prior to 1712.* Philadelphia, PA: Leary Stuart Company, 1898.

———. *History of Lancaster, Pennsylvania.* Lancaster, PA: Gilbert Hills, 1844.

Russell, William D. "King James Strang: Joseph Smith's Successor?." In Mark McKiernan, Alma Blair, and Paul M. Edwards, eds. *The Restoration Movement: Essays in Mormon History.* Independence, MO: Coronado Press, 1973, 231–56.

Russell, Samuel. Letter to Dear Lucy Ettie, Friends, and Kindred. 3 November 1882. Russell Family Correspondence. MS 4180. Fd. 2. LDS Church History Library.

Ryder, Hartwell. "A Short History of the Foundation of the Mormon Church, Based on Personal Memories and Facts Collected by Hartwell Ryder, Hiram, Ohio, at the Age of 80 Years." Ca. 1900. Typescript. Mildred Bennett Memorial Collection of Local History Materials. Box 3/C/2. Hiram College Library Archives, Hiram, OH.

Salisbury, Katharine. "Testimony of Katharine Salisbury." *Herald* 46, no. 17 (April 26, 1899): 261.

Sampson, Paul, and Larry T. Wimmer. "The Kirtland Safety Society: The Stock Ledger Book and the Bank Failure." *BYU Studies* 12, no. 4 (Summer 1972): 427–36.

Schindler, Harold. *Orrin Porter Rockwell: Son of Thunder.* Salt Lake City: University of Utah Press, 1977.

Schott, Andrew. "Andrew Schott, a Pioneer." Undated clipping from unidentified newspaper in scrapbook. "Index Rerum." Waterloo Library and Historical Society, Waterloo, NY. Quoted in Porter, "A Study of the Origins of the Church," 226.

Schweich, George W. "The Position of David Whitmer." *The Return* 3, no. 5 (December 1892): 4–5.

———. Letter to O. R. Beardsley. 17 January 1900. Holograph. MSS SC 1547. Perry Special Collections. Published in the Appendix to Edmund Clarence Stedman. *A Library of American Literature from the Earliest Settlement to the Present Time.*

———. Letter to Joseph Smith III. 30 October 1894. Published as "John C. Whitmer Dead." *Herald* 41, no. 47 (November 21, 1894): 741.

Schweich, Julia Ann Whitmer (1835–1914). *Family Bible*. Used ca. 1851–1914. Philadelphia: Thomas, Copperthwait, & Co., for the American Bible Society, 1846. MS 18735. LDS Church History Library.

Scott, Jacob. Letter to Mary Warnock. 24 March 1842. P21-1, f4, CofC Archives.

Seixas, Joshua. *A Manual Hebrew Grammar: For the Use of Beginners*. Andover, MA: Gould and Newman, 1834. Vault Collection. CofC Archives.

Senate Document 189: Testimony Given Before the Judge of the Fifth Judicial Circuit of the State of Missouri, on the Trial of Joseph Smith, Jr., and Others, for High Treason and Other Crimes Against that State. United States Congress (26th, 2nd session, 1840–1841. Salt Lake City, Modern Microfilm Co., [1965].

Shattuck, Benjamin. Letter to Mr. Howe. *Telegraph* (Painesville, OH), 2, no. 45 (April 26, 1831), 3.

Shenk, Elizabeth. Ancestry.com at: http://awt.ancestry.com/cgi-bin/igm.cgi?op= GET&db=familyhart&id=I349575. Accessed September 15, 2007.

Sherwood, Salmon. Letter to the *Illinois Journal*. 25 February 1833. Independence, MO. Reprinted in *(Columbia) Missouri Intelligencer* 17, no. 43 (April 20, 1833): [page not known]. Uncle Dale's [Dale Broadhurst] Readings in Early Mormon History: http://www.sidneyrigdon.com/dbroadhu/MO/Miss1831.htm. Accessed November 19, 2007.

Shipps, Jan, and John W. Welch, eds. *The Journals of William E. McLellin, 1831–1836*. Urbana: University of Illinois Press/Provo, UT: BYU Studies, 1994.

Shoemaker, Floyd C. "Far West." *This Week in Missouri History*, Columbia: State Historical Society of Missouri. Clipping n.d. Far West subject folder. CofC Archives.

Shook, Charles A. *Cumorah Revisited*. Cincinnati, OH: Standard Publishing Company, 1910.

Shoop, Joseph and Maria. Indenture to David Whitmer. 1 January 1845. Deed Record Book E, p. 241. Ray County Land Records. Ray County Recorders' Office, Richmond, MO.

Shurtliff/Shirtliff, Luman Andros. "Biographical Sketch." Holograph/typescript. MS 1605. LDS Church History Library.

Shurtliff, Luman Andros. "Biographical Sketch." 1870s. Holograph/typescript. BX 8670.1 .Sh93. Perry Special Collections.

Simmonds, A. J. "John Noah and the Hulets: A Study in Charisma in the Early Church." Paper presented at the annual meeting of the Mormon History Association, Lamoni, IA, May 26, 1979, 24. Photocopy in my possession.

Skousen, Royal, ed. *The Original Manuscript of the Book of Mormon.* Provo, UT: The Foundation for Ancient Research and Mormon Studies, 2001.

Smith, Don Carlos, and George A. Smith. "Appendix to History of the Prophet Joseph: A Journal Kept by Don C. Smith, When on a Mission with George A. Smith, His Cousin." *Improvement Era* 6, no. 1 (November 1902): 11–16.

Smith, Emma. *A Collection of Sacred Hymns, for the Church of the Latter Day Saints.* Kirtland, OH: Printed by F. G. Williams & Co., 1835 [1836].

———. [Emma Hale Smith Bidamon.] Interview by Joseph Smith III. February 4–10, 1879. Published as "Last Testimony of Sister Emma." *Herald* 26, no. 19 (1879): 289–90.

———. Letter to Mrs. (Emma) Pilgrim. 27 March 1876. Emma Smith Papers. P4, f43. CofC Archives.

Smith, Frederick M. Letter to Samuel A. Burgess. 15 April 1926. J. F. Curtis Papers. P22, f14. CofC Archives.

———. Letter to Oscar W. Newton. 20 June 1926. P22, f18. CofC Archives.

Smith, George A., and Thomas Bullock. "Listing of the Persons Driven from Jackson Co., Mo. in 1833." August 27, 1864. Holograph. MS 6019. LDS Church History Library.

Smith, George D., ed. *An Intimate Chronicle: The Journals of William Clayton.* Signature Books, Salt Lake City, 1991.

Smith, Heman C. "Church History." *Journal of History* 1, nos. 1, 2, 3 (January, April, July, 1908): 45–63, 135–50, 292–305. First publication (incomplete) of The Book of John Whitmer.

———. Cold Water, NE. Letter to the editor. 16 May 1882. *Herald* 29, no. 12 (June 15, 1882): 192.

———. "Editor Herald" [Letter to the editor]. *Herald* 31, no. 28 (July 12, 1884): 442.

Smith, Heman H. "Biography of David Whitmer." *Journal of History* 3, no. 3 (July 1910): 298–305.

Smith, Hyrum. "To the Saints Scattered Abroad." *Times and Seasons* 1, no. 2 (December 1839): 20–24.

———. Record Book. 24 February 1835–26 March 1844. Joseph Smith Sr. Family Collection. Perry Special Collections.

Smith, Israel A. "A 'Sealed' Book." *Herald* 89, no. 9 (February 28, 1942): 262–63.

———. "Whitmer Heirlooms." *Herald* 100, no. 11 (March 16, 1953): 245–46, 257.

Smith, John. Letter to George A. Smith. 1 January 1838. Cited in Smith, "Whitmer Heirlooms," 257.

Smith, Joseph Jr. Bible. Revision. manuscripts. Old and New Testament. Holograph. P72–3. Vault Collection. CofC Archives.

———. Blessing for Joseph Smith Sr. by Joseph Jr. December 18, 1833. Patriarchal Blessing Book 1. LDS Church History Library.

———. The Book of Moses. Chapter 1. *The Pearl of Great Price: A Selection from the Revelations, Translations, and Narrations of Joseph Smith*. Salt Lake City: LDS Church, 1965, 1–4.

———. "Ohio Journal: 1835–1836," November 27, 1835. In Dean C. Jessee, ed. *The Papers of Joseph Smith, Vol. 2: Journal 1832–1842*. Salt Lake City: Deseret Book, 1992, 2:90–91.

———. The Holy Scriptures: Inspired Version. Independence, MO: Herald Publishing House, 1974.

———. Petition to Ariel Hanson. November 7, 1836. Holograph. Lake County Historical Society, OH.

———. Revelation to Thomas B. Marsh. July 23, 1837. Holograph. P5, f5. CofC Archives.

———. "Try the Spirits." *Times and Seasons* 3, no. 11 (April 1, 1842): 743–48.

———, ed., "Be it known unto the Saints scattered abroad greeting:" *Elders' Journal* 1, no. 2 (November 1837): 27, 28.

———. "We Would Say to the Patrons of the Journal." *Elders' Journal* 1, no. 2 (November 1837): 27, 28.

———. *History of the Church of Jesus Christ of Latter-day Saints*. See *History of the LDS Church* in Short Citations.

———. *History of the Church of Jesus Christ of Latter-day Saints*. Edited by B. H. Roberts. Salt Lake City: Deseret News Press, 6 vols. 1902–12, Vol. 7 1932; 1967 printing. Cited as *History of the LDS Church*.

———. Letter. Quoted in Stevenson, Journal, 15 August 1834. MS 4806.Reel 5, fd. 5, vol. 48. LDS Church History Library.

———. Letter to John Corrill and the Church in Zion. 4 September 1837. Quoted in Dean C. Jessee, ed., *The Personal Writings of Joseph Smith*, Salt Lake City: Deseret Book, 2002, 391.

———. Letter to Edward Partridge. 2 May 1833. "Concerning Inheritances." Joseph Smith Collection. LDS Church History Library. Quoted in Arrington, Fox, and May, *Building the City of God*, 25–26.

———. Letter to W. W. Phelps, 31 July 1832. In Jessee, *The Personal Writings of Joseph Smith*, 272–73.

Smith, Joseph Jr., Oliver Cowdery, Sidney Rigdon, Frederick G. Williams, W. W. Phelps, and John Whitmer. Portion of letter to Hezekiah Peck. 31 August 1835. Retained copy in John Whitmer. The Book of John Whitmer. Manuscript history, chap. 16, p. 77.

Smith, Joseph Jr., and John Whitmer. Letter to Dearly Beloved in the Lord. 20 August 1830. Harmony, PA. In Newel Knight. Journal. LDS Church History Library.

———. Letter to Colesville Saints. 28 August 1830. In Vogel, *Early Mormon Documents*, 1:13–14.

Smith, Joseph, Sr. "We Would Say to the Patrons of the Journal." *Elders' Journal* 1, no. 2 (November 1837): 27–28.

Smith Joseph, III. "Last Testimony of Sister Emma." *Herald* 26, no. 19 (October 1, 1879): 289–90.

———. Letterpress Books. 1876–1897. 10 vols. CofC Archives.

———. Letter to James T. Cobb. 14 February 1879. Joseph Smith III. Letterbook 2:285–88. CofC Archives.

———. Letter to Dr. E. A. Kilbourne. 11 March 1879. Elgin, IL. Joseph Smith III Letterbook, 2:135, 136. CofC Archives.

———. Letter to James R. B. Van Cleave. 27 September 1878. Joseph Smith III Letterbook, 1:462–63, P6. CofC Archives.

———. Letter to David Whitmer. 2 September 1879. Plano, IL. Joseph Smith Letterbook, 2:345. CofC Archives.

———. Notes for Memoirs. Dictated to Israel A. Smith. October 13, [1914]. Joseph Smith III Papers. P70–6, f46. CofC Archives.

Smith, Joseph III, and Heman Hale Smith. *History of the Church of Jesus Christ of Latter Day Saints, 1805–1890.* See complete citation under "Short Citations."

Smith, Joseph F. Letter to Samuel Russell. 19 March 1901. Holograph. MS 5103. LDS Church History Library.

Smith, Joseph Fielding. *Essentials in Church History.* Salt Lake City: Deseret News Press, 1922.

Smith, Joseph Fielding. *Life of Joseph F. Smith, Sixth President of the Church of Jesus Christ of Latter-day Saints.* 2nd ed. Salt Lake City: Deseret Book, 1969.

Smith, Lucy Mack. "Lucy Smith History, 1845." In Vogel, *Early Mormon Documents*, 1:227–452.

Smith, T[homas] W. "Urim and Thummim." *Herald* 27, no. 1 (January 1, 1880): 67.

Smith, Vida E. "Biography of Patriarch Alexander H. Smith." *Journal of History* 4, no. 1 (January 1911): 1–19. 4, no. 2 (April 1911): 143–56. 4, no. 3 (July 1911): 265–78. 4, no. 4 (October 1911): 394–411. 5, no. 1 (January 1912): 54–68. 5, no. 3 (July 1912): 259–78. 5, no. 4 (October 1912): 477–95. 6, no. 1 (January 1913): 20–40. 6, no. 2 (April 1913): 212–32. 6, no. 3 (July 1913): 294–310. 6, no. 4 (October 1913): 394–418. 7, no. 1 (January 1914): 61–75. 7, no. 2 (April 1914): 130–45. 7, no. 3 (July 1914): 305–22. 8, no. 1 (January 1915): 8–25.

———. *Young People's History.* Lamoni, IA: Herald Publishing House, 1914. Full page reproduction of the Caractors opposite page 14.

Smith, Walter W. Letter to First Presidency. 14 September 1925. Holograph. [David] Whitmer Papers. P10, f19, item 23. CofC Archives.

———. Letter to Samuel A. Burgess. 15 April 1925. Independence, MO. In J. F. Curtis Papers. P57, f2. CofC Archives.

Smith, William B. Interview by J. W. Peterson and W. S. Pender. 4 July 1890. In "Statement of J. W. Peterson Concerning William Smith." May 1, 1921. Miscellaneous Letters and Papers. P13, f1490. CofC Archives. Also available in Vogel, *Early Mormon Documents,* 1:507–9.

———. Quoted in Peterson, "The Urim and Thummim," 6–7.

———. Letter to James J. Strang. 1 March 1846. Nauvoo, IL. *Voree Herald* 1, no. 7 (July 1846): 31.

———. "Mass Meeting at Far West, Mo." *Herald* 26, no. 22 (November 15, 1879): 355–56.

Snow, Eliza. "Eliza R. Snow: Letter from Missouri." *BYU Studies* 13, no. 4 (Summer 1973): 544–52.

Snyder, John J. Letter to Paul Hanson. 31 January 1923. Hanson Collection. P12–1, f18. CofC Archives.

Spafford, Horatio Gates. *Gazetteer of the State of New York.* Albany, NY: B. E. Packard, 1813.

"A Special Conference," *The Ensign of Liberty of the Church of Christ* 1, no. 1 (March 1847): 1, 10.

St. John, John, ed. "The Golden Bible." *Cleveland Herald* 7, no. 5 (November 25, 1830): [page not known]. SolomonSpaulding.com. http://www.solomonspaulding.com/docs/1830h11b.htm. Accessed November 5, 2007.

Staker, Mark Lyman. *Harken, O Ye People: The Historical Setting of Joseph Smith's Ohio Revelations.* Salt Lake City: Greg Kofford Books, 2009.

———. "The Relationship between Oral Tradition and Latter-day Saint Material Culture: Joseph Smith in Hiram, Ohio as a Test Case." Unpublished paper. 2001. Copy in [John] Whitmer History subject folder. CofC Archives.

Stedman, Edmund Clarence. *A Library of American Literature from the Earliest Settlement to the Present Time.* Answers.com. http://www.answers.com/topic/william-e-benjamin. Accessed May 14, 2007.

Stevenson, Edward. Journal. 1820–1896. Holograph. MS 4806. Reel 5, fd. 5, vol. 48. LDS Church History Library.

———. Letter to John Taylor. 7 January 1878. Journal History.

Stevenson, Joseph Grant. *Stevenson Family History, Vol. 1.* Provo, UT: Stevenson's Genealogical Center, 1986.

Steward, Dick. *Duels and the Roots of Violence in Missouri.* Columbia: University of Missouri Press, 2000.

Stewart, Bruce G. "Hiram Page: An Historical and Sociological Analysis of an Early Mormon Prototype." Masters thesis, Brigham Young University, 1987.

Stick of Joseph. Broadside [placard]. Perry Special Collections. In Bachman, "Sealed in a Book," 321–45, facsimile on 324.

Stott, Graham St. John. "Just War, Holy War, and Joseph Smith, Jr." *Restoration Studies* 4 (1988): 134–41.

Stowell, Lydia. Letter (addressee not identified; n.d.). Bloomington, CA. W. W. Phelps file. LDS Church History Library.

Strang, James J. "An Epistle." *Voree Herald* 1, no. 1 (January 1846): 1–4.

———. "Note 3." *Gospel Herald* 2, no. 44 (January 20, 1848): 206.

"Mr. Strang." 24 December 1847. Caldwell County, MO. *Gospel Herald* 2, no. 44 (January 20, 1848): 206.

Strassberger, Ralph B., and William John Hinke, eds. *Pennsylvania German Pioneers: A Publication of the Original Lists of Arrivals in the Port of Philadelphia from 1727 to 1803.* 3 vols. Camden, ME: Picton Press, 1992.

Swartzell, William. *Mormonism Exposed, Being a Journal of a Residence* in *Missouri from the 28th of May to the 20th of August, 1838.* Pekin, OH, 1840. Photomechanical reprint. Salt Lake City: Utah Lighthouse Ministry.

Sweitzer, Frederick (guardian of Peter Whitmer Sr.). Petition. Orphan Court Record. Court of Common Pleas for the County of Lancaster. December 11 and 31, 1792 and March 26, 1793. Lancaster County Historical Society, Lancaster, PA. Cited in Davis, *Emigrants, Refugees, and Prisoners,* 2:422.

Tamez, Jared. "The Hiram Page Stone: Tracing a Mormon Artifact." Paper for BYU History 200. April 2007. Photocopy. Whitmer History subject folder. CofC Archives.

Taylor, L. L., ed. *Past and Present of Appanoose County, Iowa: A Record of Settlement, Organization, Progress, and Achievement.* Chicago: S. J. Clarke Publishing, 1913, 2:118–19. Photocopy. [John] Whitmer History subject folder. CofC Archives.

Tanner, Jerald. Interview of unnamed granddaughter of Jacob Whitmer. 1957. Quoted in Huggins. "Jerald Tanner's Quest for Truth," 3.

Tanner, Jerald, and Sandra Tanner, eds. *John Whitmer's History.* Salt Lake City: Modern Microfilm, 1966.

———, eds. *Joseph Smith's 1835–1836 Diary.* Salt Lake City: Modern Microfilm, 1979.

———, eds. *Joseph Smith's Kirtland Revelation Book.* Salt Lake City: Modern Microfilm, 1979.

———, eds. *The Reed Peck Manuscript.* Salt Lake City: Modern Microfilm.

"Teachers Supported by the Wilmington Monthly Meeting, 1794–1842, School Committee Records and Vouchers, Wilmington Friends School safe; Wilmington Friends School Safe; Accounts of the Treasurer of the Fund for Friends Belonging to the Wilmington Monthly Meeting. Friends Historical Library. Swarthmore College, Swarthmore, PA.

Temple Lot Case. See complete citation under "Short Citations."

"Terrific Cyclone." *Richmond Conservator.* June 7, 1878, 1, 2. Reprinted in Curtis, "A Hometown Perspective on the 1878 Richmond Tornado," 7–15.

Terry, J. M. Letter to editor. 6 October 1897. Far West, MO. *Zion's Ensign* 8, no. 42 (October 14, 1897): 3.

Thompson, John E. "The Initial Survey Committee Selected to Appoint Lands for Gathering in Daviess County, Missouri (1837–38)." *Restoration Studies* 3 (1986): 305–13.

Thorp, Joseph. *Early Days in the West.* Liberty, MO: Irving Gilmer, 1924.

Thornton, Carter. Deed of Manumission. 4 September 1849. Book C, pp. 166–67. Ray County Circuit Court Records. Ray County Recorders' Office, Richmond, MO.

Thornton, Carter, and Fanny. Note to David Whitmer. 12 April 1844. Witnessed by G. A. Dunn and Iram Bisbee. Book E, p. 154. Ray County Land Records. Ray County Recorders' Office, Richmond, MO. See also [David] Whitmer Papers. P10, f2, item 19. CofC Archives.

"To His Excellency, Daniel Dunklin, Governor of the State of Missouri." Dated ca. 1 October 1833. *Evening and the Morning Star*, 2, no. 15 (December 1833): 114.

"To the Editor." *Reflector* (Palmyra, NY) 2, no. 12 (February 1, 1831): [page not known].

"To the Patrons of the Evening and the Morning Star." *The Evening and the Morning Star* 2, no. 15 (December 1833): 113–14.

"To the Saints Abroad." *The Messenger and Advocate* 2, no. 10 (July 1836): 347–50.

Traughber, John Logan. "David Whitmer: 'The Last Witness' of the Book of Mormon." John Logan Traughber Papers." Holograph. MS 666. Box 2, fd. 23. Manuscripts Division. Marriott Library. Also quoted in Palmer, *An Insider's View of Mormon Origins*, 183n22.

Traughber, John Logan, Jr. "Testimony of David Whitmer: Is it True, or False?." *Herald* 26, no. 22 (November 15, 1879): 341.

Tucker, Pomeroy. *Origin, Rise and Progress of Mormonism*. New York: D. Appleton, 1867. See also http://www.solomonspalding.com/docs1/1867tucA.htm. Accessed August 2010.

Turley, Theodore. Memoranda. 5 April 1839. Journal History. LDS Church History Library.

Turner, Jonathan B. *Mormonism in All Ages*. New York: Platt & Peters, 1842.

Unidentified correspondent. Letter to editor. 26 January 1831, *Reflector* (Palmyra, NY) 2, no. 12 (February 1, 1831): [page not known]. Uncle Dale's [Dale Broadhurst] Readings in Early Mormon History. http://www.sidneyrigdon.com/dbroadhu/NY/wayn1830.htm#020131. Accessed October 28, 2007.

US Census. New York. Uncle Dale's [Dale Broadhurst] Readings in Early Mormon History. http://www.sidneyrigdon.com/dbroadhu/NY/wayn1830.htm#020131. Accessed October 28, 2007.

US Census, 1810. New York, Seneca County, Fayette Township.

US Census, 1820. Ohio, Cuyahoga County, Mayfield Township.

US Census, 1830. Ohio, Cuyahoga County, Mayfield Township.

US Census, 1840. Missouri, Caldwell County, Rockport Township. 1840. Missouri, Appanoose County, Chariton Township.

US Census. 1850. Iowa.

US Census. 1850. Missouri, Ray County, Richmond, District 71 and 75.

US Census, 1860. Missouri, Ray County, Grape Grove. Missouri, Caldwell County, Mirabile. Missouri, Ray County, Richmond.

US Census, 1870. Missouri, Ray County, Richmond. Missouri, Caldwell County, Mirabile.

US Census, 1880. Missouri, Ray County, Richmond Township.

"Valuable Manuscript." *Richmond Conservator.* September 13, 1878, 2. Reprinted in Curtis, "A Hometown Perspective on the 1878 Richmond Tornado," 22.

Van Cleave, James R. B. Letter to Joseph Smith III. 29 September 1878. Holograph. Miscellaneous Letters and Papers. P13, f255. CofC Archives.

Van Orden, Bruce A. "William W. Phelps: Scribe to Joseph Smith in Ohio." Ca. 1990. Unpublished typescript. CofC Archives.

———. "Writing to Zion: The W. W. Phelps Kirtland Letters (1835–1836)." *BYU Studies* 33, no. 3 (1993): 572–93.

Van Wagoner, Richard S. *Sidney Rigdon: A Portrait of Religious Excess.* Salt Lake City: Signature Books, 1994.

"Viator" [wayfarer]. "Far West: The Old Mormon Settlement in Missouri, How It Appeared Thirteen Years Ago and What It Is To-day: A Sketch of Its History." *Daily Morning Herald* (St. Joseph, MO), January 1, 1875. Unpaginated clipping in newspapers folder. CofC Archives.

"A Visit to John Whitmer." *Herald* 22, no. 21 (November 1, 1875): 655. Reprinted from *Deseret Evening News* 24, no. 11 (April 14, 1875): 13.

Vogel, Dan. *Early Mormon Documents.* 5 vols. Salt Lake City: Signature Books, 1996–2003.

———. *Religious Seekers and the Advent of Mormonism.* Salt Lake City: Signature Books, 1988.

———. "The Validity of the Witnesses' Testimonies." In *American Apocrypha: Essays on the Book of Mormon.* Edited by Dan Vogel and Brent Lee Metcalfe. Salt Lake City: Signature Books, 2002, 79–121.

Walker, Jeffery N. "Mormon Land Rights in Caldwell and Davies Counties and the Mormon Conflict of 1838: New Findings and Understandings." *BYU Studies* 4, no. 1 (2008): 4–56.

Walker, John Phillip, ed. *Dale Morgan on Early Mormonism: Correspondence and a New History.* Salt Lake City: Signature Books, 1986.

Walters, George. Indenture to John Whitmer. 12 March 1840. MS 6378. Fd. 2, item 5. LDS Church History Library.

Wasson, George J., and Angeline B. Wasson. Indenture to David Whitmer. 1 May 1851. Deed Record Book G, p. 228. Ray County Land Records. Ray County Recorders' Office, Richmond, MO. Also in David Whitmer Papers. P10, f3, item 2. CofC Archives.

Wasson, George J., and Angelina B. Wasson. 1857. David Whitmer Papers. P10, f3, item 25. CofC Archives.

Watson, Elden J., comp. *The Orson Pratt Journals*. Salt Lake City: Elden J. Watson, 1975.

"We Are Pleased to Learn That Miss Josie Schweich." *Richmond Conservator* 22, no. 42 (January 1876): 3. Microfilm, Ray County Library, Richmond, MO.

Webb, Caroline Amelia Owens. "A Short Sketch of Her Life Written by Herself for the Fillmore *Contributor*." Microfilm of typescript. MS 13758. LDS Church History Library.

Webb, Robert C. *The Case Against Mormonism*. New York: L. L. Walton, 1915. Fascimile of Caractors, 22.

Welch, John W., and Larry E. Morris, eds. *Oliver Cowdery: Scribe, Elder, Witness*. Provo, UT: The Neal A. Maxwell Institute for Religious Scholarship, 2006.

West, J. B. Plat of Far West. Attributed to George M. Hinkle. Photograph by Bertha Booth. CofC Archives.

Westergren, Bruce N., ed. *From Historian to Dissident: The Book of John Whitmer*. Salt Lake City: Signature Books, 1995.

Wevodau, Edward N. *Abstracts of Lancaster County, Pennsylvania, Orphans Court Records*. Apollo, PA: Closson Press, 2001.

Whittaker, David J. "Substituted Names in the Published Revelations of Joseph Smith." Table of pseudonyms in the Doctrine and Covenants. *BYU Studies* 23, no. 1 (Winter 1983): 111.

"Whitmer & Son Have Been Adding to Their Livery Stock." *Richmond Conservator* 20, no. 16 (July 19, 1873): 3. Microfilm. Ray County Library, Richmond, MO.

Whitmer Family Bible. 1851–1914. The American Bible Society. Philadelphia, PA: Thomas, Copperthwait, & Co., 1846. MS 18735. LDS Church History Library.

Whitmer, Alexander. July 28, 1862. Enrolled Missouri Militia Record. http://www.sos.mo.gov/archives/soldiers/details.asp?id=S333017&conflict=Civil%20War&txtName=whitmer,%20Alexander&selConflict=All&txtUnit=&rbBranch=all#. Accessed February 1, 2011.

Whitmore [*sic*], Alexander P. "Volunteer Enlistment." Carded Records Showing Military Service of Soldiers Who Fought in Volunteer Organizations [from the State of Missouri] during the American Civil War. Compiled 1890–1912. Documenting the period 1861-1866. 44th Infantry, Record Group 94. National Archives Catalog ID 300398. The National Archives Publication Number M 405. Photocopies of Alexander J. Whitmore [Whitmer]'s

Enrolled Missouri Militia and Federal service records placed in Whitmer History subject folder. CofC Library.

"Whitmer and Son." *Richmond Conservator* 20, no. 43 (January 24, 1874): 3. Microfilm. Ray County Library, Richmond, MO.

Whitmer, David. *An Address to All Believers in Christ: By a Witness to the Divine Authenticity of the Book of Mormon.* Richmond, MO: privately printed, 1887.

———. *An Address to Believers in the Book of Mormon.* Pamphlet. April 1, 1887. Richmond, MO. Vault pamphlets. CofC Archives.

———. Bible. CofC Archives.

———. Indenture from David Ewing. 26 May 1843. Deed Record Book E, p. 79. Ray County Land Records. Ray County Recorders' Office, Richmond, MO.

———. Interview by George Q. Cannon. February 27, 1884. Richmond, MO. George Q. Cannon. Journal. LDS Church History Library. Quoted in Cook, *David Whitmer Interviews: A Restoration Witness*, 107.

———. "David Whitmer Interviewed." *Herald* 28, no. 22 (November 15, 1881): 347. Reprints interview by the *Chicago Times* (October 17 1881). See Cook. *David Whitmer Interviews*, 73–80.

———. "David Whitmer: The Only Living Witness to the Authenticity of the Book of Mormon." *Chicago Times* (August 7, 1875). Reprint *Salt Lake Herald* (August 12, 1875). Cited in Richardson, "David Whitmer," 156–58. Reprint of interview by the *Chicago Times*, October 17, 1881.

———. "David Whitmer, The Only Living Witness." *Kansas City Daily Journal.* June 5, 1881.

———. Interview. *Chicago Tribune.* December 15, 1885. *Chicago Tribune.* December 17, 1885. Reprinted as "David Whitmer: He Describes the Translation," *Deseret News* 34, no. 51 (January 6, 1886): 2. Also reprinted in Cook, *David Whitmer Interviews*, 171–80.

———. Interview by J. W. Chatburn, n.d. "Bro. J. W. Chatburn, of Harlan, Iowa" *Herald* 29, no. 12 (June 15, 1882): 189.

———. Interview by Zenas H. Gurley. January 14, 1885. Typescript. MS 4681. P21, f93. CofC Archives.

———. Interview by James H. Hart. March 18, 1884. "About the Book of Mormon." *Deseret News* 38, no. 12 (April 9, 1884): 14.

———. Interview by William H. Kelley. September 15, 1881. "Letter from Elder W. H. Kelley." *Herald* 29, no. 5 (March 1, 1882): 66–69.

———. Interview by James H. Moyle. June 28, 1885. *Deseret News* [Church Section]. (August 2, 1941). In Cook, *David Whitmer Interviews*, 163.

————. Interview by P. W. Poulson. "Interview with David Whitmer." *Deseret News* 27, no. 29 (August 21, 1878): 13.

————. Interview by Orson Pratt and Joseph F. Smith. September 7–8, 1878. Joseph F. Smith Collection. LDS Church History Library.

————. Interview by Orson Pratt and Joseph F. Smith. "Report of Elders Orson Pratt and Joseph F. Smith." *Millennial Star* 40 (December 9, 1878): 771–74.

————. Interview by Edward Stevenson. Saturday, December 22, 1877.MS 4806. Reel 2. LDS Church History Library.

————. Interview by James H. Hart. August 23, 1883. Seneca, MO. "David H. [*sic*] Whitmer, Etc.," *Deseret News* 32, no. 36 (September 26, 1883): 3. Reprinted in Cook, *David Whitmer Interviews,* 97–98.

————. Interview by Nathan Tanner Jr. April 13, 1886. LDS Church History Library. Reproduced in Cook, *David Whitmer Interviews,* 191.

————. Interview by Correspondent. December 15, 1885. *Chicago Tribune.* (December 17, 1885). Reprinted as "David Whitmer: He Describes the Translation," *Deseret News* 34, no. 51 (January 6, 1886): 2. Also reprinted as "David Whitmer on His Death Bed," *Herald* 33, no. 2 (January 2, 1886): 12–13.

————. Letter to Oliver Cowdery. 8 September 1847. Far West, MO. In "Important Letters." *The Ensign of Liberty* 1, no. 6 (May 1848): 93.

————. Letter to Dear Brethren. 9 December 1886. In "Letters from David and John C. Whitmer." *Herald* 34, no. 6 (February 5, 1887): 89, 90.

————. Letter to *Kansas City Journal.* Corrections to June 1, 1881 interview. *Kansas City Journal* (June 19, 1881). Reprinted in Cook, *David Whitmer Interviews,* 71–72.

————. Letter to S. T. Mouch. 18 November 1882. Whitmer Papers. P10, f10. CofC Archives.

————. Letter to J. B. Price. 9 July 1882. Biographical collection. P21, f93. CofC Archives.

————. Livery Business Record. Richmond, MO. June 13, 1846–February 5, 1849. Whitmer Papers. P10, vol. 1. CofC Archives.

————. "Mormonism: Authentic Account of the Origin of This Sect from One of the Patriarchs, Discovery of the Plates, and the Translation of the Book of Mormon" (interview). *Herald* 28, no. 3 (July 1, 1881): 197–99. Reprinted in *Kansas City Journal,* June 5, 1881.

————. "Report of Elders Orson Pratt and Joseph F. Smith." September 7–8, 1878. Richmond, MO. *Deseret News* 27, no. 43 (November 16, 1878): 2.

———. A Revelation. Received at Far West, Caldwell County, MO. July 26, 1861. Quoted in Pollard and Woods, *Whitmer Memoirs*, 30–33.

———. Tax receipts. David Whitmer's annual receipts. 1850–1890. Holograph. Whitmer Papers. P10. CofC Archives.

———. P. Letter to My Dear Cousins. 22 July 1881. Richmond, MO. Holograph. MS 6378. Fd. 1, item 8. LDS Church History Library.

Whitmer David, and Julia. Indenture to Dr. Charles Johnson. 31 January 1855. Item 21. CofC Archives.

Whitmer, Jacob D. Family Record. Original in the possession of Gerd Buntkin, Independence, MO. Photocopy in my possession. Photocopy in Whitmer Family Papers. P1, f19. CofC Archives.

———. "Jacob D. Whitmer." In *History of Caldwell and Livingston Counties, Missouri: as quoted in Richmond Conservator* 25, no. 18 (July 28, 1878): 2. Microfilm. Ray County Library, Richmond, MO.

Whitmer, John. "Address." *Messenger and Advocate* 2, no. 6 (March 1836): 285–88. See also Whitmer Family Papers. P10, f19. CofC Archives.

———. Account Book. January 5, 1832–November 20, 1832. Holograph. MS 1159. LDS Church History Library.

———. Blessing. 22 September 1835, recorded 2 October 1835, in Oliver Cowdery's handwriting. Patriarchal Blessing Book 1, p. 14. LDS Church History Library.

———. The Book of John Whitmer. 1831–1844. Holograph. CofC Archives.

———. Certificate of Enrollment. 23 October 1862. Holograph. MS 6378.Fd. 6, item 7. LDS Church History Library.

———. John Whitmer's copy of the 1835 Doctrine and Covenants. MOR M223 W 59. Perry Special Collections.

———. Elder's License. June 9, 1830. Original in Western Americana. Beinecke Rare Book and Manuscript Library, Yale University, New Haven, CT. Photostatic copy, Whitmer Papers. P10, f1. CofC Archives.

———. Exemption from Service Certificate. 1864. Holograph. MS 7062.Fd. 6, item 10. LDS Church History Library.

———. Family Bible. *The Holy Bible Containing the Old and New Testaments, Translated Out of the Original Tongues and with the Former Translation Diligently Compared and Revised.* Stereotyped by L. Johnson, Philadelphia. Philadelphia, PA: Towar, J. & D. Hogan; and Hogan & Co. Pittsburgh, PA: C. Sherman & Co. Printers, 1830. MS 13505. LDS Church History Library.

———. Indenture to Burr Riggs. 13 August 1838. Holograph. John Whitmer Papers. MS 6378. Fd. 2, item 3. LDS Church History Library.

———. Interview by Myron Bond. See Myron Bond. Letter to Henry Stebbins, 2 August 1878. Cadillac, MI. *Herald* 25, no. 16 (August 15, 1878): 253.

———. Letter to Oliver Cowdery and Joseph Smith. 29 July 1833. Joseph Smith Collection. LDS Church History Library.

———. Letter to M[ark H]. Forest [Forscutt]. 5 March 1876. Holograph. Whitmer Papers. P10, f9. CofC Archives.

———. Letter to Edward Partridge. 20 March 1840. Far West, MO. MS 6378. Fd. 1, item 1. LDS Church History Library.

———. Obituary. *Kingston Sentinel.* Quoted in *Richmond Conservator*, July 26, 1878.

———. Land Patents. September 7, 1838. Holograph. MSS SC 245. Perry Special Collections.

———. Letter to Dear Children [Sarah Elizabeth and James Johnson]. 1 March 1871. Holograph. MSS 1221. Perry Special Collections.

———. Letter to Oliver Cowdery. 29 July 1832. In Joseph Smith Papers. LDS Church History Library.

———. Letter to Oliver Cowdery and David Whitmer. 29 August 1837. Far West, MO. Postmarked September 3, 1837. McQuown Collection. Holograph/typescript. MS 143. Box 42, fd. 53. Marriott Library.

———. Letter to Heman C. Smith. 11 December 1876. Artificial Collection. P31, f8. CofC Archives.

———. License to the office of elder. June 9, 1830. Photocopy. P10, f1. CofC Archives.

———. Quoted in Gurley. "Synopsis of a Discourse," 369–71.

———. "To the Patrons of the Latter Day Saints' Messenger and Advocate." *Messenger and Advocate* 1, no. 9 (June 1835): 135–37.

———. John Whitmer Papers. MS 6378. Fd. 4. LDS Church History Library.

———. Patriarchal Blessing. Given by Joseph Smith Jr. September 22, 1835. Patriarchal Blessing Book 1. LDS Church History Library.

———. Personal Property Assessment List. Caldwell County, MO. 1875. Holograph. MS 1159. LDS Church History Library.

———. Receipt to William Jones. Administrator of the estate of Edward Partridge. December 8, 1846. MS 6378. Fd. 2, item 6. LDS Church History Library.

———. Receipts. October 6, 1841, March 4, 1843. MS 7062. Fd. 5, items 5, 6. LDS Church History Library.

Whitmer, John, and Joseph Smith Jr. Certificate of Ordination to William Smith, to Office of Teacher. October 5, 1831. Original. Miscellaneous Letters and Papers. P13, f4. CofC Archives.

Whitmer, John C. "Sayings of John C. Whitmer." *Herald* 35, no. 41 (October 13, 1888): 651.

———. "John C. Whitmer Dead." *Herald* 41, no. 37 (September 12, 1894): 582.

Whitmer, Peter. http://en.wikipedia.org/wiki/Peter_Whitmer%2C_Sr. Accessed September 15, 2007.

Whitmer, Peter [Sr.], and Mary. Indenture to Michael Collins. 31 January 1839. Deed Record Book F, 250. Jackson County Land Records. Jackson County Recorder's Office, Independence, MO.

Whitmer, Peter Jr. Journal. 13 December 1831. Holograph. MS 5873. LDS Church History Library.

Whitmer History. Subject folder. CofC Archives. MS 5873. LDS Church History Library.

Whitney, Elizabeth Ann L. Smith. "Leaf from an Autobiography." *Woman's Exponent* 7 (August 1878–February 1897): 33, 41, 51, 71, 83, 91, 105, 191.

Whitsitt, William. *Sidney Rigdon: The Real Founder of Mormonism*, 1885, unpublished manuscript. MS AC1158. Library of Congress. At SidneyRigdon. com. http://www.sidneyrigdon.com/wht/1891WhE1.htm#pg149. Accessed November 3, 2007.

Widmer, Ulrich. http://midatlantic.rootsweb.com/database/d0124/g0000066. htm#I270949. Accessed February 3, 2007.

Wight, Lyman. Journal. No longer extant. Quoted in *History of the RLDS Church*, 1:153.

Wight, Jermy Benton. *The Wild Ram of the Mountain: The Story of Lyman Wight*. Afton, WY: Thrifty Print, 1997.

Wight, Lyman. Letter written from Medina River [TX] to *Northern Islander*. July 1855. Lyman Wight Letterbook. Holograph. P13, f79, pp. 21–26. CofC Archives.

———. "Testimony of Lyman Wight." In *History of the LDS Church*, 3:441.

Wight, Orange L. "Recollections of Orange L. Wight." 1903. Typescript, not paginated. http://www.boap.org/LDS/Early-Saints/OWight.html. Accessed November 30, 2007.

Wilcox, Pearl G. "Early Independence in Retrospect, Part 8." *Herald* 106, no. 8 (February 23, 1959): 178–79.

———. *The Latter Day Saints on the Missouri Frontier.* Independence, MO: privately printed, 1972.

———. "The Saints in Northwest Missouri, Part 3" *Herald* 107, no. 42 (October 17, 1960): 1008–Part 4, 107, no. 46 (November 14, 1960): 1004–6.

———. *Saints of the Reorganization in Missouri.* Independence, MO: privately printed, 1974.

Willers, Diedrich [Jr.]. "Pennsylvania German Settlers Fayette." *Centennial Historical Sketch of the Town of Fayette, Seneca County, New York, 1800–1900,* Geneva, New York: Press of W. F. Humphrey, 1900.

Williams Brothers. *History of Geauga and Lake Counties.* Philadelphia, Pa.: Albert Gallatin Riddle, 1878.

Williams, Frederick Granger. Letter to Dear Brethren. 10 October 1833. Reprinted in *LDS History of the Church,* 1:416.

Williams, James. *Seventy-Five Years on the Border.* Kansas City, MO: Press of Standard Printing Co., 1912.

Williams, Nancy Clement. *After One Hundred Years: Meet Dr. Frederick Granger Williams.* Independence, MO: Zion's Printing and Publishing Company, 1951.

Willis/Willes, Ira J. "The Names of the Colesville Church." May 20, 1862. Holograph. MS 2014. LDS Church History Library.

Wilson, Andrew. Letter. Quoted in Max H. Parkin, "History of the Latter-day Saints in Clay County," 255.

Winget, Catherine Hulet. "A Life Sketch of Catherine Hulet Winget." Hulet History/1960. Cited in Johnson, "The Life History of Charles Hulet and His Wives," 68.

Winn, Kenneth H. "'Such Republicanism as This': John Corrill's Rejection of Prophetic Rule." In Roger D. Launius and Linda Thatcher. *Differing Visions: Dissenters in Mormon History.* Urbana: University of Illinois Press, 1994, 45–75.

Witmer, Christian. Will. Dated February 14, 1776. Probated February 7, 1777. Lancaster County Wills. Lancaster County Archives, Lancaster, PA.

Witmer, Johannes. http://midatlantic.rootsweb.com/database/d0123/g0000066.htm#I270948. Accessed February 3, 2007.

Wittmer, Peter. http://worldconnect.rootsweb.com/cgi-bin/igm.cgi?op=GET&db=lacor&id=I153559. Accessed September 10, 2007.

————. Will. Dated November 20, 1784. F–370. Wills, Lancaster County Archives, Lancaster County, PA.

Woodruff, Wilford. *Wilford Woodruff's Journal.* Edited by Scott G. Kenney. 9 vols. December 1833–September 1898. Midvale, UT: Signature Books, 1983.

Woodward, Charles L., comp. Scrapbook. New York Public Library.

Woodward, George and Nancy. Indenture to Jacob Whitmer. 30 August 1843.

Woodward, George David P. Whitmer, indenture to Jacob Whitmer, 21 October 1853, p. 4.

Woldconnect.genealogy.rootsweb.com. http://worldconnect.genealogy.rootsweb. com/cgi-bin/igm.cgi?op=AHN&db=glory43&id=I1893. Accessed September 10, 2007.

Woolley, Edwin Gordon. Autobiography. 1845–98. Quoted in Cook, *David Whitmer Interviews*, 80-81.

Young, Emily Dow Partridge. "Autobiography." *Woman's Exponent* 13, no. 14 (December 15, 1884): 105–6.

Young, Joseph Sr. Levi Edgar Young Papers. Typescript. MSS B 12. Box 8, f5. Utah State Historical Society.

Youngreen, Buddy. "And Yet Another Copy of the Anthon Manuscript." *BYU Studies* 20, no. 4 (Spring 1980): 346–47.

Zehr, Ruby Friesen *Sing the Journey! Hymnal: A Worship Book Supplement 1.* Waterloo, Ontario: Faith and Life Resources, 2005.

Zimmer, John, Andrew Jackson Zimmer, and Eliza Jackson Zimmer. Letter to Sarah and John Whitmer. 2 May 1849. Centerville, IA. MSS 1214. Perry Special Collections.

Note: Names of individuals precede those of places/businesses. Illustrations in boldface.

A

Aaron's breastplate, 32

"Adam-ondi-Ahman" (hymn), 262, 383

Adam-ondi-Ahman, MO, 364, 552

Adams, Thomas, 88

Addams, R. Jean, xviii, 442n22

Address to All Believers in Christ, An (1887),
 417, 419, 486

*Address to Believers in the Book of Mormon,
 An*, **417**, 419

alcohol, in washings and anointings, 278–79

Aldrich, Isaac N., 419

Aldridge (of Kirtland), 275

Alger, Fanny, 345, 346n28

Allen (non-Mormon in Missouri), 207–8

Allen, Charles, 213, 217

Allen, Elizabeth I., 558

Allen, Harvey, 213–14

almanac, 165–66, 166n24

American Indians. *See* Lamanites.

Amish, 2

Anabaptist background of Whitmers, 33

Anderson, George Edward, xvii, 304, 423,
 484

Anderson, John, 333

Anderson, Lavina Fielding, xviii

Anderson, Paul L., xvii

Anderson, Richard Lloyd, xvii

Anderson, Rodger I., 27

angel

 appears to Hiram Page, 57

 helps with David Whitmer's farm
  work, 30

 shows plates to the Three Witnesses,
  52

 speaks to David Whitmer, 32

Anthon, Charles, 491–42

anti-Masonry, 551

apostolic calling, 61–62

army, to retake Missouri lands (1834),
 267–68, 274. *See also* Joseph Smith,
 militarism, Mormon War, *and*
 Danites.

Arrington, Leonard, 105

Arthur, Michael, 239, 243,

 John Whitmer lives with, 244, 250, 276

 Lyman Wight builds house for, 246

 on high council, 244, 245n76

 purchases property, 382

*Articles, Covenants, and Law of the Church
 of Christ*, 154

Articles of Working Harmony, 512n17

Ashurst-McGee, Mark, 496

Atchison, David R., 298, 547

Auditorium, RLDS, historical materials
 in, 514

Austin, Emily, 194, 294, 299

authority. *See also* Church of Christ.

 challenges to, 103–4, 108–10, 162

 developments in, 106n13, 115, 161

Avard, Sampson, 284n54, 307, 350, 373

Avery, Valeen Tippetts, xvii, 21, 51

B

Backman, Milton, 358

Baldwin (Missourian), 233, 294

Baldwin, Caleb, 233, 373, 549

baptism. *See also individuals.*
  and Book of Mormon, 23
  for the dead, 580–82

Barchers, Harold, as family historian, xiiin6, xvii–xviii, 1, 5n22, 13n52, **500**

Barchers, Kay, xvii

Barchers, Lillian Merle Koontz, 59n37, **500**

Barlow, Philip L., xvii

Barney, Ronald O., xvi

Barr, John, 88n17

Barrows, Ethan, 305

Barton, William, 383n20

Bates, Alex, 576

bathing, attitudes toward, 279n29

Baubie, A. T., 450, 539

Bauder, Peter, 85

Baugh, Alexander L., xvii, xii, 505n31

Baughman, Barbara Ebersohl Witmer, 4, 6

Baughman, John, 4, 6

Beadle, John H., 209, 459, 595

Beardsley, O. R., 587

Beebe, Calvin, 244, 306, 327

Beebe, George, 230

Beliefs and Superstitions of the Pennsylvania Germans, 58

Benjamin, William Evarts, 491, 491n5, 493–94, 590

Bennett, John C., 27

Bent, Samuel, 333n26

Berge, Dale, 11

Bernard, Lewis, 310n80

Bernauer, Barbara, xvii

Bible. *See* New Translation.

Bidamon, Emma Hale Smith. *See* Smith, Emma Hale.

Big Blue, battle of, 235

Big Blue River/Valley, 187–99

Big Blue settlement (Missouri), 174–75

Big Fan. *See* Danites.

Billings, Titus, 105

Bird, Charles, 379n5

Bisbee, Iram Packard, 471

Bisbee, Mariann Whitmer, 471

bishop, office of, 105–6

Black, Joseph S., 458, 488

Black Pete, 95

Black, Susan Easton, xvii

blacks. *See* slaves.

blacksmiths, at Far West, 307

Blair, Alma R., xvii

Blair, William W., 40

blanket. *See* Book of Mormon, translated.

Blankmeyer family, and David Whitmer's trunk, 468n11, 503

Blankmeyer, Charles Harrison, 503n27

Blankmeyer, Helen Farwell Van Cleve, xviii, 497
  angel helps David Whitmer with farm work, 30
  describes Elizabeth Ann Whitmer Cowdery, 16
  donates trunk to RLDS Church, 503
  on Juliann [*sic*] Jolly Whitmer, 99
  on seer stones, 38n12
  relation to David Whitmer, 503n27

Bloomington Branch, 442n22

Blue River Branch, 188

Blue River, ferry at, 232

Bogart, Samuel, 576

Boggs, Lilburn W., 217n42, 367, 547, 550

Bolt, Darrell, 500

Bolton, John, 577

Bond, Myron, 36, 37n6, 61n46

Bonny, Alfred, 419

Book of Abraham, 269

Book of Commandments and Revelations, **223**

    and Doctrine and Covenants, 257, 261–62

    as scripture, 143

    described, 145n26

    discovery of printer's manuscript (2008), 145

    in Nauvoo, 355n53

    mixed reception of, 172

    mss in John Whitmer's possession, 251, 355n53, 507

    preserved when print shop destroyed, 212

    publication planned, 142, 161, 165, 199

    revisions to, 146, 177

    John Whitmer's copy of, xvii

Book of Ether plates, 52–53

"Book of John Whitmer, The"

    as work of faith, 593

    described, 263, 507–10

    in Community of Christ archives, xv, 501

    in John Whitmer's possession, 355n53

    microfilm exchanged with LDS Church History Department, 515

    on Sidney Rigdon, 508

    on James J. Strang, 508

    on Brigham Young, 508

    post-1838 entries, 508

    RLDS Church acquires, 494–95, 511–13

    Bruce Westergren edition of, xiv

    Jacob D. Whitmer refuses LDS efforts to acquire, 508

    John Whitmer's work on, 144

    writing history of, xiii, xiv

Book of Mormon

    antipolygamy passage, 491

    as social protest, 51

    "caractors," 425; in John Whitmer's possession, 507; published reproductions, 595–96; RLDS Church acquires, 494–95, 511

    hat, and Book of Mormon translation, 31, 45–46, 47n39

    influence on Joseph Smith, 106

    manuscript, security of, 62

    William McLellin summarizes, 131

    plates rumored to be in bank vault, 490

    printer's copy: conservation of, 515; RLDS acquires, 494–95, 511–12; to George Schweich, 490; to David Whitmer, 424; David Whitmer refuses sell or give it to LDS Church, 468–70

    public reaction to, 119

    published and mss versions compared, 480–82

    read aloud to Whitmer family, 50

    second edition, 166

    seer stone in hat, 31

    translated behind blanket/curtain, 36, 46, 56; in Whitmer home, 25, 35–47

    John Whitmer describes, 526–27

    Whitmerite edition, 493

Book of Mormon manuscript

    in Oliver Cowdery's possession, 355n53

    preserved during tornado, 465–68

Book of Mormon witnesses, 16, 384. *See also individuals.*
  alienated, xi–xii
  given "inheritances" in Missouri, 202
  testimonies of, 285
Booth, Bertha Ellis, 307, 435
Booth, Ezra
  and Johnson family, 112
  and Edward Partridge's financial difficulties, 156
  describes Independence, 153
  disaffected, 82, 137, 151, 157, 263, 593
  excommunicated, 134–35
  mission to Missouri, 130
  on Copley property, 118
  on Oliver Cowdery and Ziba Peterson's impropriety, 163
  on Hiram Page, 79
Boulton (of Far West), 544
Boyce (of Far West), 387
Boynton, John, 303, 343, 349
Bozarth, William T., 374, 545, 582
Brace, Ruby, 312
Bragg, Miles, 396, 560
Bragg, Volney, 396, 560
Branch (of Far West), 395, 560
Brand, Edmund C., 458, 507, 588
Brannan, Samuel, 369
brass plates, vision of, 52
Brazeal (in Missouri), 233
Brechbill, Anna, 3
Brewsterites, William McLellin denounces, 537
Briggs, Jason, 430
Brindle, Mark, 381
Broadbuck, Joseph, 247
Brodie, Fawn, 497

Brooke, John L., 60
Broom County, and Joseph Smith, 72, 77
Brother of Gideon. *See* Danites.
Brown, Albert, 269
Brown, Lorenzo, 72n31
Brown, William, 215–16n36
Brubaker, Hans, 3
Brubaker, Jacob, 3
Brunson, Seymour, 93, 151–52
Budick, Constance E. Johnson, 503, 503n25
Bullock, Thomas, 595
Bunnell, David Edwin, 17n69
Bunnell, Sally Heller Conrad, 17n69
Burch, Celenary, 400n14
Burch, Thomas C., 400n14
Burdick, Betty A., 505n31
Burdick, John E., 505n31
Burgess, Samuel A., 497, 513–14
Burk, John M., 358, 370
Burk Settlement, 250
Burned-Over District, The, 30
Burnes, Calvin F., 541
Burnett, Irenus/Serenus, 139
Burnett, Peter, 391
Burroughs, Philip, 80, 83n64
Burwell, H. W., 220n52
Bushman, Richard Lyman, xvii, 274, 291
Butler, John L., 364n2
Buttgen, Gerd W., 441

C

Cahoon, Reynolds
  fund-raising (1831), 139–40
  in Kirtland, 134
  in Missouri, 132–33, 147
Caldwell County, map, **300**

description of, 301; (1862–63), 440–41

established, 297

Mormons in, 290, 292–308, 542

Calif, Jemima Lindsey, 236

Call, Anson, 378

Camel, James, 210n9

Campbell, Alexander, 104

Campbell, James, 215–16n36

Campbellism

and Sidney Rigdon, 89n29, 92

bishops in, 106

Cannon, Donald Q., xvii, 435

"caractors." *See* Book of Mormon.

Carroll, John, 545

Carter family, meeting at home, 336

Carter, Jared, 132–33, 254–55, 260, 309

Carter, John S., 259

Carter, Simeon

fund-raises for Joseph Smith, 140

leather store of, 306

mission to Missouri, 133–34

on Far West High Council, 244, 327

on Kirtland apostasy, 135

payment for church officers, 330

tongues in Missouri, 190n30

Case against Mormonism, The, 596

Cavanaugh (at Far West), 382n18

cave, vision of, filled with records, artifacts, 496

Chamberlain, Oran, 83n64

Chandler, Allen, 215–16n36

Chapman, George, 17

Chardon, OH, 93

charisma. *See* Joseph Smith.

Chase, Darwin, 383n20

Chatburn, J. W., 54

Chicago Times, 509

children and youth education curriculum, 166

Childs, Joel F., 210n9

Chiles, Henry, 215–16n36

Chiles, John F., 215–16n36

cholera, and Zion's Camp, 242

Chouteau, Francois, 293

Christ's Church (Reformed German and German-speaking), 13–14

Christensen, Steven F., 59n37

Church of Christ/of Latter Day Saints (Joseph Smithism)

administrative developments, 102–3, 141

business ventures, 148

date of organization, 66n2

lists of founders/members, 65–66nn1–2

location of organizational meeting, 65–66n2

organization of, 65–83

publications, 164. *See also* Literary Firm.

records of, Oliver Cowdery's to Whitmers, 424–25

store, funding of, 161

theology, 107

Church of Christ, 470, 470n18. *See also* David Whitmer.

competition for RLDS, 480

location of members, 480

meetings of, 471, 480, 493

membership (1880), 480, 486

publishes Book of Mormon, 493

Church of Christ, Temple Lot, 442n22, 512n17

title to property, 460

typescript of John Whitmer history at, 501

Church of Jesus Christ of Latter Day Saints. *See* RLDS Church.

Clark, Hiram, 382, 383n20

Clark, John B., 375, 547

Clark, John W. 370–71, 383n20

Clark, William C., 383n20

Clark, Wycom, 109

Clay County, MO
 citizens press Mormons to move, 289, 292, 294–96
 Mormons in, 237–38, 289

Cleminson/Clemminson, John
 as county clerk, 544
 to/from Far West, 384, 545
 peace efforts of, 367, 367n10
 testifies for state, 373

Cleveland, Henry Alanson, 232–34

Cockrell, James, 215–16n36

code names, 120, 148n35

Coe, Joseph, 130, 134, 259

coffee, and Word of Wisdom, 197

Cole, Abner, 63

Colesville Branch
 confirmations in, 75, 78–79
 consecration efforts, 118–19, 128–30, 141, 174–75, 188, 232
 established, 71–72
 in Missouri, 180
 letter to, 89
 ordinations in, 266
 Joseph Smith in, 96

Collier, Fred, xviii

Coltrin, Zebedee, 154

common consent, 76, 82

communitarianism in Ohio, 92–94. *See also* Copley *and* "the Family."

Community of Christ. *See also* RLDS Church.
 archives: Book of Commandments, xvi; Book of Mormon "caractors," 596; New Translation, xvi; seer stones, 59; John Whitmer documents in, xvi–xvi;
 chapel, in Far West, 304, 306
 Independence Temple, 514

Compton, Todd M., xvii

Comstock (Missouri militia), 548

conferences
 June 1830, 71
 September 1830, 75, 78n49, 81–83
 January 1831, 90
 June 1831, 124
 August 1831, 132–33
 October 1831, 139–40
 November 1831, 145, 147
 January 1832, 153–54, 156, 162

Conor, William, 215–16n36

Conrad, Sarah, 16, 35

consecration. *See also* Colesville Branch.
 and church printing press, 147–48
 concept of, 105–7
 conflict over, 152, 167, 203, 329
 designed to fund Joseph Smith, 108
 in Jackson County, 177–78, 183, 192–94, 202
 in Ohio, 180, 201
 reinstituted in Far West, 359–60

Cook, John, 215–16n36

Cook, Lyndon, xvii, 19, 435
 on Sidney Rigdon, 176
 on United Firm, 164. *See also* Literary Firm.

on John Whitmer's baptism, 48

Cooper, Rex, 107

Cope, Nathan, 548, 552

Copley, Leman/Lemon, 118–19, 126, 128–30

cordwainer (shoemaker), 2n6

Corkins, Lucy, 218–19

Cornet, John, 215–16n36

Corrill, Isaac, 299

Corrill, John

  accuses dissenters, 335

  and School of Elders, 270

  and United Firm committee, 163n9

  as church historian, 343

  disaffected, 376

  in Independence, 188, 198, 210

  land in Caldwell County, 290, 292, 294, 297–98, 297n22

  land in Daviess County, 327

  on debts in Kirtland, 340

  on Joseph Smith's revelations, 115–16

  on spiritual excesses, 94–95, 117, 125

  on violence, 176, 221, 233, 274, 320

  ordained elder, 106

  peace efforts of, 367, 369

  second counselor to Edward Partridge, 180

  store in Far West, 306

  testifies for state, 373

council of seven high priests (Missouri), 196, 198

Cowdery, Adeline Fuller, 381

Cowdery, Elizabeth Ann (dau. of Oliver Cowdery), 381

Cowdery, Elizabeth Ann Whitmer, **190**

  at Oliver's death, 422

  baptized, 69

  biography, 6, 9, 35, 573, 575

chores caused by visitors, 26, 45

in Ohio, 136, 248, 381, 407

lives with Whitmers in Missouri, 184, 222, 226, 321, 361, 424, 442

marries, 16–17, 191

not rebaptized LDS, 415

on angel's aid with David Whitmer's farm work, 30

on Book of Mormon translation, 41, 45–46

portrait of, 283, 503n26, 572

RLDS Church acquires documents from, 503

Cowdery, Josephine Rebecca, 381

Cowdery, Julia Olive, 381

Cowdery, Lyman, 378, 415n38

Cowdery, Maria Louise (dau. of Oliver Cowdery). *See* Johnson, Maria Louise Cowdery.

Cowdery, Oliver Hervy Pliny, 16, 142, **190**

  In New York/Pennsylvania period:

  as founding church member, 65–66nn1–2, 67

  as scribe, 21–23, 25, 36, 39n12, 40–41, 42n24, 46–47, 80, 139

  baptisms by, 72

  baptism of, 103

  buys Phinney edition of KJV Bible, 72

  compensation (1831), 149

  in Harmony, PA, 71–72

  makes printer's copy, Book of Mormon manuscript, 63–64

  meets Joseph Smith, 20, 31

  one of Three Witnesses, 48, 51

  possible courtship in Ohio, 88

  role "as Aaron," 81

  seer stone, 425

  sees angels, 87

testimony of Book of Mormon, 219–20, 460, 475

In Ohio period: 87, 136, 225–26, 228, 381, 407

and Book of Commandments, 146n29, 165, 199–200

and Doctrine and Covenants, 256

and Kirtland High Council, 260

and Literary Firm, 165

and United Firm, 164, 163n9

as historian, 67, 122

as Lamanite missionary, 83n65, 84, 127

blesses children, 236

challenges wording of revelation, 75–76

commanded to correct Hiram Page, 80–81

commanded to take revelations to Missouri, 149

defends Joseph Smith, 275

family of, 571

health blessings by, 281

instructs John Whitmer in recording children's blessings, 170n40, 170

Kirtland Temple dedication, 282

ordained elder, 48

marries, 191

on Fanny Alger, 345–46

on canonizing Doctrine and Covenants, 264–65

on Egyptian papyri, 270

on presiding bishop committee, 163

on John Whitmer, 257

ordained, 49

ordains William McLellin, 140

never consecrated property, 167

patriarchal blessings, 266, 329

performs baptisms, 48, 69

performs marriage, 186

reports Independence expulsion to Joseph Smith, 222, 224

to Salem, MA, to seek funds, 298

Joseph Smith blesses, 267

In Missouri period: 132, 134

accusations against, 163, 333–34, 353n48, 355, 378

advises Mormon move to Caldwell County, 297

and press, 148, 170, 226, 318

and war department, 274

at Far West, 306, 320–21, 353, 545

edits *Messenger and Advocate*, 285, 292, 317

edits *Northern Times*, 250

in Caldwell County, 290

in Daviess County, 327

inheritance in Zion, 259

instructions to Missouri Saints, 266

leader in Missouri, 196, 198, 210, 219, 221

lives with Whitmers, 35, 321, 415–16

partner in George Hinkle's store, 323

prophecies of, 238

speaks in tongues, 189

Disaffection of:

accusations against, 336, 349

alienated by Joseph Smith's theo-politics, 27, 314–15, 319–20, 345–48, 347n32

court and excommunication, 163, 323n34, 334, 344, 388

Danites threaten, 352

letters to brothers, 346–47

records in possession of, 63–64, 355n53

sheltered by McLellins, 355–57

Post-Mormon period:

attorney, 323, 381, 415n38, 416, 416n42;
law office of, **381**

called as counselor in Whitmerite
church, 409

gives Book of Mormon printer's copy,
etc., to David Whitmer, 485, 590

in Richmond, MO, 361

on hostility in Nauvoo, 205

William McLellin on, 528

portrait of, 283, 283n53, 503, 503n26, 572

reconciles with LDS Church/
rebaptized, 414–15, 418

John Whitmer praises, 520

Death of: 422

grave in Richmond, 427, **484**, 488

scarf belonging to, 485

Cowdery, Oliver Peter Jr., 381

Cowdery, William, 283n53, 503n26

Craig, Oliver, 375

Crandall, Daniel, 189, 189n28

Crandall, John, 189n28

Crandall, Lewis, xvii

Crandall, Patrick, 189n28

Crandall, Sally/Sarah, 189

Crandall, Simeon, 189n28

Crandall, Thomas, 189n28

Crandall Historical Printing Museum, xvii

Cravin (RLDS member), 588

Crawley, Peter, 344

Crooked River, battle at, 366, 392, 547

Cross, Whitney, 30

Crow Creek Branch, 442n22

Crowley, Helen Schweich, 496n14

culture of honor, 274

Culver, Aaron, 72

Culver, Ester Peck, 72

Cummins, Robert, 215–16n36

Cumorah, Nephite takes plates to, 31;
vision of plates/artifacts inside
hill, 31, 53

Cumorah Revisited, and Book of Mormon
"caractors," 596

curses, on Jackson County enemies, 282–83

curtain. *See* Book of Mormon, translated.

Curtis, Annette, xviii

Curtis, William, xviii

Curtis, Nahum, 336

Cutler, Alpheus, 383n20

cyclone. *See* tornado.

D

Dales Boarding House, 481

Daley, John, 545

Damon, Bonnie Page, xvii

Danewood, John W., 215–16n36

Daniels, Solomon, 239

Danites

activities of, 363–64, 546

allegedly sent to kill David Whitmer,
485

and dissidents, 352, 355–57

first publication of "Book of John
Whitmer" omits chapter on, 498

William McLellin denounces, 536

organized, 350

raids by, 365

David Whitmer on, 329

Dartmouth College, and Indians, 84

Daughters of Zion. *See* Danites.

Daviess County, MO, 364, 327

Davis (of Independence), 215

Davis, John, 215–16n36

Davis, Joseph C., 215–16n36

Davis, Joshua, 451

Davis, Richard W., 2, 8

Dawson, Ann Jane, 577

Dawson, James, 577

Dawson, John, 393n1

Dawson, Mary, 577

Dawson, Sarah, 577

Dawson, William, 382n18, 393n1

De Pillis, Mario S., xviii

Dear, Cleora, xviii

Dear, Izora Beulah Whitmer, 465, 486

DeHawn, William N., 426, 436

Delano Branch, 582

Deming, Arthur Buel, 477–78, 585–86

Deming, Miner R., 477

DeMint, Gladys Evelyn Koontz, 59n37

Democratic Party, 257

Derr, Jill Mulvay, xvii

Deseret Alphabet, 434

Deseret Theological Institute, 433–34

Deshler, John, 101n66

DeWitt, MO, Mormons in, 364n5

Dibble, Philo, 166n23

    in Far West, 230, 545

    property of, 93n42

    wounded, 233–34

Dillon, Samuel, 434

dissenters, in Missouri, 201. *See also* Oliver Cowdery, David Whitmer, John Whitmer, *and* W. W. Phelps.

    character of, 358

    marginalization of, xii

    threatened, 340–58

divining stones. *See* seer stones.

Doak, Walter A., 397, 578

Doctrine and Covenants

    copies to John Whitmer as payment, 285

printed, 256, 261–62, 264, 273

Document Containing the Correspondence, Orders, & in Relation to the Disturbances with the Mormons, **372**

Dombsby/Orsby/Wamsley/Walmsley (of Far West), 543, 576, 578

Donegal Township, Lancaster County, PA, 2–3, 7

Doniphan, Alexander W.

    attorney for Mormons, 250, 298

    helps establish Caldwell County, 297n22

    in militia, 547–58

Doniphan, Atchison, Rees, and Wood (law firm), 225

Duffin, Sharalyn, 515

Duncan, Chapman, 211, 213

    biography, 319n13

    arrested, 370

    John Whitmer's employee, 319

Duncan, Rebecca Rose, 319n13

Dunklin, David, Mormons petition, 225

Dyer, Alvin R., 498

E

Eagle Creek Branch, 442n22

Eakin, Joanne Chiles, 213n25

Earl, James, 307

early church documents/artifacts. *See* RLDS Church.

Early Mormon Documents, xx, xviii

Ebersohl, Abraham, 4

Ebersohl, Barbara Detweiler, 4

Edmonds, Joel, 379

Edmund Durfee Settlement, 336

Edwards, John, 294

Edwards, Paul M., xvii

Edwards, W., 323

Eggleston, Ester, 312

Egyptian mummies, 269

Eight Witnesses, selection of, 55–58

"Elect Lady." *See* Smith, Emma.

elder, office of, 106n13

Elders' Journal, 318, 344

Elledge, Tarlton, 215–16n36

endowment, for missionaries (1831), 113–14, 117, 124–26

Engle, Catharina Brechbill, 3

Engle, Jacob, 4

Engle, Ulrich, 3

English, Charles, 252

English, Lydia Whiting, 252

Enrolled Missouri Militia, 439, 441

Ensign of Liberty, 412

Epperson, Steve, 27

Esplin, Ronald K., xvii

Evans (Missouri militia), 548

Evans, R. C., 513

Evening and the Morning Star. See also print shop.

    among John Whitmer papers, 513

    established, 132

    furniture given to another press, 211n20

    in Kirtland, 226

    paper for, 155, 161

    prospectus of, 147n33, 154–55

    publication of, 166

    westernmost newspaper, 169

Ewing, David, 400

Extermination Order, 367

F

F. G. Williams & Co., 256, 258, 281, 285

Fallis, Isaac, 152

Falls (captain), 482–43

"the Family," communal experience in Ohio, 104–5; Joseph Smith's adaptation of, 108. *See also* consecration.

Far West (newspaper), 293

Far West, MO, map, **302**

    conference at, 349

    descriptions of: (1839), 385–86; (1842), 395–96; (1862–63), 440–41; (1875), 450–51, 538–43; (1882), 477, 576–79; (1911), 560–62

    dismantling of, 383–86, 391–92, 395–96, 550, 561, 591

    growth of, 301, 304–6, 315–16

    high council, 326, 330, 334. *See also* dissenters.

    land records and plat, 317, 327, 435–37, 436n13

    plans to publish newspaper, 318

    siege and surrender, 368, **369**, 371, 577–78

    temple, 315–16, 329, 382–83, 430, 485, 538, 541, 543–44, 559–60, 576, 580–81

Far West Record

    includes Kirtland documents, 151

    on discipline of Oliver Cowdery, 163

"Far West: The Old Mormon Settlement in Missouri," 538–52

Faul, Charles, 553

Faulring, Scott H., xvii, 76n39

Fayette Branch. *See* Whitmer Settlement.

Fayette, NY, 10, 85, map of, **74**

    and church organization, 65n2

    conference at, 75

First Vision, 50

Fishing River, hostilities, 296. *See also* Zion's Camp.

Five Fingers Lakes, 9

Flanders, Robert B., xvii

Flournoy, Jones H., 211n20, 215–16n36

Flournoy, Roland, 215–16n36

Floyd, Julia Alice Page, 456

Fogel, Edward Miller, 58

folk beliefs, 47n39, 58, 60

Follett, King, 186, 293

Follett, Louisa, 186

foot-washing, 282

Forscutt, Mark H., 459–60

Foster (of Far West), 577

Founder of Mormonism, The, 491

Fox, Feramorz Y., 105

Franklin, Lewis, 210, 215–16n36

Franklin, Thomas J., 580

Frederick Granger Williams
    alienated from Joseph Smith, 324
    and Gilbert estate, 360
    and patriarchal blessings, 266
    at Far West, 307
    complaints against, 312, 352
    in Caldwell County, 290, 297
    in Missouri, 324
    in Mormon army, 274
    Kirtland Temple dedication, 282
    portrait of, 284n53
    withdraws from church, 334
    witnesses revelation, 312

Fredonia (NY) Censor, describes Book of Mormon, 63

"Free Jim," 401

Freemasonry, 217

friendship, and Joseph Smith, 29

Frisby, George, 443

Fristoe, Richard, 210n9, 215–16n36

From Historian to Dissident: The Book of John Whitmer, xiv, 511

Fruitvale Hospital (California), 56n26

Fry, Evan A., 573–75

Frye (of Far West), 387

Fugitt's Mill, 544

Fuller, Adeline, 310–11

Fuller, Edison, 93n42

Funn, I. C., 461

G

Galland, Maria Allen, 217

Gallatin, MO, 364, 367n10, 552

Gamble, Hamilton Rowan, 439

Gardner, Freeborn, 382n18

Gardner, Simeon, 382n18

gathering, renewal of, 443–44

Gause, Jesse
    and Literary Firm, 165
    and United Firm, 164
    as scribe, 139
    as Joseph Smith's counselor, 156
    disaffected, 168
    goes to Missouri, 158, 161–62
    Martin Harris replaces, 148n35, 164n14
    instructs John Whitmer in grammar, 168
    on presiding bishop committee, 163

Geddes, John, 163, 198

Geneva, NY, 10

German Reformed Church, 14

German Reformed Synod of the United States, 14

Germany, Whitmer family from, 1, 8, 10

Gibbs, Luman, 382n18

Gilbert, Algernon Sidney
  and United Firm, 163n9, 164
  estate of, 360, 382
  in business with Newel K. Whitney,
    164
  in Missouri, 130, 132, 176
  in Ohio, 194
  leader in Independence, 188, 198, 210
  never consecrated property, 167
  on presiding bishop committee, 163
  property of, 152, 360
  store, 148, 212, 221, 236–37
Gilbert, Elizabeth Van Benthusen, 360,
    360n4
  and redemption of Zion, 308
  in Far West, 130, 382, 384
Gilbert, John, 62
Gilbert, Sherman, 265n30
Giles/Jiles (colonel), 482–43
Godfrey, Kenneth, 35–36, 45n32
Golden Bible, The, 596
Goodson, John, 382n18
Goose Creek, 483
gorgets. *See* seer stones.
Goshen College (IN), 3
Gould, John, 228–29
Grandin, Egbert B., 62–64
Granger, Artemesia, 383n20
Granger, Oliver, 309
Granger, Sarah, 383n20
grape juice/wine revelation, 78
Graves, Calvin, 306
Graybill, Vivian, xviii
Green, Addison F., 373
Green, Henry, 275
Green, Hervey, 306, 306n60

Green, Jane Ann Rich, 306n60
Green, John, 220
Greene, Evan, 303
Gregg, Harmon, 215–16n36
Gregg, Josiah, 204–5
Griffiths, Gomer, 582
Griffiths, Terry, 582
Griggs (at Far West), 382n18
Grover, Thomas, 333, 327
Groves (fund-raiser), 298n28
Groves, Elisha Hurd, 272, 318
  and church's press, 320–21
  on Far West High Council, 327
  on Far West Temple committee, 330
  payment for church officers, 330
Grunder, Rick, 59n37
Gudgel (of Richmond, MO), 361
Gunn, Stanley, 20
Gurley, Zenas H.
  on David Whitmer's meeting with
    Joseph Smith, 26
  on John Whitmer's disaffection, 345
  role in Reorganization, 26n26
  visits John Whitmer, 449
  David Whitmer describes disaffection
    of, 329
  John Whitmer on Book of Mormon
    translation, 46

H

Hadley, Samuel, 379
Hale, Aroet Lucious, 343n12
Hale/Hall, Levi, 72
Hale, Isaac, 76
Hale, Reuben, 21
Hales, Jonathan H., 379n5
Half Moon Prairie Branch, 442n22

Ham, Wayne, xvii

Hamer, John C., xvii–xviii, 303n40

Hancock, Alta, 88

Hancock, Levi Ward, 88, 119, 124, 154, 346

Hancock, Pauline, 511

Hancock, Solomon, 93
 and high council, 244, 327
 mission of, 87–88, 124

Hannibal and St. Joseph Railroad, 540,
 547, 561

Hanson, Ariel, 309

Harmony, PA, 71–72, 76–77; map of, **74**

Harper, Steven C., 66n2

Harrington, John, 430

Harris, Emer, 79, 81, 140, 148

Harris, George W., 371, 524

Harris, John, 215–16n36

Harris, Lucy, 22, 22n12

Harris, Martin, xii, 139
 and church press, 147–48, 154
 and Literary Firm, 176
 as founding church member, 65–
  67nn1–2
 as one of Three Witnesses, 48, 51–52
 as scribe, 21–22
 baptism of, 68n11
 Book of Mormon printing, 62–63
 compensation (1831), 149
 consults eastern scholars, 491–92
 death of, 452, **452**
 described, 21
 donations, 259
 in Missouri, 130, 133
 in Ohio, 102
 in Utah, 451
 William McLellin commanded to
  rebaptize and reordain, 530

 on Book of Mormon translation, 41
 on Kirtland High Council, 259
 on missing 116 pages, 39–40
 on presiding bishop committee, 163
 seer stones, 43

Harris, Preserved, 100

Hart, James H., 467

Hartley, William G., xvii, 170–71, 188

Hatch, Nathan O., 51

Haun's/Hawn's Mill, 336, 367–69, 547–48

Havenaugh, Sarah, 393n1

Hayes, Beulah Elizabeth Koontz, 59n37

healing, missionaries fail, 114–15

Hebrew, church leaders study, 270, 272;
 grammar, **271**

Hedrick, Granville, 341, 442, 444

Hendricks, Drusilla Dorris, 296

Herald Publishing House
 fire at, 512
 publishes John Whitmer's history, 511

Herr, Christian, 3

Herr, Elizabeth Lotscher, 3

Herr, Isaac, 3

Herr, Magdalena Shellenberger, 3

Herr, Peter. 3

Hickman, James P., 215–16n36

Hicks, Edwin F., 215–16n36

Hicks, Russell M., 209–10n9, 215–16n36

Higbee, Elias, 206
 appointed church historian, 343
 in Far West, 327, 345, 545
 leather store, 306, 319
 payment for church officers, 330

Higbee, John, 239

high priesthood, Joseph Smith as president
 of, 196

high priests council, 197

Higley, Philander, 401n19

Hill, Henry, 294

Hill, Marvin, 50–51, 97–98, 341

Hinderks, Temme, 553

Hines, John, 576

Hines, Wesley, 576

Hinkle, George M.

    disaffection of, 376

    imprisoned, 549

    in Far West, 306, 327, 330, 432

    in state militia, 365n4, 366, 547

    investigates dissenters, 333, 335

    peace efforts of, 367, 367n10, 369

    plat of Far West, 435

    store, 323

    testifies for state, 373

Hiram (Mormon) Branch, 179, 182, 186

History of the Reorganization, 430

Hofmann, Mark W., 59n37

Holbert, William, 170, 170n40

Holman Store, 576

Holmes, Milton, 246

Holsclaw, Elizabeth, 218–19

Holzapfel, Richard Neitzel, xvii

Hor/Herr (of Far West), 319

Horton (no first name), 110

hosanna shout, 279–80

hotel, proposed for Independence, 153

House of the Lord. *See* Kirtland Temple.

Howard, Jim, 578

Howard, N., 541

Howard, Richard P., xvii, 43, 505n32, 515

Howard, Robert, 383n20

Howe, Eber D.

    critiques Mormonism, 56, 120

on Colesville Branch, 130, 130n32

on spiritual gifts, 96

reports Rigdon's return to Ohio, 101

Howlett, David, xvii

Hubble, Laura, 109

Huffaker (of Richmond), 456

Hughes (of Richmond), 466

Hughes, David, 477, 550, 576

Hughes, J., 541

Hughes Baxter Store, 577

Hulet family, in Far West, 305

Hulet, Ann Taylor, 181n5

Hulet, Catherine, 181, 181n5

Hulet, Charles, 179, 181, 181n5

Hulet, Charlotte, 179

Hulet, Electa Fidelia, 181n5

Hulet, Elizabeth, 182

Hulet, Francis, 179, 181n5

Hulet, Margaret Ann Noah, 179, 181n5, 182

Hulet, Mary (dau). *See* West, Mary Hulet.

Hulet, Mary Lewis, 179, 181n5

Hulet, Melvina, 181n5

Hulet, Orrin Taylor, 181n5

Hulet, Rhoda. *See* Mills, Rhoda Hulet.

Hulet, Sally, 179

Hulet, Schuyler, 181n5

Hulet, Sylvanus, 179, 181n5

Hulet, Sylvanus Cyrus, 181n5

Hulet, Sylvester, 186, 189, 276

Hulet Branch, 189–90, 242

Hulet Settlement, 245–46, 276

Hunt, C. J., 501, 568–70

Hunter, James M., 215–16n36

Hunter, James W., 210n9

Huntington, Oliver B., 17n69

Huntington, William, 379n5

Huntington Library, xvii

Hyde, Heman T., 246

Hyde, Orson, 140, 228–29, 260, 387, 545–46

hymns, 165, 166n23

I

Independence, MO, sketch of, **173**

  citizens' committee, 208, 210

  conflict/expulsion of Mormons, 206–47

  courthouses, 152

  described, 153

  Mormon branch in, 188

  print shop: constructed, 169; destroyed, 166

  superior status of, 198n17

  temple site, 132, 460n30

Indians, Mormons accused of inciting, 205–6

individualism in larger American society, 32

"inheritances" assigned to church leaders, 258–59. *See also* consecration.

ink, recipe for, 172

Inouye, Henry, K. Jr., xvii, 173

Inspired Version. *See* New Translation.

institutional narratives, xii–xiii

interpreters, 42n24, 44, 47, 53, 410–11. *See also* spectacles *and* seer stones.

Irwin, William L., 215–16n36

Ishem, M. C., 419

J

J. Willard Marriott Library, University of Utah, xvi

Jackman, Levi

  in Missouri, 182, 186–87, 232, 244

  map of Whitmer Settlement, 235

on Far West High Council, 327

Jackson, Albert, 217

Jackson, Andrew J. (Sarah Jackson Whitmer's brother), 127, 257, 380, 417

Jackson, Eliza, 127, 417

Jackson, Henry, 152

Jackson, James (Sarah Jackson Whitmer's brother), 127, 394, 417

Jackson, John (Sarah Jackson Whitmer's father), 127, 190, 191n32, 252, 361

Jackson, John (Sarah Jackson Whitmer's nephew), 171, 417

Jackson, Joseph H., 27, 27

Jackson, Kent P., 138

Jackson, Lewis (Sarah Jackson Whitmer's brother), 127, 251–52

Jackson, Martha F. (Sarah Jackson Whitmer's mother), 127, 190, 361, 380, 388

Jackson, Sarah Maria/Mariah. *See* Whitmer, Sarah Maria/Mariah Jackson.

Jackson, Thomas (Sarah Jackson Whitmer's brother), 127, 394, 417

Jackson County. *See also* Independence, MO.

  as Zion, 131, 135

  Mormon settlements in, **174**

  Joseph Smith's continued expectation for, 290–91, 336

Jaques, Vienna, 242

Jasinski, Peter M., 138

Jennings (Missouri militia), 548

Jennings, Warren, xvii, 505n32

Jensen, Marlin K., xvi, 145

Jensen, Richard L., xvii

Jensen, Robin Scott, xvi, 146n32, 200, 261n16

Jenson, Andrew, xvii
    attends World's Fair and Congress of
        Religions, 489
    makes holograph copy of John
        Whitmer's history, 489–90,
        509–10; makes typewritten copies,
        510
    on "Book of John Whitmer," xvii, 263
    visits David Whitmer, 483
    visits David John Whitmer and
        George Schweich, 488
    visits John Christian Whitmer, 458
Jessee, Dean C., xvii
    identifies Book of Mormon scribes, 36
    on Oliver Cowdery, 76
    on postal system, 171
John the Baptist, 23
John Whitmer Books, xviii
John Whitmer Historical Association,
    xviii, 473, 474n27, 505n32
Johnson (of Far West), 393
Johnson, Benjamin F., 346
Johnson, Charles (husband of Maria
    Louisa Cowdery), 424n4, 460
Johnson, Clark V., xvii
Johnson, Edward, 157
Johnson, Eli, 157
Johnson, Ella Edith, **285, 474**
    biography, 571
    donates family portraits to RLDS
        Church, 503n26
    in 1860 census, 434
    LDS Church acquires her inheritance,
        505
    lives with John Whitmer, 283n53, 432,
        442, 445n2, 447–48, 558
Johnson, Elsa, 112–13, 307
Johnson, Gan, 215–16n36

Johnson house, photo, **142**
Johnson, James Edward, 445n2, 571
    abandons family, 442, 446
    corresponds with John Whitmer,
        446–48
    in 1860 census, 434
    marries Sarah Elizabeth Whitmer, 432,
        441
    profession, 431–32
    sends valentine to Sarah Jackson
        Whitmer, 445
Johnson Jan/Gan, 210n9
Johnson, John
    at Far West, 307
    conversion of, 112
    farmhouse, exterior, **137**; interior, **142**
    in Literary Firm, 176
    inn, 226
Johnson, John Edward (son of Sarah
    Elizabeth), 441, 445n2, 448, **474,
    485**, 566, 571, 558
    lives with grandparents, 442
    marries Stella E. Smith, 442n21
Johnson, John, Jr., 157
Johnson, Luke, 112–13, 260, 343, 349
Johnson, Lyman E.
    complaints against, 312, 343, 349, 353n48
    disaffiliated/excommunicated, 324n38,
        334
    in Far West, 324
    leaves Far West, 353
    Mormons threaten, 352
Johnson, Maria Louise Cowdery, 381,
    382n16, 571
    and Independence Temple title, 460
    described, 396, 561
    lives with Whitmers, 422, 424

Johnson, Nancy L. Johnson, 424

Johnson, Nathan, **474**

Johnson, Robert, 210n9, 215–16n36

Johnson, Samuel, 215–16n36

Johnson, Sarah Elizabeth Whitmer (dau. of John Whitmer). *See* Kerr, Sarah Elizabeth Whitmer Johnson.

Johnson, Stella E. Smith, 442n21

Jolly, Elizabeth, 69, 281n40

Jolly, Vincent, 69

Jolly, William, 60, 281n40

Jones, John P., 505n31

Jones, Marjorie, 505n31

Jones, Sheldon, 576, 578–79

Jones, William, 390–91

Jorgensen, Danny, xvii

Joseph Smith Translation. *See* New Translation.

Joseph Smith Papers project, 515

Judd, Peter, xviii

Judd, Zadock, 365n4

Judy, Paris T., 391

K

Kansas City, MO, 186

Kansas City Post, 485

Karpowicz, Mike, xviii

Kavanaugh (of Far West), 578

Kaw Township, 174, 184

Keener, George U., 491

Keener, Sarah ("Sally") Elizabeth, 496n14

Kellar (of Far West), 578

Kelley, E. L., 494, 513

Kelley, W. H., 480

Kendig Creek, 69

Kerr (of Far West), 393

Kerr, Catharine Simpson, 558

Kerr, Christopher F., **474**

  biography of, 475, 558–59

  death of, 441. 441n21

  marriage, 571

Kerr, James, 558

Kerr, Sarah Elizabeth Whitmer Johnson (dau. of John Whitmer), 273, 432, 445n2, **474**, 477, 558, 576

  birth, 312–13, 321

  death of, 441, 441n21, 505

  denounces polygamy, 559

  divorces James Edward Johnson, 446, **447**, 571

  family information, 304n45, 402, 445n2

  flower garden, 430

  gravestone, **473**

  has first edition Book of Mormon, 559

  in Clay County, 239

  in 1847, 407

  in 1850, 424

  in 1860, 434

  inheritance from John Whitmer, 475

  lives at Far West, 446

  marries James Edward Johnson, 571

  marries Christopher F. Kerr, 441n21, 571

  on father's character, 501

  on tornado, 467

  places of residence, 441–42

  raises chickens, 448–49

  rebuffs LDS attempts to acquire papers, 471

  sends valentine to Sarah Jackson Whitmer, 445

  visit from Joseph F. Smith and Orson Pratt, 555–57

Kidder College, 540

Killebrew, Rachel, xvii, 496

Kimball, Heber C., 242, 307, 383
  in Far West, 577
  on mission, 284, 545
Kimball, Vilate, 284
King (of Richmond, MO), 361
King, Austin A., 371, 544, 549
King, Daniel, 215–16n36
King, John, 211
Kingsley, Rachel, 384
Kingston, MO
  becomes county seat, 397
  cemetery, 406
  named for Austin King, 550, 552
Kirtland, OH
  banking, failure of, 287–88, 309, 321, 324, 332,
  debts in, 295, 308, 340
  described, 286–87, **287**
  high council, 259–60
  William McLellin commanded to build church in (1847), 532, 536
  Mormons in, 93
  resistance to Joseph Smith, 286, 308–9, 314, 323–24
Kirtland Temple, **276, 381**
  and William McLellin, 410
  dedication of, 267, 277, 280; preparatory rituals, 277–82
  revelation to construct, 247
  seating in, 282
Kitchell, Ashbel, 126n22
Knecht, Stephen, 80, 121
Knight family, 19, 82, 117, 175
Knight, Joseph, Jr., 65n1, 72, 100, 188
Knight, Joseph, Sr., 66, 66n5, 72, 100n63
Knight, Lucy, 100n63
Knight, Newel/Newell

  and Colesville Branch, 174
  baptism of, 71
  blesses Philo Dibble, 235
  donates home for printing press, 344
  in Missouri, 153, 244, 294, 327
  in Ohio, 98
  leadership assignments, 142
  visits Joseph Smith (1830), 77
Knight, Polly (dau.), 72
Knight, Polly Peck, baptized, 72, 100n63
Koontz, Mayme Janetta Whitmer, 59n37, 486, 498, **500**

L

L. Tom Perry Special Collections, Harold B. Lee Library, Brigham Young University, John Whitmer papers in, xvi
Laban's sword, seen in vision, 31, 53
Lake Cayuga, 10
Lake Seneca, 10
Lamanite missionaries, 81–82, 83n65, 84, 87, 96, 127–28
Lamb, M. T., 595
Lambert, Richard J., 510n12
Lancaster County, PA, 2–3, 7
Landon, M., 380
Larson, Stan, xvi
Launius, Roger D., xvii, 511
Laurel Club, 284n53, 503n26
"Law of Consecration and Stewardship." *See* consecration.
"Law of the Church" (D&C 42), 106–8, 110–13
lawsuit in Jackson County, 301
LDS Church
  acquires Far West property, 505n31
  conserves documents, 515

facsimile of "Book of John Whitmer," 501

William McLellin denounces, 537

leather store, in Far West, 306

"Lectures on Faith," 256

Lee, David, 503–5

Leonard, Glen M., xvii

LeSueur, Stephen C., xviii

Lewellen, Ethel Johnson, 283n53, 304n45, 445n2, **474**, 503, 503n25

    letter to C. Edward Miller, 571

Lewis, John, 215–16n36

Lewis, Joshua, 132, 184, 231

Lewis, William, 461, 553–54

Liahona, seen in vision, 53

Liberal Institute, 56n26

liberalism, in larger American society, 32

Library of American Literature from the Earliest Settlement to the Present Time, A, 491n5

Life in Utah, 596

Lightner, Adam, 306–7

Lightner, Mary Elizabeth Rollins, 189, 218

Linn, William Alexander, 596

Literary Firm

    activities of, 165, 199, 265

    and press, 250

    conflicts with, 162, 162n3

    failure of, 175–76, 317

    members of, 165

    over-optimism about, 148, 167

    revived in Ohio, 226

Little Blue River, 187

Littlefield, Lyman O., 306, 385–86

Livonia, NY, 83n65

Log Creek Church (Primitive Baptist), 394, 394n2

Lord's supper, water/wine revelation, 77–78

Lovett (in Missouri), 234

Lucas, Samuel D., 210n9, 215–16n36, 366, 366n8, 368

Lyman, Amasa, 190n30, 249, 369, 549

Lyman, Mary, 255

Lynda (in John Whitmer letter), 566

Lyons (doctor), 380

M

Macedon, NY, 83n65

Maguire, Frank, 544

Mahoning Baptist Association, 105

mail. *See* postal system.

Majors, Benjamin, 215–16n36

Malinda (in John Whitmer letter), 566

Manchester, NY, 65n2, 66, 68n10

Manless, Ann, 393n1

Manless, Eliza, 393n1

Marchant, Amy, 187

Markham, Stephen, 383n20

Marks, David, 61

Marquardt, H. Michael, xviii

Marsh, Thomas B., 166n23

    accuses dissenters, 335–36

    and *Elder's Journal*, 344

    as fund-raiser, 298

    disaffected, 337, 376, 546

    gives health blessings, 281

    in Missouri, 174, 244, 319, 325–26, 342

    in Ohio, 102, 333

    on Missouri violence, 231

    on John Whitmer, 326

    pro-Joseph leader, 328

    reconciles with LDS Church, 325

    revelation to, 332n22, 355n53

Joseph Smith's expectations of loyalty, 332

speaks in tongues, 189

Marshall, Jan, xviii

Martin, David C., 59n37

Masers, William, 215–16n36

Matthews, Robert J., xvii, 72, 85

May, Dean L., 105

May, Roderick, 494, 513

Mayer, Lewis, 58

Mayfield, OH, 88, 93, 163

Maynard, Jotham, 382n18, 384

Maynard, Nelson, 382n18

McAfee, Chris, 515

McBeath, Mary J., 558

McCarty, Robert, 215–16n36

McCreary/McCray, James C., 548

McGee, James, 215–16n36

McHenery (goes to Missouri), 293

McKiernan, F. Mark, xvii, 511

McLellan [sic], James Martin, 349, 350n41

McLellin, Emeline, 325, 349

McLellin/McLellan, James Martin, 325

McLellin, William

　about dissidents, 353, 355–37

　accused of theft, 343, 349, 375, 378

　and Granville Hedrick, 442–43

　challenged to write revelation, 143

　converted, 130–31

　disaffected, 183, 183n12, 324–25

　in Far West, 307, 325

　in Missouri, 133–34, 181n5, 183, 231, 244, 443n27, **444**

　leadership of, 196

　"man of sin" revealed to, 532

　narrative of Mormon history, 412–13

　on Fanny Alger, 346

　on Book of Mormon, 42n24, 219

　on church's organization, 66

　on gathering, 209, 209n7

　on Independence, 153, 208, 212–13, 219,

　on Kirtland bank, 288

　ordained by David Whitmer, 443

　ordained high priest, 140

　revelation to (1847), 529–31

　supports David Whitmer's leadership, 243, 407–10, 528–37

　visits Whitmers in Far West, 392, 442, 529, 531

　Whitmers alienated from, 410–12, 418–19

McLerie [sic] McCleary, Sophronia, 406

McPhearson, Sally, 381

McRae, Alexander, 373

Melchizedek, Joseph Smith on, 113

Melchizedek Priesthood, ordinations to, 125

Mennonites, 2–4, 8–9

Mercantile Firm, 155, 155n15, 162, 164

Messenger and Advocate

　Oliver Cowdery edits, 256

　plans to sell, 285–86

　publication of, 250, 258

　terminated, 318

　John Whitmer edits, 256–68, 516–22

　Peter Whitmer's obituary, 300

Metcalf, Anthony, 59n37

Metcalf, Zebulon, 380, 388

Metcalfe, Erin B. Jennings, xviii, 2–3, 5n22, 148n35, 464n40

　on Jesse Gause, 168

　on Sarah Jackson Whitmer, 127n26

meteor shower, 238–39, 239n51

Methodist Episcopal minister, 490

Middaugh, Benjamin, 396, 560

Middaugh, Timothy, 396, 560

Miles, Samuel, 316n7

Miller, C. Edward, 220n52, 283n53, 445n2, 503n26

Miller, George, 382n18

Miller, Gilbert, 303

Miller, S., 374

Miller, Sinclair K., 400

Miller, William, 366n8

Milliken [*sic*] Millikin, Arthur R., 406

Milliken [*sic*] Millikin, Nancy [Lucy], 406

Millport, MO, 367n10

Mills, Elvira Pamela, 181, 181n5

Mills, Marietta Streeter, 181

Mills, Rhoda Hulet, 179, 181, 181n5

Mills, Robert Frederick, 181n5

Minerva (ship), 5

Mirabile, MO, 273, 483. *See also* Far West.

missionaries to Lamanites. *See* Lamanites.

"Missionaries Covenant," 84

missions, emphasis on in Kirtland, 110

Missouri. *See also* individual towns and counties.

    as site of New Jerusalem, 126

    attitudes toward Mormons in, 204

    branches in (1832), 188

    described, 187

    fourteen missionary teams to, 128

    leadership councils, 162

    map of northern counties, 328

    numbers of Mormons in (1832), 175, 176, 178

    route to/from Kirtland, 130

Missouri Daily Republican, 486–87

Missouri Enquirer, 211n18

Missouri Loyalty Oath (1865), 439

Missouri Mormon Frontier Foundation, 473, 474n27

Missourians, appropriate Mormon land, 375

Mitchell, Samuel, 491–92

Morey, George

    Far West high council, 327

    investigating dissenters, 333

    property stolen, 375

    store in Far West, 319

Morgan, Dale, 497

Morgan, Elizabeth Gant, 470n18

Morgan, James, 470n18

Morgan, Lucinda, 551

Morley, Isaac

    and solemn assemblies, 192

    and "the Family" (communalism), 92, 105

    and United Firm, 163n9

    as leader in Independence, 188, 198, 210, 221

    as patriarch in Missouri, 321

    buys land in Missouri, 290, 292, 294, 298–99

    preaching at home of, 95, 124

    store in Far West, 306

"Mormon/Mormonite," as derisive names, 19

Mormon War (1838), 363–77, 547–50

Mormonism, began with three extended families, 19

Morris, Nancy W., 558

Morris, Rebecca Fuller, 310n80

Morse, Michael, 40, 40n20

Morse, Tryal Hale, 40

Moses, revelation about, 72

Moss, J. J., 94

Moyle, James Henry, xi, 54

Mulholland, James, 379

Mullin, Eri, 42

Murdock/Murdoch, John

    concerned about spiritual excesses, 117

    investigates dissenters, 333n26

    mission to Missouri, 126, 133

    moves to Clay County, 297, 299

    on Far West High Council, 244, 327

Murdock, Joseph and Julia (twins), 136

Murdock, S. Reed, xviii

Musick, Samuel, 307, 358

Musselman, family, 2

Musselman, Christian, 7–8

Musselman, David, 7–8

Musselman, Elizabeth, 5, 7

Musselman, Henry, 7

Musselman, Jacob, 5, 7–8

Musselman, Mary. *See* Whitmer, Mary
    Musselman.

Musselman, Michael, 7

Myers, Jacob, 260–61

N

N. K. Whitney & Co., 165

Nading, James, 399

Nelson (Ohio) Branch, 179, 181–82, 186

Nelson, George, 382n18

Nelson, Joseph, 382n18

Nephites, appearances of, 32

New Organization. *See* Reorganized
    Church of Jesus Christ of Latter
    Day Saints *and* RLDS Church.

New Translation of Bible, 72–73, 80, 197, 513

    Peter Bauder on, 85

    conservation of, 515

    in Lorene Pollard's possession, 507

    in George Schweich's possession, 507

    in John Whitmer's possession, 355n53

    manuscript version of, 90n30

    publication planned, 138, 166

    quotations from in 1981 LDS edition
        of King James Bible, 434n5

    Sidney Rigdon works on, 151

    RLDS Church buys, 494–95, 513

    Emma Smith preserves manuscript,
        89, 379, 433–34

    Joseph Smith's work on, xvi, 64, 72–73,
        111–13n28, 120–24, 139, 151

New-York Messenger, 369

Newell, Linda King, xvii, 21, 51

Noah, John, 110

Noland, Smallwood V., 152

Nolt, Seven M., 3

North Union, OH, 126

Northern Times, 250, 257, 286

O

O'Driscoll, Jeffrey S., xviii

Ohio. *See also* individual towns.

    as stake, 201

        Lamanite missionaries in, 87–88

Old Order River Brethren (Donegal
    Township), 4

Oldham, Leonidas K., 215–16n36

"Olive Leaf" revelation, 192–93, 202–3

Olmstead, Harvey, 214n27

Olmstead, Nathan K., 215–16n36

Olson, Earl E., 515

"Our Tour West," 528–37

Overton, Aaron, 215–16n36

Owens, Abigail Cornelia Burr, 182

Owens, James Clark, 182

Owens, Samuel C., 209, 215–16n36

P

Page family, in Far West, 305

Page, Alma, 424

Page, Alonzo, 479

Page, Catharine/Catherine/Catherina Whitmer

  baptism of, 68

  biography of, , 4, 6, 8, 5n22, 15–16, 401, 573–75

  in Hulet Branch, 252

  in Missouri, 407

  in Richmond (1850), 424

  in 1880 census, 479

  mob attacks home, 230

  moves to Grape Grove, MO, 426

Page, Cora (dau. of Philander), 479

Page, David (son of Philander), 479

Page, Elizabeth, 230

Page, Hiram

  Pre-Mormon life:

  biography/family information, xvii, 401, 438, 456, 575

  marries, 16–17

  medical knowledge, 16

  Life during Mormon years:

  cuts rails, 187

  baptism of, 68

  beaten, 230–31

  defends Whitmer settlement, 234

  in Hulet Branch, 252

  on falling stars, 238

  one of Eight Witnesses/Book of Mormon, 16, 55, 57, 475

  not required to consecrate, 202

  performs weddings, 252

  revelations of, 79

  seer stones, 47n39, 58, 81, 497

  superstitious personality, 58

  Post-Mormon life:

  at Oliver Cowdery's death, 422

  death of, 419n52, 426; gravestone, 418

  corresponds with McLellin, 407–11, 418–19

  in Richmond: 377, (1847) 407; (1850), 424

  William McLellin visits, 529

  sheltered by McLellins, 355–57

  supports James Strang, 403–4

  supports David Whitmer as church leader, 407–9; present at revelations to David Whitmer (1847), 531; rebaptized/reordained (1847), 535; on Whitmer family's beliefs, 419–20

  testimony of, 419n52

Page, Hiram, Jr., 424

Page, John, 230

Page, John David, 424

Page, John E., 383, 387

Page, Julia, 468, 479

Page, Louisa, 479

Page, Marion, 479

Page, Mary, 68

Page, Mary (dau. of Philander), 479

Page, Mary Elizabeth, 424

Page, Mary May, 424

Page, Nancy L. *See* Johnson, Nancy L. Page.

Page, Oliver, 424

Page, Peter, 5n22, 470n18, 479

Page, Peter Christian, 424

Page, Philander/Phylander A.

  and tornado, 468

and John Whitmer's final illness, 471

as presiding elder, 493

biography, 401n19

in Church of Christ (Whitmer), 470

in 1850, 424; in 1880, 479

mob attacks family, 230

moves to Grape Grove, MO, 427

supervised comparison of Book of
Mormon printer's mss and
published version, 481–82

Page, Sarah (dau. of Philander), 479

Page, Sarah (wife of Philander), 479

Painesville Telegraph, 54

Palmer, Grant, 39–40

Palmyra Freeman, 40

Palmyra, NY, 10, 62

Parker, Sally, 57

Parkin, Max H, xvii

Parris, Warren W., 265n30, 312, 332, 346

Partridge, Caroline, 217

Partridge, Edward

and Colesville Branch, 126

and consecration/tithing, 178–80,
192–94, 330

and presiding bishop committee, 163

and printing press, 344

and solemn assemblies, 192–93

and United Firm, 163n9, 164

and John Whitmer's mortgage, 388–90

appointed bishop, 106

as leader in Missouri, 198, 210

blesses children, 236

conference at home, 184

conflict with Sidney Rigdon, 162, 168

duties of, 117–18

estate settled, 390–91

Far West property, 327, 338n41, 545

Far West Temple site, 317

financial difficulties, 156

hymn by, 166n23

in Independence, 152, 188

in Missouri, 130, 132, 141

in Ohio, 99, 100n63, 101

Independence Temple title, 460

inheritance assigned, 259

meets Joseph Smith, 88–90

on redeeming Zion, 268

property transactions, 154, 290, 292,
294, 298–99, 336

status of, 162, 197

tarred and feathered, 213–18, 221

Partridge, Edward, Jr., 213

Partridge, Eliza, 294

Partridge, Emily, 206–7, 213, 217

Partridge, Harriett, 213, 217

Partridge, Lydia, 213, 215, 218, 336, 460

patriarchal blessings, 266, 321

Patten, David W.

and conflict, 337, 349

and Joseph Smith, 332, 343

as leader in Missouri, 327, 342

in Kirtland, 325, 333

Johnson family lives with, 324

Patten, Phebe Ann, 375

Pearl of Great Price, 433

Peck, Hezekiah, 72, 266, 383n20

Peck, Martha Long, 72, 383n20

Peck, Mary Ann, 383n20

Peck, Reed

at Far West, 305–7, 384

disaffected, 376

excommunicated, 384n21

in Caldwell County, 296, 298–99

money appropriated in Kirtland, 289

on print shop, 345

peace efforts of, 367, 369

testifies for state, 373

peepstone. *See* seer stone.

Pement, Isleta, xvii

Pender, W. S., 41

Penney, Eli, 393–94, 430, 432

Penney, James Cash, Jr., 394n2

Penney, James Cash, Sr., 393–94, 394n2, 430

Penney, Mary ("Polly") Burris, 393

Penney, Mary Frances Paxton, 394n2

Pennsylvania, Whitmer family in, 2

Pentecost (June 1831) conference, 125, 267

Peterson, J. W., 41–42

Peterson, Richard B. ("Ziba")

    as Lamanite missionary, 83n65, 84, 127

    baptized, 69

    disaffection, 163

    in Ohio, 87

    preaches to Orson Pratt, 86n9

    prophesies, 238

Pettigrew, David, 206–7, 294, 301

Phelps, Lydia, 250

Phelps, Morris, 265, 373

Phelps, Sally

    children of, 152, 250

    leaves Independence, 211

    separates from W. W., 383

    portrait of, 284

Phelps, Waterman (son of W. W. Phelps),
    250, 251n7, 252, 254, 257n2

Phelps, William Wine (W.W.)

    accusations against, 319, 326, 333–34,
    350, 352–53, 377

    and Book of Commandments, 165, 172,
    199–201

    and Hebrew, 271–72

    and Literary Firm, 165

    and United Firm, 163n9, 164

    as leader in Independence, 152, 188, 198,
    210

    as printer, 140–41, 148, 166, 204–5, 319

    boards with Joseph and Emma Smith,
    254

    Caldwell County judge, 544

    compensation (1831), 149

    conference at John Whitmer home,
    298

    corresponds with John Whitmer, 433,
    401

    counselor in Missouri church, 244–45

    debt to John Whitmer, 319n15, 387

    Egyptian alphabet and grammar, 270

    equates "interpreters" with Urim and
    Thummim, 43

    excommunicated, 334–36, 338

    hymns, 165n23, 166n23, 257, 262

    in Far West, 315–16, 361, 383, 545, 574,
    577

    in Illinois, 386–87

    in Missouri, 128, 130, 132. *See also*
    individual towns.

    in Ohio, 252

    in Utah, 433–34

    inheritance assigned, 259

    instructions to Missouri Saints, 266

    Kirtland Temple dedication, 277

    land purchased, 290, 292, 294, 298–99

    Messenger and Advocate, 262

    never consecrated property, 167

    on consecration, 183, 192, 202

    on Doctrine and Covenants, 264–65

    on education, 166n26

on presiding bishop committee, 163

on self-defense, 337

on Joseph Smith's authoritarianism, 359

on Christian Whitmer's death, 276

peace efforts of, 367

performs ordinations, 265

performs weddings, 191

print shop destroyed, 212, 221–22

reconciles with Joseph Smith, 387

testifies for state, 373

war department, 274

John Whitmer visits, 250

Philadelphia Press, 491

Pioneer Stage Line, 101

Pitcher, Thomas, 210, 215–16n36, 237–39

Pitkin, George, 158, 186

Pixley, Benton, 203, 211

plates, seen in vision, 31

politics of definition, xii. *See also* Kirtland.

Pollard, Lorene Elizabeth Burdick, xvii–xviii, 5

and local history , 17, 26

describes Caldwell County, 301

on Far West, 305

on Sarah Elizabeth Whitmer Johnson, 448

on Sarah Whitmer's thimble, 191

on Whitmer family, 127n23

on Whitmer farming, 431

on John Whitmer's homes, 391n40

photos from, 448, 485

Pollard, Roger, xviii

polygamy

first publication of "Book of John Whitmer" omits chapter on, 498

revelation about, 585

Poorman, John, 136n2, 186

Porter, Larry C., xvii, 10, 408

Porter, Nathan, 203–4

postal system, rates, 171–72

potatoes, Peter Whitmer's method of planting, 17–18

Poulson, M. Wilford

acquires John Whitmer's Doctrine and Covenants, 273

Poulson, Peter Wilhelm

biography, 55n26

correspondence from Sarah Elizabeth Johnson Kerr 467, 472

interviews John and David Whitmer, 55, 61n46, 463_64, 526_27

on Oliver Cowdery's death, 422n3

on Jacob Whitmer gravestone, 428

treats David Hyrum Smith, 472

Powell, David, 430

Prairie Branch (MO), 174–75, 188–89

Pratt, Orson

and Pearl of Great Price, 433n3

as missionary, 79–80, 89

dedication of Far West temple site, 383

on Book of Mormon translation, 36

on high council, 244

on New Translation, 72–73

prophesies, 238

revelation to, 86

tries to acquire early records, 471, 476, 508–9, 585

visits David Whitmer, 468–69, 555–57, 590

Pratt, Parley P.

arrested/imprisoned, 369–71, 373

as Lamanite missionary, 83n65, 84, 127

complaints against, 312

concerned about spiritual excesses, 117

hymns, 166n23

in Missouri, 153, 231, 249, 296

in New York, 79

in Ohio, 87

on high council, 244

preaches to Orson Pratt, 86n9

prophesies, 238

school of elders, 188

Pratt, Thankful, 153

prayer for funding, 272–73

Presbyterians, structure of, 13n49

"president of the High Priesthood," Joseph Smith as, 162

presiding high priests, as committee, 163

priest, office of, 106n13

priesthood authority

equality, 49, 62

offices, 106n13. *See also* individual offices.

print shop

in Far West, 320, 335, 343–44, 366, 366n8

in Independence, 154, 161, 170, 210–11

in Kirtland, 226–27, 332, 333n24

property, claims that Joseph Smith's appropriated, 83n64, 98

Prophet, 595–96

Pugh, William, 215–16n36

"Pure Church of Christ," 109

Q

Quinn, D. Michael, xviii, 403

Quorum of the Twelve Apostles, called, 248

R

"radical tradition," 60

Ramsey (of Caldwell County), 544

Rathbun, Hiram, 213

Rathbun, Robert, 213, 213n26

Ray County Savings Bank, 486

rebaptism, William McLellin's revelation on, 408, 420, 530, 535

records, offered to Strang, 404–5

redemption of Zion. *See* Zion, redemption of.

Rees, Amos, 250, 298

Reflector, 63

reordination, William McLellin's revelation on, 530

Restoration Studies, 43

return to Jackson County. *See* redemption of Zion.

Return, The, **356**, 357, 487

sacrament. *See* Lord's supper.

Revolutionary War, 5

Reynolds, James, 215–16n36

Reynolds, Noel, 256n2

Rich, Leonard, 248, 530

Richards, Franklin D., 433, 590

Richards, Levi, 370

Richards, Willard, 401

Richardson, John C., 422, 422n2

Richmond Conservator, 470

Richmond High School, **455**, 456n22

Richmond, MO, map, 397

Whitmer family at, xiiin6, 283n53, 357. *See also individuals.*

hearing at (1838), 369–71

Richmond Pioneer Cemetery, 422, **423**, 485

Rickman, Robert, 215–16n36

Rigdon, Phebe/Phoebe, 157, 341

Rigdon, Sidney

absent from meeting canonizing D&C, 264
and Book of Commandments, 146, 199
and communalism, 92, 104–5
and Doctrine and Covenants, 264–65
and *Elder's Journal*, 344
and Literary Firm, 165
and Mercantile Firm, 155
and New Translation, 113, 120–24, 138–39, 157
and United Firm 164
arrested, 369–71
challenges John Whitmer's competence, 342
conflict with Edward Partridge, 156, 162, 168
conversion of, 87–89
describes John Whitmer as apostle, 91
edits *Messenger and Advocate*, 317
financial demands of, 148–49, 197
imprisoned, 373, 549
in Caldwell County, 290, 297
in Far West, 325, 342, 345, 545
in Pittsburgh, 312
influence on Joseph Smith, 120–21
inheritance in Zion, 259
instructions to Missouri Saints, 266
Kirtland publishing projects, 318
Kirtland Temple dedication, 282
leadership roles, 156, 196
mental illness, 176–77
militarism of, 274, 345, 350, 353n48, 362–63, 366, 372, 424, 524, 546–48
millennialism of, 97
on presiding bishop committee, 163
never consecrated property, 167
patriarchal blessings, 266

preaching of, 97
property stolen, 375
replaces John Whitmer, 89
Salt Sermon. *See* militarism.
seeks money in Salem, MA, 298
takes over John Whitmer's hotel, 358
tarred and feathered (March 1832), 157
teaches Hebrew, 272
to/from Missouri, 128, 130, 132–33, 379
to/from Ohio, 99–100n63, 101, 134, 136, 157, 333, 341
travels with Joseph Smith, 96
David Whitmer blames for alienation from Joseph Smith, 352
John Whitmer on, 371–72, 508
Riggs, Burr
accused of theft, 375, 378
at Far West, 307
biography, 376n30
business with John Whitmer, 361
excommunicated, 376
on Joseph Smith's rhetoric, 366
testifies for state, 373
Riggs, Gideon, 376n30
Riggs, Lovina Williams, 376n30
Riggs, Michael S., xviii
Riggs, Susan Pitcher, 376n30
Riley, I. Woodbridge, 491
Ripley, Alanson, 344, 348n37, 372, 379n5, 524–25
RLDS Church
RLDS Archives, 594
acquires John Whitmer history, parts of New Translation, Book of Commandments, printer's manuscript of Book of Mormon, and Book of Mormon "caractors," 468n11, 488–506, 513

compares Book of Mormon manuscript to published version, 480

members of, 578

pre-organization developments, 429–30

Robertson, William O., 220n52

Robinson, Ebenezer, 323, 344, **356**, 357, 382, 480

Robinson, George W.

arrested, 369

as clerk, 317, 345

on law of land, 525

threatens Whitmers and Cowdery, 352, 353n48

John Whitmer, testimony about, 372

Rockwell family, in Missouri, 175

Rockwell, Orrin (father), 232

Rockwell, Orrin Porter, 68n11, 232

Rogers, David, 323

Rogers, Eric Paul, xvii

Rogers, Joseph, 27

Rogers, Samuel, 239n51

Rollins, Mary Elizabeth. *See* Lightner, Mary Elizabeth Rollins.

Romig, Anne Holmes, xviii

Romig, Rene, xviii

Romig, Ronald E.

as director of Kirtland Temple Visitor Center, xvi

critique of Westergren's *From Historian to Dissident*, xiv–xv, 592–94

identification with John Whitmer, xiii

purpose of biography, xv

Rooker, C. Keith, 341

Ross, Charles, 548

Roundy, Shadrach/Shadrack, 379n5, 383n20

Russell (near Richmond), 393n1

Russell, Isaac, 382, 382n18, 393, 477

Russell, Mary, 382n18, 578

Russell, Samuel, 393n1, 477, 493, 576–79, 589–90

Russell, William D., xvii–xviii

Ryder, Hartwell, 136–37, 157

Ryder, Symonds, 134–35, 157

Ryland (judge), 231, 757

S

"Sabbath Hymn," 262

Salem, MA, seeking money in, 298

Salisbury, Catherine/Katherine Smith, 406

Salisbury, W. J., 406

"Salt Sermon" 350, 353n48. *See also* Sidney Rigdon, militarism.

effects of, 362–63

John Whitmer on, 372, 524

Salyards, R. S., 494, 513

Sarachek Art Galleries, 283n53, 503n26

Schenk, Elizabeth Musselman, 5n22

Scherer, Mark, xvii

school of elders (Missouri), 188

School of the Prophets (Kirtland), 227, 283n52

Schott, Anna, 15, 17

Schott, Frederick, 15, 17

Schweich, George Washington Leopold, **492**

at David Whitmer's death, 487

Book of Mormon "caractors," 596

home in Richmond, 491

in 1860 census, 437, 437n15

letter to O. R. Beardsley (1900), 587

livery business, 461–63, 490–91

on David Whitmer in Richmond, MO, 357

opinion on presiding elders, 493

photograph of, 485

permits Andrew Jenson to hand copy John Whitmer history, 489

possession of "Book of John Whitmer," Book of Mormon printer's manuscript, 490, 491n5, 509–10, 513

seer stones, 496

sells documents to RLDS Church, 493–94, 510–11

Joseph F. Smith meets, 590

tornado, 465–66

Schweich, George (father of George Schweich, John Whitmer's son-in-law), 496n14

Schweich, George (son of George Schweich), 496n14

Schweich, Josephine ("Josie") Helen. *See* Van Cleave, Josephine ("Josie") Helen Schweich.

Schweich, Julia Ann Whitmer
    at David Whitmer's death, 487
    descendants of, 503n27
    in 1860 census, 437
    in Richmond (1850), 424
    photograph of, 485
    returns to parents' home, 454

Schweich, Julia Clare, 496n14

Schweich, Julius, 437, **438**, 454

Schweich, Katherine Louise, 490, 496n14

Schweich, Paul, 496n14

Schweich, Ruby Twelves, 496n14

Schweich, Sarah Keener, 490

Schweich, Van Cleave Whitmer, 496n14

Scott, Andrew, 9

Scott, Ann, 379, 382n18

Scott, Isaac, 382n18

Scott, Jacob, Sr., 382n18, 393n1

Scott, Walter, 104n9

screen. *See* Book of Mormon, translation.

seer stones, 43, 47, 47n41, 59n39
    acquired by RLDS Church, 496
    and Book of Mormon, 38n12, 425
    in Whitmer family, 495–96, 498
    Hiram Page's, 58–59, 79, 81
    Joseph Smith's, 25, 497
    David Whitmer's, 44, 309–10, 408, 410n23, 498, **499**
    Jacob Whitmer's, **500**

Seixas, Joshua, 272

Seneca Lake, 48, 69; map, 70

Seneca Grenadiers, 15

Shakers, 93–94, 106, 118

Shanks (of Chariton, MO), 182

"Shaping of Latter-day Saint History, The," 36

Sharp, Ellen, 576

Shaver, Eleanor, 255

Shearer, Daniel, 379n5, 383n20

Shearer, Norman, 383n20

Shellenberger, Magdalena, 3

Shellenberger, Mary, 3

Shellenberger, Peter, 3

Shellenberger, Ulrich, 3

Shepherd, Jonathan, 215–16n36

Sheppard, Sam, 152

Shiley, Jacob, 69

Shipps, Jan, xii, xviii

Shoal Creek, 297, 540. *See also* Far West.

Shook, Charles A., 596

Shoop, Joseph, and Maria, 400n14

Short, Alta, xviii

Short, Edward John, 470–71

Short, Lutie Bisbee, 471

Short, Sally Bisbee, 471

Shumaker, Jacob, 360

Shurtliff, Luman, 254n20

Simpson, George W., 214–16n36

Simpson, Richard, 210n9

Simpson, Robert, 215–16n36

Skidmore, John, 544

Slade, Benjamin, 373

Slade, William, 380

slaves: Mormons accused of inciting, 205, 209; David Whitmer owns, 401

Smith family, one of three constituting early church, 19

Smith, Alexander Hale, 480–81

Smith, Caroline, 379

Smith, David Hyrum, 56n26, 472

Smith, Don Carlos

    as printer, 318, 382

    compensation (1831), 149

    fund-raising, 365

    leaves Missouri, 380

Smith, Elias, 382–83n20

Smith, Emma Hale (Bidamon)

    and Fanny Alger, 345

    and redeeming Zion, 268

    and Word of Wisdom, 197

    as scribe, 21 40–41, 85, 139; Book of Mormon translation, 37, 43; touches plates under cloth, 38

    baptized, 72

    "Elect Lady" revelation to, 75

    hymns, 165 and note 23, 166n23

    in Harmony, PA, 26, 35

    lives with Whitmers, 35

    moves to Far West, 341–42

    moves to Illinois, 379–80

    moves to Ohio, 99

    New Translation mss in her possession, 433

    sees Whitmers as honest, 483

    James Strang tries to recruit, 405

Smith, Frederick M., 494, 513

Smith, George A., 135, 332, 365–66, 382–83

Smith, Heman C.

    as historian, xvii

    documents in possession of, 512

    present at transfer of John Whitmer papers, 513

    publishes John Whitmer's history (1908), 498, 511; omissions in, 498; accuracy defended, 501

Smith, Hyrum, **323**

    advises Mormon move to Caldwell County, 297

    and Book of Mormon, 62–63, 240, 595

    and Kirtland Temple, 282

    arrested/imprisoned, 369–71, 373, 549

    as assistant president, 275, 374

    as fund-raiser, 140, 255

    as founding member of church, 65–66nn1–2

    at Colesville, 82–83n65

    baptizes William McLellin, 131

    death of, 402

    in Far West, 290, 325, 545

    in Kirtland, 325

    mission to Missouri, 133–34

    in war department, 274

    not required to consecrate, 202

    one of Eight Witnesses, 55, 57

    ordained, 49

present for Joseph Smith revelation, 312

seeks money in Salem, MA, 298

vision in Hill Cumorah of plates, Laban's sword, etc., 31

Smith, Israel A., 480, 497, 502

Smith, James, 399

Smith, Jerusha, 82

Smith, John (uncle), 259, 332, 379n5

Smith, John (of Independence), 215–16n36

Smith, Joseph, Jr., **323**. *See also* conferences.

In New York: See also Book of Mormon.

and Literary Firm, 165

and United Firm, 164

at Whitmer home, 35, 78

baptized, 103

compensation (1831), 149

in Broom County court, 72

in Harmony, PA, 76

ordination of, 49

organizes church, 65–67nn1–2

In Ohio:

absent from canonizing D&C, 264

and Fanny Alger, 345

and Bible. *See* New Translation.

and Book of Commandments, 146

and Kirtland Temple dedication, 282

and Mercantile Firm, 155

and Zion's Camp, 241–42

defends against Booth's critique, 151

described by Presbyterian visitor, 103

dissent in Kirtland, 332

expands power into secular realm, 308, 359

flees Kirtland, 333, 341

gives "patriarchal/evangelist's" blessings, 267

health blessings by, 281

in Hiram, OH, 136, 139, 157

innovations in Ohio, 201

instructions to John Whitmer, 177

keeps leaders in Ohio, 194–95

on consecration, 183, 192–93, 202; never consecrated own property, 167

on Egyptian papyri, 270

on presiding bishop committee, 163

on Sidney Rigdon's mental illness, 176–77

on spiritual gifts, 189

seeks funds in Salem, MA, 298

studies Hebrew, 272

tarred and feathered (March 1832), 157

warns against altering revelations, 200

In Missouri:

advises Jackson County Saints not to move, 224

advises Mormon move to Caldwell County, 297

arrested/imprisoned, 369–71, 373, 549

asks for John Whitmer's property, 373

conferences in Missouri, 242–43. *See also* conferences.

edits *Messenger and Advocate*, 317

gives date for redeeming Zion, 249n1

in Caldwell County, 290

in Far West, 325–39, 342, 483, 541, 545

in Missouri (April 1832), 158

inheritance in Zion, 259

instructions to Mormons in Independence, 206, 265

on dissenters, 362

on Nelson Branch, 182–83

on redeeming Zion, 268

ordains David Whitmer as president in Missouri, 407

renews consecration, 167

visits Missouri (1832), 128, 130, 132–34, 161, 168, 175

Personal qualities:

administrative innovations, 156, 195–96, 274–75n19

charisma, 28–29, 110

countenance transparent during spiritual experience, 31–32

debts/finances of, 147, 149, 161, 197, 202, 340

demands loyalty, 27 33

engagement with Whitmer family, 16, 19–34; alienation from, 319, 328; insults David Whitmer, 361–62; rebukes John Whitmer, 276, 342;

militarism of, 208–9, 267–68, 274, 348–50, 348n37, 366, 524, 546, 548; John Whitmer testifies about, 371; plans Mormon army, 248–49

slanders former friends, 27, 412–13

rebukes W. W. Phelps, 276

revelations: assigning locations to church officers, 312; on Kirtland bank, 288; on self-defense, 228

theology of Christian community, 33, 106–11

threatening language of, 365

wants John Whitmer's property, 360, 525

In Nauvoo:

death of, 402

Smith, Joseph, Sr.

as assistant president, 275

as founding member of church, 66

as one of Eight Witnesses, 55–56

baptism of, 68

illness of, 275–76

jailed for debt, 87

on Kirtland High Council, 259

operates tavern at Far West, 307, 358

ordained church patriarch, 266

to/from Missouri, 329, 379–80

Smith, Joseph, III

and Zenas Gurley, Sr., 26

and William Smith, 580

and Whitmer family, 480

as successor to Joseph Smith Jr., 406

compares Book of Mormon mss and published version, 481

corresponds with James Van Cleave, 352

corresponds with John Whitmer, 460

interviews Emma on Book of Mormon, 37, 21n11, 47n41

invites David Whitmer to conference, 476

lectures at Liberal Institute, 56n26

on presiding Whitmerite elder, 493

receives John Whitmer papers, 513

visits Far West, 341

visits David Whitmer, 480

Smith, Joseph F.

and Book of Mormon "caractors," 595

diary quoted (1878), 555–57

dismisses Book of Mormon printer's mss as valueless, 589–90

letter to Samuel Russell, 589–90

on witness signatures, 590

tries to acquire "The Book of John Whitmer," etc., 471, 493–94, 508

visits David Whitmer (1878), 468–69, 590

Smith, Joseph Fielding, 595, 595n22

Smith, Joseph Murdock, 158

Smith, Lucy Mack

angel aids David Whitmer's farm
work, 23, 23n20

as original church member, 66

at Whitmer home, 51–52

baptism of, 68n11

changing attitude toward David
Whitmer, 309–10

leaves Missouri, 379–80

moves to Ohio, 99, 102

on converts in Ohio, 88

on Oliver Cowdery as scribe, 22

operates tavern at Far West, 307–58

moves to Waterloo, NY, 86

William Smith claims Lucy supports
Strang, 406

Smith, Mary Fielding, 595

Smith, Samuel Harrison

and patriarchal blessings, 266

appointed to sell D&C, 265

as founding church member, 66–67

as missionary, 83n65

as one of Eight Witnesses, 55–56, 58

compensation (1831), 149

in Harmony, PA, 26

in Kirtland, OH, 134; on high council,
260, 309n78

in Missouri, 132

ordination of, 49

takes Oliver Cowdery to Joseph
Smith, 23

Smith, Sylvester, 260

Smith, T. W., 408, 427, 481

Smith, Vida E., 596

Smith, Walter Wayne, 494, 494n12, 513

Smith, William B. (Joseph's brother)

announces gathering at Far West,
580–84

conference resolutions (1879), 583–84

compensation (1831), 149

establishes church, 537

in Kirtland, 325, 333

leaves Missouri, 379

on Book of Mormon translation, 41

supports James Strang 405–6

Smith, William S. (not related to Joseph
Smith), 95

Snow, Eliza R., 166n23

Snow, Nelson, 503–5

Snyder, John, 223

solemn assemblies, 192–93

Sons of Dan. *See* Danites.

Sorensen, Steven, xvi

spectacles (seer stones), 40, 42, 47

Speek, Vickie Cleverley, xviii

spice, in washings and anointings, 278–79

spiritual experiences, important to
Whitmers, 23–24n20

spiritual gifts/excesses, in Kirtland, 94–95,
115–17, 188–89. *See also* tongues.

spiritualism, 56n26

Squires (of Caldwell County), 544

St. John, John (editor), 119

St. Louis Republican, 470

Staker, Mark Lyman, 116, 124, 515

stakes, in Ohio and Missouri, 196

Stanton, Daniel, 174

Staples/Steeples, Abner F., 215–16n36

Stayton, David A., 215–16n36

Stebbins, Henry A., 580

Stedman, Edmund Clarence, 491

Steeples, Abner, 210n9

Stevenson, Edward, 30–31, 65n1, 458, 484, 488

Stewart, Bruce G., xvii

Stewart/Stuart, Charles, 101n66

Stoddard, Calvin, 100

Stoner (of Far West), 393

store, in Far West, 305–6

Story of Mormons, The, 596

Strang, James J./Strangites, 403–6, 508, 537

Stringham, Esther Knight, 72

Stringham, William, 72

Strongsville, OH, 93

Strope, George, 373

Styles (RLDS missionary), 588

succession, and David Whitmer, 243, 407. *See also* Whitmer, David, Church of Christ.

Susquehanna River, and Whitmer family, 7–8

Swaringer (of Jackson County), 187

Sweet, Northrop, 109

Sweitzer, Frederick, 4

Switzerland, Whitmer family from, 1–2

T

Tamez, Jared, 497

Tanner, Anna Whitmer, 184, 424

Tanner, David T., 424

Tanner, Jerald and Sandra, 486, 511

Tanner, Nathan, Jr., 36, 45, 45n32

tavern at Far West, 307

Taylor, John (apostle), 203, 383

Taylor, Russ, xvi

tea, and Word of Wisdom, 197

teacher, office of, 106n13

temple. *See respective towns.*

Thayre/Thayer, Ezra, 99–100

Theological Seminary of the Reformed Church, 58

Thomas, Clarissa, 88

Thomas Creek, baptismal site, 69

Thompson, OH, 118, 126–27n22, 129, 180–81

Thompsonian doctors, 307

Thornton, Carter, 401

Thornton, John, 422n2

Thorp, Joseph, 304

Thorp, William, 294

Three Witnesses chosen, 51–52

Tiffin, OH, 381

Timber Branch. *See* Whitmer Settlement.

Times and Seasons, 57, 382

Tinney's Grove, 350, 355

Tippets, William, 264

tithing, 330

tobacco, and Word of Wisdom, 197

tongues, 189–90, 280

tornado, in Richmond, 465–68, 488

Traughber, John Logan, xvi, 44, 408, 457

triune baptism, 4n18

Troost Lake Park, 186

"True Followers of Christ," 19

trunk, and Whitmer papers, 465–68, 497, **502**, 503–5

Turley, Richard E., xvi

Turley, Theodore, 60, 379, 379n5, 307, 383n20, 384

Turner, Bessie, 573

Turner, Ella, 573

Twelves family, and Whitmer trunk, 503–5

Twelvites. *See* LDS Church.

Tyler, Daniel, 58

U

United Firm, 155, 163–64n14, 164, 317

Updike, Lee, xvii
Upper Missouri Advertiser, 166
Urim and Thummim, 41–44, 43n25, 46–47, 60n44. *See also* seer stones.

V

Van Cleave/Cleve, James R.
marries Josephine ("Josie") Helen Schweich, 503n27
on David Whitmer, 352
possession of "caractors," 491
Van Cleave/Cleve, James R. B.
documents in possession of, 478
interviewed by Arthur Deming, 585–86
obtains John Whitmer's papers, 586
plans to write a history of Mormonism, 477–78
Van Cleave/Cleve, James R. B.
acquires John Whitmer's papers, 509
interviews David Whitmer, 509
marries Josephine ("Josie") Helen Schweich, 456
on seer stones, 47n41
Joseph F. Smith meets, 590
Van Cleave, Josephine ("Josie") Helen Schweich, **398, 455**
at David Whitmer's death, 487
in 1860 census, 437
marries James Van Cleave, 477, 503n27, 509
newspaper mentions of, 454–56
teaches school, 456
Van Cott, John, 86n9
Van Wagoner, Richard Savage, xvii, 104
Vance, Malinda, 434
Viator (pseud.), 450–51, 538–52
violence, code of honor, 227n13
Vogel, Dan, xviii
on concept of authority, 106n13
on founding church members, 65–66nn1–2
on reliability of Three/Eight Witnesses, 53, 56
on Whitmer family origins, 1

W

W. W. Phelps & Co., 169, 175–76
wafers, for sealing letters, 170–71
Walden, Barbara, xvii
Walker, Jeffery, 375
Walker, John M., 215–16n36
Waller, Zachariah, 215–16n36
Walmsley/Dombsby/Orsby/Wamsley (of Far West), 543, 576, 578
Walter (near Richmond), 393n1
Walters, George, 382n18, 388
Walton (near Richmond), 393n1
Walton (of Far West), 578
Walton, Alf, 577
Walton, Anne, 577
Walton, Robert, 383n18, 577
Wamsley. *See* Walmsley.
Wanless, Ann, 383n18
war department (Mormon), 274
Warner, Lillian Page, 470–71
Warner, W. W., 470
Warnky, F. C., 596
Warnock, William, 383n18
washing of feet, 201
washings and anointings, 277n248, 277
Wasson, George J., 426, 416n45
Waterloo, NY, 10, 83n65
Watt, Ronald G., xvi
Webb, Caroline, 181
Webb, Robert C., 596

Webster (first name unknown), 11n46, **12**

Welber (artist), 284, 503n26

Wells, Junius, 484

West, Adaline Louise Follett, 252, 255

West, J. B., 435

West, Mary Hulet, 179, 181n5

West, Nathan, 186, 234, 252

West, Nathan Ayers, 181n5

Westergren, Bruce, xiv–xv, xvii, 263, 511, 592–93

Western Star, 382, 390

Weston, Samuel, 215–16n36

Wheaton, Clarence, 501, 512

"white stone," 60n44

Whiting, Lydia, 181n5

Whiting, William, 181n5, 182, 186

Whitlock, Harvey, 128, 130, 133, 154, 263, 593

Whitmer family. *See also individuals.*

   alienation from Joseph Smith's theo-political authoritarianism, xi, 276, 308, 314–39, 349

   attack on settlement, 234

   burial plot in Richmond Pioneer Cemetery, 485

   centrality of Missouri to, 309

   descendancy chart, 6

   established position as non-Mormon but not anti-Mormon, 374

   ethnic origins of, 1

   farm and locale, map, **15**, 70

   family Bible, xvi, **8**

   frequent gatherings, 401

   home, **12**, 35, 78

   in Hiram, OH, 136

   in Missouri, 184, 305, 357

   in New York, 9–10

   loyalty to Joseph Smith, 16, 19–34

   name variations, 2

   one of three families constituting early church, 19

   religious beliefs, 419–21

   Joseph Smith rejects and punishes, 27–28

   testimony of Book of Mormon, 588

Whitmer, Alexander Peter Jackson

   birth of, 394

   described, 441

   family information, 402, 445n2

   in 1860 census, 434

   killed in Civil War, 441

Whitmer, Anna. *See* Tanner, Anna Whitmer.

Whitmer, Anne/Anna Schott, 15, 17, 68, 276

Whitmer, Catherine. *See* Page, Catherine Whitmer.

Whitmer, Celia Ann Tattershall/Tatarshall/Tatershall, 448, 559, 567, 576

Whitmer, Charles William, 479, 496n14

Whitmer, Christian

   as county sheriff, 19–20

   as scribe, 26, 425n7

   attacked by mob, 233–34

   baptism, 68

   birth of, 6

   biography, 573

   compensation (1831), 149

   death of, 276

   father blesses, 245

   illness of, 251

   in Missouri, 184, 186–87

   in New York militia, 14

   gives Joseph Smith clothes, 27

   lived near parents-in-law, 17

member of Christ's Church, 14

not required to consecrate, 202

on high council, 244

one of Eight Witnesses, 55–56

prophesies, 238

shoemaker, 6, 13, 13n52, 187

Whitmer, Dan/Daniel E., 9n34, 424

Whitmer, David, **421, 458**

    Family background:

    biography of, 573

    death recorded, 273, 486

    grave marker, **486**, 487

    initial "D." in some records, 6, 15

    on Peter Whitmer, Sr., 12–13

    reports Oliver Cowdery's impressions of Joseph Smith, 21

    In New York:

    and Book of Mormon

    believed "caractors" were Martin Harris's, 491

        on Book of Mormon translation, 42

    on signatures of eleven witnesses, 590

        on Urim and Thummim, 43

    rejects suggestion of hallucination, 482–43

        relates Joseph Smith's inability to translate when quarreling with Emma, 37

    testimony of, 39, 41, 368, 475, 219–21, 487, 590

    angel's aid in farm work, 23, 23n20

    as founding church member, 65–66nn1–2

    as one of Three Witnesses, 48, 51–53, 553–54

    as missionary, 49

    as recorder, 83

    describes Joseph Smith, 27

    family information, 16

    in Fayette, NY, 85

    in Harmony, PA, 71–72

    leadership assignments, 142

    lives with parents, 35

    "natural" or "spiritual" view of plates, 59n40

    on church organization, 65–67

    opposed to printing Book of Commandments, 143–44, 149n38, 172

    ordination of, 49

    seer stones, 44

    In Ohio:

    appointed to sell D&C, 265

    compensation (1831), 149

    faith of, 357–58

    friendship with Oliver Cowdery, 19–20

    father blesses, 245

    in Kirtland, 325; on high council, 312; temple dedication, 282

    marries Julia Ann Jolly, 98–99

    on June 1831 conference, 125

    on Word of Wisdom, 197

    paid in books, 285

    predicts expulsion from Jackson County, 144

    raises funds for Joseph Smith (1831), 139–40

    sends material to Missouri, 293

    Joseph Smith blesses, 267

    seer stones, 47n39

    to/from Ohio, 248, 317

    to Missouri, 293, 312

    vision of additional artifacts, 52–53

    In Missouri:

as missionary, 128, 130, 133, 179

Far West Temple, 315

in Far West, 316, 414, 545

in Mormon army, 274

inheritance in Zion assigned, 259

land in Caldwell County, 304; in
    Daviess County, 327

leads Mormon defenders, 233–34

on violence in Missouri, 231

ordained church president in Missouri,
    243, 245

presiding elder/ordained president in
    Missouri, 187, 426

prophecies (1833), 238

reassures Philo Dibble, 235

refused to attack Mormons, 368

speaks in tongues, 189

to/from Missouri, 184, 186, 312

Disengages from Joseph Smith/Church:

accusations/complaints about, 326,
    333–34, 353n48, 378

alienated from Joseph Smith, xi, 83,
    310–11, 314, 319–20, 328, 361–62

blames Sidney Rigdon for Joseph
    Smith's alienation, 352

excommunication, 334–35, 338, 343, 349,
    353n49, 486

friendship with Joseph Smith, 27

Mormons threaten, 316, 352–53

on self-defense, 337

sheltered by McLellins, 355–57

uneasy with consecration, 329; not
    required to consecrate, 202

Post-Mormon life:

and James J. Strang, 403

antipolygamy position of, 469–70

as progressive farmer, 396

as Joseph Smith's successor, 406–7, 586

as whittler, 456

at Oliver Cowdery's death, 422

Church of Christ (Whitmerite),
    organizes, 356, 401n19, 456–58
    ordains William McLellin,
    443–44
    organizes, 407–14

rebaptism/ reordinations (1847), 535

condemns polygamy, 486

correspondence with Joseph III, 311–12,
    415–16

decision to stay in Missouri, 309, 407

documents and artifacts in possession
    of, 476, 497

enrolled in militia during Civil War,
    439

established position as non-Mormon
    but not anti-Mormon, 374

freighting/livery stable/horse breeder,
    361, 398–400, 437, 452–54, 462,
    561; advertisements of business,
    462–63

in 1850, 424

in 1860 census, 437

in 1880 census, 479

in Richmond, 377, **398, 399**

injured hand, 356

interviewed, xi, 53, 50, 70, 463–64, 527;
    complains about misquoting,
    67n9

performs marriage of granddaughter,
    490

portrait, 283, 284n53, 571

places early records in bank vault,
    485–86

possession of John Whitmer papers,
    513

property in Richmond, MO, 400, 416,
    426, 437

rejects Oliver Cowdery's attempt to persuade him to be rebaptized, 415

rejects LDS offers to buy records, 485, 585

revelations to, 356–57, 408; (1847), 531–36; (1861), 563–65

  about Civil War, 438–39

Don Carlos Smith meets, 365–66

tornado, injured in, **462**, 466–67

visit from Hedrickite elder, 443

wagon appropriated by militia, 368

Personal qualities:

as healer, 275–76

memories varied, 35, 67

reputation of, 459

testifies about angel, 131

valued equality of prophecies, 62

vision of locked chest, 535

Whitmer, David Alma, 479–80, 496n14

Whitmer, David, Jr., 273

Whitmer David Jacob

  and tornado, 466–67

  at David Whitmer's death, 486

  death of, 490

  family information, 238, 574

  in Richmond (1850), 424

  manages livery operation, 452; advertisements for, 453–54, **453**

Whitmer, David Peter (Jacob's son), 424, 436–37, 442

Whitmer, Edwin Franklin, 496n14

Whitmer, Elizabeth Schott (Jacob's wife)

  baptism of, 68

  children of, 9n34, 401, 457

  close to in-laws, 427, **428**

  death of, 429

  in Richmond (1850), 407, 424

  marriage, 15–16, 573–74

  property inherited, 429, 429n21

  resides near David Whitmer, 442

Whitmer, George, possibly from Prussia or Switzerland, 1

Whitmer, Harry, 464n40, 559

Whitmer, Izora Beulah, 479

Whitmer, Jacob (brother of David and John Whitmer), **428**

  and James J. Strang, 403

  as family leader, 427

  baptism of, 68

  biography of, 573

  birth of, 1

  Book of Mormon testimony, 475

  children/descendants, xvii, 9n34, 457, 496n14

  claim of "David" as middle name, xiiin6

  compensation for church work, 149, 330n14

  death of, 428; gravestone, 428, 488

  descendancy chart, 6

  family cemetery, 488

  Far West: on high council, 326; on temple committee, 330

  gives early documents to David Whitmer, 509

  in Richmond, MO, 377, 401, 424, 427–28, 566

  locations of, 184, 336, 407, 414, 488

  marries, 15–16

  William McLellin visits, 529

  member of Christ's Church, 14

  not required to consecrate, 202

  one of Eight Witnesses, 55–56

  seer stone, 58–59n37, 495, 498

sheltered by McLellins, 355–57

shoemaker, 13, 13n52, 424, 427

supports David Whitmer as church leader, 407–8; present at revelations to David Whitmer (1847), 531; rebaptized/reordained (1847), 535

Whitmer, Jacob ("Jake") David Jefferson (son of David Whitmer)

biography, 559

birth of, 402

discharged from militia, 441

in 1860 census, 434

in Far West, 391n40, 464, 576

inheritance, 475

hospitality of, 484

hotel, 484

letter to Sarah Elizabeth Johnson, 567

location of, 445n2

marries, 448

owns temple site (did not farm), 446, 476

rebuffs LDS attempts to acquire papers, 471

Joseph F. Smith and Orson Pratt visit, 555–57

Whitmer, John, **frontispiece, 421, 449**

Family background:

alleged middle name ("David"), xiiin6

biography of, 573–74

birth of, 1

descendancy chart, 6

father blesses, 245

marries, 191

Joseph Smith's friendship with, 27

lives in parents' home, 35

loyalty to Joseph Smith, 29

meets Joseph Smith, 16

member of Christ's Church, 14

In New York:

accepts Joseph Smith's theology, 33

as clerk, 112, 137, 145, 147, 149, 154, 170

as full-time church employee, 108

as historian, xiii, 122–23, 129–30, 144, 149–51, 170, 173, 328, 339, 401

"The Book of John Whitmer," **270**

copies history in bound volume, 262

copies revelations, 262

duties of, 139–40

final chapters of history, 402

includes James J. Strang, 405

as missionary, 83, 86, 112, 132, 170, 229

as scribe, 26, 36, 36nn4–5, 40–41, 40n20, 46, 75–77, 82, 86, 89

baptized, 48

Book of Commandments and Revelations, 142, 144, 165, 199–200, 240, 250; helps arrange and copy revelations, 74–75

Book of Mormon witness

testimony of, 260, 285, 384, 449, 451, 459, 459n28, 460–61, 475, 507; on Oliver Cowdery's testimony, 460

describes plates, 61

Doctrine and Covenants, testifies to, 265

elder's license, 71, 493n9

friendship with Joseph Smith, 29

in Fayette, NY, 85

in Harmony, PA, 71–72

inheritance in Zion assigned, 259

instructions to Missouri Saints, 266

Joseph Smith blesses, 267

on church organization, 66n2,
65–66nn1–2, 68
on spiritual excesses, 95
on statistical reports, 139–40
one of Eight Witnesses, 55
ordained high priest, 125
performs ordinations/ordinances, 93,
265
participation in councils and
conferences, 169
replaces Oliver Cowdery, 85
replaced by Sidney Rigdon, 89
revelations, 49, 241
witnessed Joseph Smith/Isaac Hale
land transaction, 77

In Ohio:
and Literary Firm, 165
and United Firm, 164
as conference clerk, 149
commanded to take revelations to
Missouri, 149
defends Joseph Smith, 275
financial needs, 148–49, 197
funds to redeem Zion, 308
Kirtland Temple dedication, 277, 282
New Translation, 123–24, 132, 138;
described, 90n30
not required to consecrate, 167, 202
on Book of Abraham/Joseph of Egypt,
270
on presiding bishop committee, 163
patriarchal blessing, 523
solemn assemblies, 192
studies Hebrew, 271–72
to/from Ohio, 91–92, 136, 252

In Missouri:
account book, entries (November 1831–
March 1832), **158, 159,** 160, 172–73,
253, 322, 354
as leader in Missouri, 198
birth of Sarah Elizabeth, 312
buys gardening supplies, 158
buys land in Missouri, 299, 361–62
concerned about militarism, 348
counselor in Missouri church
presidency, xiii, 244–45, 326
edits *Messenger and Advocate*, 256–68
284; first/last editorials (1835),
516–22
holds Edward Partridge notes, 375–76,
388–90
gives Joseph Smith money, 260
in Clay County, 238–39
in Far West: clerk pro tem, 329; co-
founds, xiii, 302–4; leaves, 353;
printing press, 319–21; temple site,
315
Jackson County, expelled from, 240–41
on George W. Harris's militarism, 524
on Sidney Rigdon's "salt sermon," 524
on Alanson Ripley's attitude toward
law of the land, 524–25
on self-defense, 337
on spiritual gifts, 188
on Lyman Wight autobiography,
246–47
performs ordinations, 260
prophesies, 238
takes census of Mormons, 173–75, 178
teaches school, 240
to/from Missouri, 151, 293
transfers press to Thomas B. Marsh,
343
violence in Independence, 210, 221

Disengages from Joseph Smith/Church:

accusations against, 319, 326, 333, 337, 342, 352–53, 353n48, 355; defense against, 334

excommunicated, 334–35, 338, 345

moves to Richmond, MO, 361

Joseph Smith as fallen prophet, 263

refuses Joseph Smith's request for his property, 360, 373, 525

opposes militarism, 524–25

sheltered by McLellins, 355–57

testifies for state, (1838), 371–73, 524–25

uneasy relationship to Joseph Smith, 225–26

Post-Mormon life:

acquires Far West property, 375–76, 378, 384, 388, 413–14, 426, **435**, 436–37, 545; includes temple site (did not plow), 388, 430

and Hedrickites, 443

and W. W. Phelps's debts, 387

approached by restorationists, 429

as widower, 449

builds cistern, 431

Church of Christ

 present at revelations to David Whitmer (1847), 531

 rebaptized and reordained (1847), 535

 supports David Whitmer as leader, 407–8

Civil War militia, enlisted, 439; discharged, 441

decision to stay in Far West, 380, 407

described by visitor (1875), 451

Doctrine and Covenants, personal copy, 273–74

early documents (Book of Mormon printer's manuscript, "caractors,"

etc.) in possession of, xiii, 355n53, 459n28, 477

established position as non-Mormon but not anti-Mormon, 374

farms, plants flower garden/trees, 430–31

handles Gilbert estate, 360, 390

home/hotel in Far West, **285**, 303–4, 392, **474**, 591

in 1860 census, 434

interviewed by William Lewis, 553–54

interviewed by Peter Wilhelm Poulson, 463–64, 526–27 [see question about initial under Poulson, M. Wilhelm]

letter to children (1871), 566–67

on gathering, 461

James Cash Penney, business dealings with 430

seer stone, 47n39, 59, 498

tax assessment, 451

visit from E. C. Brand, 588

visit from RLDS, 458–59

visit from travelers, 540–41

visit from David Whitmer, Jacob Whitmer, Hiram Page, and William McLellin, 529

Death and post-death documents:

"The Book of John Whitmer," provenance and publication, 498, 501

death of, 471

estate of, 475

gravestone of, **473**, 474, 559

locations of history, 507–15

Kingston, MO, fire in courthouse, 435

obituary, 472

portrait, RLDS Church acquires, 501, 569–70

RLDS Church buys documents,
494–95
Personal qualities:
closeness to David Whitmer, 401
faith expression of, 519–22
reputation of, 430, 459, 461, 542
signature of, **271**
speaks in tongues, 189
steadfastness of faith, 505–6
testifies of angels, 236
Whitmer, John, and Sarah
family Bible presented to LDS
Church History Library, 273, 501
live with David and Julia Ann
Whitmer, 254
live with Peter Jr. and Vashti Whitmer,
250–51
photographs presented to LDS
Church History Library, 501
Whitmer, John Gant, 479, 495–96, 496n14
Whitmer, John Oliver, 273, 295, 402, 406,
445n2
Whitmer, Julia Ann/Juliann Jolly, **398**
baptized, 98n60
death of, 489
first child, 238
in 1860 census, 437
in Missouri, 184, 186, 407
in Richmond, MO (1850), 424
married, 98–99, 574
portrait of, 283–84n53
Whitmer, Marianne, 184
Whitmer, Mary [*sic*] (Mayme) Janetta,
479–80
Whitmer, Mary Musselman (mother of
John Whitmer)
angel shows plates, 31
baptized, 69

burden of hospitality, 26
death of, 427
family information, 1, 5, 6, 16, 573
in Missouri, 184, 377, 407
Whitmer, Mary F., 479
Whitmer, Mary Gant, 432, 470n18
Whitmer, Nancy (dau. of Peter Whitmer
Sr.), 6, 9, 573
Whitmer, Nancy Jane (dau. of John
Whitmer), 240, 445n2
Whitmer, Nora Bell, 479
Whitmer, Peter, Jr.
as founding member of church,
65–66nn1–2, 67
as Lamanite missionary, 83–84n65,
87–88, 127, 132, 179
biography of, 573, 575
Book of Mormon
guards printer's manuscript, 62
testimony of, 87
compensation (1831), 149
Oliver Cowdery baptizes, 48
death, 300
decides to stay in Missouri, 309
defends Whitmer Settlement, 234
family information, 6, 9, 401n19
illness of, 281
in Missouri, 158, 184, 246
in Ohio, 136, 269
inheritance in Zion assigned, 259
lives with parents, 15–16, 35
marries, 184, 191
on Oliver Cowdery and Ziba Peterson,
163
on Kirtland High Council, 276
one of Eight Witnesses, 55–56
ordained, 49

nurses Heber C. Kimball, 242

prophesies, 238

studies Hebrew, 272

trained as tailor, 13, 13n54

Whitmer, Peter, Sr. (and Mary Musselman)

advises David Whitmer on farm work, 24n20

baptized, 69

blesses John and Sarah Whitmer, 251

blesses Peter Jr. and Vashti Whitmer, 251

blesses sons, 245

describes New Translation manuscript, 85

family information, 1, 3–4, 6–9, 11–12, 573

in Richmond, MO, 377, 400, **423**, 424

in Missouri, 184, 187, 407

in Ohio, 102

not required to consecrate, 202, 202n28

opposes Catharine's marriage to Hiram Page, 16

refuses to receive wounded Mormons, 234

resists Diedrich Willers Sr., 58

sells farm, 100–101

sells Jackson County property, 378

death of, 427

Whitmer, Sarah Elizabeth. *See* Kerr, Sarah Elizabeth Whitmer Johnson.

Whitmer, Sarah Maria/Mariah Jackson, **254**. *See also* Whitmer, John.

corresponds with, 171

illness and death, 445, 448, 559, 566

lives in Far West, 380

marries, 191

meets John Whitmer, 127

moves to Missouri, 178, 190

Whitmer, Vashti Higley, 184, 191, 300, 401n19

Whitmer, Virginia ("Jennie") Frances, 479

Whitmer Branch, 174, 188–89

Whitmer Settlement, 182n9, 184, 337

attacked, 229–30, 232

location of, 187–88

map, 185, 186, 235

Whitney, Elizabeth Ann Smith, 89

Whitney, Newel K.

and Mercantile Firm, 155

and United Firm, 164

bishop in Ohio, 180

borrows money using his store as collateral, 165, 167

business associate with A. S. Gilbert, 164

on presiding bishop committee, 163

on redeeming Zion, 268

purchases new press, 226

store, 194

to/from Missouri, 158

to/from Ohio, 194

Whitney, Samuel, 280n39

Whitney, Susanna Kimball, 280n39

Wichita Beacon, 490

Widmer, Heinrich, 2, 6

Widmer, Jakob, 2, 6

Widmer, Peter Hiestand, 2, 6

Wight, Jermy, 246

Wight, Lyman

and Book of Commandments, 240

arrested/imprisoned, 369–71, 373, 549

as missionary, 112, 229

at Adam-ondi-Ahman, 306

autobiography, 246

builds house for Michael Arthur, 246
in Ohio, 87
in Prairie Branch (MO), 175
in "the Family," 92, 105, 127
land in Daviess County, 327
leather store, 306
militancy, 228–29, 232, 236–37, 249, 274,
364, 364n4
on high council, 244, 327
on spiritual gifts in Ohio, 94
ordinations by, 593
Wightites, William McLellin denounces,
537
Wilcox, Pearl G., xviii, 304, 453
Wildermuth, E. M., 47n41
Willers, Didrich/Diedrich, Sr., 13–14, 14n59,
16, 58, 69, 83n64
Williams, Frederick Granger
and Gilbert estate, 382, 382n16
and Literary Firm, 176
as missionary, 127, 132, 134
as scribe on New Translation, 139
edits *Northern Times*, 257
instructions to Missouri Saints, 265–66
mission to Missouri, 132
on Oliver Cowdery and Ziba Peterson,
163
portrait of, 283
stays in Ohio, 194
Williams, James, 394, 560–62
Williams, Nancy Clement, 284n53
Williams, Peter W., 60
Williams, Rebecca, 283
Wilson ("general" in Missouri), 230
Wilson/Willson, Moses G., 210n9,
215–16n36

Wilson/Willson, Thomas W., 210n9,
215–16n36
Wilson's Store, 232–33
Wimmer, Larry T., 341
Winchester, Alonzo, 303, 399, 400
Winchester, Benjamin, 246
Winchester, Daniel, 303
Winchester, Nancy, 303
Winchester, Paulina, 303
Winchester, Stephen, 246, 303, 399
Witmer, Christian Herr, 2, 6
Witmer, Elizabeth, 6
witnesses to Book of Mormon, 48–64
Wittmer, Catharina Brechbill Engle, 6
Wittmer, Elizabeth, 3
Wittmer, Elizabeth Herr Brubaker, 3
Wittmer, Magdalena, 3
Wittmer, Magdalena Shellenberger, 6
Wittmer, Mary, 3
Wittmer, Peter (son of Christian;
identified as Peter Whitmer, Sr., 3
Wittmer, Peter/Petter, 2n6, 2n8; marriages
of, 3
Wittmer/Whitmer, Christian, 3–4
Wood, Jack, 435
Woodruff, Wilford, 246, 298n28, 382–83
Woods, Henry, 384
Woods, Rebecca, 17, 26
Woodward, George and Nancy, 427
Woolley, Edwin Gordon, 466–67
Word of Wisdom, 201, 278
accusations of, 333–34
institution of, 197

Y

Yost, Lee, 83n64
Young, Biloine Whiting, xvii

Young, Brigham
  as missionary, 545
  in Missouri, 342, 379n5, 383
  on David Whitmer, 310
  post-martyrdom leadership, 406
  John Whitmer on, 508
Young, Daniel, 58
Young, Lucy Cowdery, 422
Young People's History, 596
Young, Phineas, 414, 422, 425–26n7

Z

Zimmer, Eliza Jackson, 361, 388, 394, 417–18

Zimmer, John, 361, 388, 390, 394, 394n4
Zion, redemption of, 290–91, 299
  and Kirtland Temple, 266, 282–83n51
  blessings about, 267
  Jackson County property, 272
  redefined, 308
  revelation on, 81, 438–39
  Joseph Smith plans for, 179, 268
  David Whitmer in Missouri, 533–34
Zion's Camp, 241–42, 303
Zion's Ensign, 494n12
Zwingli, Ulrich, 14

www.ingramcontent.com/pod-product-compliance
Lightning Source LLC
Chambersburg PA
CBHW060419100426
42812CB00030B/3238/J